HUMAN
RIGHTS
WATCH

WORLD REPORT

2017

EVENTS OF 2016

ISBN-13: 978-1-60980-734-4

Front cover photo: *Men carrying babies make their way
through the rubble of destroyed buildings after an airstrike
on the rebel-held Salihin neighborhood of Syria's northern
city of Aleppo, September 2016.*
© 2016 Ameer Alhalbi/Agence France-Presse-Getty Images

Back cover photo: *Women and children from Honduras and
El Salvador who crossed into the United States from Mexico
wait after being stopped in Granjeno, Texas, June 2014.*
© 2014 Eric Gray/Associated Press

Cover and book design by Rafael Jiménez

www.hrw.org

Human Rights Watch defends the rights of people worldwide.

We scrupulously investigate abuses, expose the facts widely, and pressure those with power to respect rights and secure justice.

Human Rights Watch is an independent, international organization that works as part of a vibrant movement to uphold human dignity and advance the cause of human rights for all.

Human Rights Watch began in 1978 with the founding of its Europe and Central Asia division (then known as Helsinki Watch). Today, it also includes divisions covering Africa; the Americas; Asia; Europe and Central Asia; and the Middle East and North Africa; a United States program; thematic divisions or programs on arms; business and human rights; children's rights; disability rights; health and human rights; international justice; lesbian, gay, bisexual, and transgender rights; refugees; women's rights; and emergencies. It maintains offices in Amsterdam, Beirut, Berlin, Brussels, Chicago, Geneva, Johannesburg, Kiev, London, Los Angeles, Moscow, Nairobi, New York, Paris, San Francisco, Sao Paulo, Silicon Valley, Stockholm, Sydney, Tokyo, Toronto, Washington DC, and Zurich, and field presences in over 46 other locations globally. Human Rights Watch is an independent, nongovernmental organization, supported by contributions from private individuals and foundations worldwide. It accepts no government funds, directly or indirectly.

HUMAN RIGHTS WATCH

Table of Contents

COUNTRIES 63

Foreword

World Report 2017 is Human Rights Watch's 27th annual review of human rights practices around the globe. It summarizes key human rights issues in more than 90 countries and territories worldwide, drawing on events from late 2015 through November 2016.

The book is divided into two main parts: an essay section, and country-specific chapters.

In his keynote essay, "The Dangerous Rise of Populism: Global Attacks on Human Rights Values," Human Rights Watch Executive Director Kenneth Roth examines the rise of leaders who, claiming to speak for "the people" amid rising public discontent over the status quo, reject rights as an impediment to their perception of the majority will. Roth sees such unrestrained majoritarianism and assaults on government checks and balances as "perhaps the greatest danger today to the future of democracy in the West." The past should serve as our guide he warns: leaders who have claimed insight into the will of the majority have gone on to crush the individual who stands in their way. "We should never underestimate the tendency of demagogues who sacrifice the rights of others in our name today to jettison our rights tomorrow when their real priority—retaining power—is in jeopardy," he writes. Rather than taking on this surge of populist attacks on human rights, he says, too many Western leaders are lying low, "hoping the winds of populism will blow over." Some seem to think that echoing populists' positions will mitigate their rise rather than reinforcing their message. Others, such as Russia's Vladimir Putin, Turkey's Recep Tayyip Erdoğan, Abdel Fattah al-Sisi of Egypt, and Syria's Bashar al-Assad, appear emboldened in their repressive path by the rise of Western populism, and by the West's muted response.

This global assault on human rights, Roth says, requires "a vigorous reaffirmation and defense" of its basic values, with media, civil society, and government all having important parts to play. But the real responsibility, he says, lies with the public, who via nongovernmental organizations, political parties, and traditional and social media, offer the best antidote to demagogues' lies by demanding "a politics based on truth and the values on which rights-respecting democracy has been built." "Rights by their nature do not admit an à la carte approach," Roth says. "You may not like your neighbors, but if you sacrifice their rights today, you weaken your own tomorrow, because ultimately rights are grounded on the reciprocal duty to treat others as you would want to be treated yourself."

In the second essay, "When Exposing Abusers Is Not Enough: Strategies to Confront the Shameless," Akshaya Kumar examines the traditional human rights strategy of "naming and shaming" those who violate human rights. Increasingly, she notes, that approach is being undermined by human rights abusers who revel in their atrocities, rather than hide them, and even use them to entice new followers. Human rights activists, Kumar argues, need to adapt their own tactics accordingly, by taking on those who enable abusers— financial backers, arms suppliers, and other networks that make their rights violations possible—and drawing on the expertise of those who map such systems. "There is no one-size-fits-all approach," she concludes. But unmasking and holding to account those on whose shoulders the shameless stand is an investment the human rights movement needs to make if it is to take on those for whom exposure is a boost, not a blow.

Fears of extremist armed attacks continue to drive legal and policy change in much of the world. Suicide bombers and gunmen have killed hundreds of people and injured thousands more outside of traditional conflict areas in recent years. Governments are responsible for protecting their populations from such attacks, but, as Letta Tayler writes in "Overreach: How New Global Counterterrorism Measures Jeopardize Rights," many attempt to do so by adopting laws and policies that are dangerously overbroad or intrusive, and thus counterproductive. Tayler focuses on two recent trends: a proliferation of counterterrorism laws, many aimed at so-called Foreign Terrorist Fighters ("FTFs"); and declarations of states of emergency. Rather than providing greater security these measures to often risk violating basic rights, incarcerating the wrong people, and alienating populations that could play a positive role in helping to curtail attacks. The solutions, she says, include reforming counterterrorism laws—for example, narrowing the definition of terrorism and mandating rigorous oversight of potential abuses—and limiting the scope and duration of emergency powers to the minimum that is genuinely necessary. As Tayler concludes, effective responses to terrorism do not sideline human rights; rather they uphold them.

In "The Internet is Not the Enemy: As Rights Move Online, Human Rights Standards Move with Them," Dinah PoKempner identifies a troubling dichotomy between the principles of internet freedom that governments publicly support, and the practical steps they take back home that run counter to them, particularly intrusive surveillance. She presents three features of online speech that make it particularly powerful, and hard to regulate—its lack of inhibition, its longevity, and its cross-border reach—challenges that she says demand a "doubling down on privacy and freedom of speech, rather than giving up on them." Noting that some rights-limiting steps are sometimes warranted, indeed necessary, she stresses the evaluation of "necessity and proportionality" in regulation, as well as the requirements of transparency, independent oversight, and avenues of appeal and redress. Failure to follow these time-tested standards, she warns, can lead to discrimination, persecution, and even undermine national security or public order by eroding trust in government and protection of minorities. "Societies that deprive their inhabitants of online privacy and means of digital security are deeply vulnerable" she concludes; rights need to be part of the digital age.

Education is often a casualty for children caught up in conflict and persecution. For older children, particularly, it has become an "impossible dream." Today, less than a quarter of the world's nearly 2 million secondary school-aged refugee adolescents attend school. Girls are often most affected. In the final essay, "The Lost Years: Secondary Education for Children in Emergencies," Bassam Khawaja, Elin Martinez, and Bill Van Esveld identify the causes of these "lost years" as primary-school focused funding, and restrictive refugee policies that limit the ability of displaced children to attend and stay in school. To address them, they say, humanitarian actors and donors need to place more emphasis on secondary education, and address the physical, social, economic, policy, and linguistic barriers that make it hard for older children to get an education. The stakes, they argue, could not be higher: the personal growth, safety, and sense of hope of displaced older children, and the economic and social well-being of their host and home countries—if and when they return.

The rest of the volume consists of individual country entries, each of which identifies significant human rights abuses, examines the freedom of local human rights defenders to conduct their work, and surveys the response of key international actors, such as the United Nations, European Union, African Union, United States, China, and various regional and international organizations and institutions.

The book reflects extensive investigative work that Human Rights Watch staff undertook in 2016, usually in close partnership with human rights activists and groups in the country in question. It also reflects the work of our advocacy team, which monitors policy developments and strives to persuade governments and international institutions to curb abuses and promote human rights. Human Rights Watch publications, issued throughout the year, contain more detailed accounts of many of the issues addressed in the brief summaries in this volume. They can be found on the Human Rights Watch website, www.hrw.org.

As in past years, this report does not include a chapter on every country where Human Rights Watch works, nor does it discuss every issue of importance. The absence of a particular country or issue often simply reflects staffing or resource limitations and should not be taken as commentary on the significance of the problem. There are many serious human rights violations that Human Rights Watch simply lacks the capacity to address.

The factors we considered in determining the focus of our work in 2016 (and hence the content of this volume) include the number of people affected and the severity of abuse, access to the country and the availability of information about it, the susceptibility of abusive forces to influence, and the importance of addressing certain thematic concerns and of reinforcing the work of local rights organizations.

The World Report does not have separate chapters addressing our thematic work but instead incorporates such material directly into the country entries. Please consult the Human Rights Watch website for more detailed treatment of our work on children's rights; women's rights; arms and military issues; business and human rights; health and human rights; disability rights; international justice; terrorism and counterterrorism; refugees and displaced people; and lesbian, gay, bisexual, and transgender (LGBT) people's rights; and for information about our international film festivals.

More than 200 Human Rights Watch staff contributed to World Report 2017; Danielle Haas, Senior Editor, oversaw the editing; Aditi Shetty, Program Office Associate, managed the logistics.

The Dangerous Rise of Populism
Global Attacks on Human Rights Values

By Kenneth Roth, *Executive Director*

Human rights exist to protect people from government abuse and neglect. Rights limit what a state can do and impose obligations for how a state must act. Yet today a new generation of populists is turning this protection on its head. Claiming to speak for "the people," they treat rights as an impediment to their conception of the majority will, a needless obstacle to defending the nation from perceived threats and evils. Instead of accepting rights as protecting everyone, they privilege the declared interests of the majority, encouraging people to adopt the dangerous belief that they will never themselves need to assert rights against an overreaching government claiming to act in their name.

The appeal of the populists has grown with mounting public discontent over the status quo. In the West, many people feel left behind by technological change, the global economy, and growing inequality. Horrific incidents of terrorism generate apprehension and fear. Some are uneasy with societies that have become more ethnically, religiously and racially diverse. There is an increasing sense that governments and the elite ignore public concerns.

In this cauldron of discontent, certain politicians are flourishing and even gaining power by portraying rights as protecting only the terrorist suspect or the asylum seeker at the expense of the safety, economic welfare, and cultural preferences of the presumed majority. They scapegoat refugees, immigrant communities, and minorities. Truth is a frequent casualty. Nativism, xenophobia, racism, and Islamophobia are on the rise.

This dangerous trend threatens to reverse the accomplishments of the modern human rights movement. In its early years, that movement was preoccupied with the atrocities of World War II and the repression associated with the Cold War. Having seen the evil that governments can do, states adopted a series of human rights treaties to limit and deter future abuse. Protecting these rights was understood as necessary for individuals to live in dignity. Growing respect for rights laid the foundation for freer, safer, and more prosperous societies.

But today, a growing number of people have come to see rights not as protecting them from the state but as undermining governmental efforts to defend them. In the United States and Europe, the perceived threat at the top of the list is migration, where concerns about cultural identity, economic opportunity, and terrorism intersect. Encouraged by populists, an expanding segment of the public sees rights as protecting only these "other" people, not themselves, and thus as dispensable. If the majority wants to limit the rights of refugees, migrants, or minorities, the populists suggest, it should be free to do so. That international treaties and institutions stand in the way only intensifies this antipathy toward rights in a world where nativism is often prized over globalism.

It is perhaps human nature that it is harder to identify with people who differ from oneself, and easier to accept violation of their rights. People take solace in the hazardous assumption that the selective enforcement of rights is possible— that the rights of others can be compromised while their own remain secure.

But rights by their nature do not admit an à la carte approach. You may not like your neighbors, but if you sacrifice their rights today, you jeopardize your own tomorrow, because ultimately rights are grounded on the reciprocal duty to treat others as you would want to be treated yourself. To violate the rights of some is to erode the edifice of rights that inevitably will be needed by members of the presumed majority in whose name current violations occur.

We forget at our peril the demagogues of yesteryear—the fascists, communists, and their ilk who claimed privileged insight into the majority's interest but ended up crushing the individual. When populists treat rights as an obstacle to their vision of the majority will, it is only a matter of time before they turn on those who disagree with their agenda. The risk only heightens when populists attack the independence of the judiciary for upholding the rule of law—that is, for enforcing the limits on governmental conduct that rights impose.

Such claims of unfettered majoritarianism, and the attacks on the checks and balances that constrain governmental power, are perhaps the greatest danger today to the future of democracy in the West.

Spreading Threat and Tepid Response

Rather than confronting this populist surge, too many Western political leaders seem to have lost confidence in human rights values, offering only tepid support. Few leaders have been willing to offer a vigorous defense, with the notable exception, at times, of German Chancellor Angela Merkel, Canadian Prime Minister Justin Trudeau, and US President Barack Obama.

Some leaders seem to have buried their heads in the sand, hoping the winds of populism will blow over. Others, if not seeking to profit from populist passions, seem to wish that emulation of the populists might temper their ascendancy. British Prime Minister Theresa May denounced "activist left wing human rights lawyers" who dare to challenge British forces for torture in Iraq. French President François Hollande borrowed from the National Front playbook to try to make depriving French-born dual citizens of their nationality a central part of his counterterrorism policy, an initiative he later abandoned and said he regretted. The Dutch government supports restrictions on face veils for Muslim women. Many European leaders now back the call of Hungary's Prime Minister Viktor Orbán to close Europe's borders, leaving refugees in the lurch. Such mimicry of the populists only reinforces and legitimizes the politicians attacking human rights values.

A similar trend can be found outside the West. Indeed, the rise of Western populists seems to have emboldened several leaders to intensify their flouting of human rights. The Kremlin, for example, has eagerly defended President Vladimir Putin's authoritarian rule as no worse than the West's increasingly troubled human rights record. China's Xi Jinping, like Putin, has pursued the toughest crackdown on critical voices in two decades. President Recep Tayyip Erdoğan of Turkey took advantage of a coup attempt to crush opposition voices. President Abdel Fattah al-Sisi of Egypt intensified the crackdown begun after his own coup. President Rodrigo Duterte of the Philippines has openly called for summary executions of suspected drug dealers and users—and even of human rights activists who defend them. Prime Minister Narendra Modi of India tried to shut down critical civic groups as he closed his eyes to intimidation and hate crimes by Hindu nationalist groups against religious and ethnic minorities.

Meanwhile, confident that there is little to fear in the West's occasional protests, Syrian President Bashir al-Assad, backed by Russia, Iran, and Lebanon's Hezbollah, has shredded the international laws of war, ruthlessly attacking civilians in opposition-held parts of the country including eastern Aleppo. Several African leaders, feeling vulnerable to domestic or international prosecution themselves, have harshly criticized the International Criminal Court and, in three cases, announced their intention to withdraw from it.

To counter these trends, a broad reaffirmation of human rights is urgently needed. The rise of the populists should certainly lead to some soul-searching among mainstream politicians, but not to an abandonment of first principles, by officials or the public. Governments committed to respecting human rights serve their people better by being more likely to avoid the corruption, self-aggrandizing, and arbitrariness that so often accompany autocratic rule. Governments founded on human rights are better placed to hear their citizens and recognize and address their problems. And governments that respect human rights are more easily replaced when people become unhappy with their rule.

But if the appeal of the strongman and the voices of intolerance prevail, the world risks entering a dark era. We should never underestimate the tendency of demagogues who sacrifice the rights of others in our name today to jettison our rights tomorrow when their real priority—retaining power—is in jeopardy.

Trump's Dangerous Rhetoric

Donald Trump's successful campaign for the US presidency was a vivid illustration of this politics of intolerance. Sometimes overtly, sometimes through code and indirection, he spoke to many Americans' discontent with economic stagnation and an increasingly multicultural society in a way that breached basic principles of dignity and equality. He stereotyped migrants, vilified refugees, attacked a judge for his Mexican ancestry, mocked a journalist with disabilities, dismissed multiple allegations of sexual assault, and pledged to roll back women's ability to control their own fertility.

To make matters worse, there was also a practical emptiness to much of his rhetoric. For example, a large part of his campaign was built around attacking trade deals and the global economy, but he also scapegoated undocumented migrants as responsible for stealing American jobs. Yet the mass deportation of migrants that he threatened, including of many with established ties in the United States and a record of contributing productively to the economy, will do nothing to bring back long-lost manufacturing jobs. US job growth continues to rise, but to the extent there is economic stagnation for some, it can hardly be blamed on un-documented migrants whose net numbers have not changed significantly in re-cent years and who are often willing to perform jobs that most US citizens will not.

Candidate Trump's plan for confronting terrorism by Muslims was equally futile—even counterproductive—as he demonized the very Muslim communities whose cooperation is important for identifying tomorrow's plots. He portrayed refugees as security risks even though they are subjected to far more thorough vetting than the vastly larger number of people entering the US for business, education, or tourism. Trump also showed no willingness to limit overbroad measures such as mass surveillance, an enormous invasion of privacy that has proven no more effective than judicially supervised, targeted surveillance.

Trump even toyed with reintroducing torture such as waterboarding, apparently oblivious to the bonanza for terrorist recruiters provided by President George W. Bush's "enhanced interrogation techniques." His belated post-election discov-ery of torture's ineffectiveness after a conversation with the general he later nominated to head the Department of Defense offers little solace because he si-multaneously declared a willingness nonetheless to order torture "if that's what the American people want." He, presumably, would be the privileged interpreter of that desire, while ignoring the laws and treaties that prohibit inflicting such brutality and pain regardless of the circumstances.

The Populist Wave in Europe

In Europe, a similar populism sought to blame economic stagnation on migra-tion, both to and within the European Union. Yet those who hoped to stop migra-tion by voting for Brexit—perhaps the most prominent illustration of this trend—risk making Britain worse off economically.

Throughout the European continent, officials and politicians harken back to dis-tant, even fanciful, times of perceived national ethnic purity, despite established immigrant communities in most countries that are there to stay and whose integration as productive members of society is undermined by this hostility from above. There is tragic irony in the anti-refugee policies of some leaders, such as Hungary's Orbán: Europe welcomed Hungarian refugees from Soviet repression but today Orbán's government does everything it can to make life miserable for the latest people fleeing war and persecution.

No government is obliged to admit everyone who comes knocking at its nation's doors. But international law limits what can be done to control migration. People seeking asylum must be given a fair hearing and, if their claims are found valid, a refuge. No one should be returned to war, persecution, or torture. With narrow exceptions, immigrants who have spent many years in a country or developed family ties should be given a route to legal status. Detention should not be arbitrary, and deportation procedures must afford due process.

With those caveats, governments can bar and send home economic migrants.

Yet contrary to the appeals of the populists, immigrant communities living lawfully in a country should have their rights fully respected. No one should face discrimination in housing, education, or employment. Everyone, regardless of legal status, is entitled to protection by the police and fairness within the justice system.

Governments should invest to help immigrants to integrate and fully participate in society. Public officials in particular have a duty to reject the hatred and intolerance of populists and affirm their faith in independent and impartial courts tasked with upholding rights. Those are the best ways to ensure that, even as nations become more diverse, they maintain the democratic traditions that historically have proved the best route to prosperity.

Particularly in Europe, some politicians justify hostility toward immigrants—especially Muslims—by suggesting that these communities want to replicate the suppression of women or gays and lesbians in certain of their home countries. But the proper response to these repressive practices is to reject them—they are the reason many immigrants have fled—and to ensure that all members of society respect the rights of all others. The answer is not to reject the rights of one segment of the population—in the current climate, typically Muslims—in the name of protecting the rights of others. Such selectivity in the application of rights undermines the universality of rights that is their essence.

Rising Authoritarianism in Turkey and Egypt

Erdoğan's increasingly dictatorial rule in Turkey illustrates the dangers of a leader trampling on rights in the name of the majority. For several years, he has shown diminishing tolerance for those who would challenge his plans, whether to build over a park in central Istanbul or to amend the constitution to permit an executive presidency.

In the past year, Erdoğan and his Justice and Development Party used a coup attempt and its hundreds of victims as an opening to crack down not only on the plotters he alleged had been associated with the exiled cleric Fethullah Gülen but also on tens of thousands of others deemed to be his followers. A declared state of emergency became an opportunity to turn on other perceived critics as well, closing down much of the independent media and civil society groups. In addition, in the name of pursuing the Kurdistan Workers' Party, or PKK, the government jailed the leaders and parliamentarians of the main pro-Kurdish party in Parliament and removed its local mayors.

There was broad cross-party support for Erdoğan's government in the wake of the coup, given the collective sigh of relief that many in Turkey felt after the attempt failed. But with the precedent of repression established, and the independence of the courts and other institutions of law decimated, there was nothing to stand in the way of Erdoğan's widening crackdown. A firm and timely response from Western leaders might have been expected, but other interests, whether curtailing the flow of refugees to Europe or fighting the self-described Islamic State, or ISIS, often stood in the way.

Egypt under the Sisi government underwent a similar evolution. Unhappy with the brief rule of the Muslim Brotherhood under President Mohamed Morsy, many Egyptians welcomed the military coup that Sisi led in 2013. But he has proceeded to rule far more repressively than even the long dictatorship of President Hosni Mubarak that was overthrown during the Arab Spring. For example, Sisi oversaw the killing of at least 817 Muslim Brotherhood protesters in a single day in August 2013—one of the largest massacres of protesters in modern times.

Many Egyptians assumed that only Islamists would be targeted, but Sisi has overseen the radical closing of political space, with human rights groups, independent media, and opposition political parties all shut, and tens of thousands of prisoners held, often after torture and with little if any judicial process.

The Shallow Appeal of the Strongman

The rising tide of populism in the name of a perceived majority has paralleled a new infatuation with strongman rule that was apparent particularly prominently during the US presidential election campaign. If all that matters are the declared interests of the majority, the thinking seems to go, why not embrace the autocrat who shows no qualms about asserting his "majoritarian" vision—self-serving as it may be—and subjugating those who disagree.

But the populist-fueled passions of the moment tend to obscure the longer-term dangers to a society of strongman rule. Putin, for instance, has presided over a weakening Russian economy plagued by massive crony corruption and a failure to diversify when oil prices were high, leaving it vulnerable to the decline that followed. Fearful that popular discontent of the sort seen on the streets of Moscow and several other large cities beginning in 2011 might revive and spread, Putin has sought to preempt it, introducing draconian restrictions on assembly and expression, setting out new, unprecedented sanctions for online dissent, and crippling civil society groups.

The Kremlin bolstered Putin's autocracy and boosted his dwindling approval ratings by mobilizing public nationalism in support of Russia's occupation of Crimea, which triggered European Union sanctions and only deepened economic decline. In Syria, his military backing of Assad's slaughter of civilians, with Russian bombers joining in, made the lifting of those sanctions, as a political matter, all the more remote. Until now, the Kremlin's skilled propagandists have tried to justify increasing economic hardship by claiming the need to counter alleged efforts by the West to weaken Russia. However, as the economy deteriorates further, it gets harder for Russian apologists to sell that message to the Russian public.

China's President Xi has embarked on a similar path of repression. China enjoyed remarkable economic growth as earlier leaders freed the Chinese people economically from the whims of Communist Party rule that had brought the disastrous Great Leap Forward and Cultural Revolution. But economic liberalization was not accompanied by political reform, which was left stillborn in the crushing of the 1989 Tiananmen Square democracy movement. Ensuing governments made economic decisions guided mostly by the party's desire to sustain growth at any cost in order to keep popular discontent under wraps. Corruption flourished while social inequity soared and the environment deteriorated.

Worried as well that popular discontent would rise as economic growth slowed, Xi, too, has embarked on the most intense crackdown since the Tiananmen era, leaving his government even less accountable. Despite anointing himself with a lengthening list of leadership titles, this strongman looks increasingly fearful, while not delivering on the Chinese people's demands for cleaner air, safer food, a just judicial system, and an accountable government.

Similar tendencies have characterized other autocrats' rule. The Bolivarian revolution in Venezuela, initiated by the late President Hugo Chávez and now stewarded by his successor, Nicolás Maduro, has become an economic disaster for the worst-off segments of society whom it ostensibly serves. Their reward has been hyperinflation, severe food and medicine shortages, and a nation with the largest proven oil reserves on the planet reduced to penury. The government has also launched military and police raids in immigrant and low-income communities that led to widespread allegations of abuse, including extrajudicial executions, arbitrary deportations, evictions, and destruction of homes.

Meanwhile, President Maduro, who controls the judiciary, deployed the intelligence services to arbitrarily detain and prosecute opposition politicians and ordinary critics, undermined the ability of the opposition majority in the National Assembly to legislate, and used his allies at the electoral authority to obstruct a recall referendum.

Indeed, there is a long history of autocrats delivering results for themselves but not their people. Even supposed models of authoritarian development like Ethiopia and Rwanda are plagued upon closer examination by government-imposed suffering. The Ethiopian government forced rural farmers and pastoralists into service-deprived villages to make room for agricultural megaprojects. The Rwandan government rounded up street vendors and beggars and beat them in filthy detention centers in the name of clean streets. Central Asia is filled with strongmen whose countries have stagnated under enduring Soviet-style rule. Even relatively vibrant countries in Southeast Asia now see their economic progress put at risk by the stultifying rule of the Thai military junta and the corruption-heavy government of Malaysian Prime Minister Najib Razak.

Civic Groups and the International Criminal Court Under Attack

In Africa, some of the most alarming attacks on human rights protections stem from strongmen who, refusing to transfer power peacefully, curb criticism through violence and legislation. A disconcerting number of African leaders have removed or extended term limits—the so-called constitutional coup—while others have launched violent crackdowns to suppress opposition and public protests over flawed or unfair elections. Teodoro Obiang Nguema Mbasogo of Equatorial Guinea, Yoweri Museveni of Uganda, and Robert Mugabe of Zimbabwe—each in power for more than 30 years—have amended their nations' constitutions to remain in office.

In recent years, the wave of presidents seeking additional terms sometimes succeeded through suppression of any opposition, as in Rwanda, or through violent repression of protests, as in Burundi and the Democratic Republic of Congo. Many of these governments used similar tools to restrict civil society groups and independent media, cut access to social media and the internet, and shut down political opposition. The attacks on civic groups have targeted foremost their funding—Ethiopia was a leader in this tactic—as governments that actively solicit foreign aid, trade, and investment suddenly balk at civic groups seeking contributions from abroad.

This backdrop of strongmen refusing to relinquish power occasionally intersects with concern over potential prosecution for crimes committed while in office. Burundian President Pierre Nkurunziza was the first to announce plans to withdraw from the International Criminal Court (ICC), because violent repression under his rule had made him a prime target for prosecution. He was soon joined by Gambia's President Yahya Jammeh, a notoriously brutal dictator, although a short time later he was voted out of power, and his elected successor, Adama Barrow, said he would reverse Jammeh's decision to leave the court. South Africa had long been an African leader on human rights and justice, but President Jacob

Duterte's encouragement of summary executions could fall under her jurision.

ICC, with its mandate to deliver justice for the world's worst crimes when na-al courts fail, will inevitably rub up against powerful political interests op-ed to accountability. It needs countervailing political and practical stance from supporters to succeed.

acks on Civilians in Syria

a represents perhaps the deadliest threat to rights standards. There is no e fundamental wartime rule than the prohibition against attacking civilians. Assad's military strategy has been to fire deliberately and indiscriminately at ians who live in areas of the country held by the armed opposition, as well as ian structures there, such as hospitals.

devastating aerial bombing including "barrel bombs," cluster munitions, ery barrages, and occasional chemical weapons, Assad has laid waste to stretches of Syria's cities, with the aim of depopulating them to make it ler for opposition forces to operate there. That strategy has been supple-ted by deadly sieges designed to starve the civilian population into surren-

e September 2015, despite these blatant war crimes, Assad has been joined ussian forces that have substantially reinforced his firepower but have not red his strategy. Indeed, the strategy looks remarkably similar to the one d by the Kremlin to devastate Chechnya's capital, Grozny, in 1999 and 2000, n effort to crush an armed rebellion there.

se war-crime attacks on civilians, committed with little global effort to bring authors to justice, are the primary reason why so many Syrians have been laced. Half the population has been forced from its home, and some 4.8 mil-have fled for neighboring countries, mostly Lebanon, Turkey, and Jordan, some 1 million moving on to Europe. Yet when it comes to Syria, the West re-ns focused primarily on ISIS. ISIS is responsible for unspeakable atrocities, it represents a threat well beyond its haven in Syria and Iraq, but its civilian in Syria is vastly exceeded by Assad's. Local sources estimate that Assad's

Zuma started the process to withdraw from the ICC as he was
corruption allegations and an embarrassing domestic legal c
sion to flout a court order by letting Sudan's President Omar
country rather than answer ICC charges for genocide and crin
ity. Meanwhile, Kenya's President Uhuru Kenyatta, whose ICC
dropped amid pressure on witnesses and government obstru
cution's investigation, fueled attacks on the ICC by the Africa

That these few African leaders do not speak for all Africans w
civic groups across the continent that reaffirmed their suppo
were backed by such states as Nigeria, Tanzania, Senegal, ar
Africans saw through the fallacious claim that the ICC, led by
prosecutor who is fighting to end the impunity that has cause
people to suffer atrocities without recourse, is somehow anti

The ICC, which through 2015 had focused its investigations o
tims, is challenged by the failure of powerful states, including
China, and Russia, to have joined the court. As of November :
open formal investigations in several important non-African s
had under preliminary examination, such as those implicatin
unprosecuted torture in Afghanistan or Israeli officials for the
transferring Israelis to settlements in the occupied West Bank

If the opponents of the court really want equitable justice, the
forts to encourage completion of these investigations, or to p
China to stop using their veto at the UN Security Council to blo
over the atrocities being committed in Syria. Their silence on t
for justice reveals their main concern—undermining prospect:
home. That several African nations want to substitute an Afric
exempt sitting presidents and other senior officials speaks vo

The attacks on the ICC were not only in Africa, but they had in
est in impunity. Russia had never joined the court but deactiv:
a move of symbolic, not practical significance—after the ICC p
an investigation into crimes allegedly committed during the 2
sia conflict and placed the situation in Ukraine under examina
President Duterte dismissed the ICC as "useless" after its pro:

forces and his allies are responsible for some 90 percent of Syrian civilian deaths.

Because Assad's political survival today depends on Russia's military support, Putin has enormous potential leverage over his conduct. But there is no evidence that the Kremlin has used that leverage to stop the slaughter of civilians. On the contrary, Russian bombers have regularly joined in, as in the tragic case of Aleppo.

Yet the Obama administration in particular has been disappointingly reluctant to press Russia to use that leverage, focusing instead on Russia as a partner in peace talks—even though the negotiations have dragged on endlessly with little to show for the effort, while the attacks on civilians make the prospect of Syrian opposition forces coming to terms with the government even more remote.

Judging by his campaign rhetoric, President-elect Trump seems determined to increase this US focus on ISIS, and is even proposing to join with Putin and Assad in that effort, evidently ignoring how little of their energy has been directed to ISIS and the role their atrocities play as a driver of ISIS recruitment. Even if ISIS is ultimately defeated militarily, these atrocities could easily breed new extremist groups, just as similar atrocities helped to fuel the emergence of ISIS from the ashes of Al-Qaeda in Iraq.

The Need to Reaffirm Human Rights Values

What is needed in the face of this global assault on human rights is a vigorous reaffirmation and defense of the basic values underpinning these rights.

There are important roles for many to play. Civil society organizations, particularly groups that fight to uphold rights, need to protect civic space where it is threatened, build alliances across communities to show the common interest in human rights, and bridge North-South divides to join forces against autocrats who are clearly learning from each other.

Media outlets should help to highlight the dangerous trends underway, tempering their coverage of today's statements and conduct with analysis of the longer-term ramifications. They should also make a special effort to expose and rebut the propaganda and "fake news" that certain partisans generate.

Governments ostensibly committed to human rights must more regularly defend basic principles. That includes democracies in Latin America, Africa, and Asia that now regularly vote positively on country initiatives at the UN led by others but rarely take the lead, whether at the UN or in their direct relations with other countries.

Ultimately, responsibility lies with the public. The demagogues traffic in casuistry, building popular support by spinning false explanations and cheap solutions to genuine ills. The best antidote is for the public to demand a politics based on truth and the values on which rights-respecting democracy has been built. Populists thrive in a vacuum of opposition. A strong popular reaction, using every means available—civic groups, political parties, traditional and social media—is the best defense of the values that so many still cherish despite the problems they face.

Lies do not become truth just because propagated by an army of internet trolls or a legion of partisans. Echo chambers of falsehoods are not inevitable. Facts remain powerful, which is why autocrats go to such lengths to censor those who report inconvenient truths, especially about human rights abuse.

Values are fragile. Because the values of human rights depend foremost on the ability to empathize with others—to recognize the importance of treating others the way we would want to be treated—they are especially vulnerable to the demagogue's exclusionary appeal. A society's culture of respect for human rights needs regular tending, lest the fears of the moment sweep away the wisdom that built democratic rule.

When Exposing Abusers Is Not Enough
Strategies to Confront the Shameless

By Akshaya Kumar, *Deputy United Nations Director*

"I don't care about human rights," Rodrigo Duterte boasted in August 2016, shortly after becoming president of the Philippines. In just a few months since coming to power, Duterte's self-proclaimed anti-drug campaign has resulted in police and "unidentified gunmen" killing thousands of Filipinos, without any semblance of due process. Promising medals to those who join his effort, Duterte has compared himself to Hitler and declared that he would be "happy to slaughter" the more than 3 million Filipinos he describes as "drug addicts."

This kind of braggadocio makes it difficult to try to change Duterte's actions by simply showing how his tactics violate basic human rights. In this he is not alone. Groups like the Islamic State (ISIS), autocrats like Syria's Bashar al-Assad, and populists vying for political influence in Europe and the United States are distinguishable from one another in many important ways, but they all share a common feature with Duterte: a public embrace of policies that flout international human rights law.

"Naming and shaming," an important tool for human rights advocacy, works best if advocates can raise the reputational costs of problematic behavior by disclosing that their targets are breaking the rules or highlighting the devastating impact of their actions. But increasingly it seems that some actors are almost completely immune to this kind of pressure. The "shameless" do not seek to hide their abuses or the policies that underpin them, but instead flaunt them as electoral or recruitment tools.

This essay outlines strategies to challenge those actors by shifting the focus from them onto their networks of financial enablers and, for those implicated in violations in armed conflicts or security operations, their arms suppliers. By underscoring their enablers' complicity in abuses and seeking to impose punitive measures on these enablers directly, human rights advocates have a chance to affect the calculations of the shameless too. Some of those financing or arming abusers may be more vulnerable to being exposed publicly than their clients.

But since enabling alone can amount to a serious international crime or human rights abuse, advocates should also make clear that coercive tools like sanctions and punitive measures like prosecutions apply directly to enablers as well.

The Special Court for Sierra Leone, for example, convicted Liberian president Charles Taylor in 2012 for aiding and abetting the war crimes of a brutal rebel group in neighboring Sierra Leone. The court pointed to Taylor's role in providing arms and assistance to the abusive Revolutionary United Front (RUF) and his participation in the blood diamond trade, which helped to fund the RUF during Sierra Leone's armed conflict. More recently, US government lawyers weighing the risks of assisting the Saudi-led coalition in its aerial bombardment of Yemen, are reported to have considered the legal precedent set by the Taylor decision when evaluating their own role as enablers.

Of course, like all advocacy strategies, these tactics need to be calibrated to address the scale and nature of abuses being perpetrated and the degree to which enablers are complicit. There is no one-size-fits-all approach. But focusing on the networks of the complicit, instead of just frontline abusers or their commanders, offers an important vehicle to protect and promote rights.

"Naming and Shaming"

Human rights advocates are adept at leveraging shame to press for change. Once exposed, governments or corporations can become so ashamed to be in the spotlight they quickly switch tactics to avoid further criticism.

For example, within days of an October 2016 report on his government's role in the rape and sexual exploitation of women and girls displaced by Boko Haram, Nigeria's President Muhammadu Buhari ordered a special investigation into the allegations. Similarly, the Central African Republic government's June 2016 decision to suspend the director of an abusive police unit came after researchers documented his role in at least 18 unlawful executions.

Sometimes condemnation or abusers' fears of prosecution secure rights advocates a seat at the table to define how policy makers should remedy the situation. Extensive research on the use of child labor in mining, for example, has given advocates an opportunity to shape the due diligence guidance promulgated by the Organisation for Economic Co-operation and Development for responsible investment. In Japan, research on the harassment and bullying of youth based on their sexual orientation and gender identity laid the foundation for a push to revise the country's national curriculum to be more inclusive of the needs and perspectives of lesbian, gay, bisexual, and transgender students.

Counterintuitively, the energy that some abusive governments devote to silencing critics, even as they continue to commit abuses, also reveals that naming and shaming has power.

Bahraini human rights defender Nabeel Rajab, for example, faces up to 15 years in prison for his tweets about alleged torture in Jau prison and airstrikes by the Saudi-led coalition, of which Bahrain is part, in Yemen. And in June 2016, days after the United Nations added the Saudi-led coalition to its "list of shame" for attacking schools, and hospitals, and killing and maiming children in Yemen, Saudi Arabia and its Arab allies launched an unprecedented diplomatic campaign to get off the roster, including by threatening to stop funding key humanitarian programs. While UN Secretary-General Ban Ki-moon made this blackmail public, leaving the Saudi-led coalition with a diplomatic black eye, the campaign worked. Powerful abusers can often evade criticism, even when it is based on well-documented patterns of abuse.

More worrying is the fact that some abusers attempt to draw power from public attention to their abuses. When ISIS broadcasts its executions, it covers the faces of its fighters, but not their acts. This is not accidental. ISIS seems to have designed its fighters' rape of Yezidi women in Iraq and the brutality of its rule in Libya in part as a magnet for recruits. A recent UN report on ISIS concluded: "By publicizing its brutality, the so-called ISIS seeks to convey its authority over its areas of control, to show its strength to attract recruits and to threaten any [...] that challenge its ideology."

There are many other less egregious cases where the same principle applies. Australia's offshore detention processing centers for asylum seekers seem to be designed to be so inhumane that they dissuade others from seeking refuge on its shores.

In Hungary, Prime Minister Viktor Orbán is not shy of publicly advancing policies that violate basic norms. He emphasizes, "European identity is rooted in Christianity" and points to the so-called "right to decide that we do not want a large number of Muslim people." Orbán's government erected razor-wire fences and prosecuted asylum seekers who bypassed them. It purposely stoked anti-refugee sentiment by spending millions of taxpayers' money on a smear campaign to bolster a referendum to reject a binding EU duty to relocate asylum seekers to Hungary from overstretched Greece and Italy. These policies may appear to be aimed at keeping asylum seekers and migrants away but they also mobilize popular support for the government.

During his campaign for the US presidency, Donald Trump openly urged policies that would amount to war crimes under international humanitarian law. For example, he repeatedly lauded the benefits of waterboarding and "worse," dismissing those who disapprove of using such techniques as "too politically correct." When reminded that torture is illegal, Trump promised that he would work to change the law. Governing, of course, is different than campaigning. Following his election, Trump told "60 Minutes" and the *New York Times* that torture "is not going to make the kind of a difference that a lot of people are thinking."

Rhetoric like this is hugely problematic. Trump's focus on whether the tactic is effective misses the point. International law makes it clear that that no national emergency, however dire, ever justifies torture. Further, Trump's choice of retired Lt. Gen. Michael Flynn as his National Security Advisor demonstrates a disturbing disregard for human rights principles and the laws of war since, even when asked directly, Flynn did not repudiate proposals such as waterboarding that would constitute torture.

For many populist politicians, publicity of their tactics or condemnation as being abusive is not seen as something to avoid. Instead, it is viewed as an effective deterrence strategy and an electoral argument. These governments justify harsh policies that violate rights as necessary to counterterrorism or stem migration and dismiss rights groups' criticism by pointing to the broad-based popular support of their citizens. Indeed, leaders need followers and any comprehensive strategy to address the enablers of shameless leaders should consider how and why these messages resonate with voters, recruits and supporters.

Similarly, it is also worth considering the role of allied governments in offering shameless abusers political cover and protection from scrutiny at inter-governmental bodies, like the UN. Russia, for example, has used its power as a permanent member of the UN Security Council to cast five vetoes to shield the Assad government's crimes in Syria.

Confronting Enablers

Naming and shaming has limits when dealing with the shameless. But that does not mean that these actors are untouchable or unmovable. While condemnation in the press or public may not restrain them or change their calculations, these actors do not operate in a vacuum. In regions with effective regional human rights courts like the European Court of Human Rights, litigation can offer an important vehicle for redress. But in many other regions, to effectively confront the shameless, advocates must look beyond shining a spotlight on what abusers are doing wrong. Human rights groups need to shift some of their focus onto those who are enabling these shameless actors to continue that wrongdoing.

A dynamic whole-systems approach, which confronts enablers, is not uncharted territory. In 1997, advocates seeking to end the abuses of Joseph Kony's Lord's Resistance Army (LRA), an armed group founded in northern Uganda that also reveled in its own brutality, appealed to the government of neighboring Sudan to end its support for the group. In 2003, researchers connected the weapons being used in unlawful attacks by Liberians United for Reconciliation and Democracy (LURD) to neighboring Guinea. Pointing to these ties, which flouted a UN arms embargo on Liberia, Human Rights Watch called for a suspension of US military assistance to Guinea.

Efforts to challenge the Liberation Tigers of Tamil Elam's (LTTE) use of child soldiers did not stop at Sri Lanka's borders. In 2006, Human Rights Watch examined coercive practices the LTTE used to extract money from the Tamil diaspora in Canada. While urging the Canadian government to take steps to end that intimidation and extortion, the report also recommended that the diaspora itself seek to ensure that funds provided for humanitarian causes not be used to benefit the LTTE while it committed serious abuses.

This research strategy involved showing both that the tactics being used to extract money in Canada were abusive and that the funds themselves helped to further abuses back in Sri Lanka. The Canadian government and others subsequently prohibited LTTE fundraising on their soil. Almost a decade later, a Court of Appeals in The Hague found that five people who had raised millions of euros for the LTTE were part of a criminal organization with the intent of committing war crimes, including recruiting child soldiers. In this case, the enablers were not just exposed, they were also convicted for their role as a part of the broader "criminal organization."

Research in 2013 on abuses by armed groups in their offensive to take parts of Latakia province in Syria—dubbed "Operation to Liberate the Coast"—took this approach a step further. Researchers used social media postings to identify individuals who actively raised funds to support the operation. Unlike previous work on the LTTE, this research did not unearth any evidence of coercion or abusive tactics to extract money. Unlike the situation involving the LURD, there is no arms embargo on Syria. Nonetheless, by pointing to the abuses being conducted by groups financed by those donations, Human Rights Watch suggested restricting or blocking money transfers from Gulf residents to groups responsible for the operation. Noting that funders were potentially liable for the group's abuses if they continued to provide money after the operation's abusive tactics became public, this advocacy strategy emphasized that enablers were at risk of complicity.

Financiers of Abuses

Drawing on research into ISIS crimes in Libya, Human Rights Watch has called on the UN Security Council to impose sanctions, not just on ISIS and its members but also "those who intentionally finance or otherwise assist abuses." This recommendation is grounded in the idea that sanctions on those knowingly financing abuses might stop them from continuing to enable these atrocities.

Of course, even before human rights groups made this recommendation, global efforts to curb the spread of ISIS were already seeking to choke its financial networks. Similar tactics have been used to respond to North Korea and Iran's nuclear programs.

Some of these inter-government initiatives are motivated by policy considerations that go far beyond the scope of human rights organizations work and mandates. Others straddle both arenas. The UN Security Council's many sanctions committee panels of experts have long held mandates that included a duty to research and identify those responsible for human rights abuses and war crimes, and to investigate arms sales, the illegal exploitation of natural resources and finances.

Human rights research typically does not extend to doing the painstaking financial forensic analysis required to identify those financiers and enablers. Venturing into this area will require harnessing the research expertise of accountants, arms experts, and others who specialize in mapping these networks, and learning from effective techniques that others are using to target networks that support shameless perpetrators. For example, The Sentry, a new initiative led by George Clooney and John Prendergast seeking to explore this space, follows the money and then makes policy recommendations that seek to alter the incentive structures that let enablers benefit financially and politically from abusive conflict and mass atrocities in east Africa.

But even if human rights groups can successfully harness this expertise, there is no guarantee of success. For example, the 2015-2016 ISIS attacks in France cost relatively little, just tens of thousands of euros. The Bastille Day attack on Nice cost Mohamed Lahouaiej-Bouhlel no more than €2,700. Still, in some cases, adopting a wider lens could provide important leverage for those seeking to change the behavior of shameless abusers.

One example of the potential opened by adopting this wider lens is recent work applying the United Nations Guiding Principles on Business and Human Rights to violations of international law in the West Bank. In its January 2016 report, Human Rights Watch concluded that it is impossible to do business in Israeli settlement communities without contributing to injustice and discrimination against Palestinians. Rights campaigners have long engaged with companies to ask them to voluntarily stop their activities in settlements and screen their supply chains for settlement-related activities. Based on a business and human rights analysis, Human Rights Watch was able to join them in arguing, for example, that by advertising, selling, and renting homes in settlements, the Israeli franchise of the real estate company RE/MAX contravenes best practices for corporate social responsibility and its responsibilities to uphold human rights.

One lesson from this kind of work is the importance of piercing the veil of plausible deniability. Human rights groups have an important role to play here by informing corporations of their possible complicity in distant abuses and war crimes.

In June 2015, the Swiss government prosecutor declined to move forward with a case brought by TRIAL International, an NGO that fights against impunity for international crimes, against a Swiss gold refiner for its role in processing conflict-affected gold from the Democratic Republic of Congo. Charges that the refiner had unlawfully abetted a pillaging Congolese armed group were dropped because the prosecution did not find evidence that the refinery knew enough about abuses happening at the gold's real point of origin. If evidence had been available that the refiner was notified about abuses and proceeded with business anyway, this kind of a defense, based on ignorance of complicity, would not have been valid.

The use of tools of coercion like targeted sanctions or asset freezes inevitably raises questions about unintended consequences, possible violations of due process, and mistaken identity. These risks are heightened because enforcement actions frequently occur without any kind of legal proceeding. There are also legitimate concerns about the proportionality of these measures, particularly considering the impact that these sanctions can have on family members and business partners of sanctioned individuals and entities.

Some sanctions mechanisms, like the ones established by the UN Security Council to combat terrorism, now include a means to appeal these measures, but the appeals process remains deeply flawed. Outside the counterterrorism realm, other sanctions regimes enforced by the UN Security Council do not even have those limited safeguards.

Additionally, fear of penalties for violating sanctions restrictions can lead international businesses to aggressive de-risking, where they simply stop doing business in "high risk" jurisdictions. This can unintentionally marginalize communities by limiting their access to financial services, preventing them from accessing critical remittances and atrophying their economic development. Oxfam has campaigned against the US government's restrictions, for example, on informal money transfers to Somalia, pointing to the impact it had on Somalis access to the remittances they rely on to meet their basic needs.

There is a human rights case for caution, but also one for thoughtful sanctions enforcement against enablers who aid and abet or are knowingly complicit in abuses. These measures can play a powerful role in influencing behavior and should always be reversible, giving enablers who focus on their bottom line a reason to stop supporting abusers. Finding ways to effectively freeze assets of enablers while not giving short shrift to due process and other fundamental rights is a challenge. However, it is one that human rights advocates should see as part of their work.

Arms Suppliers

Financial backers play a role in enabling the shameless, but for those conducting abusive military campaigns in Syria, South Sudan, or Yemen, arms suppliers remain among their most important enablers.

Although not impossible, it is much more difficult to continue to commit abuses on a large scale without the influx of new weapons and ammunition, either from abroad or through domestic production. Many human rights groups' mandates do not extend to stopping wars, which conflicts with a policy of neutrality in all armed conflicts. Instead, advocates push for hostilities, when they occur, to be conducted according to international humanitarian law.

Nonetheless, in places like Syria, rights advocates have argued the UN Security Council to impose arms embargoes to stop further sales and transfers of weapons to known abusers and war criminals. In 2016, following years of advocacy at the UN by arms control, humanitarian, and human rights groups, the Security Council considered a resolution that would have imposed an arms embargo and limit future weapons transfers to South Sudan. In the US, rights advocates campaigned against a US$1.2 billion arms sale to Saudi Arabia pushing the US Congress to debate and vote on the issue in September 2016. In the United Kingdom, the Campaign Against Arms Trade brought a lawsuit challenging the export licensing of weapons sales to Saudi Arabia in light of abuses being committed by the Saudi-led coalition in Yemen.

In November 2016, Turkey decided to gradually stop sales and production of fertilizer, despite its many legitimate uses in agriculture, due to concerns about terrorism. The decision came after brisk cross-border fertilizer sales from Turkey to Syria triggered speculation that ISIS was using the fertilizer to build explosives.

In places where police or law enforcement are responsible for widespread abuses, like the Philippines, Burundi, or Egypt, rights groups have worried that bilateral donor assistance, especially to the security sector, could be contributing to abuses. In March 2015, in the wake of heavy criticism from human rights groups for resuming weapons sales to the Sisi government in Egypt, the US decided to wind down its longstanding policy of allowing the Egyptians to buy US equipment on credit starting in FY2018.

In June 2016, the UN peacekeeping mission in the Central African Republic decided to stop accepting Burundian police due to concerns about "serious and ongoing" human rights violations by police back in Burundi. The Burundian government, like many developing countries, benefits from the salaries paid to their troops and participating in UN missions. In November 2016, the US State Department suspended a planned sale of 26,000 assault rifles to Duterte's Philippines following an objection raised by US Senator Ben Cardin about Duterte's abusive "war on drugs."

Since 2012, human rights groups have pointed to the role of Russia's state-owned arms dealer, Rosoboronexport, in selling the Syrian government weapons and urged responsible governments and corporate actors to avoid all new business dealings with the company. Campaigners have also asked arms fairs in Paris and London to stop featuring Rosoboronexport as an exhibitor.

Human rights groups have also directly challenged UK-based BAE Systems and the US-based Boeing and General Dynamics for their role in supplying Saudi Arabia with weapons that enable abuses in Yemen. BAE is currently engaged in discussions around a possible five-year contract to supply Saudi Arabia with Eurofighter Typhoon combat aircraft. The recent arms sale to Saudi Arabia approved by the US Congress included Abrams tanks produced by General Dynamics to replace tanks that had been damaged as a part of combat operations in Yemen.

In August 2016, Textron, the last company manufacturing cluster munitions in the United States, decided to end its involvement in that business. Shame created by the international ban on these weapons did not achieve this victory alone. Mounting concerns over civilian casualties from the use of the weapons by the Saudi-led coalition in Yemen were instrumental. The company's own explanation of its decision to stop producing cluster munitions came on the heels of the US government's May suspension of cluster munitions sales to Saudi Arabia and made clear that it had become "difficult to obtain approvals" needed for its sales to foreign customers.

But those more conventional tools are not the only paths to halt the flow of weapons into places where they may be used to commit further abuses. In 2012, the UK invoked EU sanctions to stop the delivery of repaired attack helicopters to the Syrian government by calling on the ship's British insurer, Standard Club, to revoke its coverage of the vessel. Although an insurance company is not the first entity that comes to mind when thinking about the arms trade, by looking beyond the usual suspects, the UK was able to turn the ship around before it could deliver its cargo. Pushing the insurance company to stop its coverage of the ship due to its cargo's problematic destination required treating them as a complicit enabler.

More recently, in October 2016, NATO's secretary general warned Spain against allowing Russian warships headed for Syria to refuel in its ports. By cautioning that the ships could "be used as a platform for more attacks against Aleppo and Syria, and thereby exacerbating the humanitarian catastrophe," NATO raised the reputational stakes for the Spanish government. Although Spain did not formally rescind the permission to dock, the Spanish chose to request a clarification from Russia about the nature of their mission in light of ongoing abuses in Syria. Shortly after, Malta made clear that it was unwilling to let Russian ships stop and refuel in their ports either.

Focusing on the Complicit

One of the more frustrating moments human rights advocates face is when perpetrators issue denials. The Sudanese minister who refuses to believe that his government's troops could use chemical weapons or rape hundreds of Darfuri women, or the Chinese Communist Party official who called the Tiananmen Square massacre in 1989 "much ado about nothing" are paradigmatic examples.

Blanket denials of months or even years of painstaking research are an everyday hazard of human rights work. But the shameless do not even bother with denials of this kind. They revel in being criticized. For human rights advocates and those who fight to civilize the conduct of war, these shameless actors pose an undeniable threat. Responding will require expanding the frontiers for human rights advocacy.

Human rights research typically focuses on those who have blood on their hands or should have used their power and authority to prevent injustice. But in situations where exposing abuses alone is not enough to effect change, advocates need to consistently adopt a wider lens and devote more energy to better understanding the expansive networks of financial backers and arms suppliers who enable abusers to continue their wrongdoing. That kind of analysis may require more specialized expertise that falls outside of human rights documentation. But it is worth the investment.

Overreach
How New Global Counterterrorism Measures Jeopardize Rights

By Letta Tayler,
Senior Researcher, Terrorism and Counterterrorism

News from the terrorism and counterterrorism fronts has been grim of late. Extremists—with or without the support of armed groups—have staged a horrific run of attacks on the general population. From a stadium in Paris to a café in Dhaka, from a hotel in Bamako to a beach in Côte d'Ivoire, from a government office party in California to a gay nightclub in Florida, and from airports in Brussels and Istanbul to a park in Lahore, suicide bombers and gunmen have killed hundreds of people and injured thousands more since late 2015. On the beachfront in Nice, one man ran down 85 Bastille Day celebrants with a cargo truck.

While the group Islamic State (also known as ISIS) was seemingly in retreat from Middle Eastern battlefields at time of writing, thousands of its foreign members have begun returning to their homes around the world, including both the disillusioned and those perhaps intent on carrying out attacks on their native soil. Additional ISIS members may have never left home to begin with. Other armed groups continue deadly strikes on civilians, including Al-Shabab in Somalia, and Al-Qaeda offshoots such as Al-Qaeda in the Islamic Maghreb. So-called lone wolves, sympathizers who do not have the direct backing of extremist armed groups, remain a potent threat.

In response to these immense challenges, dozens of governments are adopting an array of counterterrorism laws and measures that are separate from any planned or potential military operations. States have a responsibility to protect their populations from harm, but many of these recent national laws and measures are dangerously overbroad, vague, or intrusive. Rather than providing greater security, they risk violating basic rights, incarcerating the wrong people, and alienating minority populations that could play a positive role in helping to curtail terrorist attacks.

Two major developments are especially pertinent today: the proliferation of counterterrorism laws, many aimed at so-called Foreign Terrorist Fighters ("FTFs"); and declarations of states of emergency to combat a terrorist threat.

In many cases, governments have rushed through such measures in the immediate aftermath of tragic attacks with scant debate, which past experience has shown creates a serious risk that exceptional measures will become norms without sufficient public scrutiny or consideration of their long-term impact.

Those who could or do bear the brunt of overly broad or vague counterterrorism measures include not only terrorism suspects but also peaceful protesters, journalists, political opponents, human rights defenders, and members of ethnic or religious groups. In operations against Islamist armed groups, many of those who risk being wrongfully targeted or stigmatized are Muslims.

A rise in xenophobia and Islamophobia in Western countries, stoked in part by political figures capitalizing on both Islamist extremist attacks and a global refugee crisis that has displaced millions—particularly from predominantly Muslim countries such as Syria, Afghanistan, and Somalia—risks further conflating Muslims with armed extremists. Yet many victims of Islamist armed attacks are themselves Muslim and many refugees are fleeing the atrocities of extremist armed groups like ISIS. And as the United Nations special rapporteur on counterterrorism and human rights has noted, there is little if any evidence to suggest that refugees or asylum seekers pose a greater security threat than other groups.

Properly conceived and implemented, many of the recent counterterrorism measures could advance both security and fundamental values. Yet too often they are framed or implemented in ways that could erode the rule of law and human rights, including in democratic governments that should be at the vanguard of protecting them.

New "Foreign Terrorist Fighter" Measures

Counterterrorism laws and regulations in a growing number of countries include one or more "FTF" provisions. Human Rights Watch research shows that at least 47 countries have passed "FTF" laws since 2013—the largest wave of counterterrorism measures since the immediate aftermath of the attacks of September 11, 2001.

While many earlier counterterrorism laws contained similar and equally problematic provisions, such as expansions of police and intelligence powers without adequate legal safeguards, this second wave exacerbates the potential for abuse.

Countries that have enacted new counterterrorism laws or toughened pre-existing ones include Algeria, Austria, Australia, Bahrain, Belgium, Bosnia and Herzegovina, Brazil, Bulgaria, Cameroon, Canada, Chad, China, Denmark, Egypt, France, Germany, Indonesia, Ireland, Israel, Italy, Jordan, Kazakhstan, Kenya, Kosovo, Libya, Macedonia, Malaysia, Morocco, the Netherlands, New Zealand, Norway, Pakistan, Poland, Portugal, Russia, Saudi Arabia, Serbia, Spain, Sweden, Switzerland, Tajikistan, Tunisia, Uganda, the United Arab Emirates, the United Kingdom, the United States, and Uzbekistan.

Many countries are enacting these measures to comply with UN Security Council Resolution 2178 of 2014, which aims to stem the "acute and growing threat" posed by "FTFs" at home and abroad. Drafted primarily by the US, Resolution 2178 requires all UN member countries to prosecute as "serious criminal offenses" an array of acts, such as training or fighting with foreign terrorist groups, recruiting for these groups, or financing their operations.

The US estimated in October 2016 that 40,000 foreign fighters from over 120 countries had gone to Syria over the preceding five years, although the flow appears to have ebbed.

In a grave omission, Resolution 2178 does not limit the actions that governments may designate as "terrorism" or "terrorist"—terms for which no universal legal definition exists. This has left governments to craft dangerously open-ended laws and regulations that could be used to criminalize internationally recognized activities including peaceful protests, critical speech, and freedom of movement and religion. They also risk infringing on due process guarantees, the right to privacy, and even the right to life.

"FTF" measures can also put humanitarian assistance at risk by criminalizing impartial aid deliveries and life-saving medical treatment by foreign volunteers and nongovernmental organizations.

Overbroad and vague laws run counter to the basic principle in international human rights law that laws should be precisely drafted and understandable, both as a safeguard against their arbitrary use and so that people know what actions would constitute a crime.

A large number of foreigners joining groups such as ISIS are teenage children, including some who were forcibly recruited. How countries apply "FTF" laws in such cases is of particular concern. Recruitment of children under the age of 15 is a war crime. Governments should generally treat child soldiers foremost as victims who need rehabilitation and social reintegration, not detention or prosecution.

Adults whose actions abroad did not include direct involvement in armed violence also should be considered for reintegration services in lieu of criminal incarceration. Such programs can involve monitoring suspects, provided the measures are not overly invasive and are subject to effective review.

Overbroad or Vague Definitions of "Terrorism"

Countries including Australia, Brazil, Canada, China, Egypt, Israel, Saudi Arabia, and Tunisia have enacted counterterrorism laws criminalizing non-violent activities that fall far short of material support or participation, such as singing a banned group's anthem or participating in anti-government protests.

China's definition of "terrorism" as of January 2016 includes a term that can mean to "propagate" but also to "advocate," potentially creating a new tool to outlaw thought or speech.

Canada's counterterrorism law of 2015 creates a criminal offense of knowingly "advocating or promoting the commission of terrorism offences in general," without defining the term "terrorism offences in general."

The list of offenses in Israel's counterterrorism law of 2016 includes expressing support for a listed terrorist group: acts such as waving the group's flag, or singing its anthem are punishable by up to three years in prison.

Countries are also creating or stepping up use of pre-existing "glorification" of terrorism offenses regardless of whether such praise amounts to incitement. In February 2016, a Spanish court charged two puppeteers with "glorifying terrorism" for staging a carnival show that included violent scenes and a puppet holding a sign that referenced Al-Qaeda and the Basque armed group ETA. A judge dismissed the charges four months later, but the puppeteers were jailed for four days in the interim and barred from leaving the country.

In the wake of the Charlie Hebdo attacks, France has applied its "glorification" of terrorism penal code provision broadly, convicting 385 people in 2015. In at least four of the cases, prosecutors interrogated children, some as young 13, for referencing ISIS in social media or during altercations with police.

Travel Bans

Many "FTF" measures include imposing travel bans—often implemented through suspending passports and national identity cards—on people suspected of intending to travel abroad to join or train with groups the government considers to be foreign terrorist organizations. Suspensions generally range from six months to two years.

The United Kingdom restricts not only departures but also returns of citizens and residents suspected of terrorism-related travel if they refuse to participate in a deradicalization program. Tunisia and Egypt have enacted sweeping foreign travel bans on males under ages 35 and 40, respectively. Countries including Egypt and Kenya have used such travel bans to bar travel of opposition figures and academics, as well as civil society members invited to training workshops.

While travel bans may be warranted in certain cases, blanket bans risk violating the international right to leave or return to one's country and could harm the suspect's family members. Of particular concern is the fact that many countries do not require prior judicial approval to ban travel or suspend passports and identity cards.

Citizenship Revocation

Countries also are passing laws that can revoke citizenship of dual nationals convicted of terrorism-related offenses.

Australia's Allegiance Act of December 2015 allows immigration authorities to strip Australian citizenship from dual nationals as young as 14, without requiring a criminal conviction, if they believe the individual engaged in serious terrorism offenses abroad. Other countries that have passed citizen-stripping laws include Austria, Australia, Bahrain, Belgium, Canada, the Netherlands, and the UK.

International law affirms that everyone has a right to a nationality. While most countries only allow for revocation of citizenship where the individual in question has a second nationality, the UK allows for revocation of citizenship from naturalized British citizens who do not hold another nationality, creating a risk of statelessness. Bahrain has reportedly revoked the citizenship of more than 300 people since 2012, including civil society activists, journalists, and religious figures—many via a 2014 counterterrorism amendment that allows authorities to strip citizenship from Bahrainis who "cause harm to the state" or fail in their "duty of loyalty." This reportedly has rendered several of them stateless.

Expanded Police and Intelligence Powers

Belgium, Canada, China, France, Israel, Pakistan, Poland, Russia, and Tunisia are among countries that have expanded police or intelligence powers in terrorism-related cases, in many instances with insufficient oversight.

Canada's counterterrorism law of 2015 allows the Canadian Security Intelligence Service (CSIS) to disrupt activities if it deems them unlawful, and even to violate the country's Charter of Rights and Freedoms so long as it obtains a warrant in a secret hearing.

Poland's counterterrorism law of 2016 allows surveillance of foreigners for up to three months without a court order. It also empowers a local security force commander to order snipers to shoot to kill to prevent a rapid attack on human life or health or when rescuing a hostage when the country is at its highest threat level. While UN principles allow police to use lethal force as a last resort to save the lives of others, Poland's measure raises the concern that a commander may issue a kill order without having determined that there is an imminent threat to human life.

Since 2013, France has passed several laws that codify sweeping authority for digital surveillance on both a targeted and mass basis. Internet service providers may be forced to install "black boxes" on their networks to search all traffic for unspecified "suspicious" patterns. These laws do not impose adequate safeguards against abuse and often do not require prior judicial approval. Russia and China also have enacted sweeping surveillance laws.

The United States and United Kingdom continue to collect data on hundreds of millions of internet users worldwide every day, three years after US whistle-blower Edward Snowden first revealed these mass violations of privacy. Reforms in the US in 2015 were insufficient, as were the reforms of intelligence powers proposed in the UK at time of writing.

Preventive Detention and Control Orders

In tandem with measures banning suspected "FTFs" from travel abroad, countries including Australia, Canada, France, Libya, and the UK have enacted or continued to use preventive detention or "control" measures for terrorism suspects that severely restrict their movements at home.

Despite US President Barack Obama's pledge upon taking office in 2009 to close the US military prison at Guantanamo Bay, the United States at time of writing continued to indefinitely detain dozens of individuals there without charge.

Preventive detention and control measures limit people's liberty on the suspicion that they may intend to commit a criminal act in the future, rather than because they are suspected or found guilty of committing a crime in the past. These measures are imposed based on a lower threshold of evidence than would be required for a criminal conviction, and in some cases on intelligence material that may be difficult for the accused to challenge. While control orders may be permissible in exceptional, narrowly defined circumstances, such as clear evidence of a potential threat, their routine use violates international human rights law.

Control orders typically include curfews, extensive home confinement, forced domestic relocation, and restrictions on where targeted people can pray, whom they can visit, what websites they can access, and even what over-the-counter substances they can consume.

Lengthy Pre-Charge and Pretrial Detention

Terrorism suspects are increasingly subjected to pre-charge or pretrial detention periods that exceed international guidelines. In some cases, the detainee is initially held incommunicado. International standards require "prompt" judicial review of detention—generally within 48 hours—as longer periods increase the risk of torture and other ill-treatment.

Chad, Egypt, France, Malaysia, Poland, Saudi Arabia, Spain, and Tunisia are among countries with excessive pre-charge or pretrial detention periods. Chad allows pre-charge detention for 30 days, renewable twice. Malaysia's 2015 Prevention of Terrorism Act allows pretrial detention of up to two years, with indefinitely renewable two-year extensions.

Special Courts and Death Penalties

Another growing trend is the use of special courts or proceedings for terrorism suspects that flout international due process standards by holding closed sessions with little or no justification, and restricting suspects' rights to consult a lawyer, examine evidence against them, and question those who testify against them.

Egypt's courts have tried hundreds of suspected Islamists in mass trials in which lawyers said they were denied the right to make their case or question witnesses.

Chad, Egypt, Pakistan, Saudi Arabia, the United Arab Emirates, and the US combine proceedings for terrorism offenses with the death penalty. Pakistan and Saudi Arabia since late 2015 have each executed dozens of people on terrorism convictions, including after trials that fell far short of international due process standards. Chad in 2015 executed 10 men in one day after convicting them in secret proceedings. The United States continues to try detainees at Guantanamo in military commissions that do not meet international fair trial standards. Six of seven men currently charged face the death penalty.

"Countering Violent Extremism"

UN Security Council Resolution 2178 also requires that states "enhance efforts" aimed at "countering violent extremism" ("CVE")—sometimes referred to as "Preventing Violent Extremism ("PVE")—through educational, social, and other activities.

Implemented with sensitivity and respect for human rights, efforts to dissuade individuals from joining or supporting terrorist groups could be a welcome addition to counterterrorism efforts. However, Resolution 2178 lists "preventing radicalization" as an "essential element" of "CVE" without any requirement that the "radical" behavior involve violence or intended violence. This raises the specter of clampdowns on peaceful expression and association, including academic freedom and religious devotion.

In France following the Bastille Day attack in Nice, mayors along the Riviera used "CVE" as a justification to ban the "burkini"—burqa-inspired swimwear—arguing that it signified potential "affiliation with religious fundamentalism." A court overturned the ban, rejecting any link between the garment and national security threats, but the debate still rages.

The UK's long-standing "CVE" program, Prevent, has been criticized for its overbroad approach, which has included police surveillance of a predominantly Muslim neighborhood in a British city. In 2015, the UK imposed a duty on primary schools, universities, and healthcare providers to "prevent" violent extremism. Reports have emerged that schools and universities are casting suspicion on lawful activities, creating the risk of a chilling effect on academic freedom.

In the United States some "CVE" programs instruct social workers, teachers, mental health professionals, religious figures, and others to report on young people they believe are heading towards radicalization based on criteria such as "perceived sense of being treated unjustly," "expressions of hopelessness, futility," and "connection to group identity (race, nationality, religion, ethnicity)."

States of Emergency

Since late 2015, Egypt, Ethiopia, France, Mali, Tunisia, and Turkey have cited terrorism as a reason to enact or extend states of emergency. Some of these emergency measures vastly increase government powers to search, detain, and monitor individuals, to shut establishments such as meeting houses and places of worship, and to ban public gatherings or free speech.

International law allows restrictions on fundamental rights and freedoms during severe crises such as those that threaten the life of a nation. However, the restrictions must be temporary, non-discriminatory, and strictly limited in scope. Certain rights are non-derogable, including the rights to life; freedom from torture, inhuman, or degrading treatment; legality and equality before the law; and freedom of thought, conscience, and religion. Many measures under such states of emergency have violated these principles.

Ethiopia in October 2016 declared a sweeping, six-month state of emergency following government crackdowns in the restive Oromia region that killed at least 500 people in largely non-violent protests during the past year. The government called the protesters "terrorists" or said they were working with "terrorist groups abroad." At time of writing the government said 1,600 people had been arrested during the state of emergency—in addition to tens of thousands of others detained in regions where residents have protested government policies in the past year. Human Rights Watch received unconfirmed reports of unlawful killings, mass arrests, and looting of houses and businesses by security forces.

Mobile phone access to the internet was blocked and Addis Standard, one of Ethiopia's few remaining independent publications, stopped publishing its print edition due to state of emergency restrictions. Ethiopia also continued to detain scores of opposition leaders, journalists, and dissenters under its overbroad counterterrorism law of 2009.

In response to a coup attempt in July 2016, Turkish President Recep Tayyip Erdoğan at time of writing had imposed a state of emergency until January 2017 to quash what he described as the "Fethullahist Terrorist Organization (FETO)," in reference to supporters of the US-based cleric Fethullah Gülen, whom he has accused of masterminding the failed putsch. Erdoğan has used his emergency powers to detain more than 40,000 people, including soldiers, policemen, judges, prosecutors, journalists, and teachers, on suspicion of involvement in the coup or membership in FETO. Erdoğan's government also has used the emergency powers to crack down on Kurdish activists, opposition elected officials, and media outlets under the guise of countering terrorism.

The emergency powers also extend pre-charge police detention for terrorism suspects from 4 to 30 days and deny detainees access to counsel for 5 days, removing crucial safeguards against torture. Not surprisingly, allegations of torture and other ill-treatment of detainees surfaced following declaration of the emergency.

France's emergency law, activated after the Paris attacks in November 2015, was renewed until January 2017; a further extension seemed likely at time of writing. The law empowers police to raid homes and other premises, search luggage and vehicles, and seize data from computers and mobile phones, without prior approval from a judge. It allows the interior minister to place people under house arrest on vague accusations, such as being a "radical," also without prior judicial approval. Human Rights Watch has documented abusive or discriminatory searches and house arrests of Muslims under the state of emergency.

Tunisia has used its state of emergency, enacted in 2015 after a series of armed extremist attacks, to disperse apparently peaceful protests against a proposed law to grant impunity to former government officials for corruption. It also has confined at least 139 people to their homes, indefinitely and without charge, since November 2015, a Human Rights Watch investigation found. Police deliver the arrest orders orally rather than in writing, making it harder for the affected person to mount a court challenge.

Egypt has cited terrorism as reason to maintain a state of emergency in North Sinai that since 2014 has made it easier for the military and police to carry out arbitrary detentions, and thousands of mass evictions and home demolitions that violate international human rights law.

***

Targeted laws and prevention programs can be important tools to address the pressing and often transnational challenges that extremist armed groups pose. But the recent spate of sweeping counterterrorism measures worldwide suggests many governments have learned little from the corrosive "Global War on Terror" that the US launched after the September 11, 2001 attacks. While many countries now reference human rights in their counterterrorism initiatives, their laws and policies continue to invite overreach, and too many dispense with judicial review and other critical checks against abuse.

A key step toward reversing that trend is for UN member states to press the Security Council to limit what acts can be considered "terrorism" in mandates such as Resolution 2178, to ensure they are fully consistent with international human rights law, refugee law, and international humanitarian law (the laws of war). These definitions should, for example, exclude acts that lack the elements of criminal intent to cause death, serious bodily injury, or the taking of hostages in order to create a state of panic and provoke a government or third-party response. Regional bodies such as the European Union and the African Union should follow suit.

Governments, for their part, should promptly repeal or revise overly broad or vague "FTF" and CVE measures, and, when facing extraordinary threats that warrant declaration of an emergency, should limit the scope and duration of emergency powers to what is truly necessary to address the crisis. They should publicly call on other countries to do the same.

Governments need effective responses to attacks, but effective responses should not and do not have to come at the expense of basic human rights. Abusive responses are not only unlawful; they also backfire by alienating local populations at a time when governments should seek to unite societies against extremist armed threats.

The Internet is Not the Enemy
As Rights Move Online,
Human Rights Standards Move with Them

By Dinah PoKempner, *General Counsel*

We are at a difficult juncture in the protection of online speech and privacy, when states resist applying principles they have endorsed internationally to their own domestic legislation and practice. It is as if all road signs to freedom of speech and privacy pointed one way, yet governments insist on taking the wrong fork, telling the alarmed passengers it is for their own safety.

Divergence between what states endorse at the United Nations and what they do at home is hardly news, though governments do not seem self-conscious when it comes to restricting rights on the internet. They seem to sense that the internet is somehow different, perhaps more powerful than older media, and reflexively reach for greater limitation.

They are right that the internet gives individuals unprecedented ability to project their communications across borders and to access the world's information. But that does not necessarily justify sacrificing privacy and speech to create un-precedented police powers.

New technology has been empowering individuals—both for good and ill—and making the world smaller for many decades, even while international human rights law grew and flourished. Typewriters may be heading towards extinction, but rights seem more important than ever. And how governments protect them in the digital age will determine whether the internet will be a force that liberates or enchains us.

What States Say and What They Do

The bifurcation between existing norms and what states really do is most evident in the unfolding debate over surveillance.

Edward Snowden, a former US government contractor, put that debate into high gear in 2013 by leaking documents to media that showed the United States and its allies were engaging in massive, indiscriminate data collection on people in the US and abroad who had no connection to wrongdoing. With the disclosures came popular and government condemnations. The UN went into high gear, with General Assembly debates and resolutions, Human Rights Council resolutions, more expert reports, and even the creation of a new expert position on privacy. Around the world, people challenged surveillance in courts and legislatures debated them.

Yet in the ensuing years, few countries curtailed surveillance powers and many instead moved to cement into their laws powers similar to what the US was shown to wield.

In the US, some reforms gained traction, though they seem unlikely to significantly curtail the breathtaking scope of data collection and real-time monitoring. Congress revised the law used to justify collecting millions of call records with another only somewhat more constraining. President Barack Obama apologized for spying on allied heads of state, but the legal authorities that undergird overseas communications surveillance still permit collection for "foreign intelligence," a vague purpose that can easily justify sweeping communications interception, including from US persons caught incidentally in the dragnet.

The United Kingdom is adopting the troubling Investigative Powers Bill, which legalizes "bulk" surveillance practices of directly tapping into undersea cables that carry internet traffic, government hacking, and thematic warrants that allow intelligence services to designate broad targets without prior judicial approval.

France also moved to place surveillance practices on a legal footing in 2015, but with deeply flawed laws, rushed through in the wake of attacks. The UN Human Rights Committee, reviewing France's compliance with the International Covenant on Civil and Political Rights (ICCPR), concluded that the intelligence law of June 2015 "grants excessively large powers of very intrusive surveillance on the basis of broad and ill-defined aims, without prior judicial authorization and without an adequate and independent oversight mechanism." Most recently, the Conseil d'Etat ruled unconstitutional the law's regime of warrantless surveillance of wireless communications.

Russia also took a retrograde path, with legislative amendments in 2016 that require companies to retain the contents of all communications for six months, data about those communications for three years, and to store all their data within Russian territory. Companies must also provide "information necessary for decoding" digital communications, a provision that may mean backdoor access to encrypted material.

China, long a leader in censoring online speech and controlling access through a national firewall, adopted a cybersecurity law in 2016 that would require companies to censor and restrict online anonymity, store user data in China, and monitor and report undefined "network security incidents," deepening fears of increased surveillance.

Even Brazil and Mexico, both critics of the mass surveillance programs of the US National Security Agency (NSA) and strong proponents of privacy at the UN, entertained cybercrime bills in 2016 that would have widened data retention requirements and constricted access to information and free speech. Germany, a leading proponent of data protection laws, approved a law in October 2016 that authorized mass untargeted surveillance of non-citizens, earning the criticism of three different UN rights experts and a legal challenge to its constitutionality.

Little wonder the UN expert on freedom of expression lamented, "One of the most disappointing aspects of the current situation … is that many States with strong histories of support for freedom of expression—in law and in their societies—have considered measures liable to abuse."

Three Ways in which the Internet is Distinctive (and How that Scares Us)

This schizophrenic state of affairs, where states pledge allegiance to international human rights online and then legislate to curtail them, reflects a deeper split in perceptions of the internet, its promise and its peril.

There was a time when discussion of the internet and human rights rang full of utopian aspiration—the internet would set speech free, remove censoring intermediaries, enable social organizing on a scale never known. To some extent, this promise came true; activists who were stifled under authoritarian governments that suppressed organizing, protest, or an independent press could move their causes forward online. Knowledge once cabined in libraries, universities, or other networks of the elite became available to remote users in villages, fields, or slums. Minds could meet in that new location, "cyberspace," making global-ized creation and impact within the reach of ordinary people.

The backlash from authorities who found this threatening was not long in com-ing. Dissidents and critics of illiberal governments who tried to avoid suppres-sion by going online soon found themselves monitored, publicly shamed or arrested, a trend in full force today in Turkey, Egypt, Vietnam, Saudi Arabia, China, or Russia's Chechen Republic. Some governments, like Egypt, have even sought harsher penalties for online speech crimes than their offline counter-parts.

When activists (as well as criminals) have tried to shield themselves through anonymity or encryption, governments have issued orders or proposed laws to force tech companies to hand over their users' data and decode communica-tions. National firewalls, wholesale blocking of social media, and even internet shutdowns are used by repressive governments in efforts to control online activ-ity.

But even in non-authoritarian settings, there is ambivalence about the internet's power of social mobilization. People may admire how democracy activists can organize online, yet worry when the Islamic State (ISIS) recruits remotely. They may applaud those who crowd source evidence of war crimes, but condemn "trolls" who expose, threaten, or harrow their victims.

To probe this growing ambivalence over the power of online speech, it is useful to consider what differentiates it from offline communication. At least three char-acteristics are distinctive: online speech can be more disinhibited—that is, less inhibiting—than speech in the real world; it persists and can be accessed on the internet for a long time unless deliberately removed; and it is inherently trans-border, both in the way it travels and is accessed. Each of these attributes can make online speech powerful. And each complicates the task of regulation.

Disinhibition in online speech is a much studied but not well-understood phe-nomenon. It accounts for greater responsiveness and "sharing" when we interact with social media, and also for greater informality, incivility and invective. While it is common to attribute disinhibition to anonymity, disinhibition is characteris-tic of attributed online speech as well, and various studies cite many factors that contribute to this quality, including the rapidity and impersonality of a medium lacking nonverbal cues and interaction. In fact, being identified (so peers can see you as the nastiest troll on the site) may worsen behavior. This complexity suggests that real-name policies are not necessarily a sure-fire way to better behavior. They are, however, a favorite requirement of authoritarian regimes that would like to identify dissenters so they can be silenced.

The persistence of online information advances all types of research and news gathering, long after first reports. Real-time fact-checking in political contests, for example, can add immeasurably to informed decision-making in elections. But malicious or false speech also persists, and even when the subject succeeds in having it retracted in one jurisdiction, it may be mirrored or available from another.

The European Court of Justice considered this problem in the 2014 Costeja judgment, and pronounced that search engines like Google had an obligation to delink to data that is "inaccurate, inadequate, irrelevant or excessive"—a standard that potentially allows for much more sweeping restrictions on public access to information than allowed under international human right standards or some national constitutions. A European view of what is "irrelevant" or "excessive" information, for example, might strike a US court as a violation of the First Amendment guarantees of freedom of speech; the information might well still be accessible in the US even if delinked from search results in Europe.

The persistence of information on the web and its global accessibility has prompted courts in Canada and France to issue orders to Google that would require the web index to delist content the world over, and not just within the court's home jurisdiction. But if Canada and France prevail, global injunctions against content or links to content can be expected to become de rigeur, including from countries that routinely punish dissent. Would more rights-respecting countries enforce such orders?

We may not even get to that question. Such injunctions would place the burden of challenge on the speaker, not on the party that wishes to suppress the speech. People who place controversial material on the internet may lack the means to challenge such orders in every country. The force of global injunctions is their chilling effect. They might reduce the amount of content some countries consider unlawful, but they might also purge the internet of much art, hetero-doxy, criticism, and debate.

Finally, the trans-border accessibility and routing of online communications em-powers those far from the social and commercial hubs where information con-centrates, be they villagers, or rebels in the hinterlands. Governments have sought to control data by requiring it be kept within their borders to facilitate surveillance, or by using firewalls to keep undesirable content out. This may seem appealing in the context of limiting the influence of terrorists, intellectual property thieves, or those who shame and expose their victims. It is less attrac-tive when considered from the point of view of dissenting authors and activists who throw their thoughts over the firewall, hoping they will live and be accessi-ble elsewhere on the net.

The combination of these attributes—prolific, often unguarded sharing, accessi-ble through time and across borders—makes possible not only scientific, artistic or even criminal collaborations as never before, but also frightening potential for comprehensive social profiling and persecution. Data mining, aggregation, and retention are increasingly in the human rights spotlight as new and potent dan-gers to freedom. This led prominent internet archivist Brewster Kahle to remark, "Edward Snowden showed we've inadvertently built the world's largest surveil-lance network with the web."

The new problems raised by the distinctive features of online speech seem to re-quire doubling down on privacy and freedom of speech, rather than giving up on them. The internet is not some unusual and threatening medium, but increas-ingly the ordinary means of transmitting every type of speech and information in our world. It is not a state of exception, and the baseline rule in human rights law is that full observance of rights such as free expression and privacy is the norm; it is limitations that must be exceptional.

When Technology Changes, Human Rights Standards Still Fit

Back in 1948, the drafters of the Universal Declaration of Human Rights had the foresight to insulate one of the most fundamental rights from obsolescence. Arti-cle 19 of this foundational UN instrument provides:

Everyone has the right to freedom of opinion and expression; this right includes freedom to hold opinions without interference and to seek, receive and impart information and ideas through any media and regardless of frontiers (emphasis added).

Since then, the principle that all rights that apply offline apply online as well has been reiterated by the Human Rights Council and the General Assembly. While new media pose new challenges, there is little support for the view that somehow the advent of the internet has made human rights less important, or subject to entirely different standards.

The basic principles for evaluating whether restrictions on free expression, access to information, association, and privacy are consistent with international human rights law are well-established and reflected in many regional and domestic legal systems. The Human Rights Committee, the UN expert body that interprets the ICCPR, in 2004 summarized the basic framework this way:

States must demonstrate their necessity and only take such measures as are proportionate to the pursuance of legitimate aims in order to ensure continuous and effective protection of Covenant rights. In no case may the restrictions be applied or invoked in a manner that would impair the essence of a Covenant right.

Consider the test of "necessary" to a "legitimate aim," that is, an aim specified in the ICCPR, such as national security, public order, or the rights of others. The state bears the burden of showing "a direct and immediate connection" between the right to be restricted and the threat. It would not be enough, for example, for personal information to be collected simply because it might be, at some undefined point in the future, useful in advancing a variety of national interests.

In the context of the most common justification for electronic surveillance, the special rapporteur stated that "States often treat national security and public order as a label to legitimate any restriction." Such interests are understood in human rights law to represent the public's interest, rather than the interest of a particular government or elite. So "national security" should be seen as public interests in maintaining national independence or territorial integrity, not some individual's or group's concern about staying in power or maintaining an edge over competitors. Invidious discrimination is never in the public's interest, and cannot be the basis of a valid limitation on rights, so surveillance measures that are directed at religious, ethnic, or national groups cannot be justified as "necessary" for "public security."

Dragnet collection and prolonged retention of masses of irrelevant personal data would normally be difficult to justify as "necessary" in the sense of directly connected to a specific threat to national security or public order. But, as noted above, international human rights law requires that laws restricting speech be "proportionate" as well as necessary, and it is even harder to show that sweeping surveillance measures meet that test.

To be proportionate, a limitation on rights must be the least restrictive means to protect the public interest that motivates the restriction. It is hard to imagine how regularly invading everyone's privacy, and monitoring everyone's communications could be proportionate to a specific threat, even the threat that a particular terrorist movement poses. Indeed, such practices would seem to "impair the essence of the right."

The special attributes of the internet can make old problems—whether terrorism, threatening speech, discrimination against minorities, or crime prevention—seem more daunting and in need of new solutions. But our obligation—if we think rights have meaning—is to still subject every solution that limits rights to rigorous consideration of necessity and proportionality.

Applying the Standards to Today's Challenges

Law enforcement figures have argued that to identify terrorists and prevent attacks, a large "haystack" of data must be assembled to search. This presumes that more data will yield more relevant data to be mined, producing more "needles" constituting true threats. This may work for problems where instances are abundant, and the risk factors are relatively easy to identify.

But terrorists and terror plots are relatively rare and quite varied in profile, motivation, and details. The danger is that false leads can overwhelm the system and divert resources from more productive actions, such as developing reliable networks of informants or mining a suspect's past criminal history for clues.

As security expert Bruce Schneier said in his recent book, Data and Goliath, "there is no scientific rationale for believing that adding irrelevant data about innocent people makes it easier to find a terrorist attack, and lots of evidence that it does not." Even the NSA has urged its personnel to "store less of the wrong data." The more irrelevant data is added to the "haystack," the harder it is to justify the collection program as proportionate. But when mass collection also leads to mass data retention, further questions arise. One is whether data collected for one purpose (say, foreign intelligence) can be later used for another (say, enforcement of drug laws).

Unless each use depends on an independent evaluation of necessity and proportionality, repurposing data cannot be sure to comply with human rights law. And simply retaining data for some hypothetical future use is difficult to justify as "necessary." As Norway's Supreme Court recently held in a case considering seizure of documentary maker's footage, the possibility that the material may contain "valuable clues" to the prevention of terrorism recruitment was not enough to make its disclosure "necessary."

Another problem is the use of biased data for predictive purposes. Corporations have long been aggregating and analyzing data on consumers to predict what advertisements, news, or job listings most suit their profile. Data protection law can offer some protection against this profiling by making what corporations do with your data more transparent, and enabling you to correct data or refuse to provide it.

But when governments use data analysis to predict where police should be directed, or whether a defendant with a particular profile is likely to recidivate, there is often little transparency as to what data was used to train the algorithm—and biased data produces biased results. Law enforcement practices all too often reflect bias, as Human Rights Watch has shown with relation to police profiling of immigrants and Muslims and racial disparities in arrest and incarceration in the US, abusive identity checks of Muslims in France, or police discrimination against transgender people in Sri Lanka. Algorithms that are trained on biased data can reinforce and even exaggerate biased profiles and policies, in a horrible self-confirming loop.

Surveillance, even when justified, involves limiting rights, but bias can turn this into discrimination or even persecution. When a person's faith, ethnicity, sexual orientation, or race are taken as indicators of potential criminality—by police or by the algorithm—their rights are violated. Programs for "countering violent extremism" can fall into this trap when they focus as much on the expression of "extremist" beliefs or opinions as on any indicator of actual violence.

The UK's "Prevent" strategy, for example, defines its objective as countering "ideology"—that is to say, ideas—and defines "extremism" as "vocal or active opposition to fundamental British values." Schools, and thus teachers, are obliged to monitor children's online activity for signs of radicalization, and intervene with those who are "vulnerable." The program has drawn widespread criticism from teachers for stifling free expression in the classroom, and from many as stigmatizing and alienating precisely the segments of the community that law enforcement most needs help from in identifying threats.

Applying the principle of proportionality, we see the more a program limits rights for the many, the less likely it is to be the least intrusive means of protecting security. Indeed, pervasive rights intrusions themselves can worsen national security or public order by eroding trust in government and protection of minorities. A case in point are laws that undermine anonymity, like Russia's, or that require companies to somehow decode encryption, like China's. No doubt some criminals use these strategies to evade detection, but ordinary people use them as well, to evade persecution, secure transactions, or simply ensure privacy in normal communications and pursuits.

Neither anonymity nor encryption are absolute rights; a court may order that a criminal suspect be identified, or require a person to decrypt their communications as part of an investigation. But disproportion is likely when governments claim it is necessary to compromise the rights and security of millions of users to catch specific bad guys by forcing companies to provide "back doors" into secure technology.

When the US Department of Justice, eager to get into the San Bernadino shooter's iPhone, tried to force Apple to re-engineer its security features, much more than that specific phone's security was at stake. This "fix" could be leaked or hacked by criminals who would seek to open the same models. Nor was there any guarantee the US government, or other governments, might not demand or use it repeatedly jeopardizing the security of all users of that model.

Governments can't evade their human rights obligations by pushing the burden onto companies to suppress uncivil speech, de-index information or retain unnecessary data. The effect on rights can be as disproportionate as if government had limited rights itself. Private companies, however, have considerable discretion to set the rules for their services, and these terms can be much harder for users to challenge than government-made laws.

Before urging internet service providers to monitor or bank all incoming traffic or provide back doors in security features, governments should consider the human rights impact. Even when civic groups urge corporations to enforce values like civility, we should consider whether these corporate rules will be transparent or opaque, capable of challenge, or driven by the sort of rights-blind algorithm that cannot tell the difference between pornography and photojournalism.

Realigning State Practice with International Standards

Limiting rights only where necessary and proportionate does not make regulation impossible. Some limits are essential, because protecting people from terrorism, incitement to violence, or revenge pornography is also a human rights obligation. We know that these principles are being taken seriously when there is transparency in law and state practice, independent oversight of executive powers, and avenues of appeal and redress.

Restrictions should apply to the fewest people and the fewest rights possible for the shortest period. And we have to consider whether some issues need state action, or are better addressed by communities, or new technology, or by enabling and promoting counter-speech. Finding the least intrusive means takes some imagination, and some collaboration between those who govern and those whose rights are at stake.

The present split between what states say and what they do cannot be sustained indefinitely. Either rights will take a beating in the digital age, or state practice must reconnect to rights protection.

Human rights and security are two faces of a single coin. When rights are consistently violated, societies become insecure, as anyone watching the destruction of Syria can tell. Societies that deprive their inhabitants of online privacy and means of digital security are deeply vulnerable—to crime, to demagogues, to corruption, to intimidation, and to stagnation. Hurtling into a digital future, it seems prudent to carry our rights along, rather than abandon them by the roadside with our typewriters.

The Lost Years
Secondary Education for Children in Emergencies

By Bassam Khawaja, *Researcher, Middle East Division;*
Elin Martinez, *Researcher, Children's Rights Division;*
Bill Van Esveld, *Senior Researcher, Children's Rights Division*

Amin, 18, became a refugee when his family fled Syria for Lebanon five years ago. He has not set foot in school since. With his father unable to get legal status or work, responsibility for supporting the family of seven fell to Amin. A seventh grader when he left his school in Homs, the then 13-year-old became a construction worker, hauling cement blocks for new apartment buildings. "I've been here five years and lost five years of my life," he said.

Every day in 2015, around 17,000 children fled their homes due to persecution and conflict. Forcibly displaced children, including refugees, have the right to available and accessible quality secondary education, without discrimination. Such access is crucial: it can protect them physically; create a normal routine vital to healing and recovery; provide a safe space at a developmentally critical age; develop problem-solving skills; pave the way for better economic possibilities; and nurture hope.

But for many older children, going to school is an impossible dream.

According to the United Nations Refugee Agency (UNHCR), half of the world's 3.5 million refugee children of primary-school age attend classes, but less than a quarter of the 1.95 million secondary-school aged children do. In Turkey—host to the largest number of refugees in the world—including nearly 3 million Syrians—just 13 percent of secondary school-age refugee children attend school. In Cameroon, 6 percent do; in Pakistan and Lebanon, just 5 percent.

And it is worse for girls: globally, just 7 girls for every 10 refugee boys go to secondary school. Although data on forcibly displaced children with disabilities is limited, they clearly face huge obstacles, and are often excluded from secondary education altogether.

While the record number of refugees and internally displaced people around the world has focused attention on the need to ensure that displaced children can enroll in school, humanitarian responses to crises have tended to focus on primary, not secondary, education.

This essay examines problems that bedevil secondary education in emergencies—especially conflicts that forcibly displace children. And it offers solutions that host countries, donors, and humanitarian actors could adopt to promote and guarantee secondary education in aid-recipient countries affected by crises or large refugee flows.

At the root of these problems, and solutions, are funding and refugee policies. Globally, less than 2 percent of donor support goes to education in emergencies; of that, far more goes to primary than secondary education. Inadequate resources coincide with restrictive refugee host-country policies that often hit children hardest just as they become adolescents.

Quality secondary education benefits societies in which forcibly displaced children have sought safety. Children with secondary education typically earn more as adults and are healthier, increasing productivity and reducing health care costs. They are more likely to find work, and escape poverty. When more girls can complete access secondary education, it can narrow the gender pay gap.

Yet despite its importance, in refugee situations and other humanitarian crises, barriers to education mount as children advance in school. Some host countries simply deny adolescent refugees the right to enroll in secondary schools outside refugee camps. Other serious barriers include hazardous labor, child marriage and sexual violence, harassment by state security forces, and targeting and recruitment by armed groups.

Failure by donors and host countries to ensure secondary education for displaced children and adolescents risks undermining economic development. For example, UNICEF estimates the lost earning potential of displaced children who miss out on secondary education due to the conflict in Syria to be in the tens of millions of dollars.

It also robs secondary school-aged children of the tools and skills they need to contribute to host and home communities if they return home—a scenario that could have severe repercussions for the security and stability of both.

Secondary Education and Conflict

Education promotes stability: it provides children with care, support, and tools for resolving disputes peacefully, and increases productivity. Quality secondary education has been shown to promote tolerance, foster a stronger belief in democracy and civic participation, and help resist recruitment to violent extremism.

High secondary school enrollment levels have even been suggested to lower the probability of civil war, while failure to provide education for displaced adolescents in crises can hamper reconstruction efforts and fuel unrest. One study indicated that if countries in which 30 percent of youth had a secondary education doubled that percentage, they could halve the risk of conflict, according to a 2014 UNESCO report.

Yet education is often a casualty when children are forced to flee for safety. In Somalia—where all parties to the conflict have kidnapped, recruited, or used children for military service—a 2012 Human Rights Watch report found that the threat of forced recruitment and abduction has led children to leave school, and often flee the country with their families. Dropout rates reportedly reached 50 percent following an offensive in 2010.

When conflict erupts, the impact may be greater on secondary than primary education, because secondary schools need specialized resources, including teachers, which are hard to get in crises, and because forcibly displaced adolescents who drop out of school are unlikely to later return.

Some governmental responses have only made matters worse for refugee and internally displaced children. After an attack by the Pakistani militant group Tehreek-i-Taliban in December 2014 killed 132 secondary school-aged schoolchildren in Peshawar, hostility towards Afghans living in Pakistan intensified, and authorities restricted Afghan refugees' access to social services, including education, according to a 2015 Human Rights Watch report on police abuses against Afghans in Pakistan.

In Nigeria, the government's response to attacks by the extremist group Boko Haram ("Western education is forbidden")—including its targeting of secondary school-age boys and its notorious April 24, 2014 abduction of more than 200 girls from a secondary school in Chibok, Borno state—has not adequately protected schools, and enrollment has plummeted among internally displaced children. One teacher told Human Rights Watch in 2015 that his own secondary school had become "a Boko Haram slaughtering ground ... anyone they caught, they will bring to the school and kill them."

Enrollment and attendance levels have dropped dramatically due to fear of attacks. In conflict-affected states in northeast Nigeria, fewer than 90,000 of nearly 590,000 displaced school-age children can access education. Even when schools remain open, parents have been too afraid to send their children; another teacher in northern Borno state said that "some parents had sent their children to Niger to be refugees there."

Compounding the problem, the government has allowed security forces to continue to use both primary and secondary schools, violating the commitment it demonstrated by signing the Safe Schools Declaration to end military use of schools in 2015.

Overlooked and Underfunded

In survey after survey, refugees identify education as a critical emergency need; many spend large portions of their incomes sending their children to school. Others take enormous risks: one woman returned to Syria after being unable to enroll her children in Lebanese schools despite the danger. "Education is the only goal," she told Human Rights Watch.

Yet education's share of donor aid is paltry and falling. In 2002, lower and middle-income countries received 13 percent of overseas development assistance, but 10 percent in 2015. Less than a quarter of that was disbursed to low-income countries, which host 86 percent of the world's refugees and are some of the most under-resourced school systems.

Many grants lasting only 12 months, often disregarding the importance of investing in early recovery interventions. Education in emergencies is also funded unequally: some countries experiencing long-term crises are permanently underfunded, affected by a humanitarian funding system that skews towards recent or ongoing emergencies, as well as those with greater media visibility.

Of the limited funds available for education, primary education receives the lion's share, with secondary an afterthought, even though it often costs more due to the need for more highly-qualified teachers, more textbooks and class-rooms, and specialized equipment and infrastructure. In 2015, for example, UNHCR allocated just 13 percent of its education budget to secondary education, one-third of what it spent on primary.

In part, this uneven distribution is because there are limited funds for education.

But agencies themselves do not necessarily have as much programming for sec-ondary education as they do for younger children, though many focus on acceler-ated learning programs and non-formal education. Humanitarian actors are still playing catch-up when it comes to providing secondary education, in both for-mal non-formal education.

In Lebanon, the Ministry of Education and the United Nations High Commis-sioner for Refugees (UNHCR) set a target last year of enrolling nearly 200,000 Syrian refugee children in public primary schools, but just 2,080 in public sec-ondary schools. And while a back-to-school public outreach campaign adver-tised free and easy enrollment for refugee and Lebanese children in grades 1-9, it did not include higher grades.

A separate UNESCO program covered secondary-school fees for Syrian children, but it was not publicly advertised, and reached just 2,280 of the 82,744 children of secondary school-age registered with UNHCR in the 2015-2016 school year.

Bureaucratic Barriers

Bureaucracy can hamper access to secondary education.

For example, in some countries, secondary school-age children who have been forcibly displaced can be barred from education if they lack official documenta-tion, as Human Rights Watch research in Turkey and Lebanon—home to 1.4 mil-lion school age Syrian refugee children—shows. In Lebanon, children turning 15 must pay $200—often a prohibitive sum— to renew their residency, and many lack the required passport or individual identification card. In Turkey, Syrian refugee children must obtain an identification document (a kimlik) to enroll in schools and access subsidized healthcare, but a "pre-screening" procedure put in place in March 2016 has created backlogs of up to six months.

Syrian adolescents in Jordan described giving up trying to re-enroll in secondary school after spending years trying to meet inflexible requirements for school certification. Amal, 20, said she had completed all her high school exams "except the very last one" before her family fled Syria, but when she tried to finish her exams in Jordan, Ministry of Education officials refused. "They said they needed proof I had passed 11th grade, but they wouldn't accept my faxed form, and told me I needed to send in the original." She would have to return to Syria to obtain it, "but the border is closed, and anyway it is dangerous for me to go back."

In Lebanon, refugee children must provide 9th grade transcripts to enroll in secondary school, which many left behind while fleeing the war in Syria. In other cases, refugee children face school officials unwilling to accommodate them. Sixteen-year-old Loreen has been out of school since heavy shelling cut her off from seventh grade in Syria. When she tried to enroll in a secondary school in Turkey, the director said she would "have to join her age group, no exceptions," even though she spoke no Turkish. When her mother asked the school about language help, she was told "there wasn't any." Loreen did not enroll and now works full-time in a dried-fruit factory.

Barriers to Girls' Education

Girls face hurdles to secondary school that can be exacerbated in crisis situations, including restrictive social norms, sexual and gender-based violence, and early pregnancy and marriage.

In Afghanistan, Taliban forces targeted girls' education after being forced from power in 2001; in 2004, only 5 percent of Afghan girls attended secondary schools, and attacks on education increased in 2005 and 2006. Taliban forces continued to distribute threatening "night letters" to school, ordering girls to stop attending school past puberty (around fourth grade), fatally shot students and teachers, threw battery acid in the faces of adolescent schoolgirls, and attacked girls' schools with rockets, arson, and improvised explosives.

The destruction or denial of access to school sanitation facilities during conflict can also force girls to miss out on education, because private, clean facilities are essential during menstruation.

In situations of forced displacement, parents may marry off girls as a way to cope with poverty or safety concerns, and most married girls stop going to school. Out-of-school girls are more susceptible to child marriage, which has leapt four-fold among Syrian refugee girls in Lebanon, Turkey, and Jordan.

Conversely, the benefits of secondary education for girls can be life-changing, with potential gains for host countries and overall development by facilitating their access to information about rights and services, and enabling participation in decision-making and accountability. It also saves lives. Ensuring girls stay in secondary education can reduce child marriage and childhood deaths because children with higher education levels are more likely to have a healthy diet and seek medical care, and girls with secondary education are less likely to marry early.

Poverty and Child Labor

For too many displaced children, poverty—exacerbated by policies that prevent parents from finding legal work—pushes school out of reach and makes child labor more likely. Pressure to earn intensifies as children grow older, and even those who do not work often cannot afford secondary-school related costs, including fees in countries where secondary education is not yet free, uniforms and notebooks. Transport costs are also often higher for secondary schools, which are fewer in number than primary schools.

Leaving school to work can lead to serious harm: exploitation, hazardous work environments, or violence. In Lebanon, humanitarian agencies documented a sharp increase in the worst forms of child labor among refugee children in 2015, and Human Rights Watch interviewed children who had been injured, attacked, or arrested while working.

When there are few opportunities for skilled work or higher education—like in Kenya's Dadaab camp, where just 13 percent of adolescents are accommodated in secondary schools—there is far less incentive to get a secondary education. A UN survey in Zaatari, Jordan's largest refugee camp, found that barriers to education included "a sense of the pointlessness of education as [Syrian children] had limited hope for their future prospects." In a smaller refugee camp in Jordan, enrollment in a high school class plummeted by half in the fall of 2015, shortly after three students were accepted to university but could not afford the fees.

Allowing refugees to work could help to ameliorate many of poverty's knock-on effects on secondary education. But host countries are often politically loath to take this step due to fears that refugees will take citizens' jobs. In fact, refugees often take jobs that nationals do not want to do, and labor protections could help stem the downward pressure on wages that results from informal work.

Even in countries that have opened access to work permits for refugees, like Turkey and Jordan, restrictions often remain, such as quotas, limits on access to more skilled jobs, geographical restrictions, and tying permits to local sponsorship. Denied the opportunity to work legally, Syrian refugees in Jordan and Lebanon largely depend on insufficient humanitarian aid and have sunk deeper into debt and poverty, making it harder to afford to send children to school.

Alternatives are possible. In Uganda, where some 500,000 refugees are allowed to work, choose where to live, and access public schools, only 1 percent rely completely on aid.

Global Response

It has taken decades for the global community to recognize the importance of education in humanitarian response, but recent promises could help staunch the loss of education for displaced children—if they are kept.

In May 2016, humanitarian donors and UN agencies launched Education Cannot Wait, a global fund that aims to support education for 75 million children and young people affected by emergencies each year by raising $3.85 billion by 2020.

In September 2016, at a US-sponsored summit on refugees at the UN, participating countries pledged commitments that, according to the White House, improved access to lawful work for 1 million refugees, and access to education for 1 million refugee children. In parallel, the UN Global Commission on Education has set out specific goals and timelines for governments to achieve free, equitable, and quality secondary education for all by 2030, a target that all UN member states pledged to meet as one of 17 Sustainable Development Goals agreed to in September 2015.

But the good news must be taken with a grain of salt. Donor attention to education has proved fickle before; in 2010, domestic investment and donor funding dedicated to education decreased dramatically when donors reduced global aid budgets or diverted existing funds to other sectors.

Greater transparency is also needed to hold donors to their promises. In February 2016, donors pledged more than $11 billion in multi-year support in response to the Syria conflict, to meet goals that include universal school enrollment in refugee-hosting countries by 2017. Hundreds of millions have been disbursed, but as of August 2016, a report found that most donors had "failed to meet even the most basic criteria for transparency."

Ways Forward

It is essential that governments affected by crises urgently protect secondary education from attack, create safe and accessible alternatives during violence, and ensure their own forces refrain from the military use of schools.

Governments and humanitarian actors need to address barriers that cause older displaced children to drop out of school, address the needs of girls and children with disabilities, and support those who need to study an unfamiliar curriculum or in a foreign language.

Humanitarian actors and donors responding to humanitarian crises should take heed of increasing long-term displacement and make secondary education an integral part of response plans. Transparent, sustained, multi-year funding is urgently needed for education programs to ensure children, and particularly girls, can access and complete secondary school.

The link between poverty and education must also be addressed. To reduce poverty and enable families to pay school-related costs, host countries should allow refugees access to lawful work. Donor countries should ensure that livelihood efforts are funded alongside education planning, so that families do not have to rely on child labor and can send secondary-age children to school.

Host countries should also revise legal status requirements and restrictions on movement that proscribe children's access to secondary education, and with it their futures. Governments hosting foreign children, regardless of their immigration status, should provide legal access to secondary education or vocational and skills training on an equal basis with nationals, and de-link immigration-related requirements such as residence permits from enrollment criteria.

Host countries should also ensure national education plans include provisions for refugee education, and accommodate children who may not have official documents with flexible enrollment requirements. Administering placement exams, in lieu of requiring transcripts, is one simple way to ensure children are not excluded from secondary education due to factors beyond their control.

Host countries must recognize that older children deserve the same protection and support offered to primary school age children, and above all need to be in school. Continuing to ignore their needs would be a grave mistake.

SILENCING TURKEY'S MEDIA
The Government's Deepening Assault on Critical Journalism

WORLD REPORT
2017

COUNTRIES

HUMAN RIGHTS WATCH

"Education on the Front Lines"
Military Use of Schools in Afghanistan's Baghlan Province

Afghanistan

As fighting continued between Taliban and government forces in Afghanistan in 2016, thousands of civilians were killed and injured in insurgent suicide and IED attacks. The Taliban claimed responsibility for many of these, but groups affiliating themselves with the Islamic State (also known as ISIS) claimed several particularly deadly attacks in Kabul.

The Afghan government continued to expand its use of illegal militias, some of which were responsible for killings and assaults on civilians. Afghan National Security Forces (ANSF) were also responsible for civilian casualties from indiscriminate aerial and mortar attacks. Both the Taliban and ANSF increasingly used schools for military purposes; such abuses, along with insecurity throughout the country, deprived many children, particularly girls, of access to education. Hundreds of thousands of Afghans became newly internally displaced, including many returned refugees and migrants.

Throughout the year, political infighting stalled progress on the National Unity Government's reform agenda, threatening a political crisis over the government's failure to hold district council and parliamentary elections on time, and meet the deadline for convening a constitutional Loya Jirga (grand assembly). The government made some progress in releasing women jailed for so-called morality crimes, but failed to end prosecutions of women for "running away." The year saw no progress in the government's vows to implement a national action plan to curb torture, or to hold accountable government officials responsible for attacks on journalists.

Armed Conflict

The United Nations documented 8,397 civilian casualties as of September 30, approximately the same as the record number set in the first nine months of 2015. The Taliban and other insurgents were responsible for 61 percent, most from IEDs and suicide attacks. Government forces, including unofficial militias, caused 23 percent of civilian casualties.

Kabul saw an increase in particularly deadly attacks, including an April 16 suicide truck bomb that detonated in a parking lot adjacent to the VIP Protection

Force Directorate. The Taliban clamed responsibility for the blast, which killed 56 civilians and injured more than 300. On July 23, multiple suicide bombings at a large protest march made up primarily of ethnic Hazaras killed at least 80 and injured more than 250; groups affiliated with ISIS claimed responsibility for the attack. On August 24, insurgents attacked the American Univeristy of Afghanistan in Kabul, killing 14 students and lecturers.

Throughout 2016 both ANSF and insurgent forces raided and attacked medical clinics and hospitals. Early on February 18, Afghan police special forces raided a clinic run by the humanitarian organization Swedish Committee for Afghanistan, assaulted medical staff, and shot dead two patients, including a 16-year-old, and a 15-year-old caregiver. Witnesses reported that international military forces accompanied the Afghan forces, although they did not enter the clinic. Wardak provincial authorities justified the raid on the grounds the clinic was treating Taliban. On September 12, Taliban fighters dressed as doctors attacked the Mirwais Hospital in Kandahar city, apparently targeting the deputy governor who was visiting the facility. In the ensuing gun battle, one patient was killed.

Civilian casualties from ANSF operations during ground offensives also increased compared to 2015; most were due to indiscriminate mortar and rocket fire in civilian-populated areas. Aerial strikes—most from attack helicopters—resulted in a 72 percent increase in civilian casualties—the highest since 2011. Most victims were women and children.

The number of people internally displaced due to the conflict surged as fighting intensified in mid-year. More than 300,000 new internally displaced persons (IDPs) in 2016 brought the nationwide total to at least 1.3 million people. Humanitarian organizations reported that many IDPs were living in informal settlements where they lacked access to safe water, sanitation, health care, and education. Many returning refugees and migrants, most from Pakistan, joined the ranks of the IDPs.

In late 2015 through at least early 2016, the Taliban stepped up their recruitment of child soldiers, particularly in northeastern Afghanistan. While the government criminalized the recruitment of Afghans under 18 years of age, the practice continued, most notably among the Afghan Local Police (ALP), a militia force. Government forces, including the Afghan National Army (ANA), Afghan National Police (ANP), and ALP increasingly occupied or used schools for military purposes in contested areas. The practice was particularly acute in Baghlan and Helmand provinces. The United Nations also reported a significant increase in attacks against schools by both Taliban and groups affiliating themselves with ISIS.

As fighting intensified in northern provinces, Afghan officials reactivated pro-government militias to bolster security. In Faryab, Kunduz, and other provinces, these militia forces were accused of killing and assaulting civilians.

These recent attacks on civilians added to decades of armed conflict and insecurity, which have taken their toll on the population's mental health. Health experts have voiced concern about the high prevalence of mental health conditions among Afghans, and the lack of community-based mental health services for those with psychosocial disabilities.

Women's Rights

Members of parliament opposed to the landmark 2009 Elimination of Violence Against Women (EVAW) law, notably the parliamentary Judicial Commission headed by Nazir Ahmad Hanafi, continued their efforts to amend the law to remove provisions regulating the minimum age of marriage, prescribing punishments for domestic assault; and providing for women's shelters. As of November 2016, the draft amendments were being considered by the parliamentary Commission on Women, Civil Society and Human Rights.

Although in December 2015 the Supreme Court issued a judicial ruling banning the imprisonment of women for running away from their families, the ban was limited to cases in which the women went to a medical provider, the police, or the house of a close male relative (mahram). As this was the practice before the ruling, the court's action represented no real change. In many cases, women running away from home are fleeing domestic violence and forced marriages. The Afghanistan Independent Human Rights Commission reported that in the first eight months of 2016, it documented 2,621 cases of domestic violence, about the same as 2015, although the number is likely much higher due to underreporting.

On March 8, the Supreme Court granted significant sentence reductions to 13 men convicted of the murder of Farkhunda, a woman who was beaten to death by a mob of men in Kabul in March 2015 in a case that sparked widespread crit-icim of the police and judiciary. The court also reduced the sentences of nine other defendants who had been convicted of assault. Many of the men involved in the attack were never arrested.

In December 2015, the Afghanistan Independent Human Rights Commission is-sued a report documenting the widespread use of so-called virginity examina-tions on female detainees. Afghan police and prosecutors routinely order such tests on women in their custody, and use the results to charge women with "morality crimes." President Ashraf Ghani reportedly ordered a review of the practice, but as of November 2016, no results had been announced.

The Afghan government reportedly finalized its implementation plan for the Na-tional Action Plan for Women, Peace, and Security, under UN Security Council Resolution 1325. However, as of November 2016, the government had not final-ized a budget for the implementation plan.

In December 2015, Sima Joyenda, one of Afghanistan's only two female gover-nors, was removed from her post in the western Ghor province after she received a number of death threats. Joyenda was reappointed as deputy governor of Kabul province, but the case illustrates the continuing threats that female public officials face in Afghanistan.

Arbitrary Detention, Torture, and Discriminatory Practices

Although President Ghani launched a national action plan to eliminate torture in early 2015, these was no progress on implementation through 2016, and the government did not make public information on investigations into cases of tor-ture. In March, a smartphone video showing police in Kandahar beating a sus-pect and dragging him behind a truck was widely circulated on social media, prompting government officials to state that the incident had been investigated and those responsible punished. However, no details were forthcoming.

Afghan law criminalizes consensual same-sex sexual conduct, and there were re-ports of harassment, violence, and detentions by police. Advocates for the les-bian, gay, bisexual, and transgender (LGBT) community function largely underground out of fear of persecution.

Freedom of Expression

The year was the bloodiest on record since 2001 for Afghan journalists, with 12 killed in the first nine months of the year. Government or pro-government elements were responsible for most of the violence against journalists, followed by the Taliban. A January 20, 2016 suicide attack on a minibus in Kabul killed seven journalists affiliated with Tolo, one of the largest national media outlets. The Taliban claimed responsibility for the attack, which it described in a statement as "revenge" for "false allegations" made against the insurgent group.

On January 30, President Ghani issued a decree for the protection of journalists, ordering the Attorney General's Office to "urgently" investigate all deaths of journalists since 2002 and publicize the results. As of November 2016, no results of any investigations had been made public.

Following an incident on August 29, in which Ghani's security detail beat nine journalists during a visit to Bamiyan city, the National Security Council approved the Procedure for Immunity and Security of Journalists and the Press, aimed at protecting journalists from violence.

The implementation of the Access to Information Law, which came into effect in 2014, remained limited. In his January 2016 media decree, President Ghani urged officials to provide information to journalists in a timely manner. But in September 2016, the Oversight Commission on Access to Information reported that the government was failing to share information with journalists.

The Media Violations Investigations Commission, which the government had dissolved in 2015 in response to demands by media watchdogs, was reinstated. The minister of information and culture oversees the commission. Powerful individuals, mostly government officials, have used the commission as a tool to intimidate and silence journalists.

Key International Actors

The US military in May 2016 released a report on the October 2015 airstrike on a Médecins Sans Frontières (Doctors Without Borders) hospital in Kunduz that killed 42 and wounded dozens more. The report concluded that US personnel had committed violations of international humanitarian law during the operation, yet because there was no showing that the personnel acted deliberately, did not recommend that any criminal charges be brought.

At the NATO Summit in Warsaw on July 8-9, member states pledged to sustain the Resolute Support mission in Afghanistan beyond 2016 and continue the mission's training and financial assistance to Afghan security forces through 2020. At the summit, NATO members endorsed a new policy for protecting civilians that included measures to monitor its own actions in conflict areas and respond to those of partner states.

The US government did not clarify the overarching military objectives of US or NATO military forces supporting Afghan security forces. As of June 15, the US authorized its forces to "more proactively support" ANSF through providing "close air support" and "accompanying and advising Afghan conventional forces."

The US continued to carry out counterinsurgency operations in Afghanistan, often partnering with Afghan Special Forces units in ground operations. The US carried out airstrikes on a level not seen since 2011 in battles in Helmand, Kunduz, and Uruzgan when Taliban forces threated to take over provincial capitals, and against Taliban and groups affiliating themselves with ISIS, particularly in Nangarhar. More than 100 civilians were reportedly killed by US airstrikes in the first half of 2016.

Noting Taliban gains and continuing insecurity in Afghanistan, on July 6, US President Barack Obama announced a revised withdrawal timetable to leave 8,400 troops in Afghanistan by the end of December 2016. Germany, Turkey, and Italy agreed to keep their deployments in Afghanistan at current levels of 850, 760, and 500 troops, respectively, after 2016. The UK increased its troop commitment, adding 100 additional forces in July 2016.

India committed to defense and counterterror cooperation and promised assistance in education, health, agriculture, empowerment of women, infrastructure and strengthening of democratic institutions, but did not call for human right protections.

The International Criminal Court continued its preliminary examination of allegations of serious international crimes in Afghanistan, which it began in 2007.

At the Brussels Conference on Afghanistan in October 2016, donors committed US$15.2 billion to the Afghan government, but specified no concrete human rights benchmarks for that assistance.

Triggered by a surge in the return of refugees and migrants from Pakistan, in September the UN high commissioner for refugees launched an emergency appeal for Afghanistan to provide humanitarian assistance to an unprecedented number of returnees, along with hundreds of thousands of those newly displaced by the expanding conflict.

Algeria

Algerian authorities increasingly resorted to criminal prosecutions in 2016 against bloggers, journalists, and media figures for peaceful speech, using articles in the penal code criminalizing "offending the president," "insulting state officials" or "denigrating Islam." They have also prosecuted labor activists who organized or called for peaceful demonstrations on charges such as "unauthorized gathering."

Parliament adopted amendments to the constitution in February 2016 that include recognition of academic freedom and press freedom without prior censorship and without prison as a punishment for press offenses. However, the constitution conditions the exercise of these and other rights to national laws that restrict them significantly.

Freedom of Assembly

Algeria's 2016 constitution states that "the right to peaceful assembly is guaranteed within the framework of the law, which sets forth how it is to be exercised" (article 49).

In practice, relying on a range of laws, Algerian authorities routinely violate the right to freedom of assembly. The penal code punishes organizing or participating in an unauthorized demonstration in a public place with up to one year in prison (article 98). Authorities in Algiers, the capital, banned public demonstrations indefinitely in 2001, when the country was under a state of emergency. Authorities did not rescind the ban when they lifted the state of emergency in 2011.

The ban on demonstrations in Algiers is strictly enforced by authorities, who mobilize large numbers of police to thwart demonstrations and detain participants, usually holding them for a few hours before releasing them. Police arrested 20 members of the National Coordination of Contractual Teachers who called for a demonstration in Algiers on March 21 and 22, and held them in detention in police stations for several hours, then released them without charge.

Police arrested relatives of the forcibly disappeared during the violence of the 90s and several human rights activists as they demonstrated on August 30, the International Day of the Disappeared, in front of the National Consultative Commission for the Promotion and Protection of Human Rights in Algiers. They held them for several hours before releasing them without charge.

Authorities have also restricted the right to assemble even in private spaces indoors. On February 6, 2016, the National Union of Public Administration Staff (SNAPAP), an independent labor union, organized a symposium on the socio-economic situation in Algeria at the House of the Unions, a private space rented by the SNAPAP. Police encircled the place, prevented people from accessing it, and arrested six union leaders for several hours, then released them without charge.

Freedom of Association and Unions

In 2012, the government enacted Law 12-06, which requires all associations—including those that had already successfully registered—to re-file registration applications and obtain a registration receipt from the Interior Ministry before they can operate legally, in a cumbersome procedure akin to a new registration.

To date, major human rights organization such as the Algerian League for Human Rights (Ligue Algérienne des Droits de l'Homme, LADDH) and Youth Action Rally (Rassemblement Action Jeunesse, RAJ,) and the Algerian division of Amnesty International, which submitted compliance applications in January 2014 as provided for by Law 12-06, have still not obtained a receipt certifying their legal existence. The absence of a receipt weakens them by making it impossible to open a bank account or rent an office in their own name, or hire a public hall for a meeting. Moreover, members of an association that is "non-accredited, suspended, or dissolved" risk prison sentences of up to six months for conducting activities in its name.

Until the 1990s, Algeria had only one lawful workers' union, the General Union of Algerian Workers (Union Générale des travailleurs algériens, UGTA). On June 2, 1990, Algeria adopted Law 90-14, allowing for the establishment of independent unions. Several autonomous unions were created in the public sector.

In practice, authorities have curtailed the work of independent unions in various ways. They withheld legal status from independent unions that applied for it, hindering their ability to collect the membership fees they would need to rent an office and organize events. Without legal status, they cannot open a bank account or file cases in court. Several union activists faced retaliation for organizing or participating in strikes. They were suspended from their positions without compensation and never rehired. In 2016, the International Labor Organization recommended that Algerian authorities end the practice of preventing the registration of autonomous unions and reinstate all workers suspended or dismissed because of their trade union activities.

Freedom of Speech

Since the 1990s, Algeria has seen a proliferation of privately owned newspapers that enjoy a certain margin of freedom to criticize public figures and state policies. The 2014 Law on audio-visual activities ended the formal state monopoly on audiovisual media. However, repressive press laws, dependence on revenues from public-sector advertising, and other factors limit press freedom. The "information code" adopted in 2012, contains several articles that constrain freedom of expression. Article 2 states that news journalism is to be "a freely practiced activity," as long as it respects "national identity, the cultural values of society, national sovereignty and national unity, as well as the requirements of national security, national defense, public order, and the country's economic interests, among others."

In 2016, authorities prosecuted a number of Algerians for critical speech. On September 6, an appeals court gave Slimane Bouhafs, a converted Christian, a three-year prison sentence for Facebook posts "offending the prophet" and "denigrating" Islam, under article 144 bis of the penal code.

On August 9, an Algiers appeals court upheld a two-year prison sentence for Mohamed Tamalt, a freelance journalist with dual Algerian and British nationality, for a video he posted on Facebook featuring a poem deemed offensive to Algeria's president.

On May 25, the Laghouat first instance court sentenced Belkacem Khencha, a labor rights defender, to six months in prison for posting a video on Facebook criticizing the judiciary for sentences imposed on other rights activists. He remained free pending an appeal scheduled for September 29.

On June 24, authorities placed in pretrial detention two executives from the privately owned television channel KBC that aired the satirical political talk show

"Ki Hna Ki Ness" (Just Like Everybody Else), five days after security forces shut down operations at the studio producing the show and confiscated production materials. *"Ki Hna Ki Ness" had* begun broadcasting on June 6.

The two executives were accused of making false statements under article 223 of the penal code and complicity in the abuse of office under articles 33 and 42 of a 2001 anti-corruption law. They spent three weeks in prison before being sentenced, on July 18, to a suspended prison term of six months, and a fine of 50,000 dinars (US$457). At time of writing the show had not resumed and production materials remain confiscated.

Women's Rights

Algeria's Constitution enshrines the principle of non-discrimination based on sex and requires the state to take positive action to ensure equality of rights and duties of all citizens, men and women. In February 2016, parliament introduced an article proclaiming that the "state works to attain parity between women and men in the job market," and "encourages the promotion of women to positions of responsibility in public institutions and in businesses."

On December 10, 2015, parliament adopted amendments to the penal code specifically criminalizing some forms of domestic violence. Assault against one's spouse or former spouse can be punished by up to 20 years in prison, depending on the victim's injuries, and the perpetrator can face a life sentence for attacks resulting in death. The amendments also criminalize sexual harassment in public places.

Despite adoption of the law, Algeria has yet to adopt the more comprehensive legal measures, such as protection orders to protect women from violence and concrete duties on law enforcement to respond to domestic violence, needed to prevent domestic violence, assist survivors, and prosecute offenders. The law, moreover, makes women vulnerable to threats from the offender or relatives, by including a provision that a pardon by the victim puts an end to prosecution.

Algeria's Family Code continues to discriminate against women despite some amendments in 2005 that improved women's access to divorce and child custody. An adult woman still requires a male guardian to conclude her marriage contract, a requirement not imposed on men. A man can divorce unilaterally, while a woman must apply to the courts. If a woman wishes to divorce without her husband's consent and without justification, she needs to pay back her dowry, or an equivalent amount of money, to her husband in return for the divorce. This is particularly problematic as the code does not recognize marital property, provisions that values women's non-monetary contributions to the marriage at the time of termination.

Accountability for Past Crimes

Perpetrators of human rights crimes and abuses during the internal armed conflict of the 1990s continued to enjoy impunity under the Charter on Peace and National Reconciliation. The charter criminalizes comments deemed to denigrate the security forces or state institutions for their conduct during the armed conflict, when both state forces and extremist Islamist groups committed torture, enforced disappearances, unlawful killings, and other serious abuses.

Associations representing the families of the disappeared continued to face denial for legal registration. Families of the disappeared alleged being subject to pressures because they refused to accept compensation from the state in exchange for accepting a death certificate for their still-missing relatives.

Sexual Orientation and Gender Identity

Algeria's penal code criminalizes same sex relations with a prison sentence of two months to two years. In 2015, several people were arrested for same-sex relations but none were prosecuted.

Sahrawi Refugee Camps

Algeria allows the Polisario Front, the liberation movement for the Western Sahara, to administer refugee camps housing some 100,000 Sahrawi refugees in the southern desert near the border with Western Sahara. During his first visit to the refugee camps as UN Secretary-General, Ban Ki-moon in March called it an "unacceptable situation" and angered Moroccan authorities by referring to the Western Sahara as "occupied" by Morocco.

In at least three cases during 2016, Sahrawi families prevented their adult daughters from exercising their right to freedom of movement by departing for Spain, where they had lived and established legal residency. The Polisario was unwilling or incapable of ending these situations of illegal confinement of women, a form of domestic violence. Algeria, despite its ultimate responsibility for protecting the human rights of all persons present on its territory, did not intervene to end their confinement.

Key International Actors

Algeria continued to deny international human rights organizations entry to conduct research missions. It also did not reply to requests, pending since 1997 and 2011, respectively, for visits by the UN special rapporteurs on torture and on freedom of peaceful assembly and of association.

Angola

Human rights in Angola suffered during 2016 due to continued government repression and the country's worst economic crisis since the civil war ended in 2002.

Sparked by the global drop in oil prices, the economic crisis slowed a decade of growth and exposed unresolved problems caused by years of corruption, mismanaged public funds, and political control of institutions. Calls to diversify the economy to create new revenue sources led to massive land acquisition by the government and private businesses, often with forced evictions and other violations, including in the capital, Luanda.

President José Eduardo dos Santos, in power since 1979, has announced that he will step down in 2018, and that he will not run for office in 2017 elections. Security forces continued to crack down on pro-democracy activists and those protesting on behalf of human rights.

Freedom of Media

Coverage in state-run media remained highly biased in favor of the government and the ruling party, the Popular Movement for the Liberation of Angola (MPLA). The government continued to restrict freedom of expression with censorship in state-run media and some private media controlled by ruling party officials, which remained the only outlets with countrywide coverage.

In 2016, state television channel TPA at times invited opposition and civil society groups to debates but those discussions mostly maintained a pro-government slant. Social media, blogs, and privately owned news websites continued to operate without interference as the main channels for independent news and debates.

In November, without public consultation, the parliament passed a new media law that gives regulatory control of all media to a new body that is controlled by the state and ruling party. The Angolan union of journalists called the law "a political tool to intimidate the press," and vowed to take the matter to the constitutional court.

Freedom of Assembly

Article 47 of Angola's Constitution permits citizens to protest without pre-authorization, provided they inform authorities in advance. However, the government consistently blocked peaceful anti-government protests with intimidation and detention, and when peaceful protests did take place, they frequently encountered excessive force and arbitrary arrests.

In March 2016, after a lengthy trial, a Luanda court sentenced 17 members of a book club to between two and eight years in prison for discussing peaceful protest and democracy at a meeting in June 2015, inspired by Gene Sharp's book, *From Dictatorship to Democracy*.

In June, in an unprecedented move, the governor of Benguela province gave permission for a group of anti-government activists called the Revolutionary Movement to protest against the arrests. Later that month, after international condemnation, the Supreme Court provisionally released the 17 people pending a final decision on their appeal. In September, they were pardoned following the approval of an amnesty law.

In May, the Supreme Court overturned the conviction of human rights defender Marcos Mavungo, who had been sentenced to six years in prison in September 2015 in relation to a planned peaceful demonstration on corruption, human rights abuses, and poor governance in oil-rich Cabinda province.

Treatment of Detainees

Prison conditions remained poor, with local activists and media highlighting corruption, overcrowding, and violence. In April, the Angolan government announced that it would open four new jails by the end of the year to help accommodate the estimated 24,000 inmates distributed among 40 prisons across the country. In July, parliament approved a new amnesty law that granted freedom to thousands of inmates with prison sentences of up to 12 years for nonviolent crimes.

Abuses by Security Forces

Security forces continued to use excessive force with impunity as the government failed to investigate and prosecute officers who committed serious human rights violations.

Authorities refused requests from local human rights groups, opposition members of parliament and the United Nations High Commissioner for Human Rights to establish an independent commission to investigate the events of April 2015, when a police operation against a religious sect left at least 22 people dead in Huambo.

In April 2016, Julino Kalupeteka, the leader of the sect, and nine of his followers were sentenced to up to 28 years in prison for the killing of nine police officers during the raid on their makeshift camp. However, to date, no security force members have been arrested or prosecuted for the killing of the sect members.

In April, police gunfire wounded at least three people during a student demonstration against an increase in school fees in Caluquembe, Huila province. Police initially denied firing live ammunition but later admitted that one officer had opened fire and said he would be punished. It is not known what steps were taken to punish him, or others.

On August 6, soldiers fired live ammunition during a peaceful protest against forced evictions in Luanda, killing a teenage boy (see below). The government announced an investigation into the case but had not published any findings at time of writing.

Right to Health

Angola's healthcare system, already under stress due to falling oil prices, struggled to respond to parallel outbreaks of malaria and yellow fever.

Angola has one of the highest child mortality rates in the world. According to the Children's Rights and Emergency Relief Organization (UNICEF), one in five children in Angola does not survive to age 5. Almost 3,000 people died from malaria, predominantly children, in the first quarter of the year—a much higher number than in previous years—because among other reasons, the healthcare system ran out of basic malaria medicines.

The healthcare system also ran out of yellow fever vaccines, essential for protecting children against this potentially deadly disease. Both basic malaria medicines and yellow fever vaccines are on the World Health Organization (WHO) Model List of Essential Medicines. Governments are therefore required to ensure their adequate availability even in times of economic crisis. Shortages of other essential medicines and medical supplies were also reported, including syringes and gloves, due to health budget cuts.

Housing Rights and Forced Evictions

Forced evictions persisted during the year with a host of associated human rights violations. In Luanda, a special force tasked with protecting government infrastructure and land forcibly evicted over 1,000 people in Zango area on the outskirts of the city, destroying their homes and property.

In July, armed soldiers with bulldozers and trucks arrived without warning or a court order and demolished homes. In August, security forces responded to a residents' protest by shooting in the air and at their feet, killing a 14-year-old boy. After growing complaints of abuses by soldiers against Zango residents, authorities ordered the operation to be stopped in late September. However, at time of writing, the forcibly evicted residents had not been relocated or compensated.

In June, 18 nongovernmental organizations signed a petition that denounced land grabbing and forced evictions in Curoca, Cunene province. The groups accused security forces of abusing their powers, using excessive force, and arbitrarily detaining activists from the local communities.

Key International Actors

Angola continued to play an important role in the region, most notably in conflicts in Africa's Great Lakes region. As president of the International Conference on the Region of the Great Lakes (ICGLR), Angola organized in October an international conference to discuss the situation in the Democratic Republic of Congo.

Following an invitation by the government, the United Nations special rapporteur on the human rights of migrants visited Angola in May. The UN official urged Angola to ratify the Optional Protocol to the Convention against Torture (OPCAT) and to establish a National Preventive Mechanism to undertake regular unannounced visits to all places of detention, including migrant detention centers. He also renewed calls for Angola to establish an independent national human rights institution.

In October, a delegation of the African Commission on Human and Peoples' Rights, led by the chairperson and special rapporteur on freedom of expression and access to information, visited Angola at the invitation of the government.

Angola's mandate as non-permanent member of the UN Security Council ended in 2016. Despite the economic crisis, Angola has thus far remained donor independent thanks to years of strong trade links with China. The health crisis has, however, forced the government to request help from the United States, with which it already had strong bilateral relations. Throughout 2016, the US provided assistance to prevent major infectious diseases and strengthen Angola's health system. The European Union also provided funding and support to develop higher education, agriculture, and sanitation.

In June, Angola endorsed the Safe Schools Declaration, thereby committing to implement and use the Guidelines for Protecting Schools and Universities from Military Use during Armed Conflict.

Argentina

Argentina faces long-standing human rights problems that include police abuse, poor prison conditions, endemic violence against women, difficulty accessing reproductive services, and obstacles keeping indigenous people from enjoying the rights afforded to them by Argentine and international law.

Impunity for the 1994 AMIA bombing, vaguely defined criminal provisions that undermine free speech, and delays in appointing permanent judges are serious concerns.

In 2016, Argentina adopted federal regulations to ensure access to official information and to prevent favoritism in government purchase of media advertisements, an important source of media revenue. Argentina continues to make significant progress protecting lesbian, gay, bisexual, and transgender (LGBT) rights and prosecuting officials for abuses committed during the country's "Dirty War" (1976-1983), although trials have been delayed.

Confronting Past Abuses

As of September 2016, 2,541 people had been charged, 723 convicted, and 76 acquitted of crimes allegedly committed by Argentina's military junta during the country's "Dirty War," according to the Attorney General's Office. Prosecutions were made possible by a series of actions taken in the early 2000s by Congress, the Supreme Court, and federal judges annulling amnesty laws and striking down pardons of former officials implicated in the crimes. As of November 2016, 121 children illegally taken from their parents during the war had been located.

In May, a federal court convicted 14 former military and intelligence chiefs from Argentina and one from Uruguay of crimes against humanity committed as part of the Condor Plan, a joint initiative targeting political opponents by the dictatorships in Argentina, Bolivia, Brazil, Chile, Paraguay, and Uruguay. In August, a federal court sentenced 28 people to life without parole for crimes that included torture, homicide, and the illegal abduction of babies in 1974—the first conviction for abuses committed before the 1976 coup.

Given the large number of victims, suspects, and cases, prosecutors and judges face challenges bringing those responsible to justice while respecting their due

process rights. In September, the Attorney General's Office reported that 489 pretrial detainees and convicted prisoners were under house arrest, a right provided for by Argentine law to people over 70 years old. In August, the government said it would not appeal judicial rulings granting house arrest to these detainees and convicted prisoners.

The fate of Jorge Julio López, a torture victim who disappeared in 2006—a day before he was due to attend the trial of one of his torturers—remains unknown.

Freedom of Expression

In January 2016, police detained Milagro Sala, a prominent social leader in Jujuy province, for participating in peaceful street protests. Sala and other demonstrators had gathered in the provincial capital to protest a decree issued by the governor that purported to regulate organizations like Sala's, which implement government-funded housing and other welfare programs.

Sala was charged with instigating protesters to commit crimes and also with sedition, an offense that Argentine law broadly defines as "publicly mobilizing to prevent implementation of national or provincial laws or resolutions of national or public officials." As of November, Sala was in prison awaiting trial on several charges, including sedition.

Upon taking office, President Mauricio Macri adopted a temporary set of decrees to regulate media, and created a new agency that reports to the Communications Ministry to implement the new rules. In July, the government said it was drafting a communications law that it claimed would respect free speech. As of November, the law was still being drafted but the new, supposedly temporary agency that lacks structural independence from the executive had already issued rulings regulating media.

In August, the Macri administration issued a resolution setting forth transparent criteria for government purchase of media advertisements, and in September, Congress passed a national law ensuring public access to information held by government bodies. Some provinces and municipalities still lack such laws, however, undermining free speech.

Police Abuse and Prison Conditions

Overcrowding, ill-treatment by guards, inadequate facilities, and inmate violence continue to be serious issues in Argentina's prisons. The National Penitentiary Office, created by Congress in 2003 to supervise federal prisons and protect the rights of detainees, reported eight violent deaths in federal prisons between January and September 2016. The office also documented 775 cases of torture or ill-treatment in federal prisons in 2015, and 446 cases between January and September 2016.

A report published in September by the Provincial Commission for Memory—an autonomous public body created by the legislature of Buenos Aires province— found that in 2015, an average of three detainees died per week in Buenos Aires province prisons, most of them due to preventable illnesses. The report highlights that more than half of detainees in prisons and police stations in the province were being held in pretrial detention.

Police abuse remains a serious problem. Security forces occasionally employ excessive force against protesters, despite a 2011 commitment by authorities in at least 19 of Argentina's 23 provinces to ensure that force is used proportionately.

In May, under a justice reform package called "Justice 2020," the Macri administration said it would create a national mechanism to prevent torture, in an effort to fulfill its obligations under the Optional Protocol to the Convention against Torture and other Cruel, Inhuman or Degrading Treatment or Punishment.

Judicial Independence

The delayed appointment of permanent judges by the Council of the Judiciary has led to temporary appointments of judges who lack security of tenure, which, the Supreme Court ruled in 2015, undermines judicial independence. As of November 2016, 254 of 979 lower-court judgeships remained vacant.

In December 2015, President Macri issued an executive decree to appoint two Supreme Court justices, without following the process established in a 2003 presidential decree that includes civil-society participation in nominating judges and Senate approval. After strong criticism by the opposition, lawyers, and non-government organizations (NGOs), the government implemented the process. In June 2016, after taking into consideration inputs from the public, NGOs, and academic and bar associations, the Senate approved President Macri's nominations and the justices took office in August.

Impunity for the AMIA Bombing

Twenty-two years after the 1994 bombing of the Argentine Israelite Mutual Association (AMIA) in Buenos Aires that killed 85 people and injured more than 300, no one has been convicted of the crime.

The investigation stalled when Iran, suspected by the Argentine judiciary of ordering the attack, refused to allow Argentine investigators to interview Iranian suspects in Argentina. In 2013, Argentina and Iran signed a memorandum of understanding (MOU) that allowed an international commission of jurists to review evidence and question Iranian suspects—but only in Tehran, which would likely have rendered the interviews inadmissible in an Argentine court. A federal court declared the MOU unconstitutional, a ruling that the Macri administration said it would not appeal. The government said further that it would ask Interpol to re-issue red notices—a form of international arrest warrant—to detain several Iranians implicated in the attack, and that it would present draft legislation to try the Iranians in absentia.

In January 2015—days after he filed a criminal complaint accusing then-President Cristina Fernández and her foreign affairs minister of conspiring with Iran to undermine the investigation—Alberto Nisman, the prosecutor in charge of investigating the bombing, was found dead in his home with a single gunshot wound to the head and a pistol beside him. In 2015, a federal court dismissed Nisman's complaint but an appeal by a federal prosecutor to reopen the investigation was pending at time of writing. As of November 2016, the courts had not determined if Nisman was a victim of suicide or murder.

In 2015, a court began the trial of several officials—including former President Carlos Menem, his head of intelligence, and a judge—for their alleged interference with the initial investigation into the bombing. The trial continued at time of writing.

Indigenous Rights

Indigenous people in Argentina face obstacles in accessing justice, land, education, health care, and basic services. Argentina has failed to effectively implement existing laws to protect indigenous peoples' right to free, prior, and informed consent when the government adopts decisions that may affect their rights—a right provided for in international law.

In May, President Macri created by decree the Advisory and Participatory Council of Indigenous People of Argentina to protect and promote indigenous rights. One of the council's tasks is to ensure that a survey of indigenous lands, required by a 2006 law, is carried out. The survey is being conducted, but slowly.

Women's Rights

Abortion is illegal in Argentina, except in cases of rape or when the life of the woman is at risk. But even in such cases, women and girls are sometimes subject to criminal prosecution for seeking abortions, and have trouble accessing such reproductive services as contraception and voluntary sterilization.

In April, a 27-year-old woman from Tucumán province was sentenced to eight years in prison for aggravated homicide after suffering a miscarriage. In August, the Supreme Court of Tucumán ordered her release, but at time of writing it had yet to adopt a final decision regarding her conviction.

Despite a 2009 law setting forth comprehensive measures to prevent and punish violence against women, the unpunished killing of women remains a serious concern. The National Registry of Femicides, administered by the Supreme Court, reported 235 femicides, but only seven convictions, in 2015.

Sexual Orientation and Gender Identity

In 2010, Argentina became the first Latin American country to legalize same-sex marriage. The Civil Marriage Law allows same-sex couples to enter into civil marriages and affords them the legal protections of marriage enjoyed by opposite-sex couples, including adoption rights and pension benefits. Since 2010, nearly 15,000 same-sex couples have married nationwide.

87

In 2012, the landmark Gender Identity Law established the right of individuals over the age of 18 to choose their gender identity, undergo gender reassignment, and revise official documents without any prior judicial or medical approval.

Key International Actors and Foreign Policy

In July, the United Nations Human Rights Committee called on Argentina to decriminalize abortion and ensure that the new Communications Law does not generate media concentration. It also urged Argentina to appoint an ombudsman to monitor human rights—a position that has been vacant since 2009.

In October, the UN Working Group on Arbitrary Detention (UNWAD) ruled that Milagro Sala's detention was arbitrary and urged the Argentine government to immediately release her. In November, the Argentine government invited the UNWAD and the Inter-American Commission on Human Rights to visit the country to assess Sala's case.

In August, the US government declassified over 1,000 documents—including some from the FBI and Pentagon—containing information about Argentina's Dirty War, an important contribution to the country's efforts to bring those responsible for abuses to justice.

At a December 2015 meeting of the regional trade bloc Mercosur, and several times afterwards, President Macri openly criticized Venezuela's poor human rights record and called for the release of its political prisoners—a much clearer stance than was taken by Foreign Minister Susanna Malcorra before the Organization of American States in May 2015.

In 2016, Argentina announced that it would host a conference on the global Safe Schools Declaration in March 2017.

Armenia

Armenia's human rights record remained uneven in 2016. Authorities used excessive and disproportionate force against peaceful protesters, assaulted journalists, and pressed unjustified criminal charges against protest leaders and participants. Ill-treatment in custody remained a persistent problem, and investigations have been ineffective.

Other concerns include domestic violence, often perpetrated with impunity, violence, and discrimination based on sexual orientation and gender identity, and unnecessary restrictions on access to pain medications for people with life-limiting illnesses.

Excessive Use of Police Force

In July, Armenian authorities used excessive force against peaceful protesters demonstrating support for a radical group opposed to the government, and assaulted journalists reporting on the demonstrations. Authorities arbitrarily detained dozens of protest leaders and participants, pressing unjustified criminal charges against them and denying some of them basic rights of detainees.

Protests erupted after armed men from the radical opposition group, "Founding Parliament," seized a police station in the capital Yerevan on July 17, killing one policeman and taking several hostages. Before the gunmen surrendered on July 31, public support for them and disaffection with the government grew into a protest movement. The protests were largely peaceful, with isolated incidents of violence from participants.

On July 29, police fired stun grenades into peaceful crowds in the neighborhood of the seized police station, causing demonstrators to sustain first and second degree burns and fragmentation wounds. Police did not attempt less violent crowd control means, and did not make any meaningful effort to warn crowds to disperse or about their plans to use force.

Police and unidentified people in civilian clothes acting with them, then charged towards the protesters, punching, kicking, and using wooden clubs and iron bars to beat some protesters, before detaining many of them.

Police warned several journalists to move away from the main crowd before using force. While most journalists complied, police fired several stun grenades in their direction, injuring at least eight. Police and unidentified men also beat some journalists and damaged and seized their equipment.

Authorities opened an investigation into police actions on July 29, sacked the Yerevan police chief, suspended four officers pending the investigation, and reprimanded 13. At time of writing, the investigation was ongoing.

Arbitrary Detentions and Ill-Treatment

In July and August, authorities arbitrarily detained dozens of people linked to the protests, beating many of them, and pressing unjustified criminal charges against some.

Police held some detainees for up to 12 hours without documenting the detention, and on at least two occasions arbitrarily held groups of people in a gymnasium on an interior troop base. Authorities primarily relied on police testimony to press criminal charges against at least 40 people for allegedly "organizing mass disorder," which carries a penalty of up to 10 years' imprisonment. Courts relied on general and abstract reasons to send many of the detainees to pretrial detention. On appeal, courts released some protest leaders from detention on their own recognizance.

Authorities denied many detainees their basic rights, including prompt access to a lawyer of their choosing and the opportunity to inform a relative of their detention and whereabouts. Police also beat many detainees, in some case severely, and did not allow some to get prompt medical care for their injuries. At time of writing, an investigation was pending into illegal detentions and beatings by police.

In a separate case, on January 1, police arrested opposition activist Gevorg Safaryan for allegedly assaulting a police officer, amid a scuffle during a public event organized by "Founding Parliament" members. Sarafyan denies he attacked the officer. A court approved Safaryan's pretrial detention despite no evidence that he posed a flight risk or risk to the investigation. Local human rights groups consider his prosecution politically motivated. Safaryan's trial was continuing at time of writing.

In June, authorities arrested "Founding Parliament" leader Jirair Selifyan and six other members on charges of planning an armed coup. Selifyan denied the accusations as politically motivated.

The gunmen involved in the July armed takeover of the Yerevan police compound demanded Selifyan's release and the president's resignation, initially in exchange for release of hostages. After the men surrendered, authorities charged them with seizure of state buildings, hostage taking, and illegal arms possession. Authorities also arrested several other "Founding Parliament" members, including on suspicion of aiding and abetting the gunmen. Among them is a US citizen of Armenian descent, Garo Yegnukyan, who participated in peaceful protests following the seizure of the police station, and considers the charges politically motivated. Yegnukyan remained in pretrial detention at time of writing.

Women's Rights

Despite evidence that violence against women remains common and sustained pressure from women's rights groups and activists, Armenia has no law criminalizing domestic violence and has not ratified the Council of Europe's Convention on Prevention and Combatting Violence against Women and Domestic Violence. The Coalition to Stop Violence Against Women published a report documenting 30 cases of women killed by intimate partners and family members between 2010 and 2015. The report notes that domestic violence is grossly underreported and largely perpetrated with impunity. Coalition members receive more than 2,000 calls about domestic violence each year.

Palliative Care

Authorities continue to discuss reforming complicated and time-consuming prescription and procurement procedures that create unnecessary obstacles in accessing essential opioid medications. Current regulations obstruct delivery of adequate palliative care, condemning most patients with life-limiting illnesses to unnecessary suffering. Lack of oral opioids, tight police controls on injectable opioids, and restrictive policies on procurement, prescription, and disbursement are inconsistent with many World Health Organization palliative care recommendations.

Sexual Orientation and Gender Identity

Activists reported that lesbian, gay, bisexual, transgender, and intersex (LBGTI) people face discrimination, harassment, and violence. The government has not addressed hate speech or discrimination against LGBTI people. Gender identity and sexual orientation are not included as protected grounds in anti-discrimination or hate speech laws, limiting legal recourse for many crimes against LGBTI people.

Following the October 2015 Rainbow forum, organized by Armenian LGBTI-friendly groups to discuss protection and promotion of minority rights, anonymous people targeted some participants with intimidation and threats, mostly on social media, including to burn and kill them. Authorities refused to launch a criminal investigation into the threats, citing lack of evidence.

In June, the LGBTI rights group, PINK Armenia, published a survey revealing that 90 percent of the population is hostile to LGBTI people and support limits on their rights. In July, PINK Armenia released a report documenting 46 cases of violence and discrimination against LGBTI people in 2015. The government has not taken meaningful steps to combat stereotypes and discrimination against LGBTI people.

Key International Actors

The observation mission of the Council of Europe's Parliamentary Assembly (PACE) called the December 2015 referendum to transform the government from a presidential to a parliamentary system "driven by political interests instead of the needs of the Armenian public." PACE criticized inaccurate voter lists, allegations of vote buying, abuse of administrative resources, an imbalanced media field, and the effective exclusion of people with disabilities in the absence of mobile voting.

The Organization for Security and Co-operation in Europe's representative on freedom of the media, Dunja Mijatović, called for an investigation into verbal and physical attacks on journalists at referendum polling stations.

In response to the July demonstrations, the European Union delegation, together with heads of mission of EU Members States in Armenia, called on the authorities to avoid using unnecessary force and for effective investigations into police actions, and urged demonstrators to protest peacefully. The United Nations in Armenia called for swift investigations and respect for peaceful assembly and free expression rights and criticized the use of force against journalists.

In a September Human Rights Council speech, United Nations High Commissioner for Human Rights Zeid Ra'ad al-Hussein criticized the authorities' denial of full access for his staff, preventing full engagement with the government and civil society.

In a report to the Human Rights Council in March, Maud de Boer-Buquicchio, UN special rapporteur on the sale of children, child prostitution, and child pornography, acknowledged Armenia's progress in combatting trafficking in persons, reducing placement of children in residential care, and limiting intercountry adoptions. However, she stated that the extent of child trafficking is unclear in the absence of relevant legislation and child-friendly complaint mechanisms, and insufficient awareness-raising among parents, professionals, and society. She urged authorities to pass domestic violence and other relevant legislation and ensure the child protection system consistently acts in the best interests of the child.

Australia

Australia is a vibrant multicultural democracy with a strong record of protecting civil and political rights, but serious human rights issues remain. In 2016, the government continued its draconian policy of offshore transfers of asylum seekers to Manus Island in Papua New Guinea (PNG) and Nauru. There were growing calls to address abusive offshore detention conditions and resettle those found to be refugees in Australia.

Indigenous Australians remain disproportionately subject to the criminal justice system. In 2016, the government of Prime Minister Malcolm Turnbull announced a royal commission into the mistreatment of children in detention facilities in the Northern Territory.

Australia does not recognize the right of same-sex couples to marry. The Australian government announced a plebiscite on the right of same-sex couples to marry, but political opponents blocked it, arguing a plebiscite is expensive and wasteful and that the issue should be determined by a parliamentary free vote.

In November, controversy over the Racial Discrimination Act—including attacks on the Australian Human Rights Commission for its handling of discrimination complaints—led the government to set up a parliamentary inquiry to examine whether the act imposes unreasonable limits on free speech. Other human rights concerns include overly broad counterterrorism laws and limits to the rights of people with disabilities.

Asylum Seekers and Refugees

Since June 2013, anyone intercepted arriving by boat and seeking refuge in Australia has been sent to Manus Island or Nauru. At time of writing, more than 900 asylum seekers and refugees lived on Manus Island and about 1,200 on Nauru.

In February 2016, the Australian High Court rejected a constitutional challenge to the offshore detention regime in Nauru. The court ruled that Australia's role in securing, funding, and participating in the detention of asylum seekers and refugees on Nauru was authorized by law. However, in April, the PNG Supreme Court ruled that the detention of asylum seekers on Manus Island was unconstitutional. In August, the Australian and PNG governments agreed to close the center, although they set no timetable.

On Nauru, refugees and asylum seekers regularly endure violence, threats, and harassment from Nauruans, with little protection from local authorities. They face unnecessary delays in, and at times denial of, medical care, even for life-threatening conditions. Many have dire mental health problems and suffer from depression. Self-harm and suicide attempts are frequent. In May 2016, two refugees self-immolated in separate incidents; one died and the other was badly burned.

At time of writing, only 25 of the 675 refugees on Manus had been allowed to move to mainland PNG, working in Lae or Port Moresby. Of this number, several returned to Manus citing threats to personal safety and poor working and living conditions. Of six refugees who resettled from Nauru to Cambodia under an A$55 million (US$43 million) deal struck between the countries in 2015, two remain. The others returned to their country of origin.

The Australian government's offshore operations are highly secretive. Service providers working for the Australian government face criminal charges and civil penalties if they disclose information about conditions for asylum seekers and refugees. In August and September 2016, the Guardian newspaper published more than 2,000 leaked documents that exposed endemic and systematic abuse, predominantly of children, at the Nauru detention center.

In 2016, the Australian navy turned back boats carrying migrants, sending them to Vietnamese and Sri Lankan waters. Both countries have poor records concerning returned migrants.

Asylum seekers or refugees perceived to be lesbian, gay, bisexual, transgender, or intersex (LGBTI) face harassment and abuse despite the recent decriminalization of same-sex conduct in Nauru; in Papua New Guinea, such conduct remains criminalized.

In November, the Turnbull Government introduced legislation that would prohibit adult asylum seekers and refugees who have attempted to arrive in Australia by boat since July 19, 2013, from ever obtaining an Australian visa of any kind. In November, the government also announced a one-off arrangement to resettle some refugees from Manus and Nauru in the United States, saying that women, children, and families would be prioritized. At time of writing, no one had been removed for resettlement to the US.

Indigenous Rights

2016 marked the 25th anniversary of the Royal Commission into Aboriginal Deaths in Custody. The commission recommended that imprisonment of indigenous convicted of crimes be a sanction of last resort. However, since 1991, the rate of indigenous imprisonment has doubled.

Indigenous Australians are significantly overrepresented in the criminal justice system. Indigenous adults are 13 times more likely to be imprisoned than their non-indigenous counterparts. Aboriginal women are the fastest growing prisoner demographic in Australia. In the state of Western Australia, some 50 percent of the female adult prison population is of Aboriginal or Torres Strait Islander origin even though such individuals make up only 3 percent of the state's population. Indigenous offenders are disproportionately detained or imprisoned for minor and poverty-related offenses, particularly public order and unpaid fines offenses.

The juvenile detention rate for indigenous youth is about 24 times the rate of non-indigenous youth. Indigenous children are often held in pre-trial detention, despite the international legal requirement that detention of children be a last resort and for the shortest appropriate period of time.

In October, the Turnbull Government instructed the Australian Law Reform Commission to report on the overrepresentation of indigenous Australians in prisons; Federal Attorney-General George Brandis called it a "national tragedy."

Children's Rights

In July 2016, the Australian Broadcasting Corporation aired disturbing CCTV footage showing the teargassing, hooding, shackling, and stripping of children at a youth detention facility in August 2014. The incident had been a subject of a 2015 report by the Northern Territory's children's commissioner that revealed serious shortcomings in juvenile detention practices in the territory. Despite the report, territory officials failed to act. Within 12 hours of the footage airing, Prime

Minister Turnbull announced a royal commission into child protection and youth detention in the territory.

In August, the Queensland attorney general announced an independent review into the practices, operation, and oversight of Queensland's youth detention facilities after the emergence of allegations of mistreatment akin to those in the Northern Territory.

Counterterrorism Laws

Since 2014, the Australian government has introduced a range of counterterrorism laws in response to the threat of "home-grown terrorism."

In September, the government introduced two further legislative measures to deter terrorist attacks. The first bill proposes legislation that would allow a judge to authorize detention for terrorist offenders who have served their sentences but who pose an "unacceptable risk" of committing a serious offense if released. Such post-sentence detention for periods of up to three years could be renewed, raising concerns about arbitrary and indefinite detention using a low standard of proof and secret evidence. The second bill, passed in November, extends control orders to 14 year olds.

Disability Rights

In November 2015, a senate committee inquiry found that violence, abuse, and neglect of people with disabilities is both "widespread and takes many forms." The committee's report detailed long-term systematic abuse of persons with disabilities in residential and institutional settings.

Women and girls with disabilities in Australia are particularly at risk of sexual violence. Studies have shown that women with disabilities face much higher rates of sexual abuse than the general population of women. Some face coerced sterilization and forced psychiatric interventions.

People with disabilities are overrepresented in prisons and are more likely to be investigated, charged, remanded to custody, or serve longer prison terms than people without disabilities. In some cases, people with disabilities have been languishing in prison for years without having been convicted of a crime, simply because the government has not provided alternatives to incarceration.

In July 2016, the government rolled out the new National Disability Insurance Scheme (NDIS). While the NDIS represents a major advancement on many fronts, in some states it harms services for people with disabilities most at risk, such as those in contact with the justice system.

Foreign Policy

Australia raises human rights concerns in other countries, but does so very selectively. It seldom raises human rights concerns publicly about countries it works closely with in interdicting asylum seekers and refugees or with which it has significant trade relations.

However, Australia supported a US-led joint statement at the United Nations Human Rights Council in March condemning China's detention of activists and enforced disappearances of citizens and foreigners. In August, Australia and Vietnam held their 13th Annual Human Rights Dialogue in Hanoi. Australia reiterated its "serious concerns about the harassment, arrest and detention of peaceful human rights activists."

In February, the government announced that Philip Ruddock would be Australia's first special envoy for human rights and would drive Australia's campaign for a seat on the UN Human Rights Council in 2018. As Australia's immigration minister from 1996 to 2003, Ruddock implemented the "Pacific Solution," Australia's abusive policy of offshore detention and processing of refugees and asylum seekers.

In May, a parliamentary committee report into Australia's advocacy for the abolition of the death penalty called on the Foreign Affairs Department to coordinate "a whole-of-government strategy for the abolition of the death penalty which has as its focus, countries of the Indo-Pacific and the United States of America."

Key International Actors

In February, the UN Committee on the Rights of the Child expressed "great concern" over the Australian High Court's finding that detaining asylum seekers offshore is legal. In May, the UN refugee agency stated that Australia's "current policy of offshore processing and prolonged detention is immensely harmful" and that the arrangements with Nauru and PNG had "proved completely untenable."

In August 2016, in response to the leaked files published in the *Guardian*, the UN High Commissioner for Human Rights again urged Nauru and Australian authorities to "put an end to the model of processing and keeping migrants offshore."

In October, UN Special Rapporteur on Human Rights Defenders Michael Forst visited Australia and expressed concern about restrictions facing civil society, freedom of expression, freedom of assembly, and access to justice. In November, UN Special Rapporteur on the Human Rights of Migrants Francois Crepeau visited Australia and Nauru and found that some of Australia's migration policies "have increasingly eroded the rights of migrants, in contravention of its international human rights and humanitarian obligations." Crepeau expressed deep concern about the impact of such policies on the mental health of many migrants.

HUMAN RIGHTS WATCH

HARASSED, IMPRISONED, EXILED

Azerbaijan's Continuing Crackdown on Government Critics, Lawyers, and Civil Society

Azerbaijan

The government continued its thorough crackdown on dissenting voices in 2016, leaving a wide gap in Azerbaijan's once vibrant independent civil society. Authorities released 17 human rights defenders, journalists, and political activists imprisoned on politically motivated charges. But at least 25 government critics remained wrongfully imprisoned, including political activists and bloggers arrested in 2016. Restrictive laws continue to prevent nongovernmental organizations (NGOs) from operating independently.

Reports of torture and other ill-treatment persisted throughout the year.

The September 2016 constitutional referendum abolished minimum age requirements for presidential and parliamentary candidates, extended from five to seven years the presidential term of office, and expanded the power of the presidency.

The Extractive Industry Transparency Initiative (EITI) declined to restore Azerbaijan's full membership in the organization and gave the government four months to reform its laws limiting space for civil society or face suspension.

Prosecuting Government Critics

In March, President Ilham Aliyev pardoned 13 journalists, human rights defenders, activists, and bloggers who had been prosecuted on politically motivated charges in previous years. Their convictions have not been quashed, and some former detainees continued to face travel and work restrictions and risk detention if they resume their work. Some led NGOs, and these groups remained closed.

Also in March, courts converted the prison sentences of journalist Rauf Mirgadirov and human rights lawyer Intigam Aliyev to suspended terms and released both. In May, the Supreme Court similarly converted investigative journalist Khadija Ismayilova's prison term and released her. All three retain a criminal record and two faced foreign travel restrictions.

Ilgar Mammadov, leader of the pro-democracy opposition movement Republican Alternative (REAL), remained in prison despite the 2014 European Court of Human Rights decision on his case and repeated demands by the Council of Europe to release him. Others who remain behind bars include youth activist Ilkin Rustamzadeh, opposition Azerbaijani Popular Front Party Popular (APFP) activist Murad Adilov, journalist Seymur Hazi, and blogger Abdul Adilov.

New Arrests and Convictions

In August, in the lead-up to the constitutional referendum, the government arrested eight activists on a range of false, politically motivated charges, including drug possession, hooliganism, incitement, and illegal business activity. The authorities also accused some activists of possessing banned or potentially illegally imported materials related to Fethulla Gülen, the US-based imam who Turkey accuses of organizing the failed July 2016 coup attempt there.

Among those arrested were Fuad Ahmadli, a well-known social media activist and senior APFP member and Faig Amirov, financial director for the leading opposition newspaper *Azadlig*. During searches following their arrests, police claimed to have found prohibited religious books and compact discs related to Gülen, but also pressed other criminal charges against them. Both were in custody at time of writing.

Police also arrested three REAL members: Natig Jafarli, the party's executive secretary, who had publicly criticized the constitutional referendum, and two other REAL activists campaigning against the referendum. A court jailed the latter two for a week for refusing to abide by a police order not to distribute campaign leaflets. In September, Jafarli was released pending trial.

Authorities continued to target leading and rank-and-file APFP activists, at least 12 of whom were either on trial or serving prison terms in 2016. Among those facing trial is Fuad Gahramanli, deputy APFP chairman, arrested in December 2015 on trumped-up charges of calling for the government's overthrow. The charges are part of the criminal conspiracy and terrorism case against religious activists in Nardaran, a Baku suburb known for its Shi'ia conservatism. Gahramanli was in pretrial custody at time of writing. In March, a court convicted Mammad Ibrahim, advisor to APFP chairman Ali Kerimli, on spurious hooliganism charges and sentenced him to three years in prison. Elvin Abdullayev, a youth activist and APFP member remained in prison since his January 2015 arrest on dubious drug possession charges. In June 2016, the Supreme Court reduced his prison sentence from six to two-and-half years.

Freedom of Media

Independent outlets faced harassment and closure, and critical journalists faced threats and intimidation aimed at silencing them.

In April, authorities launched a criminal investigation into alleged tax evasion and related economic infractions supposedly involving 15 journalists who cooperate with Meydan TV, a Berlin-based online independent Azeri-language media outlet that provides critical reporting on human rights, corruption, and similar issues. They were at liberty pending the investigation; at least seven of them face travel bans while under investigation. In December 2015 and April 2016, courts convicted three family members of Meydan TV's exiled journalists on trumped-up drug charges and paroled them in April 2016 after they had served less than a year.

In September, the state-run printing house refused to publish *Azadlig* due to the newspaper's failure to make a debt payment to the company following the detention of Faig Amirli. As a result, *Azadlig* had to indefinitely suspend its print edition.

In July, authorities first suspended and then revoked the broadcasting license of a privately owned, staunchly pro-government ANS television, following its announcement to broadcast an interview with Fethullah Gulen. The TV channels remained closed at time of writing.

Freedom of Association

Highly restrictive and punitive regulations on NGOs adopted in 2014 and 2015 make it almost impossible for independent groups to fund and carry out their work. In February 2016, new regulations went into force giving the Justice Ministry broad powers to conduct intrusive inspections of NGOs on a wide range of grounds.

In April, the Prosecutor's Office suspended the sweeping criminal investigation opened in 2014 against dozens of foreign donors and their grantees. Several organizations and their leaders that are members of Azerbaijan's coalition for the Extractive Industries Transparency Initiative (EITI) saw restrictions linked to the investigation lifted. The authorities unfroze their bank accounts, lifted travel bans against them, and stopped intrusive screenings at the Azerbaijani borders.

Despite the unfrozen bank accounts, several groups in the EITI coalition cannot access funding because authorities refuse to register their grant agreements. Azerbaijani regulations require NGOs to provide banks with proof of grant registration in order to access grant funds.

The bank accounts of at least a dozen NGOs that worked on human rights and government accountability remain blocked; the groups suspended their work or operate in exile.

Torture and Ill-Treatment

Torture and other ill-treatment continued with impunity. In August, police arrested Elgiz Gahraman, member of an opposition youth movement, and held him incommunicado for six days. Garhraman told his lawyer police beat and threatened him with sexual humiliation to force him to confess to false drug possession charges. Authorities failed to effectively investigate. Gahraman remained in custody at time of writing.

In May, police arrested youth activists Giyas Ibrahimov and Bayram Mammadov for spraying graffiti on a monument to former President Heydar Aliyev and demanded that they apologize on camera. When they refused, policemen beat and threatened to rape them with truncheons to force them to confess to drug possession. Authorities failed to conduct effective investigation into the ill-treatment allegations. In October, Ibrahimov was sentenced to 10 years' imprisonment; Mammadov's trial was ongoing at time of writing.

In July, 18 of the 68 defendants in a high-profile trial counterterrorism case told a court that police had beaten them repeatedly to elicit confessions and testimony. The case concerns state allegations that Taleh Bagirzade, a religious activist who had previously been jailed on politically motivated charges, conspired with others to overthrow the government.

A November 2015 police raid to arrest Bagirzade in Nardaran, a Baku suburb, turned violent during unclear and disputed circumstances, with shootings leaving two police and seven civilians dead. Bagirzade stated at trial that state agents beat him to induce testimony against two political opposition leaders. Authorities denied the allegations and did not thoroughly investigate.

Key International Actors

The United States, European Union, and Azerbaijan's other bilateral and international partners welcomed the release of government critics but failed to effectively leverage the potential of their relationships with the government to press for meaningful rights improvements.

In October, EITI, a prominent international coalition that promotes good governance in oil, gas, and other extractive industries, declined to restore Azerbaijan's full membership status in the organization, and gave the government four months to reform its restrictive NGO laws or face suspension.

Following its May 2016 visit, the United Nations Working Group on Arbitrary Detention noted receiving "a large number of testimonies [...] about torture and ill treatment" in custody. It also observed "dire conditions of living and high level of negligence in the institution for women," and expressed dismay "about the application of chemical restraints accompanied in the case of children with 'light' electroshocks" in one institution.

Following his September visit, the UN special rapporteur on human rights defenders, Michel Forst, urged the government to stop criminalization of human rights defenders for peaceful and legitimate activities, release all detained defenders, and rescind criminal and administrative sanctions against them and their families.

In its October concluding observations, the UN Human Rights Committee urged Azerbaijani authorities to end "the crackdown on public associations ... ensuring that they can operate freely and without fear of retribution for their legitimate activities."

In late 2015, Council of Europe Secretary General Thorbjørn Jagland launched an inquiry into Azerbaijan's failure to carry out the European Court of Human Rights' rulings. Jagland's special representative could not visit Azerbaijan throughout 2016, apparently due to the lack of government cooperation to facilitate the initiative.

In December 2015, bipartisan legislation was introduced in the US House of Representatives, calling on the Azerbaijani government to free all "political prisoners." The bill called for, among other things, visa bans on unnamed senior Azerbaijani officials responsible for the crackdown.

During her March visit to Baku, European Union High Representative for Foreign Affairs and Security Policy Federica Mogherini announced the EU's intention to speed up negotiations on a new partnership agreement with Azerbaijan, making little public mention of Baku's atrocious human rights record.

International financial institutions have continued or increased funding to the Azerbaijan government, including in the extractives industries, despite the worsening human rights situation.

Bahrain

There was a marked deterioration in the human rights situation in Bahrain in mid-2016, when authorities dissolved the main political opposition group, al-Wifaq, jailed the country's leading human rights activist, and harassed and prosecuted Shia clerics who peacefully protested the arbitrary revocation of the citizenship of al-Wifaq's spiritual leader, Sheikh Isa Qasim. This orchestrated crackdown on the rights to free expression, assembly and association undermined prospects for a political solution to Bahrain's domestic unrest.

Authorities made little progress in holding officials accountable for the mistreatment and torture of detainees, continued to arbitrarily strip citizenship from Bahrainis who have been critical of the government, and subjected civil society actors to arbitrary travel bans.

Freedoms of Expression, Assembly, and Association

Human rights activists Zainab al-Khawaja spent three months in jail after her detention in March 2016 based on four convictions that violated her right to free expression, one of which resulted from an unfair trial. Al-Khawaja left Bahrain for Denmark, where she also has citizenship, after authorities released her in June. She said Bahraini authorities were preparing to press further charges against her that could have resulted in a lengthy prison sentence.

In May, Bahrain's High Court of Appeal more than doubled the prison sentence of al-Wifaq's secretary-general, Sheikh Ali Salman, from four years to nine years. The appeal court overturned a trial court's decision to acquit him of advocating the overthrow of the government by force. It increased the sentence despite strong evidence his initial trial was unfair and the fact that two of the charges on which he had been convicted clearly violated his right to freedom of expression.

In June, authorities detained prominent human rights activist Nabeel Rajab solely on charges that violate his right to free expression. He is facing 15 years in prison on charges that include criticism of Bahrain's participation in Saudi Arabia-led military operations in Yemen, and "offending national institutions." The latter charge is based on comments about alleged torture of inmates in Jaw Prison in March 2015. On September 5, authorities charged Rajab with "undermining the prestige of the state," one day after the *New York Times* published an open letter he wrote from prison.

Also in June, the Ministry of Justice and Islamic Affairs requested that the judiciary dissolve al-Wifaq. The court issued an "expedited" ruling on June 14 ordering the group to close its headquarters and suspend activities, and confiscated its funds based on government allegations that the party was a cover for "acts associated with extremism and terrorism." Authorities produced no evidence to support their allegations.

After authorities arbitrarily stripped al-Wifaq's spiritual leader Sheikh Isa Qasim of his citizenship in June for allegedly inciting sectarianism, hundreds of people, including many Shia clerics, gathered in peaceful protest outside his home in the town of Diraz. Authorities responded with a campaign of harassment against Shia clerics, in violation of their right to free expression and peaceful assembly.

In August, a Bahraini court convicted Sheikh Ali Humaidan of "illegal gathering" and sentenced him to one year in prison for his involvement in the Diraz protests. One of the most high-profile Shia clerics charged with illegal gathering, Sheikh Maytham al-Salman, said that police insisted that he remove his clerical turban and robes, refused his request to shower and change his clothes, and kept him in interview rooms for 26 hours without sleep. He said he believed the insistence that he remove his religious attire was intended to "insult and intimidate a Shia cleric." Credible Bahraini sources told Human Rights Watch that authorities questioned or brought charges against more than 50 Shia clerics in the aftermath of the Diraz protests.

In July, a prosecutor charged Nazeeha Saeed, a Bahraini correspondent for the French news agency Agence France Presse, with violating the country's licensing law for journalists. Bahrain's Information Affairs Authority sent a letter to one of Saeed's employers citing "the unsatisfactory evaluation of her performance by our specialists" as the reason for not renewing the license.

Mistreatment of Detainees

The third annual report from the Office of the Ombudsman, released in June 2016, provided further evidence that authorities have made little progress in holding police and security forces accountable for the torture and mistreatment of detainees.

Since it was created in 2012, the Office of the Ombudsman has, according to its annual reports, referred 138 cases to the Special Investigations Unit, the body responsible for investigating and prosecuting security or other government officials allegedly involved in the torture or cruel, inhuman, or degrading treatment of detainees. Of these, the Special Investigations Unit has successfully prosecuted only one torture case, which the ombudsman's second annual report characterized as "a vicious assault" on a detainee "in an attempt to force him to confess to drug dealing."

The ombudsman's 2016 report contained no information on the status of 15 complaints relating to the alleged torture of inmates by prison officials after unrest in Jaw Prison in March 2015. In May, M. Cherif Bassiouni, the lead author of the Bahrain Independent Commission of Inquiry report into the anti-government protests of 2011 and the disproportionate response of the security forces, urged "the pursuit of investigations of those responsible for the killing of five persons under torture and the ascertainment of their superiors' responsibility."

Revocation of Nationality

As a result of a 2014 amendment to Bahrain's citizenship law, the Interior Ministry can, with cabinet approval, revoke the citizenship of any person who, according to authorities, "aids or is involved in the service of a hostile state" or who "causes harm to the interests of the Kingdom or acts in a way that contravenes his duty of loyalty to it."

In 2016, information from media reports and credible local sources indicates that the Bahraini authorities stripped 133 individuals of their citizenship, bringing the total to 341 since the beginning of 2015. They can be classified into three broad categories: human rights defenders, political activists, and journalists; Bahrainis known to be fighting alongside the Islamic State (also known as ISIS); and individuals convicted of domestic terrorism offenses.

In June 2016, the Interior Ministry said it was revoking the citizenship of Sheikh Isa Qasim, considered the spiritual leader of the main opposition group, al-

Wifaq. It accused him of "creating an extremist sectarian environment" and saying he had "encouraged sectarianism and violence."

Bahraini authorities deported seven stateless Bahrainis whom they had previously stripped of their citizenship, including Shia cleric Mohamed Khojasta in February, academic Masaud Jahromi in March, and human rights lawyer Taimoor Karimi in June.

Right to Leave the Country

Authorities have placed arbitrary travel bans on tens of individuals who have been critical of the authorities' human rights abuses. In September, an arbitrary travel ban prevented human rights activist Nedal al-Salman from attending a United Nations Human Rights Council meeting in Geneva, after earlier subjecting two of al-Salman's colleagues from the Bahrain Centre for Human Rights to similar bans.

Other Bahrainis subjected to travel bans included Mohamed al-Tajer, a human rights lawyer; Abdulnabi al-Ekry, a rights activist; Jalila al-Salman, the former vice-president of the dissolved Bahrain Teacher's Society; Rula al-Saffar, a nurse and human rights activist; Mohamed Sharaf, the president of the Bahraini chapter of Transparency International; and journalist Nazeeha Saeed.

Women's Rights, Sexual Orientation, and Gender Identity

Law no. 19 of 2009 on the Promulgation of the Law of Family Rulings regulates matters of personal status in Bahrain's Sunni courts. The law does not apply in the country's Shia courts, with the result that Shia women, who comprise the majority in Bahrain, are not covered by a codified personal status law. Both Sunni and Shia women are discriminated against. For instance, men have a unilateral right divorce their wives; Sunni men can do so orally, and Shia men must do so in writing. Women must apply to the courts for a divorce.

Adultery is criminalized, as are sexual relations outside marriage, which is prosecuted under an article that criminalizes "an act of indecency with a female." However, there is no law that prohibits discrimination on the grounds of sex, gender, sexual orientation, or gender identity.

Key International Actors

Bahrain remained a member of the Saudi Arabia-led coalition that launched air strikes in Yemen throughout 2016, causing hundreds of civilian deaths, according to the UN.

The United States, which has a permanent naval base in Bahrain, criticized the dissolution of al-Wifaq and called on the government to drop charges and free Nabel Rajab. The United Kingdom, for whom the Bahrainis are building a permanent naval base, failed to call for the release of any imprisoned activists, or to criticize the dissolution of al-Wifaq.

In September, US government officials announced that the approval of the sale of F-16 fighter jets to Bahrain would be dependent on unspecified improvements in the human rights situation in the country.

In August, five UN human rights experts issued a joint statement criticizing authorities' "systematic harassment of the Shia population."

HUMAN
RIGHTS
WATCH

"No Right to Live"
"Kneecapping" and Maiming of Detainees
by Bangladesh Security Forces

Bangladesh

Bangladesh witnessed a spate of violent attacks against secular bloggers, academics, gay rights activists, foreigners, and members of religious minorities in 2016.

On July 1, armed gunmen attacked the Holey Artisan Bakery, a café in Dhaka, killing 21 people, including foreigners, while holding Bangladeshi staff and guests hostage until security forces stormed the café the next morning. On July 8, three people were killed at a checkpoint when gunmen carrying bombs tried to attack a gathering to mark the Muslim Eid holiday.

Although Islamist extremist groups, including the Islamic State or ISIS, claimed responsibility for most of these killings, the government blamed domestic groups, and said some had links to the main opposition political parties. Thousands of people were arrested, and dozens of alleged members or supporters of extremist groups are said to have been killed in armed encounters.

Fire and safety factory inspections continued in the garment industry following agreements between big brands and the Bangladeshi government arising out of the 2013 Rana Plaza disaster. However, a September fire in a packaging factory killed at least 24 people, highlighting the need for further efforts to ensure worker rights and safety.

Security Force Abuse and Impunity

Bangladesh security forces have a long history of arbitrary arrest, enforced disappearance, and extrajudicial killing, raising concerns about recent arrests and deaths. The Detective Branch of the police, the Bangladesh Border Guards (BGB), the Directorate General Forces Inspectorate (DGFI), and the Rapid Action Battalion (RAB) have all been accused of serious violations.

In June 2016, security forces arrested nearly 15,000 people, mostly young men, in connection with a series of attacks targeting writers, minority religious leaders, and activists.

Following the July attack on the Holey Artisan Café, security forces reportedly arbitrarily detained and in many cases killed suspected militants. Two of the hostages in the attack were secretly arrested and detained for over a month until international and national pressure forced the government to admit to holding them in detention. A kitchen assistant, initially suspected to be one of the attackers, was allegedly tortured to death. The government announced several raids in various parts of the country but, due to lack of transparency about security force abuses and the ongoing government clampdown on media, details of those killed or arrested remain unclear.

Attacks on Civil Society

Human rights groups in Bangladesh face constant obstacles, including escalating harassment and surveillance by police. A new law placed strong restrictions on receiving foreign funds without approval by the NGO Affairs Bureau within the Prime Minister's Office.

Journalists are also a common target. The editor of the English-language *Daily Star*, Mahfuz Anam, faces a total of 54 criminal defamation cases and 15 sedition cases. Fifty-five cases have been filed against editor Matiur Rahman and some journalists associated with the country's highest circulation daily, *Prothom Alo*, for criminal defamation and "hurting religious sentiment."

Freedom of Expression

Several laws were proposed in 2016 to increase restrictions on freedom of expression. The Distortion of the History of Bangladesh Liberation War Crimes Act provides for imprisonment and fines if details of the 1971 war of independence are debated or disputed. The Foreign Donation (Voluntary Activities) Regulation Act, passed in October, to control nongovernmental organizations (NGOs) will hinder freedoms of expression and association. Proposed Press Council Act amendments include provisions for closing newspapers.

The government continues to use the overly broad and vague Information and Communication Technology Act against people critical of decisions and activities of senior government officials or their families.

Bloggers expressing secular views and editors and writers supporting sexual minority rights were attacked in 2016, many of them hacked to death in public spaces. While authorities condemned the attacks, some recommended that individuals holding unpopular views censor themselves, implying that the responsibility for avoiding such attacks lay with the victims.

Minorities

Several religious leaders were killed or injured in targeted attacks, allegedly by the same extremist Muslim groups that targeted secular writers. In April, the advocacy group Hindu-Buddha-Christian Oikya Parishad said there had been three times more incidents of violence against minority communities in the first three months of 2016 than in all of 2015. Hindu shrines, temples and homes were attacked over the October 2016 Diwali festival. The government responded by arresting several hundred suspects, but some sporadic attacks against the Hindu community continued. Thousands of indigenous people in the Chittagong Hill Tracts and other areas are at risk of forced displacement.

Environment

Workers in the tanneries of Hazaribagh, a residential area in Dhaka, continue to suffer from highly toxic and dangerous working conditions, while residents of nearby slums complain of illnesses caused by the tanneries' extreme pollution of air, water, and soil. The government continues its de facto policy of not enforcing labor and environmental laws with respect to the tanneries and has failed to insist on the relocation of the tanneries to a dedicated industrial zone in Savar, ignoring a High Court decision from 2001.

Some 20 years after the problem of arsenic in Bangladesh's drinking water first came to the world's attention, 20 million people in Bangladesh are still drinking water contaminated with arsenic above the national standard. Deeper wells drilled down approximately 150 meters into the ground can often supply higher-quality water without arsenic, but some politicians are diverting funds for such wells to political supporters and allies, a practice facilitated by a government policy permitting national parliamentarians to influence the siting of 50 percent of all new government water points.

HUMAN RIGHTS WATCH

NEPOTISM AND NEGLECT

The Failing Response to Arsenic in the Drinking Water
of Bangladesh's Rural Poor

Labor Rights

Bangladeshi authorities again failed to implement their commitments under the Sustainability Compact in 2016. These include amending the Labour Act and laws governing Export Processing Zones to bring them in line with international standards. Largely, factory officials were not held accountable for attacks, threats, and retaliation against workers involved with unions.

In August, a Bangladeshi court charged 18 people with murder for the 2013 collapse of the Rana Plaza textile factory, which killed 1,135 people and injured hundreds.

In September, another factory fire and building collapse in a packaging factory killed 31 workers and injured another 50.

Women's and Girls' Rights

Bangladesh government data indicates that the percentage of girls marrying before age 18 declined from 65 percent in 2014 to 52 percent in 2016, and that 18 percent of girls still marry before the age of 15, the highest rate in Asia and among the highest in the world. In 2014, the government pledged to end marriage of children younger than 15 by 2021, and marriage younger than 18 by 2041.

In 2016, the government undermined progress toward these goals by continuing to push for weakening of the law governing the minimum age of marriage. At present, the minimum age of marriage for women is 18 with no exceptions, but the government proposed to allow 16- and 17-year-old girls to marry with parental consent, a change that would constitute a de facto lowering of the age of marriage, as most marriages are arranged by parents. A national plan on ending child marriage, promised by end-2014, had still not been finalized at time of writing.

Stalking, sexual harassment, and violent retaliation against and even murder of women and girls who protest such harassment continued in 2016. Prompt investigation and prosecution in such cases continues to be rare.

Indigenous women and girls face multiple forms of discrimination due to their gender, indigenous identity, and socio-economic status; they are especially vulnerable to sexual and gender-based violence.

Overseas Workers

Millions of Bangladeshis work abroad, sending home remittances worth billions of US dollars. In 2016 alone, almost 100,000 women migrated overseas, mostly to Gulf countries, for domestic work. The government has sought to increase the recruitment of such workers without putting in place adequate mechanisms to protect them against workplace abuses. Bangladeshi workers in the Gulf continue to report being deprived of food and forced to endure psychological, physical, and sexual abuse. In some cases, such abuses amount to forced labor or trafficking. Some Bangladeshi domestic workers pay high recruitment fees and take out loans in order to migrate.

Bangladesh has set a minimum salary for domestic workers in the Gulf equivalent to roughly US$200, the lowest minimum salary of all sending countries—and its embassies in the region do not provide adequate protection and assistance to many Bangladeshi nationals there.

Refugees

Bangladesh began its first census of undocumented Rohingya refugees in June, setting off fears that it might lead to a mass relocation or forcible repatriation to Burma. About 32,000 Rohingya are sheltered in camps administered by the United Nations, but hundreds of thousands who have never been allowed to register as refugees or to lodge asylum claims live undocumented in squalid, makeshift camps, or in private dwellings scattered around southeast Bangladesh, vulnerable to human traffickers and exploited as cheap labor.

War Crimes Trials

The International Crimes Tribunal (ICT), set up to address laws of war violations committed during Bangladesh's 1971 independence movement, continued its operations in 2015 without addressing serious procedural and substantive defects. In September, the government executed Mir Qasem Ali, a senior member of the executive committee of the opposition Jamaat-e-Islaami party, for crimes he alleged committed in 1971, even as the country's chief justice criticized the attorney general, the prosecution, and investigators for producing insufficient evidence in the case. The government secretly detained Ali's son, a key member of his defense team, denied him access to his father before execution, and forbade him from participating in the funeral.

Sexual Orientation and Gender Identity

Prominent gay activists Xulhaz Mannan, the founder of *Roopbaan*, Bangladesh's first lesbian, gay, bisexual, transgender, and intersex (LGBTI) magazine, and Mahbub Rabby Tonoy, the general secretary of the group, were hacked to death in April. Al-Qaeda in the Indian Subcontinent (AQIS) claimed responsibility for the killings. Fearing for their lives, many LGBT activists sought temporary refuge outside the country.

"Carnal intercourse against the order of nature" carries a maximum sentence of 10 years in prison. The government has twice rejected recommendations to repeal the colonial-era law during its Universal Periodic Review at the UN Human Rights Council.

The Bangladesh cabinet in 2014 declared legal recognition of a third gender category for hijras—a traditional cultural identity for transgender people who, assigned male at birth, do not identify as men—but the absence of a definition of the term or procedure for gaining recognition of third gender status led to abuses in implementation of the legal change. In June and July 2015, a group of hijras were subjected to harassment and invasive and abusive physical examinations at a government hospital as a requirement to join a government employment program.

Key International Actors

India, the United Kingdom, and the United States, countries with significant influence over the Bangladesh government, remained largely silent on the country's human rights record in their public statements in 2016. The UK said nothing publicly at all.

The US Department of Justice funded and trained an internal investigations program within the RAB, but the program produced no human rights prosecutions or convictions in 2016, and US authorities said little publicly to signal the importance of holding RAB officers accountable for human rights crimes. In July, Secretary of State John Kerry offered US assistance to Bangladeshi authorities investigating the militant attack on the Holey Artisan Bakery that killed 21 people in Dhaka.

The United Nations High Commissioner on Human Rights raised concerns about the lack of fairness in the war crimes trials and about arbitrary and illegal arrests, but the Bangladeshi government ignored the statements.

Belarus

Belarus' human rights friendly rhetoric was not supported by genuine human rights improvements in 2016. The death penalty remains in use. Officials continue to prosecute human rights activists and critical journalists on spurious charges. Legislative amendments further restricted freedom of expression by expanding the definition of "extremism" and by banning dissemination of certain types of information among children under the false pretense of protecting them. International observers recognized some progress during the September parliamentary elections, but called for additional reforms.

The European Union lifted sanctions, citing releases of political prisoners and improved elections. The European Bank for Reconstruction and Development ended restrictions on lending to state entities. Authorities continue to refuse to cooperate with the United Nations special rapporteur on Belarus.

In October, the government finalized an action plan to implement recommendations made by UN human rights treaty bodies and the Human Rights Council in the country's Universal Periodic Review. The government did not consult independent civil society, and the plan lacks specifics and does not adequately address civil and political rights.

Death Penalty

Belarus remains the only European country with the death penalty. There were no steps in 2016 to introduce a moratorium or abolish it.

Ivan Kulesh and Siarhei Khmialeusk were executed in November 2016. Siarhei Ivanou, sentenced in 2015 for murder, was executed in April, although his complaint about violations of his rights was pending before the United Nations Human Rights Committee.

Death sentences were issued to Henadz Yakavitski for murder, Siarhei Khmialeuski for three murders, and Siarhei Vostrykau for rape and two murders. All three sentences were upheld on appeal.

Human Rights Defenders and Critics

Although in 2015 Belarussian President Aliaksandr Lukashenka pardoned six men sentenced in politically motivated trials, their criminal records were not expunged, preventing them from occupying governmental jobs or standing in elections; authorizing police to question them frequently; and preventing their international travel.

Elena Tonkacheva, a human rights lawyer and chair of the Legal Transformation Center who had been forced from Belarus in February 2015 with a three-year entry ban, appealed for it to be shortened, but the appeal was rejected in January 2016. A second appeal was also denied in October 2016.

Also in January, a Minsk court found youth activists Maksim Pekarski, Vadzim Zharomski, and Viachaslau Kasinerau guilty of criminal hooliganism and fined them US$300-500 for public graffiti in August 2015. Local activists consider the decision to press criminal rather than administrative charges to be politically motivated. In March, an appeals court upheld the sentence.

Mikhail Zhamchuzhny, a founder of the prisoner's rights group Platform Innovation, was sentenced in 2015 to six-and-a-half years' imprisonment for allegedly disclosing official secrets after publishing information about police abuse he obtained from a police officer. In July, he complained that prison officials denied him access to necessary medical care and interfered with his filing an appeal against his sentence.

In April, a Minsk court found Aliaksandr Lapitski, 80, guilty of insulting President Lukashenka and other authorities after numerous letters appealing against his son's 2011 conviction and accusing the president of organizing the 2011 Minsk metro bombing. The court deemed Lapitski "legally incompetent" and sentenced him to forced treatment in a closed psychiatric institution for up to one year. He began serving his sentence in November, after losing all appeals.

In September, the Prosecutor's Office denied a request by the Turkmenistan government to extradite Chary Annamuradov, a former dissident and journalist, who traveled to Belarus for a vacation. Annamuradov fled persecution in Turkmenistan in 1999 and received asylum in Sweden in 2003.

Freedom of Assembly

From January to April, police did not disperse unsanctioned assemblies or detain participants, but continued to levy administrative charges and heavy fines against them.

In late April, Minsk traffic police and riot police dispersed a monthly event of the apolitical Critical Mass cycling movement, and detained six people, including one nongovernmental monitor. Police forced detainees onto the floor of a police bus, punched them, threw their bicycles on top of them, and brought administrative charges of disorderly conduct and violating traffic violations against them. Authorities brought additional criminal charges against Stanislau Kanavalau and Dzmitry Paliyenka for allegedly resisting police and grabbing their uniforms. Kanavalau was released, while Paliyenka stayed in pretrial detention until October, when a court convicted him and handed him a suspended two-year prison sentence.

Freedom of Expression and Attacks on Journalists

In early 2016, authorities resumed targeting freelance journalists cooperating with unregistered foreign media, a practice suspended since August 2015 after President Lukashenka publicly promised to examine the cases. Law enforcement officials in southern Belarus' Homel region brought 10 administrative cases against Kanstantsin Zhukouski and Larysa Shchyrakova for cooperating with Poland-based Belsat television channel, and fined them US$250-350.

Police detained Zhukouski and Aliaksei Atroshchanka in June as the journalists prepared a video about a business where workers complained about low wages in Loyeu, Homel region. Zhukouski alleged police beat him, and filed a complaint. In response, authorities charged and fined him for disorderly conduct, insulting police, and petty hooliganism.

In January, Minsk police beat and detained Pavel Dabravolsky as he filmed how police detained two activists holding a "No to Political Prosecution!" banner outside a court. Dabravolsky sustained minor injuries. An internal police inquiry found that the use of force was justified. Dabravolsky was fined for contempt of court and disobeying police orders. Dabravolsky claimed he did not resist police.

In an August closed hearing, a Minsk court found nine publications from 1863x.com, a news and analytical website often critical of the government, to be "extremist" in nature, alleging some content contained pornography and incited ethnic hatred, but relied exclusively on a state expert's analysis. The site's administrator, Eduard Palchys, and his lawyer had to sign a non-disclosure agreement prohibiting them from speaking publicly about the trial. After the criminal investigation opened last year, Palchys fled, but Russian authorities detained him in January 2016 and extradited him in May. Palchys remained in detention until October, when he was convicted in a closed trial and sentenced to one year and nine months of supervised parole, including restrictions on his movements.

Through August, the Information Ministry blocked at least six websites for allegedly distributing information about illegal narcotics, and was able to block websites without judicial review. None of the website owners received warnings first. The ministry also issued at least twelve warnings to eight media outlets and four news websites through June. After two warnings, the ministry may request a court-ordered closure.

In April, parliament hastily adopted a bill expanding the definition of "extremist activity" and introduced new offenses, including "creation of an extremist group" and "financing the activities of an extremist group." Activists warned that the law's vague definitions may be misused to suppress legitimate speech.

Parliament adopted a vaguely worded bill in May on "protecting children from information harmful for their health and development." These provisions may be used to restrict dissemination of neutral or positive information about lesbian, gay, bisexual, and transgender (LGBT) people as "discrediting the institution of the family."

Freedom of Association

Authorities continue to enforce criminal code article 193.1 criminalizing involvement in an unregistered organization and at the same time arbitrarily deny registration to nongovernmental groups and political parties.

In March, the Supreme Court deemed lawful the Justice Ministry's fourth refusal to register the Human Rights Association "For Fair Elections." The group's founders believe this fourth denial since 2011 was arbitrary and politically motivated.

The Supreme Court in April dismissed an appeal against the Justice Ministry's sixth refusal to register the Belarusian Christian Democratic Party. Also in April, the Justice Ministry for the fifth time refused to register "Tell the Truth," an opposition political movement. No political party has been registered since 2000.

Parliamentary Elections

International observers monitoring the September parliamentary elections noted some improvements, but urged further reforms. The Organization for Security and Co-operation in Europe Office for Democratic Institutions and Human Rights (OSCE/ODIHR) found the elections "were efficiently organized but a number of long-standing systemic shortcomings remain."

The Parliamentary Assembly of the Council of Europe (PACE)'s pre-electoral statement called for reforms "to ensure a thoroughly competitive political environment." The EU echoed these concerns. The UN special rapporteur on Belarus said the "elections proved a clear lack of political will to promote and protect human rights in Belarus."

Key International Actors

Belarus continued political "rapprochement" with European governments and institutions. These actors strengthened their relations despite a lack of tangible rights improvements.

The government continued to oppose and refused to cooperate with UN Special Rapporteur on Belarus Miklos Haraszti, appointed in 2012. In June, the UN Human Rights Council renewed the rapporteur's mandate for another year.

In February, the EU lifted sanctions on 170 individuals and 3 companies, citing release of "all the remaining political prisoners" and 2015 presidential elections free from violence.

The EU's special representative for human rights, Stavros Lambrinidis, visited in March and had meetings with officials, political party representatives, and nongovernmental groups, and called on Belarus to end the death penalty at an international conference but did not publicly condemn other human rights abuses.

In June, the EU and Belarus held their third human rights dialogue, the first to occur in Minsk. Topics included freedoms of expression, assembly and association; elections; the death penalty, torture and ill-treatment; and disability rights. The concrete outcomes were not known at time of writing.

The European Bank for Reconstruction and Development reviewed its Belarus strategy in September and removed restrictions on support for state projects. The bank noted that "the situation of human rights in the country has not undergone a systemic change and remains a subject of concern," but claimed Belarus had a "constructive role" in the region and authorities showed "more openness" to discussing human rights.

The EU, the Council of Europe's secretary general, PACE rapporteurs, and ODIHR's director repeatedly criticized the application of the death penalty in Belarus and called for a moratorium.

Bolivia

Impunity for violent crime and human rights violations remains a serious problem in Bolivia. The administration of President Evo Morales has created a hostile environment for human rights defenders that undermines their ability to work independently.

Despite recent legal reforms, extensive and arbitrary use of pretrial detention—combined with trial delays—undermine defendants' rights and contribute to prison overcrowding. Threats to judicial independence, violence against women, and child labor are other major concerns.

In February, voters rejected a national referendum that would have reformed the constitution to allow President Morales—who has served as president since 2005—to run for a fourth term in 2019.

Impunity for Abuses and Violent Crime

Bolivia has prosecuted only a few of the officials responsible for human rights violations committed under authoritarian governments from 1964 through 1982, in part because the armed forces have at times refused to provide information to judicial authorities on the fate of people killed or forcibly disappeared. Despite repeated commitments to do so, the Bolivian government has yet to create a truth commission to carry out independent investigations of abuses during that period.

Those responsible for the 2008 killing of at least 19 people during protest-related clashes between supporters and opponents of President Morales have largely gone unpunished. As of September, a La Paz court had yet to rule in a case against Leopoldo Fernández, former prefect of Pando Department, and three other local officials, for their alleged roles in the deaths of 13 people.

Authorities have also failed fully to investigate alleged 2011 police abuses against protesters opposing a proposed highway in the Isiboro Secure National Park and Indigenous Territory (known as "TIPNIS") and the 2009 police killing of two Hungarians (one of Bolivian birth) and an Irishman whom the government alleged were mercenaries involved in a separatist plot.

Impunity has led to mob attacks, or lynchings, of alleged criminals. Five people died in lynchings in 2015, according to the Ombudsman's Office. In March 2016, media reported that a mob in El Alto killed a man with mental disabilities whom they suspected to be a criminal and burned parts of his body. Many lynchings go unpunished.

Military Abuses and Jurisdiction

Human rights violations against soldiers remain a problem. In January, the Ombudsman's Office reported that a soldier had been killed in a military headquarters that month and that another had died in December 2015 after being subject to an "inhumane" military exercise. Most such deaths of soldiers go unpunished, according to the Ombudsman's Office.

The Constitutional Court ruled in 2012 that a civilian court should have jurisdiction of the case of a conscript who died in 2011 following a combat training exercise during which instructors allegedly beat him on the head and chest. The high court urged lawmakers to reform Bolivia's military justice code to ensure that cases of military human rights violations are heard in civilian courts. At time of writing the code had not been reformed.

Judicial Independence

The Bolivian justice system has been plagued by corruption, delays, and political interference for years.

In June, members of the three branches of government, as well as civil society groups and other stakeholders, discussed proposals to reform the Bolivian justice system during a "National Justice Summit." The summit's recommendations included requiring that the Plurinational Assembly reform the selection process for high-court judges, creating a new body to supervise judges, and assessing the work of current judges and prosecutors. The scope of the proposed reforms and thus their impact on judicial independence remained unclear at time of writing.

Due Process and Prison Conditions

As of June, 69 percent of inmates in Bolivian prisons had not been convicted of a crime. Extended pretrial detention and trial delays have led to prison overcrowding and poor conditions. As of March, 13,940 inmates packed prisons built to hold a maximum of around 5,000.

A 2014 law decreased the maximum periods of pretrial detention in most cases. Presidential decrees adopted between 2012 and 2015 allowed the president to reduce the sentences of those convicted of minor crimes and pardon those held in pretrial detention for minor crimes. As of January 2016, more than 4,500 people had benefited from these decrees, according to official figures.

In June, the National Justice Summit recommended that pretrial detention be used "exceptionally" and that legal reforms should broaden alternatives to pretrial imprisonment. At time of writing, no legislation had been introduced to implement those recommendations.

In May, lawyer Eduardo León was detained and prosecuted for "human trafficking" after he represented Gabriela Zapata Montaño, a former lover of President Morales who claimed she had a son with him. Bolivian authorities said that Zapata and León had paid a boy to say he was Morales' son. According to the Ombudsman's Office, judges violated León's due process rights, detaining him without charge beyond the maximum period allowed by Bolivian law. Later that month, government authorities summarily withdrew Leon's license to practice law, alleging he had falsified his military service certificate in 1999 (presenting such a certificate was required to get a university degree at the time).

In October, the Attorney General's Office used a 2010 law to charge businessman and opposition leader Samuel Doria Medina with "anti-economic conduct" for mismanagement he allegedly committed in 1992 when he was minister of planning. International human rights law prohibits such retroactive application of the criminal law, unless doing so is beneficial to the defendant.

Police Response to Protests

In May 2016, several protesters and policemen were wounded in La Paz during clashes at a demonstration by people with disabilities demanding a raise in their disability allowances. In August, the UN Committee on the Rights of Persons with Disabilities urged the Bolivian government to investigate allegations by civil society groups that police used excessive force during the protest.

Human Rights Defenders

Human rights defenders continue to face harassment, including from government officials, undermining their ability to work independently.

In 2013, President Morales signed a law and adopted a decree granting the government broad powers to dissolve civil society organizations. Under the decree, any government office may request that the Ministry of Autonomy revoke the permit of a nongovernmental organization (NGO) if it performs activities other than those listed in its bylaws, or if the organization's legal representative is criminally sanctioned for carrying out activities that "undermine security or public order."

The decree also allows the Plurinational Assembly to request the revocation of an NGO permit in cases of "necessity or public interest." These measures give the government inappropriately wide latitude to interfere with the operation of independent civil society groups. In December 2015, the Bolivian Constitutional Court ruled the law and decree constitutional.

In March 2016, President Morales said that "some NGOs" were "conspiring" against his government but did not specify which ones. In September, the minister of the Presidency said that "some NGOs" sought to carry out a coup and "subdue the Bolivian People," but he neither named the NGOs nor presented evidence to support his claim.

Freedom of Expression

While public debate is robust, the Morales administration periodically lashes out against journalists, accusing them, often without presenting evidence, of publishing what it calls lies and politically motivated distortions. The government has repeatedly accused media outlets of participating in an international conspiracy against Bolivia and President Morales.

Bolivia lacks transparent criteria for using government funds to purchase media advertisements—an important source of media revenue—and some media outlets have accused the government of discriminating against those who criticize government officials by withholding advertising from them.

When the OAS special rapporteur for freedom of expression told the Bolivian media in August that under international law governments should not discriminate against media companies viewed as critical when purchasing media advertisements, President Morales accused him of being part of a "cartel of liars."

Indigenous Rights

The 2009 Bolivian Constitution includes comprehensive guarantees for indigenous groups' rights to collective land titling, intercultural education, prior consultation on development projects, and protection of indigenous justice systems.

Indigenous peoples' right to free, prior, and informed consent (FPIC) regarding legislative or administrative measures that may affect them is not fully embodied in Bolivian legislation. A current mining law limits FPIC to the exploitation phase of land concessions, but international standards call for FPIC through all stages of projects that impact on indigenous peoples' rights over land and natural resources.

Gender-Based Violence and Reproductive Rights

Women and girls in Bolivia remain at high risk of gender-based violence, despite a 2013 law that sets forth comprehensive measures to prevent and prosecute violence against women. The law created the crime of "femicide" (the killing of a woman in certain contexts, including of domestic violence) and called for the establishment of shelters for women, as well as special prosecutors and courts for gender-based crimes.

In July, the Attorney General's Office reported that that 147 "femicides" had occurred in Bolivia from January 2015 through June 2016, and that prosecutors had obtained convictions in four of these cases.

Women and girls face numerous obstacles to accessing reproductive health products, contraceptives, and services.

Under Bolivian law, abortion is not a crime when the pregnancy is the result of rape or if the procedure is necessary to protect the life or health of a pregnant women. In 2014, the Constitutional Court ruled that prior judicial authorization and prosecution of the alleged rapist were not prerequisites for post-rape abortion. In November 2015, the health ministry issued a resolution stipulating that abortion should be permitted when the mental health of the mother—not just her physical health—is at risk.

Child Labor

In 2014, the Plurinational Assembly adopted legislation allowing children as young as 10 to work, in contravention of international standards and making Bolivia the first country in the world to legalize employment at such a young age. In February 2015, the Ombudsman's Office said that 850,000 children were working in Bolivia, most of them younger than 14.

Sexual Orientation and Gender Identity

In May 2016, the Plurinational Assembly passed a bill that allows people to revise the gender noted on their identification documents without prior judicial approval.

Same-sex couples in Bolivia are not allowed to marry or engage in civil unions. The 2009 constitution defines marriage as the union of a man and a woman.

Key International Actors

In September, the Inter-American Commission on Human Rights urged Bolivia to carry out an independent and impartial investigation into the killing of 5 people, including the then-vice minister of interior, during a protest by miners in the municipality of Panduro.

In August, the UN Committee on the Rights of Persons with Disabilities urged Bolivia to abolish legislation that limits the legal capacity of people with disabilities to form a family, vote, and enter into contracts, among other things. The committee also recommended that Bolivia end the practice of sterilization without consent and take measures to deinstitutionalize children with disabilities.

Bosnia and Herzegovina

Bosnia and Herzegovina formally applied for European Union membership in February 2016, but progress on human rights remains largely stalled. Authorities failed to end political discrimination against Jews, Roma, and other minorities. There was slow progress towards accountability for war crimes in domestic courts. Journalists remain vulnerable to intimidation and threats. Lesbian, gay, bisexual, and transgender (LGBT) people face hate speech and threats.

Ethnic and Religious Discrimination

The government and assembly made no progress towards amending the constitution to eliminate ethnic and religious discrimination in candidacy for the national tripartite presidency and the House of Peoples. Currently, the constitution requires candidates for these institutions to come from one of the three main ethnic groups—Bosniaks, Serbs, and Croats, thereby excluding Jews, Roma, and other minorities from political office.

The European Court of Human Rights ruled in 2016 that the arrangements violate the European Convention on Human Rights—the third time it has done so. Implementation of prior rulings lost momentum after the EU dropped implementation of the original 2009 European Court ruling as a condition for the entry into force of the Stabilisation and Association Agreement.

Local elections were held in Bosnia and Herzegovina on October 2, 2016, for all municipalities except for the city of Mostar. Mostar has been excluded over failure by local authorities to give effect to a BiH Constitutional Court decision that its election rules are discriminatory. Residents of the city have been unable to vote in local elections since 2008.

The results of the 2013 census of BiH were finally published on June 30, 2016, showing a changed demographic picture in which the country lost almost one-fifth of its pre-war population.

Refugees and Internally Displaced Persons

According to the Ministry for Human Rights and Refugees, the official number of internally displaced persons at the end of 2015 was 98,324. The government published a revised strategy on the return of refugees and internally displaced persons in December 2015.

But a lack of reliable public information either from the Bosnia authorities or UNHCR about returns of displaced persons and refugees to their pre-war homes makes it difficult to assess what progress if any has been made under the previous 2010 strategy, and what impact the new strategy will have.

Accountability for War Crimes

There was slow progress in prosecuting war crimes in domestic courts. The goal to finish the most complex cases in the War Crimes Chamber of the State Court by the end of 2015 has not been reached. At time of writing, the Special Department for War Crimes of BiH Prosecutor's Office was still working on 346 of the most complex war crimes cases in relation to 3,383 individuals.

Bosnia and Herzegovina's national war crimes strategy was critically assessed in two separate studies published in 2016, one by the Supervisory Body for Overseeing the Implementation of the National War Crimes Strategy and the other commissioned by the Organization for Security and Co-Operation (OSCE) in Europe and International Criminal Tribunal for the Former Yugoslavia (ICTY). Both found that that authorities had failed to meet the targets in the strategy and identified a lack of strategic planning, understaffing, and poor training as contributing factors.

Between January and August 2016, the State Court War Crimes Chamber reached 13 verdicts (3 acquittals, 10 convictions) at the first instance in relation to 25 defendants, and 19 verdicts (11 upheld, 7 modified, and 1 revoked) at the second instance in relation to 26 defendants, increasing the total number of completed cases at the first instance to 169 and at the second instance to 158 since the court became fully operational in 2005.

Between January and October 2016, the cantonal courts reached 20 verdicts (5 acquittals, 15 convictions) in relation to 27 defendants. The district courts reached 5 verdicts (3 acquittals, 2 conviction) in relation to 5 persons in the same period.

In August 2016, research conducted by Balkan Investigative Reporting Network showed that cantonal courts and the Basic Court in Brcko have allowed five war crime convicts who were sentenced to up to one year in prison to pay fines to avoid going to jail.

The trial in the State Court against Naser Oric, a former Bosnia army general, and Sabahudin Muhic, a former Bosnian army soldier, started on January 26, 2016. The trial started after the Mechanism for International Tribunals rejected a request by Oric's lawyers to order the State Court to stop the case against him because he has already been acquitted of the same charges at the International Criminal Tribunal for the Former Yugoslavia (ICTY). The prosecution alleges that Oric and Muhic killed three Serb prisoners in the villages of Zalazje, Lolici, and Kunjerac in 1992.

At the ICTY in March, Bosnian Serb wartime President Radovan Karadzic was convicted of genocide, crimes against humanity, and violations of the laws or customs of war and sentenced to 40 years' imprisonment. Karadzic was convicted of genocide in the area of Srebrenica in 1995, of persecution, extermination, murder, deportation, inhumane acts (forcible transfer), terror, unlawful attacks on civilians and hostage-taking. He was acquitted of the charge of genocide in other municipalities in BiH in 1992.

At time of writing, the defense case in the trial of Ratko Mladic, the former commander of the Republika Srpska Army, was in progress at the ICTY. Mladic's case experienced a substantial slowdown due to delays in evidence presentation by the defense. Mladic is on trial for genocide in Srebrenica and seven other municipalities in Bosnia and Herzegovina, the persecution of Bosniaks and Croats throughout the country, terrorizing the civilian population of Sarajevo and taking UN peacekeepers hostage. The trial judgment was expected in November 2017.

National Security

Imad Al-Husin (also known as Abu Hamza), a naturalized Bosnian from Syria detained in 2008, was released in February 2016 from the immigration center in Sarajevo where he was held for over seven years on national security grounds without ever being indicted. The Ministry of Security announced in a press release in February 2016 that the decision to expel Imad Al-Husin still stands; until then his movement remains limited to the Canton of Sarajevo.

Zeyad Khalaf Al Gertani, an Iraqi citizen, detained without charge on national se-curity grounds from 2009 until 2014, remains under a supervision order confin-ing him to the Bosnian town of Banovici, apart from his family.

Human Rights Defenders and Civil Society

By October 2016, Civil Rights Defenders had registered 12 incidents targeting groups and individuals working to defend human rights, including six physical attacks against journalists and three incidents against one human rights organi-zation in Prijedor municipality.

Freedom of Media

Journalists continue to face threats and intimidation. In the first nine months of 2016, the national journalists' association registered 40 cases of violations of media freedom and expression, including 5 physical attacks, 2 death threats, 6 cases of pressure, 3 cases of defamation, and 3 cases of verbal threats.

Borka Rudic, general secretary of the Association of Journalists of Bosnia and Herzegovina, and the Journalists' Association itself were accused in July by Salmir Kaplan, a member of parliament and adviser to the security minister, of supporting the Gulen movement in Turkey and Rudic was called a "Chetnik" (right-wing nationalist Serb), after Rudic spoke out against curbs on media free-dom in Turkey.

In May, a Croatian television journalist Petar Panjkota was struck on the head after reporting from a demonstration in Banja Luka. Two crew from Bosnian TV station BN TV covering the same demonstration were verbally abused and a third received threats on social media.

Sexual Orientation and Gender Identity

Sarajevo Open Centre, the lesbian, gay, bisexual, and transgender rights organi-zation, documented 23 cases of hate speech and incitement of violence and hate and two crimes and incidents motivated by prejudice on the basis of sexual orientation and/or gender identity in the first three months of 2016. The reaction of authorities to these incidents is generally inadequate. There was no progress in police investigations into the 2014 attack on a film festival that Sarajevo Open Centre organized.

Key International Actors

In April, Dunja Mijatovic, the Organization for Security and Co-operation in Europe's representative on freedom of the media, urged authorities to address attacks against journalists who are experiencing a growing number of online threats. The problem is particularly severe when it comes to female journalists.

A July 2016 report prepared by the European Committee for the Prevention of Torture and Inhuman or Degrading Treatment or Punishment (CPT) noted allegations of widespread physical ill-treatment of detainees by law enforcement officials and inmates by prison staff, and was critical of the failure by prosecutors and judges to investigate such allegations.

The United States State Department annual report on human rights in Bosnia and Herzegovina, published in April 2016, underlined the issue of severe mistreatment of detainees in prisons, remand detention centers, and the harsh and sometimes life- threatening conditions in the country's prisons. Furthermore, the report highlighted the widespread violence against women, including sexual assault and domestic violence, exacerbated by ineffective, underfunded social services and an inadequate police response.

In its annual progress on Bosnia and Herzegovina published in November, the European Commission highlighted the failure of authorities to amend the constitution, in breach of the European Convention on Human Rights and to implement rulings by the Constitutional Court. The report also identified inadequate legal protection for LGBTI persons and the failure of authorities to protect adequately the rights of minorities and to ensure media freedom.

HUMAN
RIGHTS
WATCH

"Good Cops Are Afraid"
The Toll of Unchecked Police Violence in Rio de Janeiro

Brazil

Brazil suffered both economic and political crises in 2016. In August, its Congress impeached President Dilma Rousseff; Vice President Michel Temer replaced her.

Chronic human rights problems plague Brazil's criminal justice system, including unlawful police killings, prison overcrowding, and torture and ill-treatment of detainees. Some recent reform efforts aim to address these problems, but other proposed moves would exacerbate them. In 2016, the judiciary broadened a program to ensure that detainees are promptly brought before judges after their arrest, as required by international law. Congress approved a counterterrorism bill with overbroad and vague language that could be used to undermine freedom of association.

Public Security and Police Conduct

Widespread violence, often perpetrated by criminal gangs, plagues many Brazilian cities. Abuses by police, including extrajudicial executions, contribute to a cycle of violence in high-crime neighborhoods, undermining public security and endangering the lives of the police officers who patrol them. In 2015, 393 police officers were killed in Brazil, according to the latest data available at time of writing.

Police officers, including off-duty officers, killed 3,345 people in 2015, according to official data compiled by the nongovernmental organization (NGO) Brazilian Forum on Public Security. This represents a 6 percent increase over 2014, and a 52 percent increase over 2013. While some police killings result from legitimate use of force, others are extrajudicial executions, as documented by Human Rights Watch and other groups, and as acknowledged by Brazilian criminal justice officials.

After doubling in 2014, killings by on-duty police officers in São Paulo–the state with the largest population in Brazil–decreased by 17 percent in 2015 and fell by another 19 percent from January to September of 2016. But killings by on-duty police officers in Rio de Janeiro–the state with the highest rate of police killings–

increased 11 percent in 2015 and an additional 23 percent in the first 9 months of 2016.

In September, an appeals court voided the convictions of 74 police officers for their participation in the 1992 killing of 111 detainees in the Carandiru prison in São Paulo. One of the members of the three-judge panel claimed "there was no massacre" and that all killings were in self-defense, despite overwhelming evidence that police executed the detainees.

Prison Conditions, Torture, and Ill-Treatment of Detainees

Many Brazilian prisons and jails are severely overcrowded and violent. The number of adults behind bars jumped 85 percent from 2004 to 2014 and exceeds 622,000 people, 67 percent more than the prisons were built to hold, according to latest Ministry of Justice figures.

A key contributor to the dramatic increase in Brazil´s prison population has been a 2006 drug law that increased sentences for traffickers. While the law also replaced prison sentences for drug users with penalties such as community service, a measure that might have reduced the prison population, the law was worded vaguely, leaving open the possibility of users being prosecuted as traffickers. In 2005, 9 percent of those in prison had been detained on drug charges—in 2014 it was 28 percent, and among women, 64 percent, according to the latest data available.

In 2014, judges started seeing detainees promptly after arrest, as required by international law. Such "custody hearings"—currently carried out in state capitals and some other jurisdictions—help judges determine who should be in preventive detention and who should be set free pending trial. In the absence of custody hearings, detainees often wait many months to see a judge for the first time. In Brazil, 40 percent of people in prison are pretrial detainees. At time of writing, Brazil's Congress was examining a bill to make such hearings mandatory throughout the country.

Custody hearings have the potential to be a powerful weapon against police abuse of detainees because they allow judges to detect and hear about mistreatment soon after arrest. However, an analysis by the Institute for the Defense of the Right of Defense (IDDD), an NGO, of more than 700 custody hearings carried out in São Paulo in 2015 showed that judges asked detainees about their treatment in custody in only about 40 percent of cases, and took no action in a third of the 141 cases of alleged abuse they heard. Judges sent the rest to the police internal affairs divisions. The IDDD had no information about the results of any inquiries into the cases by those divisions by the time it published its report in May 2016.

A team from the government's National Mechanism for the Prevention and Combatting of Torture visited six states between April 2015 and March 2016, documenting cases of torture and cruel, inhuman, or degrading treatment in "most, if not all" of the 17 jails and prisons it inspected. In Sorocaba jail in São Paulo state, they found 50 detainees in cells designed to hold 9 people.

Children's Rights

Brazil's Senate is examining a Constitutional amendment—a version of which was approved by the Chamber of Deputies in 2015—that would allow 16 and 17-year-olds accused of serious crimes to be tried and punished as adults. If enacted, the law would violate international norms enshrined in human rights treaties that Brazil has ratified, which state that people under 18 should not be prosecuted as adults.

The Chamber of Deputies is considering a separate bill, which the Senate has already approved, to raise the maximum time of internment for children from 3 to 10 years. If enacted, the bill would aggravate overcrowding in the juvenile detention system, which was built to hold about 18,000 juveniles but held close to 22,000 in 2014, according to the latest data published by the National Council of the Prosecutor's Office.

The National Mechanism for the Prevention and Combatting of Torture found that the physical infrastructure of the nine juvenile centers it visited in three states between April 2015 and March 2016 did not comply with the Federal Government's regulations: instead of promoting rehabilitation and education, the centers served as places of isolation and punishment. In most units, children spent more than 20 hours a day—and in one unit 24 hours a day—locked in their rooms. Conditions were especially dire in the state of Ceará, where the number of children held as of January 2016 was more than double capacity in some facilities, according to CEDECA Ceara, an NGO. Some children reported that juvenile detention officers beat them and that they were kept in units infested with rats and cockroaches, and which lacked adequate sanitation, ventilation, mattresses, and basic hygiene products.

Counterterrorism

In February, the Rousseff administration won Congressional approval for a counterterrorism bill that contains vague language that endangers such basic human rights as freedom of association. The law includes an overbroad definition of "terrorism" and of "actions in preparation" of a terrorist act that could be used against peaceful advocacy groups.

Internet Freedom, Privacy, and Freedom of Expression

Brazil was at the vanguard of digital rights in 2014 with the enactment of a Digital Bill of Rights, intended to protect privacy and free expression rights online. It also co-led an initiative at the United Nation Human Rights Council in 2015 to create a new UN special rapporteur on the right to privacy. One of Dilma Rousseff's last acts as president was signing a decree in May 2016 that implemented the law.

But other developments risk setting back the right to privacy in Brazil. From February 2015 to July 2016, four judges ordered the temporary blocking of WhatsApp, the Facebook-owned messaging service, across the country, and in March 2016 federal police arrested a Facebook executive because the company refused to turn over user information to authorities.

Between March and June 2016, judicial officials filed more than 40 lawsuits against five employees of the newspaper *Gazeta do Povo* (People's Gazette) in the state of Paraná for a series of stories, based on information publicly available from government websites, revealing that judges and prosecutors were receiving more in wages and benefits than is allowed by the Constitution. In July, Brazil's Supreme Court suspended the lawsuits pending its review of the cases.

In August, a judge authorized police to wiretap a reporter's phone after he refused to reveal his sources for a story that published a list of Brazilians whom authorities suspect have Swiss bank accounts.

According to Artigo 19, a Brazilian NGO, five journalists were killed in Brazil in 2016 through October, including at least two who were attacked or threatened prior to their deaths. Since 2011, at least 21 journalists have died violently in Brazil in direct relation to their work, according to the Committee to Protect Journalists, an international press freedom group.

Women's Rights

Abortion is legal in Brazil only in cases of rape, when necessary to save a woman's life, or when the fetus suffers from anencephaly, a fatal congenital brain disorder. In 2016, conservative members of Congress promoted several bills that would eliminate those exceptions and that would make it a crime even to provide information to women about abortion.

Women and girls who abort pregnancies illegally risk not only injury and death, but face sentences of up to three years in prison, while people who perform abortions face up to four years, if convicted.

Brazilian women and girls of child-bearing age faced new health challenges from an outbreak of the Zika virus starting in 2015. The virus can cause a series of congenital conditions during fetal development, including microcephaly, or the underdevelopment of the brain. In August, the National Association of Public Defenders, with support from the NGO Anis, filed a petition before the Supreme Court to allow women infected with Zika to have abortions.

Disability Rights

In January, a disability rights law came into effect, requiring public agencies to give priority to people with disabilities when providing services related to health, education, work, housing, culture, and sport. The law also instructs cities to adapt sidewalks and public spaces for people with disabilities. In June, Brazil's Supreme Court upheld a provision in that law that requires private schools to incorporate children with disabilities in regular classrooms at no extra cost to their families.

However, a bill under discussion in Congress could set back Brazil's efforts to meet its obligation under the Convention on the Rights of People with Disabilities to ensure that persons with disabilities "enjoy legal capacity on an equal basis with others in all aspects of life." The bill would revert to a system under which some people with disabilities can be placed in guardianship arrangements that are not consistent with Brazil's human rights obligations.

Sexual Orientation and Gender Identity

Brazil's Supreme Court approved same-sex marriage in 2011 and it upheld the right of same-sex couples to adopt children in 2015. But the Chamber of Deputies was, at time of writing, debating a bill that would define a family as a union between a man and a woman.

The national Human Rights Ombudsman's Office received 1,983 complaints of violence, discrimination, and other abuses experienced by lesbian, gay, bisexual, and transgender (LGBT) persons in 2015. In the first half of 2016 the ombudsman received 879 such complaints.

Labor Rights

Since 1995, the Ministry of Labor has documented almost 50,000 cases of workers being subjected to abusive working conditions that under Brazilian law rise to the level of "slave-like," such as forced labor and degrading working conditions. More than 1,000 such cases were documented in 2015. From April 2014 to April 2016, the Ministry of Labor imposed penalties on 349 companies for employing 4,119 people in "slave-like" conditions.

Rural Violence

Rural activists and indigenous leaders involved in conflicts over land continue to face threats and violence in Brazil. According to the Pastoral Land Commission of the Catholic Church, 39 people involved in land conflicts died violently from January to August 2016.

In 2015, five indigenous people died as a result of land conflicts, according to the Indigenous Missionary Council of the Catholic Church (Cimi). Of particular concern, the council said, is the situation of the Guaraní-Kaiowá people, who continue to suffer violent attacks by militias linked to landowners as they struggle to regain their rights over ancestral lands.

After a visit to Brazil in March 2016, the UN special rapporteur on the rights of indigenous peoples said that in the last eight years there was a "disturbing" lack of progress in areas of key concern to indigenous peoples, such as the demarcation of their territories. She urged Brazil's government to address violence and discrimination against indigenous people.

Confronting Military-Era Abuses

The perpetrators of human rights abuses during military rule from 1964 to 1985 continue to be shielded from justice by a 1979 amnesty law that was upheld by the Supreme Court in 2010, a decision that the Inter-American Court of Human Rights quickly ruled was a violation of Brazil's obligations under international law. In 2014, the National Truth Commission identified 377 such perpetrators, but owing to the amnesty law, their crimes remain unpunished.

Federal courts did allow the prosecution of at least two former military officers for killings during military rule, but the Supreme Court temporarily halted those prosecutions in 2014 and 2015, pending its re-examination of the validity of the amnesty law.

Key International Actors

In a May report to the UN Human Rights Council, the UN working group on business and human rights found that mining company Samarco had failed to alert residents after the November 2015 rupture of a tailings dam, which caused one of the worst environmental disasters in Brazilian history and the death of 19 people. Prior warning might have prevented these deaths, the working group said. In November, four UN rapporteurs said in a joint statement that the measures taken so far by the government and the company are "insufficient" to deal with the "massive" environmental and human impact of the disaster.

Foreign Policy

Brazil was elected to the Human Rights Council for the 2017-2019 term. In June, the council adopted a resolution, presented by a core group of Latin American countries, including Brazil, that established the position of UN independent expert on protection against violence and discrimination based on sexual orientation and gender identity.

The total number of people with refugee status in Brazil more than doubled from 2011, when President Rousseff took office, to more than 8,800 in April 2016, according to the Ministry of Justice. About a quarter of those with refugee status are Syrian. The Temer administration has said that in 2017 it intends to receive at least 3,000 Syrians from Jordan, Turkey, and Lebanon, as well as an undetermined number of Central American refugees who are in Mexico.

The new government made a clear shift in its position toward Venezuela. In August, Foreign Minister José Serra called the Venezuelan government "authoritarian and repressive" and highlighted the plight of political prisoners there. The Rousseff administration had avoided criticizing Venezuela's persecution of political opponents and crackdown on protesters.

Burma

Burma's new government led by the National League for Democracy (NLD) took office in March 2016 after sweeping the November 2015 elections. Headed by State Counsellor Aung San Suu Kyi and President Htin Kyaw, the NLD controls a majority of both upper and lower house parliamentary seats in the country's first democratically elected, civilian-led government since 1962. However, the new government inherited deep-rooted challenges, including constitutional empowerment of the military, repressive legislation, weak rule of law, and a corrupt judiciary.

The political transition began promisingly, with the April release of over 200 political prisoners and detainees. Nonetheless, the NLD-led government has thus far not capitalized on its initial momentum in guiding the country toward substantive reform or the creation of democratic institutions.

Fighting between the Burmese armed forces and ethnic armed groups intensified or flared up in several regions during the year, resulting in abuses against civilians and massive displacement. Violent attacks by unknown insurgents against border guard posts on October 9 in Maungdaw, northern Rakhine State, resulted in the deaths of nine officials and sparked the most serious humanitarian and human rights crisis in Rakhine State since the October 2012 "ethnic cleansing" campaign against the Rohingya.

Under the deeply flawed 2008 constitution, the military retains autonomy from civilian oversight and extensive power over the government and national security, with control of the Defense, Home Affairs, and Border Affairs Ministries. It is guaranteed 25 percent of parliamentary seats, which constitutes an effective veto over any constitutional amendments, and is authorized to assume power in a national state of emergency.

Ethnic Conflict and Armed Forces Abuses

Fighting between the Tatmadaw (Burmese armed forces) and ethnic armed groups worsened over the year in Kachin, Rakhine, Karen, and Northern Shan States, displacing thousands of civilians. Government forces have been responsible for serious abuses, including extrajudicial killings, torture, sexual violence,

HUMAN
RIGHTS
WATCH

"The Farmer Becomes the Criminal"

Land Confiscation in Burma's Karen State

and destruction of property. Government shelling and airstrikes have been conducted against ethnic areas, in violation of the laws of war. Both government and non-state groups have been implicated in the use of anti-personnel landmines and forced recruitment, including of children.

The legacy of the Burmese military's "divide and rule" approach persists, as the conflict's spillover and ensuing abuses compound tensions among ethnic groups.

The Nationwide Ceasefire Agreement (NCA) orchestrated under the previous Thein Sein government was signed in October 2015 by eight non-state armed groups, fewer than half of the country's total. Since its adoption, military operations and clashes between signatory and non-signatory armed groups have continued.

From August 31 to September 3, Aung San Suu Kyi presided over the 21st Century Panglong Conference, billed as a forum for re-engaging armed groups and other national stakeholders in the country's peace process. Intensified fighting on the ground has continued unabated since the conference.

In Northern Shan State, fighting between the Ta'ang National Liberation Army and the Restoration Council of Shan State/Shan State Army-South, at times with the support of the Tatmadaw, flared throughout the year.

Fighting between the military and the Kachin Independence Army (KIA) in Kachin State increased steadily since mid-August. In September, fighting between ethnic armed groups and government forces in Karen State displaced about 5,900 civilians.

Violence over the past five years has left 220,000 people displaced nationwide—120,000 in Rakhine State and 100,000 in Shan and Kachin States.

Security threats, weak infrastructure, and restrictions imposed by government and non-state authorities regularly impeded access by humanitarian agencies to civilians displaced in conflict-affected areas. Restrictions on access to Internally Displaced Persons (IDPs) in Kachin and Shan States increased in late 2016.

Abuses against Rohingya

Muslim minorities in Burma, in particular the 1.2 million ethnic Rohingya, continue to face rampant and systemic human rights violations.

Outbreaks of violence in Maungdaw district in northern Rakhine State escalated following an October 9 attack on three border outposts that left nine police officers dead. Asserting that both the initial and subsequent attacks were carried out by armed Rohingya militants, the government initiated "clearance operations" to locate the alleged attackers while locking down the area, denying access to humanitarian aid groups, independent media, and rights monitors.

The security operations led to numerous reports of serious abuses by government security forces against Rohingya villagers, including summary killings, rape and other sexual violence, torture and ill-treatment, arbitrary arrests, and arson. The military employed helicopter gunships during a series of clashes beginning on November 11. At time of writing, the government said it had arrested over 300 alleged suspects. Local groups reported the use of torture and a number of deaths in custody.

Satellite imagery in November revealed widespread fire-related destruction in Rohingya villages, with a total of 430 destroyed buildings in three villages of Maungdaw district.

Government travel restrictions placed on humanitarian agencies have led to critical food insecurity and malnutrition, and an estimated 30,000 Muslim villagers remain displaced.

The government has continually failed to adequately or effectively investigate abuses against the Rohingya, and did not act on recommendations to seek UN assistance for an investigation into the violence.

The ongoing crisis in Maungdaw represents the most serious and widespread violence against the Rohingya since the ethnic cleansing campaign carried out in June and October 2012. Four years after the 2012 violence, about 120,000 Rohingya remain displaced in camps in Rakhine State. Humanitarian conditions for both remaining IDPs and newly resettled persons remain dire due to restrictions on movement and lack of access to livelihoods and basic services.

The effective denial of citizenship for the Rohingya—who are not recognized on the official list of 135 ethnic groups eligible for full citizenship under the 1982 Citizenship Law—has facilitated enduring rights abuses, including restrictions on movement; limitations on access to health care, livelihood, shelter, and education; arbitrary arrests and detention; and forced labor. Travel is severely constrained by authorization requirements, security checkpoints, curfews, and strict control of IDP camp access. Such barriers compound the health crisis caused by poor living conditions, severe overcrowding, and limited health facilities.

The government refuses to use the term Rohingya, which the group self-identifies as but is rejected by nationalist Buddhists in favor of the term "Bengali," which implies illegal migrant status in Burma. Aung San Suu Kyi refers to the group as the "Muslim Community in Rakhine State," and has requested that international stakeholders, including the United States, European Union, and United Nations, follow suit.

The new Burmese government established two bodies to address sectarian tensions in Rakhine State—a government committee and a nine-member national/international advisory commission led by former UN Secretary-General Kofi Annan, which initiated its year-long research mandate in September.

Freedom of Expression and Assembly

Restrictions on the rights to freedom of expression and assembly persist, amid the government's failure to contend with the range of rights-abusing laws that have been long used to criminalize free speech and prosecute dissidents.

In its final months of rule, Thein Sein's government continued arresting activists using politically motivated charges, failing to fulfill the former president's 2013 pledge to release all political prisoners by the end of his term. In April, the new NLD-led government released 235 political prisoners and detainees in a series of amnesties.

However, the nod toward a new era of openness was contradicted by the government's continued use of problematic legislation to restrict free speech. In April, two Muslim interfaith activists were convicted on charges under section 17(1) of the Unlawful Association Act and sentenced to an additional two years in prison with hard labor. Numerous activists were arrested under section 66(d) of the

HUMAN
RIGHTS
WATCH

"They Can Arrest You
at Any Time"
The Criminalization of Peaceful Expression in Burma

Telecommunications Act for "defaming" Aung San Suu Kyi, President Htin Kyaw, or the military in social media posts. These include Maung Saungkha, who was sentenced to six months in prison in May for a poem he posted on Facebook, and Aung Win Hlaing, sentenced to nine months in prison in September for calling the president an "idiot" and "crazy" on Facebook.

Parliament put forward a new Peaceful Assembly and Peaceful Procession Law in May, yet despite slight improvements the proposed revisions maintain regulations that allow for at-will crackdowns on peaceful protests, blanket prohibitions on certain protest speech, and criminal penalties for any violation of its restrictions.

Arrests and prosecutions for participation in peaceful assemblies have continued under the new administration. Police arrested 90 political activists in May, including student leaders of an interfaith peace walk in Rangoon; demonstrators against the Letpadaung mine in Sagaing Division; and 76 labor rights activists marching to the capital, Naypyidaw, to protest treatment by local factory owners. Fifty-one of the labor activists were charged with unlawful assembly, rioting, and disturbing public tranquility under the Burmese penal code; 15 were convicted in October and sentenced to between four and six months in prison.

Throughout the year, as many as 60 Arakanese men were arrested under section 17(1) of the Unlawful Association Act for alleged ties to the Arakan Army. From March to July, 28 were found guilty and sentenced to two to five years in prison with hard labor.

The criminalization of expression perceived as a threat to the armed forces also continued. In late June, the Ta'ang Women's Organization was forced to cancel a press conference in Rangoon to launch a report documenting military abuses against ethnic Palaung in Northern Shan State. In August, Khine Myo Htun, an environmental activist and member of the Arakan Liberation Party, was charged with violating sections 505(b) and 505(c) of the penal code for accusing the armed forces of committing crimes against humanity. In October, veteran activist Htin Kyaw was arrested and charged with violating section 505(a) for accusing the military of committing human rights abuses.

While the relaxation of press censorship has been a key hallmark of the democratic transition, various forms of government control remain inscribed in the legal framework and employed to restrict media freedom. In June, the Ministry of Information banned the film "Twilight Over Burma" from a human rights film festival for its depiction of a relationship it claimed would threaten ethnic and military relations.

As part of the military's "clearance operations" in northern Rakhine State, the authorities denied independent journalists access to the region since early October. The *Myanmar Times* fired a journalist who had reported on allegations of rape by security forces in Maungdaw, reportedly under pressure from the Ministry of Information.

Burma's national penal code criminalizes consensual same-sex behavior between adult men. In recent years police have arrested gay men and transgender women assembling in public places, and politicians have called for the "education" of gay people.

Women's and Girls' Rights

Justice for women and girls in Burma remains elusive, particularly with regard to violence related to armed conflict. Sexual violence by the military, and to some extent ethnic armed groups, has been frequent, and the renewed violent clashes in Kachin and Northern Shan States has exacerbated the problem. Such crimes are facilitated by a near total lack of accountability, and no institutionalized complaint mechanism. Few prosecutions have been publicly reported, despite allegations of more than 115 cases of sexual violence perpetrated by the Burmese army since fighting renewed.

In October and November, media and local groups reported numerous incidents of rape and other sexual assault of Rohingya women and girls committed by security forces during the "clearing operations" in Maungdaw district. The government denied all reports of sexual violence, and the military lockdown has prevented independent investigations into the abuses. This suppression is emblematic of the military's long-standing refusal to seriously investigate cases of sexual violence.

In May, the Tatmadaw announced that an investigation into the January 2015 rape and murder of two Kachin schoolteachers by suspected army soldiers had taken place, but no public information about charges or a trial was released.

Women in conflict zones and displaced or stateless women are especially vulnerable to abductions, enforced disappearances, sexual violence, and exploitation.

Despite their central role in human rights and democracy activism in Burma, women have been marginalized in the government's various peace process initiatives, and their concerns have been noticeably absent from the negotiations. Women made up less than 10 percent of participants in the peace process, and women's rights groups were sidelined at the 21st Century Panglong Conference.

Women hold only 13 percent of seats in the new parliament; only one woman sits on the 18-person cabinet, and only 0.25 percent of village-level administrators are women.

Key International Actors

Burma's political transition has triggered an enthusiastic response from international stakeholders. Since the new administration took office, there have been only limited attempts by foreign governments to press for genuine legal and policy reforms.

In May, the United States government relaxed a range of sanctions to ease US business investments and financial transactions in Burma. Following a visit by Aung San Suu Kyi in September, the US announced plans to lift most remaining sanctions, which was carried out by executive order on October 7.

The US also resumed the General System of Preferences (GSP) trade status with Burma, despite serious concerns that Burma's labor practices do not meet GSP conditions on labor rights. In a contradictory move, the US State Department downgraded Burma in its annual Trafficking in Persons report to Tier 3, the lowest tier, in recognition of ongoing abuses related to human trafficking, child soldier recruitment, and forced labor.

The UN Human Rights Council in March once again adopted its resolution on Burma and extended the special rapporteur's mandate, requesting that she identify benchmarks for reform. However, the EU decided not to introduce a resolution at the UN General Assembly in November, underscoring the international community's softening approach.

As Burma's immediate neighbor with significant business and military ties within the country, China continued efforts to strengthen its geopolitical engagement with the Burmese government and advance the large-scale development projects that offer access to the country's natural resources and strategic regional borders, often to the detriment of local populations.

Burundi

The political and human rights crisis that gripped Burundi the previous year deepened in 2016, as government forces targeted perceived opponents with increased brutality. Security forces and intelligence services—often in collaboration with members of the ruling party's youth league, known as Imbonerakure—were responsible for numerous killings, disappearances, abductions, torture, rape, and arbitrary arrests. Armed opposition groups also carried out attacks and killed ruling party members.

Dozens of dead bodies, some mutilated, were found across the country. The identity of the perpetrators was often unknown.

In December 2015, in the deadliest attack since the crisis began, police and military shot dead a large number of residents in the capital, Bujumbura, following attacks on four military installations, attributed to the opposition.

The justice system is manipulated by ruling party and intelligence officials and judicial procedures are routinely flouted. The prosecutor general created several commissions of inquiry into allegations of serious human rights abuses. Their reports were biased and misleading, largely exonerating security forces and failing to hold those responsible to account.

More than 325,000 Burundians have fled the country since 2015, most to Tanzania, Rwanda, Uganda, and the Democratic Republic of the Congo.

Killings by Security Forces and Ruling Party Youth

On December 11, opposition members, with support from some members of the military, attacked three military positions and a military training center in Bujumbura.

Police, military, and armed *Imbonerakure* pursued the attackers into Nyakabiga and Musaga, two neighborhoods where residents had demonstrated in large numbers against President Pierre Nkurunziza's third term in 2015. In Nyakabiga, armed opponents engaged the security forces in a sustained gun battle. It is unclear how many were killed on each side.

HUMAN RIGHTS WATCH

BURUNDI'S
HUMAN RIGHTS CRISIS
Materials Published by Human Rights Watch
Between April 2015 and April 2016

Police, military and Imbonerakure then forced their way into houses and ordered residents to show them where young men or combatants were hiding, some shouting ethnic slurs at Tutsi residents. They killed scores of people in Nyakabiga and Musaga and carried out large-scale arbitrary arrests.

The following day, some victims were found lying side by side, face down; they appeared to have been shot in the back or the head.

On December 12, 2015, police and *Imbonerakure*, accompanied by local government officials and public health workers, picked up some of the dead bodies from Musaga and took them away in local government vehicles to bury them in mass graves in and around Bujumbura.

Several witnesses said that *Imbonerakure*, wearing surgical masks and gloves, dug three or four graves in a cemetery in the Kanyosha neighborhood and buried bodies there.

Then-Prosecutor General Valentin Bagorikunda set up a commission of inquiry into the December 11 events. Summarizing its main conclusions on March 10, he did not mention killings of Bujumbura residents by the security forces. He claimed that those killed on December 11 were armed "combatants" wearing police or military uniforms.

Torture and Disappearances

There was a sharp increase in torture by the intelligence services and the police, particularly of alleged opposition sympathizers. Intelligence agents beat detainees with hammers and steel construction bars, drove sharpened steel rods into their legs, dripped melting plastic on them, tied cords around men's genitals, and used electric shocks. Many tortured or injured detainees were denied medical attention.

Disappearances and covert abductions increased in late 2015 and early 2016. In December 2015, Marie-Claudette Kwizera, of the human rights group Ligue Iteka, was driven away in a vehicle thought to belong to the intelligence services. She has not been seen again.

In late July, Jean Bigirimana, a journalist with the independent newspaper Iwacu, disappeared after leaving his home in Bujumbura for Bugarama, in Muramvya province. Unconfirmed reports indicate he was arrested by the intelligence services. In early August, two decomposed bodies were found in the Mubarazi River in Muramvya, one of which was decapitated and the other weighed down by stones. There was speculation that one of them could have been Bigiri-mana's but local authorities buried the bodies before determining their identities.

Rape and Other Abuses by Ruling Party Youth

Members of the Imbonerakure and police, sometimes armed with guns, sticks or knives, raped women whose male family members were perceived government opponents. In some cases, Imbonerakure threatened or attacked the male relative before raping the woman. Women often continued to receive threats after being raped.

Imbonerakure and police raped women who attempted to cross into Tanzania, apparently to deter them from leaving Burundi.

Imbonerakure set up roadblocks and check points in some provinces. They extorted money, harassed passersby, and, despite having no powers of arrest, arrested people they suspected of having links to the opposition. They also went door to door, extorting money from residents.

Mass Arrests

Scores of opposition party members have been arrested, ill-treated, and illegally detained, and other detainees taken to unknown destinations. Police almost never produced warrants at the time of arrest.

Ruling party officials, police, and *Imbonerakure* arrested at least 16 members of the opposition party National Liberation Forces (FNL) at a bar in Kirundo province in March. The police claimed they were conducting a political meeting without authorization. Many more FNL members were arrested in later months.

Large-scale arrests, many of them arbitrary, continued throughout the year. In May, police arrested more than 200 young men and students in Bujumbura's Musaga neighborhood. Local residents said the police ordered them to produce identity cards and "household notebooks," an obligatory register of all people living in each house. Police beat some detainees with belts and truncheons.

After a grenade attack in Bujumbura's Bwiza neighborhood in May, the police detained several hundred people. Police spokesperson Pierre Nkurikiye told a local media outlet it was "normal" to arrest people near the site of a grenade explosion and "among those arrested, there may be perpetrators of the attack." Police officials said all those arrested were later released.

Abuses by Armed Opposition Groups

Local journalists and human rights activists reported several grenade attacks and killings believed to have been committed by armed opposition groups. Other armed opposition attacks appeared to be more targeted and covert.

Unidentified people attacked several bars in Bujumbura and elsewhere with grenades. Burundian media reported that in May, an attack on a drinks depot and bar in Mwaro province killed a judicial policeman and injured several customers. During the same attack, a guard at the ruling party offices in Ndava, in Mwaro, was also killed as the attackers attempted to burn down the building. Three men were arrested in connection with the attacks.

In Bururi province, unidentified gunmen shot dead several ruling party members in April and May, including Jean Claude Bikorimana, on April 9. Three ruling party members were among four people shot dead at a bar on April 15; another attack on the same night killed a ruling party member, Japhet Karibwami, at his home.

Civil Society and Media

Most leading civil society activists and many independent journalists remain in exile, after repeated government threats in 2015 and arrest warrants against several of them. In October, the Interior Minister banned or suspended 10 civil society organizations that had spoken out against government abuses.

In February, the Burundian National Communications Council signed an agreement with Radio Isanganiro and Radio Rema FM allowing them to resume their broadcasts. Following an attempted coup d'état in May 2015, the government had closed these stations, along with Radio Publique Africaine, Radio Bonesha, and Radio-Television Renaissance, which remain off the air at the time of writing.

In August, men armed with a machete attacked a Burundian human rights activist in Nakivale refugee camp in Uganda. The activist survived.

Key International Actors

There was little progress in regional and international efforts to broker a dialogue between Burundian political actors, co-facilitated by former Tanzanian President Benjamin Mkapa.

The Burundian government reacted with hostility to statements and initiatives by the United Nations, the African Union (AU), the European Union (EU) and other governments and international institutions. Ruling party officials accused donors, foreign journalists and human rights organizations of siding with the opposition. Government officials repeatedly rebuffed diplomats' concerns about human rights.

Most major donors have suspended direct budgetary support to the Burundian government, but some maintained humanitarian assistance. The US and EU have imposed targeted sanctions on several senior Burundian officials and opposition leaders.

The Office of the Prosecutor of the International Criminal Court (ICC) announced in April that it was opening a preliminary examination into the situation in Burundi. In early October, Burundi's parliament voted overwhelmingly to withdraw from the ICC and the government officially notified the UN Secretary-General of its decision to withdraw on October 27.

At a special session in December 2015, the UN Human Rights Council (HRC) tasked a team of three independent experts to investigate human rights violations in Burundi. The team's report, presented in September, found that gross and systematic human rights violations had taken place, some possibly amounting to crimes against humanity. It suggested the HRC review Burundi's membership status. The HRC adopted a resolution presented by the EU calling for a commission of inquiry into human rights violations in Burundi since April 2015, including on whether they may constitute international crimes. The inquiry would also identify alleged perpetrators with a view to ensuring accountability.

In October, the Burundian government, angered by the UN report, stated it had suspended all cooperation with the Office of the UN High Commissioner for Human Rights in Burundi and declared the three UN independent experts persona non grata.

The UN chose in June not to replace Burundian police in its peacekeeping mission to the Central African Republic because of concerns about human rights abuses in Burundi.

In July, the UN Committee Against Torture held a special session on Burundi and raised serious concerns about torture and other violations. The Burundian delegation failed to show up on the second day to answer the committee's questions, instead sending a statement requesting more time to respond. The committee rejected this request and released its concluding observations in August.

In August, the UN Security Council passed a resolution calling for the deployment of 228 unarmed police officers to Burundi to support UN human rights monitors. Burundian authorities rejected the deployment and pro-government demonstrators protested it.

The AU authorized the deployment of 100 human rights observers and 100 military observers, but only a small number have been deployed because of disagreements between the Burundian government and the AU. The AU authorized in December 2015 the deployment of a 5,000-person African Prevention and Protection Mission in Burundi, which the Burundian government rejected, saying it would consider it an invading and occupying force. The AU did not pursue the proposal.

Cambodia

During 2016, Prime Minister Hun Sen and his ruling Cambodian People's Party (CPP) significantly escalated persecution on political grounds, targeting Cambodia's political opposition, human rights workers, social activists, and public intellectuals on the basis of their real or perceived political opposition to the government and its leader. These abuses appeared aimed to prevent victory or create conditions for overturning victory by the opposition Cambodia National Rescue Party (CNRP) in local and national elections scheduled for 2017 and 2018 respectively. The government also filed baseless charges against Rong Chhun, a member of the National Election Committee (NEC) appointed as a neutral member of the NEC as part of a political deal with the opposition.

On July 10, popular political commentator Kem Ley, who had voiced many criticisms of the government, was shot to death in Phnom Penh in broad daylight. Members of the public chased the gunman, who police took into custody. Authorities soon announced he had confessed to the crime. Media reports identified him as a former soldier from outside the capital. No genuine effort was made to identify those who ordered the killing.

Authorities systematically denied Cambodians their right to peaceful assembly by suppressing protests and issuing a series of ad hoc bans on non-violent gatherings and processions. Senior military officials backed this up with a flurry of pronouncements, including threats to deploy armed forces to prevent or suppress demonstrations by taking "absolute" action against them. These followed a memorial march on July 24, 2016, in memory of Kem Ley. Tens of thousands of people attended, despite government efforts to restrict participation.

Corruption remains a huge problem. Rather than targeting high-level official corruption, Cambodia's official anti-corruption unit has launched politically motivated investigations against the CNRP and the Cambodian Human Rights and Development Association (ADHOC), one of the country's oldest and most respected nongovernmental organizations (NGOs).

Attacks on the Political Opposition

CNRP president Sam Rainsy remained outside Cambodia in 2016, having de-cided not to return to the country in 2015 after the government announced it was going to enforce a two-year prison sentence against him on trumped-up charges. During 2016 four new prosecutions were brought against Rainsy, including one for being an accomplice to CNRP Senator Hong Sok Hour, convicted on politically motivated charges in August 2015 despite having parliamentary immunity and in violation of his right to freedom of opinion and expression. Two assistants to Rainsy fled abroad to avoid arrest on charges that carried up to 17 years in prison. The three other cases against Rainsy were for alleged criminal defama-tion of Hun Sen, CPP honorary chairperson Heng Sarmin, and a minister of state attached to Hun Sen.

On September 9, a Phnom Penh court convicted CNRP acting leader Kem Sokha of disregarding a court summons to appear as a witness against two fellow CNRP National Assembly members in another trumped-up case. In pursuing the case against Sokha, the courts violated his parliamentary immunity and sentenced him to five months in prison. Following a failed government attempt to arrest him in May, he moved to CNRP headquarters where he remained at time of writing, protected by party supporters but enduring a form of de facto house arrest.

On June 13, a Phnom Penh Court convicted without basis three CNRP activists for "insurrection." Arrested in August 2015, they joined 11 other CNRP activists found guilty on the same trumped-up charge in July 2015, in serving long prison terms for their involvement in a 2014 demonstration in Phnom Penh during which security forces attacked protesters.

CNRP parliamentarian Um Sam-an was arrested on April 11 for criticizing the gov-ernment's handling of border disputes with Vietnam. He was falsely charged with incitement and discrimination and faces up to five years' imprisonment.

Attacks on Land Activists

Government promises to end decades-old land-grabbing practices had no over-all positive effect. According to statistics compiled by NGOs working on the sub-ject statistics, land disputes in 2016 continued at the same level as in 2014-2015, affecting approximately 10,000 families per year.

165

HUMAN
RIGHTS
WATCH

DRAGGED AND BEATEN

The Cambodian Government's Role in the October 2015
Attack on Opposition Politicians

The government targeted veteran land activists for prosecution. On August 15, Phnom Penh authorities ordered the arrest of two for holding a peaceful protest vigil. In a summary trial seven days later, they were sentenced to six days' imprisonment for "insulting" government officials. On August 19, two long-dormant politically motivated prosecutions against one of the two, Tep Vanny, were suddenly revived. She was kept in detention after the other activist was released. At least three other land activists were charged in these two revived cases, both related to land rights protests. On September 19, Tep Vanny and three others were convicted and sentenced to six months in prison in one of the cases, despite no evidence connecting them to any recognizable criminal offense.

Attacks on Labor Activists

While labor unions succeeded in gaining government agreement for an increase in the minimum wage for garment workers, labor activists were under siege. In addition to NEC member and labor activist Rong Chhun, whose case is mentioned above, at least 12 other prominent trade union figures faced prosecution on baseless or frivolous charges. Although none of the 13 were in detention, all faced the prospect of jail. Trade union activists believed the prosecutions were in significant part intended to intimidate the movement's leadership during negotiations with the government that began in September 2016 over the minimum wage for garment workers.

Election-monitoring experts were concerned that prosecution of Rong Chhun aimed at pressuring him to refrain from pressing for free and fair elections. They also pointed out that convicting him would remove him from the NEC and allow the CPP to shift the balance of power there decisively in its favor.

Attacks on Human Rights Organizations

On April 28, 2016, the government's Anti-Corruption Unit (ACU) took into custody four senior staff of the Cambodian Human Rights and Development Association (ADHOC) and one former staffer, Ny Chariya, a deputy secretary-general of the NEC. They were accused of "bribing a witness" in connection with legal advice and other assistance ADHOC had been providing to a witness in the case against Kem Sokha. All five remained in detention on charges punishable by up to 10 years in prison. Authorities warned that further arrests of ADHOC staff could follow. On September 22, Ny Chariya was sentenced to six months in prison upon conviction in another case for having raised crtical questions about the conduct of a provincial court dealing with a land dispute.

Attacks on Public Intellectuals

The CPP sued political commentator Ou Virak in April in a defamation lawsuit for raising questions about the CPP's legal actions in the Kem Sokha case. Although defamation itself does not carry a custodial sentence, the damages requested were exorbitant and failure to pay could result in imprisonment.

On July 22, 2016, the Appeals Court upheld the conviction earlier in the year of student Kong Raya for advocating a "color revolution" in Cambodia, maintaining his one-and-a-half-year prison sentence.

Impunity

The May 2016 trial of three officers of Hun Sen's personal Bodyguard Headquarters for a brutal October 2015 assault against two opposition National Assembly members resulted in partly suspended prison sentences. Two of the attackers will each serve just one year. The cases appeared to be brought to pin the blame on lower-ranking individuals and avoid following up on evidence that higher-ups were involved in the crime, which had all the hallmarks of being government-orchestrated.

Similarly, according to sources with direct knowledge of the investigation into the killing of Kem Ley, the charging and detention of the alleged shooter was accompanied by an attempt by officials to falsely implicate the CNRP national leadership as having orchestrated the assassination while avoiding following up on leads that might produce evidence of CPP involvement.

The UN-supported Khmer Rouge Tribunal has been crippled since its inception in 2006 by Hun Sen-led government non-cooperation with its investigations into international crimes committed in the 1970s by Pol Pot's Khmer Rouge. In 2016, the court did not complete a second trial of two prominent ex-Khmer Rouge leaders, Nuon Chea and Khieu Samphan, and did not conclude investigations into four other, mid-level, Khmer Rouge leaders.

Arbitrary Arrest and Detention

Despite promises by Hun Sen to reform or close the Prey Speu detention center for Phnom Penh's "undesirable people," it remained operational. Security forces arbitrarily arrested hundreds of alleged homeless people, people who use drugs, sex workers, street children, and persons assumed to have a mental disability, and sent them to Prey Speu or one of the seven other so-called drug treatment centers around the country, where they are held for indefinite periods without a judicial process. At least two detainees died in Prey Speu under suspicious circumstances. The centers, many of them operated by security forces, often subject detainees to torture and other forms of ill-treatment.

Transgender women report high rates of police harassment, arbitrary arrest, and detention.

Key International Actors

China, Vietnam, and South Korea were key investors in 2016. China, Japan, and the European Union were the leading providers of development-related assistance.

In a joint statement first made before the UN Human Rights Council on September 14, 39 countries declared they were deeply concerned about escalating threats to "legitimate activities by opposition parties and human rights NGOs" in Cambodia and called on the government to ensure future free and fair elections and thus "the legitimacy of the next government." The European Parliament issued a strong resolution condemning abuses and repression. Nevertheless, foreign governments took no concrete steps to address Cambodia's deteriorating human rights situation.

HUMAN
RIGHTS
WATCH

MAKE IT SAFE
Canada's Obligation to End the First Nations Water Crisis

Canada

In October 2015, Canada's Liberal Party, led by Justin Trudeau, won power in national elections and signaled a change in Canadian politics. However, the new government faces important human rights challenges, including violence against indigenous women and girls, the rights of indigenous peoples, the impact of Canada's extractive and garment industries abroad, and children in detention.

Violence against Indigenous Women and Girls

In August 2016, the Canadian government launched a national public inquiry into the murders and disappearances of indigenous women and girls across Canada. With five commissioners and a budget of $53.86 million (US $41.13 million) over two years, the inquiry is tasked with examining the root causes and institutional responses to the high levels of violence. Although they represent just 4.3 percent of Canada's female population, 16 percent of female homicide victims are indigenous.

The inquiry comes after a change in government and stern criticism from international human rights authorities. In 2015, the United Nations Committee on the Elimination of Discrimination against Women concluded that Canada had committed a "grave violation" of the rights of indigenous women by failing to promptly and thoroughly investigate the high levels of violence they suffer.

The extent to which the inquiry will scrutinize policing practices remains to be seen. Government ministers have assured the public that the broadly worded terms of reference will provide for a critical review of policing, even though it is not referenced explicitly. Advocates have long fought for an investigation into allegations that police forces have neglected the murders and disappearances, and that some officers have committed abuses against indigenous women and girls.

Rights of Indigenous Peoples

The government has yet to pay adequate attention to severe poverty, housing, water, sanitation, healthcare, and education problems in indigenous communities, particularly those in remote and rural areas. Inadequate access to clean, safe drinking water continues to pose a major public health concern in a number of indigenous communities.

As of July, there were 132 drinking water advisories—indicating unsafe water—in effect in 92 First Nations communities across Canada, excluding British Colombia. Contaminants found in the water have been linked to negative health consequences, from serious gastrointestinal disorders to increased risk of cancer.

The UN Committee on Economic, Social and Cultural Rights voiced concern in March about the inadequate access to safe drinking water and to sanitation faced by First Nations, as well as the lack of water regulations for First Nations people living on reserves.

A June Human Rights Watch report, Make It Safe, found that this restricted access impacts the health and hygiene of families on reserve. Caregivers shoulder extra burdens to ensure that children, elders, and others avoid exposure to unsafe water.

Children in Immigration Detention

A 2016 report by the University of Toronto's International Human Rights Program found that children in Canadian immigration detention are held in facilities that resemble medium-security prisons, where they receive inadequate access to education and have insufficient recreational opportunities. Primary medical care is available, but children receive no mental health support. Outside Ontario and Québec, children are held in even less suitable facilities, in some instances in correctional facilities for young offenders.

Canadian law and policy do not prohibit immigration detention of children and do not set a limit on how long children can be held in immigration detention. An average of 242 children were held in Canadian immigration detention each year between 2010 and 2014, according to government statistics released to University of Toronto researchers.

That figure does not include all children, including Canadian citizens, who are not themselves subject to formal detention orders but stay in detention with their parents in order to avoid separating from them. The exact number of these de facto detained children is not publicly known: Canada's immigration agency considers them "guests" of the detention facilities.

They are not legally obligated to be in detention, but if their parents are held, the only alternative may be placement with a child protection agency. In 2014-15, such children spent, on average, three times as long in detention than children who are held under formal detention orders, the Canada Border Services Agency told University of Toronto researchers.

Canada's federal government and the Canada Border Services Agency have shown willingness to reform the immigration detention system but had not announced concrete steps to do so at time of writing.

Human Rights Watch and other groups called on Canadian authorities to ensure that children and families with children are not detained solely because of their immigration status; develop strong policies and guidelines about how the various alternatives to detention should be used; and review their practices to ensure that they are reflecting the best interests of the child in all decisions that affect them.

Mining Industry Abuses

Because Canada is the mining industry's most important global hub, the collective human rights impact of Canadian mining firms is enormous. In past years, our research has uncovered widespread patterns of gang rape by employees of Barrick Gold in Papua New Guinea, and the apparent use of forced labor at Nevsun Resources' Bisha mine in Eritrea. Many human rights problems linked to Canadian mining firms go underreported and unremedied because the government makes no proactive effort to monitor, let alone regulate, the human rights conduct of Canadian companies operating abroad.

Consistent with its predecessor, the Trudeau government has expressed the view to Human Rights Watch that no new oversight or regulation in this space is warranted, pointing in part to the existence of the government's Corporate Social Responsibility Counselor. This institution, however, cannot and indeed does not even purport to do what is most urgently needed—carry out any extraterritorial oversight or independent monitoring of Canadian firms.

In November 2016, the Canadian Network on Corporate Accountability proposed draft legislation that would create an ombudsman's office to hear and investigate human rights complaints against Canadian extractives firms operating in countries around the world.

Palliative Care

In June 2016, Canada enacted legislation to allow people with "grievous and irremediable medical conditions" that cause enduring and intolerable suffering to seek assistance from a physician or nurse practitioner to end their lives, acting on a February 2015 Supreme Court ruling.

While the government has discussed a number of possible measures to address the significant gaps in the availability of hospice palliative care in the country it has yet to make a clear commitment to do so, or to take the urgent steps necessary to ensure that Canadians who will die of natural causes—likely the vast majority—can live the final stretches of their lives with dignity.

Foreign Policy

The administration of former Conservative Prime Minister Stephen Harper began brokering an arms manufacturing and supply deal between Canada and Saudi Arabia in 2012. The finalized arrangement with General Dynamics Land Systems Canada resulted in a $15 billion, 15-year contract to manufacture an unspecified number of Light Armored Vehicles (LAVs), representing the largest manufacturing-export contract in Canadian history. On April 8, 2016, Foreign Affairs Minister Stéphane Dion approved six export permits covering more than 70 percent of the transaction.

Canadian law puts limits on the export of military technology to countries with a record of human rights violations against their citizens. Canadian arms export law demands indication that "there is no reasonable risk" that the arms will be used against civilians. However, the Saudis have used such vehicles to violently suppress peaceful protests in eastern Saudi Arabia in 2011 and 2012.

In addition, since a Saudi Arabia-led coalition began its military campaign against Houthi forces in Yemen on March 26, 2015, at least 3,799 civilians have been killed and 6,711 wounded, according to the Office of the High Commissioner for Human Rights (OHCHR). In addition, Saudi Arabia is arming Yemeni forces led by a controversial military commander accused of using child soldiers, in the fight to retake the north from the Houthis and forces loyal to former President Ali Abdullah Saleh, including with vehicles.

Central African Republic

On March 30, 2016 former Central African Republic Prime Minister Faustin-Archange Touadéra was sworn in as president after more than two years of an interim government. Despite the rare peaceful transition of power and relatively peaceful elections, the country remained insecure, unstable and beset by serious human rights violations.

Sectarian violence and attacks on civilians continued in central and western regions of the country, most notably in the Ouaka, Nana-Grébizi, and Ouham-Pendé provinces where predominantly Muslim Seleka rebel groups, largely Christian and animist anti-balaka militias and other armed groups remained active. Civilians continued to bear the brunt of the fighting and armed groups raped and sexually assaulted women and girls. An estimated 467,800 people, the majority of them Muslim, remained refugees in neighboring countries and a further 384,300 remained internally displaced.

The United Nations peacekeeping mission, MINUSCA, deployed about 10,050 peacekeepers and 2,000 police across many parts of the country during the year, but struggled to establish security in key areas and to sufficiently protect civilians. MINUSCA's efforts were marred by allegations of sexual exploitation and abuse by peacekeepers of civilians, including children. Credible accusations that African Union (AU) peacekeepers murdered 12 civilians in Boali in 2014 gained further strength when a mass grave was exhumed in the town in February.

Impunity for past abuses and war crimes remained pervasive. Progress toward the functioning of a Special Criminal Court in the national justice system has been slow. The International Criminal Court (ICC) prosecutor continued investigations, started in September 2014, into alleged war crimes and crimes against humanity committed in the country since August 2012.

About 2.3 million people, out of a population of 4.6 million, needed humanitarian assistance. Of those 2.3 million, some humanitarian aid reached only 1.9 million.

Attacks on Civilians

The Seleka, a predominantly Muslim rebellion made up of loosely affiliated factions, continued to attack civilians, killing scores, often under the pretext of protecting themselves from the anti-balaka. In September, fighters from the Union for Peace in the Central African Republic (*l'Union pour la Paix en Centrafrique*), a Seleka faction, attacked villages on the road between Kouango and Bianga, in Ouaka province.

In October, Seleka forces attacked and burned a displacement camp in Kaga-Bandoro, killing at least 37 civilians, despite the presence of UN peacekeepers. At least four people with disabilities were among the victims. Rising insecurity in the Nana-Grébizi province led to dozens of attacks on international humanitarian organizations by armed groups and bandits between August and October, impairing life-saving assistance.

An armed group 3R, meaning "Return, Reclamation, Rehabilitation," comprised of Muslim Peuhl, emerged in western Ouham-Pendé province under the command of General Sidiki Abass. As fighting between 3R and anti-balaka increased in 2016, scores of civilians, both Muslim Peuhl herders and non-Muslim farmers, were killed. Credible reports indicated that both sides committed rapes, reflecting the widespread problem of sexual violence in the conflict since 2013.

The Ugandan rebel group the Lord's Resistance Army (LRA) remained active in the southeast with allegations of increased killings and abductions of civilians.

While the capital Bangui stabilized in late 2015 after the violence of the previous months, armed militias raped or sexually assaulted at least 25 women and girls in and around the M'poko displacement camp between September and December 2015. In some cases, the perpetrators raping the women and girls said it was to punish them for allegedly interacting with people on the other side of the sectarian divide. Survivors of sexual violence continued to face stigma, rejection, and other barriers to accessing essential services and justice.

Refugees and Internally Displaced Persons

Conditions for internally displaced persons and refugees remained harsh. Many displaced people, such as those in Ouaka and Ouham provinces, had little or no humanitarian assistance. Persons with disabilities at displacement sites faced barriers to access sanitation, food, and medical assistance. The M'poko displacement camp in Bangui held approximately 20,000 people by the year's end.

In southwestern parts of the country, small pockets of Muslims lived in enclaves protected by UN peacekeepers. In central and northwestern parts of the country, displacement increased as a result of the violence. Attacks by Seleka in the southern Ouaka province displaced 3,500 people and fighting in Ouham-Pendé displaced between 5,000 and 10,000. Approximately 20,000 people were displaced after the Seleka attacked the displacement camp in Kaga-Bandoro in October.

Elections

In a December 2015 referendum, voters overwhelmingly approved a new constitution. Legislative and presidential elections took place two weeks later and Touadéra won a presidential runoff on February 14, 2016.

At least eight anti-balaka leaders participated in parliamentary elections, three of whom won seats, including Alfred Yékatom, also known as "Rombhot." Amnesty International accused Yékatom of having participated in and ordering killings of civilians in 2014 and the UN imposed sanctions on him in 2015. The UN Panel of Experts on the Central African Republic identified Yékatom as having intimidated voters and harassed political competitors in Mbaïki, his constituency, during the 2016 electoral campaign. Another victorious candidate, militia leader Eric Pogola, threatened staff of a political rival and allegedly sent armed fighters to polling stations on election day in the Sangha-Mbaéré province.

Peacekeeper Abuses

In early February, Human Rights Watch issued a report documenting sexual abuse and exploitation by MINUSCA peacekeepers of at least eight women and girls between October and December 2015 around Bambari in the Ouaka province, including the rape of a 14-year-old girl and the gang-rape of an 18-year-old woman. In response to the allegations, MINUSCA promptly sent home 120 peacekeepers from the Republic of Congo.

The contingent of peacekeepers from the Democratic Republic of Congo, who also faced numerous other allegations of sexual exploitation and abuse, were repatriated at the end of February for failing to meet UN standards for equipment and preparedness. Criminal proceedings by DRC authorities into sexual abuse and exploitation by peacekeepers from that country began in Kinshasa, but were adjourned in June to explore ways of interviewing victims.

In March, international media reported additional allegations of sexual exploitation and abuse by MINUSCA peacekeepers. MINUSCA announced it was investigating the cases and would take action against perpetrators.

A military trial in Paris against five French peacekeepers for beating a Central African man began in September. Military trials against French peacekeepers accused in 2015 of sexual abuse continued.

In June, the government of the Republic of Congo announced that a judicial procedure was ongoing against an unspecified number of Congolese MINUSCA peacekeepers based in Mambéré who had allegedly beaten two men to death in 2015.

In February, a mass grave exhumed at Boali appeared to contain the remains of 12 people allegedly killed by AU peacekeepers from the Republic of Congo in 2014. In December 2013, AU peacekeepers also from the Republic of Congo allegedly beat to death two anti-balaka fighters they had detained in Bossangoa and, in February 2014, allegedly executed two anti-balaka fighters in Mambéré. In June 2016, the government of the Republic of Congo announced that a judicial procedure was ongoing for the Boali and Bossangoa cases. At time of writing, no action has been taken on the 2014 Mambéré killings.

National and International Justice

Impunity remained one of the main challenges in addressing past and ongoing atrocities. In August and September, the criminal court in Bangui tried 55 cases, some of them dealing with serious crimes such as rape and murder. However, the court did not address any abuses or alleged war crimes related to the conflict.

Resource constraints and administrative hurdles impeded operationalizing the Special Criminal Court, a hybrid court with national and international judges and prosecutors that will focus on grave international crimes committed since 2003. In a positive step, the minister of justice announced in July that the court's special prosecutor would be appointed before the end of 2016. In August, the UN and the government signed a document that outlined their tasks and responsibilities related to the court.

The Office of the Prosecutor at the ICC continued its investigations throughout the year into serious crimes committed by the Seleka and anti-balaka. The ICC issued no arrest warrants in 2016.

A previous ICC investigation led to the conviction of Jean-Pierre Bemba Gombo, a former vice president of the Democratic Republic of Congo. Forces from Bemba's Movement for the Liberation of the Congo (*Mouvement pour la Libération du Congo*) were active in the Central African Republic in 2002 and 2003, acting at the behest of then-President Ange-Félix Patassé to repress a coup attempt by then-Gen. François Bozizé.

On March 21, 2016, ICC judges found Bemba guilty of rape, murder, and pillage under the legal principle of "command responsibility." On June 21, the court sentenced him to 18 years in prison. In September, Bemba's legal team filed an appeal. The prosecutor, who had sought a 25-year sentence, has indicated that her office would appeal the sentence to "reflect the totality of Bemba's culpability." On October 19, ICC judges found Bemba and four associates guilty of witness tampering because they attempted to bribe witnesses.

Key International Actors

France began withdrawing its peacekeeping forces in October. They are expected to retain approximately 300 troops in the country.

At the Brussels International Conference for the Central African Republic on November 17, the European Union, the country's largest donor, pledged €409 million (US$450 million) over five years for peace building, development and humanitarian assistance. Overall pledges from the conference totaled €2.06 billion ($2.28 billion).

In 2016, the United States provided $95 million in humanitarian aid. The total humanitarian response met only 32.2 percent of the country's funding needs.

The Netherlands, US, and the UN were the principal donors to the Special Criminal Court, but the court's five-year budget remained only partially covered.

In April, the EU approved the establishment of a military training mission, EUTM RCA, operational for an initial period of two years to train two battalions of the national army.

In August, the Ugandan military began withdrawing troops from an AU-led offensive against the LRA in the southeast. At time of writing, the US had decided to continue counter-LRA operations in the country.

Chile

Courts continue to prosecute people for abuses committed during military rule In Chile, but the Supreme Court has used its discretionary powers in many cases to reduce sentences against human rights violators, resulting in punishments incommensurate with the gravity of the crimes. Poor prison conditions and reports of excessive use of force by police also continue to be significant human rights concerns in Chile.

The National Service for Minors became the center of a scandal in 2016 when information was released indicating that more than 850 children and 448 adults had died in state custody since 2005. Reported causes of death varied, but included infants and young children drowning in their own gastric or respiratory fluids, suicides, and delayed medical attention to injuries.

Chile's parliament has debated reform of a counterterrorism law and decriminalization of abortion in limited circumstances, as promised by President Michelle Bachelet, but neither had passed at time of writing. In November, a bill was introduced to end the jurisdiction of military courts over alleged human rights abuses by *Carabineros*, Chilean police officers responsible for public order and crime prevention.

Confronting Past Abuses

According to data released by the Ministry of the Interior's human rights program in December 2015, justice authorities are investigating a total of 1,048 cases involving human rights violations committed during military rule (1973-1990). As of December 2015, 344 individuals had been sentenced for human rights crimes, including killings and enforced disappearances; 117 of them were serving prison sentences. While courts continue to prosecute abuses committed during military rule, the Supreme Court has used its discretionary powers in many cases to reduce the sentences imposed on perpetrators, sometimes even to a non-custodial sentence.

In July 2016, Juan Emilio Cheyre, former army commander-in-chief, was placed under judicial investigation for his alleged role as accomplice in the 1973 murders of 15 opponents of the Pinochet dictatorship. At the time, he was a lieutenant in the La Serena regiment, and the homicides were part of what became known as the "Caravan of Death," a military death squad that tortured, extrajudicially killed, and disappeared suspected dissidents throughout Northern Chile. Gen. Sergio Víctor Arellano Stark, who led the Caravan of Death, died in March 2016 without serving prison time, though the Supreme Court convicted and sentenced him to six years.

In October, the Supreme Court overturned the 1974-1975 convictions for sedition and treason of 12 ex-members of the Chilean air force who refused to join the 1973 military coup.

Counterterrorism Law

A bill presented by the government in November 2014 to replace Chile's counterterrorism law remained under discussion in the legislature at time of writing. The current law lacks sufficient due process protections, and its definition of terrorism is overly broad. The bill would update and narrow the definition of terrorism, excluding crimes against private property, which have formed the basis for terrorism prosecutions of Mapuche indigenous activists. It would also strengthen due process guarantees, giving defense attorneys the right to learn the identity of protected witnesses, question them about their evidence, and probe their credibility.

Military Jurisdiction

Military courts continue to exercise jurisdiction over abuses committed by Chile's uniformed police, the Carabineros. Criminal proceedings in military courts lack the independence and due process guarantees of ordinary criminal cases. Investigations are secret, the proceedings are conducted mainly in writing, and lawyers have limited opportunities to cross-examine witnesses. Many legitimate complaints of human rights abuses filed in military courts are dismissed. Sentences are often inappropriately reduced by the military appeals court. Both the Constitutional Court and the Supreme Court have opposed military jurisdiction in such cases.

In May 2014, the minister of defense promised to present draft legislation before the end of June 2015 that would end military jurisdiction over crimes committed against civilians by the armed forces (including Carabineros). In November 2016, the government introduced such a bill.

Freedom of Expression

In May 2016, President Bachelet filed criminal defamation charges against four journalists from the magazine *Qué Pasa*, after it printed the transcript of a telephone wiretap of a suspect in the Chilean Public Ministry's investigation into a business with links to one of Bachelet's relatives. In September, the ethical council of the Federation of Media of Chile (FMCS), a professional association, adopted a resolution sanctioning the magazine for breach of journalistic ethics. Bachelet subsequently withdrew her case, saying she was "satisfied" with the FMCS sanction and had never intended to "affect journalists or win money."

Police Abuses

Carabineros continue to use excessive force, according to media reports, particularly against protesters, students, and indigenous communities. Some officers have allegedly sexually harassed women and girls at protests.

A controversial law that allows what many are calling "preventive identity control" entered into force in July 2016. Article 12 of Law 20931 permits law enforcement to ask for identification from anyone who is older than 18 years of age without any suspicion of connection to a crime, which was the standard previously required to check identification. This is particularly concerning in the case of protests, as identification checks at protests in Chile have been reported as disproportionately affecting marginalized groups.

Torture

In November, President Bachelet signed into law a bill that will modify Chile's criminal code to comply with international and regional standards on torture and cruel, inhuman, and degrading treatment including by increasing penalties for torture and prohibiting amnesty.

According to the Public Ministry, complaints of torture, genocide, ill-treatment, and crimes against humanity increased 193 percent in the first nine months of

2016, compared with the same period in 2015. Most cases allegedly involve public functionaries, such as Carabineros.

Prison Conditions

Despite measures adopted in 2010-2013 to reduce the prison population, many of Chile's prisons remain grossly overcrowded. Prisons in Chile house nearly 49,000 detainees and prisoners, though their maximum capacity is less than 42,000. Conditions remain poor, and violent abuses by prison guards are common.

Children's Rights

The National Service for Minors (Sename), the government agency tasked with caring for children and adolescents whose families are unable to do so, became the center of a scandal in July when an information request through Chile's Transparency Law revealed that 185 children died in the care of state institutions from 2005 to May 2016; in October, Sename confirmed that the figure was even higher: 865 children and 448 adults (such as persons with disabilities or those in residences or outpatient programs)—a total of 1,313 deaths of people in its custody. As noted above, reported causes of death included infants and young children drowning in their own gastric or respiratory fluids, suicides, and delayed medical attention to injuries. The Chamber of Deputies questioned Minister of Justice Javiera Blanco in August, and a judicial investigation was ongoing at time of writing.

Reproductive Rights

In March, Chile's Chamber of Deputies approved a bill to decriminalize abortion in cases of rape, fetal inviability, and when a woman or girl's life is at risk. The Senate Health Commission held public hearings in August. The bill, in particular the provision that decriminalizes abortion in rape cases, has been met with near-unanimous opposition from center-right and right-wing parties in Congress, as well as from the Catholic and Evangelical Churches. At time of writing, the bill was still pending in the Constitutional Commission of the Senate.

Sexual Orientation and Gender Identity

A "civil union" bill presented by former President Sebastián Piñera in 2011 that provides legal recognition and protection for same-sex couples became law in April 2015 and went into effect in October 2015.

In September 2016, the Senate Human Rights Commission approved a bill to recognize the gender identity of transgender people, with a Senate vote expected in December.

In June 2016 Chile, on behalf of four Latin American states and 42 co-sponsors, presented a resolution at the United Nations Human Rights Council creating the first UN expert post addressing violence and discrimination based on sexual orientation and gender identity.

Human Rights Defenders

On May 13, uniformed personnel of the National Human Rights Institute (INDH)—a government agency that promotes, monitors, and reports on human rights in Chile—reported being arbitrarily detained, beaten, and verbally assaulted by Carabineros when they tried to visit detained protestors at a police station in Antofagasta. Their professional association cited the incident as part of broader police attempts to undermine their function. In 2015, the Chamber of Deputies defeated, in a two-to-one vote, a motion to dismiss Lorena Fries, then director of INDH, for alleged negligence, after the INDH distributed educational materials critical of the Carabineros. The dismissal request and chamber vote showed the agency's vulnerability to political reprisals.

Key International Actors

The special rapporteur for freedom of expression of the Inter-American Commission on Human Rights, in preliminary observations from a 2016 visit to Chile, expressed concern that President Bachelet's criminal charges against *Qué Pasa*, along with various bills under consideration in Congress, risked restricting the media, particularly from reporting on issues of public interest that involve political figures.

In June, the UN special rapporteur on freedom of assembly and association called Chile's military jurisdiction system and the impunity it engenders "the most visible parts of the legacy of dictatorship," criticized excessive use of force by police at protests, particularly against Mapuche demonstrators, and expressed opposition to the use of preventive identity controls at protests.

In April 2016, the UN Committee on the Rights of Persons with Disabilities urged the government to prohibit practices amounting to cruel, inhuman, or degrading treatment of people with disabilities in state and private institutions—such as psychosurgery, electroconvulsive therapy without consent, physical restraints, and isolation in cells—and to investigate reports of security forces mistreating people with disabilities.

China

More than three decades after pledging to "reform and open up," there are few signs the Chinese Communist Party intends to change its authoritarian posture. Under the leadership of President Xi Jinping, who will remain in power until 2022 and possibly beyond, the outlook for fundamental human rights, including freedoms of expression, assembly, association and religion, remains dire.

China made modest improvements in a few areas in 2016. These include trial regulations promulgated in February that may reduce the rate of pretrial detention, the Supreme People's Court's continued efforts to retry cases of wrongful convictions and executions, and the acceptance by courts of discrimination cases brought by lesbian, gay, bisexual, and transgender (LGBT) individuals. But such developments pale in comparison to the government's systematic efforts to silence independent civil society voices, its passage of abusive new laws, and a highly politicized anti-corruption campaign that is further undermining an already weak judicial system.

Over 16 human rights lawyers and activists—detained after a nationwide sweep of rights advocates in July 2015—were the clearest victims of the authorities' hostility towards independent civil society. Most were held in secret and not allowed to communicate with their families or lawyers of their choosing. Families, lawyers, and supporters who inquired about the cases or sought the detainees' release also became targets of the authorities' wrath.

The secrecy surrounding these detentions stood in stark contrast to the aggressive state media campaign to smear the detainees, many of them well-known for their years of activism. The publicity, which departed from the quieter treatments of past political trials such as that of Liu Xiaobo's in 2009, appears designed to punish the activists and advance President Xi's campaign to depict independent civil society as a national security threat.

Chinese authorities' enforced disappearance of critics from Hong Kong and other countries in 2016 garnered headlines globally. Beijing's decision to interfere in a politically charged court case in Hong Kong in November undermined judicial independence and the territory's autonomy. In the ethnic minority regions of Xinjiang and Tibet, Beijing continued its highly repressive rule, curtailing political activity and many peaceful expressions of ethnic and religious identity.

Authorities also moved to further limit freedom of expression. In November, the government passed a Cybersecurity Law, which will strangle online freedom and anonymity, and further clamped down on media outlets for reporting that departs from the party line. Authorities also issued multiple directives to tighten control over the internet, which has long been a beacon of hope as a relatively free public space, despite online censorship and surveillance.

The Chinese government continues to lead the world in the number of people executed, with 46 crimes eligible for the death penalty. Scholars in China claimed in September that executions had "fallen about 60 percent" to "a few thousands" in 2005, but official statistics remain state secrets.

Human Rights Defenders

As noted above, more than 16 human rights lawyers and activists were detained in a nationwide sweep of rights advocates starting in July 2015. State media aired their forced confessions, ran frontpage "exposes" about their personal lives, and disparagingly described their work as that of a "major criminal gang" aiming to "attack social stability" with the backing of "foreign forces." Authorities handpicked four Hong Kong-based and one Taiwan-based pro-Beijing media outlets to cover the trial proceedings while barring others from entering the courtroom.

In August 2016, after days of closed trials, a Tianjin court handed down heavy sentences to Beijing Fengrui Law Firm director Zhou Shifeng and veteran activist Hu Shigen, and gave suspended sentences to two other activists. Although authorities released some detainees on bail, including lawyer Wang Yu and her husband, legal advocate Bao Longjun, their lawyers and close friends have not been able to contact them. Most of the 16 remained in detention awaiting trial at time of writing.

Authorities' hostility toward those who advocate for human rights reached new heights in 2016. Some activists who had previously been able to carry out advocacy now find themselves behind bars. In June, citizen journalists Lu Yuyu and Li Tingyu, who had been documenting China's protests since 2012, were formally detained for "creating disturbances." Labor rights advocates Meng Han and Zeng Feiyang were convicted without credible evidence on vague charges including "gathering crowds to disturb public order" and "gathering crowds to disturb social order." Meng was sentenced to 21 months in jail while Zeng was given a four-year suspended sentence. According to state media, they had "used funding from abroad" to "incite workers to go on strike."

Authorities increasingly use vague public order charges against activists, including "creating disturbances" and "disturbing social order," in addition to serious political charges such as "subversion." In a disturbing trend, charges of "subversion"—which previously had been reserved for those who voiced opposition to the Chinese Communist Party—are now being extended to lawyers and activists who do not directly challenge the party, as in the case against the Beijing Fengrui Law Firm.

In January, rights activist Zhang Haitao was sentenced to 19 years in prison for "inciting subversion of state power" and "probing and illegally supplying intelligence abroad." In June, democracy activists Lu Gengsong and Chen Shuqing were slapped with over 10 years in prison for "subversion."

In January, a Guangzhou court handed down a five-year prison term to lawyer Tang Jingling; he had promoted non-violent civil disobedience. In September, a Beijing court convicted rights lawyer Xia Lin on dubious extortion charges and sentenced him to 12 years in prison. Official lawyers associations in January cancelled the license of Shandong lawyer Liu Shuqing and in May refused to renew the license of lawyer Liu Xiaoyuan. Both had supported lawyers held in the July 2015 crackdown.

Authorities continued to tighten their grip over independent groups. In January, a Swedish national who heads a nongovernmental organization (NGO) that provides funding to human rights lawyers, Peter Dahlin, was detained for 23 days, forced to confess on television, and then deported. In April, the National People's Congress approved the Foreign NGO Management Law, which gives police unprecedented power to restrict the work of foreign groups in the country, and limits domestic groups' ability to obtain foreign funding and work with foreign organizations. In August, authorities issued new rules on domestic civil society groups, requiring a "strengthening" of the party's "leadership role" over them. In September, a new charity law went into effect; it may further limit fundraising by and strengthen state control over civil society.

HUMAN
RIGHTS
WATCH

"SPECIAL MEASURES"

Detention and Torture in Chinese Communist Party's Shuanggui System

Freedom of Expression

Freedom of expression, already severely restricted through censorship and punishments, was hit particularly hard in 2016. Shortly after activist Lei Yang's May death in police custody, the Ministry of Public Security issued new rules requiring officers to film some of their operations. Few other media stories broke through official censorship to generate nationwide discussion or policy change.

In February, President Xi visited three major state media outlets and called on them to pledge absolute loyalty to the party. That month, authorities also shut down the microblogs of prominent blogger Ren Zhiqiang, who has 35 million followers, after Ren criticized Xi's media visits.

In March an anonymous letter calling for Xi's resignation was posted on the Wujie news website, prompting police to interrogate 20 people. Also in March, Guangxi police detained He Linxia, director of Guangxi Normal University Press, which is known for publishing books focused on politics. He was formally arrested for "corruption" in May. In May, the State Administration of Press, Publication, Radio, Film and Television (SAPPRFT) reportedly met with video companies to ask them to sell company equity stakes to the government as a means to increase control over content.

In June, the Cyberspace Administration issued new rules requiring app providers to keep user logs for 60 days to reduce the spread of "illegal information." It also ordered news websites to "clean up" comment sections to purge views prohibited by the government. SAPPRFT also issued new rules requiring game developers to submit their work for government pre-approval.

In July, authorities sacked two of Tencent's editors after the website ran a headline with an error seen as insulting to President Xi. That month the Beijing Cyberspace Administration shut down seven web-based news channels of Sohu, Sina, Netease, and Ifeng. In July, the CCP United Front Work Department established Bureau Number 8 to enlist the support of influential individuals in new media for the Party. In the same month, Beijing authorities sacked or demoted the editors of *Yanhuang Chunqiu*, a moderate history magazine with the backing of relatively liberal Party elders, leading to its closure.

In August, the Cyberspace Administration imposed new requirements on websites, including requiring staff to monitor content round the clock, and the SAP-

PRFT issued a notice ordering all media "not to promote western lifestyles" or to "poke fun at Chinese values" when reporting entertainment news.

In October, authorities closed the influential intellectual website Consensus, 21ccom.cn, for "transmitting incorrect ideas." In November, the Cyberspace Administration issued new rules on live streaming platforms, requiring companies to monitor user content that threatens national security.

Hong Kong

Under its Basic Law, Hong Kong is guaranteed autonomy in all matters other than foreign affairs and defense, and enjoys an independent judiciary and other civil liberties. In practice Beijing is increasingly encroaching on rights to political participation, expression, and assembly in the territory.

Between October and December 2015, five staff members of the Causeway Bay Bookstore, which publishes and sells books in Hong Kong about mainland politics, went missing. One, Swedish national Gui Minhai, was disappeared from Thailand. Another British national, Lee Po, was disappeared from Hong Kong, though his travel documents had remained at home. In March, four of five disappeared booksellers reappeared in China, confessed on television to smuggling banned books, and were released. Swedish national Gui Minhai remains detained incommunicado in an unknown location. In June, Lam Wing-kee, one of the four who was released, broke with his captors' orders and told media about his detention in the mainland. The central Chinese government has yet to explain whether, and under what circumstances, mainland security forces are operating in the territory, and Hong Kong authorities have failed to press for such information.

In July, a Shenzhen court convicted Wang Jianmin and Guo Zhongxiao, who published and sold Chinese political magazines in Hong Kong but reside in the mainland, to prison sentences of five and two years for "running an illegal business." Their lawyer had contended that the duo did not break Chinese law as the magazines were sold in Hong Kong.

Also in July, a Hong Kong court convicted student leaders Joshua Wong and Alex Chow of "unlawful assembly" and Nathan Law of "incitement," offenses under Hong Kong's Public Order Ordinance. The charges stem from their leadership of a peaceful sit-in that triggered the 79-day pro-democracy Umbrella Movement in 2014. While all three received light sentences, such as community service, their prosecution indicated a worrying trend, as peaceful protest leaders previously had rarely been prosecuted in the territory.

In July, Hong Kong's Electoral Affairs Commission announced a new requirement that candidates running for the semi-democratic Legislative Council ("LegCo") must formally declare their recognition of Hong Kong as an "inalienable part" of China. Election officers then disqualified six candidates who have peacefully advocated for the territory's independence. In August, a spokesperson for the Education Bureau warned teachers that they could lose their professional qualifications for advocating independence. In September, voters turned out in record numbers for the LegCo elections, sending to office six individuals who support Hong Kong self-determination.

In November, China's top legislature issued an interpretation of a provision of the Basic Law (Hong Kong's functional constitution) on oath-taking that seemed designed to compel the Hong Kong High Court to disqualify two recently elected pro-independence legislators from taking office. It marked the first time Chinese authorities had issued a ruling on the Basic Law while legal proceedings were ongoing in Hong Kong.

Xinjiang

Authorities made no moves in 2016 to lift restrictions on fundamental human rights and end pervasive ethnic and religious discrimination in Xinjiang, home to 10 million predominantly Muslim Uyghurs and an increasing number of Han Chinese migrants. Opposition to central and local government policies has been expressed in peaceful protests but also through bombings and other violent attacks. The Chinese government claims that it faces terrorism in the region and conducts counterterror operations there. However, details about protests, violence, and terrorism, and counterterrorism operations are scant, with few independent sources of information there.

In June, Ili police announced that applicants for passports must supply a DNA sample, fingerprints, a voice recording, and a "three-dimensional image," according to media reports. The requirement adds to already stringent restrictions on foreign travel for Xinjiang residents. Local government authorities again

HUMAN
RIGHTS
WATCH

RELENTLESS
Detention and Prosecution of Tibetans Under China's
"Stability Maintenance" Campaign

banned civil servants, students, and teachers from fasting and instructed restaurants to stay open during the Muslim holiday of Ramadan.

In August, Xinjiang authorities issued a new directive to implement China's abusive Counterterror Law, which came into effect in January 2016. In June, a group of 10 Uighur students in Guangzhou No. 75 Middle School were reportedly arrested for terrorism, but little other information was available about the case at time of writing.

Uighur economist Ilham Tohti is serving a life sentence on baseless charges of separatism for having peacefully criticized the government's Xinjiang policies. In October, he was awarded the prestigious Martin Ennals human rights award.

Tibet

Tibetans continue to face routine denial of basic freedoms of speech, assembly, and movement. In 2016 authorities prioritized rights-abusing "anti-splittism" and "stability maintenance" campaigns despite the absence of tangible threats, and forbade almost all residents of the Tibet Autonomous Republic (TAR) from foreign travel.

In August, Wu Yingjie, an ethnic Chinese Communist Party cadre, was appointed to succeed Chen Quanguo as TAR party secretary and is expected to continue Chen's policies of heavy-handed governance and social control. The 13th Five Year Plan began in 2016, and the TAR set ambitious goals for massive infrastructure construction and urban development; Tibetan areas of Qinghai and Sichuan provinces are also slated for greater resource extraction. Many reported public protests were against rural land grabs, including one in Gansu which security forces suppressed in May.

Continuing restrictions on religious freedom include a program of demolitions and evictions at Larung Gar monastic complex in Serta county, Sichuan, which will see the world's largest Tibetan Buddhist community shrink from its 2016 population of at least 10,000 to no more than 5,000 by September 2017. The Tibetan writers Shokjang and Lomik were given three and seven-and-a-half year sentences, respectively, and Lu Konchok Gyatso and Tashi Wangchuk remained in custody at time of writing, one for planning to publish a book and the other for speaking to the *New York Times* about the loss of Tibetan language teaching.

At time of writing, two more Tibetans had self-immolated in 2016, both in Sichuan. At least four Tibetans were believed to have died in custody, including Kandze nun Yeshe Lhakdron, who has not been seen since her arrest in 2008.

Freedom of Religion

The government restricts religious practice to five officially recognized religions and only in officially approved religious premises. The government retains control over religious personnel appointments, publications, finances, and seminary applications. The government classifies many religious groups outside of its control as "evil cults." Falun Gong, a meditation-focused spiritual group banned since July 1999, continues to suffer state persecution.

Zhejiang authorities released some of the individuals it took into custody in 2015 for resisting its campaign to remove crosses from churches in the province, known as China's "heartland of Christianity." In February, Zhejiang state television aired a coerced confession of human rights lawyer Zhang Kai, who had been detained incommunicado for providing legal advice to Christians affected by the cross removals. Zhang was released in March. But in Jinhua City, pastors Bao Guohua and Xing Wenxiang were sentenced to 14 and 12 years, respectively, in a case widely seen as retaliation for their opposition to the anti-cross campaign.

In April, President Xi gave a major speech on religion, during which he warned against "overseas infiltrations through religious means," and called on religions to "Sinicize" or "adopt Chinese characteristics."

In August, a Tianjin court sentenced Hu Shigen, a veteran activist and a Christian, to seven-and-a-half years in prison. Hu's crimes, according to the prosecution, included "using illegal religious activities as a platform" to "spread subversive thoughts."

In September, the Chinese government released draft revisions to its abusive 2005 Religious Regulations; these require that religion "protect national security" and prohibit individuals and groups not approved as religious bodies from attending meetings abroad on religion.

Guizhou authorities have held Pastor Li Guozhi of the Living Stones Church since December 2015, when the authorities closed down the 500-member house church and declared it "illegal."

Sexual Orientation and Gender Identity

China has no law protecting people from discrimination on the basis of sexual orientation or gender identity, and there is no legal recognition of same-sex partnership. Possibly because their activism is not considered threatening to the state, LGBT individuals enjoyed some success advancing legal cases in 2016.

In January, a Hunan court heard a case filed by Sun Wenlin against the local Bureau of Civil Affairs, which had refused to marry Sun and his male partner. Though the court ruled against Sun in April, his case—the first gay marriage lawsuit accepted by Chinese courts—attracted wide media attention. In June, a Henan court accepted a case filed by Yu Hu against a mental health hospital that had subjected him to 19 days of involuntary "therapy" to "cure" his homosexuality. Also in June, a Guangdong university student, Qiu Bai, sued the provincial education department over textbooks that depict homosexuality as an illness. Qiu filed a similar suit in 2015, though she withdrew it later because the department had promised to look into the matter. She decided to sue again after the authorities' pledge failed to materialize.

In June, China voted against a UN resolution creating an expert post dedicated to addressing violence and discrimination based on sexual orientation and gender identity.

Women's Rights

Women in China face systemic discrimination in higher education and employment, as well as domestic violence and sexual harassment. The government's response to these abuses continues to be inadequate despite its rhetorical commitment to gender equality.

Authorities' heightened hostility toward civil society extended to women's rights activists in 2016. In January, Guo Jianmei, founder of the well-known Beijing Zhongze Women's Legal Counseling and Service Center, closed the organization, citing official pressure.

In April, in a landmark case, a Guangzhou court ruled in favor of a woman who sued two companies for discriminating against her in their hiring process. Women's rights advocates criticized the paltry compensation—2,000RMB (US$300)—awarded by the court.

Disability Rights

Although China ratified the Convention on the Rights of Persons with Disabilities in 2008, persons with disabilities continue to face barriers and discrimination in areas including education and employment. The government also continues to detain activists in psychiatric facilities.

Regulations drafted in 2013 on access to education for people with disabilities have still not been adopted. Official guidelines continue to allow universities to deny enrollment in certain subjects if the applicants have certain disabilities. In July, a Henan student, Song Yichen, made headlines when he was rejected by Tianjin University of Traditional Chinese Medicine for his visual impairment.

Official guidelines on hiring civil servants continue to discriminate against those with certain disabilities. In August, Tan Jinsong, a man with visual impairment was rejected for a job with the local legislative office in Henan province despite obtaining the highest scores in the civil service exam.

Key International Actors

In February, the UN high commissioner for human rights expressed concern regarding China's continued arbitrary detention and interrogation of lawyers, harassment and intimidation of government critics and NGO workers, and the negative impact on basic rights of the new Foreign NGO Management law.

In February 2016, the European Parliament adopted a strong resolution condemning human rights abuses in China and in March, a dozen governments led by the United States signed on to an unprecedented statement condemning China's "deteriorating human rights record" at the UN Human Rights Council. Several governments, including those of Canada, the European Union, Germany, and the United States, issued statements in 2016 about the crackdown on civil society, disappearances of the Hong Kong booksellers, and the foreign NGO management law. No government, however, imposed any other concrete costs on Beijing for its deteriorating human rights record.

On his penultimate visit to China as UN secretary-general in July, Ban Ki-moon finally expressed concern about the crackdown on civil society, and urged Chinese authorities to give "citizens a full say and role in the political life of their country." US President Barack Obama failed to make any specific public statements about human rights on his last visit as president to China in September. G20 member states not only failed to condemn China's human rights record when they met in Hangzhou in September, they also failed to condemn the abuses in Hangzhou stemming from the event, such as the detention of local activists or the far-reaching restrictions China imposed to limit participation by independent civil society organizations in G20 discussions.

Foreign Policy

In July, the Permanent Court of Arbitration, an international tribunal, issued a sweeping rebuke of China's claims of sovereignty over large portions of the South China Sea, stating that Beijing's claims lacked legal validity. China responded by dismissing the legality of the court, saying it would not respect the ruling.

In 2016, China did not exercise its veto power at the UN Security Council. However in December 2015, China tried to block discussion of the human rights situation in North Korea by forcing a procedural vote. China also abstained on resolutions that authorized additional regional peacekeepers for South Sudan and UN police for Burundi. At the UN Committee on Non-Governmental Organizations and the UN Economic and Social Council, the Chinese delegation opposed granting UN accreditation to the internationally respected Committee to Protect Journalists.

In August, China allowed a visit by the UN special rapporteur on extreme poverty, Philip Alston. But consistent with past practice, authorities restricted Alston's movements and meetings, and in his departing press conference the special rapporteur noted some of the economic progress China has made but condemned the "dramatically shrinking space for civil society."

The Asian Infrastructure Investment Bank (AIIB), launched by China in 2015, held its first annual general meeting in Beijing in June. None of the governments present pushed the AIIB to adopt safeguard policies requiring the bank to identify and address human rights risks in its projects. The AIIB has not publicly addressed whether it will consult with nongovernmental groups, particularly in countries hostile to independent monitors.

In an alarming trend, Beijing pressured several governments, including Armenia, Cambodia, and Kenya, to deport Taiwanese citizens to mainland China. The people, suspected in the mainland of fraud, were given no discernible opportunity to contest their deportations before a competent court in those countries.

Chinese authorities claimed that some 500 allegedly corrupt "economic fugitives" had been returned to the mainland by September, bringing the two-year total of the "Sky Net" campaign to nearly 2,000. It was unclear at time of writing whether any of these people had access to family members or lawyers of their own choosing while awaiting trial in China, or what guarantees the returning countries sought from China prior to their return.

Colombia

The government and the country's largest guerilla group, the Revolutionary Armed Forces of Colombia (FARC), reached an agreement in 2016 to end their 52-year armed conflict. The agreement provides a historic opportunity to curb human rights abuses. Much will depend on how its justice provisions are passed into legislation, reviewed by the Constitutional Court, and then interpreted by a new "Special Jurisdiction for Peace." On October 2, an initial version of the peace deal with flawed justice provisions was rejected by a slim margin in a national plebiscite, but the parties reached a new agreement on November 12.

Violence associated with the conflict has forcibly displaced more than 6.8 million Colombians, generating the world's second largest population of internally displaced persons (IDPs), after Syria. Civilians continue to suffer serious abuses by the country's second largest guerilla group, the National Liberation Army (ELN), and by paramilitary successor groups that emerged after a demobilization process a decade ago. Human rights defenders, trade unionists, journalists, indigenous and Afro-Colombian leaders, and other community activists face death threats and violence, including from guerrillas and successor groups. Perpetrators of violence against civilians are rarely held accountable.

Since the FARC announced a unilateral ceasefire in July 2015, abuses attributed to them have declined steeply. The Colombian government and the ELN announced in March 2016 that, after almost two years of exploratory negotiations, they would start formal peace talks. These had not started at time of writing, largely owing to the ELN's unwillingness to free captives and end kidnappings.

In September, the Council of the State—one of Colombia's high courts—annulled the 2012 re-election of Alejandro Ordoñez as the country's inspector general and dismissed him from office. Under Colombian law, the inspector general is charged with protecting human rights, but during his seven years in office, Ordoñez repeatedly sought to undermine the rights of women and lesbian, gay, bisexual, and transgender (LGBT) people.

Guerrillas

Since its formation in the mid-1960s, the FARC has committed systematic atrocities against civilians, including child recruitment, abductions, and widespread crimes of sexual violence.In August, President Juan Manuel Santos and the FARC leadership declared a "definitive ceasefire" which was followed by the peace agreement approved later in the year.

The ELN continues to commit serious abuses against civilians. In the province of Chocó, for example, it has been responsible for kidnappings, killings, forced displacement, and child recruitment. In May 2016, ELN guerillas kidnapped three journalists in the northeastern province of Norte de Santander.

The ELN continued in 2016 to use antipersonnel landmines. The government reported that landmines and unexploded ordnances killed 3 civilians and injured 19 between January and October 2016.

Paramilitaries and their Successors

Between 2003 and 2006, right-wing paramilitary organizations with close ties to security forces and politicians underwent a deeply flawed government demobilization process in which many members remained active and reorganized into new groups. These successor groups continue to commit such widespread abuses as killings, disappearances, and sexual violence. They have at times benefited from the tolerance and even collusion of state agents.

Buenaventura, a largely Afro-Colombian port on the Pacific coast where successor groups continue to commit such abuses, has one of the highest rate of forced displacement in Colombia, with 12,956 residents fleeing their homes in 2015, and 1,955 fleeing from January through October 2016.

The conflict between the AGC and the ELN in the province of Chocó has severely limited the ability of many indigenous and Afro-Colombian people to leave their towns.

Implementation of the Justice and Peace Law of 2005, which offers dramatically reduced sentences to demobilized paramilitary members who confess their crimes, has been slow, despite significant progress since 2014. As of July 2016, 182 of the more than 30,000 paramilitary troops who officially demobilized had been sentenced under the law. The convictions cover a small portion of the more than 4,000 defendants seeking the law's benefits.

In October, the Attorney General's Office indicted Santiago Uribe, the brother of former President Alvaro Uribe, on charges of murder and association to commit crimes for his alleged role in the paramilitary group "The 12 Apostols" in the 1990s.

"Parapolitics" investigations of current and former members of Congress accused of conspiring with paramilitaries continued in 2016. From 2006 through August 2015, 63 legislators were convicted of crimes related to "parapolitics."

Abuses by Public Security Forces

From 2002 through 2008, army brigades across Colombia routinely executed civilians. Under pressure from superiors to show "positive" results and boost body counts in their war against guerrillas, soldiers and officers abducted victims or lured them to remote locations under false pretenses—such as promises of work—and killed them, placed weapons on their bodies, and reported them as enemy combatants killed in action. There has been a dramatic reduction in cases of alleged unlawful killings attributed to security forces since 2009, though credible reports of some new cases continue to emerge.

As of June 2016, the Attorney General's Office was investigating more than 3,600 alleged unlawful killings from 2002 through 2008, and had convicted more than 800 state agents in 210 rulings.

The vast majority of those convicted are low-level soldiers. Authorities have failed to prosecute senior army officers involved in the killings and instead have promoted many of them through the military ranks.

At time of writing, the Attorney General's Office had summoned a total of 11 active or retired generals for questioning on their alleged role in false-positive cases. In August, retired Gen. Henry William Torres Escalante, was indicted; but no meaningful progress has been achieved in other cases against generals allegedly responsible for "false positive" killings. In March 2016, prosecutors summoned the former head of the army, retired Gen. Mario Montoya Uribe, for a hearing in which he was to be charged. The hearing had yet to take place as of November.

Gen. Rodríguez Barragan continued, at time of writing, to command the armed forces, despite strong evidence implicating him in false-positive killings.

Peace Negotiations and Accountability

The peace agreement creates a Special Jurisdiction for Peace to try those responsible for gross human rights violations committed during the conflict. Individuals responsible for crimes against humanity and serious war crimes who fully cooperate with the new jurisdiction and confess their crimes will be subjected to up to eight years of "effective restraints of rights and liberties."

The November 12 agreement, while not fully addressing the flaws of the original, contains language that could make it much easier to fix at least two of the most important ones: an overly narrow conception of when superior officers can be held responsible for the crimes of their subordinates, and modest and vaguely defined definitions of the "restrictions on liberty" to be imposed on individuals who fully and promptly confess their war crimes.

Members of the armed forces would also benefit under the agreement, probably including many soldiers responsible for false-positive killings.

Internal Displacement and Land Restitution

More than 6.8 million Colombians have been internally displaced since 1985, government figures reveal. Some 35,000 people were displaced in 2016, a significant drop from the more than 140,000 displaced in 2015.

The government's implementation of land restitution under the Victims' Law continues to move slowly. The law was enacted in 2011 to restore millions of hectares of abandoned land and land stolen by armed groups and civilians to internally displaced Colombians. As of September 2016, the courts had issued rulings in just 4,100 of more than 93,000 claims received.

Gender-Based Violence

Gender-based violence (GBV) is widespread in Colombia. Lack of training and poor implementation of treatment protocols impede timely access to medical services and create obstacles for women and girls seeking post-violence care. Perpetrators of GBV crimes are rarely brought to justice.

In July 2015, "femicide"—defined, in part, as the murder of a woman because of her gender—became a crime. The law established comprehensive measures to prevent and prosecute GBV, including recognizing a victim's right to specialized legal assistance.

Human Rights Defenders, Journalists, and Trade Unionists

Rights advocates and journalists continue to be targeted with threats and attacks. Despite an Interior Ministry program that assigns protection to human rights defenders, trade unionists, and journalists, the United Nations high commissioner for human rights in Colombia documented the killings of 28 leading rights advocates and community activists from January through September 2016. During 2015, the Attorney General's Office successfully prosecuted seven individuals for killing community activists and rights advocates.

The Foundation for a Free Press, a respected Colombian nongovernmental organization (NGO) that monitors press freedoms, reported threats against 91 journalists from January through October 2016.

The National Labor School, Colombia's leading labor-rights NGO, reported 18 killings of trade unionists from January 2015 through February 2016—and the government has reported more than 120 since 2011. As of February 2015, the Attorney General's Office had obtained convictions in only six of such killings committed since 2011.

Sexual Orientation and Gender Identity

In recent years, authorities in Colombia have taken several steps to recognize the rights of LGBT people. In June 2015, the Justice Ministry issued a decree allowing people to revise the gender noted on their identification documents without prior judicial approval. In November 2015, the Constitutional Court ruled that sexual orientation could not be used to prohibit someone from adopting a child, although a legislative proposal to hold a referendum on this issue remained pending at time of writing. In April 2016, the Constitutional Court upheld the right of same-sex couples to marry.

In October 2016, FARC leaders met with conservative politicians and agreed to promote a definition of the family as formed by a man and a women. The FARC backtracked after meeting with LGBT representatives days later. Conservative politicians and evangelist leaders had attacked the peace agreement claiming that it would "destroy families."

Between January and June 2016, the Ombudsman's Office received 89 reports of cases of violence against LGBTI people.

Indigenous Rights

Indigenous peoples in Colombia suffer disproportionate limitations on their enjoyment of social and economic rights. From January through August 2016, at least 51 children—the vast majority of them belonging to Wayuu indigenous communities—died in the province of La Guajira of causes associated with malnutrition. Many of these deaths are caused by limited access to water. The Inter-American Commission of Human Rights had asked the government in December 2015 to take measures to curb these deaths.

Key International Actors

The United States remains the most influential foreign actor in Colombia. In February, US President Barack Obama announced "Peace Colombia"—a new framework for bilateral collaboration to support peace efforts—and pledged US$450 million for the 2017 fiscal year.

A portion of US military aid is subject to human rights conditions, which the US Department of State has not enforced; in September, it again certified that Colombia was meeting the conditions. Through a special envoy to the FARC peace talks, Bernard Aronson, the US has strongly supported the peace agreements reached in September and November.

Cuba has also provided key support to the peace process by hosting the talks and acting as "guarantor" of the process.

In September, before the peace agreement was rejected in the national plebiscite, UN Secretary-General Ban Ki-moon participated in the ceremonial signing of the agreement, saying it "creates the conditions for lasting peace."

The Office of the Prosecutor of the International Criminal Court (ICC) continues to monitor Colombian investigations of crimes that may fall within the ICC's jurisdiction. In September, ICC Prosecutor Fatou Bensouda welcomed the announcement of the peace deal with the FARC but highlighted the importance of "genuine accountability" and "effective punishment" for those responsible for atrocities.

In January 2016, the UN Security Council, at the government's request, established a political mission under a tripartite mechanism—the UN, the government, and FARC—to monitor and verify the peace agreement's definitive bilateral ceasefire and cessation of hostilities, and the laying down of arms.

The Office of the UN High Commissioner for Human Rights continues to play a key role in defending and promoting human rights in Colombia. On October 31, the day the office's mandate would have expired, the Colombian government agreed to extend it until 2019.

In October, President Santos was awarded the Nobel Peace Prize for his efforts to bring the Colombian armed conflict to an end.

Côte d'Ivoire

Côte d'Ivoire's continued political stability and strong macroeconomic growth provided a platform in 2016 for gradual improvement in the rule of law and the fulfillment of economic and social rights. A new constitution removed a divisive nationality clause—requiring a presidential candidate's father and mother to be Ivorian—that had contributed to over a decade of political turmoil. However, little progress was made in addressing key human rights issues at the root of political violence, such as combating impunity and delivering justice for the victims of over a decade of political violence, including the 3,000 victims of the 2010-11 post-election crisis.

The campaign in advance of an October 30 referendum on the new constitution was characterized by some violations of the rights of freedom of assembly and expression. The new constitution contains provisions that the opposition contend significantly strengthen the power of the presidency. Côte d'Ivoire was slated to hold legislative elections on December 18.

A terrorist attack on a beach resort in Grand-Bassam on March 13 killed 22 people, including three assailants. The attack, claimed by al-Mourabitoun, an offshoot of Al-Qaeda in the Islamic Maghreb, underscored the risk that Côte d'Ivoire faces from regional extremist groups.

Freedom of Assembly and Expression

Ahead of the constitutional referendum, the ability of opposition parties to explain their opposition to the draft constitution was undermined by a brief seven-day campaign period, lack of access to state media, and the suspension of two opposition-leaning newspapers.

The opposition argued that the addition of a vice president and a senate, one third of which is appointed by the president, as well as a clause stating that the constitution can be amended by a two-thirds vote of the national assembly and the senate, gave undue power to the executive.

In the weeks leading up to the vote, Ivorian security forces on at least two occasions dispersed demonstrators opposed to the constitution and briefly detained several opposition leaders. Several other opposition rallies occurred without incident. Many opposition parties boycotted the vote, which was marred by modest turnout and the vandalism of dozens of polling stations in opposition strongholds.

Accountability for Past Abuses

Progress in delivering impartial justice for victims of past political violence was slow. In January 2016, the International Criminal Court (ICC) trial began of former President Laurent Gbagbo and the former youth minister and militia leader, Charles Blé Goudé, for crimes against humanity committed during the 2010-11 crisis.

An Ivorian court tried former First Lady Simone Gbagbo for crimes against humanity and war crimes during the crisis. The ICC and national judges are investigating high-level perpetrators from pro-Ouattara forces but had yet to bring them to trial at time of writing.

The Special Investigative and Examination Cell, established in 2011, continued its investigations into human rights crimes committed during the 2010-2011 post-election crisis. The cell has charged high-level perpetrators from both sides, including several pro-Ouattara commanders now in senior positions in the Ivorian army.

The only national civilian trial for human rights crimes so far, however, is that of Simone Gbagbo, whose trial in Côte d'Ivoire's highest criminal court (*cour d'assises*) for crimes against humanity and war crimes began on May 31, 2016. Human rights groups acting on behalf of victims decided not to participate in the trial, citing violations of victims' due process rights. In May, the Ivorian Supreme Court denied Simone Gbagbo's appeal of her March 2015 conviction and 20-year sentence for offenses against the state during the post-election crisis.

The ICC has also indicted Simone Gbagbo, but the Ivorian government has refused to transfer her to The Hague. The ICC's long-delayed investigations into crimes committed by pro-Ouattara forces continued during 2016, although President Ouattara has said that all further cases related to the post-election crisis will be tried in national courts.

A military court on February 18 convicted 13 military personnel, including Gen. Dogbo Blé, the former leader of Gbagbo's Republican Guard, and Commander

HUMAN
RIGHTS
WATCH

"Justice Reestablishes Balance"
Delivering Credible Accountability for Serious Abuses in Côte d'Ivoire

Anselme Séka Yapo, former head of protection detail of Simone Gbagbo, for the 2002 assassination of former coup leader and Ivorian president, Gen. Robert Gueï and his family. Neither the special cell nor the ICC are investigating crimes committed during election-related violence in 2000 or the 2002-2003 armed conflict.

Côte d'Ivoire's reparations body had, when it submitted its report in April 2016, compiled a list of more than 316,000 victims potentially eligible for reparations, although the vast majority of victims have yet to receive assistance. The government on October 25 published the report of the Dialogue, Truth and Reconciliation Commission, which completed its work December 2014, although the report does little to identify those responsible for crimes committed during the 2002-2003 conflict or 2010-11 crisis.

Judicial System

Sessions of the *cour d'assises* were held in Abidjan and several regional courts, an essential step to clear the backlog of serious criminal cases. However, approximately 40 percent of the prison population remains in pretrial detention, often for several years. Despite the conditional release since December 2015 of some 100 pro-Gbagbo defendants arrested for their alleged role in the post-election crisis or subsequent attacks against the state, more than 200 remained in extended pretrial detention.

Most prisons are overcrowded and detainees lack adequate nutrition, sanitation, and medical care. On February 20, 2016, an uprising in Abidjan's central prison (*Maison d'Arrêt et de Correction*), led to the death of a prison guard and 10 inmates, including a gang leader responsible for systematic racketeering inside the facility.

Fear of violent crime committed by street gangs, including by children, fueled several public lynchings of suspected criminals. Although the government has taken steps to eliminate its use of the word "germ" ("*microbe*") to describe children in criminal gangs, it has yet to develop a comprehensive strategy to address the social, psychological, and economic drivers of violent crime by children.

Conduct of Security Forces

The prevalence of arbitrary arrests, mistreatment of detainees, and unlawful killings by the security forces lessened in 2016. Investigations and prosecutions of those who do commit abuses increased slightly, but were still rare. The military justice system remains severely under-resourced, and needs reform to strengthen its independence from the executive.

The security forces continued to engage in extortion, parallel tax systems and other criminal conduct to obtain revenue from the illicit exploitation of cocoa, diamonds, and other natural resources. Commanders allegedly responsible for severe human rights violations remain in positions of authority within the armed forces and several have allegedly illicitly accumulated private wealth and personal armories.

Extortion by security forces at illegal checkpoints remains an acute problem on secondary roads in rural areas. The United Nations reported that in March, in Assuéfry northeastern Côte d'Ivoire, the Ivorian army fired on protesters angry at soldiers' continued extortion, resulting in the death of three persons.

Communal Violence and Land Rights

In March, violent intercommunal clashes between pastoralists and farmers in Bouna, in the northeast, left at least 27 people dead and thousands more displaced. Armed traditional hunters, known as Dozo, intervened in the conflict and were responsible for at least 15 of the killings. The government subsequently charged the Dozo chief from Bouna with murder, and some 70 Dozos were among more than 115 people arrested for their role in the violence. More than 75 people at time of writing remained in detention awaiting trial.

Land conflicts between migrant and indigenous communities underscored episodic violence in southwestern Côte d'Ivoire, including a December 2, 2015 attack by Ivorian and Liberian militiamen in Olodio that killed seven Ivorian soldiers. The December 2015 resumption of the repatriation of refugees from Liberia, on hold during the Ebola crisis, increased competition for land in western Côte d'Ivoire.

In an effort to restore Côte d'Ivoire's dwindling forests, the government in July evicted more than 15,000 cocoa farmers from Mont Péko National Park, leaving many families without access to sufficient food, shelter, or sanitation. Smaller-scale evictions from protected forests were frequently conducted without adequate notice, and farmers were beaten and extorted during eviction operations.

Violence against Women and Girls

Gender-based violence remains widespread, particularly against girls. A July UN report found that of 1,129 rapes reported between 2012 and 2015, more than two-thirds of victims were children. Because the *cour d'assises* mandated to try rape cases rarely functions, Ivorian judges frequently reclassify rape cases to lesser offenses, although *cour d'assises* did hear at least 15 rape cases in 2016, resulting in more than a dozen convictions.

Sexual Orientation and Gender Identity

No law prohibits discrimination on the grounds of sexual orientation, gender identity, or intersex status. Côte d'Ivoire does not criminalize same-sex conduct, but the criminal code establishes higher penalties for same-sex couples convicted of public acts of indecency. Two men were in November convicted of public indecency and sentenced to three-month prison terms after being accused of same-sex sexual acts. Two gay men were assaulted in June after a photo was published of them signing a book of condolences to the victims of a shooting at a gay nightclub in Florida, US.

Human Rights Defenders

Although in June 2014 the government passed a law that strengthened protections for human rights defenders, it has so far failed to adopt a decree to facilitate the law's implementation. International and national human rights groups generally operate without government restrictions.

Key International Actors

On April 28, 2016, the UN Security Council extended the mandate of the UN peacekeeping mission, the UN Operation in Côte d'Ivoire (UNOCI), for a final time, to June 30, 2017. The UN Security Council also terminated the arms embargo and individual sanctions first imposed in 2004. UNOCI progressively reduced its military and civilian components throughout 2016, leaving France, the European Union, and the United States as the government's principal partners on justice and security sector reform.

Cuba

The Cuban government continues to repress dissent and punish public criticism. It now relies less than in past years on long-term prison sentences to punish its critics, but short-term arbitrary arrests of human rights defenders, independent journalists, and others have increased dramatically in recent years. Other repressive tactics employed by the government include beatings, public shaming, and termination of employment.

On November 25, Fidel Castro, who ruled Cuba from 1959 until handing off the presidency to his brother, Raúl, in 2006, died in Havana.

In March, US President Barack Obama visited Cuba, where he met with President Raúl Castro, as well as with representatives of Cuban civil society. President Obama gave a nationally televised address and held a joint press conference with President Castro in which he urged the Cuban government to lift restrictions on political freedoms and reiterated his call for the US Congress to end the economic embargo of the island.

Arbitrary Detention and Short-Term Imprisonment

The government continues to rely on arbitrary detention to harass and intimidate critics, independent activists, political opponents, and others. The Cuban Commission for Human Rights and National Reconciliation, an independent human rights group that lacks official authorization and is therefore considered illegal by the government, received more than 7,900 reports of arbitrary detentions from January through August 2016. This represents the highest monthly average of detentions in the past six years.

Security officers rarely present arrest orders to justify the detention of critics. In some cases, detainees are released after receiving official warnings, which prosecutors can use in subsequent criminal trials to show a pattern of "delinquent" behavior.

Detention is often used preemptively to prevent people from participating in peaceful marches or meetings to discuss politics. Detainees are often beaten, threatened, and held incommunicado for hours or days. The Ladies in White (Damas de Blanco)—a group founded by the wives, mothers, and daughters of

215

political prisoners also, like the Cuban Commission on Human Rights, lacks official authorization and is therefore considered illegal by the government. Its members are routinely harassed, roughed up, and detained by either police or state security agents before or after they attend Sunday mass.

Prior to President Obama's visit in March, police arrested more than 300 dissidents as part of a crackdown on opposition leaders.

Freedom of Expression

The government controls virtually all media outlets in Cuba and restricts access to outside information.

A small number of journalists and bloggers who are independent of government media manage to write articles for websites or blogs, or publish tweets. However, the government routinely blocks access within Cuba to these websites. Moreover, only a fraction of Cubans can read independent websites and blogs because of the high cost of, and limited access to, the internet.

Independent journalists who publish information considered critical of the government are subject to smear campaigns and arbitrary arrests, as are artists and academics who demand greater freedoms.

Lazaro Yuri Valle Roca, a blogger and videographer who often covers the Sunday demonstrations of the Ladies in White, was jailed for five days after trying to cover a protest on March 20, the day of President Obama's arrival in Cuba. Police officers apprehended Valle Roca, beat him, and took him to a nearby police station, according to Aliuska Gómez García, a member of the Ladies in White who witnessed the beating and arrest and spoke afterwards to the Committee to Protect Journalists. Valle Roca was later accused of attacking an official. While he did not face charges on this occasion, officers warned him that he might if arrested in the future.

In May, police detained journalist Daniel Domínguez López in his office at the Cuban Institute for Freedom of Speech and Press (ICLEP) after he wrote an article about a deprivation-of-property case involving a member of the National Revolutionary Police Force. Police ultimately took him to a "criminal instruction unit," where he said that they threatened to imprison or kill him and his family. Officers reportedly warned him against further distribution of his bulletin and told him that they were determined to destroy ICLEP.

Police in October detained Maykel González Vivero, a reporter of the news site *Diario de Cuba*, while he was reporting on the damage caused by Hurricane Matthew. Three days later, police arrested Elaine Díaz, director of the independent news site *Periodismo del Barrio* and four of her colleagues when they traveled to Baracoa, eastern Cuba, to report on the storm's effects. She and her team were released a few hours later, as was González, but authorities reportedly confiscated their laptop computers, cameras, and other equipment.

The government harasses artists as well. Police detained Danilo Maldonado, a graffiti artist known as "El Sexto," during a march led by the Ladies in White movement shortly before President Obama's visit in March 2016, but released him the following day. The day after Fidel Castro's death in November, police arrested Maldonado again after he posted an online video mocking Castro's death and spray painting "se fue" (he's gone) on a wall in downtown Havana. Police held him incommunicado for 72 hours, inflicting a beating that triggered an asthma attack. After his mother brought an inhaler, his detention continued. He was still detained at time of writing in early December. Two years earlier, Maldonado had been charged with "contempt for authority" for attempting to stage a satirical performance with two pigs daubed with "Raul" and "Fidel." He served 10 months in prison.

Political Prisoners

Despite the release of the 53 political prisoners in conjunction with the agreement to normalize relations with the US, dozens more remain in Cuban prisons, according to local human rights groups. The government denies access to its prisons by independent human rights groups, which believe that additional political prisoners, whose cases they cannot document, remain locked up.

Cubans who criticize the government continue to face the threat of criminal prosecution. They do not benefit from due process guarantees, such as the right to fair and public hearings by a competent and impartial tribunal. In practice, courts are subordinated to the executive and legislative branches, denying meaningful judicial independence.

Travel Restrictions

Reforms to travel regulations that went into effect in January 2013 eliminated the need for an exit visa to leave the island. Exit visas had previously been used to deny the right to travel to people critical of the government—and to their families. Since then, many people who had previously been denied permission to travel have been able to do so, including human rights defenders and independent bloggers.

Nonetheless, the reforms gave the government broad discretionary powers to restrict the right to travel on the grounds of "defense and national security" or "other reasons of public interest." Such measures have allowed authorities to deny exit to people who express dissent.

The government restricts the movement of citizens within Cuba through a 1997 law known as Decree 217, which is designed to limit migration to Havana. The decree has been used to harass dissidents and prevent those from elsewhere in Cuba from traveling to Havana to attend meetings.

Prison Conditions

Prisons are overcrowded. Prisoners are forced to work 12-hour days and punished if they do not meet production quotas, according to former political prisoners. Inmates have no effective complaint mechanism to seek redress for abuses. Those who criticize the government or engage in hunger strikes and other forms of protest are often subjected to extended solitary confinement, beatings, restrictions on family visits, and denied medical care.

While the government allowed select members of the foreign press to conduct controlled visits to a handful of prisons in April 2013, it continues to deny international human rights groups and independent Cuban organizations access to its prisons.

Labor Rights

Despite updating its Labor Code in 2014, Cuba continues to violate conventions of the International Labour Organization that it has ratified, specifically regarding freedom of association, collective bargaining, protection of wages, and pro-

hibitions on forced labor. While the formation of independent unions is techni-
cally allowed by law, in practice Cuba only permits one confederation of state-
controlled unions, the Workers' Central Union of Cuba.

Human Rights Defenders

The Cuban government still refuses to recognize human rights monitoring as a
legitimate activity and denies legal status to local human rights groups. Government authorities harass, assault, and imprison human rights defenders who attempt to document abuses.

In September, police raided Cubalex, a six-year-old organization that investigates human rights violations and provides free legal services to free-expression
activists, migrants, and human-rights defenders. Officers confiscated files, strip-
searched four men and a woman, and arrested two attorneys, one of whom was
still in detention at time of writing.

Key International Actors

In December 2014, President Obama announced that the United States would
ease decades-old restrictions on travel and commerce, and normalize diplomatic
relations with Cuba. In return, the Cuban government released 53 political prisoners and committed to allowing visits by international human rights monitors.
The two governments restored diplomatic relations in July 2015, but at time of
writing, no international human rights monitors had visited Cuba.

In January 2015, President Obama called on the US Congress to lift the economic
embargo on the island that had been imposed more than four decades earlier. In
October 2016, he used executive orders to end a few trade restrictions, including
the longstanding $100 import limit on two of Cuba's signature products: cigars
and rum.

In September 2016, the European Union approved an agreement with Cuba that
would strengthen economic and political ties and bring an end to the EU's 1996
"Common Position on Cuba," which conditions full European Union economic
cooperation with Cuba on the country's transition to a pluralist democracy and
respect for human rights. In October, the UN General Assembly adopted a resolution—for the 25th consecutive year—calling on the US to end the embargo. Only

the US and Israel did not vote in favor, but for the first time, they abstained instead of voting against.

As a member of the UN Human Rights Council from 2006 to 2012 and from 2014 to the present, Cuba has regularly voted to prevent scrutiny of serious human rights abuses around the world—opposing resolutions spotlighting abuses in North Korea, Syria, Iran, and Ukraine. However, Cuba supported a resolution adopted by the council in June 2016, establishing the post of an independent expert to combat violence and discrimination based on sexual orientation and gender identity.

In October, Cuba was re-elected to the Human Rights Council for the 2017-2019 term.

Democratic Republic of Congo

Political violence and government repression intensified in 2016 as President Joseph Kabila clung to power beyond the end of his constitutionally mandated two-term limit, which ended on December 19, 2015, despite widespread opposition and international condemnation. As authorities deliberately stalled plans to organize elections, government officials and security forces systematically sought to silence, repress, and intimidate the growing coalition of voices calling for credible, timely elections.

In eastern Congo, the security situation remained volatile as numerous armed groups, and in some cases government security forces, viciously attacked civilians.

Freedom of Expression and Peaceful Assembly

Government officials and security forces repeatedly banned opposition demonstrations, fired teargas and live bullets at peaceful protesters, shut media outlets, and prevented opposition leaders from moving freely.

More than 100 activists and opposition leaders or supporters were arbitrarily arrested between January and November 2016, and held for at least 48 hours. Some were held incommunicado for weeks or months, while others were put on trial on trumped-up charges.

On November 28, 2015, in the eastern city of Goma, police fired teargas and live bullets in the air when about 100 people were attending a peaceful protest against the government's failure to halt massacres in Beni territory. A 14-year-old girl was wounded. Authorities arrested 12 people. Three teenagers among them were released after four days while the others remained in detention for over three months on trumped-up charges.

Nine youth activists and at least 30 political opposition supporters were arrested in Kinshasa and Goma on or around February 16 in connection with a "ville morte," or general strike, to protest delays in organizing presidential elections.

On May 4, Congo's justice minister opened an investigation into one of the country's leading opposition figures, Moïse Katumbi, for alleged recruitment of mercenaries. After police fired teargas and threw rocks at demonstrators who had gathered to support Katumbi when he was called in for questioning at the prosecutor's office in the southeastern city of Lubumbashi, the national prosecutor authorized Katumbi to leave the country for health reasons.

In an unrelated case, he was later convicted in absentia for forgery regarding a real estate deal many years earlier and sentenced to three years in prison and fined US$1 million. One of the judges later described how she had been threatened by the director of the National Intelligence Agency (Agence Nationale de Renseignements, ANR), Kalev Mutond, and forced to hand down the conviction— a blatant example of the agency's interference in judicial independence.

On May 26, security forces fired teargas and live bullets as they sought to prevent demonstrations from going forward in Goma, killing at least one person and injuring at least 11 others, including four children. Opposition leaders had called for nationwide demonstrations to protest the Constitutional Court's ruling that the president could remain in office "until the installation of the new elected president."

The government also shut down media outlets close to the opposition, at least seven of which remain blocked at time of writing. In November, Communications Minister Lambert Mende issued a decree, making it increasingly difficult for foreign radio and TV stations to operate in Congo. The move came a week after authorities cut the signal of Radio France Internationale in Kinshasa altogether, and temporarily jammed the United Nations-supported Radio Okapi station.

In August 2016, the Congolese government blocked a Human Rights Watch senior researcher from continuing to work in Congo.

Nine human rights and pro-democracy youth activists were released from prison in August and September. Their release ended their wrongful detention, but in itself did not signify a shift in government policy. At time of writing, at least 29 political prisoners held since 2015 remained in detention.

Congolese took to the streets again the week of September 19 to protest the electoral commission's failure to announce presidential elections, three months before the end of Kabila's term. Security forces responded with excessive force, killing at least 56 people and setting three opposition party headquarters on fire. Some protesters also turned violent, beating or burning to death several police officers. At least seven journalists were detained in an apparent attempt to block independent reporting of the situation.

In early November, a team of UN human rights experts called on authorities to lift a ban on public political meetings in several cities in Congo.

Attacks on Civilians by Armed Groups

Dozens of armed groups remained active in eastern Congo. Many of their commanders have been implicated in war crimes including ethnic massacres, killing of civilians, rape, forced recruitment of children, and pillage.

In Beni territory, North Kivu, unidentified fighters continued to commit large-scale attacks on civilians, killing more than 150 people in 2016 according to Human Rights Watch research and credible reports from Congolese activists and the UN. Nearly 700 people have been killed since the beginning of the series of massacres in October 2014. There are credible reports that elements of the Congolese army were involved in the planning and execution of some of these killings.

Intercommunal violence increased as fighters from the armed groups Nduma Defense of Congo- Renové (NDC-R), the Union of Patriots for the Defense of the Innocent (UPDI), and the Democratic Forces for the Liberation of Rwanda (FDLR) carried out ethnically based attacks on civilians, killing at least 170 people and burning at least 2,200 homes.

Kidnappings of Congolese civilians and humanitarian aid workers continued to affect parts of Rutshuru, Lubero, and Masisi territories in eastern Congo. At least 175 people were kidnapped for ransom during 2015. In 2016, kidnappings continued, with more than 20 aid workers among the victims, further shrinking humanitarian space.

In 2015, the Congolese army unlawfully detained at least 29 children in dire conditions in the Angenga military prison in northwestern Congo. The authorities alleged that the boys were members of a rebel armed group. Most of them were released in April following pressure from Human Rights Watch and the UN. The others remain detained in Angenga.

No progress was made in bringing to justice those responsible for the summary executions of at least 51 young men and boys and the enforced disappearance of

33 others during a police campaign in Kinshasa, known as Operation Likofi, from November 2013 to February 2014, or for the summary executions during the January 2015 demonstrations.

Justice and Accountability

On December 19, 2015, two Congolese rebel leaders convicted by the International Criminal Court (ICC), Germain Katanga and Thomas Lubanga, returned to Congo to serve the remainder of their sentences in Kinshasa. While Katanga finished his sentence from the ICC ruling in January, he remains in detention and faces national war crimes charges in Congo that were filed against him before he was transferred to the ICC.

On March 21, the ICC found the Congolese politician and former rebel leader Jean-Pierre Bemba guilty of rape, murder, and pillage in neighboring Central African Republic. On October 19, the ICC found Bemba and his defense team guilty of bribing witnesses to lie in his favor at his trial. On March 23, the ICC confirmed 70 charges of war crimes and crimes against humanity for Lord's Resistance Army (LRA) leader Dominic Ongwen, a former child soldier who became a senior LRA commander. The trial was due to begin in December 2016.

In October, warlord Gédéon Kyungu Mutanga surrendered. Instead of arresting him, local officials in Lubumbashi gave Gédéon, as he is commonly known, a celebratory welcome. At time of writing it remained unclear whether he would serve the remainder of his 2009 sentence.

Regional and International Developments

On October 18, an African Union-facilitated "national dialogue" concluded, accepting that Kabila would stay in power at least until April 2018. It listed a number of challenges that could further delay the vote, and did not provide a specific election day. Most of Congo's main opposition parties either refused to participate or merely observed the dialogue. Twenty-six activists from the Filimbi and LUCHA youth movements were arrested in Goma and Kinshasa in October as they were protesting the agreement.

In response to the increased political repression, the United States imposed targeted sanctions against Kinshasa's police commissioner, Gen. Célestin

Kanyama, in June, and later against Gen. Gabriel Amisi Kumba and former police inspector John Numbi in September.

In late September, following government repression of the protests in Kinshasa, the ICC prosecutor issued a strong warning that the court was closely monitoring the escalating situation.

In October, the European Union Foreign Affairs Council instructed its high representative to initiate proceedings to impose individual sanctions against those responsible for serious human rights violations.

Ecuador

The administration of President Rafael Correa has expanded state control over media and civil society and continues to harass, intimidate, and punish critics. Other persistent concerns include limited judicial independence, poor prison conditions, and far-reaching restrictions on women's and girls' access to reproductive health care.

An earthquake on April 16 left approximately 670 people dead and thousands injured and displaced. At time of writing, 2,348 victims continued to live in official shelters. Vulnerable populations, including women and children, remained at particular risk in shelters without adequate security. Some children living in the shelters have not been able to access adequate education.

Disproportionate Criminal Charges against Protesters

Hundreds of Ecuadorians took to the streets in December 2015 to protest the National Assembly's approval of constitutional amendments granting the armed forces powers to assist police in security operations, allowing the president and other elected officials to run for office indefinitely after 2017, and declaring communications a public service—thus granting the government broad powers to regulate media. The day after the protests, a court sentenced 21 people to 15 days in prison for "issuing expressions of discredit and dishonor against policemen."

In May 2016, a court in Loja province convicted Luisa Lozano and Amable Angamarca, of the Saraguro indigenous community, of interrupting public services by closing roads during protests that called for increased protection of indigenous rights. They were sentenced to four years in prison. In October, after an appeal by the Interior Ministry, three others were sentenced to four years in prison in connection with the same incidents.

Freedom of Expression

A 2013 communications law gives the government broad powers to limit free speech. The law requires all information disseminated by media to be "verified" and "precise," opening the door to retaliation against media critical of the government as officials decide what meets these vague criteria. It also prohibits "media lynching," defined as "repeatedly disseminating information with the purpose of discrediting or harming the reputation of a person or entity." In addition, it prohibits what it terms "censorship," which, under the law's definition, includes the failure of private media outlets to cover issues that the government considers to be of "public interest."

The Superintendency of Information and Communication (SUPERCOM), a government regulatory body created by the 2013 communications law and separate from the Communications Ministry (SECOM), has in dozens of cases ordered media outlets and journalists to "correct" or retract reports, including opinion pieces and cartoons, or to apologize publicly for their content. SUPERCOM has also accused outlets of engaging in "censorship" by not publishing information officials deem important.

In August, SUPERCOM issued a written warning to journalist Janet Hinostroza and the TV channel Teleamazonas, where her daily news show airs, and ordered her to apologize publicly for repeatedly denouncing irregularities in government purchase of medicines. The sanction came eight days after the president, during his Saturday weekly broadcast, accused Hinostroza and Teleamazonas of "media lynching."

The Correa administration repeatedly used the communications law to order media outlets to publish information favorable to the government and to transmit official broadcasts responding to unfavorable news coverage. In July, SECOM ordered the TV channel Ecuavisa to transmit a 30-minute official broadcast at a time when it was scheduled to air an investigative program criticizing government funding of audiovisual propaganda. Ecuavisa aired part of the investigative program in the time that was left but viewers had to view the rest online.

In July, the brother of Vice President Jorge Glas asked a court to ban a book on their father's rape conviction. In August, the judge ordered the author to suspend circulation of the book in any form, arguing it undermined the honor of the Glas family.

Criminal defamation remains a concern, despite a 2014 legal reform narrowing the crime's definition. In June, President Correa brought a defamation complaint against Eduardo del Pozo, the vice mayor of Quito, for saying in a radio interview that Correa had manipulated the justice system to send money abroad without paying taxes. In September, del Pozo was sentenced to 15 days in prison. A higher court ratified the conviction in October.

The president, his political party and its members, state media outlets, and state agencies have repeatedly sought to exploit US copyright law in efforts to have critical images and documents removed from the internet. Users sometimes manage to restore content, after a legal process that can take weeks.

In September, after digital newspaper 4Pelagatos published an article criticizing an opinion piece by President Correa's daughter in the official newspaper *El Telégrafo*, 4Pelagatos journalist Martín Pallares received threats from various Twitter accounts, including one from a high-level SECOM official threatening a beating. The photographs, phone numbers, addresses, and geo-location of the homes of Pallares and two other journalists at the newspaper, Roberto Aguilar and José Hernandez, were posted on social networks. María Dolores Miño, a law professor who published an opinion piece referring to Correa's daughter's article, also received online threats.

Freedom of Association

In 2015, President Correa issued a decree confirming broad government powers to intervene in the operations of nongovernmental organizations (NGOs), including the power to dissolve groups on the grounds that they have "compromise[d] public peace" or have engaged in activities different from those they identified when registering with the government.

In August, the education minister dissolved the largest and oldest teachers' union for allegedly violating a legal obligation to register board members. The dissolution came after the union's president met with the International Labour Organization (ILO) and the United Nations Human Rights Committee to report on alleged violations of educators' rights. In September, UN human rights experts noted that the decision seemed "arbitrary, political and lacked any logical connection to a legitimate State interest."

Judicial Independence

Corruption, inefficiency, and political interference have plagued Ecuador's judiciary for years. President Correa received a popular mandate in a 2011 referendum on whether to overhaul the justice system to fix the problems. As part of his sweeping judicial reforms, however, the Council of the Judiciary, which in practice lacks independence from the executive, appointed and removed hundreds of judges, including all magistrates of the National Court of Justice, through highly questionable mechanisms that have undermined judicial independence.

Prison Conditions

Prison overcrowding and poor prison conditions are long-standing problems in Ecuador. Since 2012, the government has spent millions of dollars to construct new detention centers, but their remote locations and strict and limited visitation rules impede prisoners' contact with family members.

In August, after the Public Defender's Office filed a habeas corpus request on behalf of detainees at the Turi detention center in Azuay Province, a series of videos were leaked to the public showing prison guards beating inmates, some of them naked, and subjecting them to electric shocks. In September, a judge approved the habeas corpus request and ordered reparation measures for the inmates.

Migrants and Refugees

In July, approximately 150 Cubans were detained during a raid in a park where they were sleeping in tents to protest their inability to obtain a special humanitarian visa from Mexico that would allow them to travel to the US border, and from there, seek asylum in the United States. Judges conducted deportation hearings that did not comply with basic due process guarantees, and ordered the deportation of most of the detainees, including some who had sought asylum in Ecuador. The Cubans were deported before they had an opportunity to appeal the orders and, in some cases, despite judicial orders in their favor.

Accountability for Past Abuses

A truth commission set up by the Correa administration to investigate government abuses from 1984 to 2008 (from the beginning of the repressive presidency of León Febres Cordero until Correa took office) documented 136 cases involving 456 victims, including 68 victims of extrajudicial execution and 17 of enforced disappearance. Progress by a special prosecutorial unit created in 2010 to investigate the cases has been slow. According to government statistics from December 2015, judicial procedures have been initiated in only eight cases.

Reproductive Rights

The right to seek an abortion is limited to instances in which a woman's health or life is at risk, or when a pregnancy results from the rape of a "woman with a mental disability." Fear of prosecution drives some women and girls to have illegal and unsafe abortions and impedes health care and services for victims of sexual violence. Fear of prosecution also hinders detection and prevention of sexual and gender-based violence. Government statistics released in 2010, the latest available, indicate that one in four women and girls over 15 years old in Ecuador has been a victim of sexual violence.

Key International Actors

In March 2016, the government refused to participate in a hearing on freedom of association before the Inter-American Commission on Human Rights, and said it would not comply with the commission's recommendations.

In its periodic review of Ecuador in July, the UN Human Rights Committee raised concerns including violence against women, violence in detention centers, the criminalization of abortion, and threats to judicial independence and freedom of expression and association. It also called on Ecuador to carry out timely investigations of cases documented by Ecuador's truth commission, and bring those responsible to justice.

In 2015 the UN General Assembly elected Ecuador to the Human Rights Council for the 2016-2018 term.

In October, during extraordinary sessions of the Inter-American Court of Human Rights (IACHR) in Ecuador, the court's president, Roberto Caldas, enthusiastically praised Ecuador's judicial reform, which led to strong public criticism regarding the lack of judicial independence in the country.

In 2016, the Inter-American Court of Human Rights ruled against Ecuador in two cases—one determining that it is discriminatory to punish officers who allegedly have homosexual sex on military installations, and another sanctioning Ecuador for the arbitrary detention and torture of four foreigners in 1994.

In November, OAS and UN special rapporteurs on freedom of expression sent a joint letter to the Ecuadorian government stating that the Communications Law undermined free speech. The government rejected the experts' analyses.

HUMAN
RIGHTS
WATCH

"We are in Tombs"
Abuses in Egypt's Scorpion Prison

Egypt

Public criticism of the government remained effectively banned in Egypt in 2016. Police arrested scores of people in connection with protests, many preemptively. Authorities ordered travel bans and asset freezes against prominent human rights organizations and their directors and brought criminal charges against the head of the Press Syndicate and the country's top anti-corruption official. Parliament proposed a new law regulating nongovernmental organizations (NGOs) that would effectively end independent human rights work in the country.

Members of the security forces, particularly the Interior Ministry's National Security Agency, continued to routinely torture detainees and forcibly disappeared hundreds of people with little or no accountability for violations of the law. The disappearance, torture, and death of Italian doctoral researcher Giulio Regeni, probably at the hands of security services, highlighted these abuses and caused a diplomatic rift between Egypt and Italy.

Investigations by National Security officers, often without any hard evidence, formed the basis of many of the 7,400 or more military trials of civilians brought since President Abdel Fattah al-Sisi issued a decree widening the scope of military jurisdiction in 2014.

Conditions in detention remained harsh. The quasi-official National Council for Human Rights continued to report that prisons and other detention facilities were severely overcrowded. Conditions were particularly harsh in Cairo's Scorpion Prison, where inmates, most of them political prisoners, suffered abuses at the hands of Interior Ministry officers, including beatings, force feedings, deprivation of contact with relatives and lawyers, and interference in medical care that may have contributed to at least six deaths in 2015.

Security Force Abuses

Officers of the National Security Agency routinely tortured and forcibly disappeared suspects with few consequences. Many of the detainees who suffered these abuses were accused of sympathy with, or membership in, the Muslim Brotherhood, which the government named a terrorist group in 2013 but has remained the country's largest opposition movement.

Between August 2015 and August 2016, the Egyptian Commission for Rights and Freedoms, an independent group, documented 912 victims of enforced disappearance, 52 of whom had not reappeared by the time the group issued its report.

National Security officers routinely tortured suspects during these enforced disappearances. Between January and October 2016, 433 detainees claimed that police or prison officers mistreated or tortured them while they were in custody, according to a count by the Nadeem Center for the Rehabilitation of Victims of Violence and Torture based on media reports, lawyers' statements, criminal complaints, and other sources. In one case documented by Human Rights Watch, National Security officers in Alexandria forcibly disappeared and tortured 20 people, including eight children, in connection with a protest and an alleged arson attack on a garage and a traffic police vehicle.

Incidents of abuse by police officers, including fatal incidents of torture and illegal killings at protests, rarely resulted in accountability. Of the hundreds of such cases recorded in media reports and by activist groups since July 2013, when the military ousted Former President Mohamed Morsy, only 10 had gone through trial as of October 2016, resulting in six guilty verdicts against police officers.

Many convicted officers have appealed initial verdicts and won acquittals or shorter sentences. In February, Egypt's highest appeals court ordered a retrial for an officer originally sentenced to 15 years for shooting and killing political activist Shaimaa al-Sabbagh at a peaceful protest in January 2015, an incident that was photographed and videotaped. In October, the same court ordered a retrial for two officers who received five-year sentences for torturing lawyer Karim Hamdy to death in a police station in 2015.

Freedom of Assembly

A 2013 decree that effectively banned all anti-government protests remained in place, though it was subject to an ongoing legal challenge before the Supreme Constitutional Court.

Police made large, pre-emptive raids and arrests on two occasions when they anticipated protests.

234

Beginning in December 2015, police arrested dozens of people in a number of governorates whom they accused of planning protests timed for the January anniversary of the 2011 uprising. In the days ahead of the anniversary, police raided numerous downtown Cairo apartments, searched them without warrants, and arrested some activists, including Taher Mokhtar, a doctor who had advocated for better detention conditions. A court in August ordered Mokhtar released on bail pending investigation.

One official at the National Security Agency told Reuters on January 21: "We have taken several measures to ensure activists don't have breathing space and are unable to gather, and several cafés and other meeting places have been closed, while some have been arrested in order to scare the rest."

After a rare mass demonstration on April 15 against President al-Sisi's decision to cede two Red Sea islands to Saudi Arabia, activists planned a follow-up protest for April 25. Police arrested at least 382 people in the days leading up to and during the dispersal of the second protest, many from their homes or downtown Cairo cafés. Police stopped people riding public transportation or walking in the street, inspected mobile phones without warrants, and arrested phone owners if they found anti-government images.

Prominent human rights lawyer Malek Adly, arrested in May after filing a legal challenge against al-Sisi's decision to cede the islands, was released without bail in late August but still faced charges of spreading false rumors, inciting protests and attempting to overthrow the government.

Freedom of Association

Parliament and authorities took unprecedented steps to restrict independent human rights work by nongovernmental organizations (NGOs), threatening their very existence.

In September, a Cairo criminal court approved a request from a panel of investigative judges to freeze the assets of three organizations and the personal assets of five people who founded or led prominent human rights groups. The investigative judges had previously banned at least 12 NGO directors, founders, and staff members from travelling outside Egypt. Activists said the travel bans were probably a prelude to the filing of criminal charges against them for illegally receiving foreign funding.

Under penal code article 78, amended by decree by President al-Sisi in 2014, NGO workers can receive a 25-year sentence under such charges if a judge determines that they received foreign funding for "pursuing acts harmful to national interests" or other broad reasons.

In November, parliament swiftly approved a new law regulating NGOs after no public debate or input from civil society. The law would effectively eliminate independent human rights work, placing all NGOs under the effective veto power of a council dominated by representatives of the General Intelligence Service and Interior and Defense Ministries and allowing the council to dissolve NGOs based on broadly worded infractions. It would punish anyone violating the law with a prison term of one to five years and a fine of 50,000 to 100,000 pounds (US$3,160-$6,300). In late November, the law still awaited legal advice of the State Council and approval from President al-Sisi.

In February, local government authorities and security officers ordered the closure of the Nadeem Center for the Rehabilitation of Victims of Violence and Torture for allegedly violating the terms of its license, but the center remained open pending negotiations with the Health Ministry. In June, an investigative judge interrogated human rights lawyer Negad al-Borai, who had been involved in drafting an anti-torture law, on charges that he received illegal funding, established an unlicensed entity, and spread false information. Al-Borai has been interrogated on these charges six times.

Freedom of Expression

On May 29, prosecutors summoned the head of the Press Syndicate and two senior board members for questioning. The following day, they charged the men with "harboring suspects against whom an arrest warrant has been issued" and "publishing false news, which threatens public peace." The charges were related to an unprecedented police raid on the Press Syndicate headquarters on May 1, during which police arrested two journalists whom they accused of belonging to the April 6 Youth Movement.

On July 28, a Cairo court for minor offenses convicted Hisham Geneina, the country's former top corruption watchdog, for disseminating false information and gave him a suspended one-year sentence. Geneina appealed the verdict but had to pay a fine of 20,000 Egyptian pounds ($2,252) and 10,000 ($1,126) for bail. President al-Sisi removed Geneina in March after Geneina claimed to have uncovered tens of billions of dollars-worth of government corruption.

In May, police arrested four members of the Street Children satire troupe who had posted videos on YouTube mocking al-Sisi and government policies. Though a court ordered the four released in September, they still faced charges of using social media sites to undermine the country's stability by inciting citizens to protest.

In February, writer and novelist Ahmed Nagi received a two-year sentence for what the prosecution described as "sexually explicit" content in his novel, *Using Life*, parts of which appeared in a newspaper.

Freedom of Religion

In August, parliament passed a long-awaited law on church building that maintained restrictions over the construction and renovation of churches and discriminated against the country's Christian minority.

The new law allows governors to deny church-building permits with no stated way to appeal, requires that churches be built "commensurate with" the number of Christians in the area, despite the lack of official census statistics, and contains provisions that allow authorities to deny construction permits if granting them would undermine public safety, potentially subjecting decisions on church construction to the whims of violent mobs that have attacked churches in the past.

Between May and July, anti-Christian violence, prompted or preceded by suspicion among some local Muslims about actual or alleged church construction, left one person dead, several injured, and numerous Christian properties destroyed. Authorities continued to fail to protect Christian minorities from sometimes fatal attacks and imposed "reconciliation sessions" that allow Muslim perpetrators to escape prosecution and foster impunity.

In February, a juvenile minor offenses court sentenced four Christian children to five years in prison for posting a video online mocking the Islamic State (also known as ISIS). The boys fled Egypt in April. In March, an appeals court upheld a three-year sentence for contempt of religion against the writer Fatma Naout for criticizing the Muslim tradition of slaughtering livestock as a sacrifice on Eid al-Adha.

Egyptian human rights groups documented unlawful harassment of other religious minorities, including Shia Muslims and atheists, such as arbitrary travel bans and summonses for interrogations.

Violence and Discrimination against Women

In August, parliament passed an amendment to a law prohibiting female genital mutilation (FGM), increasing the penalties. The new law provided for prison terms of five to seven years for those who carry out FGM and up to 15 years if the procedure results in permanent disability or death. Anyone who escorts girls to undergo female genital mutilation will also face one to three years in prison. FGM is still widely practiced, and prosecutors have only obtained one conviction since the law was passed in 2008.

In September, a group of eight women's rights organizations released a statement commending the government for initiating its "National Strategy to Combat Violence Against Women" in 2015 but recommended creating a follow-up committee to ensure that government ministries were actually carrying out the strategy.

Sexual harassment and violence against women remained endemic. The Interior Ministry appointed Brig. Gen. Nahed Salah, a woman, to a new position in charge of combating violence against women. Salah publicly urged women to avoid talking or laughing loudly in public and to be cautious about how they dress to avoid street harassment.

Women continued to face discrimination under Egypt's personal status law on equal access to divorce, child custody, and inheritance.

Sexual Orientation and Gender Identity

Sexual relations outside marriage are criminalized. Since 2013, authorities have pursued a campaign to intimidate, track, and arrest lesbian, gay, bisexual, and transgender (LGBT) people, including entrapment using social media applications. Police regularly used forced anal examinations in prosecutions of those suspected of homosexual sex.

Solidarity With Egypt LGBTQ+, an advocacy group, said it had recorded 114 criminal investigations involving 274 LGBT individuals launched between the end of 2013 and November 2016, 66 of which involved the authorities' use of social media.

Refugees, Asylum Seekers, and Migrants

According to the United Nations High Commissioner for Refugees (UNHCR), there were 212,500 registered refugees and 38,171 asylum seekers in Egypt in 2016. Since January 2015, Egyptian authorities arrested more than 2,300 people for attempting to enter or leave the country in an irregular manner, according to the UNHCR. A report by the independent website Mada Masr stated that the UNHCR recorded 3,742 migration-related detentions on the north coast of Egypt by August.

In November, President al-Sisi signed a new law on irregular migration, stiffening penalties for smugglers and shielding asylum seekers and smuggled migrants from criminal responsibility but failing to enshrine key rights. The law provides for harsher prison terms for those who smuggle women and children and life sentences for those involved in organized crime or who smuggle a migrant who dies. But it does not guarantee non-refoulement—the principle that countries will not send migrants back to places where they risk persecution, torture, or a threat to life.

Key International Actors

In April 2016, during a visit to Cairo by President François Hollande, France signed deals to build a military telecommunications satellite, extend the Cairo metro, and finance a wind farm and solar power plant. In June, France delivered the first of two Mistral class helicopter carriers to Egypt, part of a spree of Egypt-

239

ian arms purchases from France that have also included a FREMM-class frigate, four Gowind-class corvettes and 24 Rafale fighter jets. Hollande said in a press conference that he raised issues of human rights, specifically the case of Eric Lang, a French teacher murdered in a Cairo jail cell in 2013.

In March, United States Secretary of State John Kerry criticized the reopening of the investigation into the funding of local Egyptian NGOs, saying he was "deeply concerned by the deterioration in the human rights situation in Egypt in recent weeks and months."

During two visits to Egypt in April and May, Kerry's public remarks stressed cooperation against the Islamic State extremist group and made no comment on human rights concerns. In April, a US Government Accountability Office report documented the US government's failure to fully implement required end-use monitoring and human rights vetting for US military equipment purchased by Egypt under the US' annual $1.3-billion Foreign Military Financing program. The White House issued a statement in September calling on Egypt to release US-Egyptian citizen Aya Hegazy, who ran a center for homeless children before her arrest in May 2014.

During a meeting with President al-Sisi during the United Nations General Assembly in September, two months before being elected president, Donald Trump expressed "strong support for Egypt's war on terrorism" and pledged that his administration "will be a loyal friend, not simply an ally."

The disappearance, torture and murder of Italian doctoral researcher Giulio Regeni, who was in Egypt to research labor unions, caused a diplomatic rift with Italy after media reports quoted unnamed members of the security services who said that they had arrested Regeni before his death. Italy recalled its ambassador and expressed anger at apparent Egyptian efforts to stall the investigation, which remained ongoing as of October 2016.

In April, the United Arab Emirates pledged $4 billion of aid to Egypt, adding to the $20 billion already granted or loaned by other members of the Gulf Cooperation Council since former President Morsy's 2013 ouster. In October, Ali Mamlouk, head of Syrian President Bashar al-Assad's intelligence services, visited Cairo for the second time in a year, reportedly to discuss security cooperation. Mamlouk's visit, together with Egypt's support for Russia on Syria at the United

Nations Security Council, raised diplomatic tensions with Saudi Arabia, which supports armed groups fighting al-Assad's forces.

In September, the International Monetary Fund reached a staff-level agreement with Egypt on a $12 billion loan program aimed at raising revenue and cutting spending. The agreement would require Egypt to cut subsidies, impose a new value-added tax, and float the Egyptian pound.

Equatorial Guinea

Corruption, poverty, and repression continue to plague Equatorial Guinea under President Teodoro Obiang Nguema Mbasogo, who has been in power since 1979, making him the world's longest serving non-royal head of state. Obiang won another term in April 2016 elections, which most opposition groups boycotted, citing intimidation and procedural irregularities.

Vast oil revenues fund lavish lifestyles for the small elite surrounding the president, while a large proportion of the population remains in poverty. Mismanagement of public funds, credible allegations of high-level corruption and other serious abuses, including torture, arbitrary detention, enforced disappearances, repression of civil society groups and opposition politicians, and unfair trials persist.

In March, the minister of interior suspended the Center for Development Studies and Initiatives (CEID), the country's leading civic group and a member of the national steering group of the Extractive Industries Transparency Initiative (EITI), which effectively paralyzed progress toward the country's reapplication for EITI membership.

In September, a French judged ordered Obiang's eldest son, Teodorin, to stand trial on money-laundering charges. In an apparent attempt to shield him from accountability, Obiang appointed Teodorin vice president shortly after French prosecutors concluded their investigation, and filed a complaint against France in the International Court of Justice claiming breach of immunity.

Economic and Social Rights

Equatorial Guinea is among the top five oil producers in sub-Saharan Africa and has a population of approximately 1 million people. According to the United Nations 2015 Human Development Report, the country had a per capita gross national income of $21,056 in 2014, the highest in Africa. Yet it ranks 138 out of 188 countries in the Human Development Index that measures social and economic development, by far the world's largest gap between per capita wealth and human development score.

Despite the country's abundant natural resource wealth, available data, including from the World Bank and the International Monetary Fund, reveal that Equatorial Guinea has failed to provide crucial basic services. About half of the population lacks access to clean water, according to a 2011 joint household survey by government and ICF International, a US firm specializing in health surveys.

Childhood malnutrition, as seen in the percentage of children whose growth is stunted, stood at 26 percent in 2011. Equatorial Guinea has among the world's lowest vaccination rates; 25 percent of children received no vaccinations at all, according to the 2011 survey. In 2016, 42 percent of children were not registered in primary schools, the seventh highest proportion in the world, according to UNICEF. Only half of children who begin primary school complete it.

In August 2014, Equatorial Guinea reaffirmed its commitment to rejoin EITI, an initiative from which it was expelled in 2010, for its failure to guarantee an "enabling environment" for civil society to fully participate in EITI's implementation. EITI promotes a standard by which information on the oil, gas, and mining industry is published, requiring countries and companies to disclose information on the key steps in the governance of oil, gas, and mining.

Freedom of Expression and Association

Only a few private media outlets exist in the country, and they are largely owned by persons close to Obiang. Freedom of association and assembly are severely curtailed, and the government imposes restrictive conditions on the registration and operation of non governmental organizations. The few local activists who seek to address human rights-related issues often face intimidation, harassment, and reprisals.

The minister of interior, who also headed the National Electoral Commission, suspended leading civil society group CEID on March 2, one week before the government called for elections. He alleged that comments made during a youth forum organized by CEID two months earlier constituted "messages aimed at inciting violence and civil disobedience among the Equatoguinean youth." Authorities had earlier cancelled the forum on January 29, 2016, after its first day. CEID accused the government of heavy handedness for suspending the organization because of the comments of some forum participants.

A health ministry official similarly accused a theater group working in collaboration with UNICEF of "inciting the youth" in July and ordered it to stop performing its play on HIV awareness. This was after the official attended a performance session where a member of the audience raised questions as to whether the government was committing sufficient resources to preventing and treating the disease. Last year, the government shut down a cultural center after a minister objected to lyrics of a hip-hop performance as "going against the ideals of the ruling party and unconstitutional," according to EG Justice, an independent rights group.

Elections and Political Opposition

The ruling Democratic Party (PDGE) maintains a monopoly over political life. The two-chamber parliament with a total of 170 seats has only one opposition representative in each chamber.

Elections were held on April 24, 2016, after being announced only six weeks in advance. Most opposition parties boycotted the elections citing harassment, procedural irregularities, absence of an independent electoral body, and lack of media access. Obiang's term was set to end in December 2016, but the government called elections in April, in apparent violation of a constitutional provision that says elections should be held no earlier than 45 days before the end of the president's term. Obiang ran in the elections after declaring that a 2011 constitutional amendment limiting presidents to two consecutive seven-year terms is not retroactive. He declared victory with 93.7 percent of the vote.

Nine days before the elections, police reportedly arrested the campaign manager of an opposition party that had not boycotted the elections "for disturbing the peace" while he was campaigning with a megaphone, and allegedly beat him at a military base, according to EG Justice. An opposition party also reported that its headquarters was surrounded by army personnel on April 21. The United States embassy in the capital, Malabo, criticized the restrictive atmosphere prior to elections and noted that its election day observers witnessed voter intimidation, violation of voting secrecy, and other irregularities.

Political repression was not limited to election season. In January, police reportedly arrested two members of an opposition party while advertising an authorized party meeting, and held them for nine days without charge, according to EG

Justice. A month later, police arrested the son and nephew of the leader of a political opposition party living in exile. He was detained at time of writing. Their lawyer said they were accused of revealing state secrets on a social media post by divulging a government list of "blacklisted political exiles" barred from entering the country. On May 13, police arrested the leader of yet another opposition party and allegedly beat him for several hours while questioning him about his political activities and a critical article he published.

International Corruption Investigations

On September 7, a French judge ordered that Obiang's eldest son, Teodorin, stand trial on charges of corruption, money-laundering, and embezzlement. During the investigation, French authorities seized valuables belonging to Teodorin, including a mansion reportedly worth €180 million (approximately US$196 million), 18 luxury cars, and a €22 million (approximately $24 million) art collection. At the time the purchases were made, Teodorin was minister of agriculture, for which he earned less than $100,000 annually.

French prosecutors formally requested Teodorin be brought to trial in May. Obiang responded by appointing his son vice president and suing France in the International Court of Justice for violating his immunity. The impending French trial comes on the heels of the US Department of Justice's investigation into Teodorin's alleged money laundering in the US, where he purchased a $30 million Malibu mansion and a $38.5 million private jet. That case was settled when Teodorin agreed to forfeit $30 million to US authorities that would be repatriated for the benefit of Equatoguineans. The US is expected to determine which charities will receive the funds by the end of 2016.

A Spanish corruption case against several senior government officials, including the president, remains pending. The complaint alleges that the officials purchased homes in Spain through a private company that a US senate investigation revealed had received $26.5 million in government funds at around the same time of the purchases. In September 2015, police arrested a Russian couple and their son who were accused of facilitating the transactions.

Eritrea

After 25 years of rule by unelected President Isaias Afwerki, Eritrea's citizens remain subjects of one of the world's most oppressive governments.

In May 2016, a United Nations Commission of Inquiry (CoI) established by the Human Rights Council in its final report said it found reasonable grounds to believe the government has committed numerous crimes against humanity. The government's "totalitarian practices" and disrespect for the rule of law manifested "wholesale disregard for the liberty" of Eritrea's citizens, the CoI concluded.

In turn, the council by resolution "condemn[ed] in the strongest terms" Eritrea's "systematic, widespread and gross human rights violations" and asked the General Assembly to submit the commission reports to all "relevant organs of the UN." The General Assembly took no public action on that recommendation at its October 2016 session.

Indefinite Military Service and Forced Labor

By law, each Eritrean is compelled to serve 18 months in national service starting at 18 but in practice conscripts serve indefinitely, many for over a decade. Endless conscription remains a principal driver of migration. The CoI concluded that conditions of national service rise to the crime of enslavement.

Conscripts are often assigned to arduous non-military construction and agriculture projects though some serve in the civil service, education, and other service jobs. Conscripts are used not only in government-related projects, they are used in projects personally benefitting military commanders and other officials.

Treatment of conscripts is often harsh, depending on the whim of the commander. Physical abuse, including torture, occurs frequently; so does forced domestic servitude and sexual violence by commanders against female conscripts. There is no redress mechanism for conscripts facing sexual and other abuses.

Attempts to flee are sternly punished. On April 3, new conscripts trying to escape from a convoy in Asmara were shot at by guards, killing several.

Conscript pay is insufficient to support the conscript, let alone a family. An Eritrean refugee told Human Rights Watch he fled in 2015 after 18 years of service because there was no end in sight. Another said he fled after 10 years because "my family couldn't survive." A third said he fled after serving for 12 years because "I couldn't see any future for my children."

When Eritrea was discussing a large grant from the European Union in 2015, senior Eritrean officials told diplomats and foreign visitors that the 18-month limit would be applied to new conscripts, though not to those already serving far longer. In February, the government abandoned that proposal.

Instead, President Isaias announced that conscript pay would be raised. His finance minister said pay for conscripts working in the civil service would almost triple; he made no mention of increases for others. At time of writing, there is no evidence that pay had increased for most conscripts.

Repression of Speech, Expression, and Association

President Isaias rules without institutional restraint. No national elections have been held since self-rule in 1991. Eritrea has had no legislature since 2002. The judiciary is subject to executive control and interference. A constitution adopted in 1997 remains unimplemented. Public space to question government policy does not exist. No domestic nongovernmental organizations are permitted.

The government owns all media. In September 2001, the government closed all independent newspapers and arrested its leading journalists. None were brought to trial. They remain in solitary detention, with no access to family members. Former guards have reported about half have died in detention. Eleven former high-level officials who criticized Isaias's rule were also arrested and detained since 2001. Eritrean authorities have ignored calls, including by the African Commission on Human and Peoples' Rights and the UN special rapporteur for Eritrea, for their release or at least a judicial hearing.

Less prominent citizens are also subject to arbitrary imprisonment. Very few are given a reason for their arrest. Few, if any, receive trials; some disappear. The length of imprisonment is often indefinite and conditions are harsh.

Although the government issued a new criminal procedure code in 2015, requiring warrants for arrest, access to defense counsel, and other procedural safeguards, including the right to petition for habeas corpus, there is no evidence that any of these protections has been implemented.

Interference with Religious Practices

The government persecutes citizens who practice religions other than the four it recognizes– Sunni Islam and the Eritrean Orthodox, Roman Catholic, and Evangelical (Lutheran) churches. The government interferes in the practices of the four religions it recognizes. Authorities deposed the patriarch of the Eritrean Orthodox Church in 2006, appointing a successor one year later. The deposed patriarch remains under house arrest over 10 years later.

Security personnel raid private homes where adherents of unrecognized religions meet for prayers, arresting and detaining them. Those arrested are only released after repudiating their religious affiliations.

Jehovah's Witnesses are especially persecuted. Three arrested 22 years ago, in 1994, for refusing military service remain imprisoned. Fifty-four Witnesses, arrested in 2014 for "unlawful assembly," admitted guilt in March 2016 and were released with a fine of 500 nakfa (US$35); a lone holdout was sentenced to six months and fined 7,000 nakfa ($470).

Currency Confiscation

In late 2015, the government ordered all paper currency held by citizens be turned in to government banks within six weeks. In February 2016, the government decreed that payments exceeding 3,000 nakfa ($200) could only be made by check

Although the new restrictions limit black market conversions they also create new tools closely to monitor citizens' individual expenditures and income.

Refugees

The United Nations refugee agency, UNHCR, reported 475,0624 Eritreans globally to be refugees and asylum seekers at the end of 2015, about 12 percent of Eritrea's official 3.6 million population estimate.

European countries continue to attempt to stem the flow of asylum seekers and migrants from Eritrea. A Swiss immigration fact-finding mission to Asmara, Eritrea's capital, in March, however, concluded "proof of improved human rights conditions is still missing" and that involuntary returnees could count on imprisonment and perhaps torture. In October, an appellate tribunal in the United Kingdom held that Eritreans of draft age who left the country illegally and are involuntary returned to Eritrea "face a real risk of persecution, serious harm or ill-treatment"; these abuses, the decision said, violate the European Convention on Human Rights. The UK Home Office amended its immigration policy to conform to the tribunal's holding.

In May, Sudan expelled over 400 Eritrean refugees and asylum seekers to Eritrea. Most were promptly incarcerated according to CoI witnesses.

Israel for years has refused to allow Eritreans to apply for asylum. In September, an appeals court held that Eritreans must be given individualized hearings, overruling an Interior Ministry policy that from national service evasion or desertion can never be justification for asylum.

Key International Actors

Eritrea's relations with neighboring Ethiopia and Djibouti remain severely strained. After a bloody border war in 1998-2000, Ethiopia occupies slivers of territory identified by an international boundary commission as Eritrean, including the town of Badme where the war began. President Isaias uses the pretext of "no-war, no-peace" for his repressive domestic policies.

Eritrea and Ethiopia both host each other's armed opposition groups. On June 12-13, border clashes, including artillery fire, erupted near Tsorona, a village just inside Eritrea. President Isaias blamed Ethiopia for the attack but there are conflicting reports of the cause, including that fighting began when armed Eritrean troops chased fleeing conscripts into Ethiopian territory and that Ethiopia responded to an attack by an Eritrea-based rebel group.

Also in March, Eritrea released four Djibouti prisoners-of-war captured in a border conflict in 2008. Eritrea had never before acknowledged holding POWs even after two escaped in 2013. Djibouti claims Eritrea still holds a dozen more.

249

Eritrea strengthened its relations with Saudi Arabia and the United Arab Emirates (UAE) in 2016, agreeing in December 2015 to support Saudi Arabia's military role in Yemen, as part of what Eritrea called "broad strategic cooperation to combat terrorism." Eritrea has reportedly allowed the UAE to deploy military jets and train Yemeni forces at Assab on the Red Sea coast, where the UAE is building a new port to support its military activities in Yemen.

The UN Security Council continued an arms embargo on Eritrea for another year after its Monitoring Group on Somalia and Eritrea reported Eritrea has not cooperated with the group. The group said Eritrea may have violated the embargo by arming and training anti-Ethiopia and anti-Djibouti militias, using mining income and UAE payments for military purposes, and attempting to buy military equipment in Europe.

Eritrea receives substantial foreign exchange income from foreign-owned gold, copper, zinc, and nickel mining projects in which the government holds 40 percent ownership. China's SFECO Group's Zara Mining Share Company began gold production in January. Chinese state-owned Sichuan Road & Bridge Mining Investment planned to start operations in late 2016. Canadian Nevsun's Bisha mine is in its sixth year.

Based on Nevsun's experience, it is likely that the Chinese companies use Eritrean government-owned construction firms for infrastructure development, and by so doing indirectly use national service conscript labor.

After the European Union gave Eritrea a five-year €200 million (approximately $220 million) aid package in 2015, to try to stem migration, the European Parliament in March expressed its opposition and "great concern [over] the continuing deplorable human rights situation and the complete absence of rule of law and media freedom...."

Ethiopia

Large-scale and unprecedented protests swept through Ethiopia's largest region of Oromia beginning in November 2015, and in the Amhara region from July 2016. Ethiopian security forces cracked-down on these largely peaceful demonstrations, killing more than 500 people.

Scores of people fleeing security force gunfire and teargas during the annual Irreecha festival died in a stampede on October 2 in Bishoftu, Oromia region. On October 9, following the destruction of some government buildings and private property by youths, the government announced a draconian and far-reaching six-month countrywide state of emergency, which prescribes sweeping and vaguely worded restrictions on a broad range of actions and undermines free expression, association, and peaceful assembly. The directive also effectively codified many of the security forces' abusive tactics, such as arbitrary detention.

The protests occurred against a background of nearly non-existent political space: in parliament, the ruling coalition has 100 percent of seats, there are restrictions on civil society and independent media, and those who do not actively support the government often face harassment and arbitrary detention.

Ethiopia deploys troops inside Somalia as part of the African Union mission (AMISOM). In 2016, there were reports that abusive "Liyu police," a paramilitary force, were also deployed alongside the Ethiopian Defense Forces in Somalia. In July, Ethiopian forces operating outside the AMISOM mandate indiscriminately killed 14 civilians during an operation against Al-Shabab in Somalia's Bay region. (See Somalia chapter.)

Freedom of Assembly

Concerns about the government's proposed expansion of the municipal boundary of the capital, Addis Ababa, triggered widespread protests across Oromia and a heavy-handed response by security forces in 2016. Protesters feared that the Addis Ababa Integrated Development Master Plan would displace Oromo farmers, as has increasingly occurred over the past decade. There were broad doubts about the sincerity of the government's announced cancellation of the Master Plan in January 2016, due largely to past broken promises. Protesters ex-

HUMAN
RIGHTS
WATCH

"Such a Brutal Crackdown"
Killings and Arrests in Response to Ethiopia's Oromo Protests

pressed concerns over decades of historical grievances and the wrongful use of lethal force by the security forces. There were some reports of violence by protesters, but protests were largely peaceful. Similar protests and a resultant crack-down occurred in Oromia in April and May 2014.

During the protests, security forces arrested tens of thousands of students, teachers, opposition politicians, health workers, and those who sheltered or assisted fleeing protesters. While many detainees have been released, an unknown number remain in detention without charge or access to legal counsel or family. Most of the leadership of the legally registered opposition party, Oromo Federalist Congress, have been charged under the anti-terrorism law, including Deputy-Chairman Bekele Gerba, a staunch advocate of non-violence.

In July, protests spread to the Amhara region, triggered by the arrest of Welkait Identity Committee members, a group seeking to resolve long-standing concerns over administrative boundaries. Protesters in Amhara region are primarily concerned with the unequal distribution of power and economic benefits in favor of those aligned to the government. On August 6 and 7, security forces killed over 100 people in Amhara and Oromia, including over 30 people killed in Bahir Dar alone. The town witnessed one of the largest protests. There were reports of large-scale arrests throughout Amhara.

In September, dozens of ethnic Konso were killed by security forces in the Southern Nations, Nationalities, and Peoples' Region (SNNPR) following protests over administrative boundaries in the Konso area.

The government has not shown a willingness to address the expressed grievances of the protesters in Amhara, Oromia, or Konso, blaming much of the unrest on lack of good governance and youth unemployment, exacerbated by "outside forces."

The Ethiopian government failed to meaningfully investigate the killings of protesters in Oromia, Amhara, or Konso. In a report to parliament in June, the Ethiopia Human Rights Commission, a government body, concluded that the level of force used by security forces in Oromia was proportionate to the risk they faced from protesters, contrary to available evidence.

The October state of emergency directive banned all protests without government permission and permits arrest without court order in "a place assigned by the command post until the end of the state of emergency."

The Liyu police, a Somali Regional State (SRS) paramilitary police force, continued to commit serious human rights abuses in their ongoing conflict with the Ogaden National Liberation Front (ONLF). There have been reports of extrajudicial killings, arbitrary detention, and violence against civilians accused of supporting or being sympathetic to the ONLF. Following a June 12 protest in Melbourne, Australia, against the visit of SRS President Abdi Iley, dozens of family members of protesters were arrested in Ethiopia.

Freedom of Expression and Association

Media continues to be under government stranglehold, exacerbated by the state of emergency at the end of 2016, with many journalists forced to choose between self-censorship, harassment and arrest, or exile. At least 75 journalists have fled into exile since 2010. In addition to threats against journalists, tactics used to restrict independent media include targeting publishers, printing presses, and distributors.

Scores of journalists—including Eskinder Nega and Woubshet Taye—protesters, and political opponents remain jailed under the anti- terrorism law. Journalist Getachew Shiferaw was convicted in November of criminal defamation and sentenced to one year in prison. On May 10, blogger Zelalem Workagegneu was sentenced to five years and two months under the anti-terrorism law after being detained for over 700 days. Journalist Yusuf Getachew, who was convicted in August 2015 also under the anti-terrorism law, was pardoned and released on September 10, after over four years in detention.

The government regularly restricts access to social media apps and some websites with content that challenges the government's narrative on key issues. During particularly sensitive times, including after the Irreecha festival stampede, the government blocked access to the internet.

The government also jammed the signals of international radio stations like Deutsche Welle and Voice of America in August and September. Social media and diaspora television stations played key roles in the dissemination of information and mobilization during protests. Under the state of emergency, people are banned from watching diaspora television, sharing information on social media, and closing businesses as a gesture of protest, as well as curtailing opposition parties' ability to communicate with media.

The 2009 Charities and Societies Proclamation (CSO law) continues to severely curtail the ability of independent nongovernmental organizations. The law bars work on human rights, governance, conflict resolution, and advocacy on the rights of women, children and people with disabilities if organizations receive more than 10 percent of their funds from foreign sources.

Questioning the government's development policies is deemed particularly sensitive and activists face charges for doing so. For example, the trial of Pastor Omot Agwa, who had worked as the facilitator and interpreter for the World Bank's Inspection Panel as it investigated abuses linked to a bank investment, continued in 2016. Two other individuals charged with Omot were acquitted in November. They were arrested in March 2015 at Addis Ababa airport on their way to a food security workshop in Nairobi, Kenya, and charged on September 7, 2015.

Torture and Arbitrary Detention

Ethiopian security personnel, including plainclothes security and intelligence officials, federal police, special police, and military, frequently tortured and otherwise ill-treated political detainees held in official and secret detention centers, to give confessions or provide information. Many of those arrested during recent protests said they were tortured in detention, including in military camps. Several women alleged that they were raped or sexually assaulted. There is little indication that security personnel are being investigated or punished for these abuses.

Allegations of forced displacement have arisen from commercial and industrial projects associated with Addis Ababa's expansion and the continued development of state-owned sugar plantations in the Lower Omo Valley, home to about 200,000 indigenous people. Communities in Omo have seen grazing land cleared and access to the Omo River restricted. The reservoir behind the Omo River's Gibe III dam began filling in January 2015, and there was no artificial flood in 2015 and a limited flood in 2016 contrary to government assurances. The flood is important in replenishing water levels in Kenya's Lake Turkana and the agricultural lands along the banks of the Omo River.

Key International Actors

Ethiopia continues to enjoy strong support from foreign donors and most of its regional neighbors, due to its role as host of the African Union (AU) and as a strategic regional player, contribution to UN peacekeeping, regional counterterrorism, aid, and migration partnerships with Western countries, and its stated progress on development indicators. Ethiopia is also a country of origin, transit, and host for large numbers of migrants and refugees.

The brutal crackdown against protesters and the state of emergency announcement resulted in stronger than usual public statements from many of Ethiopia's traditional allies. The AU and the African Commission on Human and Peoples' Rights both issued statements expressing concern, while the European parliament released a strong resolution, and resolutions were introduced in the US Senate and House of Representatives. The UN High Commissioner for Human Rights publicly stressed the need for an international investigation into the killings in July. Other donors, including the World Bank, have continued business as usual without publicly raising concerns.

In June, Ethiopia was elected to the UN Security Council. It is also vice president of the UN Human Rights Council despite a history of non-cooperation with UN special mechanisms. Despite these roles, Ethiopia has refused entry to all UN special rapporteurs, other than the UN special rapporteur on Eritrea, since 2006.

European Union

Faced with significant strategic challenges, including the refugee crisis, the United Kingdom vote to leave the European Union, attacks by violent extremists, and rising support for populist anti-immigration parties, EU governments and institutions responded in 2016 in ways that often undercut or set aside core values and rights protections rather than working consistently together to defend them.

Migration and Asylum

The EU as a whole failed to show leadership and solidarity in the face of the largest global displacement crisis since World War II. Much of the debate about policy responses focused on concerns about the impact on security and cultural identity and growing support for populist parties with xenophobic platforms. EU policies focused primarily on preventing arrivals and outsourcing responsibility for asylum seekers and refugees to other regions.

Border closures along the Balkans route and a March agreement with Turkey contributed to a significant decline in arrivals by sea to Greek islands in the Aegean Sea, while boat migration from North Africa to Italy kept pace with previous years. In the first 10 months of the year, almost 328,000 had crossed the sea to reach European shores, compared to 736,646 during the same period in 2015, according to the United Nations Refugee Agency (UNHCR).

Fifty-eight percent of those arriving by sea came from the world's top 10 refugee-producing countries, including Syria, Afghanistan, Iraq, and Eritrea, according to UNHCR. Nigerians, Pakistanis, Gambians, Ivorians and Guineans together made up 21 percent of the new arrivals. Nearly one-third were children, and the proportion of unaccompanied children rose over previous years.

Despite increased capacity for search and rescue operations in the Mediterranean, and numerous nongovernmental organizations (NGOs) conducting rescue missions, by mid-November 4,271 had died or gone missing at sea, making 2016 the deadliest year on record. The EU began training Libyan coast guard officers amid persistent concerns about violence and degrading conditions in Libyan detention centers and the absence of a functioning asylum system.

Border closures on the Balkans route and heightened border controls by Austria, France, and Switzerland left asylum seekers and migrants stuck in Greece and Italy. There were violent pushbacks at the Bulgaria-Turkey and the Macedonia-Greece borders. Austria, Denmark, Hungary, Sweden, and Germany were among EU states adopting more restrictive asylum laws.

There was little appetite among EU governments to share responsibility for asylum seekers more equitably across the union. By mid-November, only 7,224 asylum seekers had been relocated from Greece and Italy to other EU countries under an EU emergency plan, according to the European Commission. The commission proposed a permanent relocation mechanism to help countries experiencing disproportionate numbers, but it would allow countries to pay to avoid accepting relocations, and retain the Dublin regulation that places primary responsibility for processing asylum seekers on the first EU country of entry.

A new European Border and Coast Guard began operating in October. Replacing the external border agency Frontex, the entity has more autonomy from member states and a reinforced role in returns, as well as a complaints mechanism. It does not have an explicit search and rescue mandate.

In March, the EU signed a problematic deal with Turkey to send back asylum seekers reaching Greece by sea in exchange for billions of euros in aid and a pledge to resettle one Syrian for every Syrian returned. In June, the commission announced a new "partnership framework on migration" conditioning aid on migration cooperation, drawing criticism from development NGOs, and began implementing migration control projects with countries including Sudan and Eritrea.

EU governments made slow progress on resettlement. By July 2016, only 8,268 refugees had been brought to EU states under a July 2015 EU plan to resettle over 22,000 within two years, although some EU states resettled additional numbers through bilateral arrangements. Ten EU states failed to resettle a single person. Poor progress lowered expectations for implementation of the permanent EU Resettlement Framework proposed by the commission. The proposal would make immigration co-operation an element in the decision whether to resettle refugees out of a host country.

The European Commission issued a raft of proposals in July to reform the EU's dysfunctional asylum system. They include stronger safeguards for children and better access to a lawyer, but would punish asylum seekers for moving from one EU country to another and make it easier to summarily reject claims and revoke refugee status. The council and parliament had yet to approve them at time of writing.

Discrimination and Intolerance

The ongoing refugee crisis and attacks by armed extremists in Belgium, France, and Germany reinforced xenophobic, Islamophobic and anti-immigrant sentiment, manifest in attacks on Muslims, migrants, and those perceived as foreigners and support for populist anti-immigration parties in many EU states.

Anti-Semitism, including hate crimes, remained a serious concern in some EU states including the UK and France. In an April resolution on combating anti-Semitism in Europe, the Parliamentary Assembly of the Council of Europe noted that members of the Jewish community regularly experience insults and physical violence across Europe.

In September, United Nations High Commissioner for Human Rights Zeid Ra'ad al-Hussein warned leaders of populist parties in Europe about the corrosive effect on societies of their instrumentalization of bigotry and xenophobia for political ends.

In its May annual report, the Council of Europe's Commission against Racism and Intolerance noted an anti-immigrant and Islamophobia trend, and emphasized the need to combat racist violence. The Council of Europe's Commissioner for Human Rights Nils Muižnieks urged European countries to prioritize migrant integration, including by ensuring effective protection from discrimination.

In June, the European Commission launched the High Level Group on combating racism, xenophobia and other forms of intolerance in order to improve efforts by EU member states to prevent hate crimes. In an April report, the EU's Agency for Fundamental Rights said that hate crimes often go unreported and unprosecuted and urged member states to improve access to justice for victims.

In May, the European Network Against Racism reported that Muslim women were the main targets of Islamophobia in eight EU countries surveyed.

HUMAN
RIGHTS
WATCH

GROUNDS FOR CONCERN

Belgium's Counterterror Responses to the Paris and Brussels Attacks

In February, Council of Europe Commissioner for Human Rights Muižnieks called for an end to forced evictions of Roma in several European countries, and noted that this practice increases the vulnerability of Roma families, prevents their social inclusion, and impedes the prospects of regular schooling for their children.

In May, Council of Europe Secretary General Thorbjørn Jagland urged governments to ensure that children can study in a safe environment, free from violence, bullying and discrimination on all grounds, including their sexual orientation or gender identity.

In March, the European Commission proposed that the EU ratify the Istanbul Convention on Domestic Violence. EU Commissioner for Justice Vera Jourova said that one in three women in the EU has experienced physical or sexual violence or both, and called on the 12 remaining member states to ratify the convention.

Malta was among eight EU states that began work on a pilot for an EU disability card to secure mutual recognition of the rights and benefits of 80 million people with disabilities across the EU. In a report published in August, the EU's Agency for Fundamental Rights noted that gaps in screening prevent migrants with disabilities from receiving adequate support throughout arrival, registration and asylum procedures.

Terrorism and Counterterrorism

Attacks in Belgium, France, and Germany, many claimed by the Islamic State (also known as ISIS), together killed scores of people and injured hundreds more. The attacks prompted or reinforced measures and proposals in EU states to expand police and surveillance powers, strengthen intelligence cooperation, and revoke dual citizenship of those found to have committed terrorist acts.

In Belgium, which suffered coordinated attacks on Brussels airport and a metro station on March 22, the government proposed a raft of new counterterrorism laws to expand powers of surveillance and detention. None had become law at time of writing.

In March 2016, EU Justice and Home Affairs ministers agreed a draft directive to strengthen the EU's legal framework for preventing terrorist attacks, in particular by criminalizing preparatory acts, such as training and travel abroad for terrorist purposes. Human rights groups expressed concerns about insufficient safeguards and precision in the draft directive. The draft directive remained under consideration at time of writing.

In April, the EU Council adopted a directive to regulate the transfer of personal information on air travelers to member states' law enforcement authorities in relation to possible terrorist offences and other serious crimes.

In June, the European Parliament renewed calls for investigations into the complicity of EU states into CIA torture and secret detention on European soil, reflecting the limited progress made so far in national investigations. Poland and Lithuania's criminal investigations remained stalled and the UK's concluded with no charges brought.

Croatia

Fewer than 500 people claimed asylum in Croatia in the first nine months of 2016. Thirty-four were granted some form of protection during the same period. Restrictions on the Western Balkan migration route reduced the number of arrivals. Croatia continues to push back asylum seekers and migrants who attempt to enter via Serbia.

While the government made some progress in providing housing to the small number of people from outside the Western Balkans who were granted protection, asylum seekers and refugees from outside the region continue to face difficulties in accessing education and employment. Unaccompanied migrant and asylum seeking children continue to be placed in residential institutions, including homes for children with behavior problems, without adequate guardianship or access to education.

People with disabilities continue to face exclusion and discrimination, including barriers that prevent them from participating in society on an equal basis with others. The guardianship system denies around 18,000 people with disabilities the right to make a range of decisions about their lives.

In February, the European Court of Human Rights (ECtHR) ruled that Croatia discriminated on grounds of sexual orientation against a woman from Bosnia and Herzegovina, by denying her the right to a residence permit in Croatia to join her female partner.

In April, Council of Europe Commissioner for Human Rights Muižnieks raised concerns at the reported rise in discrimination, ethnic intolerance, and hate speech targeting members of minorities, in particular Jews, Roma, and Serbs. The commissioner also warned against the inadequate state response to physical attacks, death threats, and intimidation against journalists.

As of August 2016, more than 2,800 persons, most of them Roma, remain stateless or at risk of statelessness. They face particular difficulties accessing basic state services, such as health care, social assistance, and adequate housing. Roma children remain subject to de facto segregation in the education sector.

Estonia

According to the Interior Ministry, as of January 2016, about 6.1 percent of the country's population of 1.3 million is stateless, a slight decrease from 2015.

Statelessness disproportionately affects ethnic Russians, who lost their citizenship after Estonia declared independence from the Soviet Union in 1991 and enacted policies stripping most non-Estonians of citizenship. Stateless persons continue to face significant obstacles in accessing full employment rights and are barred from holding certain jobs, including as judges, police officers, and prosecutors.

New amendments to the Citizenship Act entered into force on January 1, 2016. They provide for automatic Estonian citizenship for children born to stateless parents, whereas before parents had to apply for it. Parents may reject the grant of Estonian citizenship to their children within a year. The amendments also exempt people 65 and older from the written portion of the mandatory Estonian language exam for naturalization.

Language requirements remain the most significant naturalization challenge for the country's Russian-speaking population. The costs of naturalization, including application and language exam preparation, and income requirements, impede naturalization of poorer long-term residents and contribute to statelessness among Russian speakers. The state reimburses language class fees only after the applicant passes the test.

The government failed to adopt amendments that would allow the Co-Habitation Act to fully enter into force in 2016. The act is progressive legislation that ex-

HUMAN
RIGHTS
WATCH

DOUBLE PUNISHMENT

Inadequate conditions for Prisoners with Psychosocial Disabilities in France

tends the rights of marriage to unmarried—including same-sex—couples, encompassing, among other things, child adoption and property rights.

Estonia maintains a minimalist refugee policy. By November, the government had relocated 66 asylum seekers from Greece under the EU relocation scheme, according to the European Commission.

France

France suffered three deadly attacks claimed by ISIS in June and July, including an attack with a truck in Nice that killed 86 people and injured hundreds. The state of emergency declared by President Francois Hollande following the November 2015 attacks in Paris and Saint-Denis was renewed by Parliament in February and May 2016.

On July 21, a few days after the Nice attacks, Parliament adopted a new law extending the state of emergency by another six months and expanding already wide police powers of search, seizure, and detention.

The new law toughens several terrorism-related provisions in France's laws and criminal code. It re-instates warrantless seizures of computer and cellphone data that France's highest legal authority earlier in the year had struck down as unconstitutional, adding safeguards that still fall short of proper judicial oversight.

The law came only weeks after an already broad counterterrorism law adopted by Parliament in June 2016, which the French National Consultative Commission of Human Rights (CNCDH) had criticized for curbing freedoms.

Between November 2015 and July 2016, under the emergency law, police carried out nearly 4,000 warrantless raids and placed 400 people under house arrest, yet those actions led to only six terrorism-related criminal investigations. Those measures targeted mostly Muslims and led to abuses of the rights to liberty, privacy, freedom of movement, and non-discrimination.

A French commission of inquiry into the Paris attacks concluded on July 5 that the state of emergency had "limited impact" on improving security. The panel described important failures in analyzing intelligence that could have helped prevent the attacks. In a May review of France, the UN Committee against Torture expressed concern about excessive use of force by police when carrying out

HUMAN
RIGHTS
WATCH

SEEKING REFUGE
Unaccompanied Children in Sweden

house searches in the context of the state of emergency, as well as during demonstrations.

In August 2016, mayors in about 30 towns adopted decrees prohibiting women from wearing full body covering swimsuits (known as "burkinis") or any other skin concealing outfits on the beach, arguing that they may pose a risk to public order.

The French Human Rights League and the Collective against Islamophobia in France contested those bans before administrative courts. In August, the Council of State, France's highest administrative court, ruled that the ban in one town illegally breached fundamental freedoms and ordered it to be suspended. Some bans were subsequently withdrawn by some towns or struck down by lower courts, while other courts upheld bans despite the Council of State ruling.

The number of migrants in a camp in Calais known as "the Jungle" in August 2016 reached 6,900, according to authorities more than double the estimate a year earlier. NGOs insisted the actual numbers were higher. On July 7, the CNCDH expressed concern regarding the increase in the number of migrants living there in conditions "contrary to human dignity."

A 2016 UNICEF survey of unaccompanied children in Calais and Dunkirk camps found they were subject to sexual exploitation, violence, and forced labour. In the last week of October, French authorities dismantled the camp. Between October 24 and 26, nearly 5,600 people were relocated to reception centers across France, with some unaccompanied children brought to the UK (see below). Arbitrary age assessment meant that some unaccompanied minors were left out of the specific process put in place for children.

France had accepted 2,091 asylum seekers relocated from Greece and 231 from Italy at time writing, the largest number of any EU state under the relocation scheme.

In July, the UN Committee on Economic, Social and Cultural Rights criticized as "substandard" reception and accommodation facilities for asylum seekers in France.

In July, the National Assembly deemed as too costly a measure that would have required police officers conducting an identity check to record it in a written document. The proposal had been seen by human rights advocates as an important means of addressing discriminatory checks.

In November, the Court of Cassation ruled against the state in three cases of police identity checks involving ethnic profiling, finding that the checks were "discriminatory" and that the state committed a "gross fault." According to a CNCDH report published the same month, there is growing evidence from separate studies that young men from visible minorities are overrepresented in police checks.

An April report by the CNCDH expressed concern about the rise in racist, anti-Semitic, and Islamophobic incidents reported to police in 2015.

French prisons continued to be severely overcrowded and the suicide rate among inmates remained high, particularly among women, drawing criticism in July from the UN Committee for the Elimination of Discrimination against Women (CEDAW). Prisoners with psychosocial disabilities often have inadequate access to mental healthcare.

Germany

In 2016, Germany continued to grapple with the implications of the arrival of 890,000 asylum seekers and migrants in 2015. A number of attacks in July, some inspired by or claimed by ISIS, put the spotlight on the country's counterterrorism policy.

Authorities sought to respond to a wave of arson attacks on asylum-seeker housing, with federal police reporting more than 850 such attacks between January and mid-November 2016.

Authorities took some steps to address the shortcomings in Germany's response to hate crimes, including training law enforcement and judicial authorities to improve the investigation and prosecution of racially motivated crimes. In March, a chief judge at a district court sentenced three people to prison for hurling a gasoline bomb into an asylum-seekers' apartment and pointed to the attackers' xenophobic and racist motives.

Several changes were made to asylum law and policy. In February, the Federal parliament passed restrictions on family reunification rights for people who do not qualify for full refugee status, and in July, passed a law aimed at integrating refugees, beneficiaries of subsidiary protection, and certain asylum seekers, conditioning access to benefits and permanent residence status on cooperation with language and other integration requirements.

After a series of attacks in July, Germany amended several existing counterterrorism-related laws in an effort to increase coordination among intelligence agencies. Germany's highest court in April struck down parts of a 2009 counterterrorism law expanding the federal police authority to investigate and gather intelligence on terrorist threats, on grounds of inadequate safeguards to protect privacy.

In October and November respectively, the lower and upper houses of parliament approved a law permitting surveillance of journalists outside the EU, despite extensive criticism of the measure by human rights groups, the OSCE representative on media freedom, and three UN special rapporteurs. Several groups subsequently announced their intention to challenge the law in the constitutional court.

Mass sexual assaults against women in Cologne, Hamburg, and other German cities on New Year's Eve prompted debate about the police failure to respond effectively to violence against women. In July, Germany made it easier to prosecute suspects of sexual violence by removing a requirement that the victim physically resist assailants in order to bring charges.

Greece

Despite reforms to address chronic deficiencies, Greece's broken asylum and reception system deteriorated. While the numbers of arrivals by sea fell after the EU-Turkey deal, border closures along the Balkans route preventing asylum seekers from leaving, limited solidarity from other EU governments and ongoing arrivals by sea left more than 60,000 asylum seekers and migrants stranded in the country.

Thousands who arrived after the EU-Turkey deal were restricted to islands in the Aegean, often in closed facilities, while tens of thousands face abysmal conditions across the country. By mid-November, only 5,654 asylum seekers had been relocated from Greece to other EU countries, out of the 66,400 initially planned, even as the European Commission pressed Greece to start accepting returns of asylum seekers who transited the country under the Dublin regulation.

HUMAN
RIGHTS
WATCH

"Why Are You Keeping Me Here?"
Unaccompanied Children Detained in Greece

A Greek law adopted in April to facilitate implementation of the EU-Turkey deal allows for expedited examination of the admissibility of asylum claims in order to determine whether asylum seekers can be safely returned to Turkey to be provided temporary protection or to have the merits of their claims assessed there. At time of writing, only 12 asylum seekers have had their cases ruled inadmissible following an appeal, but none of them had been deported to Turkey. At least one Syrian is challenging the decision at Greece's highest court, the Council of State.

More than 700 people were removed to Turkey under the deal after their claims were considered in Greece under a fast-track border procedure and rejected on the merits or because they did not file an asylum claim or agreed to return voluntarily.

Most asylum seekers entering Greece came through the Aegean islands, and were processed in EU-mandated asylum centers known as hotspots. More than 16,000 asylum seekers and migrants staying in the islands' hotspots face appalling detention and reception conditions, including severe overcrowding, significant shortages of basic shelter and unsanitary, unhygienic conditions. Women, children and people with disabilities are particularly affected.

Long lines for poor quality food, mismanagement, and lack of information contributed to a chaotic and volatile atmosphere. Fights occurred on a frequent basis, particularly in the food lines, at times with no police intervention, while women and girls were exposed to sexual harassment and violence.

Greek authorities drew criticism over their failure to put systems in place that would allow the full disbursement of EU assistance to improve reception conditions.

An estimated 4,370 unaccompanied migrant children entered Greece during the year, according to the National Center for Social Solidarity (EKKA). Unaccompanied migrant and asylum seeking children were often detained in police cells or closed facilities in the islands, due to the lack of adequate shelter accommodations. At time of writing, an estimated 1,610 were waiting to be placed in a dedicated facility.

A large-scale asylum pre-registration process between June and July aimed to improve access to asylum and speed-up relocation, benefitting 27,592 asylum seekers. Despite these efforts, access to asylum remained difficult and subject to delay.

Civil society groups reported an increase in attacks and intimidation of asylum seekers and migrants on the islands and in the mainland in the second half of the year, and an inadequate police response. In a March landmark ruling, the ECtHR criticized Greece for failing adequately to investigate a racist attack against an Afghan national in 2009.

In September, Council of Europe Commissioner for Human Rights Muižnieks urged Greece to protect the human rights of persons with intellectual and psychosocial disabilities and move them out of institutions into the community. Children with disabilities were removed from an institution in Lechaina notorious for abusive practices, but in some cases transferred to other institutions rather than into community-based care.

Hungary

Hungary saw a significant decrease in asylum applications in 2016. By early September, Hungary had registered 26,192 asylum seekers, compared to over 150,000 during the same period in 2015, according to UNHCR. The majority of asylum seekers in 2016 came from Afghanistan and Syria.

February 2016 border closures on the Western Balkan route, combined with increased restrictive measures along Hungary's border with Serbia, criminal prosecutions of irregular border crossers and pushbacks, often accompanied by violence, at Hungary's border with Serbia contributed to the decrease.

An April law restricted the rights of asylum seekers and cut integration support for recognized refugees. The same month, the government announced the closure of the largest open reception facility by the end of the year.

An accelerated fast-track border procedure effectively bars asylum seekers from meaningful access to the asylum procedure. A July law legalized push-backs to the Serbian border, enabling police officers to escort to the border anyone caught irregularly eight kilometers inside Hungary. The law, together with low daily caps on entry, leaves asylum seekers—including children, families and people with disabilities—stranded at the border for weeks in poor conditions.

During 2016, the government continued its anti-immigrant rhetoric. In February, the government announced a national referendum on the EU relocation plan requiring Hungary to accept 1,294 asylum seekers and in July launched a government sponsored and tax payer funded anti-immigrant campaign. A low turnout for the October referendum meant that the result was invalid, although most who did vote supported the government's position.

Journalists continued to work in a hostile environment. In September, the editor-in-chief of *Budapest Business Journal*, Tom Popper, resigned after being told by its publishers to stop mentioning refugee issues in the editorial column. The largest opposition daily newspaper, *Nepszabadsag*, and its website closed down without warning in October with its owner citing financial losses and plummeting circulation.

Roma continued to face discrimination in housing, education, and public health care. In September, the Council of Europe Advisory Committee on the Framework Convention for the Protection of National Minorities urged Hungary to end discriminatory segregation of Roma schoolchildren.

In August, a lower court sentenced a right-wing extremist to 10 years' imprisonment for violent attacks between 2007 and 2009, including throwing Molotov cocktails at the homes of socialist MPs and an attack on a gay bar in Budapest.

In January, the ECtHR ruled that secret surveillance by the Hungarian Anti-Terrorism Task Force had violated privacy rights. The grounds for the decision included Hungary's failure to provide judicial oversight over Task Force actions and other sufficiently precise and effective safeguards.

In July, the ECtHR ruled that Hungary had arbitrarily detained an Iranian gay man and failed to take into account his vulnerability in detention arising from his sexual orientation.

By late October, 26 homeless people had been charged with misdemeanours under local decrees banning the homeless from residing habitually in public spaces, compared to 71 in the first 10 months of 2015.

Italy

By mid-November, 164,695 migrants and asylum seekers reached Italy by sea, according to UNHCR. Nigerians, Eritreans, and Sudanese made up the largest national groups. Numbers of unaccompanied children increased significantly, with an estimated 23,000 traveling alone to Italy by mid-September compared to 12,360 in all of 2015. The International Organization for Migration estimated that 80 percent of all Nigerian women arriving in Italy had been trafficked or were at risk of being trafficked into sex work.

New asylum applications and rejection rates increased compared to 2015, as increased border controls by neighboring countries prevented onward movement. Most asylum seekers lived in temporary emergency facilities of varying standards. Concerns persisted about use of force for fingerprinting as well as overcrowding and lack of protection for unaccompanied children at hotspots. At time of writing, only 1,570 asylum seekers had been relocated to other EU countries out of the 39,600 initial target under the EU plan.

Italy intensified negotiations with countries such as Sudan, Gambia, and Libya on migration control, including to facilitate deportations. In August, after a memorandum of understanding with Sudan, Italy deported 48 Sudanese it claimed had not sought to apply for asylum amid concerns about the procedure.

A bill to make torture a criminal offence in domestic law, approved by the lower house of parliament in 2015, languished in the Senate at time of writing.

In February, the ECtHR ordered Italy to compensate an Egyptian cleric known as Abu Omar for complicity with his 2003 rendition and for failing to ensure effective punishment for those responsible. At time of writing, one of the 22 CIA agents convicted in absentia by Italian courts in the case was fighting extradition from Portugal. At issue is Italy's refusal to grant her a retrial.

Italy continued to expel terrorism suspects under a procedure that explicitly denied the right to an in-country appeal. Italy expelled 47 individuals, many of them to Tunisia and Morocco, in the first eight months of 2016.

In April, the Council of Europe's Social Rights Committee said the fact that 7 out of 10 doctors in Italy are "conscientious objectors," meaning that they refuse to provide abortion services in some or all circumstances, created serious difficulties for women accessing safe and legal abortions.

As of May, same-sex couples may have their relationships legally recognized as civil unions, though they do not have the right to adopt.

Latvia

Statelessness remains a key concern. UNHCR estimated that as of late 2015, around 252,000 of the country's population is effectively stateless (referred to by authorities as "noncitizens" or "persons with undetermined nationality"). Despite 2013 reforms, several thousand children remain stateless.

Discrimination persists against Russian speakers, particularly in employment, language use, and education. Latvian non-citizens are barred from occupying certain posts in the civil service and other professions. They also face restrictions on owning land.

Authorities continued to sanction individuals over alleged failure to use Latvian in professional communications. According to the Latvia's State Language Center, a government agency, 180 people were fined for violating the state language law in the first six months of 2016. In March, a cleaner in a Russian-language school was fired following a State Language Center inspection, for not having a sufficient level of Latvian. In June, a speech therapist was forced to resign her post in a kindergarten due to a similar inspection. In July, the State Language Center fined the mayor of Riga over Russian language use in social media posts by the Riga city administration. The mayor appealed.

In September, the Latvian parliament adopted in first reading draft amendments to the Law on Public Associations and Foundations, creating broad grounds for government oversight over NGOs deemed to undermine national security, public safety, and order.

According to Latvian LGBT activists, the authorities used a 2015 law on "constitutional morality education" to censor discussion about LGBT people in at least two schools in 2016.

At time of writing, Latvia had accepted a total 148 asylum seekers relocated from Greece and Italy under the EU relocation scheme.

Netherlands

In February, the government expanded the list of safe third countries for asylum seekers. Nationals from countries deemed safe are presumed not to need international protection and are subject to accelerated procedures, raising concerns about the quality of individual examination of asylum claims. In September 2016, the country's highest administrative court affirmed the legality of Albania's designation as a safe country of origin.

The Dutch government continued to offer support that is limited in duration and scope to rejected asylum seekers, with assistance contingent on their cooperation with removal from the country. In February, several UN special rapporteurs urged the Dutch government to provide emergency assistance to rejected asylum seekers.

Refugee rights groups criticized Dutch authorities over longer waits for asylum determinations and family reunification procedures.

At the start of 2016, NGOs reported threats and discrimination against LGBT asylum seekers at asylum facilities, and a Dutch independent monitoring body, the Dutch Board for Protection of Human Rights, found in February that LGBT asylum seekers at a large facility face discrimination.

In May, the Netherlands enacted a law allowing authorities to strip Dutch citizenship from dual nationals as young as 16 if they determine that they have joined or fought abroad with a terrorist group and pose an "immediate threat" to national security. No court conviction is required. Those whose Dutch citizenship is revoked have only four weeks to appeal.

In January, the Netherlands ratified the UN Convention on the Rights of Persons with Disabilities.

Poland

Poland faced international criticism over attempts by the newly elected parliament led by the ruling Law and Justice Party to undermine the independence of the Constitutional Tribunal, the country's highest court.

In November 2015, the parliament cancelled the appointments of all five Constitutional Tribunal judges elected under the previous government, and passed a law in December that undermined the tribunal's functioning. When the tribunal ruled in March 2016 that the changes were unconstitutional, the government refused to publish the ruling or to change the law.

In July, the parliament adopted a revised Act on the Constitutional Tribunal. Polish NGOs expressed concern the new act would paralyze the court and affect its independence. The Constitutional Tribunal ruled that part of the new law was unconstitutional. At time of writing, the Law and Justice Party was reportedly preparing yet another draft revision of the act on the Constitutional Tribunal.

In March, the Venice Commission, the Council of Europe's advisory body on constitutional issues, concluded that the December 2015 amendments endanger the rule of law and called on the government to implement the Constitutional Court's judgment. In October, the Venice Commission criticized the July revised act as limiting the tribunal's effectiveness and independence.

The crisis led the European Commission in January to activate for the first time its rule of law mechanism—created in 2014 to address rights-threatening measures by EU member states. In July, the European Commission gave the government three months to publish the Constitutional Court's rulings and implement the Venice Commission's recommendations. At time of writing it had yet to announce any follow-up action.

In January, Parliament adopted amendments to the Act on the Police that raised concerns on the protection of privacy online. In June, President Andrzej Duda signed into law a new Anti-Terrorist Act that introduces a vaguely defined "event of a terrorist nature," extends investigative powers specifically on foreigners, regulates access to online content and extends arrest and search powers.

In October, Parliament withdrew a contentious proposition supported by Polish Prime Minister Beata Szydło to impose an almost total ban to abortion, following mass protests. Amid continued protests, the Law and Justice Party pressed ahead with efforts to further limit what is already one of the most restrictive abortion laws in Europe.

There continues to be little accountability for hate crimes based on sexual orientation. Anti-migrant hate speech and violence was a growing concern. Polish NGOs accused authorities of preventing asylum seekers at the border with Belarus from entering Polish territory to seek protection.

There was no sign of progress in the Krakow appellate prosecutor's longstanding criminal investigation into a secret CIA detention and interrogation program on Polish territory.

Spain

A policy of summary returns and reinforced controls at Spain's land border with Morocco in its North Africa enclaves appeared to result in migrants increasingly trying to reach Ceuta and Melilla by boat or swimming. The number of deaths along that route tripled to 45 in the first six months of 2016 compared to 2015.

There were several group attempts to scale the fences surrounding the enclaves, followed by summary returns, though fewer than in previous years. In July, Council of Europe Human Rights Commissioner Muižnieks urged Spain to adopt border procedures to prevent refoulement and collective expulsions. An ECtHR challenge to summary returns from Melilla in 2014 was pending at time of writing.

As of mid-November, Spain had relocated only 398 asylum seekers of the 9,323 it had committed to taking from Greece and Italy. While it pledged to resettle 1,449 refugees from other regions, at time of writing it had resettled only 279.

In April, the European Commission took the first step towards legal action against Spain for failure to protect consumers against unfair mortgage terms. In July, the EU Court of Justice advocate general recommended the court uphold a 2013 Spanish Supreme Court judgment preventing consumers from suing banks for interest paid on mortgages under rules subsequently declared unlawful; the EU court had yet to rule at time of writing.

In June, Spain's Constitutional Court suspended a Catalan law with protections for those facing eviction from their homes, including for failure to mortgages, pending examination of an appeal by the central government.

In May, the ECtHR ruled Spain had failed adequately to investigate allegations of torture of a man suspected of affiliation with the armed Basque separatist group ETA, while he was held and interrogated in incommunicado detention.

At least one journalist was fined, in April, for publishing photographs of a police operation under a controversial 2015 public security law. There were several high-profile cases of charges against musicians, puppeteers, and activists for glorification of terrorism, including on social media, under strengthened provisions in the criminal code.

United Kingdom

The referendum vote in June to leave the European Union sent political shock-waves through the country, creating uncertainty about future constitutional arrangements and the residence status of the more than 3 million citizens from other EU states in the UK.

The Brexit vote was preceded by the murder of MP Jo Cox, who had campaigned vigorously on behalf of asylum seekers and for the UK to remain in the UK. Following the vote there was a marked increase in xenophobic and racist hate crimes, including assault and arson attacks, with EU citizens from eastern Europe a particular target, according to data issued by the police. Poland sent police officers in September to an English town after a Polish man was beaten to death in a possible hate crime.

In an August review of the UK, the UN Committee on the Elimination of Racial Discrimination expressed concern at the "divisive, anti-immigrant and xenophobic rhetoric" employed during the Brexit campaign and the hate crimes that followed it, and called on public officials to formally reject such speech.

The government of Prime Minister Theresa May, elected leader by the Conservative Party in July, renewed its pledge to replace the UK's domestic human rights legislation with a bill of rights, but took no discernable action towards that end. After the Brexit vote, May backed away from the suggestion the UK would leave the Council of Europe and ECtHR.

May used her first party conference speech as prime minister to say that "activist left-wing human rights lawyers" would "never again" be allowed to pursue claims on behalf of victims of human rights abuse by UK military forces. She was apparently referring to cases brought against the Ministry of Defence in relation to abuses in Iraq and Afghanistan. The government wants to exempt UK forces operating overseas from human rights law.

The UK made some progress on pledges to resettle Syrian and other refugees, but opted out of the EU asylum seeker relocation scheme. In late October, as French authorities moved to close the Calais camp, the UK finally stepped up efforts to bring unaccompanied children with family ties to the UK. By mid-November, the UK had brought around 300 children from the camp. Despite a legislative requirement that the government facilitate the relocation from Calais and elsewhere in the EU of unaccompanied asylum seeking children even without family ties in the UK, very few of the children brought from Calais lacked family ties, and the government imposed age and nationality restrictions on those it would accept.

In a June review, the UN Committee on the Rights of the Child called on the UK to stop detaining asylum-seeking and migrant children and expedite family reunification for unaccompanied children outside the UK.

In January, a government-commissioned independent review of the tied visa for migrant domestic workers recommended restoring their right to change employer—a key safeguard against employer abuse. The government restored the right but failed to permit visa extensions beyond the existing six-month limit, blunting the measure's effectiveness.

In June, prosecutors announced no UK officials would face charges for involvement in the kidnap, transfer, and torture of two Libyan dissidents and their families in 2004, effectively closing the last criminal investigation for the UK authorities' complicity in global counterterrorism abuses. A review by a parliamentary body into UK complicity in torture and rendition continued at time of writing.

The Iraq Historic Allegations Team, a body set up to investigate possible war crimes by UK forces, continued work in 2016, despite unwarranted political criticism of its existence and the principle of legal scrutiny of military operations.

In November, Parliament approved problematic legislation—the Investigatory Powers Act—entrenching and broadening state surveillance powers without adequate safeguards.

Foreign Policy

The EU's foreign policy agenda was dominated by the conflicts in Syria and eastern Ukraine, and the deteriorating relationship with the Russian government as a result of Moscow's involvement in these conflicts. Another focus of EU foreign policy appeared dictated by EU member states' desire to prevent a growing number of refugees, asylum seekers, and migrants from arriving in Europe.

The EU successfully pressed Ukraine to refer jurisdiction over grave crimes to the International Criminal Court (ICC), through a so-called article 12(3) self-referral.

Gambia

The December 2016 presidential election, won by opposition coalition leader Adama Barrow, brought hope for improved respect for human rights and the rule of law. Barrow defeated incumbent Yayah Jammeh who had held power since a 1994 coup and whose government had a long track record of using enforced disappearances, torture, intimidation, and arbitrary arrests to silence opposition voices.

While the two-week election campaign was peaceful, with security forces largely respecting opposition parties' rights to freedom of expression and assembly, the lead up to the campaign was characterized by the intimidation of political opponents and the government's use of state media and resources to promote Jammeh's candidacy.

In April, prominent opposition leader Solo Sandeng was beaten to death in state custody, ushering in an often-violent government crackdown on Gambia's largest opposition party, the United Democratic Party (UDP). More than 90 opposition activists were detained for participating in peaceful protests and 30 incarcerated for three-year terms, including the leadership of the UDP.

Gambian security forces, particularly the National Intelligence Agency (NIA) and Police Intervention Unit (PIU), also arrested and detained civil society activists who criticized the government, including religious leaders, trade unionists, and journalists.

During Jammeh's three decades in power, no members of state security or paramilitary groups are known to have been convicted or otherwise held to account for torture, enforced disappearances, or other serious violations.

Gambia's key international interlocutors, including the Economic Community of West African States (ECOWAS), the United Nations, the European Union, and the United States, were at times robust critics of the government's abuses against political opponents. But in 2016 they failed to take meaningful steps to sanction the government for its persistent abuses.

Gambia notified the UN secretary-general of its withdrawal from the International Criminal Court on November 10, to take effect on November 10, 2017. However, in December, President-elect Barrow promised to reverse it.

HUMAN
RIGHTS
WATCH

MORE FEAR THAN FAIR

Gambia's 2016 Presidential Election

Crackdown on Political Opposition

The April death in custody of the UDP national organizing secretary, Solo Sandeng, presaged a wider crackdown against political opposition and the UDP in particular. Sandeng and some 25 others were arrested by Gambian police on April 14 during a rare public demonstration in favor of electoral reform. Sandeng was taken to the headquarters of Gambia's National Intelligence Agency and brutally beaten to death.

On April 16, Ousainou Darboe, the UDP leader, was among more than 20 people beaten and arrested by police during a protest against Sandeng's treatment. Forty-five protesters were subsequently arrested by the police during a May 9 rally.

In the aftermath of these protests, Jammeh repeatedly threatened opposition groups, which he called "evil vermin," warning them: "If you want to destabilize this country, I will bury you nine-feet deep."

Darboe and 18 others, including several other high-ranking UDP members, were sentenced on July 20 to three years' imprisonment for their role in the April 16 protest. On July 21, 11 protesters arrested with Sandeng were also sentenced to three years in prison. At time of writing, 14 other protesters arrested during a May 9 protest were on trial in the Banjul High Court.

Arbitrary Arrest, Detention, and Enforced Disappearances

As well as targeting political opponents, the security services, especially the NIA, continued to arbitrarily arrest, detain, and intimidate religious leaders, trade unionists, journalists and former civil servants, seemingly targeting those critical of the government and particularly President Jammeh. Barrow promised during his election campaign to release political prisoners.

The government has forcibly disappeared three imams arrested in October and November 2015. Alhagi Ousman Sawaneh, the imam of Kanifeng South, was arrested on October 18, 2015, reportedly because he petitioned the Gambian government to free a farming cooperative leader detained by the NIA. Sawaneh was initially taken to the NIA headquarters, and then reportedly transferred to Janjanbureh prison, where, at time of writing, he remained in incommunicado detention.

The High Court on March 21 ordered that the government produce Sawaneh in court, but it had failed to do so at time of writing. Two other imams, Sheikh Omar Colley and Imam Gassama, reportedly arrested in relation to the same incident, are also believed to being held incommunicado at Janjanbureh prison.

Ousman Jammeh, a former deputy minister of agriculture, has been held without charge in incommunicado detention since being removed from his post on October 15, 2015. Gambia's former ambassador to the African Union, Sarjo Jallow, was arrested and held without charge by the NIA on September 2, 2016. Although a Gambian court on October 17 granted him bail, he remained in state custody at time of writing.

Torture, Ill-Treatment, and Neglect in Detention

Gambian security forces continued to subject detainees to serious mistreatment, including torture. Several protesters arrested in April and May were subjected to serious physical abuse while in detention. UDP activist Solo Krummah, who had been arrested on May 9, died in state custody in a Banjul hospital on August 20. His family have been given no information regarding the cause of death or the medical treatment he received.

Sheriff Dibba, the leader of Gambian National Transport Control Association, died in police custody on February 21 after being arrested following a trade union demand that the government lower fuel prices. After Dibba fell ill in police custody, the government failed to provide him with prompt and adequate medical attention.

Prisons continued to operate far below international standards. Prisoners lack appropriate housing, sanitation, food, and inadequate medical care. Detainees in the security wing of Mile 2 Central Prison, including the UDP leadership, were frequently subjected to prolonged solitary confinement.

Freedom of Expression

Since 1994, dozens of journalists have fled Gambia after being arbitrarily detained and often tortured. At least two journalists have been murdered or forcibly disappeared since 2004.

While there were fewer reports of abuses against journalists in 2016 than in previous years, the culture of impunity that has permitted abuses against journalists to go unpunished under Jammeh's government remained intact and caused many journalists to self-censor reporting.

The managing director of independent radio station Teranga FM, Alhagie Ceesay, who was arrested in July 2015, held without charge at the NIA headquarters, and tortured, remained in government custody until April 2016, when he escaped while receiving treatment at a Banjul hospital. He was convicted of sedition in absentia on November 9 and sentenced to four years' imprisonment.

In December 2015, the Federation of African Journalists and three exiled Gambian reporters filed a legal claim before the ECOWAS Community Court of Justice challenging a series of Gambian laws that curtail freedom of expression, including criminal laws on sedition, defamation and the publication of "false news." Gambia is yet to implement judgments in the favor of the plaintiffs in three other ECOWAS Court of Justice cases related to journalists: the enforced disappearance of Ebrima Manneh in 2006; the torture of Musa Saidykhan in 2006; and the unlawful killing of the president of the Gambia Press Union, Deyda Hydara, in 2004.

During the two-week campaign period for the December 1 election, the Independent Election Commission granted all political parties the right to equal air time daily on state media for election broadcasts. However, the near complete domination of state media by Jammeh and the ruling party prior to the campaign period denied opposition parties a level-playing field to contest the election.

Online diaspora media organizations remain a vital source of news for Gambians with internet connectivity. The government accuses diaspora media of fabricating stories to discredit President Jammeh and, in past years, several people have been arrested for providing information to diaspora journalists.

Women's and Girls' Rights

Gambia has very high rates of female genital mutilation (FGM). President Jammeh announced in November 2015 that Gambia would ban FGM, and the Gambian parliament enacted legislation on December 28, 2015, criminalizing the practice. Jammeh announced on July 6 that child marriage was also to be criminalized and the Gambian parliament on July 21 imposed severe penalties on parents responsible for children marrying before age 18. Women's rights advocates underscored that, as a complement to punitive measures, intensive community education campaigns would be necessary to address the centuries-old customs that underpin these practices.

Sexual Orientation and Gender Identity

The government continued to resist calls to repeal laws that criminalize homosexuality, including an October 2014 law that introduced a series of new "aggravated homosexuality" offenses that impose sentences of up to life in prison. The criminalization of same-sex conduct leaves lesbian, gay, bisexual, and transgender (LGBT) Gambians at risk of arbitrary arrest and detention, although fewer arrests and physical abuse of LGBT Gambians were reported in 2016.

Key International Actors

The government's crackdown on the opposition in advance of the election led to condemnation by the African Commission on Human and People's Rights, the United Nations secretary-general, the United States, the European Union, and the United Kingdom.

The UN high commissioner for human rights expressed alarm at Gambia's human rights situation several times during 2016, including at the UN Human Rights Council in September. Gambia has drafted legislation, with UN assistance, for the creation of a national human rights commission, although the draft bill at time of writing had yet to be presented to the National Assembly.

President Jammeh was largely dismissive of critical statements regarding his human rights record, saying in May that human rights groups and UN Secretary-General Ban Ki-moon could "go to hell."

In February 2016, the EU deployed a resident ambassador to Gambia for the first time in its history. The US also upgraded their head of mission from a chargé d'affaires to an ambassador. The EU, which had frozen development assistance in December 2014 due to concerns over human rights abuses, now channels all aid through nongovernmental organizations.

Georgia

Georgia's ruling party swept to an overwhelming victory in October 2016 parliamentary elections. The state security service's unfettered access to telecom operators' networks compromised the right to privacy. Lack of accountability persisted for abuses committed by law enforcement. Other areas of concern included media freedoms and the rights of lesbian, gay, bisexual, and transgender (LGBT) people.

The International Criminal Court (ICC) ordered an investigation into war crimes and crimes against humanity committed during the August 2008 war in Georgia.

Parliamentary Elections

The ruling Georgian Dream (GD) party won an overwhelming victory in October 8 parliamentary elections, giving it full control over the formation of a new government. International observers, led by the Organization for Security and Co-operation in Europe (OSCE), concluded that the elections were "competitive, well-administered and fundamental freedoms were generally respected."

However, they also noted procedural violations during the vote count in almost one-third of all polling stations and violent altercations in four. Local monitoring groups highlighted some cases of vote-buying, alleged political intimidation, and campaigning by unauthorized persons, but found these had no effect on the overall outcome.

Three violent incidents during the week before the vote marred an otherwise peaceful pre-election process. On October 4, an explosion hit the car of a prominent member of parliament from the opposition United National Movement (UNM) party, injuring five. An October 2 shooting during an outdoor campaign meeting for an independent candidate wounded two people. On October 1, three GD activists were assaulted while campaigning. Investigations into all three incidents were pending at time of writing.

Right to Privacy

In April, the Constitutional Court ruled unconstitutional legislation that allows state security services to have direct, unrestricted access to telecom operators' networks to monitor communications and ordered the authorities to reform surveillance regulations by March 2017. Legislation adopted in 2014 had imposed restrictions on surveillance operations by law enforcement but left in place the security agencies' operation of "black box" surveillance devices in telecommunications service providers' networks. The court found this system allows mass collection of personal information in real time without effective oversight.

The online publication of several illegally recorded personal phone conversations of opposition party members and their supporters in the run-up to the election seemed aimed at influencing the vote. Among the recordings were private conversations between former President Mikheil Saakashvili and fellow UNM party members, and a call between a pro-opposition television director and an opposition party leader. The State Security Service denied involvement, and the Interior Ministry opened an investigation.

In March, unknown persons threatened to release sex tapes implicating two cabinet members, an opposition figure, and a television journalist if they did not quit their jobs by March 31. The threats were made through YouTube videos of secretly recorded videos purportedly showing their private lives, with blurred out faces, which were quickly removed. Authorities launched an investigation.

Torture, Ill-Treatment, and Police Abuse

Georgia does not have an independent effective mechanism for investigating crimes committed by law enforcements officials.

In July, the Georgian Young Lawyers' Association (GYLA), a leading human rights group, published a report analyzing 22 cases they litigated in the past two years concerning alleged torture and ill-treatment by law enforcement officials. GYLA concluded that in most cases the investigations were ineffective. In several cases, officials retaliated against the victims who had filed complaints by pressing administrative and criminal proceedings against them.

GYLA received at least 62 allegations of torture and ill-treatment in 12 months since November 2015; 45 of them concerned abuse by police, and 17 by prison staff. According to GYLA, authorities failed to effectively investigate those allegations.

In August, Demur Sturua, 22, committed suicide, leaving behind a note stating that a local policeman was coercing him to inform on local cannabis growers. The autopsy showed that Sturua had bodily injuries, which the prosecutor said were inflicted by the policeman prior to Sturua's death. The Prosecutor's Office filed criminal charges against the policeman, and the investigation was pending at time of writing. Georgia' s public defender said the case exemplified the consequences of Georgia's "repressive drug policies."

Concerns about Politicized Justice

Several criminal cases against former officials raised questions about selective justice and politically motivated prosecution. In May, a court found five former Defense Ministry and general staff officials guilty of misspending GEL 4.1 million (roughly US$1.8 million) arising from a closed 2013 tender for the laying of fiber-optic cable, and sentenced them to seven years in prison.

For several months following the defendants arrest in 2014, authorities denied defense lawyers full access to evidence, claiming it consisted of classified documents. The court did not establish any mercenary motives behind the misspending charges. The public defender filed an amicus brief in support of the defendants' Constitutional Court claim that the definition of misspending in the criminal code is vague and allows for arbitrary interpretation. The men were arrested in 2014, which led to sacking of then-Defense Minister Irakli Alasania.

In June, the European Court of Human Rights (ECHR) issued a ruling in the case of ex-minister of interior and the UNM leader Vano Merabishvili, saying that while his initial pretrial detention in May 2013 was lawful, the remand renewal four months later lacked reasonable grounds. The court said Merabishvili's continued detention "was ... treated by prosecuting authorities as an additional opportunity to obtain leverage" over investigations into unrelated cases, including one against ex-president Saakashvili. In October, the ECHR Grand Chamber agreed to hear the Georgian government's appeal of the ruling.

Sexual Orientation and Gender Identity

In August, President Giorgi Margvelashvili blocked a referendum bid on defining marriage as a union of a man and a woman, saying that the issue is already covered in the civil code. Prime Minister Giorgi Kvirikashvili vowed to pursue a constitutional definition of marriage after the October elections, arguing that this would help counter alleged Western efforts to spread same-sex marriage "propaganda" in Georgia. Local rights groups feared this effort would further marginalize the LGBT community and intensify anti-LGBT prejudice.

Authorities declined a request by LGBT activists to hold an event to mark International Day Against Homophobia and Transphobia (IDAHO) on Tbilisi's main thoroughfare, stating it was already booked for a procession by Orthodox groups to mark Family Day, an annual event established by the Orthodox Church in 2014. Activists refused to celebrate IDAHO in the alternative venue offered.

The Women's Initiatives Supporting Group (WISG), a local LGBTI rights group, said it documented almost 20 cases of attacks against transgender people in 2016. In October, a transgender woman was beaten and stabbed in what rights groups suspected was a hate crime. Police arrested a suspect on attempted murder charges, and the public defender urged authorities to examine a possible hate motive.

Freedom of Media

The ownership dispute over Georgia's most-watched television broadcaster, Rustavi 2, continued in 2016 and raised concerns about ongoing government interference with media. In June, the Tbilisi Court of Appeals upheld a lower court ruling in favor of Kibar Khalvashi, who owned Rustavi 2 from 2004 to 2006 and sought to reclaim his shares. Khalvashi alleged that in 2006, then-UNM government leaders forced him to sell the shares. Rustavi 2's current owners appealed the appeals court decision, alleging Khalvshi's lawsuit is a government-orchestrated move to take over the opposition-minded station. In September, the Supreme Court found the appeal admissible. A decision was pending at time of writing.

Key International Actors

The Association Agreement between the European Union and Georgia went into force on July 1, strengthening political and economic ties between the two. The agreement requires Georgia to fulfill extensive commitments in the areas of democracy, human rights, and the rule of law. The EU pledged €100 million ($ 107.8 million) per year to support Georgia's reform agenda, including in areas relating to human rights and the rule of law.

Following her February visit, the United Nations special rapporteur on violence against women issued a report highlighting widespread violence against women both in private and public spheres, caused by "entrenched patriarchal attitudes and gender stereotypes."

She noted ongoing and disquieting levels of domestic violence, including femicide/killings of women, and police failure to provide adequate protection in reported cases as well as the persistent belief that such violence is a private matter. She also raised concerns about the high number of child and forced marriages resulting from lax enforcement of laws prohibiting such marriages and social attitudes and practices that foster the practice. Georgia has signed but not yet ratified the Council of Europe Convention on Violence against Women and Domestic Violence (Istanbul Convention).

The US-Georgia bilateral working group on democracy and governance under the strategic partnership charter met in June in Tbilisi. The US delegation underlined the importance of a peaceful pre-election environment and reiterated concerns over the Rustavi 2 ownership dispute. The April US Department of State's annual human rights report noted among other things "significant shortcomings in the administration of justice, including pressure on judiciary in selected cases."

In January, the ICC authorized its prosecutor to open an investigation into war crimes and crimes against humanity allegedly committed in the lead up to, during, and after the August 2008 war between Russia and Georgia over South Ossetia.

Guatemala

Guatemala continued to make progress in prosecuting human rights and corruption cases, due in significant part to the collaboration of the Attorney General's Office with the United Nations-backed International Commission against Impunity in Guatemala (CICIG), which was established in 2007 to investigate organized crime and reinforce local efforts to strengthen the rule of law.

In September 2015, after being implicated by CICIG in a million-dollar tax-fraud scandal, Guatemalan President Otto Pérez Molina resigned and was arrested on charges of customs fraud, racketeering, and bribery.

President Jimmy Morales took office in January, and in April, asked the UN to extend CICIG's mandate—which had been set to expire in 2017—until September 2019.

Accountability for Past Human Rights Violations

In February, a court convicted two former military officers on charges of crimes against humanity in the form of sexual violence and domestic and sexual slavery. It was the first time that a Guatemalan court had prosecuted a case of sexual violence related to the country's 36-year internal armed conflict. The victims were 15 Maya Q'eqchi' women.

In addition to the sexual violence convictions, the court found Lt. Col. Esteelmer Reyes Girón, former commander of Sepur Zarco military base, guilty in the homicides of three females, and Heriberto Valdez Asig, former military commissioner, guilty in the enforced disappearance of the husbands of seven of the female victims. They were sentenced to 120 years and 240 years in prison respectively.

Former Guatemalan head of state Efraín Ríos Montt was found guilty in May 2013 of genocide and crimes against humanity. He was sentenced to 80 years in prison, but several days later the Constitutional Court overturned the verdict on procedural grounds. The retired general had led a military government from 1982 to 1983, when the military carried out hundreds of massacres of unarmed civilians.

In August 2015, a trial court declared Ríos Montt mentally unfit for retrial, ruling instead that he should be represented by his lawyers in a special closed-door proceeding. In October 2015, an appellate court rejected a two-year-old petition by Rios Montt's attorneys to apply a 1986 amnesty decree that would put an end to his prosecution. The court ruled that the decree, applicable to "all political and related common crimes" committed between March 1982 and January 1986, does not apply to genocide and crimes against humanity. A retrial of Rios Montt began in March 2016, behind closed doors.

In May, the First Court of Appeals issued a provisional ruling that the former dictator should be separated from his co-defendant, José Mauricio Rodríguez Sánchez, the former intelligence director. A new trial for each defendant had yet to be scheduled at time of writing.

In recent years, the Attorney General's Office has obtained convictions in several other cases involving human rights crimes committed during the war. In 2011, four army Special Forces soldiers received lengthy sentences for their role in the 1982 Dos Erres massacre of more than 250 people. In 2013, former National Police Chief Héctor Bol de la Cruz received a 40-year sentence for ordering the disappearance of a student activist in 1984. In January 2015, former Police Chief Pedro Garcia Arredondo was sentenced to 90 years in prison for a raid on the Spanish embassy in 1980, in which 37 people burned to death.

In July 2014, Fermín Felipe Solano Barillas became the first ex-guerrilla to be convicted in connection with atrocities. Found guilty of ordering the massacre of 22 residents of the town of El Aguacate in 1988, he was sentenced to 90 years in prison.

Public Security, Corruption, and Criminal Justice

Violence and extortion by powerful criminal organizations remain serious problems in Guatemala. Corruption within the justice system, combined with intimidation against judges and prosecutors, contributes to high levels of impunity. Gang-related violence is an important factor prompting people, including unaccompanied youth, to leave the country.

Despite these problems, prosecutors in recent years have made progress in cases of violent crime, as well as some cases of extrajudicial killings and corruption.

In April 2015, a CICIG investigation uncovered a US$130 million tax fraud scandal involving more than 50 high-ranking members of the government. This led to charges against then-President Otto Pérez Molina, Vice President Roxana Baldetti, and 35 others.

In April 2016, prosecutors brought additional charges against Pérez Molina in connection with a $30 million commission on a Spanish company's contract to operate a new, Pacific-coast container terminal in Puerto Quetzal.

In June, the CICIG announced arrests in connection with a clandestine structure that operated behind the façade of the Partido Patriota (PP), ex-President Pérez Molina's political party. The PP allegedly designed a financial scheme whose main objective was the illicit enrichment of its members through state contracts worth more than $35 million. At time of writing, more than 57 members of the Guatemalan business elite, from bankers to Congressmen, had been arrested.

Key International Actors

The UN-backed CICIG, established in 2007, plays a key role in assisting Guatemala's justice system in prosecuting violent crime. The CICIG works with the Attorney General's Office, the police, and other government agencies to investigate, prosecute, and dismantle criminal organizations operating in the country. It is empowered to participate in criminal proceedings as a complementary prosecutor, to provide technical assistance, and to promote legislative reforms.

The US Congress approved $750 million in assistance for 2016 for the Plan of the Alliance for Prosperity in the Northern Triangle, a five-year initiative announced in 2014 that intends to reduce incentives to migrate from Guatemala, El Salvador, and Honduras. The Obama administration requested the same amount for the plan for 2017. At time of writing, Congress had not yet approved the final budget.

The aid aims to reduce violence, strengthen governance, and increase economic opportunity. Fifty percent of it is conditioned on the US Department of State annually certifying progress by the beneficiary countries in strengthening institutions, fighting corruption and impunity, and protecting human rights. In 2016, Guatemala received certification for continued full funding under the plan. The assistance for 2016 included $7 million for CICIG in Guatemala, and funding for similar commissions, if established, in El Salvador and Honduras. The US Department of State announced in June that, since 2008, the US had invested $36 million in the CICIG's work.

The Guatemalan government is implementing a reparations plan, required for certification to receive US aid, to address human rights violations suffered by communities displaced by construction of the Chixoy Hydroelectric Dam in 1975. Distribution of $2.8 million in reparations started in March 2015. Reparations are expected to total $156 million by 2029, the dam's planned completion.

The Office of the UN High Commissioner for Human Rights has maintained an office in Guatemala since 2005. The office monitors the human rights situation in the country and provides policy support to the government and civil society.

Guinea

During 2016, the government of President Alpha Conde, who won a second term as president in flawed elections in late 2015, made some gains in consolidating the rule of law and addressing security force violations. A national dialogue between the ruling and opposition parties reduced ethnic and communal tensions and led to a roadmap for long-delayed local elections to be held in early 2017.

However, continued deficiencies within the police and judiciary, along with several risk factors—notably high unemployment, organized crime, and regional insecurity— highlighted the fragility of these gains.

Reports of human rights violations by security forces declined, and authorities demonstrated increased willingness to investigate and sanction those implicated in violations, notably those which had been widely reported in the local media.

Though the government allowed several opposition demonstrations to take place, thereby improving its respect for the right to freedom of assembly, little progress was made on improving access to key economic rights, including health care and primary education. Violence against girls and women remained high.

The judiciary made progress in the investigation into the 2009 stadium massacre of unarmed demonstrators by security forces, but largely failed to investigate other past episodes of state-sponsored violence. The justice ministry embarked on a major reorganization of the judiciary to improve the dispensation of justice, but concerns over prison overcrowding, unprofessional conduct by judicial personnel, and lack of judicial independence remain.

International actors—notably the European Union, United Nations, France, and the United States—focused on ensuring political dialogue between the ruling party and the opposition, though they infrequently pushed for progress on accountability. Donors supported programs to strengthen the rule of law, address unemployment, and improve discipline within the security sector.

Security Force Abuses

Discipline within and civilian control over the security forces appeared to improve as those mandated to respond to civil unrest—the police and gendarmerie—did so with increasing proportionality. However, in several cases, members of the security forces mistreated and at times tortured detainees as they responded to protests and criminality. There were also numerous allegations of unprofessional conduct, including theft and extortion.

In March, a widely circulated cell phone video of a criminal suspect being tortured by members of an elite anti-crime unit in Conkary was condemned by the public and government. In May, several officers from the police and the gendarmerie were questioned by investigating judges for physical violence against demonstrators in April. In June, an army colonel was removed from his post after he and several subordinates severely beat and shot residents who they accused of stalling their convoy. In August, a police captain was detained and, at time of writing, was under investigation for excessive use of lethal force that killed a bystander and injured several protestors during a demonstration.

In sharp contrast to the lack of government response following similar incidents in previous years, these cases in 2016 elicited administrative sanctions, investigations, and commitments to deliver justice. However, at time of writing, none of the alleged perpetrators in these cases had yet been held to account.

Justice for the 2009 Stadium Massacre

More than seven years on, Guinea has yet to deliver justice for the grave crimes committed in September 2009, when security forces massacred some 150 opposition supporters and raped over 100 women. The crimes were committed during the military rule of then-Cpt. Moussa Dadis Camara.

The panel of judges appointed in 2010 to investigate the massacre has made important strides despite political, financial, and logistical obstacles. They have interviewed more than 400 victims and charged some 15 suspects, including several high-level members of the security forces and the former junta leader, Camara.

While the investigation appeared to enjoy increased political and financial support from the government, the failure to suspend high-level suspects from their government posts, the March appointment of accused Gen. Mathurin Bangoura to the position of governor of Conakry, and the failure to close the investigation, raised concern.

At time of writing several investigative aspects remained outstanding, including the questioning of key witnesses and locating mass graves believed to contain the bodies of some 100 victims who remained unaccounted for.

Accountability for Election-Related Crimes

During 2016, there was little progress in investigating or holding to account members of the security forces or mobs allegedly involved in numerous episodes of political and electoral violence, perpetrated both before and after President Conde took office in 2010.

These include the alleged killing by the security forces of some 130 unarmed demonstrators in 2007, some 60 opposition supporters protesting the delay in holding parliamentary elections in 2013-2014, and at least 10 people in the run-up to the 2015 presidential poll.

There was similarly no accountability for other 2015 election-related abuses including the beating to death of two men and rape of one woman by mobs linked to the opposition, or the extensive looting and destruction of property in markets by mobs associated with the ruling party, at times allegedly in complicity with the security forces.

However, in October, the government agreed to pay reparations to victims of the 2013 political violence, including to the wounded, the families of those killed, and victims of looting and pillage.

Truth-Telling Mechanism and National Human Rights Commission

In August, the Provisional Commission on National Reconciliation (CPRN) submitted its final report to President Conde. The CPRN was established by presidential decree in 2011 to explore the roots of decades of political and communal violence and present a roadmap for addressing them. The report made 22 recommendations, including the creation of an independent truth-telling commission, justice for key perpetrators, and reparations for victims of political and communal violence.

The National Human Rights Commission (INIDH), established in 2015 and mandated by Guinea's 2010 constitution, largely failed to fulfil its mandate and suffered from a lack of credibility as a few commissioners quit amid concerns over lack of fiscal transparency.

Judiciary and Detention Conditions

The year saw the beginning of a major reorganization of the justice system aimed at strengthening its independence, impartiality, and efficiency. The changes are part of a multi-year justice sector reform project and were mandated by a 2015 law which reorganized the judiciary. However, there were concerns that the low budgetary allocation for the judiciary—around 0.5 percent of the national budget—would slow down the implementation of the plan, which mandates the construction and staffing of several new courthouses.

Guinean prisons and detention centers operate far below international standards, with severe overcrowding due to the systematic use of provisional detention, weak case management, and the failure of the courts to meet regularly. Overcrowding and conditions in Guinea's largest detention facility in the capital Conakry, designed for 300 detainees, worsened in 2016 as it regularly accommodated more than 1500. The construction of a new prison to address overcrowding stalled. An estimated 60 percent of prisoners in Guinea are held in prolonged pretrial detention. Unprofessional conduct in the judicial sector, including absenteeism and corruption, contribute to persistent detention-related abuses.

The Superior Council of Judges (Conseil Supérieur de la Magistrature), established in 2015, continued to fulfill its mandate to investigate and discipline judges. During 2016, some 20 cases were investigated by the CSM, and several judges sanctioned for corruption and unprofessional conduct.

Women's and Children's Rights

In September, the Guinean government and local organizations launched a campaign to combat female genital mutilation (FGM). An estimated 97 percent of women and girls aged 15 to 49 years have undergone FGM, despite laws banning and criminalizing the practice. In a rare case in January 2016, three women were tried and convicted in a court in Kankan for performing FGM.

In May, UNICEF, OHCHR, and UNFPA reported that since 2015 more than 50 children have been raped, the majority less than 5 years old.

Legislative and Institutional Framework for Human Rights Protection

In April, Guinea acceded to the Optional Protocol to the Convention on the Rights of the Child on the involvement of children in armed conflict. In July, Guinea's National Assembly passed a new criminal code that abolished the death penalty and, for the first time, criminalized torture.

However, the new code failed to codify several abuses as torture, including electric shocks, stress positions, mock executions, and simulated drowning, defining them instead as "inhumane and cruel" treatment. The new code also retained laws criminalizing and carrying penalties of up to five years for defamation and "insults" directed at public figures, as well as laws criminalizing "unnatural acts," carrying terms of 6 months to 3 years in prison.

Key International Actors

The EU, Guinea's biggest donor, continued to fund programs to strengthen judicial reform and fight impunity, including by supporting victims of the September 2009 crimes. The country office of the UN High Commissioner for Human Rights regularly documented abuses, monitored detention conditions, and supported the human rights and interim reconciliation commissions, but rarely publicly denounced human rights concerns. The UN Peacebuilding Commission funded programs supporting security sector reform, reconciliation, and employment.

UN Special Representative on Sexual Violence in Conflict Zainab Bangura—whose office continued to support accountability for rapes and crimes committed during the 2009 stadium massacre—visited Guinea twice: in April, jointly with US Under Secretary of State for Civilian Security, Democracy, and Human Rights Sarah Sewall, and in August to encourage progress on investigation.

The International Criminal Court (ICC), which in October 2009 confirmed that the situation in Guinea was under preliminary examination, continued to engage the national authorities on progress in the investigation.

Haiti

The continuing political crisis in Haiti, spurred by contested presidential elections in 2015, led to a power vacuum at the head of state. President Michel Martelly's term of office expired in February 2016, and the 120-day term of provisional President Jocelerme Privert expired in June, though he remained in office at time of writing. A new parliament took office in January 2016, after effectively shutting down in 2015, but continued protracted stalemates over presidential and remaining parliamentary elections hampered legislators' ability to tackle pending priorities.

The crisis hindered the Haitian government's ability to meet the basic needs of its people, resolve longstanding human rights problems, or address continuing humanitarian crises, even as a new crisis emerged. In October 2016, Hurricane Matthew, a devastating storm, hit Haiti's southwest. President Privert estimated the losses surpassed the entire national budget and warned of an impending serious food crisis, driven by the loss of crops from the storm.

As of August, authorities had failed to assist many of the 61,000 individuals still living in displacement camps since the 2010 earthquake to resettle or return to their places of origin, and many continued to face environmental risks and the threat of forced evictions. An ongoing drought affecting much of the country pushed the number of people living with food insecurity to one-third of the population.

Haiti's cholera epidemic has claimed more than 9,300 lives and infected more than 780,000 people in five years. There were more than 21,000 suspected cases and, as of July, 200 deaths in 2016. Cholera cases surged in October in the communities most impacted by Hurricane Matthew. In November, an ambitious campaign aimed to vaccinate more than 800,000 people in seven days.

Electoral Crisis

Presidential and run-off parliamentary elections in October 2015 were contested, and second-round elections were deferred multiple times. To thwart a constitutional crisis when President Martelly's term ended on February 7 without an elected successor, Martelly signed an agreement with the president of the Senate and the Chamber of Deputies that established a short-term solution. Prime Minister Evans Paul served in the presidency until the National Assembly selected a provisional president, Jocelerme Privert, to serve for a 120-day term, during which new presidential elections were scheduled. But the April elections were postponed, and Privert's term expired before a successor was elected. At time of writing, Privert was still acting as president.

In June, a special commission confirmed fraud and irregularities in the 2015 presidential and run-off parliamentary elections and scheduled a new first-round presidential election to be held in October. Presidential campaigning began in September. Due to Hurricane Matthew, the elections were further postponed and finally took place November 20. They proceeded without major reported incidents. At time of writing, the outcome of the November elections was not known. If none of the 27 candidates received more than 50 percent of the vote, a run-off election was scheduled for January 29, 2017.

Criminal Justice System

Haiti's prison system remained severely overcrowded, with many inmates living in inhumane conditions. According to United Nations Secretary-General Ban Ki-moon, nearly all of the almost 11,000 inmates in Haiti's national prison system have access to less than one square meter of space and most face 23 hours of confinement a day. Overcrowding is attributed to high numbers of arbitrary arrests and overuse of pretrial detention. According to Ban, more than 70 percent of suspects are held pending trial. Although the UN and international donors have supported several initiatives to reduce the percentage, it barely budged in 2016.

Illiteracy and Barriers to Education

Approximately one in two Haitians age 15 and older is illiterate. The UN independent expert on Haiti said in 2015 that action to eradicate illiteracy is one of the top human rights priorities in Haiti.

More than 200,000 children remain out of primary school in the country. The quality of education is generally low, and 90 percent of schools are run by private entities that charge school fees that can be prohibitively expensive for low-income families. In March, the UN Committee on the Rights of the Child called on Haiti to establish a comprehensive regulatory framework for—and to monitor regularly—private education providers, to ensure that, among other recommendations, they comply with quality standards and regularly report to relevant authorities on their financial operations, including on school fees and salaries.

Accountability for Past Abuses

The Human Rights Committee and the UN independent expert on Haiti have both called on Haiti to continue investigations into financial and human rights crimes allegedly committed during former President Jean-Claude Duvalier's tenure as president from 1971 to 1986. They have called on Haiti to bring to justice all those responsible for serious human rights violations committed during Duvalier's tenure. Allegations of violations include arbitrary detentions, torture, disappearances, summary executions, and forced exile.

Duvalier died in 2014, six months after the Port-of-Prince Court of Appeal ruled that the statute of limitations could not be applied to crimes against humanity and ordered that investigations against him should continue. At time of writing, a reopened investigation into crimes committed by Duvalier's collaborators remained pending.

Violence against Women

Gender-based violence is a widespread problem. Haiti does not have specific legislation domestic violence, sexual harassment, or other forms of violence targeted at women. Rape is only criminalized according to a 2005 ministerial decree. In March, the UN Committee on the Elimination of Discrimination Against Women called on Haiti to expedite the adoption of a draft law on violence against women. The political crisis prevented progress towards consideration of the bill or a similarly pending criminal code reform that would address gaps in protection.

Children's Domestic Labor

Widespread use of child domestic workers—known as restavèk—continues. Restavèks, most of whom are girls, are sent from low-income households to live with wealthier families in the hope that they will be schooled and cared for in exchange for performing light chores. Though difficult to calculate, some estimates suggest that between 225,000 and 300,000 children work as restavèks. These children are often unpaid, denied education, and physically or sexually abused. Haiti's labor code does not set a minimum age for work in domestic services, though the minimum age for work in industrial, agricultural, and commercial enterprises is 15. In March, the UN Committee on the Rights of the Child called on Haiti to criminalize the practice of placing children in domestic service.

Deportation and Statelessness for Dominicans of Haitian Descent

At least 135,000 Dominicans of Haitian descent and Haitian migrants working in the Dominican Republic reentered Haiti between July 2015 and August 2016, after Dominican officials deported more than 27,000 people and another 24,254 were deported without official documentation, others fled under pressure or threat. This occurred in accordance with a controversial 2015 regularization plan for foreigners in the Dominican Republic. Many deportations did not meet international standards and many people have been swept up in arbitrary, summary deportations without any sort of hearing.

Some of the poorest arrivals live in unofficial camps in the Anse a Pitres area, in harsh conditions with little or no access to basic services. Humanitarians relocated 580 families from these camps into housing in April and May 2016.

Key International Actors

The UN Stabilization Mission in Haiti (MINUSTAH) has been operating since 2004 and has contributed to efforts to improve public security, protect vulnerable groups, and strengthen the country's democratic institutions. The UN Security Council has extended MINUSTAH's mandate through April 15, 2017.

In August, prompted by a report of the UN special rapporteur on extreme poverty and human rights, a spokesperson for the UN secretary-general said that MINUSTAH needed "to do more regarding its own involvement in the initial outbreak and the suffering of those affected by cholera."

In October, the special rapporteur formally issued his report, criticizing the UN's Office of Legal Affairs and alleging that the office came up "with patently artificial and wholly unfounded legal pretense for insisting that the [UN] must not take responsibility for what it has done." The same month, the UN deputy secretary general announced the UN's new approach to cholera in Haiti, which included both an intensification to treat and eliminate cholera, and plans to develop a framework for material assistance to those most affected by cholera.

In a special session of the UN General Assembly in December, the UN secretary-general apologized on behalf of the UN. "We simply did not do enough with regard to the cholera outbreak and its spread in Haiti. We are profoundly sorry for our role," he said. He called the provision of material assistance a "concrete expression" of the UN's "regret" for the suffering of many Haitians. Initial responses from victims were positive, although they highlighted that consultations for implementing the UN plans needed to be robust.

In August, an appeal filed in 2013 by the Institute for Justice and Democracy in Haiti and the Bureau des Avocats Internationaux on behalf of 5,000 victims of the epidemic was dismissed in United States federal court. At time of writing, no petition to the US Supreme Court had been filed. To date, there has been no independent adjudication of the facts surrounding the introduction of cholera and the question of the UN's involvement.

According to figures from the UN Office of Internal Oversight Services, at least 102 allegations of sexual abuse or exploitation have been made against MINUSTAH personnel since 2007.

Honduras

Rampant crime and impunity for human rights abuses remain the norm in Honduras. Despite a downward trend in recent years, the murder rate is among the highest in the world. Journalists, peasant activists, and lesbian, gay, bisexual, and transgender (LGBT) individuals are among those most vulnerable to violence. Berta Cáceres, a prominent environmental and indigenous-rights activist, was killed in March 2016; police had failed to investigate threats on her life.

Efforts to reform the institutions responsible for providing public security have made little progress. Marred by corruption and abuse, the judiciary and police remain largely ineffective.

In April, members of a commission created by an agreement between the Organization of American States (OAS) and the government—the Mission to Support the Fight against Corruption and Impunity in Honduras (MACCIH)—began operating in Honduras. The commission's mandate includes selecting and overseeing a group of judges, prosecutors, police officers, and forensic scientists to pursue corruption cases.

Police Abuse and Corruption

The use of lethal force by the national police is a chronic problem. Investigations into police abuses are hindered by inefficiency and corruption; little information about them is made public, and impunity is the rule. Efforts to address endemic corruption have made little progress.

In April, police files surfaced showing that high-level commanders, acting under orders from Winter Blanco, a cartel leader from the Caribbean coast, had ordered the 2009 assassination of the chief of the Anti-Drug Directorate, Julián Arístides González Irías, and, two years later, of his adviser, Alfredo Landaverde. A police-reform commission appointed in response to the revelations announced the removal from active duty of 27 police commanders, including two former chiefs of the national police. Foreign Minister Arturo Corrales, a former security minister, resigned.

President Juan Orlando Hernández has expanded the military's role in combating violent crime. The National Human Rights Commission (CONADEH), in a December 2015 report, listed complaints it has received against the Military Police and Army personnel, alleging abuses that include killings, abductions, torture, rapes, and robberies.

Judicial Independence

Judges face politically motivated intimidation and interference. In December 2012, Congress voted to remove four of the five justices in the Supreme Court's Constitutional Chamber after the justices ruled that a law aimed at addressing police corruption was unconstitutional.

The replacement of the four justices was part of a broader pattern of interference. By December 2014, the Council of Judiciary, established in 2011 with authority to appoint and dismiss judges, had fired 29 and suspended another 28, according to the Inter-American Commission on Human Rights (IACHR), although the basis for disciplinary action and the applicable penalties had yet to be defined by law.

Attacks on Journalists, Lawyers, Human Rights Defenders, Environmental Activists

The IACHR described Honduras in August as "one of the most hostile and dangerous countries for human rights defenders." Journalists, lawyers, and human rights defenders suffer threats, attacks, and killings. Twenty-one journalists were murdered from 2014 through May 2016, according to the National Human Rights Commission (CONADEH). Almost all killings of journalists go unpunished.

In 2015, the government enacted a law that created a 14-member National Council for the Protection of Human Rights Defenders (NCPHRD), as well as a "protection system" headed by the Secretariat of Justice, Human Rights, Governance, and Decentralization. The Committee against Torture (CAT) noted that the NCPHRD is moving slowly on 38 petitions for protection received through May 2016.

In March, Berta Cáceres, an indigenous land rights and environmental defender, was shot dead in her home. Although she had reported to police 33 threats on her life, none were investigated. Cáceres, a member of Honduras' largest indigenous group, the Lenca, had waged a campaign to stop the building of the Agua

Zarca Dam, which the activists condemn as a threat to the Gualcarque River. Five men, including an army major and the manager for social and environmental matters for Desarrollos Energéticos (DESA), the firm contracted to build the dam, were arrested in early May for alleged participation in Cáceres's murder, which prosecutors said was part of a conspiracy with DESA. A sixth suspect was arrested in September.

Criminal Defamation

In July, Honduran television journalist Ariel Armando D'Vicente was convicted of defamation, sentenced to three years in prison, and banned for three years from working as a journalist. The charges arose from a series of reports in 2014, in which D'Vicente linked the police commander of Choluteca Department to cattle smuggling gangs. D'Vicente remains free pending appeal of his conviction.

Sexual Orientation and Gender Identity

Homophobic violence is a major problem in Honduras. In June, several United Nations agencies working in Honduras urged the government to investigate killings of LGBTI activists and noted that sexual violence against LGBTI individuals forces them into "internal displacement" or to flee the country in search of international protection.

Violence against Children

Fear of gang violence drives hundreds of children every year to leave the country and head north, often unaccompanied. According to a report by UNICEF and the National Violence Observatory of the Universidad Nacional Autónoma de Honduras (UNAH), the number of child homicides rose from 434 in 2014 to 570 in 2015.

Prison Conditions

Inhumane conditions, including overcrowding, inadequate nutrition, and poor sanitation, are endemic to Honduran prisons. Designed to hold up to 8,600 inmates, the country's lockups held more than 16,000 in December 2015. Prison guards in many facilities have effectively relinquished control and discipline to the inmates.

Key International Actors

In January, the OAS signed an agreement with the Honduran government creating the Mission to Support the Fight against Corruption and Impunity in Honduras (MACCIH). President Hernández had proposed the collaboration in July 2015, after protests demanding a commission similar to Guatemala's International Commission Against Impunity (CICIG). MACCIH began operating in April.

In November 2015, the Inter-American Court of Human Rights found that Honduras violated the rights of four judges who were dismissed for opposing the 2009 military coup against former President Zelaya. The ruling obligated Honduras to reinstate three of the judges—one had already been reinstated—or, if the government could show reinstatement was not possible, compensate them for lost pay. In response to the ruling, the government claimed that lack of vacant posts prevented reinstatement of the judges, and opted to pay reparations.

The US Congress allotted US$98.3 million in bilateral aid for fiscal year 2016, of which 75 percent was contingent on certification of the government's progress on issues including the protection of human rights, the combatting of corruption, and the strengthening of public institutions.

On September 30, 2016, the Department of State certified to the US Congress that Honduras has taken effective steps to meet the criteria specified in the Fiscal Year 2016 appropriation legislation.

In June, Honduras signed an agreement with the UN High Commissioner for Refugees (UNHCR) for the opening of a UNHCR office to aid in the protection of people internally displaced by violence, as well as refugees who are returned by the US and Mexico.

In May, in response to Cáceres' killing and the filing of charges against an employee of DESA, the Dutch development bank, FMO, and the Finnish Fund for Industrial Cooperation, Finnfund, announced they would withdraw their financing for the Agua Zarca Dam.

India

Limits on free speech and attacks on religious minorities, often led by vigilante groups that claim to be supporters of the ruling Bharatiya Janata Party (BJP), are an increasing concern in India. In 2016, students were accused of sedition for expressing their views; people who raised concerns over challenges to civil liberties were deemed anti-Indian; Dalits and Muslims were attacked on suspicion they had killed, stolen, or sold cows for beef; and nongovernmental organizations (NGOs) came under pressure due to India's restrictive foreign funding regulations.

A crackdown on violent protests in Jammu and Kashmir beginning in July killed over 90 people and injured hundreds, fueling further discontent against government forces. Impunity for police and security forces largely continued amid new allegations of torture and extrajudicial killings, including reports of sexual assault and other abuses by security forces in the central Indian state of Chhattisgarh.

There were also some positive developments in 2016. The Narendra Modi government took steps toward ensuring greater access to financial services such as banking, insurance, and pensions for economically marginalized Indians and launched a campaign to make modern sanitation available to more households. In July, the Supreme Court of India took a strong stand against impunity for security forces, ruling that the Armed Forces (Special Powers) Act (AFSPA) does not protect soldiers from prosecution for abuses committed while deployed in internal armed conflicts. The court also gave new life to a challenge to a discriminatory colonial-era law criminalizing homosexuality.

Security Forces Abuses and Lack of Accountability

Indian law makes it difficult, if not impossible, to prosecute public officials. Section 197 of the Criminal Procedure Code bars courts from recognizing any offenses (except sexual offenses) alleged to have been committed by public servants in the discharge of their official duties unless the central or a state government permits prosecution. In August, a special court discharged Gujarat police officer Rajkumar Pandian from a 2005 extrajudicial killing case under this provision. Pandian was the 12th defendant to be discharged in the case.

HUMAN
RIGHTS
WATCH

"Bound by Brotherhood"
India's Failure to End Killings in Police Custody

In rare cases in 2016, police were held accountable for abuses. In January, four policemen in Mumbai were sentenced to seven years in prison for their role in the death of a 20-year-old man in police custody. In April, 47 policemen were sentenced to life in prison for involvement in the killing of 11 Sikhs in 1991 in the Pilibhit district of Uttar Pradesh state.

Despite calls for repeal of the Armed Forces Special Powers Act, soldiers continue to have immunity from prosecution when deployed in areas of internal conflict. In July 2016, however, the Supreme Court of India, in a decision ordering an investigation into 1,528 cases of alleged extrajudicial killings in Manipur state, ruled that the AFSPA does not provide immunity to security force personnel who use excessive or retaliatory force, and that every alleged extrajudicial killing should be investigated. The confession of a Manipuri policeman in January that he had acted on orders to kill more than 100 suspected militants between 2002 and 2009 exposed how police had adopted illegal practices long associated with the army and paramilitary forces.

In October, authorities resisted calls for investigation into the killing of eight prisoners who escaped a high security prison in Madhya Pradesh state, fueling concerns that any wrongdoing by police would go unpunished.

Violent protests erupted in July after the killing of Burhan Wani and two other Hizb-ul-Mujahedin militants in an armed exchange with government forces in Jammu and Kashmir. In all, over 90 protesters and two police officers were killed, and hundreds of others were injured. The Central Reserve Police Force, a paramilitary unit, defended the use of shot guns that fired pellets and resulted in hundreds of eye injuries, even as it told the Jammu and Kashmir High Court that "it was difficult to follow the standard operating procedure given the nature of the protests."

Security forces operating against Maoist insurgents continue to be accused of serious human rights violations, including sexual assault. Numerous tribal villagers have been arbitrarily arrested as Maoist sympathizers. In July, security forces in Odisha killed five tribal villagers, including a 2-year-old child, claiming they were killed in crossfire during anti-Maoist operations, an assertion disputed by the National Commission of Scheduled Tribes.

In June, after 21-year-old tribal woman Madkam Hidke was killed in an alleged gunfight with armed Maoists in Chhattisgarh's Sukma district, family members and rights activists alleged that security personnel had forcibly picked her up from her home, gang raped her, and then killed her. In August, security forces killed a 19-year-old in Bastar region in Chhattisgarh in what activists alleged was an extrajudicial killing.

Treatment of Dalits, Tribal Groups, and Religious Minorities

Hindu vigilante groups attacked Muslims and Dalits over suspicions that they had killed, stolen, or sold cows for beef. The violence took place amid an aggressive push by several BJP leaders and militant Hindu groups to protect cows and ban beef consumption.

In March 2016 in Jharkhand state, a Muslim cattle trader, Mohammed Mazlum Ansari, 35, and a 12-year-old boy, Mohammed Imteyaz Khan, were found hanging from a tree, their hands tied behind their backs and their bodies bruised. In August, a man was killed in Karnataka state by members of a nationalist Hindu group while transporting cows.

In July, four men in Gujarat were stripped, tied to a car, and publicly beaten with sticks and belts over suspicions of cow slaughter.

The government's continuing failure to rein in militant groups, combined with inflammatory remarks made by some BJP leaders, has contributed to the impression that leaders are indifferent to growing intolerance.

A 2016 report on caste-based discrimination by the UN special rapporteur on minority issues noted that caste-affected groups continue to suffer exclusion and dehumanization. In January, the suicide of Rohith Vemula, a 25-year-old Dalit student, drew renewed attention to entrenched caste-based discrimination in Indian society, and sparked nationwide protests by students and activists calling for reforms in higher education.

In June, a special court in Gujarat convicted 24 people for their involvement in the mass killing of 69 people by a Hindu mob in Gulberg Society, a Muslim neighborhood in Ahmedabad, during the 2002 Gujarat riots. While pronouncing the verdict, the court called the killings the "darkest day in the history of civil society." But some victims' families, lawyers, and rights activists criticized the acquittals of senior BJP leaders and a police official.

Freedom of Speech

Authorities continue to use sedition and criminal defamation laws to prosecute citizens who criticize government officials or oppose state policies. In a blow to free speech, the government in 2016 argued before the Supreme Court in favor of retaining criminal penalties for defamation. The court upheld the law.

In February, authorities arrested three students at the Jawaharlal Nehru University in Delhi under the sedition law for alleged anti-national speech, acting on complaints by members of the Akhil Bharatiya Vidyarthi Parishad (ABVP), the student wing of the ruling BJP. These arrests led to widespread protests over the arbitrary use of the sedition law.

In August, police in southern Karnataka state filed a sedition case against Amnesty International India based on a complaint by ABVP, alleging that anti-Indian slogans were raised at a meeting organized by Amnesty on abuses in Kashmir. Police later claimed, however, that they did not have sufficient evidence to proceed with charges. The same month, an actor-turned-politician in the state also faced sedition charge after she praised the friendship and courtesy she received in Pakistan.

In August, the Karnataka High Court called the state government "clearly paranoid" for pressing sedition charges against three people, including two former policemen, for organizing a protest seeking better police wages and working conditions.

In Chhattisgarh, journalists, lawyers, and civil society activists faced harassment and arrest. In March, the Editors Guild of India reported that media in Chhattisgarh state were "working under tremendous pressure" from authorities, Maoist rebels, and vigilante groups.

Civil Society and Freedom of Association

The Modi government continues to use the Foreign Contribution Regulation Act (FCRA), which regulates foreign funding for civil society organizations, to cut off funds and stymie the activities of organizations that question or criticize the gov-

HUMAN
RIGHTS
WATCH

STIFLING DISSENT
The Criminalization of Peaceful Expression in India

ernment or its policies. In April 2016, Maina Kiai, the UN special rapporteur on freedom of assembly and association, analyzed the FCRA and said that restrictions imposed by the law and its rules "are not in conformity with international law, principles and standards."

In May, the government temporarily suspended the FCRA status of the Lawyers Collective, an organization founded by Indira Jaising, a former additional solicitor general, and her husband, Anand Grover, a former UN special rapporteur on the right to health. The Lawyers Collective accused the government of attempting to disempower and weaken the organization because of its work assisting people in cases challenging Modi government policies. In June, three UN special rapporteurs released a statement raising concerns over the suspension and calling on the government to repeal FCRA. In November, the government refused to renew FCRA for 25 NGOs, including several prominent human rights groups.

Even as authorities were using FCRA to tighten restrictions on NGOs, the government amended the law in March to retroactively legalize funding by foreign entities to political parties.

Women's Rights

Despite some high-profile rape and sexual assault prosecutions, new reports of gang rapes, domestic violence, acid attacks, and murders of women in 2016 continued to spotlight the need for concerted government action to improve women's safety and ensure prompt police investigation of such crimes. Women and girls with disabilities in particular continue to face barriers to accessing justice for violence against them.

In March, the Bombay High Court directed the Maharashtra state government to ensure that women are not denied entry to any place of worship that allows men access. Following the decision, two temples in the state opened their inner sanctum to women. In August, the High Court further ordered that women be allowed to enter the Mumbai-based Muslim shrine, Haji Ali. A case pending before the Supreme Court at time of writing will determine whether women of menstrual age are allowed to enter the Kerala-based Sabarimala Ayyappa Hindu temple. Sabarimala is one of the few Hindu temples to restrict entry of women aged 10 to 50, saying menstruating women are impure. In April, the Supreme Court had observed that "[g]ender discrimination in such a matter is unacceptable."

In October, the government told the Supreme Court that the practice of triple talaq (giving Muslim men the right to unilaterally divorce their wives by uttering the phrase "I divorce you" three times), a part of Muslim personal law, violates fundamental constitutional rights and inhibits gender equality. The government's statement was made in response to petitions filed by the organization Muslim Women's Quest for Equality and others seeking to have triple talaq deemed unconstitutional.

Children's Rights

In January 2016, the new Juvenile Justice Act came into force, permitting prosecution of 16- and 17-year-olds in adult court when charged with serious crimes such as rape and murder. The law was enacted despite strong opposition from children's rights activists and the National Commission for Protection of Child Rights.

In July, the parliament approved a new law against child labor that bans all forms of employment of children below age 14, with an exception for children of all ages who work in family enterprises where such work does not interfere with their schooling. Indian activists opposed the law saying it left children from poor and marginalized communities open to exploitation in the absence of effective implementation of the right to education law, emphasizing that most child labor occurs invisibly within families.

Violent protests in Kashmir that began in July 2016 led to disruption in children's education as schools were forced to close for months; at least 32 schools were burned down and several were taken over by paramilitary forces who set up temporary camps inside.

Sexual Orientation and Gender Identity

In February 2016, the Supreme Court of India allowed a challenge to section 377 of the penal code to proceed, referring the case to a five-judge bench. The colonial-era provision, which the court had upheld in 2013, criminalizes same-sex relations between adults. In June, several well-known LGBT professionals filed a petition in Supreme Court arguing that section 377 violates the right to life and personal liberty.

In August, the government introduced a new bill in parliament on the rights of transgender persons. The bill was flawed, however, by provisions that were inconsistent with the 2014 Supreme Court ruling that recognized transgender individuals as a third gender and found them eligible for quotas in jobs and education.

Rights of People with Disabilities

Women and girls with psychosocial or intellectual disabilities in India continue to be locked up in overcrowded and unsanitary state mental hospitals and residential institutions, without their consent, due to stigma and the absence of adequate community-based support and mental health services. After a Human Rights Watch report revealed the range of abuses such women face in institutions, the National Commission for Women took up its first-ever study of the issue.

India's Upper House of Parliament passed a new mental health bill in August 2016. The law fails, however, to comply fully with the United Nations Convention on the Rights of Persons with Disabilities, including its provision that people with disabilities should enjoy legal capacity on an equal basis with others in all aspects of life, with appropriate measures to provide support they may require in exercising their legal capacity.

Death Penalty

There were no executions in 2016, but some 385 prisoners remained on death row. Most of the prisoners belong to marginalized communities or religious minorities. Indian courts have recognized that the death penalty has been imposed disproportionately and in a discriminatory manner against disadvantaged groups in India.

Foreign Policy

Relations between India and Pakistan deteriorated in 2016. Following the outbreak of renewed violence in Jammu and Kashmir in July, the government of Pakistan called on the UN secretary-general for an independent inquiry and plebiscite under UN supervision.

The Indian government rejected Pakistan's allegations and request, accusing Pakistan of stirring up trouble in the region and of using terrorism as an instrument of state policy. Meanwhile, Prime Minister Narendra Modi called attention to what he called "atrocities" committed by Pakistan in Balochistan and Pakistan-administered Kashmir in his speeches, including on India's Independence Day. Tensions further escalated in September after the Indian government claimed its security forces had attacked militant sites inside Pakistan in response to an attack on an Indian army base in Jammu and Kashmir that killed 19 soldiers.

India's voting record on rights issues at the UN was disappointing. In May, the government abstained from voting on a bid by the Committee to Protect Journalists, an international press freedom group, for UN accreditation. In July, the government abstained on a resolution that created a UN expert post to address discrimination against LGBT persons and voted in favor of amendments to weaken the mandate, saying India's Supreme Court was still to decide on the issue of lesbian, gay, bisexual, and transgender (LGBT) rights.

India pushed Nepal to adopt an inclusive constitution that accommodated the aspirations of minority groups in the southern plains adjoining the Indian border. India continued to press Sri Lanka to address the demands of minority Tamils.

India and US strengthened security collaboration. In July, Modi addressed a joint session of the US Congress, noting a shared commitment to combating climate change and terrorism.

In October, India hosted the BRICS (Brazil, Russia, India, China and South Africa) summit. While the prime minister spoke of partnering to address security challenges and economic uncertainties, there was no mention of working to uphold international human rights principles.

In October, India ratified the Paris agreement on climate change, which 195 countries adopted in December 2015.

Key International Actors

A US Congressional Commission held a hearing in July 2016 on the human rights situation in India, coinciding with Modi's visit to Washington. The hearing spotlighted issues of violence against marginalized communities and religious minorities such as Muslims and Christians.

A 2016 report by the US Commission on International Religious Freedom said religious tolerance had "deteriorated" and "religious freedom violations" had increased in India. During his visit to India in June, US Senator Ben Cardin, a ranking member of the Senate Foreign Relations Committee, expressed concerns over religious intolerance, anti-conversion laws, and extrajudicial killings in the country. In August, during his India visit, US Secretary of State John Kerry emphasized the need to protect the rights to freedom of expression and peaceful protest.

In a joint statement following the India-European Union summit in March attended by Modi and the heads of European Council and European Commission, the leaders "highlighted the need for efforts to ensure gender equality and respect for women and girls' human rights."

In August, UN High Commissioner for Human Rights Zeid Ra'ad al-Hussein expressed regret at the failure of Indian and Pakistani authorities to grant his office access to Jammu and Kashmir for a fact-finding visit. "Without access, we can only fear the worst," he said.

HUMAN
RIGHTS
WATCH

LIVING IN HELL
Abuses against People with Psychosocial Disabilities in Indonesia

Indonesia

President Joko "Jokowi" Widodo's rhetorical support for human rights has yet to translate into meaningful policy initiatives to address the country's serious rights problems. In 2016, Jokowi notably failed to speak out against or otherwise address discriminatory statements and policies issued by senior government and military officials that have fueled violations of the rights of religious minorities and the country's lesbian, gay, bisexual, and transgender (LGBT) population.

Religious minorities in Indonesia continue to face discriminatory regulations and violent attacks by Islamist militant groups. Impunity for the security forces in the provinces of Papua and West Papua also remains a serious problem and dozens of Papuans remain imprisoned for nonviolent expression of their political views.

In April 2016, the government broke a decades-long taboo on open discussion of the state-backed massacres of up to 1 million alleged Communists and others in 1965-1966, hosting a symposium for survivors and victim's families to challenge the official narrative that the killings were a heroic defense of the nation against a Communist plot to overthrow the government.

However, the government has provided no details of an officially mooted accountability process for the massacres, including when it might begin operations. Jokowi's decision in July 2016 to appoint as security minister former General Wiranto, indicted by a UN-supported tribunal for crimes against humanity, has heightened concerns about his administration's commitment to human rights and accountability.

Jokowi continues to be outspoken in his support for the death penalty, making execution of convicted drug traffickers a symbol of his resolve as a leader. Indonesia executed four convicted drug traffickers in July 2016, but ordered a last-minute delay in the executions of 10 other death row prisoners pending a "comprehensive review" of their cases. The government has indicated that executions will continue in 2017.

Freedom of Religion

In January, Indonesian officials and security forces were complicit in the violent forced eviction of more than 7,000 members of the Gerakan Fajar Nusantara religious community, known as Gafatar, from their homes in East and West Kaliman-tan.

Human Rights Watch research found that security forces failed to protect mem-bers of Gafatar, standing by while mobs from the ethnic Malay and Dayak com-munities looted and destroyed properties owned by group members, many of whom originally came from Java. Government officials transferred Gafatar mem-bers to unofficial detention centers and then to their home towns, not as a short-term safety measure, but apparently to end their presence on the island and dissolve the religious group.

In March 2016, the Jokowi administration issued a decree banning Gafatar activi-ties; punishments for violations include a maximum five-year prison term. The government also arrested three Gafatar leaders who face possible prison terms of life imprisonment on charges of blasphemy and treason.

In January 2016, local government authorities banned the activities of the Ah-madiyah religious community in Subang, West Java. Neither Jokowi nor other na-tional officials spoke out or intervened to lift the ban. That same month, local government officials on Bangka Island, located off the east coast of Sumatra, in-structed the island's Ahmadiyah community to convert to Sunni Islam or face forcible expulsion from the area. Neither Jokowi nor other central government of-ficials spoke out in defense of the beleaguered Ahmadiyah communities.

In July 2016, a mob in the city of Tanjung Balai in northern Sumatra attacked and inflicted serious damage on three Buddhist temples associated with the city's ethnic Chinese community. Police deny that the attack was sectarian and ar-rested seven suspects in the attack.

Women's and Girls' Rights

In June 2016, Indonesia's Minister of Home Affairs Tjahjo Kumolo backtracked on his commitment to abolish rights-violating local and regional Sharia (Islamic law) regulations. Although his office annulled 3,143 other "problematic regional regulations" for violating the country's credo of "unity in diversity" and although Indonesian law stipulates that regulation of religion is for national, not regional or local authorities, the ministry left in place all existing Sharia provisions, many of them discriminatory.

Indonesia's official Commission on Violence against Women reported that, as of August 2016, the number of discriminatory national and local regulations targeting women had risen to 422, from 389 at the end of 2015. They include local laws compelling women and girls to don the hijab, or headscarf, in schools, government offices, and public spaces. While many of these laws require traditional Sunni Muslim garb both for women and men, research by Human Rights Watch indicates they disproportionately target women.

A local bylaw implemented in August in Sumedang, West Java, forbids anyone with an "eye-catching appearance" from going out alone at night. The municipal government justified the regulation on the basis that it would help discourage sexual activity.

Papua

The Jokowi administration has repeatedly said it intends to take a new approach to Indonesia's easternmost provinces, Papua and West Papua ("Papua"), home to a low-level insurgency and a peaceful pro-independence movement, including by addressing human rights concerns. The reality has not matched the rhetoric.

In April 2016, the government announced that it would seek accountability for 11 high-priority past human rights cases in Papua. They include the Biak massacre in July 1998 when security forces opened fire on participants at a peaceful flag-raising ceremony on the island, the military crackdown on Papuans in Wasior in 2001 and Wamena in 2003 that left dozens killed and thousands displaced, and the forced break-up of the Papuan People's Congress in October 2011 that left three people dead and hundreds injured. However, the government has not provided any details as to when, where, and how the cases would be addressed.

Indonesian authorities continue to restrict access by foreign journalists and rights monitors to the region. In January 2016, the Indonesian Embassy in Bangkok informed Bangkok-based France 24 correspondent Cyril Payen that it had denied his application for a journalist's visa for a reporting trip to Papua.

Indonesian government officials justified the visa rejection on the basis that Payen's previous reporting, which focused on pro-independence sentiment in the region, was "biased and unbalanced." Rather than engaging with Payen and France 24 to publicly challenge any inaccuracies in the previous reporting, au-

HUMAN
RIGHTS
WATCH

"These Political Games
Ruin Our Lives"
Indonesia's LGBT Community Under Threat

thorities threatened to deny visas to Payen and any other France 24 journalists seeking to report from the country. Payen's case highlights the gap between Jokowi's announced "opening" of Papua to foreign media and the reality facing journalists still blocked from reporting there.

On May 2, Indonesian police detained more than 1,500 supporters of Papuan independence for "lacking a permit to hold a rally." Police released the detainees after several hours without charge, but their detention underlines the official lack of tolerance for peaceful expression of political aspirations in Papua. At the end of August 2016, 37 Papuan activists remained imprisoned after being convicted of rebellion or treason (*"makar"*), many for nonviolent "crimes" such as public display of the pro-independence Morning Star flag.

Sexual Orientation and Gender Identity

Starting in January 2016, high-ranking Indonesian officials made a series of vitriolic anti-LGBT statements and policy pronouncements, fueling increased threats and at times violent attacks on LGBT activists and individuals, primarily by Islamist militants. In some cases, the threats and violence occurred in the presence, and with the tacit support, of government officials or security forces.

State institutions, including the National Broadcasting Commission and the National Child Protection Commission, issued censorship directives banning information and broadcasts that portrayed the lives of LGBT people as "normal" as well as so-called propaganda about LGBT lives. Ministries proposed discriminatory and regressive anti-LGBT laws.

In July and August, the Constitutional Court heard a petition that proposed amending the criminal code to criminalize sex outside of marriage and same-sex sexual relations. During the initial hearings, the petitioners—led by a group called the Family Love Alliance—put forward ill-informed and bigoted testimony similar to the anti-LGBT rhetoric espoused by Indonesian officials and politicians earlier in the year. The government, the respondent in the case, said criminalizing sex out of wedlock would make "the sinner a criminal, and the government authoritarian," a view echoed in testimony by the National Commission on Violence Against Women and other groups opposed to the petition. At time of writing the court had not yet ruled on the petition.

HUMAN
RIGHTS
WATCH

"The Harvest is in My Blood"
Hazardous Child Labor in Tobacco Farming in Indonesia

Military Reform and Impunity

Indonesia's Attorney General Muhammad Prasetyo announced in May 2015 that the government would form a "Reconciliation Commission" to seek a "permanent solution for all unresolved human rights abuses" of the past half century. Prasetyo said the cases would include the state-sanctioned massacres of 1965-1966, in which the military and military-backed vigilantes killed up to 1 million people.

The government provided no further details of when the "Reconciliation Commission" might begin operations or how the process of accountability would proceed. Paramilitary and nationalist groups that oppose accountability have criticized calls for redress for past rights abuses as an attempt "to revive communism."

Jokowi's July 2016 decision to appoint Wiranto, indicted as a crimes against humanity suspect by a UN-backed tribunal, as security minister heightened concerns about the Jokowi administration's commitment to human rights and accountability.

Children's Rights

Thousands of children in Indonesia, some just 8 years old, are working in hazardous conditions on tobacco farms. Child tobacco workers are exposed to nicotine, handle toxic chemicals, use sharp tools, lift heavy loads, and work in extreme heat. The work can have lasting consequences for their health and development. Indonesian and multinational tobacco companies buy tobacco grown in Indonesia, but none do enough to ensure that children are not doing hazardous work on farms in their supply chains. Human Rights Watch has called on the Indonesian government and tobacco companies to prohibit children from work that involves direct contact with tobacco, inspect farms to ensure children are not in danger, and carry out an extensive public education and training program to raise awareness of the health risks to children of work in tobacco farming.

Disability Rights

Despite a 1977 government ban on the practice, more than 18,000 people with psychosocial disabilities (mental health conditions) in Indonesia are currently subjected to *pasung*—being shackled or locked up in small confined spaces— sometimes for months or years at a time.

Due to prevalent stigma and the absence of adequate community-based support services or mental health care, people with psychosocial disabilities often end up locked-up in overcrowded and unsanitary institutions without their consent, where they face abuse ranging from physical and sexual violence to involuntary treatment including shackling, electroshock therapy, isolation, and forced contraception.

The Rights of Persons with Disabilities Bill was passed by the Indonesian parliament in March 2016. While the bill represents a major advancement, it does not fully comply with the UN Convention on the Rights of Persons with Disabilities, which Indonesia ratified in 2011.

During a meeting with Human Rights Watch in April 2016, Indonesia's minister of health, Nila Moeloek, orally committed to providing mental health medication in all 9,500 community health centers (*puskesmas*) across the country. Government implementation of this commitment could help turn the tide against shackling.

Refugees and Asylum Seekers

In June, the government acceded to international pressure and allowed a boatload of 44 Sri Lankans stranded on a beach in northern Aceh province to come ashore and receive assistance from UN and International Organization for Migration personnel. The decision followed a 10-day standoff in which Indonesian authorities refused to allow the group to disembark and instead insisted that the boat leave Indonesian waters after being resupplied and refueled.

According to UN refugee agency data, as of February 2016 there were 13,829 refugees and asylum seekers in Indonesia, all living in legal limbo because Indonesia is not a party to the Refugee Convention and lacks an asylum law. This number included 4,723 people detained in immigration centers, including unaccompanied children.

Key International Actors

Jokowi's support for the use of the death penalty against convicted drug traffickers has strained ties over the past year with close bilateral allies, including Australia. The likelihood of more executions in 2017 will continue to make that issue a sore point in Indonesia's foreign relations.

A July 2016 decision by a UN-backed tribunal in The Hague against China's claims in the South China Sea will bolster and ensure the continuance of joint military exercises and intelligence sharing with the United States in 2017. Indonesia's own claims of an exclusive economic zone in that area may fuel more disputes between Indonesian navy patrols and Chinese fishing boats in the coming year. However, the Indonesian government's passive and active complicity in hateful anti-LGBT rhetoric and moves toward discriminatory legislation over the past year will likely continue to be an irritant in US ties.

In August, the US government called on Indonesia to "respect and uphold international rights and standards" after Jokowi's spokesman Johan Budi declared that there was "no room" for the LGBT community in Indonesia.

Iran

Despite three years in his office, President Hassan Rouhani has not delivered on his campaign promise of greater respect for civil and political rights. Executions, especially for drug-related offenses, continued at a high rate. As Rouhani faces elections for a second term in May 2017, the hardline factions that dominate the security apparatus and judiciary continued to crackdown on citizens for the legitimate exercise of their rights, in blatant disregard of international and domestic legal standards. Iranian dual nationals and citizens returning from abroad were at particular risk of arrest by intelligence authorities, accused of being "Western agents."

Executions, Freedom from Torture, and Inhuman Treatment

Despite an initial slowdown in executions in the first months of 2016, authorities had executed at least 203 individuals by October 25. Human rights groups, however, report that the number might be as high as 437, with most executions taking place in the second half of the year. According to government authorities, individuals convicted of drug charges constitute the majority of those executed in the country.

Under Iranian law, many nonviolent crimes, such as "insulting the Prophet," apostasy, same-sex relations, adultery, and drug-related offenses, are punishable by death. In December 2015, members of Parliament introduced a bill to eliminate the death penalty for drug offences that do not involve violence. However, the initiative, while welcomed by several authorities, has not moved forward.

On August 2, authorities announced that they had executed at least 20 alleged members of a group Iran considers a terrorist organization on charges of *moharebeh*, or "enmity against God." Rights groups believe that these individuals were among a group of 33 Sunni Kurdish men arrested in 2009 and 2010, and sentenced to death in unfair trials after enduring abuses and torture in detention. In August, authorities in Khuzestan province executed three Arab citizens on alleged terrorism charges.

New amendments to Iran's penal code allow judges to use their discretion not to sentence children to death. However, Iran continued to execute children in 2016. On July 18, Amnesty International reported that authorities had hanged Hassan Afshar, who was arrested when he was 17 years old and convicted of "forced male to male anal intercourse" (*lavat-e be onf*). At least 49 inmates on death row were convicted of crimes committed when they were under 18 years old.

In March, the United Nations Children's Rights Committee noted that flogging was still a lawful punishment for boys and girls convicted of certain crimes. The committee noted reports that lesbian, gay, bisexual, transgender, and intersex (LGBTI) children had been subjected to electric shocks to "cure" them.

On May 25, Iranian media reported that authorities had flogged 17 miners in Western Azarbaijan province after their employer sued them for protesting the firing of fellow workers.

Fair Trials and Treatment of Prisoners

Iranian courts, and particularly the revolutionary courts, regularly fell short of providing fair trials and allegedly used confessions obtained under torture as evidence in court. Iranian law restricts the right for a defendant to access a lawyer, particularly during the investigation period.

According to Iran's criminal procedure code, individuals charged with national or international security crimes, political and media crimes, and those charged with crimes that incur capital punishment, life imprisonment, or retributive punishment (*qisas*), can be denied legal counsel under detention for up to a week. Moreover, they have to select their counsel from a pool of preapproved lawyers determined by the head of the judiciary.

Several political prisoners and individuals charged with national security crimes suffered from a lack of adequate access to medical care under detention. In April, Omid Kokabee, a young physicist who was sentenced to 10 years in prison in 2012, underwent surgery to remove his right kidney due to complications from cancer after authorities unduly delayed his access to appropriate medical treatment.

Freedom of Expression and Information

Space for free speech and dissent remained highly restricted, and authorities continued to arrest and charge journalists, bloggers, and online media activists for exercising their right to freedom of expression.

In April, a revolutionary court sentenced journalists Afarin Chitsaz, Ehsan Mazandarani, and Saman Safarzaei to terms of ten, seven, and five years, respectively, and Davoud Assadi, the brother of Houshang Assadi, a journalist who lives in France, to five years. Mazandarani's and Chitsaz's sentences were reduced to two and five years, respectively, by the appeals court. The intelligence branch of the Revolutionary Guards Corps (IRGC) arrested the four individuals, along with journalist Issa Saharkhiz, accusing them of being part of an "infiltration network" colluding with foreign media.

In June, the country began implementing a political crime law which, while a step forward in granting fair trials, could still limit free speech. According to the law, insulting or defaming public officials, when "committed to achieve reforms and not intended to target the system, are considered political crimes." However, political prisoners have to be detained separately from ordinary criminals and have to be tried publicly in the presence of a jury unless doing so is deemed detrimental to family disputes, national security, or religious and ethnic sentiment.

Hundreds of websites, including social media platforms such as Facebook and Twitter, remained blocked in Iran. The intelligence apparatus heavily monitored citizens' activities on social media. Hundreds of social media users, in particular on the Telegram messaging application and Instagram have been summoned or arrested by the IRGC for commenting on controversial issues, including fashion.

In the past year, the police and judiciary prevented dozens of musical concerts, particularly those featuring female vocalists and musicians, in different provinces.

Freedoms of Association, Assembly, and Voting

In February, millions of Iranians participated in elections for Parliament and the Assembly of Experts. In the lead-up to these elections, the Guardian Council, the body in charge of vetting candidates, disqualified the majority of candidates associated with the reformist movement based on discriminatory and arbitrary criteria. After the election, in an unprecedented move, the council disqualified Minoo Khaleghi, who had been elected in the city of Isfahan, on allegations of shaking hands with a man.

Authorities continue to target independent unionists and restrict freedom of assembly and association.

On February 22, a revolutionary court sentenced Ismail Abdi, secretary general of the Teachers' Association who has been detained since June 2015, to six years in prison, in part for organizing a teachers' demonstration in front of the Parliament on May 15.

On July 27, 92 student organizations published a letter to President Rouhani criticizing the persistent "atmosphere of fear and intimidation" in Iran's universities following the cancelation of student programs or the unlawful interference in the agendas of these programs by non-university authorities. While student and women's rights activist, Bahareh Hedayat was released from prison after six-and-a-half years in September, Zia Nabavi a prominent student activist remained in prison. Both had been jailed since 2009 for their peaceful activism following the presidential election that year.

Human Rights Defenders and Political Prisoners

Scores of human rights defenders and political activists such as Abdolfattah Soltani remained in prison for their peaceful activities. In May, a revolutionary court sentenced prominent Iranian human rights activist Narges Mohammadi, who had been detained for a year, to a total of 16 years in prison for charges including "membership in the banned campaign Step by Step to Stop the Death Penalty."

In 2010, a revolutionary court sentenced Mohammadi to six years in prison for her rights-related activities, but authorities released her due to a serious medical condition from which she still suffers.

In May, prominent Kurdish human rights defender Mohammad Sediq Kaboudvand, the former president of the Human Rights Organization of Kurdistan, embarked on a hunger strike in his ninth year of detention to protest new charges that were brought against him.

Prominent opposition figures Mir Hossein Mousavi, Zahra Rahnavard, and Mehdi Karroubi have remained under house arrest without charge or trial since February 2011. Tehran's prosecutor, who has banned media from publishing the name of Iran's former president, Mohamad Khatami, also prohibited him from attending several public gatherings.

Women's Rights

Iranian women face discrimination in personal status matters related to marriage, divorce, inheritance, and child custody. A woman needs her male guardian's approval for marriage regardless of her age and cannot pass on her nationality to her foreign-born spouse or their children. Married women may not obtain a passport or travel outside the country without the written permission of their husbands.

The UN Children's Rights Committee reported in March that the age of marriage for girls is 13, that sexual intercourse with girls as young as nine lunar years was not criminalized, and that judges had discretion to release some perpetrators of so-called honor killings without any punishment. Child marriage—though not the norm—continues, as the law allows girls to marry at 13 and boys at age 15, as well as at younger ages if authorized by a judge.

Authorities continue to prevent girls and women from attending certain sporting events, including men's soccer and volleyball matches.

On July 31, 2016, President Rouhani suspended the hiring exam for public sector jobs to investigate apparent discrimination against women in the job market.

Treatment of Minorities

The government denies freedom of religion to Baha'is and discriminates against them. At least 85 Baha'is were held in Iran's prisons as of October 2016. Security forces also continued to target Christian converts of Muslim heritage, as well as members of the "house church" movement who gather to worship in private homes.

In August, a number of Sunni figures in Kurdish areas were summoned and interrogated after they criticized the executions of at least 20 individuals on August 2.

The government restricted cultural as well as political activities among the country's Azeri, Kurdish, Arab, and Baluch minorities. However, in August participants in the national entrance examinations for universities in Iran were allowed to choose Kurdish and Turkish languages as their majors at the bachelor level. Last year, the University of Kurdistan reportedly accepted 40 students to study the Kurdish language at the bachelor level.

Key International Actors

On January 16, Iran and its international partners announced the "implementation day" of the nuclear agreement, known as the Joint Comprehensive Plan of Action, and the subsequent lifting of economic and financial sanctions related to Iran's nuclear activities. Since the agreement, several trade delegations have shuttled between Iran and other countries, particularly in Europe.

The Iranian government continued to provide the Syrian government with military assistance in 2016. Human Rights Watch has documented a pattern of deliberate and indiscriminate attacks on civilians as well as torture by the Syrian government. On August 15, media reports claimed that Russia had used an Iranian military base in city of Hamedan for its airstrikes in Syria.

On April 16, European Union High Representative and Vice-President of the European Commission Federica Mogherini and Iranian Foreign Minister Mohammad Javad Zarif announced in a joint statement that the EU and Iran intend to cooperate on human rights, migration, and drugs.

On October 25, the EU Parliament adopted the report on EU strategy towards Iran after the nuclear agreement in which it expressed concerns about the alarming rate of executions in Iran and called for the release of all political prisoners.

In September, the United Nations Human Rights Council elected Asma Jahangir as the new special rapporteur on the situation of human rights in Iran. Iran did not allow Jahangir's predecessor, Ahmed Shaheed, who was appointed in 2011, to visit the country.

339

HUMAN
RIGHTS
WATCH

MARKED WITH AN "X"
Iraqi Kurdish Forces' Destruction of Villages, Homes
in Conflict with ISIS

Iraq

Clashes with the Islamic State (also known as ISIS) intensified in 2016, including operations to retake Ramadi in February and Fallujah in June, and the beginning of operations in October to retake Mosul, where fighting displaced over 45,000 Iraqis as of November 11. Credible allegations emerged of summary executions, beatings of men in custody, enforced disappearances, and mutilation of corpses by government forces during the operation in Fallujah.

ISIS executed hundreds in and around Mosul, and used civilians there as human shields.

According to the United Nations Assistance Mission in Iraq (UNAMI), since January 2016 airstrikes, explosions, gunfire, or suicide attacks killed at least 9,153 Iraqis. A 2016 International Federation of Journalists report deemed Iraq the deadliest country in the world for journalists and a UNICEF report deemed it one of the deadliest for children.

ISIS Abuses

A joint UNAMI and Office of the United Nations High Commissioner for Human Rights (OHCHR) report from January said that ISIS had kidnapped between 800 and 900 children in Mosul for religious and military training.

ISIS carried out over a dozen suicide and car bombings throughout 2016. In its deadliest attack on July 3 a car bombing in Baghdad killed over 200 people and injuring hundreds more. On July 7, ISIS carried out a triple suicide attack on a Shia shrine in Balad, 100 km north of Baghdad, killing at least 35 and wounding over 60.

In September and October, ISIS launched at least three chemical attacks on the Iraqi town of Qayyarah, south of Mosul. The use of toxic chemicals as a means of warfare is a serious threat to civilians and combatants and is a war crime.

As the operation to retake Mosul began, ISIS started forcibly evacuating civilians under their control with its fighters apparently using them as human shields.

There were regular, but for the most part unconfirmed, media reports during the year of executions carried out by ISIS. In November in Hammam al-Alil, 30 kilometers southeast of Mosul, authorities discovered an ISIS mass grave containing the remains of between 50 and 100 bodies. As the battle for Mosul intensified, Human Rights Watch received reports of ISIS carrying out hundreds of executions of former Iraqi Security Forces in territory still under their control.

ISIS's Diwan al-Hisba (Moral Policing Administration) and online media apparatuses have publicly announced 27 executions of allegedly gay men, at least nine of them in Iraq. The main method ISIS used to execute these men has been to throw them off the roofs of high-rise buildings.

Women and girls reported severe restrictions on their clothing and freedom of movement in ISIS-controlled areas. They told Human Rights Watch that they were only allowed to leave their houses dressed in full face veil (niqab) and accompanied by a close male relative. These rules, enforced by beating or fines on male family members or both, isolated women from family, friends, and public life.

They also reported restricted access to health care or education because of discriminatory ISIS policies, including rules limiting male doctors from touching, seeing, or being alone with female patients. In more rural areas ISIS has banned girls from attending school. ISIS fighters and female ISIS "morality police" hit, bit, or poked women with metal prongs to keep them in line, making them afraid to try to get services they needed.

ISIS also continues to torture, rape, murder, and sexually enslave Yezidi women and children, many of whom were captured in Iraq and taken to Syria. According to a June United Nations commission of inquiry report, ISIS still holds about 3,200 Yezidi women and children, most of whom are in Syria. Such abuses are war crimes and may amount to crimes against humanity, and possibly genocide.

Abuses by Government Forces

On May 24 Prime Minister Haider al-Abadi stated that the government would take measures to protect civilians during the operation to retake Fallujah from ISIS. Nevertheless, the next day an airstrike on Fallujah General Hospital damaged the emergency room. Over the next two weeks of fighting Human Rights Watch documented summary executions, beatings of men in custody, enforced disappearances, and mutilation of corpses by government forces.

As of mid-November, according to local officials, there were still at least 643 men and boys missing, and possibly as many as 800. They said they believed that at least 49 others had been summarily executed or tortured to death while in the custody of Hezbollah Brigade, a prominent group within the government-affiliated Popular Mobilization Forces (PMF).

On June 4, 2016 Prime Minister al-Abadi announced that he had ordered an investigation into allegations of abuse in the Fallujah operations and three days later announced an unspecified number of arrests. Government officials, however, at time of writing had not responded to requests for further information about the status of the investigation, who is conducting it, or steps taken so far.

In August, authorities implemented al-Abadi's Office Order 91 from February, making the PMF an "independent military formation" within Iraq's security forces.

Despite government assurances that only the Iraqi Security Forces would screen the thousands of civilians fleeing Mosul for possible ISIS affiliation, on at least one occasion a Shabak militia, part of the PMF, arbitrarily detained men after screening hundreds of families. The Kurdistan Regional Government (KRG) and Iraqi authorities have in some cases detained men and boys for weeks arbitrarily as part of the screening process. In many cases, families of detainees did not know where they were being held, for how long, or why.

During the Mosul operation, tribal militias unlawfully detained and mistreated residents of areas retaken from ISIS.

Displacement and Movement Restrictions

Since 2014 and over the course of 2016, Human Rights Watch has documented a pattern of unlawful destruction of Arab homes and sometimes of entire Arab villages, in tandem with the deportation of residents, in areas of Kirkuk and Nineveh governorates where there was no imperative military necessity for such measures. The destruction of homes in many cases amounted to a war crime. Authorities have not allowed internally displaced people to freely move in the Kurdistan region of Iraq and the disputed territories, requiring internally displaced people to stay in camps with severe restrictions on their movement.

Freedom of Media

A 2016 International Federation of Journalists report deemed Iraq the deadliest country in the world for journalists—with more than 300 journalists killed between 1990 and 2015. In August, journalist Wedad Hussein Ali, who was allegedly affiliated with the armed Turkey-based Kurdistan Workers Party (PKK), was abducted and killed in Dohuk. KRG Asayish forces had repeatedly interrogated him over the previous 12 months about his writings critical of Kurdish authorities.

In addition to these killings, authorities continue to limit press freedom. In March, Iraq's specialized Media and Publishing Court summoned *al-Alam al-Jadeed*'s website editor, Mountadar Nasser, for questioning over a story published a month earlier which accused a regulatory telecommunication committee of corruption. Ultimately the court acquitted Nasser and dropped the defamation charges brought against him.

Also in March the Iraqi Communications and Media Commission shut down the Cairo-based, privately owned al-Baghdadia TV. A month later, the commission withdrew Qatar-based Al Jazeera's operating license for 2016 because of "media rhetoric that incites sectarianism and violence."

Women's Rights, Sexual Orientation, and Gender Identity

Many of the Yezidi women and girls who escaped ISIS and are displaced in the Kurdistan Region of Iraq lack adequate access to mental health and psychosocial services. Although some services have been provided for women who became pregnant during their captivity, safe and legal abortion services are not available. Iraqi law allows abortion only in cases of medical necessity such as a risk to a mother's life but not in cases of rape.

Women have few legal provisions and protection mechanisms to shield them from domestic violence. Iraq's penal code includes provisions on physical assault but lacks any explicit mention of domestic violence. While sexual assault is criminalized, article 398 provides that such charges will be dropped if the assailant marries the victim. A 2010 United Nations factsheet stated that one in five Iraqi women were subject to domestic violence, and a 2012 Ministry of Planning study found that at least 36 percent of married women have experienced some form of abuse at the hands of their husbands.

In 2015, Iraqi officials published a draft law on protection against domestic violence that parliament has yet to pass. The law has serious flaws, among others that it prioritizes reconciliation over justice for abuse victims and does not stipulate crimes of domestic violence nor adequate penalties. The law does not set out duties for police and prosecutors to respond to domestic violence, and does not provide for long-term protection for the victims.

Iraq's penal code does not prohibit same-sex intimacy, although article 394 makes it illegal to engage in extra-marital sexual relations. Due to the fact that the law does not expressly allow same-sex marriage, it effectively prohibits all same-sex relations. In July Moqtada al-Sadr, the prominent Shia opposition cleric, stated that although same-sex relationships are not acceptable, individuals who do not conform to gender norms suffer from "psychological problems," and should not be attacked.

Children in War Zones

In a June report UNICEF warned that Iraq was "one of the most dangerous places in the world for children," with 3.6 million children at risk of death, injury, sexual violence, and exploitation.

In March, when Fallujah was still under the control of ISIS, a medical source at Fallujah General Hospital said that starving children were gathering at the local hospital, as there were no more food sources available and families were left eating flat bread made from ground seeds and soup made from grass.

UNICEF estimated that the number of Iraqi children working had doubled since 1990, to more than 575,000.

In 2016, Iraqi government-backed tribal militias, known as Hashad al-Asha`ri, recruited at least 10 children from the Debaga IDP camp in Erbil governorate to fight against ISIS.

Death Penalty

Iraqi courts continued to impose the death penalty. In 2016 there were at least 63 confirmed executions. In late August 2016 Iraqi authorities executed 36 men convicted in a sham group trial for participating in the 2014 ISIS execution of between 560 and 770 Shia army recruits stationed at Camp Speicher, outside Tikrit.

Key International Actors

A US-led coalition of states including Australia, Belgium, Canada, Denmark, France, the Netherlands, and the United Kingdom carried out over 9,000 airstrikes on ISIS targets since late 2014.

The United States was the largest provider of equipment to the Iraqi military, and Germany the largest provider to the KRG's Peshmerga forces.

In September, the US deployed an additional 615 US troops, bringing the total number of US troops stationed there to at least 5,180, in order to assist in the operation to retake Mosul.

Lebanon's Hezbollah group and Iran's Islamic Revolutionary Guard Corps-Al-Quds Force sent forces into combat in Iraq against ISIS.

Since 2015, the Turkish airforce has carried out airstrikes on PKK positions in northern Iraq. In 2016, Turkish groundtroops entered northern Iraq and attacked ISIS positions near Mosul.

Israel/Palestine

Israel continued in 2016 to enforce severe and discriminatory restrictions on Palestinians' human rights, to facilitate the transfer of Israeli civilians to the occupied West Bank, and to severely restrict the movement of people and goods into and out of the Gaza Strip.

In 2016, a new escalation of violence that began in October 2015 continued, characterized by demonstrations, some violent, in the West Bank and at the Gaza border with Israel that Israeli forces have suppressed, often using live fire. There was a wave of stabbings and attempted stabbings by Palestinians against Israeli passersby and security forces, both in the West Bank and Israel, mostly by people acting without the sponsorship of any armed group.

Israeli security forces used lethal force against suspected attackers in more than 150 cases, including in circumstances that suggest excessive force and at times extrajudicial executions. Overall, between January 1 and October 31, 2016, Palestinians killed at least 11 Israelis, including 2 security officers, and injured 131 Israelis, including 46 security officers, in the West Bank and Israel. Israeli security forces killed at least 94 Palestinians and injured at least 3,203 Palestinians in the West Bank, Gaza, and Israel as of October 31, including suspected assailants, protesters, and bystanders, according to the United Nations.

Palestinian authorities in the West Bank and Gaza restricted freedom of expression, tortured and ill-treated detainees, and in Gaza executed at least four people, including one person accused of same-sex relations.

In the West Bank, including East Jerusalem, Israeli settlers attacked and injured 26 Palestinians and damaged their property in 66 incidents as of October 31, the UN reported.

In January 2016, an Israeli man and teenage boy, in custody since their arrest in December 2015, were indicted for their role in an arson attack that killed a Palestinian couple and their toddler son in 2015. In May 2016, an Israeli man was sentenced to life imprisonment for the burning to death of a Palestinian child in July 2014.

Also in the West Bank, Israeli authorities destroyed homes and other property under discriminatory practices that severely restrict Palestinians' access to construction permits and forcibly displaced, as of October 17, 1,283 Palestinian residents in West Bank areas under direct Israeli administrative control.

Israel maintained severe restrictions on the movement of people and goods into and out of Gaza, exacerbated by Egypt's closure of its own border with Gaza most of the time, and by Israel's refusal to allow Gaza to operate an airport or seaport.

Palestinian armed groups launched 20 rockets indiscriminately into Israel from Hamas-controlled Gaza in 2016 as of October 31, in violation of the laws of war. Hamas authorities have failed to prosecute anyone for alleged serious crimes committed during Israel's 2014 military campaign in Gaza. Israel has received more than 500 complaints stemming from the military campaign but has prosecuted only three soldiers, for theft.

The Palestinian Authority (PA) and Hamas arrested activists who criticized their leaders, security forces or policies, some of whom alleged torture in detention. The Independent Commission for Human Rights in Palestine, a statutory commission charged with monitoring human rights compliance by the Palestinian authorities, received 150 complaints of torture and ill-treatment by PA security forces and 204 such complaints against Hamas security forces as of October 31.

Gaza Strip

Israel

In the same period, Israeli forces killed 8 people in Gaza during demonstrations at the border fence, and injured at least 188. The Israeli authorities have declared an area inside Gaza but near the border with Israel to be a "no-go" zone, and Israeli soldiers fire at people who enter it. They also continued to shoot at Palestinian civilians in the "no-go" zone that Israel imposes just inside Gaza's northern and eastern borders and at fishermen who venture beyond six nautical miles from the shore—the area to which Israel restricts Gaza fishing boats. In April, Israel expanded the fishing zone to nine miles but reinstated the six-mile limit in June. Israel says it restricts access to the sea to prevent weapons smuggling and restricts access to the no-go zone to prevent cross-border attacks.

Israel's military advocate general has received over 500 complaints from individuals and human rights groups with regard to 300 incidents that occurred during the 2014 Israel-Gaza fighting, and he launched criminal investigations into 37 incidents. So far, however, criminal charges have been filed against only three soldiers, for theft. According to the UN, 1,462 Palestinian civilians, including 551 children, and 6 civilians in Israel, including a child, were killed during the fighting.

Closure

Israel's closure of the Gaza Strip, particularly restrictions on movement of people and on outgoing goods, continued to have severe consequences for the civilian population, separating families, restricting access to medical care and educational and economic opportunities, and perpetuating unemployment and poverty. Approximately 70 percent of Gaza's 1.9 million people rely on humanitarian assistance.

Travel through the Erez Crossing, Gaza's passenger crossing to Israel, the West Bank, and the outside world, is limited to what the Israeli military calls "exceptional humanitarian cases," meaning mostly medical patients, their companions, and prominent businesspersons. In the first half of 2016, an average of about 500 Palestinians crossed through Erez each day, compared to the average of more than 24,000 Palestinians who crossed each day in September 2000, just before the second "Intifida" or Palestinian uprising began. Outgoing goods in the first 10 months of 2016 averaged 158 truckloads per month, mostly produce to be sold in the West Bank and Israel, just 15 percent of the 1,064 truckloads per month prior to the June 2007 tightening of the closure.

Israeli restrictions on the delivery of construction materials to Gaza and a lack of funding have impeded reconstruction of the 17,800 housing units severely damaged or destroyed during Israel's 2014 military operation in Gaza. About 65,000 people who lost their homes remain displaced. Israel says construction materials can be used for military purposes, including fortifying tunnels, and it allows only limited quantities to enter under the supervision of international organizations.

Egypt also blocked all regular movement of goods at the crossing with Gaza that it controls and imposed increased restrictions on the movement of people. In

2016, the crossing was mostly closed, with narrow exceptions mostly for medical patients, those holding foreign passports, residencies or visas, including students, and pilgrims to Mecca. In the first 10 months of 2016, a monthly average of about 3,196 people crossed through Rafah in both directions, compared with an average of 40,000 per month in the first half of 2013, prior to the overthrow of Egyptian President Mohamed Morsy.

Hamas and Palestinian Armed Groups

In 2016 Palestinian armed groups launched 20 rockets into Israel from Gaza as of October 31, causing no casualties but generating fear and disruption in affected cities and towns. These rockets cannot be accurately aimed at military objectives and amount to indiscriminate or deliberate attacks on civilians when directed at Israeli population centers, as was the case in many instances. A UN Commission of Inquiry last year found that such attacks are serious violations of the laws of war. Hamas, which has internal control over Gaza, is responsible for policing the border and the territory it controls and acting to ensure that unlawful attacks do not take place.

The Hamas internal security agency and police allegedly tortured or ill-treated 204 people in their custody as of October 31, according to complaints received by the Independent Commission for Human Rights (ICHR), the statutory Palestinian rights body.

In Gaza, whose laws differ somewhat from the laws in the West Bank, having "unnatural intercourse" of a sexual nature, understood to include same-sex relationships, is a crime punishable by up to 10 years in prison. In February 2016, Hamas's armed wing executed one of its fighters ostensibly for "behavioral and moral violations," which Hamas officials acknowledged meant same-sex relations.

In addition, Gaza's civilian authorities executed three men convicted of murder in May, amid concerns of due process violations.

West Bank

Israel

In the West Bank, as of October 31, Israeli security forces and settlers fatally shot at least 83 Palestinians and wounded at least 3,015, including passersby, demonstrators and those suspected of attacking Israelis, according to UN monitoring. In some cases, video footage and witness accounts strongly suggest that excessive force was used.

In March, an Israeli soldier fatally shot Abdel Fattah al-Sharif, who along with another Palestinian had stabbed a soldier at a checkpoint in Hebron. Soldiers fatally shot one of the assailants and wounded al-Sharif. A few minutes after the incident, as al-Sharif lay unmoving on the ground, a video shows the soldier shooting him in the head. A military court is trying the soldier.

As of October 31, the UN reported 26 attacks in which Israeli settlers injured Palestinians and 66 attacks in which they damaged Palestinian property. Israeli authorities are required to protect Palestinians in the West Bank, but they often fail to apprehend or prosecute Israeli settlers who attack Palestinians and destroy or damage Palestinian mosques, homes, schools, olive trees, cars, and other property. According to the Israeli human rights group Yesh Din, between 2005 and 2014, police closed 92 percent of cases of reported settler violence without prosecuting anyone.

In 2015, an arson attack against two houses in the Palestinian village of Duma killed a toddler, Ali Dawabshe, and both his parents. In January 2016, a man, 21, and a teenage boy, 17, both in police custody, were charged with three counts of murder for that incident.

Settlements, Discriminatory Policies, Home Demolitions

Israel continued to provide security, administrative services, housing, education, and medical care for about 560,000 settlers residing in unlawful settlements in the West Bank, including East Jerusalem. International humanitarian law bars an occupying power's transfer of its civilians to occupied territory.

Israel also increased its settlement activity, authorizing construction work to begin on more than 1,000 new housing units in settlements in the West Bank,

HUMAN
RIGHTS
WATCH

OCCUPATION, INC.

How Settlement Businesses Contribute to Israel's Violations
of Palestinian Rights

excluding East Jerusalem, in the first half of 2016, an increase of 17 percent over the same period in 2015, according to Israel's Central Bureau of Statistics.

Building permits are difficult, if not impossible, for Palestinians to obtain in East Jerusalem or in the 60 percent of the West Bank under exclusive Israeli control (Area C). This has driven Palestinians to construct housing and business structures that are at constant risk of demolition or confiscation by Israel on the grounds of being unauthorized. Palestinians in these areas have access to water, electricity, schools, and other state services that are either far more limited or costlier than the same services that the state makes available to Jewish settlers there.

As of October 31, Israeli authorities demolished 925 Palestinian homes and other buildings in the West Bank (including East Jerusalem), mostly for failure to have a building permit. Israel also destroyed the homes of family members of alleged attackers in reprisal for attacks on Israelis, a violation of the international humanitarian law prohibition on collective punishment. In total, the demolitions displaced 1,347 people.

Freedom of Movement

Israel maintained onerous restrictions on the movement of Palestinians in the West Bank, including checkpoints and the separation barrier, a combination of wall and fence that Israel said it built for security reasons but often placed well within the West Bank rather than on the Green Line separating the West Bank from Israel. Israeli-imposed restrictions designed to keep Palestinians far from settlements forced them to take time-consuming detours and restricted their access to agricultural land.

Israel continued construction of the separation barrier around East Jerusalem. Some 85 percent of the barrier falls within the West Bank, isolating 11,000 Palestinians on the western side of the barrier who are not allowed to travel to Israel and must cross the barrier to access their own property as well as services in the West Bank.

Arbitrary Detention and Detention of Children

Israeli military authorities detained Palestinian protesters, including those who advocated nonviolent protest against Israeli settlements and the route of the separation barrier.

Israeli security forces continued to arrest children suspected of criminal offenses, usually stone-throwing; question them without a family member or a lawyer present; and coerce them to sign confessions in Hebrew, which they did not understand. The Israeli military detained Palestinian children separately from adults during remand hearings and military court trials, but often detained children with adults immediately after arrest.

As of April 2016, Israel held 692 Palestinian administrative detainees (including 2 women and 13 children) without charge or trial, based on secret evidence. Israel jails Palestinian detainees inside Israel, violating international law requiring that they be held within the occupied territory and thus leading to restrictions on the ability of family members to visit them, due to Israel's requirement that visiting family members clear security screenings and receive permits to enter Israel. A number of Palestinian prisoners have gone on hunger strikes to protest their detention without trial.

Palestinian Authority

Complaints of torture and ill-treatment by West Bank Palestinian Authority security services persisted. The ICHR reported 150 complaints in 2016 as of October 31.

PA security services arrested activists for political criticism, and some of those arrested alleged mistreatment in detention. In arresting, abusing, and prosecuting Palestinian journalists and activists engaging in peaceful speech under long-standing laws whose penalties include incarceration, the PA violated its obligations under international treaties, ratified in 2014, respecting free expression and detainee rights.

Israel

As part of an escalation of violence that began in 2015, in 2016 Palestinians killed 11 Israelis, including two security officers, and injured 131 people in Israel and the West Bank as of October 31, including 46 security officers, according to the United Nations.

Within Israel, as of October 31, Israeli security forces or bystanders killed 3 Palestinians, including those suspected of attacking Israelis.

A law passed in July imposes onerous reporting requirements on nongovernmental organizations (NGOs) receiving most of their funding from foreign governmental entities. By exempting from these requirements NGOs that receive private foreign money, the law effectively targets human rights groups, groups run by or for Arab citizens of Israel, and anti-occupation political groups.

Bedouin citizens of Israel who live in "unrecognized" villages suffered discriminatory home demolitions on the basis that their homes were built illegally, even though most of those villages existed before the State of Israel was established, and others were created in the 1950s on land to which Israel transferred Bedouin citizens. Israeli authorities refused to prepare plans for the communities or approve construction permits, and rejected plans submitted by the communities themselves that would allow them to build lawfully. Many Bedouin communities were uprooted by the establishment of Jewish towns and cities, and a succession of Israeli governments has moved them from place to place, failing to provide adequate housing.

In al-Araqib, an unrecognized village that has been embroiled in a years-long legal battle with the state, authorities demolished all the residents' shacks 10 times between January 1 and August 18, according to the Negev Coexistence Forum for Civil Inequality. Israeli authorities demolished 28 Bedouin structures in the Negev, excluding al-Araqib, and destroyed the crops of unrecognized Bedouin villages 14 times, between January 1 and August 18.

Israel continued its openly stated policy of applying coercive measures designed to render miserable the lives of the roughly 40,000 Eritrean and Sudanese asylum seekers present in the country. These measures include prolonged detention; restrictions on freedom of movement; ambiguous policies on permission to work; and restricting access to health care. Israel does not deport Eritrean and

Sudanese nationals, but it has granted asylum to only four Eritreans to date. In June, for the first time, Israel granted asylum to a Sudanese national.

Key International Actors

Under commitments stemming from the 1978 Camp David accords, the United States allocated US$3.1 billion in military aid to Israel in 2016. It also allocated $400 million in assistance to Palestinian security forces and economic support to the PA. In September, the United States and Israel signed a 10-year, $38 billion military aid deal, mostly to be spent on US-made military supplies. In January, the US Customs Authority issued a reminder of its requirement, originating in 1995, to label imports from Israeli settlements as produced in the West Bank, not in Israel.

The International Criminal Court (ICC) Office of the Prosecutor is conducting a preliminary examination into the situation in Palestine to determine whether the criteria have been met to merit pursuing a formal investigation into crimes committed in and from Palestine. In October, a delegation from the ICC prosecutor's office visited Israel and the West Bank and held meetings with Israeli and Palestinian officials.

Japan

Japan is a strong democracy with rule of law and an active civil society. Basic freedoms of expression, association, and assembly are well-respected. However, in February 2016 the Internal Affairs and Communications minister prompted an outcry when she said the government may shut down broadcasters if they repeatedly air programs that run counter to political impartiality. The United Nations special rapporteur on freedom of expression voiced concerns during his visit in April that the Broadcast Act gives regulatory authority to the government instead of an independent third party.

The ruling Liberal Democratic Party (LDP) and its allies scored a sweeping victory in Upper House elections in July, appearing to pave the way for Prime Minister Shinzo Abe to realize his longstanding ambition to initiate significant constitutional amendments. LDP proposals in 2012 for constitutional amendments would significantly weaken human rights articles of the current constitution.

Japanese criminal procedure law allows suspects to be detained for up to 23 days prior to prosecution without the possibility of release on bail. It also prohibits lawyers from being present during interrogations, increasing the prospect of coercive means being used to extract confessions. In May, a law requiring video and audio recording of interrogations was passed, but it allows broad exceptions such as giving interrogators discretion to determine that a recording will prevent suspects from providing a full statement. It also applies to just a small segment of criminal cases, such as serious cases to be tried by the lay judge system.

Refugees and Asylum Seekers

Japan ratified the Refugee Convention in 1981. While the number of asylum applications has increased dramatically in recent years (7,586 in 2015 and 5,011 in the first half of 2016), only 27 asylum seekers were recognized as refugees in 2015 and 4 in the first half of 2016. In May, just before the G7 Summit, Japan announced a plan to accept up to 150 Syrian youths, including refugees as international students, over five years. However, only six asylum seekers from Syria had been recognized as refugees at time of writing.

The Immigration Control and Refugee Recognition Act allows for asylum seekers facing deportation orders to be detained for an unlimited period, deterring asylum applications.

Migrant Workers and Human Trafficking

Since 2010, the labor law has fully applied to Technical Intern Trainees—about 200,000 people who mainly come from China and Vietnam and often work in factories and areas including agriculture, fishery, and construction. However, weak legal protections for migrant workers still resulted in abuses in 2016. These include illegal overtime, unpaid wages, dangerous working conditions, confiscation of passports, prohibitions on having cell phones and staying elsewhere overnight, forced return, and forced payments to sending agencies in home countries in case the training period does not finish successfully. Such limitations combined with the current system that generally prohibits trainees from changing employers, deter trainees from making complaints to their employers.

The most recent statistics show that in 2015, the Labor Standards Bureau recognized 3,695 cases of labor standards violations, the largest number since 2003, when records were first kept.

While the Labor Standards Act does not apply to domestic work, 2015 guidelines on migrant domestic workers attempt to protect workers by requiring them to be employed by housekeeping service companies instead of by the household. However, migrant domestic workers are generally prohibited from changing employers.

Racial and Ethnic Discrimination

Japan does not have an anti-discrimination law to protect racial or ethnic minorities. However, in May, a so-called anti-hate speech law was passed, reflecting the increase in recent years of hate speech against Korean residents (*Zainichi*) in Japan. The new law requires the government to take measures to address hate speech, although it excludes undocumented migrants and indigenous people.

Women's Rights

In December 2015, the Supreme Court ruled that article 750 of the Civil Code, which requires a husband and wife to adopt the same surname, is constitutional. Ninety-six percent of women change their surnames at the time of marriage. The United Nations Committee on the Elimination of Discrimination against Women (CEDAW) has repeatedly recommended that the article be amended.

In December 2015, Japan and South Korea announced an agreement to resolve the issue of "comfort women" "finally and irreversibly." Japan agreed to acknowledge responsibility and anew apologies for its role. Based on the agreement, Japan provided 1 billion yen (approximately US$10 million) to the Foundation for Reconciliation and Healing established by the South Korean government. Women's rights advocates widely criticized the agreement for reasons including the lack of proper consultations with victims.

In March, CEDAW published concluding observations on the combined 7th and 8th periodic reports of Japan. The report included about 50 concerns and recommendations, many repeating previous concluding observations. The committee also expressed concerns related to the issue of comfort women, including the lack of a full victim-centered approach, and the need for "full and effective redress and reparation" for all victims, including those from countries not covered by the agreement with South Korea. Comfort women were also from countries such as the Philippines, China, Taiwan, the Netherlands, Indonesia, and East Timor.

The rights of female workers made some advances, including a March legal reform requiring that employers take measures to prevent their unfair treatment due to pregnancy, childbirth, maternity leave, family care leave, and the April enforcement of the 2015 Act on Promotion of Women's Participation and Advancement in the Workplace.

Japan has the second lowest proportion of female managers among OECD countries. In December 2015, Japan's Cabinet adopted a new five-year "Fourth Basic Plan for Gender Equality," lowering the target set in 2003 to ensure that at least 30 percent of leadership positions are held by women in all areas by 2020. Under the new target, the female leadership ratio goal was reduced to 7 percent

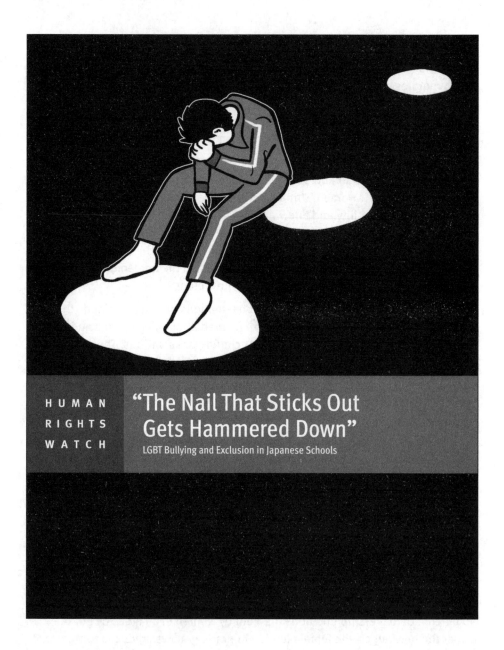

for middle managerial positions in the central government and 15 percent for the same in the private sector.

Sexual Orientation and Gender Identity

A bipartisan parliamentary group established in March 2015 continued to discuss legislation to address discrimination based on sexual orientation and gender identity, but at time of writing it had yet to come up with an agreed draft bill.

Japanese law treats those requesting legal recognition as transgender as having a "Gender Identity Disorder" and requires obtaining such medical diagnosis. It also requires forced sterilization, compulsory single status, not having any underage children, and being 20 years or older.

While same-sex marriage is not legally recognized in Japan, Tokyo's Shibuya ward in April 2015 became the first municipality to pass a regulation recognizing same-sex partnerships, with more municipalities recognizing such partnerships in 2016.

Bullying is a problem in Japanese schools generally, and particularly so against lesbian, gay, bisexual, and transgender (LGBT) students. A 2016 Human Rights Watch report found that many students face discrimination and disregard for gender identity, including mandatory gender-based uniforms. In April, the Ministry of Education, Culture, Sports, Science and Technology (MEXT) for the first time released a guidebook for teachers regarding sexual orientation and gender identity.

Disability Rights

In April, the Act on the Elimination of Discrimination against Persons with Disabilities, which the Japanese government enacted as part of ratification of the Convention on the Rights of Persons with Disabilities, came into effect. The law prohibits unfair discriminatory treatment by governments and private entities based on disability. It also requires that government-related agencies provide reasonable accommodation to enable the elimination of social barriers, unless the expense is "excessive."

In July, a 26-year-old man stabbed 19 men and women to death and wounded another 27 in a state-funded institution for people with disabilities in Sagamihara, southwest of Tokyo, approximately five months after he was discharged from involuntary psychiatric hospitalization. The suspect was quoted as saying, "It is better that disabled people disappear" moments after the attack. Following the incident, the Japanese government began examining the practice of involuntary hospitalization in psychiatric hospitals. However, at time of writing, no major reform had been proposed to address stigma against people with disabilities, including by guaranteeing their right to live independently by supporting their inclusion in the community.

Children's Rights

In May, the Diet passed an amendment of the Child Welfare Act that for the first time explicitly refers to children as rights holders, in accordance with the Convention on the Rights of the Child. As noted in a 2014 Human Rights Watch report on the over-institutionalization (nearly 90 percent) of children in Japan's alternative care system, the revised law envisions a major shift from institutions to families. Article 3.2 lays out a new principle for family-based care although there are questions about the government's commitment to enforce the new act.

Death Penalty

Japan continued to use the death penalty in 2016, executing convicted criminals by hanging. Two people in March and one in November were executed, bringing the total to 17 since Abe returned to power in December 2012. Anti-death penalty advocates have long raised concerns about death row inmates having inadequate access to legal counsel and only being notified of their execution on the day it takes place.

Foreign Policy

Prime Minister Abe started his second cabinet by announcing in January 2013 "diplomacy based on the fundamental values of freedom, democracy, basic human rights, and the rule of law," partly to contrast his foreign policy from that of China.

However, in practice Japan rarely speaks publicly about human rights, with Foreign Ministry officials and diplomats sticking to their longstanding policy of quiet diplomacy. This is aimed at maintaining good relations, particularly in Asia, in part to compete with China, maintain access, and promote trade. In his 2016 speeches, Abe only vowed to deepen ties with countries sharing these values. The one country that Japan has been willing to criticize publicly is North Korea, which gets exceptional domestic attention because of Pyongyang's past abductions of Japanese nationals.

In February 2016, Japan and Iran held their 11th Human Rights Dialogue in Tehran. Like other human rights dialogues that Japan has convened, the announcement came only a few days before the meeting, without any briefing opportunities before, during, or after the meeting. This prevented any meaningful input from human rights activists and organizations. The post-meeting online announcement only noted that the two sides had "exchanged views" on human rights.

Jordan

King Abdullah II dissolved Jordan's lower house of parliament on May 29, 2016, after the resignation of Prime Minister Abdullah Ensour, who had been in office since October 2012. Elections for Jordan's 130-seat House of Representatives took place on September 20 under a new list-based electoral system, resulting in the election of 20 women, including five who won competitively outside the women's quota.

In March 2016, under instruction by King Abdullah, Jordanian authorities launched the Comprehensive National Plan for Human Rights, a 10-year initiative that calls for changes to numerous laws, policies, and practices. Positive changes included a commitment to allow suspects the right to a lawyer at the time of arrest and to move jurisdiction over crimes of torture and ill-treatment from the police court to regular courts. Bassel Tararwneh, Jordan's governmental human rights coordinator, facilitated government interaction with local and international nongovernmental organizations (NGOs) and held open consultation sessions on human rights issues.

In March 2016, Jordanian authorities proposed sweeping amendments to the country's association law that, if implemented, will hamper the ability of NGOs to form and operate.

Freedom of Expression and Belief

Jordanian law criminalizes speech deemed critical of the king, foreign countries, government officials and institutions, as well as Islam and speech considered to defame others.

On June 14, Jordanian authorities detained university professor and popular Islamic preacher Amjad Qourshah in connection with an October 2014 video posted to his Facebook page in which he criticized Jordan's participation in the US-led coalition bombing of the Islamic State, or ISIS. Authorities released him on bail in early September, but at time of writing he remained on trial before the State Security Court charged with exposing Jordan to the danger of hostile acts, a counterterrorism law provision. Authoriites defended Qourshah's arrest as a measure to combat hate speech and extremist thought.

On August 14, authorities detained writer Nahed Hattar after he posted a cartoon on his Facebook page critical of ISIS. The cartoon depicted an ISIS fighter in bed with two women ordering God to bring him wine. Authorities charged him with insulting religion under article 278 of the penal code. Authorities stated that Hattar's arrest was intended to prevent defamation of religion. Hattar was later murdered on September 25 while entering an Amman court to attend a trial session.

Jordanian authorities increasingly relied on press gag orders in 2016 to prevent public reporting on sensitive issues. In 2016, authorities imposed gag orders on news stories such as: a complaint by orphans against the Ministry of Social Development; a street assault on an Egyptian worker in Jordan; a security operation in the northern town of Irbid in March in which seven militants and one policeman were killed; an attack on a General Intelligence Directorate (GID) office north of Amman that led to four deaths; and the cases of Amjad Qourshah and Nahed Hattar.

On August 29, Jordan's media commission prohibited local press outlets from publishing any news about the king or the royal family other than information circulated by the royal court.

A legislative overhaul of the penal code was put to parliament in 2015 proposing to amend at least 180 articles of the 1960 code. At time of writing, lawmakers had still to pass the reforms. For the first time, the draft amendments provided alternatives to imprisonment, such as community service.

Freedom of Association and Assembly

In March, Jordan's Ministry of Social Development issued a group of amendments to Jordan's 2008 Law on Associations. If enacted, the changes would severely hamper the ability of NGOs to form and operate. The amendments place onerous restrictions on the establishment of civil society groups and grant the government legal authority to dissolve groups on vague grounds or deny their ability to obtain foreign funding without justification. By November, the amendments were still under consultation and had not been submitted to parliament.

Since the amended Public Gatherings Law took effect in March 2011, Jordanians no longer require government permission to hold public meetings or demonstrations. However, Amman hotels and other venues continued to seek permission

PREVENTING A LOST GENERATION: JORDAN

"We're Afraid For Their Future"

Barriers to Education for Syrian Refugee Children in Jordan

HUMAN
RIGHTS
WATCH

to host public meetings and events. In April, authorities cancelled a concert by the popular Lebanese music group Mashrou` Leila, reportedly over the claim that their songs "contain lyrics that do not comply with the nature of the Jordanian society." Authorities reversed the decision the day before the concert was to be held, but organizers said they did not have time to stage it.

Refugees and Migrants

Between 2011 and 2016, over 656,000 persons from Syria had sought refuge in Jordan, according to the United Nations High Commissioner for Refugees (UNHCR). Of these, approximately 79,000 were housed at the Zaatari Refugee Camp in northern Jordan,; 54,000 were registered in Azraq Camp, 100 kilometers east of Amman; and 7,300 were at the Emirates Jordan Camp in Zarqa Governorate. The rest were living outside refugee camps.

Jordanian officials stated that the country did not receive enough international financial assistance in 2016 to cope with the effects of the refugee crises on its public infrastructure, especially in the areas of public education and health. The UNHCR Jordan office, which coordinates the refugee response, said that by November it had raised only 57 percent of its US$1.1 billion budget goal for 2016.

In February, authorities announced the Jordan Compact at the "Supporting Syria and the Region" conference in London, which aims to promote economic growth in Jordan and improve the livelihoods of Syrian refugees by granting new legal work opportunities. By November, at least 28,000 work permits for Syrians had been issued by labor authorities.

Between January and June 21, Jordanian authorities severely restricted the Rukban and Hadalat informal border crossings with Syria in the eastern part of the country. These restrictions stranded tens of thousands of Syrian asylum seekers at an earthen berm just inside Jordan's border for days and weeks in harsh desert conditions with limited access to food, water, and medical assistance. Between March 9 and June 21, authorities transported over 20,000 Syrians from the berm to a fenced area of Azraq Camp for additional security processing.

On June 21, a suicide car bomb attack on a Jordanian military base near Rukban killed seven Jordanian soldiers and security officers, prompting authorities to classify the Jordan-Syria border as a closed military zone and halt humanitarian assistance to nearly 70,000 Syrians at the berm, other than water. Authorities allowed the resumption of humanitarian assistance in late November at a new distribution point seven kilometers northwest of the Rukban camp.

In 2016, around 80,000 Syrian children in Jordan were not in formal education. Jordan's Ministry of Education took steps to address obstacles to access to education such as relaxing documentation requirements, doubling the number of schools operating "double shifts" to create spaces for up to 50,000 more Syrian students, and establishing a "catch-up" program to reach another 25,000 children ages 8 to 12, who have been out of school for three or more years.

Jordan hosted around 80,000 migrant domestic workers in 2016, mostly from the Philippines, Sri Lanka, and Indonesia. NGOs repeatedly referred domestic workers who had suffered multiple abuses to labor ministry investigators. Abuses included non-payment of salaries, unsafe working conditions, long hours, document confiscation, and sometimes physical, verbal and sexual abuse.

Women's and Girls' Rights

Jordan's personal status code remains discriminatory, despite a 2010 amendment that included widening women's access to divorce and child custody. Marriages between Muslim women and non-Muslim men, for instance, are not recognized.

Article 9 of Jordan's nationality law does not allow Jordanian women married to non-Jordanian spouses to pass on their nationality to their spouse and children. By September 2016, Jordanian authorities distributed at least 56,000 special ID cards to non-citizen children of Jordanian women, but affected persons reported officials' lack of follow-through on other "privileges" for these children announced in 2014, especially acquisition of work permits and drivers' licenses.

Penal code articles 98 and 340, which allow reduced sentences for perpetrators of "honor crimes," remained in force. According to the Sisterhood is Global Institute/Jordan, news reports indicated that at least 26 women and girls were killed between January and November, some of which perpetrators claimed were "honor crimes".

Criminal Justice System and Police Accountability

Jordanian authorities did not carry out any executions between January and November 2016, down from 2 in 2015 and 11 in late 2014, when it ended an eight-year defacto moratorium.

In January, police court prosecutors filed torture charges under penal code article 208 against five policemen in connection with the September 2015 death in detention of 49-year-old Omar al-Nasr. It is only the second known instance in which torture charges have been filed against police, and the trial was ongoing as of September. In July, following a three-year trial, the Police Court cleared seven drug squad officers accused of involvement in the March 2013 death in detention of 33-year old Sultan al-Khatatba.

Local governors continued to use provisions of the Crime Prevention Law of 1954 to place individuals in administrative detention for up to one year in circumvention of the Criminal Procedure Law. The National Center for Human Rights reported that 19,860 persons were administratively detained in 2015, some for longer than one year.

In September, Jordan's council of ministers approved amendments to the Crime Prevention Law that institutionalize informal tribal practices including the *jilwa*, which involves banishing family members of the alleged perpetrator of a murder from their area of residence as part of a settlement between tribes.

Authorities justified the change on the pretext that it would limit the *jilwa* to direct family members rather than extended family members, but the move nevertheless gives officials the authority to punish individuals for a crime they did not commit. The draft amendments had not been submitted to parliament for approval at time of writing.

Key International Actors

Jordan received approximately US$1.4 billion in economic and military assistance from the United States in 2016 according to the Congressional Research Service. The assistance is part of a three-year memorandum of understanding in which the US pledged to provide $1 billion in aid to Jordan annually, up from $660 million in recent years. The US did not publicly criticize human rights violations in Jordan in 2015, except in annual reports.

In February, the EU pledged €1 billion ($1.2 billion) in assistance to Jordan for 2016 and 2017, of which nearly €700 million ($873 million) was allocated by July.

In April, Jordan, and Saudi Arabia announced the formation of a joint investment council to oversee investments in Jordan by the Saudi Public Investment Fund, which are expected to total billions of dollars. The two countries are also reportedly working on agreements over nuclear power cooperation and uranium extraction.

Kazakhstan

Against the backdrop of an economic downturn, Kazakh authorities in 2016 jailed peaceful protesters, targeted outspoken activists on vague and overbroad criminal charges, and prosecuted independent journalists. Parliament adopted laws placing unjustified burdens and restrictions on nongovernmental organizations (NGOs).

Opposition leader Vladimir Kozlov was released on parole in August, but two activists faced politically motivated charges in connection with peaceful land reform protests. Impunity for torture persists. Authorities continued to restrict workers' rights. Kazakhstan took a rotating seat on the United Nations Security Council and signed a strategic partnership agreement with the European Union, despite lack of progress on human rights.

Parliamentary Elections

The Organization for Security and Co-operation in Europe's Office for Democratic Institutions and Human Rights (OSCE/ODIHR) monitoring mission found that March parliamentary elections "were efficiently organized, with some progress," but identified "serious procedural errors and irregularities ... during voting, counting and tabulation," and concluded Kazakhstan's "legal framework restricts fundamental civil and political rights."

Freedom of Assembly

The government took no steps to amend a restrictive public assembly law which authorities regularly used to deny permits for peaceful protests, and to fine and jail peaceful demonstrators.

In advance of countrywide protests planned for May 21 against proposed land code reforms, authorities jailed over two dozen people, including activists Maks Bokaev and Talgat Ayan, each sentenced to 15 days' detention for administrative offences.

Authorities brought criminal charges against Bokaev and Ayan while serving those sentences. At time of writing they were on trial on charges of violating the public assembly law, inciting national discord, and disseminating false information. The men deny the charges, calling them retaliation for their activism.

On May 21, police aggressively broke up attempted peaceful gatherings against land reforms in multiple cities, detaining hundreds of people, sometimes using force, and sanctioned 51 of them on administrative charges.

On May 26, the EU called on authorities to "release without delay all remaining arrested peaceful activists, and to drop all criminal charges or penalties." Four UN special rapporteurs urged Kazakhstan to "halt the clampdown on land reform protesters."

Civil Society

In January 2016, an Almaty court found civil society activists Ermek Narymbaev and Serikzhan Mambetalin guilty of "inciting national discord" for material posted on Facebook that some felt insulted the Kazakh people, and sentenced them to three and two years' imprisonment, respectively. In March, an appeals court conditionally released them, with restrictions on their movement.

Also in January 2016, an Astana court found civil society activist Bolatbek Blyalov guilty of "inciting social discord" for online videos of him discussing Kazakh nationalism and other topics, and restricted his freedom of movement and association for three years.

On August 20, opposition leader Vladimir Kozlov was released on parole. He served four-and-a-half years of a seven-and-a-half-year prison sentence after an unfair trial in 2012. He remained subject to restrictions on his movement and freedom of association, and was required to report to police monthly.

In May, a court ordered government critic Natalya Ulasik undergo psychiatric observation after her ex-partner accused her of defamation. Authorities detained her in August. In October, a court found her mentally incompetent and placed her in forced psychiatric detention.

Civil society activist Vadim Kuramshin continued to serve a 12-year prison sentence, despite fair trial violations and concerns that his December 2012 conviction was retribution for government criticism.

Kazakh government critic and former banker Mukhtar Ablyazlov remained in detention in France pending review of an executive decree ordering his extradition to Russia. Rights groups fear that, if extradited, Ablyazov could be forcibly returned to Kazakhstan.

In December 2015, President Nursultan Nazarbaev signed into law amendments to nongovernmental organization-related legislation, imposing burdensome reporting obligations and state regulation of funding through a government-appointed body. A February EU statement expressed concern that the "newly created government controlled body could have a negative impact on NGO activities." International Legal Initiative (ILI), a rights group in Kazakhstan, unsuccessfully contested the law's legality in an Astana court.

In July, parliament adopted amendments introducing new financial reporting obligations for individuals and legal entities, such as NGOs, on foreign funds receipt and expenditure.

Media Restrictions and Freedom of Expression

Independent journalists and media outlets face harassment and interference, including criminal prosecution on dubious or excessive charges. Media watchdog group Adilsoz reported an increase in defamation lawsuits in the first half of 2016. Libel remains a criminal offense. In January, OSCE Representative on Freedom of the Media Dunja Mijatović called the situation for free expression and media freedom in Kazakhstan "deeply worrying."

Authorities detained over 50 journalists reporting on the May land protests, and blocked access to some websites, including Radio Free Europe/Radio Liberty's Kazakh branch. In May, a court found journalist Gyuzal Baidalinova criminally liable for "disseminating false information" for information she published about a Kazakh bank, imprisoning her for 18 months. In July, she was released on parole.

On October 3, an Astana court sentenced Seitkazy Mataev, head of the National Press Club, a platform for critical voices, to six years' imprisonment on embezzlement and tax evasion charges, and his son, Aset, also a journalist, to five years in prison for embezzlement. They said the investigation—which media watch-

HUMAN
RIGHTS
WATCH

"We Are Not The Enemy"
Violations of Workers' Rights in Kazakhstan

dogs criticized for its lack of integrity—was retaliation their critical views of the government.

Kazakh authorities sued Respublika, a critical website, in United States and Australian courts, over leaked government documents seeking to capitalize on those countries' anti-hacking laws.

Torture

Kazakhstan's prosecutor general acknowledged in August that torture remains a problem, despite some efforts to tackle it. In September a court convicted one prison official of rape and sentenced him to nine years in prison after a female inmate alleged he was one of four prison officials who raped her. Following its September visit, the UN Subcommittee on the Prevention of Torture noted that despite improvements in conditions, the prison system overemphasizes restrictions and punishment, rather than reintegration and rehabilitation.

Despite a 2014 UN Human Rights Committee decision finding that officials tortured Rasim Bayramov, detained in 2008 on suspicion of robbery and beaten in custody, authorities have repeatedly declined to investigate citing "lack of evidence of a crime," most recently in July.

Authorities have not credibly investigated torture allegations by people detained in Zhanaozen in December 2011, following an extended labor strike that ended in violent clashes. In its August concluding observations, the UN Human Rights Committee called on the government to ensure "an independent, impartial and effective investigation … into all allegations of torture and ill-treatment" related to the Zhanaozen events.

Freedom of Religion

Authorities continue to fine and convict people for violating a restrictive 2011 religion law. Since December 2014, 40 people have faced criminal charges for membership in the banned Tabligh Jamaat movement, according to Forum18, an international religious freedom watchdog.

On March 25, police executed search warrants at five New Life church buildings in Almaty and at several church leaders' homes under a criminal investigation into fraud charges, which church leaders deny. An appeals' court ordered Sev-

375

enth-day Adventist Yklas Kabduakasov, convicted in November 2015 for "inciting religious discord" and initially given a seven-year suspended sentence, to serve two years' imprisonment in a labor camp.

Counterterrorism

President Nazarbaev called for harsher counterterrorism measures after 19 people were killed in an armed attack in Aktobe in June, and other gunman killed four people in Almaty in July. In September, the government proposed amendments to 24 laws relating to counterterrorism and extremism.

The UN Human Rights Committee criticized the overly-broad definitions of "extremism," "inciting social or class hatred," and "religious hatred or enmity," and use of extremism legislation "to unduly restrict freedoms of religion, expression, assembly and association."

Labor Rights

The trade union law and collective bargaining regulations restrict workers' rights, including the right to strike. After repeated registration denials, the Confederation of Independent Trade Unions of Kazakhstan registered under a new name in February, but was unable to confirm its status, the second step in a burdensome two-step registration process.

The International Labour Organization again criticized Kazakhstan at its June conference for limiting freedom of association and for failing to amend its restrictive labor union law.

Sexual Orientation and Gender Identity

Surveys of lesbian, gay, bisexual, and transgender (LGBT) people reveal that many hide their sexual orientation or gender identity—including to healthcare providers—out of fear of reprisals or discrimination. When LGBT people report abuse, they often face indifference and hostility from authorities.

Transgender people must undergo humiliating and invasive procedures—including coerced sterilization—to change gender on official documents. Without identity documents, transgender people struggle to access employment, healthcare, and education. The UN Human Rights Committee called on the government to end discrimination and violence against LGBT people and review gender-reassignment surgery procedures.

Key International Actors

A December 2015 Enhanced Partnership and Cooperation Agreement gives Kazakhstan upgraded trade and economic relations with the EU, despite the lack of meaningful rights improvements in Kazakhstan. When negotiations began, the EU had linked successful negotiations to reforms.

In March, EU Commission President Jean-Claude Juncker met with President Nazerbaev and downplayed human rights concerns, calling reforms in Kazakhstan "promising."

In a March resolution on Freedom of Expression in Kazakhstan, the European Parliament noted "the serious deterioration of the climate for media and free speech" and called on Kazakhstan to review legislation and stop harassing journalists.

Following Kazakhstan's second periodic report, the UN Human Rights Committee called on the government to redouble efforts to prevent violence against women, eradicate torture, guarantee liberty and security of person, and safeguard independent judiciary.

The United States Department of State's top counterterrorism official, Sarah Sewall, visited Kazakhstan in August to discuss strengthening counterterrorism cooperation. In October, the US Embassy in Kazakhstan issued a rare statement on media freedom, expressing concern about the convictions and prison sentences handed down to journalists Seitkazy and Aset Mataev.

In June 2016, Kazakhstan became an elected member of the UN Security Council for the 2017-2018 term.

Kenya

Respect for human rights in Kenya remained precarious in 2016, with authorities failing to adequately investigate a range of abuses across the country and undermining basic rights to free expression and association. Human rights activists and journalists working on a range of issues face increasing obstacles and harassment. Human rights organizations continue to implicate Kenyan police and military in disappearances and killings of individuals allegedly linked to Al-Shabab.

With elections scheduled for August 2017, questions remain over the credibility and competence of the judiciary to arbitrate electoral disputes fairly. The ability of Kenya police to respond effectively and lawfully should violence occur before, during, or after the 2017 elections remains a concern.

In a positive step, four police officers were charged with murder in late June 2016 of an International Justice Mission lawyer, his client and their cabdriver. The case illustrates the risks human rights defenders and others face when pushing for police accountability.

Industrial developments in neighboring Ethiopia have led to a drop in the water levels of lake Turkana. These, combined with climate change, have negatively impacted the livelihoods of about 300,000 indigenous people in Turkana county, but the Kenyan government has failed to raise this issue with Ethiopia. The Climate Change Law passed in May, if rigorously implemented, is expected to improve coordination and governance of national and local policies related to climate change.

Conduct of Security Forces

Kenyan and international human rights organizations documented military and police units, including the Directorate of Military Intelligence, carrying out enforced disappearances, torture and beating of individuals suspected of links with Al-Shabab.

Kenyan authorities have not acknowledged, publicly condemned or investigated at least 32 cases of enforced disappearances and 11 unexplained deaths of people last seen in state custody in Nairobi and northeastern Kenya. Witnesses observed police and military drive with detainees into military bases and camps in Garissa, Wajir, and Mandera for detention and interrogation. Two of the 34 missing people were in late July located in state custody, with one now facing terrorism related charges. Kenya National Commission on Human Rights, a statutory human rights body, documented at least 100 cases of extrajudicial killings and enforced disappearances of those allegedly linked with Al-Shabab and continue to press for investigations.

The Commission on Administrative Justice received at least 25,000 reports of killings by police across the country since 2013. Kenyan authorities have very rarely investigated the killings or held anyone to account. In September, the Office of the Director of Public Prosecutions and the Kenya National Commission on Human Rights separately announced intentions to initiate inquests in killings by police in Kisumu in 2013 and security forces abuses at the coast, respectively.

Accountability

The collapse of the last International Criminal Court (ICC) case directly related to the 2007-2008 post-election violence devastated victims' hopes for justice. National authorities made no progress to address these crimes.

The ICC vacated charges against Deputy President William Ruto and Joshua arap Sang, a former radio journalist, in April 2016 for lack of evidence. For one judge, the combination of witness interference and political obstruction warranted a mistrial. The case's collapse followed that of cases against four others, including President Uhuru Kenyatta.

Three men wanted by the ICC since 2013 and 2015 for witness interference have yet to be surrendered. Although Kenyan authorities have issued arrest warrants, Kenyan authorities are currently challenging, in Kenyan courts, the arrest warrant of one individual. There have been no publicly available results of national investigations into the apparent murder in late 2014 of Meshack Yebei, named by the Ruto ICC defense team as its witness.

In September, an ICC trial chamber referred Kenya's lack of cooperation in the Kenyatta case to the ICC's Assembly of States Parties.

The government continues its campaign to press the AU to consider calling on its member countries who also belong to the ICC to leave the court, but several countries blocked consensus at a July 2016 summit. A bill related to Kenya's withdrawal from the ICC remains pending in parliament.

The government continues to ignore the plight of thousands of women and men who were raped during the post-election violence in 2007-08. It has failed to provide livelihood support, as well as medical and psychosocial care to them, including for children who were born from rape and face violence and discrimination. The government has not established a restorative justice fund that was promised to survivors of historical injustices, including post-election violence.

Hearings continued over the course of 2016 in the Kenyan high court on a petition brought by survivors of election-related sexual violence seeking to compel the government to investigate. A second case, related to shootings by police during the violence, is also pending.

Threats to Civil Society and Media

Nongovernmental organizations (NGOs) working on a range of issues face hostile rhetoric from public officials, including draconian administrative measures and attempts at introducing repressive amendments to the NGO law. In October 2015, the NGO regulatory body announced plans to deregister more than 900 NGOs over, among other reasons, alleged failure to comply with regulatory requirements and links to terrorism. The cabinet secretary later suspended the plan.

On September 9, the cabinet secretary for devolution announced plans to implement the Public Benefits Organizations (PBO) Act, first signed into law by President Kibaki in January 2013. The announcement came just weeks after parliament voted to compel the executive to implement the law without proposed repressive amendments, such as capping NGO funding from foreign sources at 15 percent.

The government continues to enforce laws that undermine media freedom. The Kenya Information and Communication Act (KICA), the Media Act of 2013, and the Security Laws Amendment Act of 2014 contain repressive provisions, which introduce new harsh offences and penalties, that should be repealed. In 2016, at least eight journalists and bloggers were arrested and charged under vaguely

HUMAN
RIGHTS
WATCH

"I Just Sit and Wait to Die"

Reparations for Survivors of Kenya's 2007-2008 Post-Election
Sexual Violence

worded provisions in the new laws, including "misuse of a communications gadget," "annoying a public official" or "undermining the authority of a public officer." In May 2016, a High Court judge declared section 29 of KICA, which creates an offense of misusing a communications gadget, unconstitutional.

Coerced Return of Refugees

In April, authorities announced that Kenya would no longer grant Somali refugees prima facie refugees status and in May, disbanded the Department of Refugee Affairs (DRA), a statutory government body responsible for registration of asylum seekers, issuing of travel permits and movement passes. At the same time, Kenyan officials announced plans to close Dadaab refugee camp. The government justified the closure of the camp on the grounds that terrorist attacks were mounted from Dadaab, without providing evidence.

At time of writing, Kenya's repatriation program does not meet international standards for voluntary refugee return. Refugees in Dadaab camp told Human Rights Watch of intimidation by Kenyan officials, silence over alternative options that would allow them to remain in Kenya, cuts in rations and inadequate and misleading information on conditions in Somalia. In November, Kenyan authorities postponed the closure of Dadaab camp by six months.

Sexual Orientation and Gender Identity

Kenya's penal code prohibits "carnal knowledge against the order of nature," generally understood as consensual sex between men, and "indecent practices between males." Civil society organizations and activists filed two landmark constitutional petitions against these sections in April and June 2016, arguing that the laws violate constitutional rights, including the rights to equality and non-discrimination, human dignity, freedom and security of the person, privacy, and health.

Kenya continued the prosecution of two men on charges of "carnal knowledge" after police arbitrarily arrested them in Kwale County in February 2015. The case remained open but was suspended pending the ruling of a constitutional petition filed by the two men, asserting that state officials had violated their rights by subjecting them to a forced anal examination. The High Court rejected the petition on the grounds that the men consented to the examination, ignoring that the men were in police custody and not able to provide free and informed consent. The men have appealed the ruling.

The government appealed a 2015 High Court decision ordering the Non-Governmental Organizations Board to register the National Gay and Lesbian Human Rights Commission (NGLHRC), a civil society group. Parties were awaiting a hearing date at time of writing.

The Kenya Film Classification Board overstepped its jurisdiction in asking YouTube to remove a locally produced video addressing same-sex relationships, prohibiting a lesbian speed-dating event, and attempting to ban a podcast with alleged lesbian content.

Key International Actors

Kenya plays a prominent regional role particularly regarding counterterrorism efforts in East Africa. Kenyan forces remain in Somalia as part of the African Union mission. President Kenyatta also participated in various attempts at peace negotiations in South Sudan and Burundi.

Kenya's criticism of its Western partners has become less vociferous following the end of its ICC cases, but there remain serious concerns about the human rights situation in the country. Both US Secretary of State John Kerry and Japanese Prime Minister Shinzo Abe held talks with President Kenyatta in Nairobi. Kerry raised human rights concerns.

International partners, including China, the UK, Turkey, Israel, Italy, and the US pledged support for Kenya's counterterrorism efforts and economic development. The US consistently raised concerns—publicly and privately—about abuses related to Kenya's counterterrorism efforts and took steps to restrict assistance to certain units. There was little indication that other international partners expressed similar concerns.

Kuwait

Kuwait took further steps to improve migrant worker rights in 2016, including enacting a minimum wage for domestic workers, easing employer transfer rules, and passing implementing regulations for a 2015 law that gave domestic workers enforceable rights for the first time.

Unlike many of its Gulf neighbors, Kuwait continued to allow Human Rights Watch access to the country and engaged in constructive dialogue with the organization on a range of human rights issues.

Provisions in Kuwait's constitution, the national security law and other legislation continue to restrict free speech, and were again used in 2016 to prosecute dissidents and stifle political dissent.

The emir also ordered authorities to amend a 2015 law, the first of its kind, that requires all individuals in Kuwait to provide DNA samples in violation of their right to privacy.

Kuwait continued to exclude thousands of stateless people, known as Bidun, from full citizenship despite their longstanding roots in Kuwaiti territory.

Migrant Workers

Two-thirds of Kuwait's population is comprised of migrant workers. Kuwait continues to reform aspects of the *kafala* or sponsorship system, which ties a migrant worker's legal residence and valid immigration status to an employer.

Kuwait issued a new standard contract for migrant workers in 2015 and an administrative decision that allows some migrant workers to transfer their sponsorship to a new employer without their current employer's consent after three years of work in 2016. Previously, migrant workers required their contract to end and their employer's consent to transfer employers. These reforms do not extend to migrant domestic workers.

In 2015, the National Assembly passed a law that gave domestic workers the right to a weekly day off, 30 days of annual paid leave, a 12-hour working day with rest, and an end-of-service benefit of one month a year at the end of the contract, among other rights. In July, the Interior Ministry passed implementing regulations for the law, including clarifying that employers must pay overtime compensation. The same month, the ministry issued a decree that established a minimum wage for domestic workers of KD60 (US$200).

Protections in the domestic workers law are still weaker than those in the labor law, which provides for an eight-hour work day with one hour of rest after every five hours of work and detailed provisions for sick leave. The domestic worker law also falls short by failing to set out enforcement mechanisms, such as labor inspections of working conditions in households, which can be done with due regard to privacy.

Migrant workers remain vulnerable to abuse, forced labor, and deportation for minor infractions including traffic violations and "absconding" from an employer. Authorities deported 14,400 migrants in the first four months of 2016, according to local media.

During a September visit to Kuwait, the UN special rapporteur on trafficking welcomed Kuwait's establishment of a shelter for domestic workers, but urged the government to continue its reforms and abolish the *kafala* system.

Freedom of Expression

Kuwaiti authorities have invoked several provisions in the constitution, penal code, Printing and Publication Law, Misuse of Telephone Communications and Bugging Devices Law, Public Gatherings Law, and National Unity Law to prosecute journalists, politicians and activists over the last few years for criticizing the emir, the government, religion, and rulers of neighboring countries in blogs or on Twitter, Facebook, or other social media.

Dozens of prosecutions for protected speech are ongoing in Kuwaiti courts. Kuwaiti officials and activists reported that many, if not most, initial complaints in these cases are filed by individuals, underscoring the need to further amend broadly written or overly vague Kuwaiti laws to ensure adequate protections for speech and expression. Kuwaiti courts continued to issue deportation orders in some of these cases, including against members of the Bidun population, although Kuwaiti officials reported these orders would not be implemented.

In June 2016, Kuwait amended the election law to bar from running or voting in elections all those convicted for "insulting" God, the prophets, or the emir. The law is likely to bar some opposition members of parliament from contesting or voting in future election rounds.

The Cybercrime Law, which includes far-reaching restrictions on internet-based speech, such as prison sentences and fines for insulting religion, religious figures and the emir, went into effect in 2016.

Treatment of Minorities

At least 105,702 Bidun residents of Kuwait remain stateless.

After an initial registration period for citizenship ended in 1960, authorities shifted Bidun citizenship claims to administrative committees that for decades have avoided resolving the claims. Authorities claim that many Bidun are "illegal residents" who deliberately destroyed evidence of another nationality in order to receive benefits that Kuwait gives its citizens.

Members of the Bidun community have taken to the streets to protest the government's failure to address their citizenship claims, despite government warnings that Bidun should not gather in public. Article 12 of the 1979 Public Gatherings Law bars non-Kuwaitis from participating in public gatherings.

In 2016, a Comoros Island official told Gulf News that the Comoros Island was open to Kuwaiti officials' suggestions that Kuwait may pay the Comoros Islands to grant the Bidun a form of economic citizenship, thus regularizing Bidun as foreign nationals and rendering them liable to legal deportation from Kuwait—possibly violating their right to family life.

Terrorism

The 2015 DNA law, requiring all citizens, visitors and residents to provide DNA samples to the authorities, was introduced after the June 2015 suicide bombing of the Imam Sadiq Mosque, which killed 27 people and wounded 227. Authorities reported to local media that anyone failing to comply with the law would be subject to sanctions, including cancelling their passports and a possible travel ban. In July, the United Nations Human Rights Committee found the law imposed "unnecessary and disproportionate restrictions on the right to privacy." In 2016, the emir directed the authorities to amend the law in line with constitutional standards.

Women's Rights, Sexual Orientation, and Gender Identity

Kuwaiti personal status law, which applies to Sunni Muslims, the majority of Kuwaitis, discriminates against women. For instance, some women require a male guardian to conclude her marriage contract; women must apply to the courts for a divorce on limited grounds unlike men who can unilaterally divorce their wives; and women can lose custody of their children if they remarry someone outside the family. The rules that apply to Shia Muslims also discriminate against women.

Kuwait has no laws prohibiting domestic violence or marital rape. A 2015 law establishing family courts set up a center to deal with domestic violence cases, but requires the center to prioritize reconciliation over protection for domestic violence survivors. Article 153 of the Kuwaiti penal code stipulates that a man who finds his mother, wife, sister or daughter in the act of adultery and kills them is punished by either a small fine or no more than three years in prison.

Kuwaiti women married to non-Kuwaitis, unlike Kuwaiti men, cannot pass citizenship to their children or spouses.

Adultery and extramarital intercourse are criminalized, and same-sex relations between men are punishable by up to seven years in prison. Transgender people can be arrested under a 2007 penal code provision that prohibits "imitating the opposite sex in any way."

Death Penalty

Kuwait maintains the death penalty for non-violent offenses, including drug-related charges, and carried out five executions in 2013, the first time the country had applied the death penalty since 2007. In 2015 and 2016, courts sentenced at least nine people to death.

Key International Actors

Kuwait joined the Saudi-led coalition that began attacking Houthi and allied forces in Yemen on March 26, 2015. Human Rights Watch documented 58 unlawful coalition airstrikes in Yemen, some of which may amount to war crimes, that killed nearly 800 civilians and repeatedly hit markets, schools and hospitals.

Kuwait-hosted peace talks between Yemeni parties to the conflict broke down in August.

In 2016, the United States classified Kuwait as a Tier 2 country in its annual Trafficking in Persons report. After classifying Kuwait as a Tier 3 country for nine consecutive years, the report credits the improvement to the passing of the 2015 domestic workers law and an unprecedented number of convictions of traffickers under the 2013 anti-trafficking law. The report found that Kuwait continued to have a rampant forced labor problem and that victims of trafficking were still being arrested, detained, and deported.

In August 2016, the United Nations Committee against Torture expressed its concern at reports of prolonged arrest and torture by Kuwaiti police and security forces of protesters, members of minorities, and persons suspected of terrorist activites. The committee also urged Kuwait to reinstate its de facto moratorium on applying the death penalty.

Kyrgyzstan

There were few meaningful improvements in Kyrgyzstan's human rights record in 2016. Authorities failed to implement a March 2016 decision by the United Nations Human Rights Committee calling for imprisoned human rights defender Azimjon Askarov's immediate release. As in recent years, the government did not take any steps to provide justice for the victims of interethnic violence in 2010. Impunity for ill-treatment and torture remains the norm. Violence and discrimination against women and lesbian, gay, bisexual, and transgender (LGBT) people continues.

Although parliament rejected a draft law on "foreign agents," another bill discriminating against LGBT people is pending. In December 2015, Kyrgyzstan's national security service banned a Human Rights Watch researcher from the country without reason.

Kyrgyzstan became a member of the UN Human Rights Council in January 2016.

Constitutional Reforms

An attempt in 2016 to amend the constitution was met by widespread criticism from civil society and opposition politicians. Despite substantive and procedural concerns, parliament approved legislation for authorities to hold a constitutional referendum. It was due to be held on December 11, 2016.

In its joint opinion, the Organization for Security and Co-operation in Europe's Office for Democratic Institutions and Human Rights (OSCE/ODHIR) and the Venice Commission found in August that the proposed constitutional amendments "would negatively impact the balance of powers by strengthening the powers of the executive, while weakening both the parliament and, to a greater extent, the judiciary."

Access to Justice

Authorities continue to deny justice to victims of the June 2010 interethnic violence in southern Kyrgyzstan and took no steps to review torture-tainted convictions handed down in the aftermath of the violence. Ethnic Uzbeks were disproportionately killed, and victims of arbitrary detention, ill-treatment, and torture, and house destruction during that violence.

Following a November 2015 visit to Kyrgyzstan, the OSCE high commissioner on national minorities, Astrid Thors, in May 2016 noted that "ethnic Uzbeks—the biggest minority in the country—remain severely under-represented in the Parliament." The commissioner "encourage[d] the authorities to step up activities aimed at increasing the participation and representation of national minorities as well as ensuring full access to justice."

Torture

Although the government acknowledges the problem of torture, impunity remains the norm. Criminal investigations into ill-treatment and torture allegations are rare, delayed, and ineffective, as are trials. After a five-year trial, a Bishkek appeals court in July upheld the acquittal verdict of four policemen charged in connection with the death in August 2011 of Usmanjon Kholmirzaev, an ethnic Uzbek who died of injuries sustained in police custody. At time of writing, no one had been held accountable for the torture leading to his death.

In its annual report issued in May, the National Center for the Prevention of Torture (NPM), an independent anti-torture body, concluded that "the Kyrgyz Republic does not fully ensure either in law or practice freedom from torture," and noted some interference in its work. Authorities in 2015 registered 199 claims of torture, but initiated criminal investigations in only 34 cases, the NPM reported. Parliament in March rejected in its second reading a draft law that would have curbed the NPM's independence.

Civil Society

In its March decision, the UN Human Rights Committee found that Askarov was arbitrarily detained, held in inhumane conditions, tortured, and otherwise mistreated without redress and not given a fair trial. The committee called on Kyrgyzstan to quash his conviction and release him immediately. The Office of the High Commissioner for Human Rights and human rights groups, including Human Rights Watch, echoed calls for Askarov's immediate release. Kyrgyzstan's Supreme Court in July considered the UN's decision as new evidence in the case,

and ordered a retrial, but did not order Askarov's release. The retrial was underway at time of writing. Authorities in May ordered that Askarov's house be confiscated, but his lawyer contested the order, which the state later withdrew.

After sustained efforts by Kyrgyzstan's civil society and others against the adoption of a "foreign agents" bill, which would have required organizations that receive foreign funding and engage in broadly defined political activities to
register as "foreign agents," parliament voted in May to reject the bill.

Rights lawyer Nurbek Toktogunov in January sued President Almazbek Atambaev
after the president publicly claimed that civil society had acted to destabilize the
nation and upend 2015 parliamentary elections, but the court declined to consider his complaint. In June, rights defenders Aziza Abdurasulova and Tolekan Is-
mailova similarly sued the president for publicly smearing them in a May
speech. A Bishkek court ruled in Atambaev's favor, declining to award damages.
In September, the decision was upheld on appeal.

In a February 2016 report, UN Special Rapporteur on the Situation of Human
Rights Defenders Michel Forst expressed "his deep concern at the increase of
verbal attacks, intimidation and harassment against civil society groups" and
urged the government to "ensure that human rights defenders are able to carry
out their legitimate work in a safe and enabling environment without fear of
threats or reprisals of any sort."

In December 2015, Kyrgyzstan denied entry to a Human Rights Watch Central
Asia researcher based in Bishkek, informing her at the airport that she had been
banned from the country. No written explanation was given for the ban to date,
nor has the researcher been allowed to return. In late December 2015, UN special
rapporteurs on the rights to freedom of peaceful assembly and association and
the situation of human rights defenders sent a joint letter to the government expressing "serious concern."

Violence against Women

Domestic violence against women and girls continues to be a serious problem.
Limited services and police hostility obstruct survivors' access to protection and
justice. Pressure to keep families together, stigma, economic dependence, and
fear of reprisals by abusers hinder some women from seeking assistance. Few

domestic violence complaints reach the courts and police do not systematically enforce protection orders.

A new domestic violence bill, which aims to strengthen protections for domestic abuse survivors, was adopted in its first reading on June 30, after a parliamentary hearing in mid-June. The bill was put on the parliament's agenda for November 2016, but had not been considered at time of writing.

On November 18, Kyrgyzstan's president signed into law a bill that would introduce criminal sanctions of three to five years' imprisonment for parents found responsible for allowing their underage children to marry, religious leaders for carrying out religious ceremonies for minors, and adults for marrying minors.

Freedom of Expression

Parliament approved in its first reading on June 22 contentious amendments to Kyrgyzstan's media law that ban foreigners from setting up media outlets in Kyrgyzstan and limit foreign funding of local media. Journalists and rights groups spoke out against the law. A second reading in parliament remained pending at time of writing.

In mid-December 2015, OSCE Representative on Freedom of the Media Dunja Mijatović called on Kyrgyz authorities to refrain from imposing disproportionate, excessive fines for civil defamation after a court upheld the ruling that Dayirbek Orunbekov, a journalist, pay 2 million som (US$27,750) in damages to the president. The journalist had written about the June 2010 events. In August 2016, the Prosecutor's Office opened a criminal case against Orunbekov for failing to pay damages. In November 2016, the case was sent to court for consideration.

Sexual Orientation and Gender Identity

LGBT people in Kyrgyzstan experience ill-treatment, extortion, and discrimination by both state and non-state actors. There is widespread impunity for these abuses. On May 24, the law, order and fighting crime parliamentary committee returned Kyrgyzstan's anti-LGBT bill, which would ban "propaganda of nontraditional sexual relations," for a repeat second reading, where it then stalled. The bill appears aimed at silencing anyone seeking to openly share information about same-sex relations in Kyrgyzstan.

Following a live debate on LGBT rights on national television, Kyrgyzstan's State Committee on National Security on June 14 summoned the editor-in-chief of Kloop.kg, an online media portal, for questioning about its coverage of the show. The television's supervisory board also formally reprimanded its general director for airing the content. Also in June, Kyrgyzstan voted against a resolution at the UN Human Rights Council establishing the mandate of an independent expert to address violence and discrimination against LGBT people.

Key International Actors

In late October 2015, US Secretary of State John Kerry visited Kyrgyzstan in part to try and improve relations with Kyrgyzstan after the Kyrgyz government revoked a 1993 cooperation agreement in response to the US State Department granting Askarov its Human Rights Defender award in July 2015. Kyrgyzstan and the US have not signed a new cooperation agreement.

During a March 31 visit to Kyrgyzstan in his capacity as OSCE chairperson-in-office, German Foreign Minister Frank-Walter Steinmeier downplayed human rights concerns and focused on cooperation and counterterrorism. Steinmeier noted Kyrgyzstan's "dynamic parliamentary democracy" enables it to play a "crucial role in bringing about stability."

German Chancellor Angela Merkel on July 14 visited Kyrgyzstan to discuss bilateral relations with President Atambaev. Her visit came three days after the Supreme Court review of Askarov's case. In her public comments, Chancellor Merkel did not comment on Askarov's continued wrongful imprisonment, but said she hoped Kyrgyzstan would give Askarov a fair trial.

The European Union in January 2016 granted Kyrgyzstan GSP+ status, an instrument of the EU's trade policy that grants tariff reductions for improved human and labor rights and environmental protections. The EU continued to use its annual human rights dialogue as the near-exclusive forum to raise human rights concerns, but issued a rare stand-alone rights statement on Askarov in April. The EU iterated that it "expects the Kyrgyz Republic to fully implement the recommendations of the Human Rights Committee."

Lebanon

Lebanon elected a president on October 31, 2016, ending a 29-month presidential vacuum during which political institutions remained paralyzed. A draft law to improve treatment of migrant domestic workers stalled in parliament. The government failed to take steps to end discrimination against women under Lebanese personal status laws.

The government's failure to provide basic services, including garbage removal, continued to spark protests, with some protesters being prosecuted before military tribunals. Others who spoke out against the government were subject to criminal defamation laws. Detainees continued to suffer from ill-treatment and torture, but in one welcome development, parliament in October established a National Human Rights Institute and national preventative mechanism against torture.

As the Syrian refugee crisis continued, new residency policies introduced in January 2015 caused an estimated 70 percent of Syrians to lose legal status, restricting their movement and their ability to work, access healthcare, and send their children to school. With limited international support, the government struggled to meet refugees' needs.

Lengthy Pretrial Detention, Ill-Treatment, and Torture

Amid protracted security threats, suspects suffered from lengthy pretrial detention and reported ill-treatment and torture. Following the death of a man detained in Roumieh prison on May 25, prisoners launched a protest amid allegations of negligent care.

In October, Parliament passed legislation creating a national preventative mechanism to monitor and investigate the use of torture, as required under the Optional Protocol to the Convention against Torture, which Lebanon ratified in 2008.

Hannibal Gaddafi, son of the late Libyan leader Muammar Gaddafi, has remained in "precautionary" pretrial detention since December 2015. He is facing charges of withholding information, allegedly in relation to the disappearance of Imam Musa Sadr in 1978. Gaddafi's lawyer has expressed concern about his possible extradition to Libya, where he faces a risk of imprisonment and torture.

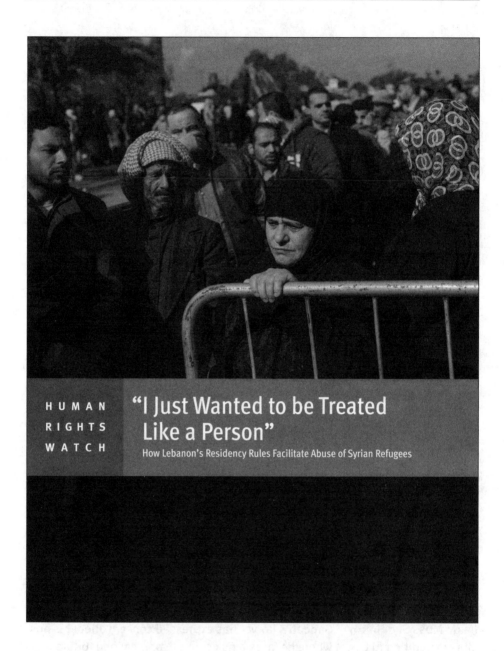

**HUMAN
RIGHTS
WATCH**

"I Just Wanted to be Treated Like a Person"

How Lebanon's Residency Rules Facilitate Abuse of Syrian Refugees

Freedom of Assembly, Freedom of Expression, and Use of Military Courts

While freedom of expression is generally respected in Lebanon, defaming or criticizing the Lebanese president or army is a criminal offense. On August 22, 2016, a woman was sentenced by a military court to a month in prison for "offending the military institution," after alleging that military intelligence members raped and tortured her in detention in 2013. Such retaliation may further deter other survivors from reporting abuse.

The Lebanese penal code also criminalizes libel and defamation of public officials, authorizing imprisonment of up to one year. Lebanese authorities arrested a lawyer and human rights activist, Nabil al-Halabi, on May 30, 2016, over Facebook posts criticizing government officials. He was detained for three days and released after signing a "document of submission."

Fourteen protesters, arrested for demonstrating against the government's failure to resolve a trash crisis, as well as corruption, in 2015, have been referred to military courts for rioting, violence against police, and destruction of property. Their trials are set to take place in January 2017. If found guilty, they face up to three years in prison. Military courts typically do not meet international fair trial standards and should not be used to prosecute civilians for criminal offenses.

Migrant Workers

An estimated 250,000 migrant domestic workers, primarily from Sri Lanka, Ethiopia, the Philippines, Nepal, and Bangladesh are excluded from labor law protections. The *kafala* (sponsorship) system subjects them to restrictive immigration rules and places them at risk of exploitation and abuse.

The most common complaints documented by the embassies of labor-sending countries and civil society groups include non-payment or delayed payment of wages, forced confinement, refusal to provide time off, and verbal and physical abuse. Migrant domestic workers suing their employers for abuse face legal obstacles and risk imprisonment and deportation due to the restrictive visa system. Several migrant domestic workers in Lebanon committed suicide or attempted to commit suicide in 2016.

Women's Rights

Despite women's active participation in all aspects of Lebanese society, discriminatory provisions remain in personal status laws, nationality laws, and the criminal code.

A lack of coordination in the government's response to sex trafficking continues to put women and girls at risk. Syrian women appear to be at particular risk of trafficking into forced prostitution and sexual exploitation. In March 2016, security officers freed as many as 75 Syrian women from two brothels. Although the country's 2011 anti-trafficking law directs the Ministry of Social Affairs to establish a trust fund for victims, the ministry has yet to establish such a fund.

A 2014 Law on the Protection of Women and Family from Domestic Violence established important protection measures and introduced policing and court reforms. But it failed to criminalize all forms of domestic violence, including marital rape. The law called for family violence units within the police and a fund to assist victims of domestic violence. But these have not yet been established. Some women continued to face obstacles in pursuing criminal complaints of domestic violence, mostly due to lengthy delays. In 2016, a man convicted for beating his wife to death was sentenced to just three years and nine months in prison. The case was under appeal at time of writing.

Women also continue to suffer discrimination under 15 Lebanese personal status laws, dependent on each individual's religious affiliation, including unequal access to divorce, residence of children after divorce, and property rights. Unlike Lebanese men, Lebanese women cannot pass on their nationality to foreign husbands and children and are subject to discriminatory inheritance laws.

Sexual Orientation and Gender Identity

Sexual relations outside of marriage—adultery and fornication—are criminalized under Lebanon's penal code. Furthermore, article 534 of the penal code punishes "any sexual intercourse contrary to the order of nature" with up to one year in prison. In recent years, authorities conducted raids to arrest persons allegedly involved in same-sex conduct, some of whom were subjected to torture including forced anal examinations.

In February, a Syrian refugee, arrested by Lebanese Military Intelligence officers apparently on suspicion he was gay, was allegedly tortured while detained at Military Intelligence, Ministry of Defense, Military Police, and Jounieh police centers.

Refugees

There are more than 1 million Syrian refugees registered with the United Nations High Commissioner for Refugees (UNHCR) in Lebanon. The government estimates the true number to be 1.5 million.

Lebanon's residency policy makes it difficult for Syrians to maintain legal status, heightening risks of exploitation and abuse and restricting refugees' access to work, education, and healthcare. An estimated 70 percent of Syrians in Lebanon now lack legal residency. Lebanon is not a signatory to the 1951 UN Refugee Convention, and refugees lacking legal status risk detention for illegal presence in the country.

Approximately 250,000 school-age Syrian children were out of school during the 2015-2016 school year, largely due to parents' inability to pay for transport, child labor, school directors imposing arbitrary enrollment requirements, and lack of language support. Secondary-school age children and children with disabilities faced particular barriers—only 5 percent of Syrians aged 15-18 were in enrolled in secondary schools last year.

Individual municipalities have imposed curfews on Syrian refugees and security services have arrested hundreds of Syrians for lack of residency documents. Several reports of attacks against Syrians by state and non-state actors emerged following a spate of eight suicide bombings in Al-Qaa on June 27, and July 2016 photos appeared to show municipal police in Amchit humiliating Syrian refugees. Five officers were questioned, but all were released and the head of the Amchit municipality reportedly stated "they didn't carry out any violations."

Human Rights Watch has also documented isolated forcible deportations of Syrians and Palestinians back to Syria, putting them at risk of arbitrary detention, torture, or other persecution. In January 2016, Lebanese authorities, in violation of their international obligations, sent hundreds of Syrians traveling through the Beirut airport back to Syria without first assessing their risk of harm upon return.

HUMAN
RIGHTS
WATCH

PREVENTING A LOST GENERATION: LEBANON

"Growing Up Without an Education"
Barriers to Education for Syrian Refugee Children in Lebanon

In 2016, Lebanon continued to impose entry regulations for Syrians that effectively barred many asylum seekers from entering Lebanon.

Approximately 45,000 Palestinians from Syria live in Lebanon, joining the estimated 260-280,000 Palestinian refugees already in the country, where they face restrictions including their right to work.

Legacy of Past Conflicts and Wars

In October 2012, Justice Minister Shakib Qortbawi put forward a draft decree to the cabinet to establish a national commission to investigate the fate of those "disappeared," during the country's 1975-1990 civil war and its aftermath but no further action was taken. In September 2014, the government finally provided the families of the disappeared with the files of the Official Commission of Inquiry appointed in 2000 to investigate the fate of the kidnapped. These showed that the government had not conducted any serious investigation.

Key International Actors

Syria, Iran, and Saudi Arabia maintain a strong influence on Lebanese politics through local allies and proxies, and increasingly so as the conflict in neighboring Syria drags on.

Many countries, including the United States, United Kingdom, members of the European Union, Canada, and various Gulf countries, have given Lebanon extensive, albeit insufficient, support to help it cope with the Syrian refugee crisis and to bolster security amid spillover violence.

Lebanese armed forces and police also receive assistance from a range of international donors, including the US, EU, UK, France, and Saudi Arabia. Some of these actors have tried to ensure the forces adhere to international human rights law, but compliance remains weak.

HUMAN
RIGHTS
WATCH

"We Feel We Are Cursed"
Life under ISIS in Sirte, Libya

Libya

The United Nations-backed, internationally recognized Government of National Accord (GNA) struggled in 2016 to assert itself in the capital Tripoli, as two authorities—one also based in Tripoli and another in eastern Libya—continued to compete for legitimacy and control over resources and infrastructure.

Forces aligned with all governments and dozens of militias continued to clash, exacerbating a humanitarian crisis with close to half-a-million internally displaced people. The civilian population struggled to gain access to basic services such as healthcare, fuel, and electricity.

Militias and armed forces affiliated with the two governments engaged in arbitrary detentions, torture, unlawful killings, indiscriminate attacks, abductions, and forcible disappearances. Criminal gangs and militias abducted politicians, journalists, and civilians—including children—for political and monetary gain. The domestic criminal justice system remained dysfunctional, offering no prospects for accountability, while the International Criminal Court, despite having jurisdiction over Libya provided by the UN Security Council, failed to open any new investigation into ongoing crimes.

The United States, United Kingdom, France, and the United Arab Emirates reportedly expanded their military activities in Libya to support forces in fighting extremists in Sirte and Benghazi.

The Islamic State (also known as ISIS) lost control over large parts of its self-proclaimed capital in Sirte, where it had been based since June 2015, and remained embroiled in fighting with Libyan and foreign forces. ISIS groups summarily executed people for alleged witchcraft and "treason" and imposed a severe and restrictive interpretation of Sharia law in areas under their control.

Tens of thousands of migrants, asylum seekers, and refugees from Africa and the Middle East transited through Libya on their way to Europe, with 4,518 drowning or going missing while crossing the Mediterranean in unsafe vessels. While in Libya, armed groups and guards at migrant detention facilities subjected many to forced labor, torture, sexual abuse, and extortion.

Political Transition and Constitution

The Presidential Council (PC), the highest body of the GNA, arrived in March in Tripoli to take control of ministries and government facilities that had previously been under the control of the self-proclaimed National Salvation Government, which stepped down in April to make way for the GNA .

In October, the former prime minister of the National Salvation Government announced a comeback together with the rump General National Congress, the former legislature, and took over the Tripoli premises of the State Council, the advisory body attached to the GNA.

The Interim Government, meanwhile, refused to recognize the cabinet proposed by the Presidency Council and continued to operate as a rival authority from al-Bayda and Tobruk in eastern Libya. Despite enjoying international recognition, the GNA struggled to win support domestically and gain authority and control over territory and institutions.

The so-called Libyan National Army (LNA), under the command of General Khalifa Hiftar and allied with the Interim Government, gained control of substantial territory in 2016, including in the oil crescent, where they took over major terminals. Libya's legislative body, the House of Representatives, remained allied with the Interim Government . Throughout the year, deputies opposing the UN-backed GNA obstructed voting for a proposed cabinet.

In June, the president of the House of Representatives, Agilah Saleh, declared martial law, a de facto state of emergency, in the eastern region and appointed the LNA chief of staff, Abdulrazeq al-Nadhouri, as military governor for that region. Since then, al-Nadhouri has replaced several elected civilian heads of municipal councils with military governors.

In September, Abdurrahman Swehli, head of the High Council of State, declared that, in light of the inability of the House of Representatives to confirm a cabinet, the High Council of State would exercise all powers, including legislative ones.

Libya's Constitution Drafting Assembly failed to finalize a preliminary draft constitution and remained embroiled in internal disagreements.

Security and Armed Militias

In the absence of a state authority exercising control over the national territory, dozens of rival militia groups and military forces, with varying agendas and allegiances, continued to flout international law with impunity. They indiscriminately shelled civilians, abducted and forcibly disappeared people, tortured, arbitrarily detained, and unlawfully killed people and destroyed civilian property.

In the first half of 2016, fighters loyal to ISIS controlled the central coastal town of Sirte and subjected residents to a rigid interpretation of Sharia law that included public floggings, amputation of limbs, and public lynchings, often leaving the victims' corpses on display.

Armed Conflict and War Crimes

Warring factions continued to indiscriminately shell civilian areas, mostly in Benghazi and Derna in the east and in Sirte. From March until August, 141 civilian were killed in the violence, including 30 children, and 146 injured, including 28 children, according to the UN Support Mission In Libya (UNSMIL).

In the east, the LNA and allied forces made substantial advances against the Benghazi Revolutionaries Shura Council, an alliance of groups including Islamist militias such as Ansar al-Sharia. As of November 2016, fighting remained concentrated in the Ganfouda neighborhood of Benghazi, where several hundred civilians, including Libyans and foreign nationals, remained trapped by a standoff between LNA and militants since 2014. Civilians, including children, struggled with limited access to medical care, electricity, and food.

In February, two Serbian civilians held by ISIS died in a US air strikes on targets in the western coastal town of Sabratha, which also killed dozens of fighters. The same month, unidentified aircraft attacked a hospital compound in the city of Derna, killing at least two civilians and causing extensive damage.

In May, armed groups allied with the GNA, backed by US airstrikes, launched a military offensive against ISIS fighters in Sirte. Hostilities continued at time of writing.

In Derna, the LNA continued to fight against the Derna Revolutionaries Shura Council, an alliance of militias that participated in the ousting of ISIS from the city in 2015.

In July, 14 unidentified bodies were found close to a dumpster in Benghazi with gunshot wounds, and in October, 10 unidentified bodies with gunshot wounds and torture marks were found in a nearby neighborhood of Benghazi. Both incidents took place in areas under LNA control. To date, authorities have not publicly announced any conclusion to their investigations. In October, shelling by unidentified forces killed one woman and injured six others in a camp for internally displaced people from Tawergha, in Tripoli.

Arbitrary Detention, Torture, and Deaths in Custody

Prison authorities and militias continued to hold thousands of detainees, including some women and children, in long-term arbitrary detention without charges or due process. While conditions varied, most prisons lacked a functioning medical facility and hygienic sanitary installations. Guards and militia members mistreated and tortured detainees with impunity.

In June, unidentified armed groups killed 12 detainees upon their conditional release from al-Baraka prison in Tripoli. All 12 were members of the former Gaddafi government and had been accused of taking part in the violence against anti-government protesters in 2011. According to the families, the bodies were found in various locations around Tripoli. At time of writing, no investigation had been conducted into these crimes.

Judicial System

Ongoing insecurity led to the collapse of the criminal justice system in Libya. Courts in the east remained mostly shut, while elsewhere they operated at a reduced level. The Supreme Court failed to issue judgments on all cases that were heard before it due to political divisions. In Sirte and environs, ISIS groups implemented their own interpretation of Sharia law in areas under their control including punishing people for smoking, wearing "immodest" dress, and adultery.

International Criminal Court

The ICC has the mandate to investigate war crimes and crimes against humanity in Libya pursuant to UN Security Council Resolution 1970 passed on February 27, 2011. The ICC prosecutor has failed to open any new investigations into the grave and ongoing crimes in Libya, citing resources limitations.

Libyan authorities failed to surrender Saif al-Islam Gaddafi, son of former leader Muammar Gaddafi, to the ICC where he is wanted for committing crimes against humanity during the 2011 uprising. Gaddafi was held by a militia in Zintan since his arrest in 2011, and was last seen by UN monitors in Zintan in June 2014.

In her November 9 update to the Security Council, ICC Prosecutor Fatou Bensouda announced her office would expand the Libya investigations in 2017 to include recent and ongoing serious crimes.

Death Penalty

The penal code contains more than 30 articles that provide for the death penalty. Since Gaddafi's overthrow in 2011, civil and military courts around the country have imposed death sentences, including against eight former officials in the Gaddafi government in a flawed trial in 2015. No death sentences are known to have been carried out since 2010.

Internally Displaced People

The UN High Commission for Refugees (UNHCR) estimated at 435,000 Libya's population of internally displaced people. UNHCR was unable to conduct vital activities such as child protection services at detention centers due to inadequate funding for its humanitarian programs.

In what amounts to a crime against humanity, militias and authorities in Misrata continued to prevent 40,000 residents of Tawergha, Tomina, and Karareem from returning to their homes in relation for alleged crimes during the 2011 revolution attributed to people from those cities against anti-Gaddafi activists and fighters.

In August, representatives of Misrata and Tawergha signed a reconciliation agreement that aims to ensure return home of the displaced from Tawergha as well as compensation for both sides and reconstruction of damaged structures.

The deal also foresees accountability for serious crimes. It has yet to come into force.

Freedom of Speech and Expression

In June, an ISIS fighter allegedly shot dead freelance reporter Khaled Al Zantani in Benghazi. In Sirte, an ISIS fighter allegedly shot and killed photojournalist Abdelkader Fassouk in July, and in September, an ISIS fighter allegedly shot and killed Dutch photojournalist Jeroen Oerlemans.

The fate of Sofiane Chourabi and Nadhir Ktari, two Tunisian journalists who went missing in September 2014 while on assignment in Libya, remained unknown.

Armed groups kidnapped and disappeared other journalists. According to RSF, in January, a unit allied with the LNA in Benghazi arrested and tortured a local correspondent for a TV station, Libya HD, Badr Al Rabhi, for three days.

Women's Rights, Sexual Orientation, and Gender Identity

The penal code permits a reduced sentence for a man who kills or injures his wife or another female relative because he suspects her of extramarital sexual relations. Libyan law inadequately prohibits domestic violence and its personal status laws continue to discriminate against women, particularly with respect to marriage, divorce, and inheritance.

Same-sex relations are prohibited and punished with up to five years in jail.

Abductions and Enforced Disappearances

Militias continued to abduct and disappear civilians, including politicians, and journalists, with impunity. Criminal groups abducted residents, including children, demanding large ransoms from their families and often killing their victims if relatives failed to come up with the money.

Those still missing include Tripoli civil society activist Abdelmoez Banoon and Benghazi prosecutor Abdel-Nasser Al-Jeroushi, both abducted by unidentified groups in 2014. Saif al-Islam Gaddafi, wanted by the ICC for crimes against humanity and sentenced to death in absentia by a Tripoli court for crimes committed during the 2011 revolution, was last seen in June 2014, in Zintan. Gaddafi was held by the Abu Baker al-Siddiq Brigade in Zintan following his arrest in 2011.

Migrants, Refugees, and Asylum Seekers

Refugees, asylum seekers, and migrants, continued to flock to Europe via Libya. As of November, UNHCR recorded over 342,774 arrivals to Italy by sea from North Africa since January mostly from Libya. According to UNHCR, at least 4,518 died or went missing while crossing the Mediterranean from Libya to Europe. The International Organization for Migration estimated that 771,146 migrants and asylum seekers were in Libya as of November.

Members of the Libyan Coast Guards or Navy intercepted boats and returned the migrants and refugees back to land and into detention centers, often subjecting the migrants they intercepted to physical and verbal abuse. While the Department for Combating Illegal Migration (DCIM), which is part of the Ministry of Interior, managed the majority of migrant detention centers, militias and smugglers controlled other unofficial detention facilities.

Conditions at migrant detention facilities remained abysmal. Officials and militias held migrants and refugees in prolonged detention without judicial review and subjected them to poor conditions, including overcrowding and insufficient food. Guards and militia members subjected migrants and refugees to beatings, forced labor, and sexual violence.

Key International Actors

The United States, European Union, and regional states all played significant roles in the armed conflicts occurring in Libya. The US, France, and United Kingdom reportedly participated in military activities in support of Libyan forces against militant groups, most notably ISIS in Sirte and Benghazi.

Efforts to reach a political settlement between warring factions, led by the UN envoy to Libya Martin Kobler, and backed by members of the international community most notably the US, UK, France, and Italy, failed to achieve the desired results as parties remained engaged in hostilities, competing for legitimacy.

On March 8, the UN Panel of Experts on Libya, established pursuant to UN Security Council resolution 1973 (2011), issued its final report which said that several countries, individuals and companies were responsible for violations of the arms embargo against Libya. According to the report, the UAE, Egypt, Qatar, Turkey, Ukraine and Sudan have all violated the arms embargo against Libya since 2011, by transferring weapons, ammunitions, aircraft or armored vehicles to the conflict parties.

Also in March, a leaked document revealed that British special forces had been actively fighting extremist groups in Libya since January. In July, France announced that three of its soldiers were killed in Libya after a helicopter crashed during an intelligence-gathering operation. In August, the US expanded its air campaign in Libya at the request of the GNA to include targets in the ISIS stronghold of Sirte.

The Office of the High Commissioner for Human Rights (OHCHR) released a report in February documenting widespread violations and abuses committed in Libya since 2014 that included unlawful killings; indiscriminate attacks; torture and ill treatment; arbitrary detention; abductions and disapperances; and violations against women, journalists, human rights defenders, migrants, and children.

Despite a recommendation by the High Commissioner that the Human Rights Council consider establishing an independent expert on Libya to report on the human rights situation and progress towards accountability, the council's resolution only requested a further report from the high commissioner in March 2017. In a September update, the high commissioner's office reported to the council that the situation has not improved and that impunity prevails, and reiterated the recommendation that the council create an independent expert mandate.

The UN Security Council extended for another 12 months in March an arms embargo on Libya. In June, the council unanimously authorized the inspection of vessels off Libyan high seas in an effort to crackdown on illicit weapons smuggling. The council also passed a resolution in July that authorized moving Libya's category 2 chemical weapons out of the country and destroying them. In October, the council renewed its authorization for the interdiction of vessels used for smuggling migrants on the high seas off the coast of Libya.

The Rule of Law and Human Rights division at UNSMIL, which operates from Tunis and visits Libya only rarely due to security concerns, scaled down its public reporting on human rights violations. However, in March, it started producing a monthly bulletin on civilian casualties in Libya.

In June, the EU extended its anti-smuggling naval operation in the central Mediterranean, Operation Sophia, to include training for the Libyan Coast Guard and Navy. In July, NATO committed to supporting Operation Sophia by providing intelligence, surveillance, and reconnaissance, as well as capacity-building for the Libyan coastguard and navy.

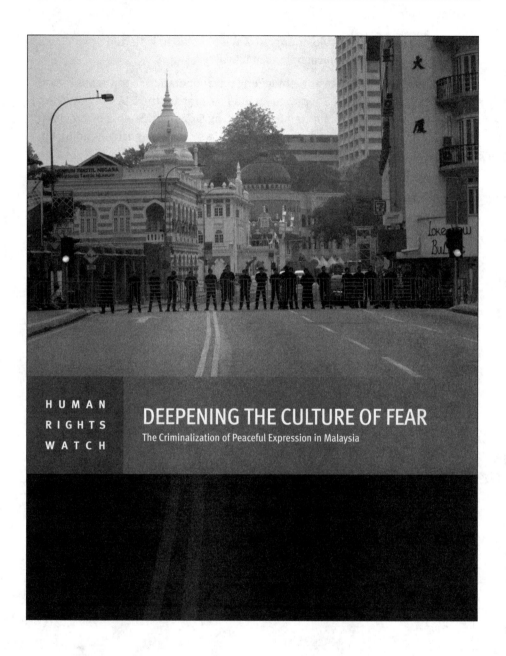

HUMAN
RIGHTS
WATCH

DEEPENING THE CULTURE OF FEAR
The Criminalization of Peaceful Expression in Malaysia

Malaysia

Malaysia's human rights situation continued to deteriorate in 2016, with human rights defenders, activists, political opposition figures, and journalists facing harassment and politically motivated prosecution. Those criticizing the administration of Prime Minister Najib Razak or commenting on the government's handling of the 1 Malaysia Development Berhad (1MDB) corruption scandal have been particular targets.

Freedom of Expression

The Sedition Act and the Communications and Multimedia Act (CMA) continue to be the laws most frequently used against critical speech. In August 2016, vice president of the Parti Amanah Negara (PAN) Youth, Mohd Fakhrulrazi Mohd Mokhtar, was sentenced to eight months in prison for sedition for calling for the release of jailed opposition leader Anwar Ibrahim at a rally in February 2015. In April, a court sent activist Haris Ibrahim to prison for eight months on a sedition charge for a speech he gave in May 2013 challenging the results of the 2013 general election.

Section 233(1) of the CMA provides criminal penalties of up to one year in prison for a communication that "is obscene, indecent, false, menacing or offensive in character with intent to annoy, abuse, threaten or harass another person." The broadly worded law has been repeatedly used against those who allegedly insulted Najib or Malaysia's royalty on social media, and against individuals calling for Najib to resign.

Graphic artist Fahmi Reza is facing two counts under section 233 for posting an online image of Najib in clown make-up. Social media posts allegedly insulting to the royal family of Johor led to at least a dozen criminal prosecutions in 2016. In June 2016, a court sentenced 19-year-old Mohammed Amirul Azwan Mohammad Shakri to a year in prison after he pled guilty to 14 counts of insulting the sultan of Johor on Facebook. Prosecutors charged activist Khalid Ismath with 11 counts of violating section 233 of the CMA and three counts of sedition for posts on a solidarity page for Kamal Hisham Jaafar, a former legal adviser to the Johor royal family who was detained on allegations of corruption.

On November 14, vice president of the opposition Parti Keadlian Rakyat, Rafizi Ramli, was convicted of violating the Malaysian's Official Secrets Act for disclosing a page of the auditor-general's report on the 1MDB scandal, which remains classified as an official secret despite having been submitted to parliament in April. He was sentenced to 18 months in jail, which disqualifies him from serving in parliament for five years after his sentence finishes.

Although successive prime ministers have pledged not to censor the internet, authorities have repeatedly used the CMA to block websites, including those reporting on allegations of corruption. Censors blocked the UK-based website *Sarawak Report* in June 2015, and the website Medium, which was printing *Sarawak Report*'s articles, in January 2016. Also blocked were the *Malaysia Chronicle*, regional news website *Asia Sentinel*, and at least four local blog sites commenting on political matters.

On February 25, 2016, the government blocked the online news portal the *Malaysian Insider* under section 233 of the CMA for publishing "unverified information." While the Malaysian Multimedia and Communications Commission (MCMC) did not specify what articles led to the blockage, the *Malaysian Insider* had recently published an article citing a source in the Malaysian Anti-Corruption Commission stating that the commission had "credible evidence" to charge Najib with corruption. On March 14, still blocked by authorities, the *Malaysian Insider* shut down, citing commercial reasons. The portal's editor, Jahabar Sadiq, told the BBC that the site had been losing money since it was blocked, with advertisers holding off buying ads until the block was lifted.

Freedom of Assembly and Association

The government continues to prosecute individuals for participation in peaceful assembly, in violation of international human rights law. Those holding a demonstration without giving notice or participating in "street protests" are routinely arrested or called in for questioning, and many charged with criminal offenses. In August 2016, after the US Department of Justice issued a civil forfeiture complaint seeking to seize assets purchased with funds allegedly looted from 1MDB, a group of students organized a rally calling for the individual referred to as "Malaysian Official No. 1" in the complaint and widely believed to be Prime Minister Najib, to be identified and arrested. Although police did not interfere with the rally, they called in the organizers and several political figures who spoke at the event for questioning for sedition, "activity detrimental to parliamentary democracy," and violation of the overly restrictive Peaceful Assembly Law.

The Societies Act restricts the right to freedom of association by requiring that organizations with seven or more members register with the registrar of societies. The law gives the minister of home affairs "absolute discretion" to declare an organization illegal, and also provides the government supervisory authority over political parties. According to the Registry of Societies' website, as of September the registrar had rejected more than 36 percent of applications to form organizations submitted in 2016.

Police Abuse and Impunity

Police torture of suspects in custody, in some cases resulting in deaths, and excessive use of force in apprehending suspects remained serious problems in 2016, as did a lack of accountability for such offenses. In January 2016, Malaysian human rights NGO Suara Rakyat Malaysia (SUARAM) released letters from six individuals detained without trial under the Security Offenses (Special Measures) Act detailing the torture and ill-treatment they had suffered while in custody, including beatings and sexual humiliation.

To date, no one has been held accountable for the mistreatment. In April 2016, the Enforcement Agencies Integrity Commission (EAIC) found that N. Dharmendran, who died in police custody in 2013, was beaten to death and recommended that the officers responsible be held to account. In June 2016, however, a court acquitted all four officers of all charges, continuing the longstanding impunity for such offenses.

Criminal Justice System

On August 1, the controversial National Security Council Act came into force. The law gives sweeping powers to a council headed by Prime Minister Najib to declare regions, including the entire country, as security areas to protect "any interest of Malaysia." Once a region is declared a security area, the law suspends

415

many restraints on police powers there, allowing the authorities to conduct arrests, searches, and seizures without warrants.

Malaysia continues to detain individuals without trial under restrictive laws. Both the 1959 Prevention of Crime Act and the 2015 Prevention of Terrorism Act give government-appointed boards the authority to impose detention without trial for up to two years, renewable indefinitely, to order electronic monitoring, and to impose other significant restrictions on freedom of movement and association, with no possibility of judicial review. The similarly restrictive Security Offenses (Special Measures) Act allows for preventive detention of up to 28 days with no judicial review.

Malaysia retains the death penalty for various crimes, with the sentence mandatory for 12 offenses, including drug trafficking. Nearly 1,000 people are estimated to be on death row. The government is not transparent about when and how decisions are made to carry out executions, and in March executed three men after giving only two days' notice to their families. The government has said it is considering amending the law to change the mandatory death penalty provisions, but has yet to take steps to do so.

Refugees, Asylum Seekers, and Trafficking Victims

Malaysia is not a party to the 1951 Refugee Convention, and refugees and asylum seekers have no legal rights in the country. Over 150,000 refugees and asylum seekers, the vast majority of whom come from Burma, have registered with UNCHR in Malaysia but are unable to work, travel, or enrol in government schools. The lack of status leaves them highly vulnerable to abuses. Many of those who seeking refuge are treated as "illegal migrants" and locked up in overcrowded and unsanitary immigration detention centers. Female refugees are particularly vulnerable to abuse, and there is evidence of large numbers of coerced and forced marriages of ethnic Rohingya women and girls from Burma.

No progress has been made in identifying and investigating suspects involved in the deaths of over 100 suspected victims of trafficking whose bodies were found in mass graves on the Thai-Malaysian border in 2015. The Malaysian government has failed to effectively implement the amendments passed in 2014 to Malaysia's 2007 anti-trafficking law, in particular by taking the necessary administrative steps to provide assistance and work authorization to all trafficking victims who desire it, while ensuring their freedom of movement.

Despite these failures, Malaysia inexplicably remained on the Tier 2 "watch list" in the annual Trafficking in Persons Report prepared by the United States Department of State as a country viewed as making a "significant effort" to meet the standards of the Trafficking Victims Protection Act.

Judicial Freedom

The government has said it intends to introduce amendments to the Legal Profession Act that would allow the government to interfere with and obstruct the bar's actions. The proposed amendments would empower the minister in charge of legal affairs to appoint two members of the Bar Council, and to issue rules and regulations governing bar association elections.

In addition, they would increase the quorum needed for a general meeting from 500 to 4,000 members, or 25 percent of the bar's 17,000 membership, making it virtually impossible for the bar to take action at its general meetings. The bill to amend the Legal Profession Act is likely be introduced when parliament next sits in March 2017.

Discrimination Based on Gender, Sexual Orientation, and Gender Identity

Discrimination against lesbian, gay, bisexual, and transgender (LGBT) people is pervasive in Malaysia. Article 377A of the penal code criminalizes same-sex activity between men with punishments of up to 20 years in prison and whipping. Numerous Sharia-based laws and regulations prohibiting a "man posing as a woman," sexual relations between women, and sexual relations between men effectively criminalize LGBT people.

Child marriage is permitted under Malaysian law, and the government's failure to collect data on age of marriage of women and girls presents an obstacle to even discussing the problem. An effort in 2016 by activists to raise the age of marriage to 18 was blocked in the lower house of parliament.

Key International Actors

Malaysia positions itself in the United Nations and the international community as a moderate Muslim state prepared to stand up to Islamist extremism, and this year established a Regional Digital Counter-Messaging Communications Centre to counter Islamic State propaganda, earning support from the US and its allies. Nevertheless, both the US Department of State and the European Parliament have expressed concern about the country's deteriorating human rights situation.

In December 2015, the European Parliament passed a resolution deploring "the deteriorating human rights situation in Malaysia and in particular the crackdown on civil society activists, academics, media and political activists" and expressing concern about the number of people facing charges or arrest under the Sedition Act."

In March 2016, the US State Department issued a statement expressing its concern about "actions to restrict access to domestic and international reporting on Malaysian current affairs" and calling on the Malaysian government to ensure that its laws fully respect the right to freedom of expression.

In 2016, Malaysia served as a non-permanent representative to the UN Security Council, where it acted as the chair of the Working Group on Children and Armed Conflict. Malaysia continued its close engagement with China, its largest trading partner. In November, Malaysia agreed to buy four Chinese naval vessels and pledged with Beijing to handle disputes in the South China Sea bilaterally.

Mali

Malian civilians endured a situation of "no war, no peace" in 2016, as implementation of the previous year's peace accord to end the military and political crisis in the north stalled, and armed groups linked to Al-Qaeda launched dozens of attacks on Malian security forces and international peacekeepers, extending their operations south.

The attacks, and the failure to disarm thousands of combatants from Mali's 2012-2013 armed conflict, deepened a security vacuum, creating a precarious human rights climate for civilians in central and northern Mali. Civilians suffered increasing incidents of criminality, and the fall-out from clashes between armed groups. Long-delayed local elections were held on November 20, but violence and threats from armed groups prohibited voters in dozens of local administrative areas from taking part.

The insecurity undermined efforts by the Malian government and its international partners to strengthen the rule of law and deliver basic health care, education, and humanitarian assistance. Persistent intercommunal conflicts in central and northern Mali left dozens dead and were exploited by armed groups to garner support and recruits.

Government forces responded to attacks by Islamist armed groups with counterterrorism operations that often resulted in arbitrary arrests, executions, and torture and other ill-treatment.

Malian authorities made scant effort to investigate and hold accountable those implicated in recent abuses or those committed during the 2012-2013 armed conflict. Rule of law institutions remain weak. Corruption was endemic at all levels of government, further impeding Malians' access to basic health care and education.

French forces and United Nations peacekeepers attempted to fill the security vacuum. The failure of the Malian government and armed groups to implement the 2015 accord and the spread of militant attacks to Burkina Faso and Cote d'Ivoire generated impatience and growing diplomatic engagement by the international community.

Abuses by Armed Groups in North and Central Mali

Throughout 2016, armed groups linked to Al-Qaeda, opposing ethnic Tuareg and Arab groups, and government-supported militia attacked each other, Malian soldiers and neutral peacekeepers, and to a lesser extent aid workers and other civilians. The increasing presence of Islamist armed groups in central Mali generated fear and engulfed more civilians in the conflict.

During 2016, Islamist armed groups executed at least 25 men, including civilians and members of armed groups, allegedly for being informants for the government and French engaged in counterterrorism operations.

Several civilians were killed by landmines and improvised explosive devices planted by some of these groups on major roads. In 2016, there were scores of attacks, the vast majority by bandits, on humanitarian agencies.

At least 23 UN peacekeepers with the Multidimensional Integrated Stabilization Mission in Mali (MINUSMA) were killed and 108 wounded in attacks by Islamist armed groups in 2016, bringing the total to 67 killed since MINUSMA's creation in 2013. Armed groups linked to Al-Qaeda in the Islamic Maghreb (AQIM) took responsibility for most of these incidents, including a February attack that killed seven peacekeepers from Guinea, and two incidents in May that killed five peacekeepers from Togo and five from Chad.

AQIM claimed responsibility for the January kidnappings of a Swiss missionary in Timbuktu and an elderly Australian doctor in Burkina Faso. In October, an American aid worker was kidnapped from Niger, bringing the number of foreign hostages believed to be held by Islamist armed groups in Mali to six.

Abuses by State Security Forces

Government forces committed numerous violations against suspected supporters and members of Islamist armed groups in 2016, including the summary killing of at least five detainees, the torture of over a dozen suspects, and the mock execution and ill-treatment of many more.

Army soldiers and members of a pro-government militia, Groupe Autodéfense Touareg Imghad et Alliés (GATIA), meted out the most frequent and serious abuse. The abuses usually stopped after detainees were handed over to government gendarmes.

Some 20 men accused of crimes against the state and terrorist-related offenses were held outside the protection of the law within the headquarters of the state security services. Members of the security forces were also implicated in frequent acts of extortion, bribe taking, and theft, including from detainees. Security forces used excessive force to respond to demonstrations in Gao and Bamako, leaving at least four dead.

The military made little effort to investigate and hold to account soldiers or militiamen implicated in violations against civilians. However, progress was made in staffing and equipping the Military Justice Directorate in Bamako.

Accountability for Abuses

Progress in addressing impunity was evident in the trial of former coup leader Gen. Amadou Haya Sanogo and 17 co-defendants, many members of the Malian security services, for the 2012 abduction and killing of 21 elite "Red Beret" soldiers, which began on November 30.

However, the Malian government made scant progress in holding to account those responsible for many other violations committed during Mali's 2012-2013 armed conflict. Serious crimes include the summary execution by armed Islamists of approximately 150 Malian soldiers in Aguelhok, sexual violence, and widespread pillage by various armed groups in the north, as well as the extrajudicial execution, enforced disappearance, and torture of suspected Islamist rebels by Mali's security forces. With a few exceptions, judicial authorities failed to investigate over 100 complaints filed by victims and their family members.

The judiciary investigated some cases of sexual violence perpetrated in 2015 and 2016 by armed groups in the north, as well as a deadly incident of communal violence near the central Malian town of Dioura.

On September 27, the International Criminal Court (ICC) sentenced Malian Ahmad al-Faqi al-Mahdi, formerly with Ansar Dine, to nine years in prison for his role in destroying historical and religious monuments in Timbuktu in 2012. The trial was the ICC's first prosecution for this war crime and the first time an ICC defendant pleaded guilty. ICC investigations in Mali are ongoing, but are limited in part because of the precarious security situation.

Truth and Reconciliation Mechanism

The Truth, Justice and Reconciliation Commission, established by executive order of the president in 2014 with a three-year mandate, made progress in 2016. In December 2015, the Council of Ministers approved the appointment of 14 commission members, and in May, an additional 10 commissioners were appointed. During 2016, the 25-member commission developed a work plan and commenced research into past violations. The credibility of the body was undermined by the government's failure to consult sufficiently with a wide variety of stakeholders on the commission's membership, mandated powers, and degree of independence. The commission's inclusion of nine members of armed groups and lack of inclusion of those representing victims' groups drew sharp criticism from Malian civil society.

Judiciary and Legal Framework for Human Rights

The Malian judiciary countrywide was plagued by neglect and mismanagement, including insufficient staffing and logistical constraints. These shortfalls hindered efforts to address impunity for perpetrators of all crimes, contributed to violations of the right to due process, and led to incidents of vigilante justice. Due to the courts' inability to adequately process cases, hundreds of detainees are held in extended pretrial detention.

In April, the government adopted a bill providing greater independence for the National Commission for Human Rights, and in September, adopted a five-year action plan to strengthen human rights and access to justice. In July, the National Assembly extended the state of emergency, first declared on November 21, 2015 in the aftermath of an attack on a hotel in Bamako, until March 2017.

Recruitment of Child Soldiers

Armed groups in the north, including those allied with the government, continued to recruit and use child soldiers. During 2016, at least seven schools in the north were at various times occupied by members of the armed groups. At least six children suspected of supporting armed groups were detained in state run detention centers, in contravention of a 2013 protocol stipulating that children were to be placed in a care center managed by the UNICEF, the UN children's rights agency.

Key International Actors

France and the United States took the lead on military matters, the European Union led on training and security sector reform, and the UN led on rule of law and political stability, though these actors were largely reluctant to publicly call for investigations into past and ongoing crimes.

The UN and several members of the international mediation team that negotiated the accord threatened targeted sanctions against those threatening Mali's security.

In light of deteriorating security, the UN Security Council in June authorized an additional 2,500 personnel for MINUSMA to a maximum strength of 13,289 military and 1,920 police, included a more robust civilian protection mandate, and authorized French forces to intervene in support of MINUSMA forces in imminent danger.

MINUSMA forces on a few occasions engaged in excessive force, which in one occasion led to the death of a detainee near Aguelhok. At time of writing, the results of the UN boards of inquiry into the cases were pending.

Operation Barkhane, the 3,000-strong French regional counterterrorism operation launched in 2014 continued operations in Mali, Mauritania, Burkina Faso, Niger, and Chad. The US military provided logistical support to Barkhane and is building a major military and drone hub in Niger.

The EU Training Mission in Mali (EUTM) began its third two-year mandate to train the Malian army, and the EU Capacity Building Mission (EUCAP) continued training the Malian national guard, gendarmerie, and police forces. Since 2013, the UN Peacebuilding Fund has allocated $12 million to address unemployment, access to justice and education, and communal tension.

MINUSMA, the UN Development Programme, the EU, the Netherlands, and Canada took the lead in programs to support the justice sector and address corruption. The United States supported reform of military justice.

The UN independent expert on the situation of human rights in Mali, Suliman Baldo, conducted two missions to Mali.

HUMAN RIGHTS WATCH

CLOSED DOORS
Mexico's Failure to Protect Central American Refugee and Migrant Children

Mexico

During the administration of President Enrique Peña Nieto, security forces have been implicated in repeated, serious human rights violations—including extrajudicial killings, enforced disappearances, and torture—during efforts to combat organized crime. The government has made little progress in prosecuting those responsible for recent abuses, let alone the large number of abuses committed by soldiers and police since former President Felipe Calderón (2006-2012) initiated Mexico's "war on drugs."

In April, the Interdisciplinary Group of Independent Experts (GIEI), which was established through an agreement between the government and the Inter-American Commission on Human Rights (IACHR), issued its final report on the case of the 43 disappeared students from Ayotzinapa, Guerrero State. The report documented egregious flaws in the government's investigation of the case, refuted key conclusions by the Attorney General's Office, and called on authorities to pursue fresh lines of investigation. Other continuing problems in Mexico include attacks on journalists and limited access to reproductive rights and health care.

Enforced Disappearances

Since 2006, Mexico's security forces have participated in widespread enforced disappearances.

In August 2016, the government reported that the whereabouts of more than 27,000 people who had gone missing since 2006 remain unknown. Prosecutors and police routinely fail to take basic investigative steps to identify those responsible for enforced disappearances, often telling the missing people's families to investigate on their own. Authorities have failed to identify remains of bodies or body parts found in various locations, including in clandestine graves, throughout the country.

The federal government has pursued potentially promising initiatives to find people who have gone missing, but they have produced limited results. In 2013, it created a unit in the Attorney General's Office to investigate disappearances, which became a Special Prosecutor's Office in October 2015. However, when consulted in April, members of that office said that they had brought charges in only four of a total of 830 cases of disappearances into which they had opened investigations.

In 2015, Congress approved a constitutional reform giving it authority to pass general laws on enforced disappearance and torture that would establish a single nationwide definition for each of the crimes and facilitate their prosecution in all 31 states and Mexico City. At time of writing, President Peña Nieto had submitted the bills to Congress but neither had been enacted.

Only one of the 43 missing students from the teachers college in Ayotzinapa, disappeared in 2014 and believed killed, has been positively identified among remains that the government says are those of the students. As of July, more than 100 people had been charged with alleged involvement in the abductions and killings; at time of writing, none had been convicted.

Extrajudicial Killings

Unlawful killings of civilians by Mexican security forces "take place at an alarmingly high rate" amid an atmosphere of "systematic and endemic impunity," according to the United Nations special rapporteur on extrajudicial, summary, or arbitrary executions in 2014.

In August 2016, the National Human Rights Commission (CNDH) concluded that federal police arbitrarily executed 22 of 42 civilians who died in a confrontation in 2015 in Tanhuato, Michoacán State. Police fatally shot at least 13 people in the back, tortured two detainees, and burned a man alive, the CNDH concluded, then altered the crime scene by moving bodies and planting guns to justify the illegal killings.

At time of writing, a federal investigation into the Tanhuato killings remained open.

Military Abuses and Impunity

Mexico has relied heavily on the military to fight drug-related violence and organized crime, leading to widespread human rights violations by military personnel. As of July, the CNDH had received almost 10,000 complaints of abuse by the army since 2006—including more than 2,000 during the current administration. It found in more than 100 cases that military personnel committed serious human rights violations.

In 2014, Congress reformed the Code of Military Justice to require that abuses committed by members of the military against civilians be handled by the civilian criminal justice system rather than the military system, which had a history of routinely failing to hold members of the military accountable for abuses. Under the reform, abuses committed by military personnel against other soldiers remain subject to military justice.

In May 2016, provisions included in a new Military Code of Criminal Procedure and in reforms to the Code of Military Justice granted military prosecutors and judges broad powers to search homes and public buildings, and to listen to private telecommunications, without a judicial order issued by a civilian judge. In June, the CNDH challenged the constitutionality of these provisions, and at time of writing a Supreme Court decision was pending.

In the case of Tlatlaya, where soldiers killed 22 civilians in 2014—witnesses and the CNDH reported that they extrajudicially executed at least 12 of them—nobody has been convicted of the killings. In May 2016, a civilian, federal court absolved the last of eight soldiers charged with homicide at Tlatlaya.

Torture

Torture is widely practiced in Mexico to obtain confessions and extract information. It is most frequently applied in the period between when victims are detained, often arbitrarily, and when they are handed over to civilian prosecutors, a period in which they are often held incommunicado at military bases or illegal detention sites. Common torture techniques include beatings, waterboarding, electric shocks, and sexual abuse.

In its second report on the Ayotzinapa case, the Interdisciplinary Group of Independent Experts, established through an agreement between the government and the Inter-American Commission on Human Rights (IACHR), concluded that 80 percent of the suspects detained in connection with the case showed bodily injuries possibly due to ill treatment and torture.

According to the CNDH, Mexico State prosecutors sought to cover up military wrongdoing in the Tlatlaya case by using torture to coerce false testimony from witnesses. In July, authorities said they would fire seven or eight investigators and suspend 22 others—for as little as a month—for misconduct, but nobody has been convicted in connection with the cover-up.

Despite a constitutional prohibition on using evidence obtained through torture, some judges continue to disregard torture complaints and accept allegedly coerced confessions.

Criminal Justice System

The criminal justice system routinely fails to provide justice to victims of violent crimes and human rights violations. Causes of failure include corruption, inadequate training and resources, and complicity of prosecutors and public defenders with criminals and abusive officials. The failure of law enforcement has contributed to the emergence of armed citizen self-defense groups in several parts of the country.

In 2013, Mexico enacted a federal Victims Law intended to ensure justice, protection, and reparations for crime victims. After Senate approval in November 2016, reforms to the law, intended to reduce bureaucracy and improve access to aid and reparations for victims, moved to the Chamber of Deputies for consideration.

Freedom of Media

Journalists, particularly those who report on crime or criticize officials, face harassment and attacks. Journalists are often driven to self-censorship by attacks by authorities or criminal groups.

The Attorney General's Office documented 124 killings of journalists from 2000 through July 2016. The nongovernmental organization (NGO) Article 19 documented seven cases of journalists killed from January through June 2016.

By April 2016, 509 people had requested protection under a 2012 law to protect human rights defenders and journalists. Protection has been slow to arrive or, in some cases, insufficient. At time of writing, authorities had yet to bring charges under the law against anyone believed responsible for threats or attacks.

Authorities routinely fail to investigate crimes against journalists adequately, often preemptively ruling out their profession as a motive. The CNDH reported in

2016 that 90 percent of crimes against journalists in Mexico go unpunished, in-cluding 82 percent of killings and 100 percent of disappearances. The Special Prosecutor's Office for Crimes against Freedom of Expression, created in 2006, had by April 2016 opened 790 preliminary investigations, concluded 633, and brought charges in 93, none of them involving disappearances or homicides.

Women's and Girls' Rights

Mexican laws do not adequately protect women and girls against domestic and sexual violence. Some provisions, including those that make the severity of pun-ishments for some sexual offenses contingent upon the "chastity" of the victim, contradict international standards.

Eighteen states have passed laws establishing that there is a right to life from the moment of conception. Although the Supreme Court ruled in 2010 that all states must provide emergency contraception and access to abortion for rape victims, many women and girls face serious barriers to accessing abortions after sexual violence, including official intimidation.

Sexual Orientation and Gender Identity

Same-sex marriage has been legal in Mexico City since 2010. Since then, nine states have legalized it; in 2015, the Supreme Court opened the door to recogni-tion in all states by ruling that the definition of marriage as a union only between a man and a woman constitutes discrimination and thus violates Mexico's Con-stitution.

In May 2016, President Peña Nieto introduced a bill to legalize same-sex mar-riage, to remove sexual orientation and gender identity as barriers to adoption, and to recognize gender identity through the reissuance of birth notices, without a doctor's involvement. Two committees in the Chamber of Deputies voted against the initiative in November.

Palliative Care

The lack of access to palliative care results in needless suffering for large num-bers of Mexicans with serious illnesses. In 2016, the National Commission for Social Protection in Health added palliative care as a covered health service under Seguro Popular, a public health insurance scheme that covers more than 55 million people. By late 2016, more than 2,000 physicians were using the new system, introduced in mid-2015, for prescribing strong pain medicines. Despite such strides, obstacles remain, including a paucity of facilities offering palliative care in many states.

Disability Rights

The UN Committee on the Rights of Persons with Disabilities, in a 2014 report, found that, despite new laws and programs protecting the rights of the disabled, serious gaps remained, including in access to justice, legal standing, and the right to vote; access to buildings, transportation, and public spaces; violence against women; and education.

In 2015, Disability Rights International reported that Mexican women with psychosocial disabilities were at high risk of being denied reproductive rights; that state-run clinics in Mexico City sometimes pressured them into being sterilized or, when pregnant, undergoing abortion; and that conditions were inhumane in Mexico City's government-funded facilities for people with disabilities, including one institution that locked children in cages.

Key International Actors

The IACHR published a report in March documenting a wide range of abuses in Mexico—including disappearances; extrajudicial executions; torture; and insecurity for women, children, migrants, human rights defenders, and journalists—which they concluded amounted to a "crisis of gross human rights violations." The government criticized the report, responding that there was no "human rights crisis" in Mexico. Later that month, Mexican authorities denied UN Special Rapporteur on Torture Juan Méndez permission to return before the end of his term, rejecting his conclusion that torture was widespread and accusing him of acting "unethically."

In April, the UN special rapporteurs on human rights defenders, freedom of expression, and freedom of assembly and association expressed concern regarding a targeted campaign in the Mexican media accusing human rights defenders and civil society organizations of fraud, corruption, and the promotion of impunity through allegedly false claims about detainees being tortured. They urged the government to ensure "a safe environment" in which such individuals and organizations could operate "free of harassment."

In October, the Office of the UN High Commissioner for Human Rights issued 14 recommendations to Mexico on the need to address impunity for human rights violations, adopt laws to regulate the use of force and eliminate torture and enforced disappearances, and establish an independent forensic institution with adequate resources. In May, the UN special rapporteur on extrajudicial, summary, or arbitrary executions released a report on Mexico identifying continuing serious violations, including extrajudicial killings and excessive use of force by security forces, impunity, and lack of reparations for victims. The UN Committee on Enforced Disappearances has issued dozens of urgent actions on cases in Mexico since 2012.

In September, the IACHR referred to the Inter-American Court of Human Rights the case of 11 women who were arrested at a protest of flower growers in Mexico State in 2006, when President Peña Nieto was governor there. The commission described their arrest as "illegal and arbitrary" and said it "considered it proved" that state agents subjected the women to physical and psychological torture and raped seven of them. The Inter-American Court is scheduled to hear the case in 2017.

Since 2007, the United States has allocated more than US$2 billion in aid through the Merida Initiative to help combat organized crime. In 2015, the US secretary of state withheld $5 million in security aid, saying the State Department could not confirm that Mexico had met the agreement's human rights criteria, but in September 2016 certified that Mexico had made sufficient human rights progress to justify receiving its full Mérida aid of about $155 million.

Morocco and Western Sahara

Morocco enacted laws in 2016 that advanced free expression and the rights of domestic workers, victims of human trafficking, and person with disabilities. However, authorities restricted the activities of local human rights associations and extended restrictions on international human rights groups. Many persons continued to serve long prison terms after unfair trials for politically motivated offenses. While authorities often tolerated protest demonstrations, in Western Sahara they systematically prevented gatherings supporting self-determination for the contested territory.

Morocco granted temporary legal status to United Nations-recognized asylum-seekers and thousands of economic migrants, pending an overhaul of its laws on asylum and foreigners on Moroccan soil.

Freedom of Expression

On July 26, parliament adopted a new Press and Publications Code. One advance over the 2002 press code was the elimination of prison time as punishment. But the new code still punishes many nonviolent speech offenses with fines and court-ordered suspensions of publications or websites.

Separately, the penal code maintains prison as a punishment for a variety of nonviolent speech offenses. Five days before adopting the new press code, parliament added to the penal code provisions, imposing prison on those who cross Morocco's long-standing "red lines"—"causing harm" to Islam, the monarchy, the person of the king and the royal family, and Morocco's "territorial integrity" (a reference to its claim to Western Sahara).

The legal overhaul left intact prison as punishment for insulting state institutions and for "praising" terrorism, while eliminating prison for defaming persons and insulting foreign dignitaries, and for malicious publication of "false news."

Ali Anouzla, editor of the independent news website Lakome2.com, faced prosecution for harming Morocco's "territorial integrity" after an interview with a German newspaper in 2015 quoted him as referring to Western Sahara as "occupied." The court dropped the case in May after the newspaper confirmed that this was a translation error.

Authorities require but often refuse to issue permits for foreign broadcast media to film in Morocco. On April 3, police detained and then expelled a crew of the French news program "Le Petit Journal" as it tried to film in a neighborhood of Beni Mellal, a city 220 kilometers southeast of Casablanca where a gay-bashing assault had taken place.

In November 2015, authorities expelled Rik Goverde, a freelance journalist for the Dutch dailies NRC and AD, on the grounds that he lacked a press card. Goverde had applied repeatedly for a card since moving to Morocco in October 2013 but never received a response.

Moroccan state television allows some space for debate and investigative reporting but none for direct criticism of the palace or dissent on key issues.

Freedom of Assembly and Association

Authorities tolerated numerous marches and rallies demanding political reform and protesting government actions while forcibly dispersing some, despite their being peaceful.

Officials continue to arbitrarily prevent or impede many associations from obtaining legal registration, although the 2011 constitution guarantees freedom of association. On March 31, an Agadir Appeals Court upheld a decision closing the Ifni Memory and Rights Association, partly on grounds that the association harmed Morocco's "territorial integrity" by the way that it asserted the rights and identity of the population in the Ifni region.

Among the many associations arbitrarily denied legal registration were scores of charitable, cultural, and educational associations whose leadership included members of al-Adl wal-Ihsan (Justice and Spirituality), a nationwide movement that advocates an Islamic state and questions the king's spiritual authority. Authorities have kept sealed since 2006 houses belonging to the movement's leader and another member in eastern Morocco, without providing a legal basis.

Authorities frequently impeded events organized by local chapters of the Moroccan Association for Human Rights, by denying access to planned venues. They also prevented the efforts by many chapters of the association to file documents as required by the law, placing them in legal jeopardy.

An effective ban, imposed in 2015, remained in place on research missions by Amnesty International and Human Rights Watch. This ban reversed relatively unimpeded access that the two organizations had enjoyed for nearly 25 years. On February 21, authorities expelled without explanation the lawyer directing the Morocco office of Lawyers Without Borders-Belgium, which led the group to reduce its activities in the country. In June, the International Institute of Nonviolent Action (NOVACT), announced it would close its Morocco office after authorities expelled one staff member in 2015 and refused entry to two others in 2016, and declined to grant the Spanish association legal recognition.

In 2015, authorities charged historian Maâti Monjib, and four other associational activists with accepting foreign funding "to harm internal security," punishable by up to five years in prison. The trial, delayed repeatedly and scheduled to begin in January 2017, centers on a foreign-funded workshop to train Moroccans in the use of a smartphone application to practice "citizen journalism."

Authorities expelled several foreign visitors who came to witness human rights conditions in Western Sahara or attend human rights events there. For example, on October 9, they expelled Carlos Beristain, a Spanish expert on human rights in Western Sahara, and two other Spaniards who the Saharan Association of Victims of Grave Human Rights Violations had invited to participate in the first public event the association had organized since obtaining legal recognition in 2015. The police agent who intercepted Beristain at the airport told him his presence "endangered the public order."

Police Conduct, Torture, and the Criminal Justice System

Courts failed to uphold fair trial rights in political and security-related cases. The Code of Penal Procedure, amended in 2011, gives a defendant the right to contact a lawyer after 24 hours in police custody, or a maximum of 36 hours if the prosecutor approves this extension. In cases involving terrorism offenses, the prosecutor can delay access to a lawyer for up to six days. The law does not give detainees the right to a have a lawyer present when police interrogate or present them with their statements for signature.

The 2003 counterterrorism law contains an overly broad definition of "terrorism" and allows for up to 12 days of *garde à vue* (pre-charge) detention in terrorism cases.

Twenty-five Sahrawis won a retrial in civilian court after the Court of Cassation on July 27 quashed their 2013 conviction before a military court. That court had imposed on 23 of them prison sentences of between 20 years and life. The men, who include a few well-known activists, had been charged in connection with violence that erupted in 2010 when authorities dismantled the Gdeim Izik protest camp in Western Sahara and 11 security officers died. The military court failed to investigate defendants' allegations that police had tortured or coerced them into signing false statements, on which it relied almost exclusively for their convictions.

Prisons held hundreds of Islamists arrested in the wake of the 2003 Casablanca bombings and since. Courts convicted many on charges of belonging to a "terrorist network," recruiting, undergoing military training, or preparing to join jihadists abroad. Often the main, if not only, evidence against the defendants was their "confessions" to police incriminating themselves and their co-defendants, which they later recanted in court.

Courts continued, when convicting defendants, to invoke article 290 of the Penal Procedure Code, which deems police statements inherently credible as evidence unless the contrary is proven. The United Nations Working Group on Arbitrary Decision in 2014 criticized this law, which applies to infractions occasioning prison sentences shorter than five years, as contrary to the presumption of innocence.

Leftist activist Wafae Charaf was freed in July after completing a two-year prison sentence for slander and "falsely" reporting an offense after she filed a complaint alleging that unknown men abducted and tortured her following a workers' protest in Tangiers. Oussama Husn, a youth reform movement activist, was serving a three-year prison sentence imposed in 2014 on similar charges after he put online a video in which he recounts having been abducted and tortured by unknown men. These sentences could have a chilling effect on people wishing to file complaints of abuse by security forces.

Moroccan courts continued to impose the death penalty, but authorities have not carried out executions since the early 1990s.

435

Right to a Private Life

Moroccan courts continued to jail persons for same-sex conduct under article 489 of the penal code, which prohibits "lewd or unnatural acts with an individual of the same sex." A Beni Mellal court convicted two men of homosexuality after a group of youths on March 9 burst into the home of one and pushed the two men naked into the street, filming the assault and later posting the clip online. The two men were freed after spending one month in prison; in April, a court imposed prison terms on two of their attackers. On October 27, police in Marrakesh arrested two girls aged 16 and 17 who were reported for cuddling in a private home. They were jailed for one week and then provisionally released prior to a trial scheduled for November 25 on charges under article 489.

Criminalization of adultery and sex outside marriage has a discriminatory gender impact, as rape victims face prosecution if they file charges that are not sustained. Women and girls also face prosecution if they are found to be pregnant or have children outside marriage.

Migrants and Refugees

Implementation continued of a 2013 national strategy to overhaul national policies toward migrants and asylum-seekers, including by providing certain basic rights. While a draft of Morocco's first law on the right to asylum had yet to be adopted, Morocco's refugee agency granted one-year renewable residency permits to more than 500 UNHCR-recognized refugees. At time of writing, Morocco had not determined the status of more than 1,700 Syrians whom UNHCR recognizes as prima facie refugees.

Morocco also granted one-year renewable residency permits to thousands of sub-Saharan migrants who were not asylum-seekers but who met criteria set forth in the 2013 plan. Some Syrians also obtained one-year residency permits under this procedure.

Parliament adopted in May a law that defines and criminalizes human trafficking and provides measures to protect its victims.

Women's and Girls' Rights

The 2011 constitution guarantees equality for women, "while respecting the provisions of the constitution, and the laws and permanent characteristics of the Kingdom."

The 2004 Family Code, which improved women's rights in divorce and child custody, discriminates against women with regard to inheritance and procedures to obtain divorce. The code raised the age of marriage from 15 to 18, but judges routinely allowed girls to marry below this age. There is no law that specifically criminalizes domestic violence or establishes protections for domestic violence victims.

Domestic Workers

Parliament adopted on July 26 the first labor law that applies to domestic workers. It requires written contracts and sets 18 as the minimum age for domestic workers, after a five-year phase-in. It limits weekly working hours and guarantees 24 continuous hours of rest per week and a minimum wage that is 60 percent of the minimum wage for jobs covered under the labor law. The law also provides for financial penalties for employers who violate the law.

Despite a prohibition on the employment of children under the age of 15, thousands of children under that age—predominantly girls—are believed to work as domestic workers. According to the UN, nongovernmental organizations (NGOs), and government sources, the number of child domestic workers has declined in recent years.

People with Disabilities

Parliament in February adopted Framework Law 97.13 on the rights of persons with disabilities, a step toward harmonizing legislation with the Convention on the Rights of Persons with Disabilities (CRPD), which Morocco ratified in 2009. However, the Framework Law fell short in some areas, such as in guaranteeing access to inclusive education for children with disabilities, and in affirming the right of legal capacity.

Key International Actors

In December 2015, the European General Court ruled to annul application of the European Union-Morocco trade agreement on agricultural and fishery products insofar as it applied to Western Sahara. The court held that the agreement was flawed because it does not "guarantee an exploitation of the natural resources of Western Sahara that is beneficial to its inhabitants." The EU has appealed the ruling.

In March, UN Secretary-General Ban Ki-moon traveled to the Sahrawi refugee camps in Algeria, where he referred to the Western Sahara as "occupied" and raised the possibility of a referendum to determine the territory's future, positions that are anathema to Morocco. In response, Morocco expelled the civilian personnel of the peacekeeping mission in Western Sahara, MINURSO. At time of writing, only some staff had been able to return.

The United States publicly acknowledged and corrected one small error, but stood by the substance of the Morocco chapter of its Country Reports on Human Rights Practices for 2015, after Morocco's interior minister in May denounced it as "truly scandalous, moving from semi-truths to invention pure and simple, from misinterpretations to flagrant lies."

Pursuant to legislation passed by Congress for 2016, the US allowed its aid allocated to Morocco to be spent in Western Sahara, despite the US's non-recognition of Morocco's sovereignty over the territory. The International Republican Institute, an American NGO, received in April a US$1 million government grant to conduct a two-year program in Western Sahara on civil society and participative governance.

Mozambique

Human rights violations in Mozambique increased in 2016 due to rising tension and armed clashes between the government and the former rebel group, now political party, Resistência Nacional Moçambicana (Mozambican National Resistance or RENAMO).

Security forces were credibly implicated in abuses in operations against RENAMO, including summary executions and sexual violence that forced tens of thousands of people to flee the country. RENAMO also committed abuses in 2016, including raids on health clinics. At least 10 high-profile figures were attacked or killed in apparently politically motivated attacks, with incomplete investigations by authorities.

The country also suffered an economic crisis due to the fall in commodity prices and disclosure of the government's enormous debt to state-owned companies. The economic crisis had a significant impact on the country's finances, making it harder for people to enjoy basic economic and social rights.

Summary Executions

Government security forces at times apparently conducted summary executions of people they believed to be linked to RENAMO. In April, the Office of the United Nations High Commissioner for Human Rights said it received reports of at least 14 RENAMO officials who had been killed or abducted around the country by unidentified individuals or groups since the beginning of the year.

Mozambican refugees in Malawi said that soldiers in uniform, some driving army vehicles, had summarily executed male villagers in Tete province in February 2016, or tied and taken them to undisclosed locations. Refugees also reported soldiers torching homes, granaries, and cornfields of local residents whom the soldiers believed were feeding or otherwise supporting RENAMO fighters.

In August, the country's leading human rights group, Liga Dos Direitos Humanos (LDH), published a report accusing security forces of summary executions, destruction of property and other human rights violations. LDH also documented human rights abuses committed by RENAMO fighters against people whom they believed were cooperating with government security forces.

Politically Motivated Attacks

At least 10 high-profile figures, including senior opposition members, state prosecutors and investigators, and prominent academics, were either killed or injured in apparently politically motivated attacks.

Among those targeted were constitutional lawyer Gilles Cistac, who was shot dead outside a Maputo café after receiving threats for publicly defending the disputed constitutionality of RENAMO's petition to create autonomous provincial authorities; Manuel Bissopo, secretary general of RENAMO, who was shot and severely wounded in Beira city center, Sofala province; José Manuel, a RENAMO member of the National Council for Defence and Security, who was shot dead outside Beira international airport; Jeremias Pondeca, a former member of parliament from RENAMO and a member of the peace talks team, who was shot dead on a Maputo beach; and Jaime Macuane, a political commentator and academic, who was shot multiple times in the legs by men who told him they had been ordered "to teach him a lesson."

Unresolved Killings

In May, local residents discovered at least 15 unidentified bodies under a bridge in a remote area between the central provinces of Manica and Sofala. Local authorities at first ignored calls for a prompt and thorough investigation. They then announced that decomposition had made it impossible to conduct autopsies, and that the bodies had since been buried. Facing pressure from human rights groups and media, the government announced it would exhume the bodies and investigate. At time of writing, no findings had been announced and a parliamentary commission that established its own investigation team had not published a detailed account of its findings.

Forced Displacement

Since October 2015, at least 10,000 people have fled to neighboring Malawi and Zimbabwe because of abuses committed by the army and RENAMO fighters. The United Nations High Commissioner for Refugees said that most of those who fled had returned home by late 2016, following assurances of safety by the Mozambican government. In 2016, the number of internally displaced people continued to grow, forcing the government to set up camps in Manica province, where authorities said over 1,000 families were living.

Attacks on Health Facilities

In the first half of 2016, armed men linked to RENAMO conducted raids on at least four hospitals and health clinics in Zambezia and Niassa provinces, looting medicine and supplies, and destroying medical equipment. The raids threatened access to health care for tens of thousands of people in remote areas. The authorities claimed that RENAMO gunmen carried out over a dozen attacks on health clinics since the beginning of the year in other places, including Sofala, Manica, and Tete provinces.

Attacks on People with Albinism

Killings, kidnappings, and physical attacks against persons with albinism continued to grow, despite government efforts to stop the violence. According to local civil society groups, over 100 people with albinism have disappeared since 2014, when the attacks were first reported.

Authorities say the attacks are fueled by the witchcraft-linked belief that potions made of body parts of persons with albinism can produce wealth and success. In August 2016, the UN Independent Expert on the enjoyment of human rights by persons with albinism, Ikponwosa Ero, visited Mozambique and praised the government's efforts to stop attacks on persons with albinism. At the same time, Ero expressed concerns over the authorities' inability to identify and arrest perpetrators of such crimes.

Child Marriage

Mozambique continued to be among the countries with the highest rates of child marriage in the world. According to UNICEF, 48 percent of girls marry before they turn 18 and over 14 percent before they turn 15. In 2016, the government unveiled its national strategy to end child marriage by 2019, which includes improving girls' access to education, sexual and reproductive health services, and legal reforms.

Key International Actors

Once one of the fastest growing economies in the world following the discovery of huge reserves of coal, oil, and gas, Mozambique continued to suffer from low commodity prices, drops in foreign investment, and a debt crisis. In May 2016, a group of 14 donor countries, including the United Kingdom and European Union, and multilateral institutions that included the International Monetary Fund and World Bank, suspended direct support to the state budget after revelations that the government has more than US$1 billion in undisclosed loans.

In June, the UK high commissioner in Maputo, Joanna Kuenssberg, expressed concerns over rising political violence in the country, and the threat it poses to freedom of expression and the press.

In July, the EU and other international groups agreed to mediate talks between the government and RENAMO. In September, Mozambican President Filipe Nyusi visited the United States and met Secretary of State John Kerry and National Security Advisor Susan Rice, with whom he discussed the country's ongoing violence. It is unclear whether they discussed human rights concerns.

During the opening statement at the 33rd session of the UN Human Rights Council in September, UN High Commissioner for Human Rights Zeid Ra'ad al-Hussein warned that Mozambique was showing signs of sliding into violence. He urged the government to hold perpetrators to account and to address the corruption that deprives many people of their economic and social rights.

Nepal

Political instability persisted through 2016, with yet another change in government. A new political coalition, led by Maoist Prime Minister Pushpa Kumar Dahal, took over in July, offering some hope for a breakthrough in the political stalemate. It was the ninth government to be formed over the last eight years, damaging efforts to implement human rights protections.

A new constitution was adopted in September 2015 but violent protests over the failure to address demands for greater inclusion by minority communities, particularly in the southern plains, stalled efforts to enforce rights or provide justice for wartime abuses.

There was little progress on relief for the victims of the devastating earthquakes in 2015, which left an estimated 9,000 people dead, nearly 20,000 injured, and over 100,000 displaced.

Two transitional justice commissions set up to deliver justice to victims of the country's 1996-2006 civil war received a reported 59,000 submissions, but the terms of reference of their future work remained unclear.

Government efforts to halt the country's high rate of child marriage inched forward, but were stalled by lack of political will and buy-in across government ministries.

Failures in Earthquake Relief and Reconstruction

The earthquakes in 2015 left some 2.8 million people remain in need of humanitarian assistance in 14 of Nepal's most severely affected districts. Many affected communities live in rural areas that are difficult to access, and received minimal assistance for emergency housing and other relief.

Although the government received over US$4 billion in aid for earthquake assistance, none of the funds had been paid out as late as August 2016. Political infighting led to delays in setting up an earthquake reconstruction authority; even though the body has been announced, parliament failed to legitimize it over ongoing political stalemates. As a result, earthquake victims spent two monsoons and one winter surviving in makeshift shelters they managed to put together on their own, or with the help of local initiatives.

**HUMAN
RIGHTS
WATCH**

"Our Time to Sing and Play"
Child Marriage in Nepal

The new government announced an increase in rehabilitation funds for earthquake victims, but as of October 2016, there was little information as to how and when the money would be disbursed.

Accountability and Justice

A hastily drafted constitution, promulgated after only one week of public consultations, led to months of violent protests, particularly along Nepal's southern border with India. In some districts, the government responded by deploying the army and in others by instituting curfews. Although some deaths were blamed on excessive use of force by security forces, at time of writing the state had yet to investigate, let alone prosecute, those responsible for killing civilians, some of whom were children.

A tense political stalemate between rival political parties was largely responsible for this failure to provide redress. The then-ruling coalition, led by former Prime Minister Khadja Prasad Oli, was deeply reluctant to accept responsibility for the violence and humanitarian crisis arising from the new constitution. Following the transition to a new government in July 2016, the government announced the formation of an independent commission of inquiry to investigate and report on protest-related violence. As of October, the terms of reference and the commission's composition and mandate had not yet been made public.

Women's and Girls' Rights

Although child marriage has been illegal in Nepal since 1963, 37 percent of girls are married by age 18, and 10 percent married before age 15. Recent research by Human Rights Watch found that police rarely act to prevent a child marriage or bring charges, and almost never do so unless a complaint is filed. Government officials often officially register child marriages.

Human Rights Watch found that poverty, lack of access to education, child labor, social pressures, and dowry practices are among the factors driving child marriage. The government has pledged to end child marriage by 2030, and in 2016 adopted a broad strategy on ending child marriage. Still missing, however, is a practical plan, and a promised process to develop one has been slow and undermined by lack of coordination and political will.

Migrant Workers

More than 2 million Nepalis work abroad, although the numbers are believed to be higher as many workers migrate through irregular channels including the porous border of India. In 2015, Nepal introduced a "free visa, free ticket" policy, whereby the employer in Gulf countries or Malaysia bears the costs of visas and flights tickets for the Nepali worker.

The Nepal Association of Foreign Employment Agencies (NEFEA) has pushed back, insisting it should be able to charge higher fees. Some workers reported to migrant rights organizations that agencies continue to charge high fees but show a receipt of the government-approved maximum fee rates.

Nepal lifted its ban on women traveling to the Gulf states for employment as domestic workers. Though motivated by protection concerns, the ban was discriminatory and forced women desperate for work to migrate through irregular channels, putting them at greater risk of exploitation. Nepal issued new guidelines allowing women over the age of 24 to migrate for domestic work in Gulf states and Malaysia with approved recruitment agencies.

The guidelines require that every domestic worker is entitled to accommodation, health and life insurance, a weekly rest day, 30 days of annual leave, regular contact with their families, and a minimum salary of $300. Such measures are important but limited as host Gulf governments continue to retain the *kafala* (visa sponsorship) system, which can trap domestic workers in abusive conditions as they cannot change jobs without their employer's consent, and are punished with imprisonment and deportation if they flee.

Statelessness

The new constitution failed to address the rights of Nepal's estimated 4 million people who are without any official status and at risk of statelessness. Despite promises of reform, many people, particularly women, children born out of wedlock, or children of a refugee or naturalized parent, remain unable to secure drivers' licenses, passports, bank accounts, voting rights, higher education, and other government welfare schemes.

Transitional Justice

Nepal made little concrete progress on justice for serious abuses committed by both sides during its civil war that ended in 2006. At least 13,000 people were killed and over 1,300 were forcibly disappeared during the decade-long conflict. Efforts to ensure prosecutions in civilian courts for serious human rights and humanitarian law violations during the conflict remain stalled.

While Nepal has delivered interim monetary and in-kind compensation to the families of those who were "disappeared" or killed during the conflict, others, such as survivors of sexual violence or torture, have received no compensation from the state.

Despite victims groups and civil society protests against the lack of transparency and consultation in the appointment of commissioners to the Truth and Reconciliation Commission and the Disappearances Commission, the two commissions started public hearings; as of August 2016, they had received nearly 59,000 complaints.

Contrary to Supreme Court orders, the previous government had directed authorities to withdraw all wartime cases and to provide amnesty to alleged perpetrators. The new government has pledged to amend the laws and ensure justice for conflict-era victims but had yet to come up with a concrete roadmap at time of writing.

Tibetan Rights

In late February, a Chinese security delegation urged Nepali counterparts to remain on high alert during March, when Tibetans mark a number of key political anniversaries. In March, Nepali authorities attempted to prevent Tibetans from participating in elections for the Tibetan government in exile. Despite previous negotiations between the Tibetan community and Nepali authorities, Nepali police in July attempted to stop celebrations of the Dalai Lama's birthday in Boudhanath, briefly detaining 30 people.

Sexual Orientation and Gender Identity

In line with a 2007 Supreme Court decision and a subsequent court order, the government in 2015 began issuing passports in three genders: "male," "female," and "other." Some with "other" passports have successfully traveled abroad with their travel documents recognized by foreign governments. The new constitution recognizes that citizenship is available in three genders, and protects "gender and sexual minorities" in clauses related to equality before the law and social justice. Activists remain frustrated with the lack of implementation of a Supreme Court-mandated committee recommendation that the government recognize same-sex relationships.

Key International Actors

Relations with India became tense over the failure of the new constitution to address the demands of the southern Terai communities, which have close kinship ties to India. The Nepal government insisted that India was responsible for instigating protests and blocking supplies. Relations between the two countries improved after a new government led by Prime Minister Pushpa Kamal Dahal took charge, but India has failed to press for effective transitional justice for victims of the civil war.

The international community remained largely silent on the failure of the Nepali government to disburse the billions of dollars in aid received to help the earthquake affected community. The United Nations has been critical over delays in the transitional justice process.

The international community similarly remained silent on the contentious constitution drafting process, as well as on the transitional justice mechanisms.

Nigeria

The euphoria and optimism that followed the relatively peaceful 2015 elections that brought in the administration of President Muhammadu Buhari gradually gave way to concern in 2016. Many of the grave human rights challenges he promised to address in his inauguration speech remain largely unaddressed and unresolved. Changes in military leadership and improved regional coordination resulted in a consistent push back against the insurgent group, Boko Haram, forcing it to cede most of the territory it controlled in the northeast. The group however continues to commit crimes against civilians, including abductions and forced recruitment.

The waning intensity of Boko Haram attacks is overshadowed by an inadequate response to the humanitarian crisis. Most of the 2.5 million internally displaced people (IDPs) lack basic rights such as rights to food, shelter, education, health-care, protection from harm, as well as the right to freedom of movement. Displaced women and girls suffer rape and sexual exploitation perpetrated by fellow IDPs, members of vigilante groups, policemen, and soldiers.

In December 2015, the army killed 347 members of the Shia Islamic Movement of Nigeria (IMN) after a road blockade by the group in Zaria. Hundreds of IMN members including the leader, Ibrahim El Zakzaky, and his wife remained in custody without charges at time of writing.

The ban imposed on the IMN by the Kaduna State government in October 2016 triggered a wave of bans against Shia in four northern states. Since then, Shia religious activities have been met with mob and police violence leading to the death of scores of IMN members in Kaduna, Kano, Katsina, Plateau, Sokoto, and Yobe States.

Elsewhere in the country, deadly communal violence between farmers and pastoralists, previously limited to north-central states spread southward in 2016. The lack of justice for victims helped fuel reprisal attacks leading to cycles of violence. In the south, government response to agitation for a separate state of Biafra and militant activities in the Niger Delta left scores of people dead and entire communities destroyed.

HUMAN
RIGHTS
WATCH

"They Set the Classrooms on Fire"
Attacks on Education in Northeast Nigeria

Abuses by Boko Haram

The seven-year old Boko Haram conflict is winding down as military operations by Nigerian forces and its northeastern neighbors intensified against the insurgents. An estimated 550 civilians died in Boko Haram attacks in 2016 compared to almost 3,500 in 2015. Insurgents resorted to suicide bomb attacks in crowded places, like IDP camps, markets and mosques, using mostly women and girls to bypass security. On February 11, two young women detonated suicide bombs in a Dikwa, Borno camp, killing about 58 IDPs. A third girl confessed to security agents that she backed out of the suicide assignment when she recognized her relatives sheltering in the camp.

Security forces recovered most areas controlled by the group, and rescued thousands of residents. However, 197 of the 276 Chibok schoolgirls abducted in April 2014, as well as over 300 elementary school students abducted from Damasak, Borno, in November 2014 are still missing. Apart from Maiduguri, Borno state capital, which has been largely free from attacks, many parts of the state remain unsafe and inaccessible. In July, a team of United Nations humanitarian aid workers were attacked by suspected insurgents as they traveled the 53 mile Bama to Maiduguri road. Two people were injured in the attack and UN temporarily suspended aid deliveries following the incident. Aid supplies resumed a few days later.

The naming in August by the Islamic State (ISIS) of Abu Musab Al-Barnawi as the new leader of Boko Haram, spurred a rift between his followers and those of Abubakar Shekau who insists he remains the leader. The Nigerian military declared in late August that Shekau had been killed in a military air raid. Previous claims of Shekau's death proved untrue.

Conduct of Security Forces

Across the country, allegations of abuses including arbitrary arrests and detention, torture, forced disappearance, and extrajudicial killings continue to trail security operations.

In July, a state government-instituted commission of inquiry recommended that soldiers involved in the killing of 347 members of the Shiite Islamic Movement of

451

Nigeria in Zaria, Kaduna state between December 2015 12 and 14, be prosecuted. Authorities have yet to implement the commission's recommendations.

In February and May, security forces were accused of killing at least 40 members of the Indigenous People of Biafra (IPOB), and Movement for the Actualization of the Sovereign State of Biafra (MASSOB). The groups are advocating for the separation of Biafra—mainly made up of Igbo-speaking people in the southeast—and the release of Nnamdi Kanu, the IPOB leader detained and undergoing trial for treason since October 2015.

In the crude oil-rich Niger Delta, media reports say that on September 8, soldiers seeking to arrest members of the militant group—Niger Delta Avengers—destroyed 43 houses and other properties in Peremabiri, Akamabugo, and Tikogbene communities in Bayelsa State.

The army seemingly yielded to the pressure for reform by establishing a yet-to-be operational human rights office in February to receive complaints of abuses against civilians, and in August the military trial of 20 soldiers for offences, including human rights abuses committed in the northeast, commenced. In October, one of the indicted soldiers was convicted for abuse against a civilian in a non-conflict related incident.

Local vigilante groups assisting Nigerian security forces to repel Boko Haram attacks and apprehend insurgents are also implicated in the recruitment and use of children, and the ill-treatment and unlawful killing of Boko Haram suspects. At least 280 members of the groups were formally recruited into the security forces in 2016.

Inter-Communal Violence

Impunity for cycles of uncontrolled and unpunished violence between nomadic and farming communities in the conflict prone "Middle-Belt" region has encouraged its spread to other areas. For two weeks in February, armed herdsmen allegedly in revenge for the killing of their cattle, attacked 11 communities, killing scores of people in Benue State. Similar attacks left 12 people dead in Ukpabi Nimbo, Enugu on April 25, while six died in Taraba's Korum, Orawua and Gidan Bature communities on May 7.

Solutions proffered by Nigerian federal authorities to end the clashes, including enacting laws to specify cattle grazing routes, have been rejected by some state governments allegedly for inequitably favoring rights of herders.

Public Sector Corruption

Endemic corruption and mismanagement of public resources directly impact on the enjoyment of basic rights by Nigerians, about 54 percent of whom live in dismal poverty. One-third of school-age children are out of school, while one in five children under five years die from treatable and preventable diseases. The government alleges that between 2006 and 2013, 55 public officials stole US$9 billion, amounting to more than 25 percent of the annual national budget. Many officials of the previous Goodluck Jonathan administration are facing prosecution for corruption.

President Buhari said in May that corruption was largely responsible for previous failure to end the Boko Haram insurgency. The Economic and Financial Crimes Commission (EFCC), is prosecuting former government officials for embezzling $2 billion allocated for the purchase of arms to prosecute the northeast conflict. Political opponents however accuse the president of using the campaign against corruption to carry out a political vendetta against previous administration officials.

Sexual Orientation and Gender Identity

The passage of the Same Sex Marriage (Prohibition) Act, SSMPA in January 2014, has far reaching effects on members of the lesbian, gay, bisexual and transgender (LGBT) community. The law is used to legitimize abuses against LGBT people, including mob violence, sexual abuse, unlawful arrests, torture and extortion by police.

On February 13, the police arrested a homosexual couple in the federal capital for allegedly attempting to conduct a wedding. The wedding sponsors and the hotel venue owner were also arrested. The penalty for entering into a gay marriage under the SSMPA is 14 years.

Ironically, former President Jonathan who defied global pressure before signing the bill into law, said belatedly in June 2016 that "with the clear knowledge that the issue of sexual orientation is still evolving, the nation may, at the appropriate time, revisit the law."

Freedoms of Expression, Media, and Association

Nigeria's strong civil society and media play robust roles in lobbying for openness and accountability in public office. It is this vibrancy, perceived as a challenge to unbridled exercise of government authority, which recent legislation appear to target.

The "Bill to Prohibit Frivolous Petitions and Other Matters Connected Therewith" introduced in the Senate in December 2015 specifically targets users of social and electronic media. The June 2016 "Bill to provide for the Establishment of Non- Governmental Organizations (NGOs) Regulatory Commission in Nigeria" seeks to monitor and control activities and funding of civil society organizations.

The NGO regulation bill passed second reading at the federal House of Representatives in July, and was referred to the committee on civil society organizations and development partners for review. Concerted advocacy by activists may have aborted the passage of the "social media" bill, but regular display of high levels of intolerance by government agents continue to imperil free speech.

On August 8, blogger Abubakar Usman was detained for two days in Abuja by the EFCC for writing a piece critical of Ibrahim Magu, chairman of the commission. Barely a month later, another blogger, Emenike Iroegbu was arrested and his computer and phones seized by Department of State Security agents in Uyo, Akwa Ibom state, for criticizing state government officials in a publication. He was released the following day without charges.

On a positive note, the Federal House of Representatives introduced in June, a Digital Rights and Freedom bill, which aims to protect the rights and freedoms of internet users.

Key International Actors

International actors, notably the United Kingdom, United States, European Union, and United Nations significantly improved their support to the Nigerian government in dealing with the Boko Haram conflict. Increased assistance in form of military training, supply of intelligence, surveillance, and communication equipment might be an indication of confidence in President Buhari's promise of military reform.

In an apparent reversal of the former assistance policy to the Nigerian military suspected of rights violations, the US donated 24 mine-resistant and armor-protected vehicles valued at about $11 million to the army in January. In mid-September, Congress was notified of plans to sell 12 A-29 Super Tucano light attack aircraft and weapons, including laser guided rockets and unguided rockets, valued at over $592 million. Critics of the move have expressed concern about the human rights implications of this sale, given the absence of genuine reform in the Nigerian military.

The UK also stepped up support to the Nigerian military in 2016, sending 300 personnel to provide medical, infantry, air defense and counter insurgency training. During the visit of then UK minister of state, Foreign and Commonwealth Office, Baroness Anelay to Nigeria in February, the UK government announced a donation of £6.7 million (US$8.4 million) to support humanitarian assistance in the northeast. The EU, UN, and World Bank established a tripartite recovery program for the six insurgency-affected northeast states.

A Post-Insurgency Recovery and Peace-building Assessment commissioned by the group in January valued the cost of repairing damage to the region at $5.9 billion. In January, the head of the EU delegation in Nigeria, Michel Arrion, said the EU had set aside a trust fund to assist in the rehabilitation and reconstruction of the beleaguered northeast.

In a November 2016 report, the Office of the Prosecutor of the International Criminal Court (ICC), found that none of the allegations of crimes committed by so-called Fulani herdsmen or by government forces against pro-Biafarn protesters and civilians caught in the fight against Niger Delta Avengers were within the ICC's jurisdiction. The office continues an analysis of the Zaria incident involving members of the IMN as well as the assessment of national efforts to prosecute crimes committed in the Boko Haram violence as part of a preliminary examination of the situation in Nigeria.

In November 2015, the African Commission on Human and Peoples' Rights urged the Nigerian government to review the SSMPA in order to prohibit violence and discrimination on the basis of sexual orientation and gender identity and ensure access to HIV prevention, treatment, and care services for LGBT individuals.

Foreign Policy

Nigeria took a stand in support of justice for grave crimes at the International Criminal Court (ICC) during the African Union's (AU) July summit in Kigali, Rwanda. Nigeria joined Cote d'Ivoire, Tunisia, and Senegal in opposing an AU call for African members of the ICC to withdraw from the court.

Despite domestic intolerance of online criticism of public officials, Nigeria co-sponsored UN Human Rights Council (HRC) Resolution 32/20 on the Promotion, Protection and Enjoyment of Human Rights on the Internet in July.

The country however took retrogressive steps against human rights when it voted alongside five other members—including China, Russia, and Cuba—against HRC 31/32 on protecting human rights defenders addressing economic, social, and cultural rights at the council's 31st session in March. This follows a previous vote against the first ever UN General Assembly Resolution Recognizing the Role of Human Rights Defenders and the Need for their Protection in November 2015.

A similar vote at the council's 32nd session in July, against Resolution 32/31 on civil society space, which "urges States to create and maintain, in law and in practice, a safe and enabling environment in which civil society can operate free from hindrance and insecurity," signals a disturbing pattern of anti-human rights and civil society rhetoric in the current Nigerian administration.

North Korea

North Korea remains one of the most repressive authoritarian states in the world, ruled for seven decades by the Kim family and the Worker's Party of Korea. During his fifth year in power, Kim Jong-Un continued to generate fearful obedience by using public executions, arbitrary detention, and forced labor; tightening travel restrictions to prevent North Koreans from escaping and seeking refuge overseas; and systematically persecuting those with religious contacts inside and outside the country.

A 2014 United Nations Commission of Inquiry (COI) report on human rights in North Korea stated that systematic, widespread, and gross human rights violations committed by the government included murder, enslavement, torture, imprisonment, rape, forced abortion, and other sexual violence, and constituted crimes against humanity.

On December 10, 2015, the UN Security Council discussed North Korea's bleak human rights record as a formal agenda item for the second year in a row, following the COI's recommendations.

On March 23, the UN Human Rights Council adopted a resolution condemning human rights abuses in North Korea. It authorized the creation of a group of independent experts tasked with finding practical ways to hold rights violators in North Korea accountable and recommending practical accountability mechanisms, including the International Criminal Court, to secure truth and justice for victims. Lawyers Sonja Biserko and Sara Hossain joined the panel, supporting Tomas Ojea Quintana, the new special rapporteur on human rights in North Korea.

North Korea has ratified four key international human rights treaties and its constitution includes rights protections. In reality, the government curtails all basic human rights, including freedom of expression, assembly, and association, and freedom to practice religion. It prohibits any organized political opposition, independent media, free trade unions, and independent civil society organizations. Arbitrary arrest, torture in custody, forced labor, and public executions maintain an environment of fear and control.

North Korea discriminates against individuals and their families on political grounds in key areas such as employment, residence, and schooling through "songbun," the country's socio-political classification system that from its creation grouped people into "loyal," "wavering," or "hostile" classes. This classification has been restructured several times, but continues to enable the government to privilege or disadvantage people based largely on family background, personal performance, and perceived political loyalty.

However, pervasive corruption enables some room to maneuver around the strictures of the songbun system, even while it burdens people as government officials regularly demand and receive bribes from those seeking permissions, pursuing market activities, or wishing to travel inside or outside the country.

Tighter Border

In 2016, Kim Jong-Un's government increased efforts to stop North Koreans from crossing into China without permission. Some tactics included building barbed-wire fences on the northern border; persecuting those caught in North Korea using Chinese cellphones to communicate with people in China or South Korea; and increasing efforts to block Chinese cell phone services near the border.

Both North Korea and China have increased patrols and established barriers to crossing the border. The Chinese and North Korean governments have also targeted and broken up broker networks in China, meaning fewer people are willing to guide North Koreans on the arduous journey to escape through China.

China is a state party to the Refugee Convention of 1951 and its 1967 protocol, but it considers all North Koreans in China to be "illegal aliens" and routinely repatriates them without consideration of their claim to asylum. Human Rights Watch believes all North Koreans fleeing into China should be considered refugees, whatever their motivation for flight, because of the certain prospect of severe punishment if they are returned.

Fleeing North Korean women are frequently forced into marriages with Chinese men, or into the sex trade. Even if they have lived in China for years, they face possible arrest and repatriation at any time. Many children from these unrecognized marriages lack legal identity or access to education or health services in China.

Former security officials who left North Korea told Human Rights Watch that North Koreans handed back by China face interrogation, torture, sexual abuse, and forced labor. North Koreans in exile with contacts inside the country told Human Rights Watch that people caught trying to reach South Korea are treated as enemies of the state, and sent to political prison camps.

Freedom of Expression and Access to Information

All domestic media and publications are strictly state-controlled, and foreign media allowed inside the country are tightly controlled as well. Internet and international phone calls are heavily monitored.

Unauthorized access to non-state radio, newspapers, or TV broadcasts is severely punished. North Koreans face punishment if they are found with mobile media, such as Chinese mobile phones, SD cards or USBs containing unauthorized videos of foreign news, films, or TV dramas.

Inhumane Treatment in Detention

The government practices collective punishment for alleged anti-state offenses, effectively enslaving hundreds of thousands of citizens, including children, in prison camps and other detention facilities. Detainees face deplorable conditions, sexual coercion and abuse, beatings and torture by guards, and forced labor in dangerous and sometimes deadly conditions.

Those accused of serious political offenses are usually sent to political prison camps, known as kwanliso, operated by North Korea's National Security Agency. These camps are characterized by systematic abuses, including meager rations that imperil health and can lead to starvation, virtually no medical care, lack of proper housing and clothes, regular mistreatment including sexual assault and torture by guards, and public executions. Political prisoners face backbreaking forced labor, including in logging, mining, and agricultural.

UN officials estimate that between 80,000 and 120,000 people are imprisoned in political prison camps.

Those whom authorities suspect of illicitly trading goods from and into China, transporting people to China, and minor political infractions, such as watching or selling South Korean films, may receive lengthy terms in detention facilities known as *kyohwaso* (correctional, reeducation centers). Detainees there face forced labor, food and medicine shortages, and regular mistreatment by guards.

People suspected of involvement in unauthorized trading schemes involving non-controversial goods, shirking work at state-owned enterprises for more than six months, or those unable to pay bribes to officials for various reasons are sent to work in short-term forced labor detention facilities (*rodong danryeondae*, literally labor training centers). Beatings are common in these facilities, and dangerous working conditions purportedly result in significant numbers of injuries.

Forced Labor

The government systematically uses forced labor from ordinary citizens to control its people and sustain its economy. A significant majority of North Koreans must perform unpaid labor at some point in their lives.

Former North Korean students who left the country told Human Rights Watch that their schools forced them to work for free on farms twice a year, for one month at a time, during ploughing and seeding time, and again at harvest time. A former school teacher who escaped North Korea in 2014 said his school forced its students (aged between 10 and 16) to work every day to generate funds to pay government officials, maintain the school, and make a profit.

Ordinary North Korean workers, both men and unmarried women, are required to work at government-assigned enterprises. Although they are theoretically entitled to a salary, they usually are not compensated. All North Korean families also have to send one family member for at least two hours per day, six days a week, to support local government construction or public beautification projects, like building structures, fixing roads, collecting raw materials like crushed stone, or cleaning public areas.

The government launched a 70-day "battle" to prepare for North Korea's most important political event in 36 years, the 7th Korean Workers Party Congress, which took place between May 6 to 10. The government forced people across the country to produce more goods and crops in order to cover the costs of the congress. Posters, billboards, and media broadcasts demanded that North Koreans complete their "battle plans," and counted down the days until the congress opened.

Labor Rights

North Korea is one of the few nations in the world that has not joined the International Labour Organization. Workers are systematically denied freedom of association and the right to organize and collectively bargain.

Since Kim Jong-Un's rise to power, the government has sent more workers overseas to earn foreign currency salaries, most of which the government seizes. Although the country does not release official data, some observers estimate that more than 100,000 North Koreans worked overseas in 2015.

The treatment of North Korean workers overseas falls short of international labor standards, with no right to freedom of association or expression, control by minders who limit freedom of movement and access to information from the outside world, long working hours and no right to refuse overtime.

Key International Actors

Japan continues to demand the return of 12 Japanese citizens whom North Korea abducted in the 1970s and 1980s. Some Japanese civil society groups insist the number of abductees is much higher.

South Korea has also stepped up its demands for the return of its citizens, hundreds of whom were reportedly abducted during the decades after the Korean War. The North Korean government has also kidnapped individuals from China, Thailand, Europe, and the Middle East.

On February 10, the South Korean government closed down the Kaesung Industrial Complex (KIC), a special joint venture industrial zone at the southern border of North Korea. In March, South Korea passed the North Korean Human Rights Act, to improve human rights and provide humanitarian aid for current and former North Korean citizens.

In July 2016, US President Barack Obama imposed targeted sanctions for human rights abuses on five institutions and ten North Koreans, including Kim Jong-Un. The list included individuals responsible for hunting down North Korean escapees, and running labor and political prison camps.

Oman

The government of Oman continued in 2016 to restrict the rights to freedom of expression, association, and assembly. Authorities continued to prosecute journalists, bloggers, and social media activists.

Oman's *kafala* (sponsorship) immigrant labor system and lack of labor law protections leaves the country's more than 140,000 migrant domestic workers exposed to abuse and exploitation by employers, whose consent they need to change jobs. Those who flee abuse—including beatings, sexual abuse, unpaid wages, and excessive working hours— have little avenue for redress and can face legal penalties for "absconding."

Freedom of Expression

Authorities, particularly from the Internal Security Service (ISS), continued to target pro-reform activists, particularly for views they expressed on social media platforms like Facebook and Twitter. Several bloggers and online activists were harassed, arrested, and sometimes detained up to several months for criticizing the authorities' policies. Courts across the country sentenced activists to prison terms on the basis of vaguely defined laws that limit free speech, including through criminalizing "insulting the Sultan" and "undermining the prestige of the state."

Authorities often have relied on provisions in the 2002 Telecommunications Act and 2011 Cybercrime Law to restrict freedom of expression online.

On February 8, a court of first instance in Sohar, northern Oman, sentenced Hassan al-Basham, a former diplomat and online activist, to three years in prison for insulting God and Sultan Qaboos bin Said al Said, who has led the country for over 45 years, in a series of Facebook and Twitter posts in which he discussed religious, political, economic, and social topics. On June 13, the Court of Appeals upheld al-Basham's sentence, but struck down a fine related to the charge of "insulting the Sultan." Al-Basham has been detained since May 3, 2016. Authorities had arrested al-Basham several times before, in 2011 and 2015.

On April 15, authorities arrested Abdullah Habib,a poet and film critic, after he appeared for investigation before the Special Division of the Omani Police General Command in the capital, Muscat, for his online posts. He was reportedly detained incommunicado, but was released from detention on May 4 without charge.

On April 28, Sulaiman al-Ma'mari, a journalist and human rights defender, was arrested and detained in Muscat without access to his family or a lawyer. Rights groups reported that al-Ma'mari's arrest appears to be related to his calling for the immediate release of his friend and colleague, Abdullah Habib.

In August, authorities ordered the immediate closure of the *Azamn* newspaper and arrested at least three journalists affiliated with the paper following the publication of articles accusing senior judicial officials of corruption.

Ibrahim al-Ma'mari, *Azamn*'s editor-in-chief, was arrested on July 28, and Zaher al-Abri, who oversees the newspaper's local coverage, was arrested on August 3. Yousef al-Haj, the deputy editor, was subsequently arrested on August 9.

In September, the court of first instance in Muscat sentenced al-Maamari and al-Haj to three years in prison on charges that included disturbing public order, misuse of the internet, publishing details of a civil case, and undermining the prestige of the state. The court also sentenced al-Abri to one year in prison and ordered the permanent closure of the paper. Previously, *Azamn* and its journalists had been targeted for their peaceful dissent. In 2011, a court issued ordered *Azamn* to shut down for a month, and sentenced al-Ma'mari and al-Haj to five-month suspended jail sentences for insulting the justice minister and other officials.

On August 26, prominent Omani human rights defender Saeed Jaded was released after serving a one-year prison sentence. In November 2015, Jaded was arrested and transferred to Raza Prison, west of Shalala, to serve a one-year prison sentence for "inciting to break national unity and spreading discord within society" in relation to a blog post he wrote in October 2014. In this post he compared the 2011 protests in Shofar to the 2014 protests in Hong Kong.

In March 2015, in a separate case, a Muscat court sentenced Jaded to three years in prison on charges of "undermining the prestige of the state," incitement to "illegal gathering," and "using information networks to disseminate news that would prejudice public order" based on his online activities. These activities included a public letter he wrote to United States President Barack Obama asking

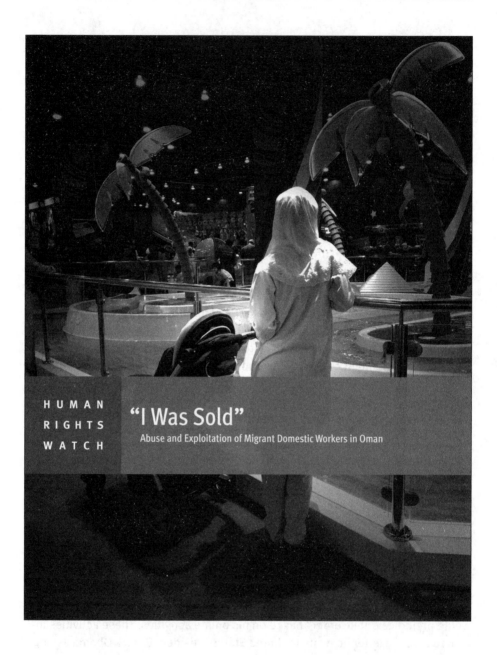

HUMAN
RIGHTS
WATCH

"I Was Sold"
Abuse and Exploitation of Migrant Domestic Workers in Oman

him to press for human rights improvements in Oman. The Court of Appeals in Muscat later upheld his three years' prison sentence, suspended for three years, and payment of a 2000 Omani Rails fine (US$5,200).

Freedom of Assembly and Association

All public gatherings require official approval in advance; authorities arrest and prosecute participants in unapproved gatherings. Some private gatherings are also prohibited under article 137 of the penal code, which prescribes a punishment of up to three years in prison and a fine for anyone who "participates in a private gathering including at least 10 individuals with a view to commit a riot or a breach of public order." Authorities sharply increased the penalties under article 137 after the pro-reform demonstrations of 2011.

Maina Kiai, the United Nations special rapporteur on the rights to freedom of peaceful assembly and of association, had characterized the "legal environment for the exercise of the rights to freedom of peaceful assembly and of association in Oman" as problematic during his visit to the country in 2014.

On May 4, Dr. Talia al-Maamari, a former Shure Council member from Lia, in Al Bettina Region, northern Oman, was released from prison three months prior to the end of his prison sentence, reportedly by a royal decree from Sultan Qaboos. In August 2014, a court of appeals in Muscat sentenced him to four years in prison on charges of "illegal gathering" and calling for anti-government demonstrations. The case stemmed from an incident in August 2013 in Lia, when police used tear gas to disperse people blocking the port's entrance to protest industrial pollution at the nearby port of Sohar. Authorities arrested al-Maamari two days after the protest, denying him access to a lawyer for over two weeks.

The United Nations Working Group on Arbitrary Detention in December 2014 characterized Dr. Talia al-Ma'mari's detention as arbitrary and stated that the government should release him immediately and compensate him.

Women's Rights

Article 17 of the Basic Law states that all citizens are equal and bans gender-based discrimination. In practice, however, women continue to face discrimination. The Personal Status Law discriminates against women on matters such as divorce, inheritance, child custody, and legal guardianship. For instance, women can lose child custody if they re-marry, and men continue to hold guardianship of the child regardless of whether they have custody.

Oman has no laws prohibiting domestic violence and marital rape. Cases can only be brought under general assault or battery charges.

Oman's penal code criminalizes sexual relations outside marriage and provides three months to one-year imprisonment when the person is unmarried, and one to three years' imprisonment when the person is married. Criminalization of such offenses apply disproportionately to women whose pregnancy can serve as evidence of the offense.

Migrant Workers

Migrant workers remained vulnerable to exploitation and abuse, due in part to the *kafala* (visa sponsorship) system that ties migrant workers to their employers and precludes them from changing employers without their current employer's consent.

Human Rights Watch found female domestic workers in particular at high risk of abuse, since Oman's labor law currently excludes domestic workers from its protections, and those who flee abuse have little avenue for redress.

Human Rights Watch documented abuse and exploitation of domestic workers, including employers frequently confiscating workers' passports despite a legal prohibition; not paying workers their salaries, in full or at all; forcing them to work excessively long hours without breaks or days off; and denying them adequate food and living conditions. In some cases, workers reported physical and sexual abuse. Migrant domestic workers who fled abusive employers reported facing "absconding" charges that can lead to imprisonment and deportation, trumped-up criminal charges by employers to force them to drop their cases, and lengthy delays when pursuing cases against employers.

Sexual Orientation and Gender Identity

The Omani penal code punishes consensual sex between men or between women with six months to three years in prison.

Key International Actors

Oman has yet to ratify key international human rights treaties, including the International Covenants on Civil and Political Rights and on Economic, Social and Cultural Rights, although the government agreed to ratify the latter when the UN Human Rights Council last considered Oman under its Universal Periodic Review (UPR) process in 2015.

In March, Oman accepted, in full or in part, 169 recommendations out of the 233 recommendations it received during its second UPR cycle in November 2015. However, authorities rejected 36 recommendations, including those on freedom of expression, assembly, allowing women to pass their nationality on to their children, and ratifying the Covenant on Civil and Political Rights.

Both the US and the United Kingdom provide significant economic and military aid to Oman. Oman's Western allies offered muted, if any criticism, of its human rights abuses in 2016, except in annual reports. In 2016, the US Trafficking in Persons report downgraded Oman to its Tier 2 Watch List category, citing a decrease in the government's anti-trafficking law enforcement efforts.

HUMAN RIGHTS WATCH

"This Crooked System"
Police Abuse and Reform in Pakistan

Pakistan

While there were fewer incidents of militant violence in 2016 than in previous years, scores of people were killed in bombings that targeted courts and mosques. Law enforcement and security agencies remained unaccountable for human rights violations and exercised disproportionate political influence, especially on matters of national security and counterterrorism. The military continued to control implementation of a national plan to address terrorism, largely without civilian oversight.

At least 85 people on death row were executed in 2016. Secret military courts continued to operate and hand down death sentences.

The government muzzled dissenting voices in nongovernmental organizations (NGOs) and media. It passed vague and overbroad cybercrimes legislation installing new curbs of freedom of expression and criminalizing peaceful internet use.

Women, religious minorities, and transgender people faced violent attacks, insecurity, and persecution, with the government failing to provide adequate protection and hold perpetrators accountable.

Police pressure and abuses compelled thousands of Afghans living in Pakistan to return to Afghanistan or flee elsewhere in 2016.

Counterterrorism and Law Enforcement Abuses

Suicide bombings, armed attacks, and killings by the Taliban, Al-Qaeda, and their affiliates targeted nearly every sector of Pakistani society, including religious minorities, security personnel, health workers, lawyers, and journalists, resulting in hundreds of deaths. Military courts sentenced at least 100 people to death in connection with the attacks. Shrouded in secrecy, the proceedings raised fair trial concerns.

In May, Aftab Ahmad, a member of the Karachi-based political party, Mutahidda Qaumi Movement (MQM), was killed while in the custody of the Pakistan Rangers, a federal paramilitary force. An autopsy report found that over 35 percent of his body was covered in bruises and abrasions inflicted while he was still alive, indicating torture. In an unusual step, the chief of army staff, Gen. Raheel Sharif, ordered a military inquiry into the death.

Dr. Asim Hussain, a member of the Pakistan People's Party (PPP), detained on August 26, 2015, on charges including "harboring and treating terrorists and gangsters" at his hospital, remained in custody. Local groups expressed serious concerns about Hussain's treatment in Rangers' custody and its impact on his mental health.

In April, Pakistani authorities used anti-terrorism laws and excessive force to prevent tenant farmers in Okara district, Punjab province, from demonstrating in favor of land rights.

Religious Minorities

At least 19 people remained on death row after being convicted under Pakistan's draconian blasphemy law and hundreds awaited trial. Most of those facing blasphemy are members of religious minorities, often victimized by these charges due to personal disputes.

The government continued to actively encourage legal and procedural discrimination against members of the Ahmadiyah religious community by failing to repeal discriminatory laws.

In March, at least 74 people were killed and 338 others injured in a suicide bombing in a public park in Lahore. The primary target of the attack was Christians celebrating Easter.

Freedom of Expression and Attacks on Civil Society

Many journalists increasingly practice self-censorship, fearing retribution from security forces, military intelligence, and militant groups. Media outlets in 2016 remained under pressure to avoid reporting on or criticizing human rights violations in counterterrorism operations. The Taliban and other armed groups threatened media outlets and targeted journalists and activists for their work.

In January, the Pakistan Rangers entered and, without a warrant, searched the Karachi house of Salman Masood, a New York Times journalist. The Interior Ministry issued an apology and ordered an inquiry, while other members of the administration claimed the raid was part of a broader search operation in the area. However, only one other house was searched, raising concerns that the raid's aim was to harass and intimidate Masood.

In May, four unidentified gunmen killed Khurram Zaki in Karachi. Zaki had been publicly critical of extremist cleric Abdul Aziz and militant sectarian groups, and had been receiving threats. He had confided to friends that he was on several militant "hitlists."

In August, MQM supporters attacked the office of ARY, one of the country's largest news broadcasters, after Altaf Husain, the party chief, publicly encouraged them to attack media outlets for not covering party protests.

Militant groups targeted lawyers, courts, and teachers. In January, armed militants attacked Bacha Khan University in Khyber Pakhtunkhwa, killing at least 20 people. In March, a suicide bombing at the district courts in Charsadda, Khyber Pakhtunkhwa, killed 17 people. In August, a suicide attack in Quetta, Balochistan, killed 70 people, most of them lawyers gathered at a hospital emergency room following the shooting of Bilal Kasi, president of the Balochistan bar association. The Islamic State (ISIS) and Jamat-ul-Ahrar, a Pakistani Taliban offshoot, claimed responsibility for the attacks. In September, a Jamaat-ul-Ahrar suicide bombing at the district courts in Mardan killed 14 people.

In August, the Prevention of Cybercrimes law was enacted, which allows the government to censor online content and to criminalize internet user activity under extremely broad and vague criteria. The law also sanctions government authorities to access data of internet users without judicial review or oversight.

A year after the government announced a policy for "Regulation of INGOs in Pakistan," there were credible reports of the policy being used to harass and impede the work of international humanitarian and human rights groups. In March, three Islamabad-based human rights groups had to stop work for not complying with regulatory requirements. Numerous nongovernmental organizations (NGOs), particularly in Punjab province, were intimidated, harassed, and in some case had their offices sealed on the pretext of implementation of the national plan against terrorism.

Women's and Girls' Rights

Child marriage remains a serious concern in Pakistan, with 21 percent of girls marrying before the age of 18. In January 2016, a proposal submitted to parliament by WHOM aimed to raise the legal minimum age to 18 for females and introduce harsher penalties for those who arrange child marriage. However, on January 14, 2016, the proposal was withdrawn following strong pressure from the Council of Islamic Ideology, a body that advises the parliament on Islamic law. The council criticized the proposal as "anti-Islamic" and "blasphemous."

Violence against women and girls—including rape, murder through so-called honor killings, acid attacks, domestic violence, and forced marriage—remained routine. Pakistani human rights NGOs estimate that there are about 1,000 "honor killings" every year.

The government continued to fail to address forced conversions of women belonging to Hindu and Christian communities.

In June, Zeenat Rafiq, 18, was burned to death in Lahore by her mother for "bringing shame to the family" by marrying a man of her choosing. In May, family members tortured and burned to death a 19-year-old school teacher in Murree, Punjab, for refusing an arranged marriage. In May, the body of Amber, 16, was found inside a vehicle that had been set on fire in Abbottabad, Khyber Pakhtunkhwa, after a jirga, or traditional assembly of elders, ordered her death for helping her friend marry of her own choice. In July, Qandeel Baloch, a well-known Pakistani model was killed by her brother in a so-called honor killing.

Pakistani law allows the family of a murder victim to pardon the perpetrator. This practice is often used in cases of "honor" killings, where the victim and perpetrator frequently belong to the same family, in order to evade prosecution. The 2004 Criminal Law (Amendment) Act made "honor killings" a criminal offense, but the law remains poorly enforced. An anti-honor killing bill seeking to eliminate the option of murder committed in the name of "honor" to be "forgiven" was passed by the parliament in October.

Children's Rights

Use of child suicide bombers by the Taliban and other armed groups continued in 2016.

In May, the United Nations Committee on the Rights of the Child concluded its review of Pakistan and expressed concern about a number of issues affecting children, including executions, the impact of sectarian violence and terrorism, and alleged torture and ill-treatment in police custody.

Refugees

The Pakistan government failed to meet its international legal obligation to protect more than 2 million Afghans in the country, including those not registered as refugees, from harassment and other abuses.

The number of Afghans repatriating from Pakistan increased in 2016 due to coercive pressure from local governments; at the end of August, about 70,000 registered refugees had been repatriated.

The uncertain residency status of Afghan refugees in Pakistan encouraged police harassment, threats, and extortion, particularly in the Khyber Pakhtunkhwa. Statements by senior Pakistani officials in 2016 raised concerns of new government actions to restrict the rights of Afghan refugees in the country.

Sexual Orientation and Gender Identity

Pakistan's penal code criminalizes sexual behavior between men with possible life imprisonment. In 2009, Pakistan's Supreme Court called for improved police response to cases involving transgender people, and to ensure the rights of transgender people to basic education, employment, and protection. However, despite the court order, violent attacks on transgender and intersex women in Khyber Pakhtunkhwa province surged in 2016, with unknown assailants frequently targeting those involved in activism.

Official responses have been inadequate. Since January 2015, human rights groups in Khyber Pakhtunkhwa have recorded dozens of threats to, and attacks on, people and property, including abuses while in police custody. In a widely publicized case in May, Alisha, a 23-year-old transgender activist, was shot eight times in Peshawar, and died in hospital while staff debated whether to put her in the male or female ward. In September, the National Commission for Human Rights called on the government to investigate the attacks.

Death Penalty

Pakistan has more than 8,000 prisoners on death row, one of the world's largest populations of prisoners facing execution. Pakistani law mandates capital punishment for 28 offenses, including murder, rape, treason, and blasphemy. Those on death row are often from the most marginalized sections of society, including people with disabilities. At least 85 people were executed in 2016.

Key International Actors

Pakistan's volatile relationship with United States, the country's largest development and military donor, deteriorated amid signs of mistrust. US foreign assistance to Pakistan fell to the lowest level since 2007. In August, the US stopped payment of US$300 million in military reimbursements to Pakistan for not taking adequate action against the Haqqani network, a Taliban-affiliated group that is accused of planning and carrying out attacks on civilians, government officials, and NATO forces in Afghanistan.

Pakistan and China deepened extensive economic and political ties, and work continued the China-Pakistan Economic Corridor, a project consisting of construction of roads, railways and energy pipelines.

The United Nations high commissioner for human rights expressed concern after historically tense relations between Pakistan and India further deteriorated in 2016, with both countries accusing each other of facilitating unrest and militancy. Scheduled talks to resolve longstanding disputes over security, territory, and sharing river water resources stalled.

In September, an armed group attack on an Indian military base in the Indian state of Jammu and Kashmir heightened tensions between the two sides. India claimed that the attackers were backed by the Pakistan government. Pakistan denied involvement.

The United Nations high commissioner for refugees termed Pakistan's treatment of Afghan refugees as a "concerted push" to repatriate a large number of refugees. Relations with Afghanistan remained characterized by mutual hostility and mistrust. The Afghan government accused Pakistan of allowing the Haqqani network to operate from Pakistan to carry out attacks in Afghanistan. Pakistan maintained that the network had been dismantled.

Papua New Guinea

Despite Papua New Guinea's (PNG) economic boom led by extractive industries, almost 40 percent of the country's population lives in poverty. The government has not taken sufficient steps to address gender inequality, violence, corruption, or excessive use of force by police. Rates of family and sexual violence are among the highest in the world, and perpetrators are rarely prosecuted.

The government led by Prime Minister Peter O'Neill was the focus of sustained protests throughout 2016, including student boycotts and acts of civil disobedience across a number of sectors of the economy, over allegations of corruption. In July, O'Neill survived a parliamentary no-confidence vote. In June, police opened fire on a student protest in Port Morseby, injuring 23.

Women's and Girls' Rights

Papua New Guinea is one of the most dangerous places in the world to be a woman, with the majority of women experiencing rape or assault in their lifetime and women facing systemic discrimination. While such acts have long been criminalized and domestic violence was specifically proscribed under the 2013 Family Protection Act (FPA), few perpetrators are brought to justice. Three years since the FPA was passed, it has not been implemented.

Police and prosecutors rarely pursue investigations or criminal charges against people who commit family violence—even in cases of attempted murder, serious injury, or repeated rape—and instead prefer to resolve such cases through mediation and/or payment of compensation.

Police also often demand money ("for fuel") from victims before acting, or simply ignore cases that occur in rural areas. There is also a severe lack of services for people requiring assistance after having suffered family violence, such as safe houses, qualified counselors, case management, financial support, or legal aid.

Violent mobs have attacked individuals accused of sorcery or witchcraft, the victims mostly being women and girls. In February, a mob killed a family of four over accusations of sorcery. In August, reports emerged of villagers attacking a number of women suspected of involvement in sorcery in PNG's Enga province, including one woman who had her hand chopped off.

PNG has one of the highest rates of maternal death in the world, second only to Afghanistan in the Asia Pacific region. Only slightly more than 50 percent of women and girls give birth in a health facility or with the help of a skilled birth attendant, and although the PNG government supports universal access to contraception, two out of three women still are unable to access and use it.

Abortion remains illegal in PNG, except in cases where the mother's life is at risk. In October 2015, a husband and wife were found guilty of killing their unborn child and were each sentenced to four years in prison, the first convictions under PNG's 1975 abortion law. The woman had experienced difficulties in previous pregnancies and an obstructed labor during the second, leaving her afraid and traumatized. The two were released in June and August 2016, with the remainder of their sentences suspended.

Government Corruption

In 2016, the government continued to weaken the country's most successful anti-corruption agency, Task Force Sweep, by starving it of funding.

Since 2014, the National Fraud and Anti-Corruption Directorate (Anti-Corruption Directorate), led by Matthew Damaru, has had a warrant for the arrest of the prime minister on corruption charges, but a court ordered a stay of execution and the warrant still had not been executed at time of writing. In April 2016, PNG's Supreme Court dismissed a suit brought by Prime Minister O'Neill that sought to prevent anti-corruption police from investigating him.

Following a number of high profile arrests in April by the Anti-Corruption Directorate—including of a Supreme Court judge, the attorney-general, and the prime minister's lawyer—Police Commissioner Gari Baki suspended Damaru and ordered the closure of the directorate. The police commissioner said it was closed for "administrative reasons" and "a lack of accountability." In May, the unit was reopened after the PNG Supreme Court urged Baki to do so.

Police Abuse

In January, Baki declared 2016 as the year to discipline police officers responsible for abuse. Baki stated that more than 1,600 complaints of police abuse were filed between 2007 and 2014, with 326 classified as criminal cases. It is unclear how many, if any, resulted in criminal convictions of police officers. Police abuse, including of children, continues to be reported with little accountability even for fatalities or egregious physical abuse.

In June, police opened fire on protesting university students in Port Moresby as they attempted to march on the national parliament. Police confirmed that at least 23 students were injured. In a statement, O'Neill blamed "agitators" for the violence and announced an inquiry "to determine the underlying reasons for continued student unrest promoted by individuals outside the student body." O'Neill maintains that the protests were funded by the political opposition.

Asylum Seekers and Refugees

Australia transfers asylum seekers that arrive in Australian waters by boat to PNG's Manus Island for refugee status determination and settlement. More than 900 asylum seekers and refugees remain on Manus Island. Approximately 872 of these are held in a center on a naval base, of whom about 675 are recognized refugees.

In April, the PNG Supreme Court ruled that the detention of asylum seekers and refugees on Manus Island was unconstitutional. O'Neill asked that Australia find alternative arrangements for its detainees and for recognized refugees who do not wish to stay in PNG. Australia resisted the decision but in August, both governments announced they would close the center.

Since April 2016, the center has remained fenced off and guarded, but at time of writing center staff were allowing refugees and asylum seekers to leave the center at scheduled times by bus or on foot under security escort.

To date, neither Australia nor PNG has taken steps to close the center. Many refugees are afraid to leave the center due to acts of violence in the community. For instance, in August, Manus locals robbed and assaulted three refugees; one of the locals attacked them with an iron bar.

Children's Rights

Even though the government has officially abolished school fees, primary education is not compulsory and barriers remain, including long distances to school, insecurity, lack of water and sanitation facilities, and limited access for children with disabilities. Thirteen percent of primary school-aged students and 60 percent of secondary school students were out of school in 2012, the latest year for which information is available. The adult literacy rate was an estimated 63 percent.

Disability Rights

Despite the existence of a national disability policy, people with disabilities are often unable to participate in community life, go to school, or work because of lack of accessibility, stigma, and other barriers associated with disability. Access to mental health care is limited, and traditional healers are the only option for many people with psychosocial disabilities.

Sexual Orientation and Gender Identity

The PNG criminal code outlaws sex "against the order of nature," which has been interpreted to apply to consensual same-sex acts, and is punishable by up to 14 years' imprisonment. Gay asylum seekers on Manus Island have reported being shunned, sexually abused, or assaulted by other asylum seekers.

Key International Actors

Australia remains PNG's most important international partner, providing over 70 percent of the country's total overseas development aid. The Australian government will provide A$558.3 million (approximately US$430 million) in total overseas development aid to PNG in 2016-17.

In May 2016, the Australian government issued the report of a parliamentary inquiry into the delivery and effectiveness of its aid to PNG, recommending that it "renew" and "increase" its commitment to PNG's development.

In May, during the periodic review of PNG's human rights record at the UN Human Rights Council, countries made more than 150 recommendations on issues including ratification of international treaties, establishing a national human rights commission, promoting gender equality, addressing domestic violence and sorcery-related violence, decriminalizing consensual same-sex relations, and abolishing or placing a moratorium on the death penalty.

In September, PNG responded that it would ratify all core human rights treaties "on the basis of priorities" and that, while there are challenges to implementing reforms, it is committed to establishing a human rights commission, improving gender equality, and addressing domestic violence and sorcery-related violence. It also noted, however, that "LGBT is currently not a priority of the Government" and that the "death penalty is in our national law, however despite this, the current government directive is not to implement until further directions are issued."

Peru

In recent years, security forces have repeatedly wounded and killed civilians when responding to occasional violent protests over mining and other large-scale development projects. These killings steeply decreased in 2016.

Efforts to prosecute grave human rights abuses committed during the 20-year armed conflict that ended in 2000 have had mixed results.

Despite a 2015 law intended to eradicate violence against women, thousands took to the streets of the capital Lima and other cities in August, demanding that the government do more to protect the lives and rights of women.

Police Abuse

In August 2016, Interior Minister Carlos Basombrío convened a special commission to investigate what he called "overwhelming indications" that members of the National Police (PNP) engaged in extrajudicial killings. Later that month, Vice Minister of Interior Rubén Vargas confirmed "serious indications" that a group of police officers, including a general, had carried out at least 20 extrajudicial killings between 2009 and 2015, and falsely reported the victims as criminals killed in combat, in order to receive promotions and awards. At time of writing, at least nine PNP members remained under criminal investigation for involvement in the killings.

Security forces reportedly shot dead two protesters in 2016, compared to 12 in 2015. According to local human rights groups, police killed Pedro Valle Sandoval and another unidentified protester on November 6, after protestors blocked a highway in the province of Pataz. Since 2006, security forces have killed at least 130 people during protests in Peru; at least 50 during the administration of Ollanta Humala (2011-2016), and 80 during the second administration of Alan Garcia (2006-2011).

In August 2015, then-President Humala issued a decree that limits the use of force by police. Under the decree, police are permitted to employ lethal force only when it is "strictly necessary" in the face of a "serious and imminent risk" of grave harm. However, Law 30151, passed in January 2014, still grants legal immunity to "armed forces and police personnel who in fulfillment of their duty and using their weapons or other means of defense, cause injury or death." This amendment to the criminal code eliminated language that made immunity conditional on police using lethal force in compliance with regulations. The law may make it impossible to hold police officers who use lethal force unlawfully accountable.

Confronting Past Abuses

Peru's Truth and Reconciliation Commission estimated that almost 70,000 people died or were subject to enforced disappearance during the country's armed conflict between 1980 and 2000. Many were victims of atrocities by the Shining Path and other insurgent groups; others were victims of human rights violations by state agents.

In a landmark trial, former President Alberto Fujimori was sentenced in 2009 to 25 years in prison for killings and "disappearances" committed in 1991 and 1992. In July 2016, he requested a pardon on humanitarian grounds, but withdrew it in September after newly elected President Pedro Pablo Kuczynski said he would likely reject it. Fujimori's intelligence advisor, Vladimiro Montesinos, three former army generals, and members of the Colina group, a government death squad, are also serving sentences ranging from 15 to 25 years for the 1991 assassination of 15 people in the Lima district of Barrios Altos, and for six "disappearances."

Courts have made much less progress in addressing violations, including extra-judicial killings, disapeareances, and torture, committed during the earlier administrations of Fernando Belaúnde (1980-1985) and Alan García (1985-1990).

Only a tiny percentage of the human rights violations committed during the armed conflict had been brought to trial, according to Human Rights Trials in Peru, a project based at George Mason University that monitors human rights prosecutions. In 2016, court hearings continued into their sixth year in the case of torture and disappearances at the Los Cabitos military base in Ayacucho in 1983. Abuses committed in that military base in 1984 and 1985 have been under criminal investigation for over 10 years, but had not been brought to trial at time of writing.

481

In September 2016, a court convicted 11 former soldiers—including a commander—of a 1985 massacre at Accomarca in which an army unit killed more than 60 civilians. The case had been under criminal investigation for 11 years, including almost 6 years of trial.

In July 2016, a trial began against 11 soldiers accused of raping 14 women in the municipalities of Manta and Vilca between 1984 and 1998.

Also in July, a prosecutor decided to close the investigation against former President Alberto Fujimori for forced sterilizations of mostly poor and indigenous women committed during his administration. A month later, a higher-ranking prosecutor requested that the closure be reconsidered, but a ruling on his request remained pending at time of writing. More than 2,000 forced sterilizations have been reported to authorities, but human rights groups contend that these represent only a small portion of such cases.

In November 2015, then-President Humala signed a decree creating a national registry of victims of forced sterilizations. In June 2016, he signed into law a bill to search for victims of disappearances committed during the armed conflict. The law creates a national registry of the disappeared and orders that the Justice Ministry approve and implement a national search plan.

In May 2016, a court ordered that the government pay reparations to victims of abuses committed by both sides of the conflict and their relatives for each of the abuses they suffered, overturning the limits on reparations established by the Peruvian legislature.

Freedom of Expression

Journalists investigating corruption by regional government officials, mayors, and business people are frequent targets of physical attack, threats, and criminal defamation suits.

In April 2016, a court in Lima convicted the then-director of the newspaper Diario 16, Fernando Valencia Osorio, of defamation and sentenced him to 20 months in prison—which it suspended—and over US$30,000 in fines and compensation in a case brought by former President Alan García. In 2013, Diario 16 suggested that when President Humala said in a speech that that "thieves should be in prison, not in power" he was referring to García.

In May 2016, a court convicted local journalist Carol Villavicencio Lizarraga of defamation and sentenced her to a suspended year in prison and a fine of almost $1,500. She had written a piece in the local magazine *El Huacón* arguing that a lawmaker had evaded taxes.

The same month, a court convicted reporter Rafael León of defamation and sentenced him to a suspend year in prison and a fine of almost $1,800. León had written a satirical article about how Meier Miró Quesada, a journalist and former editor of newspaper El Comercio, had criticized a former mayor of Lima in an article. A higher court overturned the ruling in September.

Women's Rights

Women and girls in Peru remain at high risk of gender-based violence. More than 700 women have been killed in Peru in "femicides" (the killing of a woman in certain contexts, including domestic violence and gender-based discrimination) between 2009 and August 2015, according to official statistics.

In September 2015, Peru's Congress passed a law that provides for comprehensive measures to prevent and punish violence against women. The law builds on existing judicial measures to protect women at risk, and mandates the creation of shelters to provide temporary refuge from abuse.

Still, in August 2016, thousands demonstrated in Lima and other cities calling on authorities to do more to curb gender-based violence.

In August, a Lima court ordered the national government to distribute free emergency contraceptive pills in public health facilities throughout the country. In 2009, the Constitutional Court had forbidden the free distribution of emergency contraceptive pill, undermining the reproductive rights of women. In its ruling, the court had stated that the decision could be changed if there was "consensus" that pills are not abortive, something the Lima court found in more recent decisions by international courts and statements by the World Health Organization (WHO).

Women and girls in Peru have the right to access abortions only in cases of risk to their health or lives. In July 2014, the Committee on the Elimination of Discrimination Against Women asked Peru to decriminalize abortion when pregnancy was the result of rape and severe fetal impairment. A broad bill to reform the criminal code, which remained pending in Congress at time of writing, would continue to prohibit abortion in these cases. In October, lawmakers from three political parties introduced a bill in Congress to decriminalize abortion in cases of rape and severe fetal impairment.

Sexual Orientation and Gender Identity

In March 2015, Congress rejected a bill to recognize civil unions for same-sex couples. In September 2016, a Congressional supporter of President Kuczynski announced that he would introduce a new legislative proposal to recognize same-sex civil unions.

People in Peru are required to appear before a judge in order to revise the gender noted on their identification documents. In an August 2016 report, the human rights ombudsman noted that courts had rejected most of these requests, often applying inconsistent criteria.

Key International Actors

In June, the United Nations Working Group on Enforced or Involuntary Disappearances commended the passage of the bill to search for victims of disappearances committed during the armed conflict.

President Kuczynski has been one of the few leaders in the region who has consistently expressed concern over the human rights situation in Venezuela. In July, days before taking office, he said that leaders in the region should work to address "the lack of respect for human liberties and the humanitarian crisis" in Venezuela.

Philippines

Rodrigo Duterte took office as president of the Philippines on June 30, 2016. Duterte campaigned on an explicit platform to "kill all of you who make the lives of Filipinos miserable," including criminal suspects, as part of his vow to "solve drugs, criminality, and corruption in three to six months." At his inauguration, he pledged that his administration would "be sensitive to the state's obligations to promote, and protect, fulfill the human rights of our citizens … even as the rule of law shall at all times prevail." During the government's campaign against illegal drugs, however, Duterte has publicly praised the extrajudicial killing of suspected drug dealers and drug users.

Philippine human rights groups have linked the campaign and Duterte's often-fiery rhetoric to a surge of killings by police and unidentified gunmen since he took office, with nearly 4,800 people killed at time of writing. Police say that individuals targeted by police were killed only after they "resisted arrest and shot at police officers," but have provided no evidence to support the claim. The killings have highlighted the country's long-standing problem of impunity for abusive state security forces.

Other key issues confronting the Philippines this past year include the rights of indigenous peoples, violations of reproductive health rights, child labor, and stigma and discrimination related to the HIV/AIDS crisis.

Extrajudicial Killings

The Philippines has seen an unprecedented level of killing by law enforcement since Duterte took office. Police statistics show that from July 1 to November 3, 2016, police killed an estimated 1,790 suspected "drug pushers and users." That death toll constitutes a nearly 20-fold jump over the 68 such police killings recorded between January 1 and June 15, 2016. Police statistics attribute an additional 3,001 killings of alleged drug dealers and drug users to unknown vigilantes from July 1 to September 4. The police categorize those killings as "deaths under investigation," but there is no evidence that police are actively probing the circumstances in which they occurred.

In August, Philippine National Police Director-General Ronald Dela Rosa stated that he did not "condone" extrajudicial killings. In September, police Internal Affairs Service sources said they were "overwhelmed" by the scale of police killings could only probe "a fraction" of the deaths.

Duterte has ignored calls for an official probe into these killings. Instead, he has said the killings show the "success" of his anti-drug campaign and urged police to "seize the momentum." Key senior officials have endorsed this view. Duterte's top judicial official, Solicitor-General Jose Calida, defended the legality of the police killings and opined that the number of such deaths was "not enough."

Attacks on Indigenous Peoples

In March 2016, some 6,000 protesters, primarily indigenous peoples, farmers, and their supporters from drought-stricken areas in North Cotabato and Bukidnon provinces gathered in Kidapawan City in Mindanao to call for government food aid and other assistance. The police response included shooting live ammunition into the crowd, killing two people. At time of writing, neither the Senate and nor police have released the results of their respective investigations into the incident.

Reproductive Health Rights

In his July 25 State of the Nation Address, President Duterte pledged to "put into full force and effect" the Responsible Parenthood and Reproductive Health Law (the RH Law). Such support is greatly needed because on January 8, 2016, the Philippine Congress eliminated funding in the 2016 national budget for contraception guaranteed under the RH Law, cutting vital support for lower-income individuals. Millions of Filipinos rely on state-provided contraceptive services and supplies for protection from sexually transmitted infections, and for safe birth-spacing and family planning. The United Nations Population Fund has criticized the congressional action as a threat to "the basic human right to health as well as the right to reproductive choices."

Human Rights Watch has also documented policies implemented by local governments designed to derail full enforcement of the RH Law. In Sorsogon City in the Bicol region, Mayor Sally Lee issued an executive order in February 2015 that declared the city a "pro-life city." Although the order does not explicitly prohibit family planning services and contraceptive supplies, health workers and advocates said that the city government gave oral guidelines to the city's public clinics to cease the distribution of family planning supplies and instead promote only "natural" family planning methods such as the Catholic Church-approved "rhythm method."

In Balanga City, the municipal government banned local public health officials and clinics from procuring or distributing contraceptives. That interruption compelled low-income people to either buy them from pharmacies or clandestinely from local government-employed midwives at relatively high cost.

Children's Rights

In November 2015, the Philippine government detained more than 140 children in advance of the Asia-Pacific Economic Cooperation (APEC) summit in Manila. The arbitrary detentions were part of so-called clearing operations aimed at beautifying the city ahead of the summit. Police detained the children under guard in government facilities for the homeless and orphans and then released them without charge when the summit concluded.

Child labor in small-scale gold mines remains a serious problem. Children work in unstable 25-meter-deep pits, dive underwater to mine, and process gold with mercury. Small steps taken by authorities to tackle child labor—such as vocational training for former child miners in one mining town—have been undermined by continued lack of regulation of the small-scale gold mining sector, and by the government's failure to address child labor systematically.

HIV Epidemic

Although national prevalence is still low, the country has experienced a sharp rise in new HIV infections in recent years. Prevalence among men who have sex with men (MSM) has increased 10-fold since 2010. In 2015, the Department of Health reported that at least 11 cities registered HIV prevalence rates among MSM of more than 5 percent, with one—Cebu City, the second largest city—recording a 15 percent prevalence rate in 2015. That compares to a 0.2 percent

HIV prevalence rate for the Asia-Pacific region and a 4.7 percent HIV prevalence rate in Sub-Saharan Africa, which has the most serious HIV epidemic in the world.

There has also been an increase in Cebu City in HIV among pregnant women, and in newly recorded infections among people who inject drugs in Cebu City, where the prevalence rate among such people has been recorded at between 40 and 50 percent. Many of these new infections among people who inject drugs are due to sharing contaminated needles.

The growing HIV epidemic is driven by a legal and policy environment hostile to evidence-based policies and interventions that could help prevent HIV transmission. Such restrictions are found in national, provincial, and local government policies, and are compounded by the resistance of the Catholic Church to sexual health education and condom use. Government policies create obstacles to condom access and HIV testing, limit educational efforts on HIV prevention, and have ended harm reduction programs in Cebu City that were previously distributing sterile injecting equipment to people who inject drugs.

Sexual Orientation and Gender Identity

The House of Representatives began consideration of House Bill 267, the "Anti SOGI (Sexual Orientation or Gender Identity) Discrimination Act" in June 2016. If approved, it will criminalize discrimination in the employment of lesbian, gay, bisexual, and transgender (LGBT) individuals, and prohibit schools from refusing to register or expelling students on the basis of sexual orientation or gender identity. The Senate has introduced companion legislation, Senate Bill No. 935, otherwise known as the Anti-Discrimination Bill (ADB), which had its first hearing in August.

House Bill 267 will also sensitize police and law enforcement officers on LGBT issues and train them to attend to complaints. These initiatives are essential given that LGBT rights advocacy groups have warned that hate crimes against LGBT people are on the rise and that the Philippines has recorded the highest number of murders of transgender individuals in Southeast Asia since 2008. The bill would also prohibit anti-LGBT discrimination in access to health care.

Key International Actors

The United States remains a key source of military financial assistance, with the Obama administration allotting US$120 million for 2016. Earlier military financing was conditioned on improvements of the human rights situation in the Philippines but this conditionality has been lifted as part of the Obama administration's so-called "Asia pivot." President Duterte has expressed dissatisfaction with US-Philippines relations, even saying he is willing to expel US military personnel stationed in the Philippines, but conceded that the country still needs US military help because of the South China Sea dispute with China.

Other countries such as Canada and Australia, as well as the European Union, continue to provide assistance to the Philippines for, among other things, capacity-building programs to improve the human rights situation. Spain has given funds and resources to the national Philippine Commission on Human Rights.

In November, the US State Department announced that it had suspended the sale of 26,000 military assault rifles to the Philippine National Police due to human rights concerns raised by Duterte's abusive "war on drugs." The EU has transitioned its rule of law program called EPJUST II, which involved training the police and other law enforcement agencies, into GOJUST, which is tasked with instituting justice sector reforms.

Qatar

Low-paid migrant workers continued to face abuse and exploitation, and reforms that took effect in 2016 leave the exploitative elements of the old *kafala* (sponsorship) system in place and do not cover domestic workers. Qatar-based journalists criticized the manner in which the authorities applied the provisions of a 2014 cybercrime law.

Migrant Workers

Less than 10 percent of Qatar's population of 2.1 million are Qatari nationals. The country has been increasingly dependent on migrant labor as Qatar continued to build stadiums and develop infrastructure in preparation for hosting the 2022 FIFA World Cup.

Low-paid migrant workers, mostly from Asia and to a lesser extent Africa, continued to face abuse and exploitation. Workers typically pay exorbitant recruitment fees. Employers regularly take control of workers' passports when they arrive in Qatar. Many migrant workers complain that employers failed to pay their wages on time, and sometimes not at all.

In December 2016, changes to Qatar's *kafala* system came into force. Law No. 21 of 2015, on the regulation of the entry and exit of expatriates and their residency, referred to "recruiters" instead of "sponsors" but left the fundamentally exploitative characteristics of the *kafala* system in place, whereby a migrant worker's legal residence in the country continues to be tied to their employer or sponsor.

The new law still requires foreign workers to obtain a "No Objection Certificate" from their current employer in order to transfer legally to another employer before the end of their contracts, as well as permission from an unspecified "competent authority" along with the Interior and Labor and Social Affairs Ministries.

If the contract does not specify any time frame, under the new law workers must wait five years before leaving an employer. The workers also must still obtain exit permits from their employers to leave Qatar. The new law provides for a grievance committee for workers in cases in which sponsors refuse to grant exit visas, but the arbitrary restriction on the workers' right to leave the country remains in place. In practice, this enables employers to arbitrarily prevent their employees from leaving Qatar and returning to their home country.

Qatar's labor law prohibits migrant workers from unionizing or engaging in strikes, although they make up 99 percent of the private sector workforce.

The new labor law explicitly excludes domestic workers from its remit, and leaves them still more vulnerable to abuse and exploitation. In addition to labor abuses, many domestic workers faced physical and sexual abuse. A law on domestic workers continued to remain in draft form and has not been made public.

Freedom of Expression

In March, Qatar's emir pardoned and released the poet, Mohamed al-Ajami, whom an appeal court had sentenced to 15 years in prison in 2013 on the basis of the content of poems posted online that criticized Qatar's ruling family and other Arab rulers.

Qatar issued a law "on the suppression of electronic crimes" in September 2014. The 2014 law criminalizes the spreading of "false news" on the internet and provides for a maximum of three years in jail for anyone who posts online content that "violates social values or principles," or "insults or slanders others."

Authorities used the law to detain a journalist from an independent news website, Doha News, after he wrote an article naming a man convicted of a serious criminal offence. Authorities did not press charges, but a Doha News editorial published in October criticized the manner in which authorities were applying the law, and quoted a Qatari attorney who said the law was "like a knife held close to the necks of writers, activists and journalists."

Qatar's penal code provides for a maximum of five years in jail for criticism of the emir.

Women's Rights, Sexual Orientation, and Gender Identity

Qatar's Law No. 22 of 2006 on family and personal status continues to discriminate against women. Under article 36, a marriage contract is valid when a woman's male guardian concludes the contract and two male witnesses are present. Article 58 states that it is a wife's responsibility to look after the household and to obey her husband.

Other than Article 57 of the family law forbidding husbands from hurting their wives physically or morally, and general provisions on assault, the penal code does not criminalize domestic violence or marital rape.

Qatar's nationality law does not allow Qatari women, unlike Qatari men, married to non-Qatari spouses to pass on their nationality to their children.

Qatar's penal code punishes "sodomy" with one to three years in prison. Muslims convicted of *zina* (sex outside of marriage) can be sentenced to flogging (non-married persons) or the death penalty (married persons). Non-Muslims can be sentenced to imprisonment. According to media reports, authorities have flogged dozens of people since 2004, including at least 45 between 2009 and 2011. In 2016, according to media reports, a Dutch woman was arrested after she reported that she was raped. A court handed down a suspended one-year imprisonment sentence for engaging in extramarital sex, and deported her. It also sentenced the man accused of raping her with 100 lashes for having extramarital sex and 40 lashes for drinking alcohol.

Key International Actors

Qatar maintained ground troops in Yemen, where they have been assisting the Saudi-led military campaign against Houthi forces, also known as Ansar Allah. In March, France approved the sale of 24 Dassault Rafael fighter jets to Qatar, in a deal worth US$7.5 billion. In September, the US approved the sale to Qatar of 36 Boeing F-15 fighter jets valued at around $4 billion.

Russia

The government in 2016 further tightened control over the already-shrinking space for free expression, association, and assembly and intensified persecution of independent critics. Parliament adopted laws expanding the power of law enforcement and security agencies, including to control online speech. The parliamentary vote in September resulted in the ruling party, United Russia, gaining a constitutional majority in the State Duma, the parliament's lower chamber. Russia continued to support rebels who commit abuses in eastern Ukraine. Russia's actions in occupied Crimea created a human rights crisis.

Freedom of Association

The authorities used a 2012 law to demonize as "foreign agents" dozens of non-governmental organizations (NGOs), including leading rights groups and independent think tanks. At time of writing, the "register of foreign agents" by Russia's Ministry of Justice includes 148 NGOs. Between 2012 and 2016 at least thirty groups closed rather than accept the label.

In June, authorities for the first time criminally prosecuted an activist under the law, charging Valentina Cherevatenko, chair of Women of the Don, a human rights and peace-building group, with "malicious evasion" of registration as a "foreign agent." If found guilty, she faces up to two years' imprisonment.

In February, a court dissolved AGORA, an association of lawyers defending civil and political activists, after the Justice Ministry alleged AGORA violated the "foreign agents" law and undertook work beyond its mandate.

Authorities fined many groups for failing to display "foreign agent" labels on publications. In October 2015, an appeals court upheld a 600,000 ruble ($10,000) fine against Human Rights Center "Memorial," a leading human rights group, for not labeling materials actually produced and published by a different group.

Russia's prosecutor general designated three more foreign organizations "undesirable" under the 2015 law authorizing bans on foreign or international groups that allegedly undermine Russia's security, defense, or constitutional order, bringing the total number of banned groups to seven. All seven are American democracy promotion or civil society capacity-building organizations. Russians maintaining ties with "undesirables" face penalties ranging from fines to up to six years in prison.

Freedom of Assembly

Authorities increasingly refused to sanction public protests organized by government critics and political opposition and punished protesters participating in unsanctioned peaceful gatherings and single-person pickets.

In December 2015, a Moscow court sentenced peaceful protester Ildar Dadin to three years' imprisonment, later reduced to two-and-a-half, for repeated breaches of public assembly regulations. Dadin is the first activist imprisoned under this criminal provision. In fall 2016, Dadin alleged beatings, threats, and degrading treatment by staff of the Segezha penal colony in northern Russia where he is serving his sentence. An investigation into his allegations was pending at time of writing.

Authorities launched similar proceedings against several others, including Vladimir Ionov, 76, an outspoken critic of Russia's role in eastern Ukraine. Ionov fled Russia in August.

New Restrictive Laws

In December 2015, parliament passed a law empowering Russia's Constitutional Court to determine whether international human rights bodies' rulings, including the European Court of Human Rights (ECtHR) judgments, contradict the Russian Constitution and could therefore be deemed "non-executable." A ruling deemed "non-executable" will not be implemented unless the constitution is amended. In April, the court found unconstitutional a July 2013 ECtHR ruling finding the absolute ban on prisoner voting a violation of the right to choose one's government.

In December, parliament adopted amendments requiring media outlets, broadcasters, and publishers to report funding from all international sources, including Russian NGOs designated as "foreign agents," or face fines.

In June, parliament adopted legislation holding internet search engine owners with more than 1 million daily users accountable for content appearing on their sites and requiring Russian-language search engines and those advertising for Russian audiences be owned by Russian companies or citizens. Dunja Mijatović, the Organization for Security and Co-operation in Europe representative on freedom of the media, said the vaguely worded legislation would "result in governmental interference of online information and introduce self-censorship in private companies."

A June law empowers law enforcement agencies to place on watch lists individuals allegedly engaging in "anti-social behavior," or "actions that run contrary to commonly accepted norms of behavior and morality."

In July, President Vladimir Putin signed into law counterterrorism and counterextremism amendments known as the "Yarovaya Law," after their key author. The law requires that cellular and internet providers store all communications data for six months and all metadata up to three years for potential access by security services. The law also bans religious activities outside of "specially designated places," such as officially recognized religious institutions; criminalizes "failure to report a crime" without specifying when such a requirement would apply; increases penalties for vaguely defined "public justification of terrorism" online; and severely penalizes "inducing, recruiting, or otherwise involving" others in so-called mass unrest.

Prosecutions for Online Speech

From mid-2014 through 2016, Russian courts delivered at least five guilty verdicts, with at least 15 cases pending, on criminal separatism charges for material posted online. Most charges pertained to remarks about Crimea being part of Ukraine, not Russia.

For example, in May, officials charged and placed under a travel ban Ilmi Umerov, formerly a local official in Crimea and deputy chairman of the Crimean Tatars' elected representative body, the Mejlis, after his March interview criticizing Russia's occupation of Crimea. In August, authorities forcibly confined Umerov to a psychiatric hospital for three weeks. At time of writing, his case was pending.

In May, a court sentenced Andrei Bubeev to two years and three months in prison for extremist and separatist calls based on two posts on Vkontakte, Russia's largest social network: a photo with a toothpaste tube saying "Squeeze Russia out of you," and an article "Crimea is Ukraine."

In November, Russia's Supreme Court recommended that law enforcement authorities exercise good judgement and take into account relevant context, when launching criminal extremism cases based solely on reposts in social media.

North Caucasus

Armed confrontations between Islamist insurgents and law enforcement agencies continued in the North Caucasus, particularly in Dagestan. Russia media continued to report on North Caucasus residents leaving Russia and joining the Islamic State (also known as ISIS) as well as on cases of detentions of North Caucasus residents allegedly affiliated with ISIS.

Salafi Muslim communities in Dagestan were subject to intense scrutiny and harassment as law enforcement largely equated them with insurgents or their collaborators. Authorities placed Salafis on watch lists, repeatedly detained and questioned many of them without specific grounds; raided Salafi mosques; and carried out mass detentions of believers. They closed several Salafi mosques, including in Makhachkala, Dagestan's capital.

Chechnya's strongman, Ramzan Kadyrov, asserted that Salafis have no place in Chechnya, instructing police to punish those who stray from Sufi Islam, traditional for the region. Police raids against Salafis were widespread. Authorities also pursued collective punishment, including punitive house burnings, against relatives of alleged insurgents.

Ahead of September elections for the head (governor) of Chechnya, local authorities targeted critics and those deemed disloyal to Kadyrov, including through abductions and enforced disappearances, ill-treatment, death threats, and threats of violence against relatives.

Chechnya's authorities also attacked critical journalists and human rights defenders. In March, a group of masked men believed to be Chechen officials' proxies, attacked a minibus carrying Russian and foreign journalists traveling to Chechnya, beat the journalists, and burned the bus.

The following week, thugs apparently acting as Chechen authorities' proxies physically attacked the leader of Joint Mobile Group for Human Rights Defenders in Chechnya (JMG). JMG withdrew its team from Chechnya for security reasons.

In May, Chechen police arbitrarily detained and threatened a Russian journalist researching a punitive house-burning. In September, following an unfair trial, a Chechnya court sentenced 23-year-old local journalist Zhalaudi Geriev to three years' imprisonment on fabricated drug possession charges, apparently in retaliation for his work with Caucasian Knot, known for critical coverage of Chechnya.

In Beslan, North Ossetia, during events commemorating victims of the September 2004 school hostage-taking, police roughed up and detained several activists wearing T-shirts and holding a sign saying: "Putin is the Slaughterer of Beslan." Thugs apparently acting as proxies of local law enforcement attacked journalists Elena Kostyuchenko, of *Novaya Gazeta*, and Diana Khachatryan, of *Takie Dela*. Doctors diagnosed Kostyuchenko with a brain contusion afterwards.

Sexual Orientation and Gender Identity

Authorities continued to implement discriminatory policies and laws against lesbian, gay, bisexual, and transgender (LGBT) people.

In March, police found journalist and theater critic Dmitry Tsilikin dead in his St. Petersburg apartment from stab wounds. The perpetrator, arrested a week later, confessed that he planned to blackmail Tsilikin about his homosexuality, but killed him during a confrontation. The police did not categorize the killing as a hate crime.

In January, a court in Murmansk, northwestern Russia, found LGBT activist Sergei Alekseenko guilty of violating the discriminatory "gay propaganda" law which prohibits allowing children access to positive information about LGBT relationships. The court called several publications on the website of an LGBT organization formerly run by Alekseenko "gay propaganda" and fined him 100,000 rubles (US$1,300).

Authorities continued legal action against Deti-404, an online support group for LGBT children. In April, a court in the Siberian town of Barnaul ruled to ban the website. As of November, Deti 404's website remained blocked.

In September, a court in Siberia ruled to block BlueSystem.ru, a highly popular LGBT news site. As of November, the site was blocked.

Palliative Care

According to Russian experts, 1 million Russians need effective pain treatment, and at least 300,000 die annually without it. A July government roadmap sets out plans to improve access to and quality of pain relief, including for children. However, access to morphine, an inexpensive and effective pain remedy, remains overly restricted.

Disability Rights

In March, the European Court of Human Rights found the government violated the right to family life of Vitalii Kocherov and his daughter, Anna. In 2007, St. Petersburg authorities placed Anna, born while Kocherov and Anna's mother lived in a state institution, in an orphanage shortly after birth and denied Kocherov parental rights, citing his intellectual disability. The family was reunited.

Reports of serious physical and emotional abuse against children and adults with disabilities in state institutions persist. For example, prosecutors monitoring an institution in Ulyanovsk region in July found that an employee had punished a 13-year-old boy with an intellectual disability by burning him with an iron. Authorities opened a criminal investigation. In June, the Ministry of Labor and Social Affairs proposed reforms intended to improve conditions in institutions for adults with disabilities but has no immediate plans to expand community-based living for adults with disabilities.

Federal curricular standards on primary education for children with disabilities, mandatory for all educational institutions, including mainstream schools, went into effect in September. The standards require a more individualized approach and reasonable accommodations based on children's educational requirements and aim to increase inclusion of children with disabilities in mainstream schools, but children may continue to be placed in specialized classrooms, special schools, or receive home education. The number of children with disabilities enrolled in education increased although many, including those living in institutions, do not receive a quality and inclusive education.

Russia and Ukraine (see also Ukraine chapter)

The government provides political and material support to rebels in eastern Ukraine, but Russian authorities took no measures to rein in abuses by rebels. Russia's actions in occupied Crimea created a human rights crisis. (See Ukraine chapter for details.)

In March, a court in southern Russia found Nadezhda Savchenko—a military pilot and a member of Ukraine's parliament—guilty of premeditated murder in the deaths of two Russian journalists in a 2014 shelling attack in eastern Ukraine. In an unfair trial the court sentenced her to 22 years' imprisonment. In May, authorities exchanged Savchenko for two Russian servicemen captured by Ukrainian authorities.

Oleg Sentsov, a Ukrainian filmmaker from Crimea, continued to serve a 20-year prison sentence in a penal camp in Yakutia, northern Russia. A court convicted Sentsov in 2015 on politically motivated charges of running a "terrorist organization" in Crimea.

Russia and Syria (see also Syria chapter)

Russia continued combat in Syria, mainly through air strikes. Civilian casualties increased, including from unlawful aerial attacks. While it is challenging to determine whether Russian or Syrian aircraft conducted any particular attack, Russia, because it plays an active role in joint military operations, shares responsibility for violations even when its aircraft were not directly involved.

Unlawful attacks included attacks on schools and hospitals, the use of air-dropped cluster munitions, and use of incendiary weapons in populated areas. Despite repeated official denials, convincing evidence indicates that Russia used both cluster munitions and incendiary weapons in attacks on opposition-controlled areas.

In September, airstrikes hit a United Nations aid convoy and a Red Crescent warehouse in Aleppo. Only Syrian and Russian air forces are known to be active in this part of Syria. Russia denied responsibility for the attack.

At a special session held in October, the UN Human Rights Council adopted a resolution calling for an end to aerial bombardments and mandating the Syria

Commission of Inquiry to conduct a "comprehensive, independent special inquiry into the events in Aleppo."

Russia presented a series of hostile amendments that would have removed all references to aerial bombardments, suppressed reference to the responsibility of the Syrian government "and its allies," limited the focus of the special inquiry to only the actions of opposition and terrorist groups, and removed references to the International Criminal Court. All were rejected.

Despite its involvement in the conflict, Russia has not offered to resettle any Syrian refugees, but only to provide scholarships for 300 students. As of April 2016, only two Syrian asylum seekers in Russia had been granted asylum since the conflict began in 2011, and another 1,300 temporary asylum. About 2,000 reportedly have some other form of legal basis for residence, but thousands more live in limbo.

Key International Actors

In January 2016, International Criminal Court judges authorized the court's prosecutor to conduct an investigation into crimes allegedly committed during the August 2008 Russia-Georgia conflict over South Ossetia. On November 15, the ICC's Office of the Prosecutor, in its annual report, characterized the armed conflict in eastern Ukraine and Russia's occupation of Crimea as international armed conflicts to which Russia is a party.

The next day, President Putin issued an order to notify the UN that Russia was withdrawing its signature from the Rome Statute, the founding treaty of the ICC. The European Union high representative for foreign affairs and security policy issued a statement to express regret over Russia's decision "not to become a party to the Rome Statute."

Russia's role in the Syria conflict, sanctions against Russia for occupying Crimea, and engagement with the Russian authorities to end hostilities in eastern Ukraine, dominated the agenda of key international actors. Some raised concerns about the human rights crackdown.

In September, the EU External Action Service's spokesperson urged the authorities to stop branding NGOs "foreign agents," and said the law is "clearly aimed at restricting their independence and threatening their very existence." Also in September, the EU made a similar statement at the UN Human Rights Council.

In June, the European Commission for Democracy through Law (Venice Commission) stated that the law enabling Russia's Constitutional Court to block European Court rulings "is in direct conflict with Russia's international obligations ... and should be removed." The commission also found the law on "undesirable" organizations interferes with freedom of expression and assembly, and should be significantly amended.

The US commission on international religious freedom condemned the "Yarovaya Law" and warned that "under the guise of confronting terrorism, [it] would grant authorities sweeping powers to curtail civil liberties, including ... religious practices."

Numerous international actors criticized the deteriorating human rights situation in Russia-occupied Crimea, particularly the crackdown on Crimean Tatars. The European Parliament called for an "immediate reversal" of the April ruling of the Crimean Supreme Court banning the Mejlis.The Council of Europe urged the government to re-open Crimea to its monitoring mechanisms. The US called on Russia to "advocate for the dignity and rights of the people of Crimea, and to hold human rights violators to account."

In July, the UN high commissioner for human rights urged the government to ensure investigations into all allegations of disappearances and killings in Crimea and provide "direct and unfettered access to the Crimea for the High Commissioner's office and other international human rights monitoring mechanisms."

Foreign Policy

Russia played an increasingly obstructive role at the UN Human Rights Council. It opposed the long-standing practice of NGOs proposing language during negotiations on resolutions and presented more than 30 amendments to a Norwegian resolution on human rights defenders that were designed to strip previously-agreed resolution language. Russia also used procedural tactics such as points of order to attempt to block the appointment of UN Human Right Council experts. In October, the UN General Assembly declined to re-elect Russia to the Human

Rights Council for 2017, likely reflecting deep concern over how its aerial bombardments have been carried out in Syria.

In December 2015, Russia voted for a UN Security Council resolution that called on all parties to the conflict in Syria to "immediately cease any attacks against civilians and civilian objects," but in October 2016 vetoed a resolution that would have demanded safe delivery of humanitarian assistance to people trapped in Aleppo and an end to unlawful attacks on the city. Russia's staunch support for the government of Bashar al-Assad government and opposition to an arms embargo in South Sudan made progress on issues like sanctioning the Syrian government or taking meaningful steps on South Sudan nearly impossible.

For nine months, Russia suppressed the publication of a report by the Security Council's sanctions monitoring panel for Darfur, which found the Sudanese government in violation of international law. The report was eventually published in September. The Russian delegation also blocked the UN from appointing new experts to the Darfur sanctions monitoring panel.

Rwanda

In a referendum in December 2015, Rwandan citizens overwhelmingly voted in favor of constitutional amendments that allow President Paul Kagame to run for a third term in 2017 and two additional five-year terms thereafter. Very few voices inside the country publicly opposed the move.

The referendum took place in a context of tight restrictions on freedom of expression. The Rwandan government continues to limit the ability of civil society groups, media, and international human rights organizations to function freely and independently and criticize its policies or practices.

Military and police arbitrarily arrested and detained people in unofficial detention centers, torturing and ill-treating some of them.

Civil Society

Civil society in Rwanda is very weak, due to many years of state intimidation and interference. The government remains hostile to criticism of its human rights record and strongly favors service-delivery over independent human rights reporting or advocacy.

Onerous registration requirements and bureaucratic obstacles have also prevented human rights groups from operating effectively. The regional human rights group Human Rights League in the Great Lakes Region (LDGL) struggles to work effectively, partly because of the arduous official registration process. The organization only obtained its nongovernmental organization (NGO) registration in November. In May, immigration services ordered Epimack Kwokwo, LDGL's former executive secretary and a Congolese national, to leave the country.

Freedom of Media

Few Rwandan journalists challenge official government narratives or policies or investigate allegations of human rights abuses, especially against senior government officials. Many journalists engage in self-censorship. However, some radio and television debates and call-in programs have occasionally allowed space for discussion of more sensitive topics, such as the constitutional changes, the role of journalism, and illegal detention in so-called transit centers.

John Williams Ntwali, one of Rwanda's few investigative journalists, was arrested in late January 2016 and accused of allegedly raping a minor. Judicial officials later changed the charge to indecent assault and eventually dropped the case for lack of evidence. Ntwali was released after 10 days. Prior to his arrest, he had been investigating a number of sensitive issues, including the circumstances surrounding the 2015 death of prominent businessman Assinapol Rwigara.

On February 3, police confiscated the computers of *East African* newspaper journalists Ivan Mugisha and Moses Gahigi. They had been investigating cases of alleged tax evasion and corruption. The police briefly detained and questioned Mugisha.

On August 8, John Ndabarasa, a journalist at Sana Radio, went missing. The police said they had opened an investigation, but his whereabouts remained unknown at time of writing. Ndabarasa is a family member of Joel Mutabazi, a former presidential bodyguard sentenced to life imprisonment in 2014 for security-related offenses.

Rwandan media organizations are advocating for the decriminalization of press offences and stronger self-regulation in the context of an ongoing review of the penal code and media laws.

The BBC Kinyarwanda service remains suspended since 2014.

Political Pluralism

All parties represented in parliament supported the constitutional amendments and the 2015 referendum. Only one registered party, the Democratic Green Party of Rwanda (DGPR), opposed the moves. There was limited competition during local elections in February and March. Political space remains very limited in advance of the 2017 presidential elections.

The DGPR and several unregistered opposition parties continue to face serious challenges, including arrests and harassment of members, preventing them from functioning effectively. Victoire Ingabire, president of the FDU-Inkingi, a party which has been unable to register, and several other opposition party members remain in prison.

Illuminée Iragena, a nurse and member of the FDU-Inkingi, went missing on March 26. People close to her fear she was detained and may have died in detention, although authorities neither confirmed nor denied her detention, reinforcing concerns that she may have been forcibly disappeared.

Just hours before Iragena went missing, Léonille Gasengayire, another FDU-Inkingi member, was arrested after visiting Ingabire in prison. The police detained her for three days, beat her, questioned her, and denied her access to a lawyer. She told the police that Iragena had helped to arrange the delivery of a book to Ingabire. The police released her without charge, but re-arrested her on August 23, and charged her with inciting insurrection or disorder among the population. They also accused her of stirring up local opposition to the expropriation of local residents and of promoting the FDU-Inkingi. She remained in pretrial detention at time of writing.

On September 18, Théophile Ntirutwa, Kigali representative of the FDU-Inkingi, was arrested, allegedly by military, in Nyarutarama, a Kigali suburb. He was detained, beaten, and questioned about his membership of the FDU-Inkingi. He was released two days later. Ntirutwa had complained several times to authorities about threats and harassment by local officials.

Several other opposition party members have also been arrested and briefly detained.

Justice

On February 29, the Rwandan government withdrew its declaration allowing individuals to file complaints with the African Court on Human and Peoples' Rights, on the grounds that the declaration was being exploited by convicted genocide fugitives. The court was due to hear a complaint against Rwanda, brought by Victoire Ingabire. On September 5, the court ruled that the withdrawal would only take effect after one year and would not affect pending cases.

On March 31, a military court sentenced Col. Tom Byabagamba, former head of the presidential guard, and retired Brig. Gen. Frank Rusagara, former secretary general of the Defense ministry, to 21 and 20 years in prison respectively, including for inciting insurrection and tarnishing the government's image. The prosecution had accused them of criticizing the government, alleging state involvement in assassinations of opponents, and complaining about foreign and economic policy. A prosecution witness said he was forced to testify against

Rusagara and Byabagamba. Co-accused retired Sgt. François Kabayiza was sentenced to five years and said in court that military personnel had tortured him in detention.

Arbitrary Detention and Ill-Treatment

As in previous years, authorities rounded up street vendors, sex workers, street children, and other poor people and detained them in so-called transit centers across the country. The conditions in these centers are harsh and inhumane, and beatings are commonplace. Authorities made a few changes to a center in Gikondo, in the capital Kigali, resulting in improvements to some facilities and infrastructure, but overall conditions did not significantly improve. Similar degrading conditions prevail in transit centers in Muhanga (Muhanga district), Mbazi (Huye district), and Mudende (Rubavu district).

Three security agents were sentenced to 10 years in prison for killing a street vendor in Kigali's Nyabugogo bus station in May. The government opened several designated market places for former street vendors and said it would impose fines on street vendors and their customers operating outside these places.

Police, intelligence, and military officials also detained and ill-treated people in other unofficial detention centers, such as Chez Gacinya, a police detention center in Kigali, and military detention sites.

Justice for the Genocide

In December 2015, the International Criminal Tribunal for Rwanda (ICTR) closed its doors after delivering its final judgement against former minister Pauline Nyiramasuhuko and five co-accused. Former mayor Ladislas Ntaganzwa, indicted by the ICTR , was arrested in December 2015 in the Democratic Republic of Congo and extradited to Rwanda, where his trial started in April.

Jean-Bosco Uwinkindi, a pastor, and Léon Mugesera, an academic and former government official, were sentenced to life in prison, respectively in December 2015 and April 2016, for genocide and crimes against humanity. Uwinkindi was the first case referred by the ICTR to Rwanda.

In July, a French court found Octavien Ngenzi and Tito Barahira, two former mayors, guilty of genocide and crimes against humanity, and sentenced them to life imprisonment. It was only the second time that Rwandan genocide suspects were convicted in France, a close ally of the Rwandan government before and during the genocide. A German court convicted another former mayor, Onesphore Rwabukombe, to life imprisonment for his role in the genocide in December 2015, and a Swedish court sentenced Claver Berinkindi to life imprisonment in May.

A court in London in December 2015 denied an extradition request for five genocide suspects (Vincent Brown or Bajinya, Charles Munyaneza, Célestin Mutabaruka, Emmanuel Nteziryayo, and Célestin Ugirashebuja). In the Netherlands, an appeal court in July overruled an earlier decision and allowed the extradition of Jean-Claude Iyamuremye and Jean-Baptiste Mugimba to Rwanda, which took place on November 12. Léopold Munyakazi, a professor, was extradited from the United States to Rwanda in September, and Jean Claude Seyoboka, a former military official, was transferred from Canada to Rwanda in November.

Key International Actors

The US and European Union expressed concern about the lack of sufficient time and space for debate about the proposed amendments to the constitution and the conduct of the referendum. After President Kagame announced he would run again in the 2017 elections, the US expressed "deep disappointment" and called upon the Rwandan government to ensure and respect citizens' rights to exercise their freedom of expression, conscience, and peaceful assembly.

In March, the UN Human Rights Council adopted the outcome of the Universal Periodic Review (UPR) of Rwanda. Rwanda accepted recommendations to ensure freedom of opinion and expression and promised to strengthen its policy on human rights defenders. In June, Rwandan authorities presented a roadmap on the implementation of the recommendations to civil society and donors.

The Human Rights Committee reviewed civil and political rights in Rwanda in March, expressing concern about torture in unofficial detention centers, government interference in the judiciary and enforced disappearances.

In October, the European Parliament adopted a resolution on Rwanda, focusing on the case of Victoire Ingabire. A European Parliament delegation that visited Rwanda in September 2016 was denied access to Ingabire.

Saudi Arabia

Deputy Crown Prince and Minister of Defense Mohammad Bin Salman emerged as the most visible Saudi leader in 2016 and launched Vision 2030, an ambitious government road map for economic and developmental growth that aims to reduce the country's dependence on oil. Vision 2030 was later accompanied by the National Transformation Program (NTP), which sets specific benchmarks to achieve by 2020.

Through 2016 the Saudi Arabia-led coalition continued an aerial campaign against Houthi forces in Yemen that included numerous unlawful airstrikes that killed and injured thousands of civilians. Saudi authorities also continued their arbitrary arrests, trials, and convictions of peaceful dissidents. Dozens of human rights defenders and activists continued to serve long prison sentences for criticizing authorities or advocating political and rights reforms. Authorities continued to discriminate against women and religious minorities.

Yemen Airstrikes and Blockade

As the leader of the nine-nation coalition that began military operations against the Houthis and allied forces in Yemen on March 26, 2015, Saudi Arabia has committed numerous violations of international humanitarian law. Since coalition airstrikes began, more than 4,125 civilians have been killed and 7,207 wounded; according to the OHCHR, air strikes are the single largest cause of civilian casualties.

Human Rights Watch has documented 58 unlawful airstrikes by the coalition, some of which may amount to war crimes, killing nearly 800 civilians and hitting homes, markets, hospitals, schools, and mosques. An airstrike on a crowded funeral in October killed at least 100 people and wounded 500. Human Rights Watch also documented how the Saudi Arabia-led coalition repeatedly attacked civilian factories, warehouses, and other protected sites in violation of the laws of war.

The conflict exacerbated an existing humanitarian crisis. By early 2016 an estimated 14.4 million Yemenis were unable to meet their food needs, according to the United Nations.

Human Rights Watch documented at least 16 coalition attacks using internationally banned cluster munitions, which killed and wounded dozens of civilians. Saudi Arabia is not a party to the Convention on Cluster Munitions, which bans the weapon. The Saudi military spokesman denied the use of cluster bombs in Yemen's capital, Sanaa, but admitted their use in one attack in Hajjah.

In 2016 the Saudi-led coalition was added to the UN Secretary-General's "list of shame" for children in armed conflict for its role in killing and maiming children and attacking schools and hospitals in Yemen. After Saudi Arabia and its allies threatened to withdraw hundreds of millions of dollars in assistance to the UN, the coalition was removed from the list "pending review." The Houthis have been on the list since 2011 for their use of child soldiers.

In July, the Saudi-led coalition announced findings of preliminary investigations into eight widely publicized coalition airstrikes causing civilian casualties. The coalition-appointed panel of investigators recommended compensation for victims of only one attack. In another, the panel found the coalition should have warned medical staff at a Doctors Without Borders (MSF)-supported hospital in Saada governorate, but dismissed the severity of the hospital attack by concluding there had been no "human damage." In August, the coalition struck another MSF facility, killing 19, and the organization withdrew staff from six hospitals in northern Yemen.

In September, the UN Human Rights Council adopted a resolution expressing "deep concern" at the killing of civilians and attacks on civilian infrastructure in Yemen, and requested that the high commissioner strengthen his in-country presence in order to "establish the facts and circumstances of alleged violations and abuses" and report back to the council.

Freedoms of Expression, Association, and Belief

Saudi Arabia continued to repress pro-reform activists and peaceful dissidents. In 2016 over a dozen prominent activists convicted on charges arising from their peaceful activities were serving long prison sentences.

Prominent activist Waleed Abu al-Khair continued to serve a 15-year sentence imposed by Saudi Arabia's terrorism court that convicted him in 2014 on charges stemming solely from his peaceful criticism in media interviews and on social media of human rights abuses. Prominent blogger Raif Badawi served the fourth year of his 10-year sentence, but authorities did not flog him in 2016, as they previously did in January 2015.

In March, Saudi Arabia sentenced journalist Alaa Brinji to five years in prison and an eight-year travel ban for tweets in which he criticized religious authorities and voiced support for the right of women to drive and jailed human rights activists.

By mid-2016 Saudi Arabia had jailed nearly all the founders of the banned Saudi Civil and Political Rights Association (ACPRA). In April and May, Saudi Arabia's Specialized Criminal Court, the country's terrorism tribunal, convicted ACPRA activists Abd al-Aziz al-Shubaily and Issa al-Hamid to eight and nine years in prison respectively, in addition to lengthy travel bans based solely on their peaceful pro-reform advocacy.

In December 2015, the Saudi Cabinet approved a new law permitting the establishment of civil society organizations for the first time, and authorities published the law's implementing regulations in 2016. The new regulations permit authorities to dissolve or deny registration to any nongovernmental organization on vague grounds, including "contradicting Islamic Sharia, infringing upon public order, contradicting public morals, breaching national unity, or contradicting other laws and regulations." By September, Human Rights Watch was unaware of any registration of an independent human rights group under the new law.

Saudi Arabia does not tolerate public worship by adherents of religions other than Islam and systematically discriminates against Muslim religious minorities, notably Twelver Shia and Ismailis, including in public education, the justice system, religious freedom, and employment. Government-affiliated religious authorities continued to disparage Shia Islam in public statements and documents.

In February, a Saudi court reduced Palestinian poet Ashraf Fayadh's punishment from the death penalty to eight years in prison for alleged blasphemous statements in a book of his poetry and during a discussion group.

Saudi Arabia has no written laws concerning sexual orientation or gender identity, but judges use principles of uncodified Islamic law to sanction people suspected of committing sexual relations outside marriage, including adultery, extramarital and homosexual sex, or other "immoral" acts. If such activity occurs online, judges and prosecutors utilize vague provisions of the country's anti-cybercrime law that criminalize online activity impinging on "public order, religious values, public morals, and privacy."

In February, the *Saudi Gazette* reported that the Bureau of Investigation and Public Prosecution is considering requesting the death penalty for anyone "using social media to solicit homosexual acts."

Criminal Justice

Saudi Arabia applies Sharia (Islamic law) as its national law. There is no formal penal code, but the government has passed some laws and regulations that subject certain broadly-defined offenses to criminal penalties. In the absence of a written penal code or narrowly-worded regulations, however, judges and prosecutors can criminalize a wide range of offenses under broad, catch-all charges such as "breaking allegiance with the ruler" or "trying to distort the reputation of the kingdom."

Detainees, including children, commonly face systematic violations of due process and fair trial rights, including arbitrary arrest. Authorities do not always inform suspects of the crime with which they are charged, or allow them access to supporting evidence, sometimes even after trial sessions have begun. Authorities generally do not allow lawyers to assist suspects during interrogation and sometimes impede them from examining witnesses and presenting evidence at trial.

Judges routinely sentence defendants to floggings of hundreds of lashes. Children can be tried for capital crimes and sentenced as adults if there are physical signs of puberty.

During 2016 authorities continued to detain arrested suspects for months, even years, without judicial review or prosecution.

As of September, Ali al-Nimr, Dawoud al-Marhoun, and Abdullah al-Zaher remained on death row for allegedly committing protest-related crimes while they were children in 2011 and 2012. Saudi judges based the capital convictions primarily on confessions that the three defendants retracted in court and said had

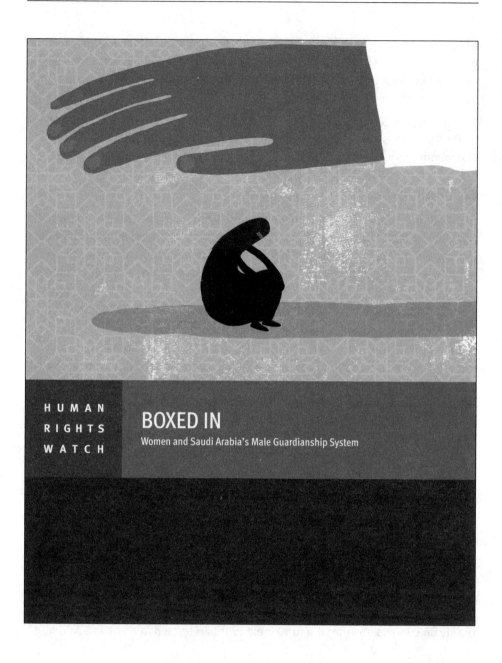

HUMAN
RIGHTS
WATCH

BOXED IN
Women and Saudi Arabia's Male Guardianship System

been coerced, and the courts did not investigate the allegations that the confessions were obtained by torture.

In April, Saudi Arabia's Council of Ministers issued a sweeping new regulation curtailing the powers of the Committee for the Promotion of Virtue and the Prevention of Vice, or religious police, to arrest, pursue, or request documents or ID cards from suspects.

In February 2016, Saudi Arabia began a high-profile trial of 32 men for allegedly spying on behalf of Iran, but the charge sheet contained numerous allegations that do not resemble recognizable crimes, including "supporting demonstrations," "harming the reputation of the kingdom," and attempting to "spread the Shia confession." All but one of the detainees have been in detention since 2013.

On January 2, 2016, Saudi Arabia carried out a mass execution of 47 men for "terrorism offenses." Forty-three were associated with Al-Qaeda attacks in the 2000s, and four were Shia allegedly involved in protest-related crimes in 2011 and 2012. It was Saudi Arabia's largest mass execution since 1980. Among those executed were Ali Sa'eed al-Ribh, whose trial judgement indicates that he was under 18 when he allegedly committed some of the crimes for which he was sentenced to death, and Sheikh Nimr al-Nimr, a prominent Shia cleric sentenced to death in 2014 after a Saudi court convicted him on a host of vague charges, apparently based largely on his peaceful criticism of Saudi officials.

According to Interior Ministry statements, Saudi Arabia executed 144 persons between January and mid-November, mostly for murder and terrorism-related offenses. Twenty-two of those executed were convicted for non-violent drug crimes. Most executions are carried out by beheading, sometimes in public.

Women's and Girls' Rights

Saudi Arabia's discriminatory male guardianship system remains intact despite government pledges to abolish it. Under this system, adult women must obtain permission from a male guardian—usually a husband, father, brother, or son—to travel, marry, or exit prison. They may be required to provide guardian consent in order to work or access healthcare. Women regularly face difficulty conducting a range of transactions without a male relative, from renting an apartment to filing legal claims. All women remain banned from driving cars in Saudi Arabia.

Following municipal elections in December 2015, 38 women were elected or appointed to councils with a total of 3,159 members across the country for the first time. In February, however, authorities ordered that the councils must be segregated by sex, with women members sitting in separate rooms away from their male colleagues and participating only by video link.

Saudi Arabia continues to discriminate against women and girls by denying them the same opportunities to exercise and play sports as men and boys. As of July 2016, most public schools did not offer physical education for girls and women were not allowed to attend or participate in national tournaments or state-organized sports leagues. But, in a positive move, on August 1, the General Authority for Sports, which functions like a sports ministry, announced a new female department. In August, four women represented Saudi Arabia in the Rio Olympics.

Migrant Workers

Over 9 million migrant workers fill manual, clerical, and service jobs, constituting more than half the workforce. Some suffer abuses and exploitation, sometimes amounting to conditions of forced labor.

The *kafala* (sponsorship) system ties migrant workers' residency permits to "sponsoring" employers, whose written consent is required for workers to change employers or exit the country under normal circumstances. Some employers illegally confiscate passports, withhold wages, and force migrants to work against their will. Saudi Arabia also imposes an exit visa requirement, forcing migrant workers to obtain permission from their employer to leave the country. Workers who leave their employer without their consent can be charged with "absconding" and face imprisonment and deportation. Such a system can trap workers in abusive conditions, and punish victims who flee abuse.

Faced with a domestic unemployment rate of 12 percent that may rise as the domestic population increases, Saudi authorities have introduced labor reforms since 2011 that create a tiered quota system for the employment of Saudi citizens in the private labor sector that differs according to the nature of the business. As a part of these reforms, Saudi labor authorities in 2016 allowed foreigners working in firms that do not employ the required percentage of Saudis to change jobs without employer approval.

During 2016, low oil prices and an economic downturn dramatically undermined Saudi Arabia's major construction companies, leaving them unable to continue projects or pay salaries of migrant construction workers. By August, tens of thousands of workers— mainly from south Asian countries—were stranded without salaries and unable to return to their home countries due to restrictions such as the exit visa requirement. Many were reportedly living in makeshift camps, relying on humanitarian assistance from their embassies.

Police and labor authorities continued to arrest and deport foreign workers found in violation of existing labor laws, targeting workers without valid residency or work permits, or those found working for an employer other than their legal sponsor.

Saudi Arabia is not a party to the 1951 Refugee Convention and has not established an asylum system whereby people who fear being returned to places where their lives or freedom would be threatened may apply to prevent their forced return.

Domestic workers, predominantly women, faced a range of abuses including overwork, forced confinement, non-payment of wages, food deprivation, and psychological, physical, and sexual abuse without the authorities holding their employers to account. Workers who attempted to report employer abuses sometimes faced prosecution based on counterclaims of theft, "black magic," or "sorcery."

Key International Actors

The United States offered only muted criticism of Saudi human rights violations. Meanwhile, as a party to the armed conflict in Yemen, the US provided logistics and intelligence support to Saudi-led coalition forces, which reportedly included assistance with military targeting. In August, the US approved a US$1.15 billion arms sale to Saudi Arabia, despite significant opposition from members of Congress concerned about Saudi conduct in Yemen.

In March, Human Rights Watch called on the US, United Kingdom, France, and other arms- exporting countries to suspend weapons sales to Saudi Arabia until it curtails its unlawful airstrikes in Yemen and credibly investigates alleged violations. In June, a coalition of nongovernmental organizations (NGOs), including Human Rights Watch and Amnesty International, called on the United Nations General Assembly to suspend Saudi Arabia's membership rights on the UN Human Rights Council over its engagement in "gross and systematic violations of human rights" in Yemen.

NGOs including Human Rights Watch similarly opposed Saudi Arabia's bid to be re-elected as a Human Rights Council member for the 2017-2019 term. In early October, in the face of strong opposition by Saudi Arabia, the UN Human Rights Council passed a new resolution on Yemen mandating the UN to work with an existing Yemen-led effort to investigate abuses related to the conflict.

Serbia

Progress in human rights protection was limited in 2016. Asylum seekers and migrant arrivals decreased, but the asylum system remains flawed with inadequate protections for unaccompanied children. Attacks and threats against journalists remain a problem. War crimes prosecutions progress remains slow. The Roma minority continue to face housing discrimination and lesbian, gay, bisexual, and transgender (LGBT) activists are subject to threats and attacks.

Migrants, Asylum Seekers, and Displaced Persons

Numbers of asylum seekers and migrants in Serbia significantly decreased in 2016 due to border closures along the entire Western Balkan migration route, including by Serbia. During the first eight months of 2016, Serbia registered 8,003 asylum seekers compared to 103,891 during the same period in 2015. Afghans comprised the largest national group (3,359), followed by Syrians (1,579). At time of writing there were 4,800 registered asylum seekers and migrants in Serbia, according to UNHCR estimates.

As of October 31, Serbia had granted refugee status to a mere 17 asylum seekers and subsidiary protection to 17 others in 2016. In addition to low recognition rates, there are significant backlogs in the country's asylum procedure with thousands of pending claims.

During the first seven months of 2016, the Ministry of Interior registered 127 unaccompanied children in Serbia, most from Afghanistan, compared to 4,112 during the same period in 2015. Serbia lacks formal age assessment procedures for unaccompanied children, putting older children at risk of being treated as adults instead of receiving child protection. Only three institutions exist in Serbia for unaccompanied children and have a total of 32 places. Other unaccompanied children stay in temporary shelters known as "refugee aid centers" together with unrelated adults or open reception centers, where in some cases unaccompanied children can be accommodated separately from unrelated adults.

Progress in finding durable solutions for refugees and internally displaces persons (IDPs) from the Balkan wars living in Serbia was insignificant. According to UNHCR, as of July 1, there were 35,300 refugees in Serbia, most from Croatia—

432 fewer than one year earlier—while the Serbian government recorded 203,140 internally displaced people, the majority from Kosovo—the same number as last year.

Freedom of Media

Journalists in Serbia continue to operate in a hostile environment. Between January and July, the Independent Journalists' Association of Serbia (NUNS) registered 33 incidents of assaults, threats or other pressure against journalists.

The killing of radio journalist Luka Popov in June drew international calls for an investigation, including by the Organization for Security and Co-operation in Europe's representative on media freedom. Police arrested three suspects. It is unclear whether the killing was connected to Popov's work as a journalist.

Smear campaigns by pro-government media and members of the government against independent media and journalists continued. In one case, Prime Minister Aleksandar Vucic targeted the independent online news site Balkan Investigate Reporting Network (BIRN) for criticism, and the pro-government media outlets TV Pink and Informer accused it of being an enemy of the state.

The work of a commission established to investigate the murders of three prominent journalists—Dada Vujasinovic in 1994, Slavko Curuvija in 1999, and Milan Pantic in 2001— progressed slowly. The ongoing prosecution of four state security officials suspected of involvement in Curuvija's murder was stalled during 2016 as a key witness failed to appear at the trial. The deaths of the other two journalists remained unsolved.

Accountability for War Crimes

War crimes prosecutions progressed slowly in 2016 due to a lack of political support, resources or staff at the Office of the War Crimes Prosecutor and inadequate witness support. Few high-ranking officials have been prosecuted for war crimes in Serbian courts. Between January and August, the War Crimes Prosecutor's Office indicted 15 people for war crimes.

During the same period, four people were convicted by the first instance court for war crimes, and given sentences of between 8 and 10 years' imprisonment. The Appeals Court sentenced six people to imprisonment for between 6 and 12 years. One person was acquitted on appeal. Eighteen cases were pending at first instance and 15 cases were still at investigation stage. Since the establishment of the War Crimes Prosecution Office in 2003, 110 judgments have been issued: 75 convictions and 35 acquittals.

The March 2015-ordered retrial against nine defendants, most of them low ranking officials, for the wartime killing of 118 Albanians in Kosovo in 1999 has been hampered by delays and progressed slowly. No high-ranking officials have been indicted for involvement in the killings.

The High Court in Belgrade started proceedings against a former Bosnian Serb army officer charged with killing four civilians and raping two women in Bosnia and Herzegovina in 1992. The case was transferred to Serbian authorities by the Bosnian state court under a war crimes cooperation protocol between Serbia and Bosnia and Herzegovina.

In February, the Serbian government adopted a war crimes strategy which sets out criteria for prioritizing cases and commitment to prosecute high ranking officials suspected of war crimes, while failing to specify how. The war crimes strategy is part of the EU requirements under negotiating Chapter 23 that focuses on rule of law, and part of EU's enlargement process with Serbia. The War Crimes Prosecutor's Office separately was drafting another strategy concerning war crimes prosecutions. The chief prosecutor of the International Criminal Tribunal for the former Yugoslavia (ICTY) Serge Brammertz expressed concern in June that Serbia had failed to appoint a new chief war crimes prosecutor after almost a year. At time of writing, Serbia had still yet to do so.

In March the ICTY acquitted Serbian Radical Party leader Vojislav Seselj on nine counts, including crimes against humanity, citing insufficient evidence. A prosecution appeal filed in May was pending before the ICTY appeals chamber at time of writing.

In June, ICTY President Carmel Agius said that Serbia had not fully cooperated with the tribunal when failing to extradite three members of the Serbian Radical Party indicted for contempt.

Human Rights Defenders

Attacks and harassment of human rights defenders continued. According to local LGBT and human rights organizations, the majority of attacks and threats against

HUMAN RIGHTS WATCH

"It is My Dream to Leave This Place"

Children with Disabilities in Serbian Institutions

members of the LGBT community go unreported with only known LGBT activists filing complaints.

In June, in Vojvodina in Northeast Serbia, an LGBT activist was attacked and kicked in the head by four unidentified perpetrators. No one had been prosecuted at time of writing. In August, LGBT activist Boban Stojanovic, one of the Belgrade Pride organizers, was punched and called a "fag" in downtown Belgrade by two unidentified men. Police were investigating at time of writing.

Hundreds of police officers deployed in Belgrade to protect the LGBT Pride march in September, which occurred without violence. This was a marked improvement from previous years when protesters attacked the parade, or the government had cancelled the event citing security concerns instead of providing adequate security.

Treatment of Minorities

Roma face discrimination and harassment primarily in areas of housing. Forced evictions of Roma living in informal settlements continued without prior consultation with families concerned, with insufficient recourse to challenge decisions, and with inadequate provision of alternative accommodation. Serbian authorities failed to provide adequate housing solutions for the approximately 50 Roma families evicted from the informal Belvil settlement in Belgrade in 2012 despite designated funds.

The Council of Europe human rights commissioner in a letter to the Serbian government in February expressed his concerns with respect to forced evictions and the lack of legal safeguards and failure to provide adequate alternative housing. The commissioner called on Serbian authorities to halt further evictions of Roma without providing alternative housing.

UN Special Rapporteur on Right to Housing Leilani Farha in February expressed concerns about aspects of a new housing law that fails to guarantee consultation with affected communities prior to evictions; lacks adequate provisions with respect to the period of notice prior to evictions; and fails to outline appeals.

Disability Rights

In April 2016, the UN Committee on the Rights of Persons with Disabilities expressed deep concerns about the number of children and adults with disabilities living in institutions and about the poor living conditions in institutions in Serbia. The committee urged Serbia to deinstitutionalize people with disabilities and to ensure access to inclusive and quality education. The committee also called on Serbia to replace its guardianship system and ensure all people with disabilities have access to services and support in the community of their own choice and preference.

Key International Actors

In July, Federica Mogherini, European Union high representative for foreign affairs and security, said that the opening of EU accession negotiating Chapters 23 and 24, on rule of law and justice, freedom and security, would allow Serbia to develop a track record of implementing reforms in the area of the rule of law, but failed to emphasize the need for improving the country's human rights record. Croatia, an EU member, in August blocked Serbia from opening Chapter 23, citing Serbia assertion of its right to prosecute war crimes committed anywhere in the former Yugoslavia during the Balkan wars.

The European Commission's annual progress report on Serbia expressed concerns about interference with press freedom, pointing to continued attacks and threats against journalists. The commission called on authorities to create an environment enabling journalists to work without interference and to investigate and adjudicate threats and attacks. The report also called on authorities to tackle political influence on the judiciary as well as addressing the backlog of cases in the courts and adopting a free legal aid system. The report raised concerns about the government's failure to appoint a new war crimes prosecutor and Serbia's lack of full cooperation with the ICTY.

During a visit to Belgrade in August, US Vice President Joe Biden offered condolences to victims killed by the NATO bombing campaign against Serbia and encouraged Serb authorities to take responsibility for their involvement in the 1990s wars in former Yugoslavia.

Kosovo

Human rights protections progressed slowly in Kosovo in 2016, though serious abuses persisted. Talks over the ratification of a border demarcation agreement with Montenegro were marred by repeated tear gas attacks in the Kosovo Assembly by the political opposition, blocking free debate, impeding the passage of legislation and halting progress on the Kosovo's s visa liberalization agreement with the European Union.

A special court based in the Netherlands to try serious crimes committed during and just after the 1998-1999 Kosovo war was awaiting final approval by the Dutch parliament. Journalists faced threats and intimidation, and prosecutions of crimes against them remained slow. Tensions between Serbs and Kosovo Albanians continued, particularly in the north. Roma, Ashkali, and Balkan Egyptian communities continued to face discrimination. The process of normalizing relations with Belgrade made limited progress.

Accountability for War Crimes

In January, Kosovo and the Netherlands signed a host-state agreement for the Netherlands to host a special court with international judges and prosecutors that will try serious crimes allegedly committed during and immediately after the Kosovo war by members of the Kosovo Liberation Army against ethnic minorities and political opponents. The Dutch parliament was expected to ratify the agreement by year's end so the court could begin its work. In September, the EU appointed former US prosecutor David Schwendiman as the court's lead prosecutor.

The mandate of the European Rule of Law Mission (EULEX), which terminated on June 14, was extended on June 30 for another two years. EULEX's mandate was modified to focus mainly on monitoring, mentoring, and advising, while continuing its work on ongoing cases but may only deal with new cases in exceptional circumstances and with the approval of the Kosovo judiciary.

In January, Oliver Ivanovic, a former Serbian government official and the head of a Kosovo Serb political party, was convicted of war crimes at the Basic Court in Mitrovica and sentenced to nine years' imprisonment. Ivanovic was found guilty of ordering the murder of nine ethnic Albanians in Mitrovica in 1999 during the NATO bombing of Yugoslavia.

In March, the Appeals Court in Pristina upheld the convictions against three men charged with organized crimes in connect with organ trafficking at Kosovo's Medicus clinic in 2008, but acquitted two others due to insufficient evidence. One of the convicted men failed to present himself at the prison facility to serve his sentence at the March 25 deadline; his whereabouts were unclear at time of writing.

In November, the Appeals Court in Pristina cleared former KLA commander and mayor of Skenderaj, Sami Lushtaku, of the murder of an Albanian civilian dating to the 1998-1999 war. The court upheld the conviction on other charges of war crimes but reduced the sentence from 12 to 7 years imprisonment. Lushtaku declared in November that he will appeal to the Supreme Court.

By early September, mixed panels consisting of the EULEX and local judges handed down two decisions related to war crimes at first instance level, two cases at Court of Appeals level, and were involved in three decisions at Supreme Court level. EULEX has been involved in a total of 38 verdicts since it was established in 2008.

Accountability of International Institutions

The Human Rights Review Panel, an independent body set up in 2009 to review allegations of human rights violations by EULEX, did not rule on any cases between January and September. Forty-nine cases were pending before the panel at time of writing.

The Human Rights Advisory Panel (HRAP), an independent body set up in 2006 to examine complaints of abuses committed by or attributable to the United Nations Interim Administration Mission in Kosovo (UNMIK), ceased its operations on July 1. In a critical July report, HRAP found that UNMIK had violated human rights; had not properly investigated serious allegations of wrongdoings, and had failed to comply with the panel's recommendations.

Abuses by UNMIK include lack of adequate criminal investigations in relation to disappearances, abductions, killings, and excessive use of force by UNMIK police during a crowd control operation in 2007, resulting in deaths and serious injuries of four protesters. The panel found violations in all nine cases that it addressed between January and July.

Treatment of Minorities

Roma, Ashkali, and Balkan Egyptians continue to face problems acquiring personal documents, affecting their ability to access health care, social assistance, and education. A lack of political will and insufficient allocation of funds resulted in the failure to adequately implement the 2009-2015 Strategy and Action Plan for the Integration of Roma, Ashkali, and Egyptian communities.

During 2016, a new strategy and action plan for the integration of Roma, Ashkali, and Egyptian communities was drafted, aiming to replace the former strategy that came to end in 2015. The new strategy focuses on improving civil registration, access to housing, education, health care, and employment.

In February, the Human Rights Advisory Panel held UNMIK responsible for placing Roma, Ashkali, and Egyptian families in five camps highly contaminated with toxic lead, where residents subsequently suffered lead poisoning. HRAP recommended that UNMIK issue a public apology and pay compensation to the victims.

In April, the UN special rapporteurs on internally displaced persons and minority issues, urged UNMIK to implement the panel's recommendations. UNMIK expressed regret for the communities' suffering. However, at time of writing, no compensation has been paid to the affected families.

Inter-ethnic tensions continued during 2016, particularly in Kosovo's divided north. In August, two unknown suspects torched a popular café terrace in north Mitrovica, in the Serb populated part of the city. No injuries were reported and police were investigating at time of writing.

In August, a Kosovo Serb attempted to demolish the minaret of a mosque in Gjilan municipality. The suspect was in pretrial detention at time of writing. Also in August, several hundred Albanians prevented 150 Kosovo Serbs from visiting an Orthodox church in the village of Mushtisht, throwing rocks and stones at Kosovo police trying to secure safe passage for the Serbs. In June, a Kosovo Serb man was attacked in Mitrovica by a gang of Albanians and sustained injuries requiring hospital treatment. Police were investigating at time of writing.

Kosovo police registered eight cases of inter-ethnic violence between January and July 2016, without specific references to whether incidents involved physical and/or material violence, making effective scrutiny of police response to inter-ethnic violence difficult.

The Kosovo Constitution protects against sexual orientation-based discrimination and a 2015 anti-discrimination law enumerates protections for both sexual orientation and gender identity; however, implementation remains weak.

Women's Rights

Domestic violence is widespread in Kosovo. According to a November 2015 survey by the Kosovo's Women Network, a nongovernmental organization, 68 percent of women respondents have experienced domestic violence in their lifetime.

Inadequate police response, few prosecutions and failure by judges to issue restraining orders against abusive spouses contribute to the problem. At time of writing, the government was drafting a new National Strategy and Action Plan against Domestic Violence replacing a 2011-2014 strategy.

Asylum Seekers, Displaced Persons, and Returning Deportees

During the first nine months of the year, the United National High Commissioner for Refugees registered 307 voluntary minority returns, including people from outside Kosovo and internally displaced persons, down from 619 during that period in 2015.

The Kosovo Ministry of Internal Affairs registered 4,534 forced returns between January and August 31, including 370 Roma, 224 Ashkali, and 46 Egyptians. Among those forcible deported, 1,474 were children. Most minorities were deported from Germany and returnees are provided limited assistance upon return.

Freedom of Media

Threats and attacks against journalists continued in 2016; investigations and prosecutions were slow. Between January and July, the Association of Journalists of Kosovo registered eight cases of threats and violence against journalists.

In March, Vehbi Kajtazi, an investigative journalist, stated that Kosovo Prime Minister Isa Mustafa threatened him over the phone, saying that Kajtazi would "pay heavily" for a piece Kajtazi had written criticizing the Kosovo health service, including a reference to Mustafa's brother and his health treatment abroad. Mustafa denied making threats. Kajtazi reported the threat to the police and the case was under investigation at time of writing.

In August, the home of the head of public broadcaster Radio TV Kosova (RTK) was fire bombed. Nobody was injured in the attack. The incident was under investigation at time of writing.

Key International Actors

European Union High Representative Federica Mogherini, following a meeting in June with President Hashim Thaci, welcomed the extension of the EULEX mandate and stressed the need for continuing normalizing relations between Kosovo and Serbia but failed to raise human rights or rule of law concerns in Kosovo. The EU has supported, and is funding, the special court for serious crimes that is expected to begin operating soon in The Hague.

US Assistant Secretary of State Victoria Nuland, during a Balkan tour in July, called on Kosovo authorities to strengthen the rule of law, the justice system, and the fight against corruption and organized crimes. In an August visit to Kosovo, US Vice President Joe Biden stressed the importance of normalizing relations with Serbia in order to make progress towards joining the EU, and called on Kosovo authorities to fight corruption but failed to mention work on improving the country's human rights and rule of law record. The US government has supported the special court to be based in the Netherlands, providing the former and current lead prosecutor.

The November EU Commission progress report on Kosovo stated that administration of justice is slow and inefficient, there is insufficient accountability for judicial officials, and the judiciary is subjected to undue political influence. The report stated that threats and attacks against journalists continued and called on authorities to effectively investigate and prosecute cases. The report also stated that while some progress was made in human rights protection, particularly on lesbian, gay, bisexual, and transgender (LGBT) issues, authorities must significantly strengthen the rights of minorities and people with disabilities.

In a May quarterly UN report on the situation in Kosovo, UN Secretary-General Ban Ki-moon stated that much work is needed to ensure the protection of minority rights, facilitate the return of displaced persons, and safeguard religious traditions.

The UN special rapporteur on human rights for internally displaced persons, Chaloka Beyani, in September urged authorities in Kosovo to intensify efforts to achieve durable solutions for the 16,000 IDPs with displacement related needs.

The US State Department Human Rights Report on Kosovo, published in June, raised concerns about opposition parties violently obstructing parliament, resulting in the blocking of free debate and passage of legislation, endemic government corruption, and lack of accountability for corruption. The report also noted violence and discrimination against minorities, police mistreatment of detainees, intimidation of media, and violence against displaced persons seeking to return to their homes.

Singapore

Singapore's political environment is stifling, and citizens continued in 2016 to face severe restrictions on their basic rights to freedom of expression, association, and peaceful assembly. The government effectively controls print media, and online media outlets are forced to register with the government and post a significant bond. Bloggers and online media that comment on political issues are targeted for prosecution with vague and overly broad legal provisions on public order, morality, security, and racial and religious harmony.

Freedom of Peaceful Assembly, Association, and Expression

The government maintains restrictions on the right to freedom of peaceful assembly through the Public Order Act, which requires a police permit for any "cause-related" assembly if it is held in a public place, or if members of the general public are invited. Permits are routinely denied for events addressing political topics.

An area of Hong Lim Park known as the "Speaker's Corner" is the only place in Singapore where an assembly can be held without a police permit, but only citizens may speak there, and only citizens or permanent residents may participate in assemblies there. The government forbids speeches about religion or religious belief, or about anything "that may cause feelings of enmity, hatred, ill-will or hostility between different racial or religious groups in Singapore." Violation of any of these restrictions is a criminal offense.

Associations of more than 10 people are required to register with the government, and the Registrar of Societies has broad authority to deny registration if he determines the group could be "prejudicial to public peace, welfare or good order." The Registrar of Societies has refused to allow any lesbian, gay, bisexual, or transsexual (LGBT) organization to register as a society on the ground that "it is contrary to the public interest to grant legitimacy to the promotion of homosexual activities or viewpoints."

The government's Media Development Authority (MDA) compels online news websites covering domestic political issues to register under the Broadcasting Act. Registration requires posting a monetary bond, paying fees, undergoing annual registration, and, on notification, immediately removing anything the MDA deems to be against "public interest, public order or national harmony" or to offend "good taste or decency." Registered websites are also prohibited from receiving any foreign funding.

Criminal laws are also used against online speech. The two co-editors of the news portal *The Real Singapore* were charged with sedition for publishing articles with allegedly "anti-foreign" content. Ai Takagi pled guilty to four counts of sedition in March 2016 and the court sentenced her to 10 months in prison. Yang Kaiheng, who co-founded the website with Takagi, pled guilty in June 2016 and was sentenced to 8 months in prison.

On May 26, 17-year-old blogger Amos Yee Pang Sang was charged with six counts of "wounding religious feelings" in violation of penal code article 298 for online posts authorities allege were derogatory of Islam and Christianity. Yee, who represented himself in court, pled guilty to six counts of wounding religious feelings. On September 29, he was sentenced to six weeks in prison.

In August 2016, the government passed new legislation codifying the law of contempt. The new Administration of Justice (Protection) Act provides penalties of up to S$100,000 (US$70,000) and three years in prison for several forms of contempt of court, including the archaic offense of "scandalising the court." The latter prohibition has been repeatedly used to penalize those who criticize the judiciary or judicial opinions.

Government officials continue to use criminal and civil defamation as a means to silence critics. In December 2015, a court ordered Roy Ngerng Yi Ling to pay Prime Minister Lee Hsien Loong 150,000 Singapore dollars (US$105,000) in damages and S$29,000 (US$20,300) in legal costs for a single blog post criticizing the management of the government's central provident fund.

All films and videos shown in Singapore must be pre-approved by the Board of Film Censors. Theater productions must also obtain a license under the Public Entertainment and Meetings Act, and to do so must submit their scripts for approval. In June 2016, a production of "Les Miserables" was forced to delete a scene containing a same-sex kiss.

Outspoken activists are subject to government harassment. In May 2016, the police interrogated and searched the homes of political activist and blogger Roy

Ngerng Yi Ling and long-time activist Teo Soh Lung, seizing phones and computers. The two were investigated for posts on their personal Facebook pages that allegedly violated an election law restricting political campaigning during a "cooling-off period" before a by-election. The law, however, specifically permits "the transmission of personal political views by individuals to other individuals, on a non-commercial basis, using the Internet," and this use of it against private individuals was unprecedented.

Criminal Justice System

Singapore uses the Internal Security Act (ISA) and Criminal Law (Temporary Provisions) Act to arrest and administratively detain persons for virtually unlimited periods without charge or judicial review. On October 6, the Ministry of Home Affairs stated that 17 individuals were currently detained under the ISA, and an additional 25 had been issued with restraining orders under the law. There is little publicly available information about those detained or the basis for their detentions, but the family of Zulfikar Mohamad Shariff, detained under the ISA in 2016, has publicly contested the alleged grounds for his detention.

Singapore retains the death penalty, which is mandated for many drug offenses and certain other crimes. Under provisions introduced in 2012, however, judges have some discretion to bypass the mandatory penalty and sentence low-level offenders to life in prison and caning. Malaysian Kho Jabing, whose death sentence for murder was reduced to life in prison and 24 strokes of the cane pursuant to the new provisions, was executed in May 2016 after the Court of Appeal overturned the resentencing and Singapore's highest court rejected his appeal of that decision.

Use of corporal punishment is common in Singapore. For medically fit males ages 16 to 50, caning is mandatory as an additional punishment for a range of crimes, including drug trafficking, violent crimes (such as armed robbery), and even some immigration offenses. Sentencing officials may also order caning for some 30 additional violent and non-violent crimes.

Sexual Orientation and Gender Identity

The rights of Singapore's LGBT community are severely restricted. Sexual relations between two male persons remains a criminal offense, and there are no legal protections against discrimination on the basis of sexual orientation or gender identity. The Media Development Authority effectively prohibits all positive depictions of LGBT lives on television or radio.

The annual Pink Dot Festival in support of LGBT rights celebrated its eighth year in Hong Lim Park in June 2016, supported by the sponsorship of corporations including Google, Barclays, J.P. Morgan, Goldman Sachs, BP, Bloomberg, Twitter, Apple, and Facebook. A few days after the event, the Ministry of Home Affairs warned multinational companies to stop funding the event, saying such support constitutes "foreign interference" with domestic affairs. In October, the Ministry of Home Affairs announced that, under newly promulgated rules, any entity that is not incorporated in Singapore and does not have a majority of Singapore citizens on its board is now required to apply for a permit to sponsor an event in Hong Lim Park.

Migrant Workers and Labor Exploitation

Foreign migrant workers are subject to labor abuse and exploitation through debts owed to recruitment agents, non-payment of wages, restrictions on movement, confiscation of passports, and sometimes physical and sexual abuse. In March 2016, a Singapore couple was convicted of starving their domestic worker, who lost more than 20 kilograms during her 15 months of employment.

The work permits of migrant workers in Singapore are tied to a particular employer, leaving workers vulnerable to exploitation. Foreign domestic workers are still excluded from the Employment Act and many key labor protections, such as limits on daily work hours. Labor laws also discriminate against foreign workers by barring them from organizing and registering a union or serving as union leaders without explicit government permission. Local nongovernmental organizations have reported an increase in the past year in underage domestic workers, particularly from Burma.

Key International Actors

Singapore is a regional hub for international business and maintains good political and economic relations with both the United States and China. The country is a key security ally of the United States and a staunch supporter of the Trans-Pacific Partnership.

In August, the UN special rapporteur on freedom of expression, David Kaye, criticized Singapore's "broadening crackdown on controversial expression, as well as political criticism and dissent," noting that the increased criminalization of speech was in breach of Singapore's international obligations. No governments publicly criticized Singapore's poor human rights record.

Somalia

Civilians in Somalia, enduring abuses by all warring parties and dire humanitarian conditions, continue to bear the brunt of the country's long-running conflict. Government commitments to improve security in areas under its control, and build capacity of rule-of-law institutions, bore limited results in 2016.

Targeted attacks on civilians and civilian infrastructure, particularly by the Islamist armed group Al-Shabab, with suicide bombings and improvised explosive devices (IEDs), continue to have a devastating impact. Over 1 million Somalis remain internally displaced, facing serious abuses and very limited access to basic services. Fighting, linked both to military operations against Al-Shabab and clan fighting over resources and political power, and forced evictions resulted in new civilian displacement and casualties.

Much of the focus of the Somali authorities and their international partners has been on the electoral process. Tight deadlines as well as ongoing political maneuvering and infighting around the electoral process, including between the federal and regional authorities, largely detracted from progress in justice and security sector reform.

The Somali president took a positive step in August by signing a law establishing a national human rights commission. The government also made important commitments to human rights protections during its Universal Periodic Review at the United Nations, but in practice it failed to address violations against the internally displaced and attacks on journalists, among other serious abuses.

Abuses by Government and Allied Forces

Somalia's national intelligence agency, NISA, continues to conduct mass security sweeps despite having no legal mandate to arrest or detain. NISA held detainees for prolonged periods without charge or judicial review and on occasion beat suspects during interrogations. On July 21, NISA agents arrested five members of a policy center, Mogadishu Center for Research and Studies, held them without charges or legal counsel until September 6, before releasing them.

Security forces continue to arbitrarily detain and recruit children. Media reported that NISA used children in their custody as informants to identify Al-Shabab members. According to the UN, a government investigation later corroborated the allegations.

The military court in Mogadishu continues to try cases that are not legally within its jurisdiction and in proceedings falling short of international fair trial standards. According to the UN, at least 64 death sentences were issued in 2016. The majority of these were handed down in Puntland, following a large-scale Al-Shabab offensive in Puntland and Galmudug, when a military court sentenced 43 people to death for their association with Al-Shabab in June. According to the UN, 12 of those on death row are believed to be children.

Large-scale forced evictions of internally displaced persons, including by government forces, continued. According to UN figures, during the first eight months of 2016, over 80,000 people were forcibly evicted by government forces and private actors, primarily in Mogadishu.

Inter-clan and inter-regional fighting primarily linked to tensions around the creation of new federal states resulted in civilians deaths and injury and the destruction of property. Fighting broke out in October between the Galmudug interim administration, which was established in 2015, and Puntland forces. At least 22 civilians were killed and dozens injured, and according to the UN, nearly 90,000 people were displaced.

Al-Shabab Abuses

Al-Shabab committed targeted killings, beheadings, and executions, particularly of those accused of spying and collaborating with the government. The armed group continues to administer arbitrary justice, forcibly recruits children, and severely restricts basic rights in areas under its control. Some young men and boys who returned from Kenya's refugee camps to Al-Shabab-controlled areas, including Buale and Sakoow, have faced pressure to join Al-Shabab.

Al-Shabab regularly targets civilians and civilian structures, with an increase in attacks on schools, hotels, and restaurants in Mogadishu, resulting in numerous casualties. On January 21, Al-Shabab conducted a complex attack on popular restaurants in Mogadishu's Lido beach, in which over 20 people were killed and dozens injured, including women and children.

Al-Shabab controls and carries out attacks along many supply routes and imposes blockades on towns captured by AMISOM and government forces, restricting movement of goods and assistance.

Al-Shabab continues to threaten and target journalists in government-controlled areas and bans independent media from reporting in areas it controls. It claimed responsibility for a December 3, 2015 car bomb that killed 31-year-old reporter Hindiya Haji Mohamed, who worked for the state-run media.

Abuses by Foreign Forces

Reports persist of indiscriminate killings of civilians by AMISOM and other foreign forces, including during operations against Al-Shabab and airstrikes.

On July 17, Ethiopian forces indiscriminately killed 14 civilians during an operation against Al-Shabab in Somalia's Bay region. So far, despite public commitments from AMISOM's leadership, the incident has not been investigated.

Airstrikes by Kenya in the Gedo region following the January 15 attack on its base in El Adde resulted in significant civilian deaths, displacement, and destruction of livestock and civilian property. The UN raised concerns of use of cluster munition by Kenya in the Gedo region, which Kenya denied.

The UN Security Council repeatedly called on troop-contributing countries to share information with AMISOM's Civilian Casualty Tracking Analysis Research Cell, but this has not regularly occurred in practice.

Sexual Violence

While the full scope of sexual violence in Somalia remains unknown, internally displaced women and girls are particularly vulnerable to rape by armed men, including government soldiers and militia. Protection of the most vulnerable communities is largely non-existent.

AMISOM took measures to strengthen its capacity to follow up on sexual exploitation and abuse. However, this capacity remains at the headquarters' level with restricted reach within the missions' sectors thus limiting its ability to investigate abuses. The UN reported allegations of gang-rape by 14 AMISOM soldiers of two girls in the Galgudud region; an AMISOM investigation found the allegations were unfounded.

Displaced Persons and Access to Humanitarian Assistance

According to the UN, there are currently 1.1 million internally displaced people in Somalia, an estimated 400,000 living in Mogadishu alone, who remain very vulnerable and reliant on assistance. Human Rights Watch and other organizations continue to document serious abuses against displaced people living in government-controlled areas including rape and forced evictions. A number of refugees returning from Kenya as part of a UN-supported repatriation drive ended up in informal displacement camps.

Humanitarian agencies faced challenges accessing needy populations due to insecurity, restrictions imposed by parties to the conflict and targetted attacks.

Attacks on Media, Human Rights Defenders, and Political Opposition

Targeted attacks on media, including harassment, and intimidation by federal and regional authorities and the Al-Shabab continue.

Sagal Salad Osman, working for the state-run media, was killed on June 5, and Abdiaziz Mohamed Ali, a journalist at Radio Shabelle, was killed on September 27, by unknown gunmen.

The Somali authorities rarely investigate cases of killings or attacks on journalists or prosecute perpetrators; the authorities have only investigated and prosecuted attacks attributed to Al-Shabab, relying on the national intelligence agency, and the country's military court, whose investigations and trials do not meet international due process standards.

On March 3, the military court sentenced Hassan Hanafi, a journalist who worked for Al-Shabab's Radio Andalus, to death for his alleged involvement in the killing of at least five journalists; he was excuted on April 11. Hanafi had been held without being brought before a court for over a year, was filmed "confessing" prior to his trial on the state-run media and only met the lawyers representing him on the day of his sentencing.

HUMAN
RIGHTS
WATCH

"Like Fish in Poisonous Waters"
Attacks on Media Freedom in Somalia

In January, President Hassan Sheikh signed a new media law that risks further hampering freedom of expression by including many vague media restrictions.

In Puntland, on June 23, the minister of information ordered the closure of Daljir's FM radio stations throughout the region, reportedly as a result of an interview with a critic of the government. Daljir was off air for 12 days.

Somaliland

Somaliland authorities continue to restrict public criticism of their governance and policies. In May, the justice minister revoked the license of human rights lawyer, Guleid Ahmed Jama, on dubious grounds that his work as a lawyer and as the chairman of a human rights organization were incompatible. The chief justice later revoked the suspension. Authorities regularly detained journalists; some resulted in criminal charges.

Somaliland continued with its negative trend of executions with seven people executed in 2016.

Somaliland authorities have failed to sufficiently control and regulate private mental health centers that have confined patients involuntarily and subjected them to chaining, and, on occasion, beatings. One private center improved it treatment of those with mental disabilities by closing its inpatient facilities and providing support to patients in their communities.

Key International Actors

Foreign and regional partners continued to provide financial and other assistance to AMISOM, and the United States and United Kingdom paid the salaries of the Somali national army. Donors also provided direct support to regional security and police forces. In addition to Turkey's ongoing humanitarian, political, and economic engagements, the Gulf states, primarily the United Arab Emirates, increased their military and political support to Somalia.

US airstrikes and ground operations against Al-Shabab significantly increased in 2016. In November, the US Defense Department acknowledged a September 28 strike had killed local militia forces and not Al-Shabab members, as they had initially claimed.

At the political level, much of the international and regional community has focused on the electoral process, despite limited progress in key reform areas.

In September, the US imposed partial military sanctions on Somalia due to its continued recruitment and use of child soldiers, barring commercial arms sales and several other categories of military assistance for the 2017 fiscal year.

South Africa

In South Africa, public confidence in the government's willingness to tackle human rights violations, corruption, and respect for the rule of law has eroded. The government has failed to ensure that an estimated half-million children with disabilities have access to basic education. Rights groups expressed concerns about the government's failure to develop a national strategy to combat the high rate of violence against women and the continued underreporting of rape. In November, the Claassen Board of Inquiry into suspended National Police Commissioner Victoriah Phiyega's fitness to hold office completed its inquiry. Its recommendations were not made public.

In March, the Supreme Court of Appeal of South Africa ruled that South Africa had acted unlawfully when the government failed to arrest Sudanese President Omar al-Bashir when he visited South Africa in June 2015 for an African Union (AU) summit. Al-Bashir is subject to arrest warrants for the International Criminal Court on charges of genocide, war crimes, and crimes against humanity in connection with crimes committed in the conflict in Darfur.

South Africa continued to face a number of human rights challenges, as the government failed to hold accountable those responsible for xenophobic attacks on the businesses and homes of refugees, asylum-seekers, and migrants between March and May, 2015. The South African Human Rights Commission (SAHRC) on September 30 said Zulu King Goodwill Zwelithini's March 2015 speech calling for foreign nationals to "pack their bags and go home," was hurtful but did not incite xenophobic violence.

South Africa has taken significant steps to improve coordination between government and civil society in combatting violence (including rape and murder) against lesbians and transgender men. To protect the human rights of lesbian, gay, bisexual, and transgender (LGBT) people, in September, the government declared homophobic United States pastor Steven Anderson an undesirable person and barred him and his associates from entering the country.

Right to Education

In September, widespread countrywide student protests for the government to provide free education, the sometimes violent #FeesMustFall demonstrations, resulted in many institutions suspending their academic programs. President Jacob Zuma on October 3, hosted a consultative meeting with stakeholders to find a solution. President Zuma said the purpose of the consultation was to "seek the wisdom of all sectors including parents, students, business and labour, to seek solutions, given that education is a societal issue."

South Africa became the first country to endorse the Safe Schools Declaration at a global conference in Norway in May 2015. By joining the declaration, it agreed to protect students and education during conflict, and to avoid using educational buildings for military purposes.

Access to Education for Children and Adults with Disabilities

The South African government has failed to guarantee the right to education for many children and young adults with disabilities, affecting an estimated half-million children. Contrary to the government's international and domestic obligations, many children with disabilities do not have equal access to primary or secondary education and face multiple forms of discrimination and barriers when accessing schools. They are turned away from mainstream schools, denied access to inclusive education, and referred instead to special schools by school officials or medical staff simply because they have a disability. The referrals system needlessly forces children to wait for up to four years at care centers or at home for placement in a special school.

While education in mainstream government schools is free, children with disabilities who attend special schools are forced to pay school fees, and many who attend mainstream schools are asked to pay for their own class assistants as a condition to stay in mainstream classes. Once in school, many children with disabilities do not have access to the same curriculum as children without disabilities. Many children with disabilities are exposed to high levels of violence and abuse by teachers and students.

The government has not implemented key aspects of a national policy to provide inclusive education for all children with disabilities adopted in 2001. South

Africa has not adopted legislation that guarantees the right to inclusive education for children with disabilities. The majority of the government's limited budget for learners with disabilities is allocated to special, segregated schools rather than to inclusive education.

Accountability for Xenophobic Attacks on Foreign Nationals

On September 30, SAHRC cleared Zulu King Goodwill Zwelithini of inciting xenophobic violence, that left seven people dead and over 5,000 displaced between March and May 2015. The Africa Diaspora Forum, Lawyers for Human Rights, and some individuals filed a complaint against Zwelithini to the SAHRC, stating that Zwelithini's statement to media on March 21, 2015, that foreigners should "pack their bags and go home," had incited violence against foreign nationals and led to xenophobic attacks that started in KwaZulu-Natal and spread to other provinces. The government did not publicly condemn Zwelithini's reckless and inflammatory statements.

The SAHRC found that Zwelithini's speech was hurtful towards foreigners and could perpetuate discrimination, but did not amount to hate speech. It gave Zwelithini 60 days to reconcile with foreign nationals and migrants in the KwaZulu Natal province, but he has not said or done anything to comply. Authorities neither thoroughly investigated nor successfully prosecuted those involved in the attacks.

Inquiry into National Police Commissioner's Fitness to Hold Office

On June 3, the Claassen Board of Inquiry into suspended National Police Commissioner Victoriah Phiyega's fitness to hold office completed its investigations. President Zuma established the Board of Inquiry in line with a recommendation of the Farlam Commission of Inquiry into the August 2012 Marikana killings of 44 people, including the police killing of 34 miners. The Farlam Commission called for an inquiry into whether Phiyega, and the North West Provincial Police Commissioner, Lieutenant Zukiswa Mbombo, were fit to hold office. On October 14, 2015, President Zuma suspended Phiyega.

Lawyers who investigated the case told the Claassen Board of Inquiry that evidence showed Phiyega breached the constitution and police code of conduct, is unfit for office, and is unable to carry out her duties in accordance with the law. They asked the board to recommend Phiyega's removal from office. Phiyega refused to testify before the board, which was expected to present its findings and recommendations to president Zuma in August. At time of writing, the Claasen Board of Inquiry had completed its investigations but had not yet submitted its report and recommendations to President Zuma.

Women's Rights

Violence against women, including rape and domestic violence, remained widespread and underreported. Although annual crime statistics released by the South African Police Services showed that sexual offences decreased slightly by 3 percent, many gender activists and human rights groups expressed concerns about the continued under-reporting of rape and the government's failure to introduce a national strategy to combat violence against women.

Sexual Orientation and Gender Identity

South Africa has a progressive constitution that prohibits discrimination on the basis of sexual orientation and protects the human rights of LGBTI people. The Department of Justice and Constitutional Development has taken significant steps to improve coordination between government and civil society in combatting violence (including rape and murder) against lesbians and transgender men.

On September 6, Home Affairs Minister Malusi Gigaba announced that due to widespread homophobic attitudes within South African society, and to protect the rights of LGBTI people, homophobic US pastor Steven Anderson and members of his church were banned from entering the country because they promote hate speech and advocate social violence. He said constitutional and legislative guarantees, including the rights of LGBTI persons, must be respected by all. Domestic LGBTI groups lauded the decision.

Foreign Policy

During 2016, South Africa missed key opportunities to consistently place respect for human rights at the center of its foreign policy practice. While South Africa played an active mediation role, as part of the Southern African Development Community (SADC), in the Lesotho political crisis that followed a failed military coup in August 2014, it remained silent in the face of a rapidly deteriorating human rights situation in Zimbabwe. South Africa did not press Zimbabwe to end police brutality and respect the rights of protesters. Instead, in July, Secretary General of the ruling African National Congress (ANC) party Gwede Mantashe labeled the protesters in Zimbabwe "sponsored elements seeking regime change."

Some of South Africa's votes at the United Nations were contrary to the country's stated human rights principles. For example, in July, South Africa voted against a UN Human Rights Council resolution on the protection of human rights on the internet and abstained on a key HRC vote to appoint an independent expert on sexual orientation and gender identity. The abstention went against the country's strong constitutional protections and domestic laws around sexual orientation and gender identity. But on November 21, in the UN General Assembly committee, South Africa voted to allow Vitit Muntabhorn, the newly appointed UN expert on sexual orientation and gender identity, to continue his work. The vote was taken after the African Group put forward a resolution to stop the operations of the UN expert who was appointed in September by the Human Rights Council.

On October 21, 2016, Foreign Minister Maite Nkoana-Mashabane announced that South Africa had submitted a notice to the UN Secretary-General Ban Ki-moon of its intent to withdraw as a party to the Rome Statute, the treaty that established and governs the International Criminal Court (ICC). Notification is necessary to trigger the withdrawal, which comes into effect a year after such notice is given. The move comes after it hosted the Sudanese president at the AU Summit in June 2015. Al-Bashir is the subject of two ICC arrest warrants on charges of genocide, crimes against humanity, and war crimes allegedly committed in Darfur. South African courts confirmed the government had a duty to arrest al-Bashir.

Various individuals and organizations, including human rights activists and ju-
rists, in South Africa expressed dismay that their government submitted a notification of withdrawal without parliamentary authorization. Former South African
Constitutional Court judge Richard Goldstone called the move unconstitutional.
Goldstone was the first chief prosecutor of the International Criminal Tribunal for
the Former Yugoslavia and the International Criminal Tribunal for Rwanda. The
Democratic Alliance, one of South Africa's main opposition parties, and the
Southern Africa Litigation Centre, a prominent human rights organization, chal-
lenged the move in South Africa's courts.

South Sudan

South Sudan's civil war, which began in December 2013, continued in 2016 with serious abuses against civilians by both government forces and opposition fighters despite a peace agreement signed in August 2015.

Government soldiers killed, raped, and tortured civilians as well as destroying and pillaging civilian property during counterinsurgency operations in the southern and western parts of the country, and both sides committed abuses against civilians in and around Juba and other areas. An additional 200,000 people were forced to flee their homes, bringing the total displaced to 2.4 million. Those left behind, including people with disabilities, have faced serious abuses.

The conflict began in December 2013 when soldiers loyal to President Salva Kiir, a Dinka, and those loyal to former Vice President Riek Machar, a Nuer, fought in the capital following months of growing political tensions. In December 2015, President Kiir dissolved South Sudan's 10 regional states and created 28 new states, fueling conflict in many areas.

Although the two sides formed a national unity government in April 2016, following the August 2015 peace agreement, they continued to fight in various locations. In July, clashes in the capital, Juba, caused Machar to flee the country. President Kiir then appointed a former ally of Machar, Gen. Taban Deng Gai, as first vice president, prompting Machar's group to call for a return to war.

In November, UN Special Advisor on the Prevention of Genocide Adama Dieng said the ongoing violence had transformed the conflict into an "ethnic war" and warned of a "potential for genocide."

Lack of accountability for grave crimes by both sides since 2013 has fuelled the current conflict. Government investigations have rarely led to concrete and lasting accountability measures. A hybrid court envisioned by the peace agreement to investigate and prosecute international crimes committed during the recent conflict has yet to be established by the African Union and the South Sudanese government.

Attacks on Civilians and Civilian Property

Government forces clashed with rebel groups and conducted counterinsurgency operations in the Equatoria and Western Bahr el Ghazal regions throughout 2016.

During operations in Yambio, Wau and Yei towns, soldiers targeted and killed dozens of civilians and committed a range of other abuses, including enforced disappearances, arbitrary detentions in poor conditions, beating and torture of detainees, and sexual violence. Soldiers pillaged civilian property and burned homes, forcing hundreds of thousands of civilians to flee.

Government forces clashed with rebel groups in various other locations in the Equatorias, with both sides committing abuses against civilians. In Wau, tensions and abuses by soldiers flared again in June after the president sacked and jailed the governor, Elyas Waya Nyipuoch, for criticizing abuses committed by the army.

In Juba, government and opposition forces clashed from July 8 to 11, when the government declared a ceasefire after opposition leader Riek Machar fled the town. Both forces fired and shelled indiscriminately in densely populated areas, injuring and killing scores of civilians. A clinic in a displaced person's camp located in the main United Nations base in Juba was also hit by shelling, forcing patients to relocate. South Sudan's army restricted the movements of United Nations Mission in South Sudan (UNMISS) peacekeepers during and after the July fighting.

On February 17 and 18, in Malakal, Upper Nile State, a group of armed Dinka SPLA soldiers and civilians attacked a UN base hosting more than 45,000 mostly Nuer and Shilluk displaced people, killing at least 30 civilians. The attackers systematically burned thousands of shelters to the ground. A UN special investigation concluded that armed Dinka men in SPLA uniforms had breached the UN compound and were responsible for violence and destruction.

Sexual and Gender-Based Violence

On July 11, shortly before the ceasefire that followed Riek Machar's retreat from the capital, government soldiers attacked a residential compound in Juba hosting expatriate and national staff of humanitarian organizations, executed a prominent Nuer journalist, beat staff members and raped or gang raped several women. In the days following the ceasefire, soldiers raped hundreds of mostly Nuer displaced women near the main UN base in Juba.

In other parts of the country, government soldiers reportedly continued to rape women and girls selected as targets based on their ethnicity.

While some survivors were able to access basic physical and mental healthcare, many did not due to insecurity and limited availability of services. No SPLA soldiers were prosecuted for the sexual violence crimes committed in July.

Recruitment and Use of Child Soldiers

Both government and opposition forces have used child soldiers since the beginning of the conflict. In April, the UN secretary-general's report on children and armed conflict noted a sharp increase in the number of incidents of child recruitment, with more than 2,500 children recruited or used, mostly by government forces. Forces aligned with the opposition also continued to recruit and use children.

The UN also reported that hundreds of children were forcibly recruited in August by government affiliated politicians in Unity state. Child soldiers were also reportedly used by opposition fighters in Western Equatoria and Western Bahr el-Ghazal.

Soldiers or armed actors often use schools as homes, preventing children from accessing the premises and attending classes.

Restrictions on Freedom of Expression

South Sudan's government authorities, especially the National Security Services (NSS), continued to harass, intimidate, and arbitrarily arrest and detain journalists.

In March, Joseph Afandi, a writer with the Arabic daily *Al-Tabeer* was found beaten and bearing signs of torture in a Juba cemetery after being abducted by security forces. In October, Malek Bol, a journalist with *Al-Maugif*, was abducted for two days, tortured, and later dumped at a graveyard.

On July 16, Alfred Taban, a veteran journalist and editor of the *Juba Monitor*, was arrested and detained for 13 days for publishing an op-ed calling for the replacement of the South Sudanese leadership. His newspaper was shut down for a day following his arrest. The *Nation Mirror* was shut down indefinitely on September 14 for publishing texts critical of President Kiir.

Civil society actors were also harassed and threatened by security forces. Shortly before a visit to Juba by the UN Security Council in September, the government threatened to shut down or deny registration to a number of civil society organizations, including the Community Empowerment for Progress Organization (CEPO) and the South Sudan Action Network on Small Arms (SSANSA).

Legislative Developments

In a contested decision in December 2015, President Kiir dissolved South Sudan's 10 states and created 28 new ones, raising fears that the new disposition would benefit certain ethnicities over others.

On February 1, 2016, the South Sudan Legislative Assembly (SSLA) passed a bill, amid controversy, which gives the government sweeping powers to regulate, shut down, and seize assets of nongovernmental and civil society organizations based on declarations or activities deemed political.

Accountability and Justice

Despite official investigations ordered by President Kiir into alleged crimes and human rights violations committed in 2016 by soldiers in Juba, Malakal, and Wau, the government has rarely made the reports of such investigations public, acted on their recommendations, thoroughly investigated, or held perpetrators to account in civilian courts.

The government has not prosecuted soldiers for crimes against civilians in civilian courts in accordance with human rights norms. Two dozen soldiers were tried for crimes committed in Wau and Juba in July and August, but these trials did not meet international fair trial standards. Victims could hardly access the proceedings and the accused were barely investigated prior to their trials. The SPLA reported that at least two soldiers were executed in late July following their conviction by a military court for murder in Wau.

The African Union Commission has yet to establish the hybrid court envisioned in the August 2015 peace agreement to investigate and prosecute international crimes committed in the conflict. The government expressed renewed commitment to the court during a visit by the UN Security Council that followed the Juba fighting in July.

Key International Actors

The Intergovernmental Authority on Development (IGAD), as well as China, the European Union, Norway, the United Kingdom, and the United States continued to support and monitor the implementation of the peace agreement signed in August 2015.

In March 2016, the UN Human Rights Council established a UN human rights mission to South Sudan to monitor the human rights situation and efforts to promote transitional justice.

UNMISS continued to shelter more than 200,000 civilians forced to flee their homes because of the fighting. UNMISS peacekeepers struggled to protect civilians outside their bases.

There was a marked increase in attacks against the property and staff of UNMISS and humanitarian organizations throughout 2016, amid increasingly hostile rhetoric against the international community.

In early August 2016, following fighting in Juba, the UN Security Council authorized the deployment within UNMISS of a 4,000 strong Regional Protection Force (RPF) tasked with protecting civilians and key infrastructure in the capital. The council threatened to impose an arms embargo should South Sudan continue to restrict the movement of UN peacekeepers or block the deployment of the RPF. At time of writing, no RPF member has been able to enter the country.

In October, following a damning report from an independent UN investigation into the peacekeepers' failure to respond to the July crisis in Juba, the UN secretary-general sacked the Kenyan force commander of UNMISS. Kenya retaliated by pulling out its entire contingent from the mission.

The UN secretary-general reported continued obstructions to the peacekeeping mission by government forces and authorities. In November, the United States Mission to the United Nations announced it would submit a proposal for an arms embargo over South Sudan, as well as additional targeted individual sanctions. At time of writing, the Security Council had yet to approve a draft resolution.

Sri Lanka

Sri Lanka acted to address some longstanding demands for accountability and political reconciliation linked to the 27-year civil war with the Liberation Tigers of Tamil Eelam, which ended in 2009. The government conducted two public consultations, one on constitutional reform and another on implementing an October 2015 United Nations Human Rights Council resolution on transitional justice.

Although the government, elected in January 2015, did not deliver all reformist promises made during the election campaign, media and civil society groups in the country largely enjoyed continued freedom from surveillance, harassment, and attacks. A long-promised Right to Information bill was enacted in June 2016. There was some progress on emblematic cases linked to the civil war, such as the murder of a prominent newspaper editor, the enforced disappearance of a political cartoonist, and the killing of five youths by state security forces in the eastern district of Trincomalee.

However, despite its pledges, the government failed to abolish the draconian Prevention of Terrorism Act (PTA), and instead used the preventive detention law during a series of arrests in April and May. A draft version of a law intended to replace the PTA retained many problematic clauses including troubling expansions of police powers. The government's unwillingness to consult adequately before enacting legislation to establish a permanent Office of Missing Persons damaged public trust during the transitional justice process.

The newly appointed Constitutional Council moved rapidly through the year to appoint members to the National Human Rights Commission and the Police Commission, and is expected to continue to work towards restoring the independence of other public service commissions.

Constitutional Reforms

A government-appointed independent task force on constitutional reform, constituted in December 2015, conducted nationwide public consultations that ended in May 2016. The taskforce heard from over 2,500 individuals, and received several hundred other submissions. Despite government-imposed time limits, it published a comprehensive public report on its findings on May 31.

The task force recognized some contentious political issues, such as whether Sri Lanka should be a unitary or a federal state, the exact nature of devolution of powers from the center, and the supremacy of Buddhism. Importantly for the protection of fundamental rights, the task force recommended that the constitution be regarded as the supreme law of the land and that the judiciary be tasked with ensuring all legislation complies with the constitution.

Accountability for Past Abuses

In October 2015, the UN Human Rights Council adopted a consensus resolution in which Sri Lanka pledged to undertake many human rights reforms, including resolving the many transitional justice demands arising out of the civil war. Under the resolution, Sri Lanka promised to establish four transitional justice mechanisms, including a special court "integrating international judges, prosecutors, lawyers and investigators" with an independent investigative and prosecuting body. The resolution also called for an office on missing and disappeared persons, a truth-telling mechanism, and a mechanism designed to guarantee non-recurrence and reparations.

A government task force designed to hold public consultations nationally on the four transitional justice mechanisms was slow to get off the ground. Shortly after, the government announced a framework to create an office to discover the fate of those missing and forcibly disappeared, leading to an outcry over inadequate public consultations. This lack of trust has marred the ongoing public consultations on the other three mechanisms.

The government failed to properly implement important recommendations to improve the human rights situation in the country, including a repeal of the PTA and reforms to the Witness and Victim Protection Law. Other undertakings, such as broader reform of the security sector and return of private lands confiscated by the military, were halting at best. An update from the UN High Commissioner for Human Rights in June 2016 mentioned the need for greater progress, and was due to provide a more comprehensive report to the Human Rights Council in early 2017.

Senior members of government continued issuing contradictory statements on the need to have international participation in the four transitional justice mechanisms, with the president and prime minister both claiming these would be wholly domestic processes, contrary to the Human Rights Council resolution.

Police Torture and Ill-Treatment

Sri Lankan police are not held accountable for routine torture and ill-treatment of individuals taken into custody. Sometimes torture is carried out to extract "confessions," but it is also used for personal vendettas or to extort funds. Police often used methods designed to leave no visible marks, suggesting a level of institutionalization. The National Human Rights Commission, though limited in resources, visited and actively monitored prisons and detention centers in 2016, and issued directives on procedures to be followed following arrest.

In April and May 2016, the UN special rapporteur on torture, Juan Mendis, visited Sri Lanka and reported that torture by the police Criminal Investigation Department was common. The rapporteur also found an increase in torture in cases of real or perceived threats to national interests by the Terrorism Investigation Division. He reported a near total impunity in both old and new torture cases.

Prevention of Terrorism Act and Politically Motivated Torture

The government attempted a redraft of the Prevention of Terrorism Act but was forced to withdraw it when it failed to meet international standards. A second draft forwarded in October did not ease concerns about ensuring rights of detainees and protecting against custodial torture. The special rapporteur on torture expressed particular concern about detainees held under the PTA and called for its unequivocal repeal.

The PTA allows for arrests for unspecified "unlawful activities" without warrant and permits detention for up to 18 months without the suspect appearing before a court. It has facilitated thousands of abuses over the years, including torture, enforced disappearances, and extrajudicial executions.

While especially problematic during Sri Lanka's long civil war, authorities continued to use the PTA even after the war ended. Following the discovery of suicide vests in Chavakchcheri in the north, security forces reportedly arrested 11 men in April and May. Many of the arrests were first undeclared, with families reporting only that security forces had abducted the men. Following pressure, particularly from the National Human Rights Commission, security forces admitted to holding them under the PTA.

Overseas Migrant Workers

More than 1 million Sri Lankans are employed overseas, mostly in the Middle East, and many remained at risk of abuse at every stage of the migration cycle, from recruitment and transit, to employment, repatriation, and reintegration. More than a third of Sri Lanka's migrants are domestic workers, almost exclusively female.

The government took some steps to protect their rights abroad, but many continued to face long working hours with little rest, delayed or unpaid wages, confinement in the workplace, and verbal, physical, and sexual abuse. The *kafala* (sponsorship) systems in the Middle East ties workers' visas to their employers; in several countries they cannot transfer jobs without employer consent, and can be punished with imprisonment and deportation if they leave employers.

In June, the government announced that it appointed a committee to study strategies to reduce the number of domestic workers abroad.

In 2016, the UN Committee on Migrant Workers reviewed Sri Lanka's record under the International Convention on Migrant Workers and their Families. Among other recommendations, the committee called on Sri Lanka to withdraw the Ministry of Foreign Employment Promotion and Welfare January 2014 circular that required a "family background report" for women migrants, as it discriminated against women and denied them the right to seek employment abroad instead of providing support they may need.

Sexual Orientation and Gender Identity

State and non-state discrimination and abuses against the lesbian, gay, bisexual, transgender, and intersex (LGBTI) population persist. Sections 365 and 365A of the Sri Lankan Penal Code prohibit "carnal knowledge against the order of nature" and "gross indecency," commonly understood in Sri Lanka to criminalize all same-sex relations between consenting adults.

Sri Lankan law does not specifically criminalize transgender or intersex people. But no laws ensure that their rights are protected, and police have used several

HUMAN RIGHTS WATCH

"All Five Fingers Are Not the Same"
Discrimination on Grounds of Gender Identity
and Sexual Orientation in Sri Lanka

criminal offenses and regulations to target LGBTI people, particularly transgender women and men who have sex with men (MSM) involved in sex work. These include a law against "cheat[ing] by personation," and the vaguely worded Vagrants' Ordinance, which prohibits soliciting or committing acts of "gross indecency," or being "incorrigible rogues" procuring "illicit or unnatural intercourse."

Some trans women and MSM said that repeated harassment by police, including instances of arbitrary detention and mistreatment, had eroded their trust in Sri Lankan authorities, and made it unlikely that they would report a crime. The community also reported abuse and harassment at the hands of medical authorities, leading many transgender people to self-medicate rather than seeking professional assistance.

Women's Rights

Allegations of sexual and other violence committed against women during the civil war are expected to be addressed through the transitional justice mechanisms, although there are concerns that many women will be reluctant to come forward absent an independent victim and witness protection program.

Key International Actors

The Sri Lankan government continued its engagement with the international community in stark contrast to the hostility of the previous government, with key actors such as the United States and European Union voicing cautious optimism regarding the government's efforts to implement the 2015 Human Rights Council resolution.

There were several visits by UN special mandate holders over the course of the year. The commissioner for human rights, Zeid Ra'ad al-Hussein, visited the country in February, and Secretary-General Ban Ki-moon visited in September. Both lauded the progress made by the government, although Zeid called for speedier implementation of the resolution, for greater efforts at confidence-building with the minority populations, and the need for international participation in transitional justice mechanisms.

The Human Rights Council resolution remained largely unimplemented although the government was able to report progress on certain aspects and did seek technical expertise from the relevant branches of the UN and other countries.

The Sri Lankan government initiated discussions with the UN and other stakeholders on the possibility of incorporating Sri Lankan security forces in international peacekeeping operations, although the mechanism for doing so had yet to be finalized given the difficulty of vetting forces who might have been engaged in war crimes.

In November, Sri Lanka appeared before the UN's Commission Against Torture to respond to allegations of abuse, where it denied allegations of torture and abuse.

Sudan

Sudan's human rights record remains abysmal in 2016, with continuing attacks on civilians by government forces in Darfur, Southern Kordofan, and Blue Nile states; repression of civil society groups and independent media; and widespread arbitrary detentions of activists, students, and protesters. The ruling National Congress Party proceeded with a national dialogue process to pave the way for a new constitution and government, following the independence of South Sudan in 2011, despite a boycott by several opposition parties.

Conflict and Abuses in Darfur

In January, Sudan's armed forces, including the Rapid Support Forces and allied militia, launched coordinated ground and air attacks on populated villages in Jebel Marra, the rebel stronghold in Central Darfur. These attacks continued for much of the year, following Sudan's "Operation Decisive Summer" campaigns in Darfur in 2014 and 2015.

Government forces killed civilians, raped women and girls, and destroyed hundreds of villages. In September, the United Nations found the violence had displaced up to 190,000 people, many of whom are not accessible to humanitarian agencies. Elsewhere in Darfur, attacks on civilians by government forces and inter-communal fighting over land and resources also resulted in deaths, destruction and displacement.

Amnesty International alleged that the government used chemical weapons against civilians. However, Sudan, a party to the Chemical Weapons Convention since 1999, denied the findings and limited the scope of investigation by the Organization for the Prohibition of Chemical Weapons (OPCW).

Government authorities continued to block the African Union/United Nations peacekeeping mission, UNAMID, from much of the Jebel Marra region, undermining the mission's ability to protect civilians.

Amid the ongoing violence and abuses, authorities held a referendum on the administrative status of Darfur in April in which voters opted to keep Darfur's current five states. Displaced communities and opposition groups boycotted the

561

process, arguing the administrative divisions serve to undermine Darfur's ethnic groups and empower Sudan's ruling party.

Conflict and Abuses in Southern Kordofan and Blue Nile

For the fifth year, armed conflict continued between government forces and armed rebels in Southern Kordofan and Blue Nile, despite a declared ceasefire. In the Nuba Mountains, government forces and allied militias attacked civilians in villages and other populated areas in ground offensives and through indiscriminate bombing, particularly from March through June.

In May alone, attacks killed six children in Heiban, injured several more at their funeral and destroyed part of a school in Kauda, wounding a teacher. Government forces burned crops, looted food, and displaced people from farming areas. The attacks caused unjustified civilian deaths, including children, many injuries and destruction of civilian property.

The government has barred humanitarian agencies from working in rebel-held areas of Southern Kordofan and Blue Nile, and has failed to agree terms for humanitarian access with the rebel group (SPLM-N).

Arbitrary Detentions, Ill-Treatment, and Torture

Sudan's National Intelligence and Security Service (NISS)—known for its abusive tactics, including torture, against real or perceived political opponents—detained activists, students, lawyers, doctors, community leaders and those perceived to be critical of the government.

In April, security officials detained dozens of students and activists in Khartoum, some for more than two months without charge, during violent crackdowns on protests at university campuses. In early May, armed security officials raided the offices of a prominent lawyer, Nabil Adeeb, and beat and arrested a group of students, their family members, and office staff. In July, security officers detained around 20 displaced community members who spoke to the United States special envoy in Niertiti, South Darfur. In October, security officials detained 14 doctors and summoned scores more for protesting working conditions and violence against medical professionals.

Many detainees were beaten and subjected to other forms of ill-treatment. Some female activists reported being sexually harassed by national security officers while in detention—exemplifying a pattern Human Rights Watch has documented of authorities using arbitrary detentions, sexual violence and public order codes to restrict or silence female human rights activists.

Freedoms of Peaceful Assembly, Association, and Expression

In January, security forces used live ammunition to disperse a protest in West Darfur over an attack on a village there. At least seven people including a child were killed in the incident.

In April, security forces violently suppressed student protests, using rubber bullets and tear gas to break up protests at the University of Khartoum and used live ammunition to disperse protests in North Kordofan and Omdurman, killing two students and injuring dozens.

To date, there has been no accountability for the victims of the violent crackdown on protests that took place in September 2013, when more than 170 individuals were killed, many by gunshot wounds to the chest or head.

Authorities also restricted civil society and blocked their participation in international events, including Sudan's Universal Periodic Review (UPR) at the UN Human Rights Council in Geneva. In February, for the second time in a year, national security officers raided the Khartoum-based Tracks for Training and Human Development, confiscating equipment and detaining and interrogating staff. Criminal charges—including crimes against the state, which carry the death penalty—are pending against several affiliated activists, including three men who were detained in May and remained in detention at time of writing.

Security officials restricted media freedom, threatened journalists, and regularly confiscated newspapers throughout the year. In May, editions of the daily newspaper *Al Jareeda* were confiscated five times, most likely because of its reporting on the student demonstrations. In October, *al-Watan* was confiscated for its coverage of a countrywide medical workers' strike.

Sudan also restricted religious freedoms and detained clerics. Three pastors and a Darfuri activist detained since December 2015 face espionage and other charges that carry the death penalty.

HUMAN
RIGHTS
WATCH

"Good Girls Don't Protest"
Repression and Abuse of Women Human Rights Defenders,
Activists and Protesters in Sudan

Refugees and Migrants

The head of Sudan's Rapid Support Forces, implicated in wide-ranging abuses, announced that his forces intercepted migrants on the Libyan border, raising concerns that European Union support to East African states on migration, known as the Khartoum Process, may provide resources to abusive forces.

In August, the Italian government deported 48 Darfuris back to Sudan as part of a new agreement between Sudan and Italy to curb migration, in proceedings that appeared not to adequately protect the rights of asylum-seekers.

In December 2015, Jordanian authorities deported 800 Sudanese back to Sudan, and in July, Egypt deported 36 Sudanese without assessing their claims to asylum. In May 2016, Sudanese officials deported hundreds of Eritreans, again without assessing their protection claims as required under international law, to likely abuses in Eritrea.

Legal Reform

The National Security Act of 2010 and laws governing media, voluntary organizations, and public order regime are especially problematic and violate international human rights norms to which Sudan is bound.

The NISS has broad powers to arrest and detain people for up to four-and-a-half months without judicial review, months beyond the international standard. Constitutional amendments in January 2015 further empowered the NISS by designating it as a regular force with a mandate to combat a wide range of political and social threats.

Authorities continued to apply Sharia (Islamic law) sanctions that violate international prohibitions on cruel, inhuman, or degrading punishment. The penalties are applied disproportionately to women and girls, typically for morality "crimes" such as adultery or violations of the public order regime.

Sudan continues to criminalize consensual same-sex sexual activity and other behavior that impacts lesbian, gay, bisexual, and transgender (LGBT) communities, including anal sex between males with penalties as harsh as life imprisonment or death, and "indecent" or "immoral" behavior with a fine or up to 40 lashes.

Child Soldiers

In September, Sudanese authorities released 21 children allegedly associated with armed groups. Sudan signed an Action Plan with the UN to protect children from recruitment and use in conflict.

Key International Actors

The African Union's High-Level Implementation Panel for Sudan and South Sudan continued to mediate peace talks for Southern Kordofan, Blue Nile, and Darfur with little success.

Sudan effectively expelled the fourth senior UN official in two years when authorities declined to renew the visa for the head of UN's Office for the Coordination of Humanitarian Affairs (OCHA) in June. Sudan shut down an international aid agency in December 2015 and expelled three other humanitarian officials in early 2016.

In October, the European Parliament adopted an urgency resolution on Sudan calling on the EU to impose targeted punitive sanctions against those responsible for continued war crimes and non-cooperation with the International Criminal Court (ICC).

The UN Security Council renewed UNAMID's mandate through June 2017, despite efforts by Sudan to restrict and even end the mission's operations, and extended the mandate of the UN Interim Security Force for Abyei through mid-May 2017

In September, the Human Rights Council extended the mandate of the independent expert for one year. The UN Panel of Experts on the Sudan released the findings of its monitoring of the Darfur sanctions regime in 2015, citing evidence of continued aerial bombardments, use of cluster munitions, and other violations of international humanitarian and human rights law.

Since June 2005, the ICC has conducted investigations into crimes committed in Darfur. The ICC has issued arrest warrants for five individuals, including for President Omar al-Bashir, for war crimes, crimes against humanity, and genocide. At time of writing, all remain outstanding, and Sudan has refused to cooperate with the court in any of the cases. Al-Bashir remains a fugitive, but his travel has been restricted. A number of anticipated trips abroad have been cancelled, rescheduled, or relocated amid diplomatic and public outcry, particularly by African civil society groups.

Swaziland

Swaziland, ruled by absolute monarch King Mswati III since 1986, continued to repress political dissent and disregard human rights and rule of law principles in 2016. Political parties remained banned, as they have been since 1973; the independence of the judiciary is severely compromised, and repressive laws continued to be used to target critics of the government and the king despite the 2005 Swaziland Constitution guaranteeing basic rights.

In September, the High Court of Swaziland ruled that sections of the Suppression of Terrorism Act and the Sedition and Subversive Act were unconstitutional and violated freedom of expression and association. The government has appealed the judgement to the Supreme Court, which was pending at time of writing.

Proposed amendments to the Public Order Act and the Suppression of Terrorism Act are under consideration in Parliament but rights activists say that these amendments are insufficient to curb the security services, which have been given sweeping powers by the two laws to halt pro-democracy meetings and protests and to curb any criticism of the government.

Freedom of Association and Assembly

Restrictions on freedom of association and assembly continued in 2016. The government took no action to revoke the King's Proclamation of 1973, which prohibits political parties in the country. Police used the Urban Act, which requires protesters to give two weeks' notice before a public protest, to stop protests and harass protesters. In February, police arrested Mcolisi Ngcamphalala and Mbongwa Dlamini, two leaders of the Swaziland National Association of Teachers (SNAT), when they participated in a protest action. Two days later, the police raided their homes.

In February, the police blocked a Trade Union Congress of Swaziland (TUCOSWA) march to parliament to present a petition. In April, the police twice invaded and searched the offices of the leaders harassed leaders of the Swaziland Union of Financial Institutions and Allied Workers (SUFIAWU) without the necessary search warrant. In the same month, the commissioner of police threatened trade unionists with death for unspecified reasons. In June the police assaulted Gladys Dlamini, a trade union activist.

Human Rights Defenders

Political activists faced trial under security legislation and charges of treason under common law. The Suppression of Terrorism Act of 2008 placed severe restrictions on civil society organizations, religious groups, and media. Under the legislation, a "terrorist act" includes a wide range of legitimate conduct such as criticism of the government. The legislation was used by state officials to target perceived opponents through abusive surveillance, and unlawful searches of homes and offices.

Two leaders of a banned political party, the People's United Democratic Movement (PUDEMO), Mario Masuku and Maxwell Dlamini, remained on bail in 2016 pending finalization of their trial on charges under the Suppression of Terrorism Act for allegedly criticizing the government by singing a pro-democracy song and shouting "Viva PUDEMO" during a May Day rally in 2014. The Swaziland High Court granted them bail in July 2015 after more than a year in custody. The trial continued at time of writing. If convicted, they could serve up to 15 years in prison. Both men attended the May Day rally of TUCOSWA in 2016, but their bail conditions prohibited them from addressing the workers.

Freedom of Expression and the Media

The Sedition and Subversive Activities Act continued to restrict freedom of expression through criminalizing alleged seditious publications and use of alleged seditious words, such as those which "may excite disaffection" against the king. Published criticism of the ruling party is also banned. Many journalists practice self-censorship, especially with regards to reports involving the king, to avoid harassment by authorities.

On September 16, the High Court of Swaziland ruled that sections of the Suppression of Terrorism Act and the Sedition and Subversive Act were unconstitutional and violated freedom of expression and association. The invalid provisions relate to the definition of the offences of sedition, subversion, and terrorism. Classification of organizations as terrorist, which the government had used to ban political parties like the People's United Democratic Movement (PUDEMO), was also ruled to be unconstitutional.

Eight trade union leaders and human rights defenders, including Masuku and Dlamini, had challenged the constitutionality of the Suppression of Terrorism Act before the High Court in September 2015. An appeal by the government against the decision was pending before the Supreme Court.

Rule of Law

Although the constitution provides for three separate organs of government—the executive, legislature, and judiciary—under Swaziland's law and custom, all powers are vested in the king. Swaziland's prime minister is supposed to exercise executive authority, but in reality, King Mswati holds supreme executive power and controls the judiciary. The king appoints 20 members of the 30-member senate, 10 members of the house of assembly, and approves all legislation passed by parliament.

The constitution provides for equality before the law, but also places the king above the law. In 2011, the then Swaziland Chief Justice Michael Ramodibedi issued a directive which protected the king from any civil law suits, after Swazi villagers claimed police had seized their cattle to add to the king's herd.

Women's Rights

Swaziland's dual legal system where both Roman Dutch common law and Swazi customary law operate side by side, has resulted in conflicts leading to numerous violations of women's rights, despite constitutionally guaranteed equality. In practice, women, especially those living in rural areas under traditional leaders and governed by highly patriarchal Swazi law and custom, are often subjected to discrimination and harmful practices.

The government has yet to enact the Sexual Offences and Domestic Violence Bill developed in 2009 to protect women's rights. Neither has the government amended the Girls' and Women Protection Act, concerned with sexual abuse of girls under 16, but excludes marital rape. Violence against women is endemic. Survivors of gender-based violence have few avenues for help as both formal and customary justice processes discriminate against them.

Civil society activists have criticized the widely held view among traditional authorities that human rights and equal rights for women are foreign values that should be subordinated to Swazi culture and tradition.

Key International Actors

In August, Swaziland took over the leadership of the Southern African Development Community (SADC), the 15-nation regional economic institution, for a year. Swaziland's poor and deteriorating human rights record could weaken further the regional body's ability to press for human rights improvements across southern Africa.

Neighboring South Africa and regional bodies, the SADC and the African Union, have done little to press Swaziland to improve respect for human rights.

The United Nations Human Rights Council assessed Swaziland's human rights record under the Universal Periodic Review. In May 2016, Swaziland accepted 121 of 181 recommendations made by council member states to improve the human rights environment in the country. Authorities committed to improve protections of freedom of expression and association, and to take action to end child marriage. Swaziland rejected recommendations to end the death penalty and on the protection of migrant workers.

The International Labour Organization (ILO) provided technical assistance to reform repressive laws within the framework of the UN Universal Periodic Review, but achieved little progress towards desired reforms to guarantee freedom of association. The ILO, the Southern African Trade Union Co-ordination Council (SATUCC), and the International Trade Union Confederation visited Swaziland in February to push for reforms.

In 2016, the European Union said it continued to monitor progress towards the implementation of recommendations of the May 2015 European Parliament resolution that called on the government of Swaziland to immediately and unconditionally release Thulani Maseko and Bheki Makhubu, and all political prisoners, including Mario Masuku, President of the People's United Democratic Movement, and Maxwell Dlamini, Secretary-General of the Swaziland Youth Congress.

The resolution further urged Swaziland authorities to take steps to respect and promote freedom of expression, guarantee democracy and plurality, and establish a legislative framework allowing the registration, operation and full participation of political parties.

Syria

Greater United States and Russian engagement on Syria and efforts to reach a political settlement in 2016 failed to significantly reduce egregious violations of human rights and humanitarian law that have come to characterize the armed conflict there.

According to the Syrian Center for Policy Research, an independent Syrian research organization, the death toll from the conflict as of February 2016 was 470,000. The spread and intensification of fighting has led to a dire humanitarian crisis, with 6.1 million internally displaced people and 4.8 million seeking refuge abroad, according to the UN Office for the Coordination of Humanitarian Affairs. By mid-2016, an estimated 1 million people were living in besieged areas and denied life-saving assistance and humanitarian aid.

More than 117,000 have been detained or disappeared since 2011, the vast majority by government forces, including 4,557 between January and June 2016, according to the Syrian Network for Human Rights. Torture and ill-treatment are rampant in detention facilities; thousands have died in detention.

The Islamic State (also known as ISIS), and the former Al-Qaeda affiliate in Syria, Jabhat al-Nusra, which changed its name to Jabhat Fath al-Sham, were responsible for systematic and widespread violations, including targeting civilians with artillery, kidnappings, and executions. Non-state armed groups opposing the government also carried out serious abuses including indiscriminate attacks against civilians, using child soldiers, kidnapping, unlawfully blocking humanitarian aid, and torture.

In its fourth report, released this year, the Joint Investigative Mechanism between the Organisation for the Prohibition of Chemical Weapons (OPCW) and the UN concluded that Syrian government forces used chemicals in an attack in Idlib in March 2015. The inquiry also identified the military units responsible for flights connected to the attacks but could not name the commanders of the units due to the Syrian government's failure to respond to crucial queries. In an earlier report, the joint inquiry had reached the same conclusion for two other attacks, in 2014 and 2015. The inquiry also previously found that ISIS had used sulfur mustard gas in an attack on areas held by armed opposition groups in August 2015.

On October 28, Russia lost its seat at the Human Rights Council after failing to secure enough votes for re-election from UN member states. Several human rights and humanitarian relief organizations, including Human Rights Watch, had urged UN member states to hold Russia accountable for its involvement in possible war crimes.

Targeting Civilians, Indiscriminate Attacks, Use of Incendiary Weapons, Cluster Munitions, and Chemical Weapons

The number of civilian deaths from airstrikes and artillery decreased slightly following internationally brokered ceasefires in February and September, but only briefly, and unlawful attacks on civilians by all parties to the conflict persisted throughout the year. Syrian and Russian airstrikes continued to target, or indiscriminately strike civilian areas, including homes, markets, schools, and hospitals, using wide-area explosives, barrel bombs, cluster munitions, and flammable incendiary weapons.

In 2016, Human Rights Watch documented several attacks on homes, medical facilities, markets, and schools that appeared to be targeted, including a major airstrike by the Syrian-Russian coalition that hit al-Quds Hospital and surrounding areas on April 27, 2016, killing 58 civilians and patients. In August alone, there were several attacks on health facilities including in Idlib, Aleppo, Hama, and Homs.

Government forces used at least 13 types of internationally banned cluster munitions in over 400 attacks on opposition-held areas between July 2012 to August 2016, killing and injuring civilians, including children. The Syrian-Russian joint military operations, which began on September 30, 2015, have also extensively used internationally banned cluster munitions. Cluster munitions have been outlawed by most countries since their submunitions fall over a wide area, failing to distinguish between fighters and civilians and because many submunitions fail to explode and become de facto land mines that can explode, if disturbed, even after many years if they are not cleared.

Government forces, and their allies, also increasingly resorted to the use of incendiary weapons, with at least 18 documented attacks on opposition-held areas in Aleppo and Idlib between June 5 and August 10. In June, Russia Today broadcasted footage of incendiary weapons—specifically RBK-500 ZAB-2.5SM bombs—being mounted on a Russian Su-34 fighter-ground attack aircraft at a Syrian airbase. Incendiary weapons induce a chain of chemical reactions that ignite fires which are hard to extinguish and cause excruciatingly painful burns that are difficult to treat. A total of 113 countries including Russia (but not Syria) have ratified the Convention on Conventional Weapons protocol prohibiting the use of air-delivered incendiary weapons in areas with a "concentration of civilians."

While Russia continues to deny its involvement in incendiary weapons attacks in Syria, Syria has persistently ignored calls to sign the protocol and its military forces' use of incendiary weapons has been documented since the end of 2012.

Government forces also continued using toxic chemicals in several barrel bomb attacks in violation of the Chemical Weapons Convention. Syrian government helicopters dropped barrel bombs with toxic chemicals on residential neighborhoods in opposition-controlled parts of Aleppo city on August 10 and September 6.

In a report issued on August 24, 2016, a UN-appointed investigation attributed two chemical weapon attacks earlier in 2016 to the Syrian government and one to ISIS, which is already under UN sanctions.

Unlawful Restrictions on Humanitarian Assistance

The siege of civilian areas by government and pro-government forces and by armed opposition groups and blocking of humanitarian aid continued in 2016. The Syrian government continued requiring aid agencies to go through a bureaucratic approval system to obtain permits before accessing these areas. The UN secretary-general said that even in areas where aid was allowed in, the Syrian government has removed life-saving items from convoys. In February alone, the government prevented 80,000 medical treatment items, including diarrhea kits, emergency health kits, antibiotics, and other medicines, from going into besieged areas, the UN said.

Humanitarian conditions in areas besieged by government and pro-government forces rapidly deteriorated, forcing civilians to leave these areas. Residents of Daraya, Damascus countryside, were forced to evacuate the city following a four-year siege on August 25.

On September 19, 2016, airplanes struck a UN humanitarian aid convoy and a Syrian Red Crescent warehouse in Urum al-Kubra in Aleppo, killing 20 civilians and one staff member as they unloaded trucks. Most of the aid, including food and medical supplies, was to be distributed to at least 78,000 people, according to a Syrian Red Crescent statement. The UN said that the convoy had received proper permits from the Syrian government in advance to cross from government-controlled Aleppo to parts of opposition-held western Aleppo to deliver the aid.

Arbitrary Arrests, Enforced Disappearances, Torture, and Deaths in Custody

Arbitrary detention, ill-treatment, torture, and forced disappearances by government forces continue to be widespread and systematic in Syria, and take place within a climate of impunity. Deaths in government detention from widespread torture, abuse, starvation, beatings, and disease is also extensive with at least 12,679 persons dying in custody between March 2011 and June 2016, according to local monitors.

A September report by the UN Independent International Commission of Inquiry on Syria noted that while stigma and trauma has led to an underreporting of sexual violence, they were able to document some cases of sexual violence against male and female detainees by government officials.

Government security forces used excessive force to quell a riot inside the Hama Central Prison that began on May 1, resulting in some injuries, according to prisoners who spoke to Human Rights Watch.

On April 1, Judai Abdallah Nawfal, director of the Syrian Center for Civil Society and Democracy, was arrested by Syrian forces at a border checkpoint on his way to Lebanon. He was previously detained in 2014 and 1992. He was being held by the Military Intelligence Branch 235, barred from meeting lawyers and his family. Likewise, the fate of Bassel Khartabil, a 34-year-old free speech advocate, remains unknown with unconfirmed information indicating that he might have been tried and sentenced to death by a military court in the al-Qaboun Syrian Military Police headquarters, notorious for closed-door proceedings that lack fairness.

Jabhat al-Nusra and ISIS Abuses

In July 2016, Jabhat al-Nusra announced it was splitting from Al-Qaeda and forming Jabhet Fath al-Sham. Jabhat al-Nusra and ISIS were responsible for abuses including intentionally bombing civilian targets, abductions, arbitrary detentions, executions, and unlawful sieges in 2016. While information about ISIS and Jabhat al-Nusra abuses is hard to obtain because of the difficulties independent monitors have accessing areas under their control, both groups have publicized their unlawful attacks.

ISIS claimed responsibility for several car bombings and suicide attacks in Latakia governorate on May 23, including near bus stations and a hospital, announcing that it was targeting areas where "Alawites gather." The attacks killed 145 civilians, according to the Syrian Observatory for Human Rights.

On February 21, a series of ISIS bombings also targeted a Shia religious site in Damascus and a civilian neighborhood in Homs, according to media reports, killing 109 and injuring 235, including children.

On July 27, ISIS also claimed to have bombed Qamishli, northeast Syria, which is held by the People's Protection Units (YPG) military forces and Kurdish police (the Asayish). A truck bomb exploded near a PYD security center, killing 48 people and injuring about 140 others.

ISIS and Jabhat al-Nusra have also both targeted and executed civilians when conducting military operations in Syria. On January 17, according to media reports, ISIS killed at least 85 civilians and 50 Syrian soldiers during an offensive in the city of Deir al-Zour.

Women and girls continue to face discrimination and severe restrictions including on their freedom of movement in ISIS-held areas. A September report by the UN Independent International Commission of Inquiry on Syria noted that ISIS fighters forcibly married Sunni women living in ISIS-controlled areas.

ISIS also continues to torture, rape, murder, and sexually enslave Yezidi women and children, many of whom were captured in Iraq and taken to Syria.

News reports in 2016 also indicate that ISIS continues to execute men accused of homosexuality. In one reported case from Deir al-Zour governorate, a 15-year-old boy was stoned to death on January 3 after he was accused of being gay. At least 25 men have been murdered by ISIS in Syria on suspicion of homosexuality or for sodomy, according to the Syrian Observatory for Human Rights.

Abuses by Other Non-State Armed Groups

Non-state armed groups have launched indiscriminate mortar and other artillery strikes from areas under their control killing civilians in neighborhoods under government control in Aleppo, Damascus, Idlib, and Latakia. These attacks repeatedly hit known civilian objectives, including schools, mosques, and markets.

According to the Syrian state news agency SANA, 16 civilians were killed and 41 injured when an opposition armed group shelled a mosque on April 29 during Friday prayers in Aleppo city. On June 5, SANA reported that five people were killed and 77 injured when opposition armed groups fired rockets on government-held parts of Aleppo, including al-Ramouseh, the Electricity Company, al-Midan, and the public park, also hitting an Armenian church. Opposition armed group shelling also hit a maternity hospital in a government-held district of Aleppo on May 3, according to media reports.

Areas under Kurdish Democratic Union Party (PYD) Control

The Democratic Union Party (PYD) and allied parties have set up local governance structures in large parts of northern Syria.

Despite some progress in the demobilization of child soldiers in 2014 and 2015 and disciplining officers who allowed children to serve, the People's Protection Units (known as the YPG affiliated with the PYD) is still not meeting its commitment to demobilize children and to stop using boys and girls under the age of 18 in combat. Concerns also remain over the creation of a YPG "non-combatant category" for children aged 16 and 17.

Displacement Crisis

Relentless airstrikes, shelling, and widespread and systematic arbitrary detention, ill-treatment, torture, and forced disappearances have exacerbated a displacement crisis, both internally and externally, which has been further aggravated by shortfalls in international humanitarian aid funding.

Neighboring countries, including Lebanon, Jordan, and Turkey, sought to curb the massive inflow of refugees with unlawful administrative, legal, and even physical barriers. Despite a bilateral open-door treaty, Lebanon since early 2015 has imposed visa-like restrictions for Syrians seeking entry and maintains stringent residency renewal regulations, negatively impacting refugees' freedom of movement, access to education, and access to healthcare. During the year, Jordanian border authorities blocked entry of migrants and asylum seekers along the eastern stretch of its border with Syria, except for a period in the early summer when it allowed 20,000 to enter for security screening.

Following a June 21 attack by ISIS on the Rukban crossing, Jordan allowed no one to enter and blocked humanitarian assistance to nearly 70,000 Syrians stranded at the border, except for one delivery of aid lowered from a crane in early August. Turkish border authorities, likewise, continue to push back refugees. In March and April, Turkish border guards killed five Syrian asylum seekers, including a child, and smugglers trying to enter the country.

The Supporting Syria and the Region conference, held in London on February 4, raised over US$12 billion, half of which was for 2016. Countries attending UNHCR's Geneva Conference on March 30, however, failed to commit to more than a modest increase in resettlement places for refugees.

The lengthy procedures and limited number of resettlement places, coupled with dwindling aid resources and restrictions on access to the European Union by land, led many Syrian refugees to choose to attempt to enter the EU by sea.

Key International Actors

Efforts to push the UN Security Council to take more meaningful action in Syria failed. Peace talks held by the International Syria Support Group, meant to resolve the conflict in Syria, stalled in February 2016 with only some bilateral meetings between Russia and the United States (the ISSG co-chairs) resuming. A cessation of hostilities was negotiated for the end of February, which saw the decrease of civilian casualties, but it collapsed rapidly. Another cessation of hostilities was negotiated in September but broke down after an airstrike hit a UN aid convoy killing at least 20 people.

The Syrian government continued to repeatedly violate Security Council resolutions demanding safe and unhindered humanitarian access—including across conflict lines and across borders; that all parties cease "indiscriminate employment of weapons in populated areas, including shelling and aerial bombardment, such as the use of barrel bombs;" and an end to the practices of arbitrary detention, disappearance, and abductions, and the release of everyone who has been arbitrarily detained.

In addition to persistently discouraging or pre-emptively rejecting suggestions for meaningful Security Council action to curb violations by the Syrian government, Russia, along with the Iranian government, continued to provide the Syrian government with military assistance in 2016.

The United States also continued to lead a coalition of other states targeting ISIS in Iraq and Syria. France promised to increase its airstrikes in ISIS-controlled areas after ISIS claimed a series of attacks in Paris in November.

On October 21, the UN Human Rights council held a special session to discuss the grave human rights situation in Aleppo, adopting a resolution which calls for an end to aerial bombardments, affirms the need for humanitarian access, highlights the need for accountability, and mandates the Syria Commission of Inquiry to conduct a "comprehensive, independent special inquiry into the events in Aleppo," identifying perpetrators of alleged violations and abuses, and reporting to the council no later than March 2017.

Tajikistan

Tajikistan's human rights situation deteriorated sharply in 2016, as authorities sentenced the leadership of the country's main opposition party to lengthy prison terms, imprisoned human rights lawyers and other perceived government critics, and predetermined the result of a constitutional referendum that will allow authoritarian President Emomali Rahmon to remain president for life.

Authorities organized and led numerous acts of retaliation, including incidents of mob violence, against relatives of government critics abroad. Activists reported cases of torture and deaths in custody of persons imprisoned on politically motivated charges. The government continued its multi-year campaign to enforce severe restrictions on religious practice.

While the government took steps to enforce a 2013 law on the prevention of domestic violence, activists and service providers report that implementation of the law's core legal protections, including prosecutions of those who repeatedly engage in domestic violence, are lacking.

Harassment of Critics

The Tajik government has imprisoned more than 150 activists on politically motivated charges since the middle of 2015. Most are lawyers, perceived critics, and members of the Islamic Renaissance Party of Tajikistan (IRPT)—the country's largest opposition party before the government banned it in September 2015. It also continued to seek the extradition of peaceful opposition activists living abroad, mainly those from the opposition movement Group 24.

In February, following pressure from human rights groups and various governments, Belarusian authorities released Tajik activist Shabnam Khudoydodova, who had been detained in June 2015 in Brest, Belarus, pursuant to a Tajik extradition request and Interpol warrant. Khudoydodova, who had called in a series of online posts for democratic reforms and was living in St. Petersburg, was detained after Polish border guards refused her entry to Poland where she planned to seek asylum. Tajik authorities have charged her with extremism and are still seeking her extradition.

In May, a Dushanbe court sentenced businessman and government critic Abubakr Azizkhojaev to two-and-a-half years' imprisonment. Azizkhojaev, a successful entrepreneur, made public allegations of government corruption. He was detained on February 26, at his home in the capital, Dushanbe, initially, as a witness, but later was charged with "inciting national, racial, regional, or religious hatred" under article 189 of Tajikistan's criminal code for his remarks about Rahmon's son-in-law.

Friends and family who were able to visit Azizkhojaev in early May said they had seen burns on his body, and Azizkhojaev told relatives that jail officials had beaten him. A lawyer for Azizkhojaev told Human Rights Watch that his corruption allegations against the government formed the basis of the charges.

In June, Tajikistan's Supreme Court sentenced IRPT leaders to lengthy prison terms on charges of attempting to overthrow the government. The sentences followed an unfair trial initiated in retaliation for their peaceful political opposition and reflect the government's pervasive manipulation of the justice system and egregious violations of the right to freedom of expression.

The court sentenced the IRPT's first deputy and deputy chairmen, Saidumar Husaini and Mahmadali Hayit, to life in prison. Rahmatulloi Rajab, Sattor Karimov, Kiyomiddini Azav, and Abdukahhori Davlat, other party leaders, were all sentenced to 28 years in prison. Senior IRPT legal adviser, Zarafo Rahmoni, the only woman among the defendants, was sentenced to two years.

Other sentences for senior party members were: Zubaidullohi Rozik 25 years; Muhammadalii Fayzmyhammad, 23 years; while Vokhidhoni Kosiddin and Sadiddini Rustam, 20 years; Hikmatulloh Sayfullozoda, editor of the now-banned IRPT newspaper *Najot*, 16 years; Muhammadsharif Nabiev and Abdusamad Gayratov, 14 years.

The trial, which began on February 24, was closed to observers and according to their lawyers marked by serious violations of due process. Sources told Human Rights Watch that several defendants were subjected to torture or ill-treatment in pretrial detention. A lawyer who represented one of the defendants and was present in court throughout the trial stated that the government presented no evidence of the defendants' guilt, citing the allegations made in the indictments as established facts.

On June 2, the day the verdict was handed down, wives of several defendants announced they would hold a peaceful protest and walk to the local United Nations office to seek a consultation on the sentences. As the women proceeded toward the UN building, police detained them. They were fined for an administrative violation of "failure to obey police."

In September, during the Organization for Security and Co-operation in Europe (OSCE) Human Dimension Implementation Meeting (HDIM) in Warsaw, opposition activists staged peaceful protests to raise attention to human rights issues in Tajikistan and also spoke at the conference's several public sessions. In response, mobs attacked homes belonging to relatives of the activists over the next several days in the cities of Kulob, Khujand, Rudaki, Dushanbe, and Dangara. The government organized rallies among college students labeling the activists "enemies of the people."

The coordination and timing of these attacks across several cities on the same days, and authorities' failure to unequivocally condemn them, pointed to tacit endorsement, if not outright coordination, by the government.

Imprisonment and Harassment of Lawyers

In 2016, authorities continued a pattern of arresting, imprisoning, and intimidating numerous attorneys in retaliation for representing political opponents or their willingness to take on politically sensitive cases.

Since 2014, authorities have arrested or imprisoned at least six human rights lawyers: Shukhrat Kudratov, Fakhriddin Zokirov, Buzurgmehr Yorov, Jamshed Yorov, Nuriddin Makhkamov, and Dilbar Dodojonova. Zokirov was released after two lengthy periods of imprisonment, charges were ultimately dropped against Dodojonova, and Kudratov was amnestied in September. But the others remain behind bars, after dubious convictions or awaiting trial on specious charges. Others, including a well-known human rights lawyer Fayzinisso Vohidova, have been harassed and threatened with spurious criminal charges.

On February 11, 2016, a Vakhdat court sentenced Firuz Tabarov to 13-and-a-half years in prison for various crimes, including "extremism" (article 307) and "facilitating mercenary fighters" (article 401). He is the son of a prominent attorney Iskhok Tabarov, the only member of imprisoned opposition figure Zayd Saidov's legal team who did not face criminal charges. Tabarov was arrested on July 3, 2015, and, his father said, was tortured in pretrial detention and forced to make a false confession. He said authorities had provided no evidence of his son's involvement in extremist or mercenary activity and that the case was in retaliation for the father's role in defending Saidov.

On March 14, 2016, journalists reported that police arrested Firuz's brother, Daler Tabarov, on charges of failing to report a crime (article 347). He was in pretrial detention in Dushanbe awaiting trial at time of writing.

In October, following a largely closed trial, a Dushanbe court sentenced lawyers Buzurgmehr Yorov and Nuriddin Makhkamov to 23 and 21 years in prison, respectively, on various charges, including fraud and "extremism," in what appeared to be retaliation for their legal representation of IRPT members. Yorov's arrest on September 28, 2015, came one day after he gave an interview in which he said that officers from the Police Unit for Combating Organized Crime had beaten his client IRPT, deputy party chairman Umarali Hisaynov, following arrest.

On August 23, authorities arrested Buzurgmehr's brother, lawyer Jamshed Yorov, on charges of "disclosing state secrets," accusing him of defying an order forbidding the publication of the June 2016 sentence of the IRPT leaders. He was released in September but was denied access to a lawyer or his relatives throughout his detention.

The Tajik government has also taken steps to extend its control over the legal profession, significantly curtailing its independence. In November 2015, authorities approved a new law requiring all lawyers to renew their legal licenses with the Justice Ministry, instead of the independent bar association or licensing body, and to retake the bar examination every five years.

Lawyers told Human Rights Watch and the Norwegian Helsinki Committee that the exam included questions on a broad range of subjects unrelated to law, such as history, culture, and politics, and that they are concerned it is being used to exclude those who take on politically sensitive cases.

Freedom of Expression

Under the pretext of protecting national security, Tajikistan's state telecommunications agency regularly blocks websites that carry information potentially critical of the government, including Facebook, Gmail, Radio Ozodi, the website of Radio Free Europe's Tajik service, and opposition websites. In early November, authorities forced the closure of *Nigoh*, one of Tajikistan's last independent newspapers after it had ostensibly insulted president Rahmon by misspelling the word "president." Also in November, another news outlet, TojNews, shut down also citing political pressure.

Domestic Violence

By September 2016, authorities had taken several steps to combat domestic violence against women and children, operating at least 12 police stations staffed by female police inspectors who underwent training in gender-sensitive, community policing. The Ministry of Internal Affairs also developed further guidelines on the implementation of Tajikistan's 2013 law on the prevention of violence in the family.

However, survivors of domestic violence, lawyers, and service providers reported that the law remains largely unimplemented and that victims of domestic violence continue to suffer inadequate protection.

Key International Actors

With a few notable exceptions, the response of key international partners to Tajikistan's crackdown on the opposition and perceived critics has remained largely muted.

In June, the European Union held its annual human rights dialogue with Tajikistan, raising concerns about torture and restrictions on freedom of expression and religion. On June 9, in a resolution on the "situation of prisoners of conscience" in Tajikistan, the European Parliament called specifically for the release of all those "imprisoned on politically motivated charges."

On April 15, the US State Department designated Tajikistan a "country of particular concern" with respect to religious freedom, highlighting "systematic, ongoing, [and] egregious violations of religious freedom." The designation allows the US government to sanction Tajikistan, although the Obama administration declined to do so based on national security concerns.

Following a country visit to Tajikistan in March, the UN special rapporteur on the right to freedom of opinion and expression stressed his "grave concern about increasing restrictions on opposition parties, civil society and the media over the past year." In June, he expressed his dismay at the lengthy sentences imposed on the IRPT leadership.

Following its Universal Periodic Review in May, the Tajik government accepted recommendations to ensure fair trials for activists, political leaders, and lawyers on trial, which contrasted sharply with authorities' actions on the ground, but rejected recommendations to release activists and lawyers detained on politically motivated grounds.

Thailand

The year was tumultuous for Thailand with the passing of King Bhumibhol Adulyadej on October 13 after a reign of 70 years. The Thai government, led by Prime Minister Gen. Prayut Chan-ocha, repeatedly failed in 2016 to fulfill pledges made to the United Nations General Assembly and Human Rights Council to respect human rights and restore democratic rule. A new constitution, which will entrench unaccountable and abusive military power, was adopted in a referendum marked by repressive tactics against critics of the proposed constitution.

Referendum and New Constitution

In the lead up to the constitutional referendum on August 7, the ruling National Council for Peace and Order (NCPO) junta curtailed the rights to freedom of expression, association, and peaceful assembly through repressive laws such the Referendum Act, the Computer Crime Act, and article 116 of the penal code on sedition, as well as NCPO orders censoring media and preventing public gatherings of more than five people.

Thai authorities arrested at least 120 politicians, activists, journalists, and supporters of political movements who had criticized the proposed constitution, publicly announced they would vote "no," urged voters to reject the draft constitution, or sought to monitor voting.

The government also did not provide equal access to state media for opponents of the proposed constitution, and failed to ensure that the election commission overseeing the referendum acted impartially. The constitution passed with support from 61 percent of voters.

The 2014 interim constitution permitted the NCPO to wield unlimited administrative, legislative, and judicial power without effective oversight or accountability, including for human rights violations. The new constitution endorses such powers, and ensures that the junta cannot be held accountable for abuses it has committed since taking power in the May 2014 coup. Instead of paving the way for a return to democratic civilian rule as promised in its so-called road map, the junta has created and imposed a political structure that appears designed to prolong the military's grip on power.

Censorship and Restrictions on Free Expression

The junta continued to censor public discussions related to human rights, democracy, the monarchy, and the NCPO's performance. On September 28, Amnesty International cancelled its Bangkok press conference to launch a report on torture in Thailand after authorities threatened to arrest senior Amnesty International staff for working illegally as foreigners in the country.

The NCPO granted power to the National Broadcasting and Telecommunications Commission to punish critical media. Outspoken news analysts at Voice TV and Spring News channels were suspended because of their critical reporting about military rule. In July 2016, Peace TV channel was forced off the air for 30 days.

The junta regularly exercises its power to ban political assembly of more than five persons. Protesters who take part in peaceful protests to express disagreement with the junta face up to two years in prison.

The junta also broadly used sedition charges, which carry up to seven years in prison, to prosecute those who express opposition to military rule. In March, the military in Chiang Mai province arrested and charged Theerawan Charoensuk with sedition for posting a photo on Facebook of her holding a red bowl inscribed with Thai New Year greetings from former Prime Ministers Thaksin Shinawatra and Yingluck Shonawatra. Since the coup, at least 38 people have been charged with sedition.

The junta continues to prosecute people under the *lese majeste* (insulting the monarchy) laws, an offense punishable by up to 15 years in prison. Since the May 2014 coup, Thai authorities have charged at least 68 persons with *lese majeste*, mostly for posting or sharing comments online.

The crackdown has intensified since the death of King Bhumibhol Adulyadej on October 13, with the authorities arresting 10 people and investigating 194 new cases. There were at least seven cases of vigilante violence targeting those accused of making negative comments about the late king or Crown Prince Maha Vajiralongkorn, or not wearing black during the 30-day mourning period.

The government in 2016 also requested that the United States, United Kingdom, Sweden, France, Australia, New Zealand, Japan, Cambodia, and Laos send back Thai citizens who sought political asylum from persecution under *lese majeste* charges.

Arbitrary Detention and Military Courts

On September 12, General Prayut revoked three NCPO orders that empowered military courts to try civilians for national security offenses, including sedition and *lese majeste*. However, the action is not retroactive and does not affect the more than 1,800 cases already brought against civilians in military courts. The military also retains power to arrest, detain, and interrogate civilians for a wide range of offenses without safeguards against abuse or accountability for human rights violations.

The NCPO summarily dismissed allegations that the military has tortured and ill-treated detainees, even after the death of fortune-teller Suriyan Sucharitpolwong and Police Maj. Prakrom Warunprapa—both charged with *lese majeste*—during their detention at the 11th Army Circle military base in Bangkok in November 2015.

At time of writing, 45 civilians were detained at the remand facility inside the 11th Army Circle military base in Bangkok without effective safeguards against abuse.

The NCPO has summoned members of the Pheu Thai Party and the United Front for Democracy against Dictatorship (UDD), known as the "Red Shirts," as well as other activists accused by authorities of opposing military rule, for "attitude adjustment." Failure to report to the NCPO's summons is considered a criminal offense. The NCPO compelled persons released from "attitude adjustment" programs to sign an agreement stating they will not make political comments, be involved in political activities, or travel abroad without permission. Failure to comply with such agreements can result in a new detention or two years in prison.

Lack of Accountability for Politically Motivated Violence

Despite evidence showing that government security forces were responsible for the majority of casualties during the 2010 political confrontation, which left at least 90 dead and more than 2,000 injured, no policymakers from the then Abhisit Vejjajiva government or military personnel have been charged for unlawfully killing and wounding protesters or passersby.

While UDD leaders and supporters faced serious criminal charges for the 2010 street protests, there has been little progress in investigating or prosecuting alleged criminal offenses by the People's Alliance for Democracy (PAD), knowns as the "Yellow Shirts," during political confrontations in 2008 or the People's Democratic Reform Committee (PDRC) in 2013-2014.

Violence and Abuses in Southern Border Provinces

Since January 2004, more than 6,000 ethnic Malay Muslims and Thai Buddhists have been killed in the armed conflict in Thailand's southern border provinces.

An ongoing peace dialogue between the government and the Barisan Revolusi Nasional and other separatist groups in the loose network of Majlis Syura Patani made little progress. Insurgents continue to violate the laws of war by targeting civilians in bombings, roadside ambushes, drive-by shootings, and assassinations. Evidence strongly suggests that separatist groups expanded their operations beyond Thailand's southern border provinces and carried out a string of explosions and arson attacks in seven tourist towns on August 11 and 12.

On September 6, a bomb detonated outside a school in Narathiwat province as parents dropped off their children, killing a father and his 4-year-old daughter. The blast also wounded at least 10 teachers, parents, and traffic police. Since 2004, alleged insurgents have torched or bombed more than 200 schools, and killed at least 184 teachers.

The government still failed to prosecute security force personnel responsible for illegal killings, torture, and other abuses against ethnic Malay Muslims. In many cases, Thai authorities provided financial compensation to victims or their families in exchange for their agreement not to pursue criminal prosecution of abusive officials.

Enforced Disappearances

Thailand signed the International Convention for the Protection of All Persons from Enforced Disappearance in January 2012, but has yet to ratify the treaty. The penal code still does not recognize enforced disappearance as a criminal offense.

Since 1980, the UN Working Group on Enforced or Involuntary Disappearances has recorded 82 cases of enforced disappearance in Thailand. Many of these cases implicated Thai officials—including the disappearances of prominent Muslim lawyer Somchai Neelapaijit in March 2004, and ethnic Karen activist Por Cha Lee "Billy" Rakchongcharoen in April 2014. None have been successfully resolved.

Human Rights Defenders

The killing and enforced disappearance of more than 30 human rights defenders and other civil society activists since 2001 remains a serious blot on Thailand's human rights record. Even high-profile cases investigated by the Justice Ministry's Department of Special Investigation rarely result in prosecution. Police made no progress in investigating the fate of land rights activist Den Khamlae, who went missing in a forest near his home in Chaiyaphum province in April 2016. Government pledges to develop measures to protect human rights defenders remained unfulfilled.

Thai authorities and private companies continue to use defamation lawsuits to retaliate against those reporting human rights violations. On September 20, the Bangkok South Criminal Court found British labor rights activist Andy Hall guilty of criminal defamation and violating the Computer Crime Act and sentenced him to four years in prison (which the judge suspended because Hall's work was considered beneficial to Thai society).

Hall's conviction was based on a complaint filed by Natural Fruit Co. Ltd.—one of Thailand's biggest pineapple processors—regarding a report alleging serious labor rights abuses at one of its factories. Hall left Thailand on November 7, saying he feared for his safety amid legal problems and growing harassment.

In July, the military filed a complaint against prominent activists Somchai Homlaor, Pornpen Khongkachonkie, and Anchana Heemmina, accusing them of criminal defamation and violating the Computer Crimes Act for reporting about torture and other ill-treatment of insurgent suspects in the southern border provinces. In September, the military accused Sirikan Charoensiri, a key member of Thai Lawyers for Human Rights, of sedition for accompanying and providing legal assistance to activists from the New Democracy Movement during their peaceful anti-coup protest in Bangkok in June 2015.

Refugees, Asylum Seekers, and Migrant Workers

Thailand has not ratified the 1951 Refugee Convention and its 1967 Protocol. Thai authorities continued to treat asylum seekers, including those whom the UN recognized as refugees, as illegal migrants who are subject to arrest and deportation.

The government has failed to provide information regarding the current whereabouts and well-being of the over 100 ethnic Uighurs and Chinese dissidents deported to China in 2015, in violation of international law.

The government announced in June that it needed more time to put in place a process, in collaboration with Burma and the UN, to repatriate more than 120,000 refugees living in the nine camps on the Thai-Burma border.

The government did not allow the office of the UN High Commissioner for Refugees to conduct refugee status determination screenings for ethnic Rohingya from Burma. Rohingya men, women, and children have been placed in indefinite detention in immigration detention centers and government shelters across Thailand.

Migrant workers from Burma, Cambodia, Laos, and Vietnam are vulnerable to physical abuses, indefinite detention, and extortion by Thai authorities; severe labor rights abuses and exploitation by employers; and violence and human trafficking by criminals, sometimes in collaboration with corrupt officials.

The government declared combating human trafficking to be a "national priority," including by enforcing the Human Trafficking Criminal Procedure Act, with mixed results. At time of writing, efforts by the Command Center to Combat Illegal Fishing to suppress human trafficking in fishing and seafood food processing sectors were still limited.

There was little progress in the trial of Lt. Gen. Manas Kongpa—together with 52 local politicians, community leaders, businessmen, and alleged criminals—for trafficking ethnic Rohingya to Malaysia. Migrant workers remain fearful of reporting trafficking crimes or cooperating with Thai authorities due to lack of effective protection.

Anti-Narcotics Policy

The government has failed to pursue criminal investigations of extrajudicial killings related to anti-drug operations, especially the more than 2,800 killings that accompanied then-Prime Minister Thaksin Shinawatra's "war on drugs" in 2003.

In June, the government announced a plan to remove methamphetamine from category 1, the most serious substance on the controlled substance list, in order to ease prison overcrowding and facilitate drug users' access to rehabilitation. While the government indicated in September that it would transfer drug dependency treatment to the Ministry of Public Health, alleged drug users are still held in drug detention centers operated by the Ministry of Interior and the military without due process and subject to an exhausting regime of exercise and military-style drills the government claims constitute "treatment."

Environment

The Pollution Control Department received a budget allocation in January 2016 to clean up Klity Creek in Kanchanaburi province. The creek is contaminated by lead from a badly regulated and now-defunct lead processing factory that presents a health threat to hundreds of ethnic Karen families living downstream. In a landmark 2013 ruling, the Supreme Court ordered the government to clean up the site. At time of writing, however, no clean-up had begun.

Key International Actors

In June, Thailand was defeated by Kazakhstan in a bid to seek a non-permanent seat on the UN Security Council for 2017-2018.

UN bodies and Thailand's major allies continued to urge the junta to respect human rights and return the country to democratic civilian rule through free and fair elections. During the Human Rights Council's Universal Periodic Review of Thailand in May, the Office of the High Commissioner for Human Rights and many countries expressed concerns regarding violations of fundamental rights and freedoms since the May 2014 coup.

In January 2015, based on recommendations from the International Coordinating Committee of National Institutions for the Promotion and Protection of Human

Rights, Thailand's National Human Rights Commission was downgraded due to the lack of independence in selecting commissioners and its own poor performance.

The US State Department upgraded Thailand from a Tier 3 ranking to Tier 2 (Watch List) in its annual Trafficking in Persons Report despite concerns by human rights groups about the lack of significant progress in government actions. The European Commission raised human trafficking and forced labor on Thai fishing boats when putting Thailand on formal notice for possible trade sanctions connected to illegal, unreported, and unregulated fishing.

Tunisia

Six years after ousting its authoritarian president, Zine el-Abidine Ben Ali, Tunisia continued to consolidate human rights protections, even as serious violations continued.

A reform of the code of criminal procedures gave detainees the right to a lawyer in pre-charge detention, thus improving their protection against torture, ill-treatment, and coerced confessions.

Tunisian lawmakers adopted laws establishing the High Judicial Council, a step that should enhance judicial independence and the constitutional court, a body that will have the power to strike down laws that are not in harmony with the constitution, including its chapter on rights and freedoms.These two institutions had not yet been set up at time of writing.

Serious human rights violations continued, including torture, arbitrary house arrests, and travel restrictions under a state of emergency declared in November 2015. Violations of lesbian, gay, bisexual, and transgender (LGBT) rights, as well as lack of accountability for past human rights violations, also persisted.

President Beji Caid Essebsi declared the state of emergency after a suicide attack on a bus killed 12 presidential guards; it remained in effect at time of writing after being renewed on September 16, 2016. The state of emergency is based on a 1978 decree that empowers authorities, after declaring a state of emergency, to ban strikes or demonstrations deemed to threaten public order, and to prohibit gatherings "likely to provoke or sustain disorder." It gives the government broad powers to restrict media and to place persons under house arrest.

Constitution

The 2014 constitution upheld many key civil, political, social, economic, and cultural rights. However, the constitution does not abolish the death penalty, even though authorities have observed a de facto moratorium on its application since the early 1990s.

Authorities made progress in harmonizing legislation with the constitution. For example, on February 2, 2016, parliament adopted revisions to the Code of Criminal Procedure granting suspects the right to a lawyer from the onset of deten-

HUMAN
RIGHTS
WATCH

"All This for a Joint"

Tunisia's Repressive Drug Law and a Roadmap for Its Reform

tion, and shortening the maximum duration of pre-charge detention to 48 hours, renewable once, for all crimes except for terrorism cases where pre-charge detention can last up to 15 days.

The 2014 constitution guarantees judicial independence and calls for establishing a Supreme Judicial Council (SJC). On November 16, 2015, parliament approved a law creating the SJC, whose functions will include making judicial appointments and overseeing discipline and the career progression of judges. The president, justice minister, and other executive branch officials are all barred from sitting on the SJC, unlike the discredited High Judicial Council (HJC) of the Ben Ali era.

Despite these positive steps, Tunisia had yet to carry out other extensive reforms to bring its legislation in line both with the constitution and international standards.

The constitution envisages the creation of a constitutional court that is empowered to rule on the constitutionality of laws, and that can invalidate laws that are not in conformity with human rights standards affirmed in the constitution. On December 3, 2015, the parliament adopted law No.50 creating the Constitutional Court, which is empowered to invalidate laws that are not in conformity with the constitution's human rights provisions. However, at time of writing, authorities had yet to set up the court and appoint its members.

Freedom of Expression

In 2011, the transitional authorities liberalized the press code and law pertaining to the broadcast media, eliminating most of the criminal penalties these laws impose on speech offenses. However, the penal code, Code of Military Justice, and the Telecommunications Law still contain articles that impose prison terms as a punishment for speech offenses.

On September 26, a military prosecutor charged journalist Jamel Arfaoui with "offending the army," under article 91 of the Code of Military Justice, which provides for up to three years in prison for this offense. His accusation stems from an article he published on July 30, in which he questioned the lack of investigation by the army into a military plane crash that killed two officers. He was free pending trial at time of writing.

Penal code article 125 that criminalizes "insulting a public official" has served, in practice, as a means by which the police can arrest individuals—some of whom ended up being prosecuted and imprisoned—merely for arguing with police, for being slow to heed orders, or when they filed a complaint or were suspected of being likely to file a complaint against police.

A journalist and a blogger were prosecuted in 2016 under article 125. Moez Jemai, who works for an online newspaper, was arrested in Gabes, on September 18, and charged the following day with insulting the police. On September 19, well-known blogger Lina Ben Mhenni appeared before the first instance tribunal in Mednine on a charge of insulting the police. The case goes back to 2014 when she alleged she was beaten up by police in front of the Jerba police station.

Transitional Justice and Accountability

Although ex-President Ben Ali's security forces used torture extensively, authorities have failed in the five years since his overthrow to investigate or hold anyone accountable for the vast majority of torture cases. They also have held no one accountable for the politically motivated long-term imprisonment of thousands of persons after unfair trials during his tenure.

On December 24, 2013, the National Constituent Assembly (NCA) adopted the Law on Establishing and Organizing Transitional Justice.

The law sets out a comprehensive approach to addressing past human rights abuses. It provides criminal accountability via specialized chambers within the civil court system for human rights violations that occurred between July 1955 and December 2013.

The law also established a Truth and Dignity Commission tasked with uncovering the truth about abuses committed between July 1955, shortly before Tunisia's independence from France, and the law's adoption in 2013. The NCA elected 15 of the commission's members on May 15, 2014. The commission declared that it had received 62.065 complaints from people alleging human rights abuses and had begun processing them. On November 17 and 18, the Truth and Dignity Commission held the first public hearings of victims of human rights violations. The hearings were aired live on national TV and radio stations.

The family and friends of ex-President Ben Ali diverted public funds and lands for their benefit, instrumentalizing state institutions such as public banks, the judiciary, and the police to benefit themselves and to punish those who resisted their business initiatives, according to the 2012 report of the National Commission to Investigate Corruption and Embezzlement.

In June 2016, parliament started debating the Law on Economic and Financial Reconciliation, which the government approved in 2015 with strong support from President Caid Essebsi. The bill, if adopted would halt ongoing and future prosecutions and trials of public servants and business people for financial corruption or misuse of public funds, provided that the person negotiates a "reconciliation" agreement with a state-run commission to repay unlawfully obtained money to the state treasury.

Counterterrorism and Security

Tunisian security forces continued to clash sporadically with Islamist militants, causing casualties on both sides. On March 7, a group of militants attacked the town of Ben Guerdane, close to the border with Libya, targeting an army barracks and the homes of military officers. Thirty-six militants were killed in the battle that followed, along with 7 civilians and 12 members of the security forces.

In terrorism cases, a law adopted on February 2 gives to the investigative judge and prosecutor the authority to delay access to a lawyer for 48 hours after the beginning of detention, and empowers police to hold a terrorism-related suspect for up to 15 days.

Since the emergency law came into force in November 2015 at least 139 Tunisians have been confined without charge pursuant to indefinite house arrest orders that the police deliver orally, providing no document and thus hindering the ability of the affected person to mount a court challenge. The measures have created economic hardship, stigmatized those targeted and prevented them from pursuing their study or business.

Torture and Ill-Treatment

The National Constituent Assembly in October 2013 approved legislation to create the High Authority for the Prevention of Torture. Parliament elected its 16 members only on March 30, 2016. The High Authority has the mandate to carry out unannounced inspections of detention sites.

In its concluding observations, after considering the third periodic report of Tunisia during its sessions held on April 19 and 21, 2016, the UN Committee against Torture welcomed constitutional and legislative progress in the fight against torture. However, it also noted with concern the persistence of torture in police custody, and the consistent reports of the lack of due diligence exercised by judges and judicial police during investigations into torture or ill-treatment.

Women's Rights

Tunisia, long viewed as the most progressive Arab country with respect to women's rights, marked additional strides in this field. The adoption of a gender parity requirement in the new electoral law required political parties to alternate male and females on each of their lists of candidates. This resulted in the election of 68 women to parliament in 2014, out of 217 seats. In June 2016, parliament adopted an amendment to the electoral law that required political parties to have at least half of their electoral lists headed by women, in future local and regional elections.

Parliament adopted a law on November 10, 2015 that allows women to travel with their minor children without getting permission from the children's father.

While Tunisia's personal status code gives women a wide array of rights, the code retains some discriminatory provisions, especially with respect to inheritance.

Sexual Orientation and Gender Identity

The penal code punisheds consensual same-sex conduct with up to three years in prison. Anal testing is used as the main evidence in order to convict men for homosexuality. In two high-profile cases in 2015, at least seven young men were arrested and subjected to anal examinations by forensic doctors, whose reports were used as evidence to convict them of sodomy and imprison them, even though it is well-documented that such exams lack medical value.

On appeal, their sentences were reduced to two months in the first case, and one month in the second.

The United Nations Committee against Torture, in its most recent evaluation of Tunisia, condemned the use of anal examinations as to prove homosexual conduct.

Key International Actors

On September 22 and 23, the UN Committee on Economic, Social and Cultural Rights examined the third periodic report of Tunisia during its 59th session. In its concluding observations, the committee inquired about the steps being taken to increase equality among regions and refugees' access to education, employment, and basic services. It also expressed concern about the high rate of school dropouts, among other issues. The committee recommended that Tunisia increase accountability for social and economic rights violations by raising awareness among judges, prosecutors, and lawyers about these rights.

On September 14, the European Parliament adopted a resolution that voiced concern about the "current economic and budgetary difficulties inherent to the instability of the transition period" and called for increased financial support to Tunisia. It expressed concern at overcrowding, lack of food, and insanitary conditions in prisons, among other issues.

On October 28, Tunisia was elected to the UN Human Rights Council for a three-year term beginning in 2017.

Turkey

On July 15, 2016, elements of the military attempted to carry out a coup d'état against President Recep Tayyip Erdoğan and the Justice and Development Party (AKP) government. The attempted coup left at least 241 citizens and government law enforcement dead. During the attempted coup fighter jets bombed Turkey's parliament. In the aftermath, the government declared a state of emergency, jailed thousands of soldiers and embarked on a wholesale purge of public officials, police, teachers, judges, and prosecutors. Most of those jailed, dismissed, or suspended were accused of being followers of the US-based cleric Fethullah Gülen. The government, with the support of main opposition parties, accuses the Gülen movement of masterminding the coup and labels it a terrorist organization. However, the crackdown also extended to the pro-Kurdish opposition party, with two leaders and other MPs arrested and placed in pretrial detention, along with many of its elected mayors, denying millions of voters their elected representatives.

The war in Syria continues to impact Turkey, which hosts an estimated 2.7 million Syrian refugees. There have been regular bomb attacks in Turkey by individuals allegedly linked to the Islamic State (also known as ISIS). Authorities blamed ISIS for a June attack in which three suicide bombers targeted Istanbul airport killing 45, and an August attack on a Kurdish wedding party in Gaziantep that killed 57.

In August, Turkish military forces entered the ISIS-occupied Syrian border town of Jarablus and attacked Syrian Kurdish forces in the area, apparently because of their links to the Turkey-based armed group the Kurdistan Workers' Party (PKK). The PKK and a related armed group, the Kurdistan Freedom Falcons (TAK), stepped up attacks in 2016, including a March suicide attack killing 37 in central Ankara, and a June attack in Istanbul killing 11, as well as regular attacks on military and police targets.

Crackdown after the Attempted Coup

The crackdown that followed the coup attempt was symptomatic of the government's increasing authoritarianism. Under the state of emergency, the president presides over the cabinet, which can pass decrees without parliamentary scrutiny or possibility of appeal to the constitutional court. Many decrees passed contain measures that conflict with basic human rights safeguards and Turkey's obligations under international and domestic law.

These include provisions allowing for dismissal from public service without an investigation, confiscation of property without judicial review, police custody of up to 30 days, and the reintroduction of incommunicado detention in which detainees can be denied access to a lawyer in the first five days of custody, giving rise to heightened risks of ill-treatment.

Turkey temporarily derogated from (asserted the right to place extraordinary restrictions on) many of the protections in the European Convention on Human Rights and International Covenant on Civil and Political Rights, although it is prohibited from derogating from core obligations, including the absolute prohibition on torture or ill-treatment of detainees.

The weakening of safeguards against abuse in detention under the state of emergency was accompanied by increased reports of torture and ill-treatment in police detention, such as beating and stripping detainees, use of prolonged stress positions, and threats of rape, as well as threats to lawyers and interference with medical examinations. While many allegations arose in relation to members of the military and police detained in connection with the coup, they were not the only groups who reported ill-treatment post-coup, and Kurdish detainees in the southeast had reported similar abuses over the past year.

The scale of dismissals and prosecutions in connection with the coup and weakened safeguards gave rise to serious concerns that the legitimate prosecution of those suspected of involvement in the coup attempt is being conducted without due process.

Over 100,000 public officials and civil servants have been dismissed or suspended. These include around 28,000 teachers alleged to be Gülen supporters and labelled by the government to be part of a terrorist organization.

Many detainees—including teachers, police, public officials—are placed in pretrial detention despite a lack of evidence of criminal wrong-doing or compelling grounds for custody. At least 2,200 judges and prosecutors were jailed pending investigation, reportedly because their names appeared on a list of alleged Gülen supporters. With 3,400 permanently dismissed for the same reason, their assets frozen, over one-fifth of Turkey's judiciary has been removed. Around 11,000 teachers in the southeast who were mainly members of the left-leaning Eğitim Sen trade union were also suspended.

Freedoms of Expression, Association, and Assembly

Government-led efforts to silence media criticism and scrutiny of government policy in Turkey involved five main trends: the prosecution and jailing of journalists; takeover of media companies—including the daily *Zaman* newspaper—by appointing government-approved trustees and seizing assets and the closing down of media; removal of critical television stations from the main state-owned satellite distribution platform and their closure; physical attacks and threats against journalists; and government pressure on media to fire critical journalists and cancel their press accreditation. Blocking of news websites critical to the government also increased. Turkey made the highest number of requests to Twitter of any country to censor individual accounts.

In January 2016, over 1,000 university lecturers who signed a petition criticizing government policy in the southeast and calling for a return to political negotiations with the PKK, were harshly targeted by Erdoğan in speeches and then subjected to a criminal investigation for "insulting" the Turkish state. The investigation had not been concluded at time of writing. Some universities dismissed signatories of the petition, and 68 were fired by decree in September and October.

International pressure, including from the UN Secretary General, helped to secure the release of some journalists from unjustified detention, including Reporters Sans Frontieres (RSF) representative Erol Onderoğlu in June. However, following the coup attempt such pressure appeared to have less effect.

Following the coup attempt, the government closed down by decree over 160 media outlets, most linked to the Gülen movement or Kurdish media. The number of journalists in pretrial detention on the basis of their writing and journalistic activities surged to 144 by mid-November, making Turkey once again a world leader in jailing journalists. Presenting no evidence of criminal wrongdoing, authorities detained many reporters and columnists employed by media outlets allegedly linked to Gülen. Among those jailed pending investigation were veteran journalists and commentators who have been prominent government critics such as Nazlı Ilıcak, Şahin Alpay, Ahmet Altan, and Mehmet Altan.

Authorities detained journalists and writers on charges of links with the PKK but again presented no evidence to support the charges. Among this group were novelists Necmiye Alpay and Aslı Erdoğan. Authorities closed down the pro-Kurdish daily *Özgür Gündem* in August and placed dozens of journalists who had participated in a solidarity campaign with the newspaper under investigation for "spreading terrorist propaganda."

Cumhuriyet daily newspaper editor Can Dündar and the Ankara bureau chief Erdem Gül were convicted in May and sentenced to over five years' imprisonment for revealing state secrets by publishing evidence of arms being sent to Syria. Dündar and Gül have appealed the verdict. Dündar is outside Turkey. In November, authorities arrested Murat Sabuncu who became *Cumhurıyet* editor after Dündar, as well as nine writers and board members from the newspaper.

Using state of emergency powers, in November the government suspended by decree the activities of 370 nongovernmental associations, among them a children's rights group, three lawyers' associations with a human rights focus, and women's rights and humanitarian organizations in the southeast.

Authorities frequently impose arbitrary bans on public assemblies and violently disperse peaceful demonstrations. For the second year running, the Istanbul governor's office banned the annual Istanbul Gay and Trans Pride marches in June 2016, citing concerns about security threats and public order.

Escalating Conflict in the Southeast

The breakdown in 2015 of a two-and-a-half-year ceasefire with the PKK and the Turkish government's peace process with the PKK's imprisoned leader Abdullah Öcalan triggered a rapid escalation of violence in 2016.

Intense security operations in the period January to May in towns in the southeast where the city militias linked to the PKK had become entrenched resulted in displacement of up to 400,000 residents. Amidst heavy clashes, hundreds of residents, police, soldiers and PKK-linked militants died.

In Cizre security forces' attacks killed and injured unarmed residents including children and destroyed civilian homes. Around 130 wounded militants and unarmed activists sheltering in three basements surrounded by the security forces were killed in circumstances which the state has neither explained nor effectively investigated.

Blanket curfews continued for many months during security operations in Cizre and other towns and neighborhoods, impeding access for journalists and human rights investigators. Authorities demolished large areas of the majority Kurdish cities of Diyarbakır, Şırnak, Nusaybin, and Yüksekova.

In June, the government introduced a law making any prosecution of the military and public officials, including the police, engaged in counterterrorism operations dependent on administrative permission. The law effectively grants immunity from prosecution to the security forces for abuses committed in the recent operations in the southeast in violation of Turkey's duty to investigate such abuses.

In May, the government secured the lifting of the parliamentary immunity of 148 deputies, 53 of them members of the pro-Kurdish Peoples' Democracy Party (HDP) facing investigation on terrorism charges. In August, the government introduced a decree appointing trustees to take over 28 municipalities (24 of them in the southeast), removing elected mayors and council members from office. By mid-November, 53 had been dismissed and 39, including Gültan Kışanak and Fırat Anlı, co-mayors of Diyarbakır, arrested pending investigation. In November, nine HDP members of parliament including party leaders Selahattin Demirtaş and Figen Yüksekdağ were arrested and placed in pretrial detention.

Refugees and Migrants

Turkey continued to host large numbers of refugees, asylum seekers, and migrants, primarily from Syria, but also from Afghanistan, Iraq, and other countries. The number of asylum seekers transiting to Greece fell after the March EU-Turkey migration deal (see European Union chapter). Despite increased aid and some efforts by authorities, most refugees and asylum seekers lack effective protection, education, or formal employment, with high rates of child labor and a particularly precarious situation for non-Syrians. Hundreds of thousands of Syrian children are still not attending school. A January decree allowing some Syrians to apply for work permits has had little effect to date.

Turkey's border gates and entire land border with Syria remain closed although people seriously injured in fighting are admitted to Turkey for medical treatment. Syrian refugees attempting to cross into Turkey at unofficial crossing points are summarily pushed back into Syria and some asylum seekers and smugglers attempting the crossing have been shot dead or beaten by Turkish border guards.

Women's Rights

Following its July review of Turkey, the UN Committee on the Elimination of Discrimination against Women (CEDAW Committee) made many recommendations to the government to address gender inequality and remove obstacles for women and girls to access education, employment, justice, and reproductive health. It noted particular obstacles for Kurdish women and women and girl refugees and asylum seekers. The committee called on authorities to ensure full access in state hospitals to legal abortion services that many currently do not offer. It also noted concerns about changes to the ministry responsible for women, and the increasing emphasis on women's role in the family rather than women's rights and gender equality.

Despite the Turkish government's ratification of the Council of Europe Convention on Violence against Women and Domestic Violence (Istanbul Convention), violence against women remains a serious concern, including deaths due to domestic violence and so-called "honor" killings.

Key International Actors

There was international support for the Turkish government in the face of the coup attempt, although the Turkish government criticized what it saw as late and weak responses by the European Union and United States.

The EU-Turkey migration deal and desire for Turkey to host asylum seekers who would otherwise travel to the EU, reinforced the EU's reluctance to use its declining leverage with Turkey. In their relationship with Turkey, the EU and its member states largely appeared to prioritize strategic interests over the promotion of human rights, while issuing repeated statements expressing concern over the growing crackdown. The European Commission progress report described negative developments over the year yet failed to capture the severity and extent of the human rights crisis in Turkey.

With the Obama administration primarily focused on seeking Ankara's cooperation in the fight against ISIS and other armed militant groups, human rights were also not a primary focus of relations in 2016.

The United Nations Office of the High Commissioner for Human Rights, Zeid Ra'ad al-Hussein, spoke out against curbs on media freedom and human rights abuses committed in the context of security operations in the southeast, pressing for a UN fact-finding team to investigate the latter. The Turkish government extended an invitation to Zeid himself, while repeatedly blocking a fact-finding mission. Zeid strongly condemned the coup attempt in Turkey while urging Turkey "to refrain from turning the clock back on human rights protections."

After the coup attempt, UN Secretary-General Ban Ki-moon urged Turkish authorities to do their utmost to ensure that the constitutional order and international human rights law are fully respected in line with Turkey's international obligations, including freedom of expression, freedom of movement and peaceful assembly, independence of the judiciary and of the legal profession, right to fair trial, and strict adherence to due process.

The UN Committee against Torture, in its April review of Turkey, expressed serious concern about "numerous credible reports of law enforcement officials engaging in torture and ill-treatment of detainees while responding to perceived and alleged security threats in the southeastern part of the country."

After the Turkish government postponed his planned October visit, outgoing UN Special Rapporteur on Torture Juan Mendez issued a statement expressing deep disappointment about a decision saying it "sends the wrong message" in light of the thousands of arrests after the coup attempt. The visit was scheduled again for late November under the mandate of the incoming rapporteur. In August, a group of 19 UN experts and three UN working groups issued a joint call to emphasize to Turkey that "one cannot avoid, even in times of emergency, obligations to protect the right to life, prohibit torture, adhere to fundamental elements of due process and non-discrimination, and protect everyone's right to belief and opinion."

In October, the Council of Europe's commissioner of human rights issued a memorandum on the serious human rights implications of the measures taken under Turkey's state of emergency.

Turkmenistan

Turkmenistan is among the world's most repressive and closed countries, where the president and his associates have total control over all aspects of public life. A new draft constitution approved in 2016 allows lifetime presidency.

The government ruthlessly punishes any alternative political or religious expression and exerts total control over access to information. Independent critics and their families, including in exile, face constant threat of government reprisal. Authorities continue to impose informal and arbitrary travel bans on activists and relatives of exiled dissidents, and others. Dozens of people remain forcibly disappeared presumably in Turkmen prisons.

Cult of Personality

Authorities continue to forcibly mobilize citizens to be present for state events and often take extreme measures in preparation for President Gurbanguly Berdymuhamedov's visits within the country. According to the Turkmen Initiative for Human Rights (TIHR), a Vienna-based group, in April four families in Akhal region were not allowed to bury their deceased relatives and hold funerals until after the president's visit ended.

Constitutional Reform

In September, parliament approved a new constitution that allows President Berdymuhamedov to remain in power for life by removing the 70-year age limit for presidential candidates and extending the presidential term of office from five to seven years. There are no presidential term limits.

The new constitution does not ban censorship and does not provide for the right to travel abroad. The Turkmen government did not incorporate recommendations on the draft made by the Office for Democratic Institutions and Human Rights of the Organization for Security and Co-operation in Europe (OSCE).

Civil Society

The government does not allow independent groups to carry out human rights work inside the country. Independent local organizations cannot register, and unregistered work by nongovernmental organizations (NGOs) is illegal. International human rights groups are not allowed to enter Turkmenistan.

Civil society activists face constant threat of government reprisal. In October alone, authorities arrested three activists. Two had monitored forced labor; authorities released on of them after 10 days, and in November a court sentenced the other to three years on bogus fraud charges. The third, Galina Vertryakova, was arrested on bogus extortion charges after she had posted comments critical of the government on Russian social media. At time of writing she was in custody pending investigation and trial.

In August, an independent activist reported invasive, humiliating airport searches by customs officials, and repeated, anonymous telephone threats. Activists' families also received anonymous threats of violence, linking the threats directly to their relatives' activism.

Unknown individuals, presumably acting as government proxies, sought to intimidate exiled activists into silence. In August, two masked men in Moscow attempted to abduct Akmukhammet Baikhanov, a Turkmen dissident, one month after he published a book exposing abuses in Ovadan-Tepe, a prison notorious for torture, horrific conditions, and for holding political prisoners. In April, authorities in Turkmenistan briefly detained his brother, making clear the detention was related to Baikhanov's criticism.

Authorities harassed family members of Geldy Kyarizov, a prominent horse breeding expert who fell out of favor with the government. Kyarizov had served nearly six years in prison in the 2000s, following a conviction on fabricated charges, and was allowed to leave the country in 2015. In November 2015, after Kyarizov's first public interview about his prison ordeal, authorities blocked his family's communication with him and threatened his brothers, detaining one on false drug charges and then releasing him. In March, Kyarizov received repeated verbal threats against him and his family.

Freedom of Media and Information

There is no media freedom in Turkmenistan. The state controls all print and electronic media. Foreign media outlets can very rarely access Turkmenistan, and local stringers for foreign outlets face harsh government retribution.

Saparmamed Nepeskuliev, a freelance correspondent for RFE/RL and Alternative News of Turkmenistan, an exile-run news website, continued to serve a three-year prison sentence, issued in August 2015, following his conviction on fabricated narcotics charges. In December 2015, the United Nations Working Group on Arbitrary Detentions recognized Nepeskuliev as a victim of arbitrary detention for having peacefully exercised his right to freedom of expression.

In October, police questioned another RFE/RL journalist, Soltan Achilova, after she took photographs of a supermarket line. Shortly thereafter unknown assailants attacked and robbed her, taking her camera. She suffered light injuries. The day after Human Rights Watch published a news release about her ordeal, other unknown people tried to assault her, warning her to stop taking photographs.

In August 2016, Turkmen authorities requested that Belarus extradite Chary Annamuradov, a former dissident and independent journalist. Annamuradov is a citizen of Sweden, where he has had asylum since 2003, after fleeing persecution in Turkmenistan. Belarusian authorities arrested Annamuradov upon arrival for vacation in July, pursuant to an international arrest warrant, and in September denied the extradition request.

In September, unknown individuals kidnapped Annamuradov's brother, Altymurad, from his home in Turkmenistan and held him for four days, during which they severely beat him and questioned him about his brother. Altynmurad Annamuradov died shortly after his kidnappers returned him home.

The Turkmen government has forcibly dismantled most private satellite dishes, and internet access in Turkmenistan remains limited and heavily state-controlled. Internet in Turkmenistan is among the most expensive worldwide, according to Stay Mobile, an independent internet industry news aggregator. Throughout 2016, users faced constant obstacles accessing mobile internet. In June, access to Skype and Line messengers was jammed. The government monitors all means of communications.

Freedom of Movement

In June, authorities allowed Aitzhamal Rejepova, the daughter of an exiled dissident, and her two young children to travel abroad for a family visit, after dropping a 13-year travel ban.

However, in most other cases, dissidents' relatives remain barred from foreign travel in 2016. Examples include the Ruzimatov family, relatives of an exiled former official, and Aidogdy Kurbanov, son of an exiled, politically active Turkmen businessman.

Freedom of Religion

A new religion law adopted in March further tightens requirements for registering religious organizations, for example by increasing from 5 to 50 the number of required founders. Unregistered congregations or religious groups are banned. Religious literature is subject to obligatory state censorship. There is still no alternative military service and objectors are subject to persecution.

In February, several congregants of the Greater Grace Church, a Protestant group, were fined 500 manats (US$140) each for possessing "illegal religious literature," and four others were detained, held for questioning, and released. State service officers confiscated their religious literature, phones, and money.

Political Prisoners, Enforced Disappearances, and Torture

The number of those jailed on political grounds is impossible to determine because the justice system is utterly opaque, trials are closed in sensitive cases, and severe repression precludes independent monitoring of these cases.

Political dissident Gulgeldy Annaniazov, arrested in 2008, continues to serve an 11-year prison sentence on charges that are not known even to his family. There had been no information about Annaniazov's whereabouts in custody until September 2015, when a Turkmen official publicly stated that he had been transferred to a prison facility where he could be visited. At time of writing, Turkmen authorities had not directly informed Annaniazov's family about his transfer.

Dozens of people, many of whom were imprisoned under former President Saparmurad Niyazov, remain victims of enforced disappearance. Following their arrest, the government denied them access to families, and the fate of many remains unknown. In 2014, the UN Human Rights Committee recognized Boris Shikhmuradov, the former foreign minister, as a victim of enforced disappearance and stated that the Turkmen government must release him. The Turkmen government has not replied to the committee or carried out its recommendations.

Prove They Are Alive, an international campaign against enforced disappearances in Turkmenistan, confirmed the deaths in custody of three forcibly disappeared people. Their bodies were returned to their families. Yolly Gurbanmuradov, a former deputy minister overseeing the gas industry, died in December 2015. Annadurdy Annasakhedov, the former head of the department of counterintelligence, died in February, and Vekil Durdyev, a former state security officer, died in August. Both had been sentenced in closed trials in 2003 relating to an alleged coup attempt in 2002.

Torture is a grave problem, particularly in high-security facilities. The International Committee for the Red Cross does not have full and independent access to Turkmen prisons and individual prisoners.

In January, the government approved a National Human Rights Action Plan that makes no mention of torture. The plan commits to facilitating visits by the UN special rapporteurs on human rights defenders and on the independence of judges and lawyers by 2018. They are among the 13 UN experts who have requested, but not received, access to the country.

Sexual Orientation and Gender Identity

Under Turkmen law homosexual conduct is punishable by up to two years in prison. Widespread prejudice leads to homosexuality being treated as a disease, including by medical institutions and judicial authorities. Law enforcement officials and medical personnel subject persons detained and charged with sodomy to forced anal examinations, with the purported objective of finding "proof" of homosexual conduct.

Key International Actors

Turkmenistan's vast gas reserves dominate the country's relationships with its international partners whose response to the human rights situation in Turkmenistan has remained overly muted. In a rare exception to this approach, in May, the European Parliament Committee on Foreign Affairs (AFET) postponed final ratification of the Partnership and Cooperation Agreement (PCA) that governs bilateral relations and cooperation between EU and Turkmenistan, citing human right concerns.

In August, German Chancellor Angela Merkel met with President Berdymukhamedov in Berlin. Merkel publicly called for international expert review of the draft constitution and noted that the two had agreed to allow foreign diplomats to visit prisons in Turkmenistan, pending further negotiations.

The United States flagged general concerns about human rights during its October 2015 US-Turkmenistan Annual Bilateral Consultations. During his November 2015 visit to Turkmenistan—the first US secretary of state visit since 1992—John Kerry merely noted that he discussed the "human dimension" with President Berdymukhamedov.

During its annual human rights dialogue with Turkmenistan in May, the European Union raised a range of issues, and urged Turkmenistan to provide information about the fate and whereabouts of disappeared prisoners and to free a number of specific prisoners whose names were not made public.

Uganda

In February, President Yoweri Museveni, in power for more than 30 years, was declared the winner of the presidential elections. Local observers said the elections were not free and fair, and international electoral observers argued the process failed to meet international standards.

Violations of freedom of association, expression, assembly, and the use of excessive force by security officials continued during campaigns and into the post-election period. Opposition presidential candidate Dr. Kizza Besigye from the Forum for Democratic Change (FDC) was held in preventative detention at his home for over a month while trying to challenge election results.

The police used unlawful means including live ammunition to prevent peaceful opposition gatherings and protests, at times resulting in loss of life.

After nine years, the Constitutional Court finally ruled in November on a challenge to a limitation on the mandate of the Equal Opportunities Commission, which barred it from investigating any matter involving behavior "considered to be immoral and socially harmful, or unacceptable by the majority of the cultural and social communities in Uganda." The judges determined the limitation was unconstitutional and violated the right to a fair hearing. Perversely, this provision had meant that the very mechanism designed to protect people from discrimination could blatantly discriminate against women, lesbian, gay, bisexual, transgender and intersex (LGBTI) people, sex workers, and anyone else who might not have been perceived to reflect the views of the majority.

Freedom of Assembly

The police used unnecessary and disproportionate force in 2016 to disperse peaceful assemblies and demonstrations, sometimes resulting in the death of protesters and bystanders.

Police selectively enforce laws, including the 2013 Public Order Management Act, and unjustifiably arrest, detain, and interfere with the movement of opposition politicians. While blocking and dispersing FDC supporters in Kampala, police fired live bullets, killing one person, and injuring many others. Police also shot and killed 13-year-old Kule Muzamiru in Kasese town while dispersing crowds gathered to hear election results. No one had been arrested at time of writing.

Police prevented Besigye from accessing campaign venues in Kampala, in the run up to the February elections on allegations that he was going to "disrupt business." Police arrested and briefly detained him several times during campaigns before returning him to his home without charge.

Between February and May, police raided and sealed off the FDC headquarters, arrested party officials, and beat supporters on several occasions. The day after the general elections, police closed the party offices and arrested Besigye, as well as other party officials. Police confiscated results declaration forms and computers. FDC party offices remained under police guard as other opposition officials and supporters were arrested countrywide. Some were held incommunicado for weeks and released without charge.

Besigye declared a "defiance campaign" against the government after the election and held a ceremony swearing himself in as president. Police then prevented Besigye from leaving his home for 44 days, under a "preventive arrest" law. Access to Besigye's home was restricted, and visitors had to seek permission from police leadership.

Eventually in May, Besigye was charged with treason and sent to prison. In July, after the High Court granted bail, police brutally beat Besigye's supporters and other bystanders with sticks and batons. Opposition activists brought a private prosecution for torture against police leadership, but the case eventually failed.

In June, a newly elected member of parliament for FDC, Michael Kabaziguruka, and 34 others, including soldiers, were charged with treason. The charges were pending at time of writing.

Freedom of Expression and Media

Government officials and police arrested and beat over a dozen journalists, in some cases during live broadcasts. On election day, the Uganda Communication Commission, the telecommunications regulator, directed all telecom companies to block social media networks for "security reasons." The ban lasted five days.

In January, a local television station was temporarily banned from covering Museveni's campaign rallies after editors did not use aerial video provided to them

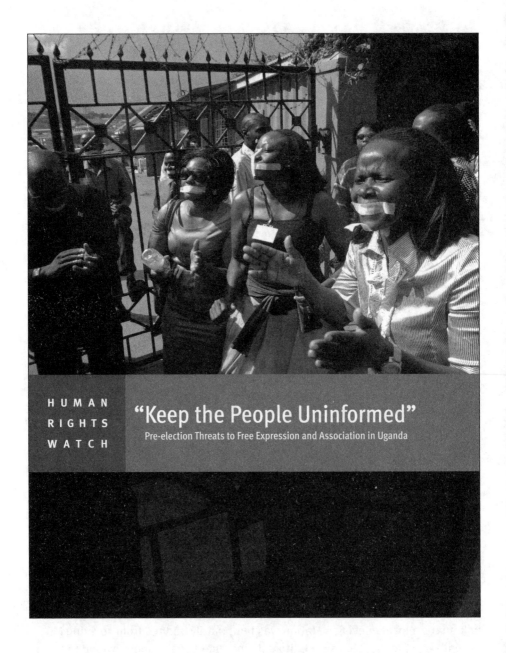

HUMAN
RIGHTS
WATCH

"Keep the People Uninformed"
Pre-election Threats to Free Expression and Association in Uganda

by his campaign team. Soldiers from the Special Forces Command stopped the station's reporters from covering some campaign meetings.

In February, police in Abim, northern Uganda, arrested and detained a BBC correspondent and three others for filming a dilapidated government-run health center. All were released without charge.

Opposition candidates were at times blocked from accessing radios, either for talk shows or after paying for airtime. In January, police blocked opposition presidential candidate Amama Mbabazi from going on the station, Voice of Karamoja. The management told him that the District Security Committee had resolved not to allow him on air.

In April, a court of appeal judge issued a temporary injunction stopping the FDC from carrying out any "defiance campaign" activities pending the hearing of the government's motion challenging the campaign's constitutionality. To implement the injunction, the government banned media from reporting on all FDC activities. The ban eventually ended with the expiry of the court interim order.

Extrajudicial Killings and Absence of Accountability

Security forces continue to use excessive force while policing demonstrations and conducting other law enforcement operations. Between February and April, inter-communal fighting prompted in part by local elections in Rwenzori region, western Uganda, led to the deaths of at least 30 people. Human Rights Watch investigations into subsequent law enforcement operations concluded that the police and army killed at least 13 people during alleged arrest attempts. Multiple witnesses said victims were unarmed when killed. There had been no investigations at time of writing.

Freedom of Association

In February, Museveni signed the Non-Governmental Organisations bill into law. Despite undergoing significant improvement during parliamentary debates, the law still includes troubling and vague "special obligations" of NGOs, including a requirement that groups should "not engage in any act which is prejudicial to the interests of Uganda or the dignity of the people of Uganda." Another provision criminalizes activities by organizations that have not been issued with a permit by the government regulator, fundamentally undermining free association rights. A separate provision provides that violations of the act can lead to jail sentences of up to three years.

Police have not responded to demands for investigations into more than two dozen break-ins at the offices of NGOs, all known for work on sensitive subjects—including human rights, corruption, land rights, and freedom of expression—and for criticizing government policies. In two instances, guards were killed, but no one has been arrested. NGO leadership and relevant government bodies held nationwide consultations to draft implementing regulations for the NGO law, which remained under discussion at time of writing.

Sexual Orientation and Gender Identity

Same-sex conduct remains criminalized under Uganda's colonial-era law, which prohibits "carnal knowledge" among people of the same sex. The new NGO law raises concerns about the criminalization of legitimate advocacy on the rights of LGBTI people.

In August, police unlawfully raided a peaceful pageant that was part of Gay Pride celebrations in Kampala. Police locked the venue's gates, arrested activists, and beat and humiliated hundreds of people, violating rights to association and assembly.

Police continue to carry out forced anal examinations on men and transgender women accused of consensual same-sex conduct. These examinations lack evidentiary value and are a form of cruel, inhuman, and degrading treatment that may amount to torture.

Lord's Resistance Army

The rebel Lord's Resistance Army (LRA) remains active in central Africa but with allegations of killings and abductions on a significantly lesser scale than in previous years.

Former LRA commander Dominic Ongwen is in the custody of the International Criminal Court's (ICC). Ongwen is charged with 70 counts of war crimes and crimes against humanity as part of attacks on internally displaced persons' camps, including murder, enslavement, sexual and gender-based crimes, and the conscription of child soldiers. Ongwen's trial was scheduled for December 2016. Warrants for four other LRA commanders have been outstanding since 2005; three are believed to be dead. Joseph Kony is the only LRA ICC suspect at large.

Former LRA fighter Thomas Kwoyelo, charged before Uganda's International Crimes Division (ICD) with wilful killing, taking hostages, and extensive destruction of property, has been imprisoned since March 2009. His trial has been postponed, first to hear challenges to the constitutionality of his prosecution, and then due to delays in operationalizing ICD regulations, problems in disclosure to the defense, lack of funding, and a backlog of electoral petitions. The trial was scheduled to begin by the end of 2016.

Key International Actors

Electoral observers from the European Union (EU) and the Commonwealth expressed concerns over intimidation and harassment of voters and candidates and a lack of independence and transparency during elections.

The United States publicly raised serious concerns over intimidation and abuse during the elections, but no changes to assistance occurred. The US provides over US$440 million annually to support Uganda's health sector, particularly provision of anti-retrovirals. The US supports the Ugandan army with at least US$70 million for logistics and training for the African Union Mission in Somalia and counter-LRA operations in the Central African Republic, among other efforts. Additional support goes to the Ugandan police's counterterrorism efforts.

The World Bank committed US$105 million to projects in Uganda in 2016, a dramatic decrease from US$664 million in 2015. In December 2015, the World Bank cancelled funding for a US$265 million road-building project and suspended two others after allegations emerged that construction workers sexually abused children. On August 22, 2016, the World Bank suspended all new lending to Uganda.

"You Don't Exist"

Arbitrary Detentions, Enforced Disappearances, and Torture in Eastern Ukraine

AMNESTY INTERNATIONAL

HUMAN RIGHTS WATCH

Ukraine

The situation in eastern Ukraine remained tense in 2016 despite the Minsk II Agreements forged a year earlier that called for a ceasefire and withdrawal of heavy weapons by all sides. Civilians in both Ukrainian and Russia-backed separatists' detention were subjected to serious abuses. Abuses in conflict-affected areas remain largely unaddressed. The government did not adequately respond to attacks on journalists by nationalist groups. In Crimea, Crimean Tatars face further persecution for their peaceful opposition to Russia's occupation of the peninsula.

Hostilities in Eastern Ukraine

The 2015 Minsk II Agreements significantly reduced hostilities, but frequent skirmishes and exchanges of artillery fire continued during the year.

According to the United Nations Human Rights Monitoring Mission in Ukraine (UNHRMMU), mortar, rocket, and artillery attacks between April 2014 and May 2016 killed over 9,000 people and injured more than 21,000—including civilians and combatants on all sides—in Donetsk and Luhansk regions. The UNHRMMU reported a 66 percent increase in civilian casualties from May to August compared to earlier in 2016, and documented 28 civilian deaths in the summer, many of which resulted from shelling and landmines.

Cruel and Degrading Treatment and Arbitrary Detention

Ukrainian government authorities and Russia-backed separatists in eastern Ukraine detained dozens of civilians for collaborating with the other side and held them in prolonged, arbitrary detention, depriving them of contact with lawyers and family. Most of those detained suffered torture or other forms of ill-treatment; some were denied needed medical attention. Both sides have been implicated in sexual violence, although few cases have been fully documented due to victims' reluctance to come forward.

Human Rights Watch, jointly with Amnesty International, found that 18 people had been held in secret detention on the Security Service of Ukraine (SBU) premises in Kharkiv through the end of July, one for as long as 16 months. Thirteen were later released: at time of writing five remained in detention. The SBU denied allegations of secret detention. The military prosecutor's office pledged to investigate. At time of writing, the investigation had yielded no tangible results.

In the self-proclaimed Donetsk People's Republic (DNR) and Luhansk People's Republic (LNR), local security services operate in a total vacuum of rule of law, which deprives people in their custody of their rights and leaves them without recourse to any remedies.

Accountability for Conflict-Related Abuses and Political Violence

In July, parliament passed a controversial amnesty law, absolving combatants involved in the "security operations" in eastern Ukraine of criminal responsibility for non-grave crimes. In August, President Petro Poroshenko vetoed the law.

In July, authorities arrested the head of Aidar battalion, Valentin Liholit, on charges of abduction, robbery, and other violent crimes against civilians. At Liholit's remand hearing, Aidar battalion members blocked the court building, while several members of parliament disrupted the hearing inside, demanding his release. The court released him, pending further investigation.

Also in July, a former member of the Tornado police battalion was sentenced to six years' imprisonment for torture and rape. Twelve other former members of the battalion, including the commander, were under investigation for sexual violence, robbery, and other violent crimes. At an August court hearing, Tornado supporters clashed with law enforcement, injuring 27 law enforcement officers.

Authorities have made some progress toward accountability for abuses during the 2014 Maidan protests by government forces against protesters. In June, authorities charged four members of the Berkut riot police battalion with killing 3 protesters and injuring 35. At time of writing, the investigation was ongoing.

Trials continued in connection with the 2014 political violence in Odesa. In May and June, when courts ruled to release "pro-federalism" defendants from pretrial detention, "pro-unity" activists temporarily blocked the courts and threatened to harm the defendants. On both occasions police eventually rearrested the defendants. "Pro-unity" activists were not held accountable for disrupting court proceedings, and in one case, some were invited to testify against the defendant.

Freedom of Expression and Media

The government continued to take controversial steps restricting media freedom, justifying them mostly by the need to counter Russia's anti-Ukraine propaganda.

In May, Ukrainian authorities banned 17 Russian journalists and media executives from entering Ukraine.

Inter, a television station widely perceived as pro-Russia, was attacked several times in 2016. The most serious attack occurred in early September, when a group of protesters tried to set Inter's building on fire. Several staff had to be evacuated and treated for carbon monoxide poisoning; one sustained a spinal injury. Several days prior to the attack, Interior Minister Arsen Avakov, through his Facebook page, accused the channel of being anti-Ukrainian.

Media ownership structure remained opaque, despite a 2015 law promoting media ownership transparency. Most television channels are believed to be controlled by oligarchs, and President Poroshenko continued to own Channel 5.

Nationalist groups attacked journalists for their work in eastern Ukraine. In May 2016, the website Myrotvorets published the names and personal data of hundreds of journalists and others who had been accredited by the DNR press center, accusing them of "cooperat[ing] with terrorists." Authorities launched an investigation, but top government officials applauded the publication. Several reporters received threats after the data dump.

The Ukrainian Institute of Mass Media, an independent monitoring group, recorded 113 physical attacks against journalists in Ukraine in the first part of 2016.

In July, a bomb car bomb killed Pavel Sheremet, a prominent investigative journalist. At time of writing, investigative authorities had not identified suspects. The trial of suspects in the 2015 killing of Oles Buzina, a journalist known for his pro-Russian views, continued.

In a positive development, in July, an appeals court acquitted journalist and blogger Ruslan Kotsaba, who had been previously convicted on treason charges for calling for boycotting conscription.

Sexual Orientation and Gender Identity

Since 2014, the government has introduced several progressive policies supporting lesbian, gay, bisexual, and transgender (LGBT) people, but anti-LGBT sentiment remains strong among high-level government officials and the public.

In March 2016, about 200 anti-gay, far-right supporters attacked a venue in Lviv hosting a LGBT equality festival, eventually causing the event to be cancelled. The Kyiv LGBT Pride march held in June took place without the violence against participants that had marred it in previous years. Ultra-nationalist groups had threatened to make the march a "bloody mess." Around 6,000 police officers protected the 1,500 march participants.

The first LGBT Pride march took place in Odesa in August. Local authorities initially attempted to ban it, but relented when organizers changed the route. Police arrested four ultra-nationalists who attempted to disrupt the event.

A new draft of the amended labor code does not include an anti-discrimination provision that would protect LGBT people in the workplace.

Crimea

Russia continued to prosecute people for publicly opposing its occupation of Crimea, further shrinking space for free speech and freedom of association.

Under the pretext of combating extremism or terrorism, authorities harassed and took arbitrary legal action against some Crimean Tatar activists in apparent retaliation for their peaceful opposition to Russia's occupation. In February 2016, authorities arrested human rights defender Emir Usein Kuku on charges of terrorism and involvement in Hizb ut-Tahrir, a Muslim political organization that is banned in Russia but not Ukraine. At time of writing he was in custody pending trial. In October, the Crimean Office for Juvenile Affairs approached Kuku's 9-year-old son and asked him questions about Kuku, implying that his father was neglecting his parental duties while in detention. Since 2014, fourteen people were detained on charges of involvement in Hizb ut-Tahrir; in September, four were sentenced to prison terms ranging from five to seven years.

In April, the Supreme Court in Crimea ruled to shut down Mejlis, the Crimean Tatars' elected representative body, on grounds of involvement in "extremist" activities. In September, Russia's Supreme Court upheld the ruling.

Akhtem Chiygoz, a deputy chairman of Mejlis arrested in 2015 on charges of allegedly organizing mass disturbances, remained in custody; his trial was ongoing at time of writing. Another Mejlis deputy chairman, Ilmi Umerov, was charged with separatism for stating in a media interview that Crimea should be returned to Ukraine. In August, Umerov was confined in a psychiatric hospital for evaluation. He was released on September 7 and at time of writing was at liberty, pending trial.

In April, Russia's Federal Security Service in Crimea arrested journalist Nikolai Semena and searched his home, confiscating computer equipment. He is currently banned from leaving Crimea and faces criminal separatism charges for articles criticizing Russia's occupation.

In May, Ervin Ibragimov, a Mejlis member, went missing. Security camera footage showed a group of men forcing him into a van and driving away. His passport was later found in Bakhchisaray. An investigation was ongoing.

Key International Actors

The European Union and the United States issued statements recognizing the territorial integrity of Ukraine. The US State Department called for an investigation into Pavel Sheremet's death and criticized the Russian court's ban of Mejlis. It also called for an end to human rights abuses in Crimea.

In February, the United Nations Children's Fund reported that 1 in 5 schools had been damaged in the armed conflict. Some 215,000 children have been displaced, significantly affecting their access to education. UNICEF called on all parties to the conflict in eastern Ukraine "to ensure safe movement and unhindered humanitarian access to help children in need."

The Parliamentary Assembly of the Council of Europe (PACE) sent rapporteurs to Ukraine in February and April to meet with key leaders to discuss the conflict and the human rights situation in eastern Ukraine while also assessing access to legal remedies for human rights violations since the onset of the war in eastern

HUMAN
RIGHTS
WATCH

STUDYING UNDER FIRE

Attacks on Schools, Military Use of Schools during
the Armed Conflict in Eastern Ukraine

Ukraine. In October, PACE adopted a resolution highlighting the lack of remedies for victims of abuses in Ukrainian territories "under effective control" by Russia.

On August 11 and 12, the UN Committee on Elimination of Racial Discrimination reviewed Ukraine's compliance with the International Convention on the Elimination of All Forms of Racial Discrimination. The committee expressed concerns over "underdeveloped" institutional framework for dealing with minority issues, noted a rise in hate speech by public figures and racist propaganda by such groups as Right Sector, Azov Civilian Battalion, and the Social National Assembly.

The Organization for Security and Co-operation in Europe's (OSCE) Special Monitoring Mission to Ukraine released several statements raising concern about civilian casualties in eastern Ukraine due to the conflict, as well as about the plight of internally displaced persons (IDPs). The chief monitor of the OSCE Special Monitoring Mission in Ukraine declared violence to be a "violation of children's rights" and emphasized the importance of abiding by a ceasefire at the beginning of the school year on September 1.

In May, the UN torture prevention body had to suspend a visit to Ukraine to inspect detention conditions due to travel restrictions in several locations under SBU authority, but returned in September to complete the visit after Ukrainian authorities granted full access.

In September, the UN high commissioner for human rights expressed concern over lack of protection for civilians living in the conflict-affected area, access to basic services and humanitarian aid, freedom of movement, and limited accountability for human rights violations.

Although Ukraine is not a member of the International Criminal Court (ICC), it has accepted the court's jurisdiction over alleged crimes committed on its territory since November 2013. The ICC prosecutor's preliminary examination as to whether it should open an investigation into abuses committed during the armed conflict remained ongoing. In June, parliament adopted a constitutional amendment package that would permit ratification of the ICC treaty, but included a transitional provision that delays the relevant amendment from taking effect for three years.

In November, the ICC's Office of the Prosecutor, in its annual report, characterized the armed conflict in eastern Ukraine and Russia's occupation of Crimea as international armed conflicts to which Russia is a party. The laws of international armed conflict would continue to apply, the report concluded, and the situation in Crimea and Sevastopol amounts to an ongoing state of occupation under those laws.

United Arab Emirates

The United Arab Emirates' intolerance of criticism continued in 2016 with the prosecution of an Emirati academic and a Jordanian journalist, among others, for exercising their right to free expression.

UAE courts acquitted several Libyan nationals whom they forcibly disappeared in 2015, and who had made credible allegations of torture in state security detention. Further evidence emerged regarding the frequent mistreatment of detainees.

The UAE deployed expensive surveillance software to target leading human rights activists. The government continued to ban international human rights organizations from visiting the country. Draconian counterterrorism laws continued to prevent victims and their families from speaking out publicly against abuses.

Freedom of Expression

UAE residents known to have spoken with international rights groups are at serious risk of arbitrary detention and imprisonment. The UAE's 2014 counterterrorism law provides for the death penalty for people whose activities are found to "undermine national unity or social peace," neither of which are defined in the law.

The trial of Emirati academic Nasser bin-Ghaith, whom authorities forcibly disappeared in August 2015 and whose whereabouts remained unknown at time of writing, began at the Federal Supreme Court in April 2016. Media reports on the trial indicate that he is accused of violating various provisions of the penal code, a 2012 cybercrime law, and a 2014 counterterrorism law. Some of these charges, according to local media reports, relate to "six tweets and images ridiculing the Egyptian president and government."

UAE-based Jordanian journalist Tayseer al-Najjar informed his family that his detention in 2016 related to his online criticism of Israeli military actions in Gaza and Egyptian security forces' destruction of tunnels between Gaza and the Sinai region of Egypt.

Arbitrary Detention, Torture, and Mistreatment of Detainees

In February, a group of United Nations human rights experts, including the special rapporteur on torture, the special rapporteur on the independence of judges and lawyers, and the chair of the Working Group on Arbitrary Detention, criticized the UAE's treatment of five Libyan nationals who had been held in arbitrary detention since 2014. The special rapporteur on torture said he had received credible information that authorities subjected the men to torture. In May 2016, the Federal Supreme Court acquitted the men of having links to armed groups in Libya.

In another case involving the UAE's state security apparatus, the son of an adviser to former Egyptian President Mohamed Morsy claimed that UAE authorities subjected him to "brutal physical and psychological torture" to get him to confess to membership in the Muslim Brotherhood. The allegation echoes numerous others that state security detainees have made since 2012.

In March, a Dubai court acquitted British businessman David Haigh of charges brought under the UAE's cybercrime laws. Haigh claimed after his release that Dubai police had punched and tasered him in an unsuccessful effort to make him confess to accusations of fraud. Haigh said that he regularly witnessed prison officers beating inmates during his two years of incarceration. Haigh said he was not able to see the evidence against him at his trial and that he was not able to give evidence or cross-examine witnesses.

Surveillance of Dissidents

A June report from Citizen Lab, a research institute at the University of Toronto that focuses on internet security and human rights, identified a series of digital campaigns against UAE dissidents, dating back to 2012. Citizen Lab described the operator of these campaigns as "a sophisticated threat actor," and said that it was implausible that a state-actor was not behind the campaign. The research identified several pieces of information suggesting a connection between the operator and the UAE government.

In August 2016, Apple issued a software update to all iPhone users after Citizen Lab identified flaws in its operating system that an Israel-based software company, NSO, had exploited in an attempt to place spyware on the phone of leading Emirati human rights activist Ahmed Mansoor.

Migrant Workers

Foreigners account for more than 88.5 percent of UAE residents, according to 2011 government statistics and many low-paid migrant workers remain acutely vulnerable to forced labor, despite some reforms.

A Labor Ministry decree outlining the rules for terminating employment and granting work permits to new employees took effect in 2016. These rules partly govern how the *kafala* visa-sponsorship system operates in the UAE and should theoretically make it easier for workers to change employers before their contract ends if their rights are violated.

Another Labor Ministry decree that took effect in January 2016 could help protect low-paid migrant workers from the practice of contract substitution, in which workers receive lower wages than those they initially agreed to, a practice that can lead to forced labor. The new decrees do not apply to domestic workers, who are explicitly excluded from UAE labor law protections.

Women's Rights

Discrimination on the basis of sex and gender is not included in the definition of discrimination in the UAE's 2015 anti-discrimination law.

Federal law No. 28 of 2005 regulates matters of personal status in the UAE, and some of its provisions discriminate against women. For instance, the law provides that, for a woman to marry, her male guardian must conclude her marriage contract; men have the right to unilaterally divorce their wives, whereas a woman who wishes to divorce her husband must apply for a court order; a woman can lose her right to maintenance if, for example, she refuses to have sexual relations with her husband without a lawful excuse; and women are required to "obey" their husbands. A woman may be considered disobedient, with few exceptions, if she decides to work without her husband's consent.

In 2010, the Federal Supreme Court issued a ruling—citing the penal code—that sanctions husbands' beating and inflicting other forms of punishment or coercion on their wives, provided they do not leave physical marks.

631

UAE law permits domestic violence. Article 53 of the UAE's penal code allows the imposition of "chastisement by a husband to his wife and the chastisement of minor children" so long as the assault does not exceed the limits prescribed by Sharia, or Islamic law.

Children's Rights

The law on juvenile offenders provides that the punishment of whipping may be imposed on children over the age of 16 for murder, assault and battery, alcohol-related offences, theft, or sexual intercourse outside marriage.

Sexual Orientation and Gender Identity

The UAE's penal code does not explicitly prohibit homosexuality. However, article 356 of the penal code criminalizes (but does not define) "indecency," and provides for a minimum sentence of one year in prison. In practice, UAE courts use this article to convict and sentence people for zina offenses, which include consensual sexual relations outside heterosexual marriage and other "moral" offenses, including same-sex relations.

Different emirates within the UAE have laws that criminalize same-sex sexual relations, including Abu Dhabi where "unnatural sex with another person" can be punished with up to 14 years in prison, and Dubai which imposes 10 years of imprisonment for sodomy.

Foreign Policy

The UAE maintained its military involvement in Yemen, where it is assisting in the Saudi-led military campaign against Houthi forces, also known as Ansar Allah. It is unclear if the UAE air force is still taking part in coalition airstrikes, but Emirati troops remain on the ground in the south of the country.

United States

The United States has a vibrant civil society and strong constitutional protections for many civil and political rights. Yet many US laws and practices, particularly in the areas of criminal and juvenile justice, immigration, and national security, violate internationally recognized human rights. Those least able to defend their rights in court or through the political process—members of racial and ethnic minorities, the poor, immigrants, children, and prisoners—are the people most likely to suffer abuses.

The election of Donald Trump as president in November 2016 capped a campaign marked by misogynistic, xenophobic, and racist rhetoric and Trump's embrace of policies that would cause tremendous harm to vulnerable communities, contravene the United States' core human rights obligations, or both. Trump's campaign proposals included deporting millions of unauthorized immigrants, changing US law to allow torture of terrorism suspects, and "load[ing] up" the Guantanamo Bay detention facility.

President-elect Trump also pledged to repeal most of the Affordable Care Act, which has helped 20 million previously uninsured Americans access health insurance and to nominate "pro-life" Supreme Court justices who would "automatically" overturn Roe v. Wade, which would allow individual states to criminalize abortion.

Death Penalty

At time of writing, the United States had executed 18 people in 2016, the lowest number since 1992.

Thirty-one states still allow for the death penalty, though in 2016 only five states carried out executions, led by Texas and Georgia. The Delaware Supreme Court ruled unconstitutional the state's death penalty statute, and the Delaware Attorney General announced that he would not appeal the decision. Nebraska reinstated its death penalty because of a November popular referendum. California residents voted to retain the state's death penalty.

HUMAN
RIGHTS
WATCH

EXTREME MEASURES
Abuses against Children Detained as National Security Threats

Harsh Sentencing

2.3 million people are behind bars in the United States, the largest reported incarcerated population in the world. Of those, 211,000 are in the federal system, and 2 million are in state prisons and local jails.

Congress continues to debate limited reform of federal sentencing laws, but it passed no significant reforms in 2016.

At time of writing, President Barack Obama had commuted the sentences of 944 people in 2016 in federal prison for drug offenses; 12,405 other petitions for commutation were pending. More than one-third of the commutations were for life sentences—no parole is available for federal crimes committed after 1987.

The US Sentencing Commission amended its sentencing guidelines in 2016 to broaden its "compassionate release" criteria, expanding eligibility for release both on health grounds and for family reasons.

Policing

Police killings of Alton Sterling in Baton Rouge, Louisiana, and Philando Castile in Falcon Heights, Minnesota, among others, drew renewed attention to US police use of excessive force in interactions with black people. Similar to the progression of events in Ferguson, Missouri, after the shooting of Michael Brown in 2014, protesters in Baton Rouge responding to the shooting of Sterling were confronted by police in riot gear.

Five police officers were ambushed and killed in Dallas by a lone gunman in July.

Youth in the Criminal Justice System

On any given day, approximately 50,000 children in the United States are held in correctional facilities. This number represents a 50 percent drop from 1999, but is still one of the highest rates of juvenile detention in the world. Every US state allows children to be tried as adults under some circumstances, and approximately 5,000 child offenders are held in adult jails or prisons at any point in time.

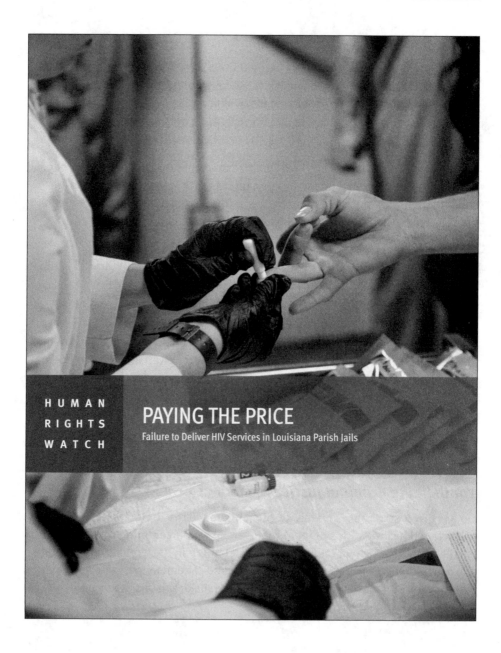

HUMAN
RIGHTS
WATCH

PAYING THE PRICE
Failure to Deliver HIV Services in Louisiana Parish Jails

Iowa, Utah, and South Dakota banned sentences of life without the possibility of parole for child offenders—17 states now ban life without parole sentences for child offenders.

California's Proposition 57, which gives judges the sole power to grant or deny a prosecutor's request to remove a child from juvenile court to be tried in adult court, passed in 2016. A similar legislative reform in Florida failed for the second year in a row.

Prison and Jail Conditions

Federal agencies submitted proposed reforms to solitary confinement policies to the White House following a directive from President Obama in March. The Bureau of Prisons also halved the average duration of placements in special management units, a form of solitary for people believed to have gang ties or with a history of serious disciplinary infractions.

At the state level, Maryland passed a bill that requires the collection of data on people in correctional facilities placed in solitary confinement. North Carolina banned the use of solitary confinement for all offenders under age 18. New York, New Jersey, Delaware, and other states considered legislative proposals to reform the use of solitary. New York City's main jail complex, Rikers Island, ended the use of solitary confinement for 16- to 18-year-olds, and New York Mayor Bill de Blasio announced in October the end to punitive solitary confinement for people under age 21.

The US Justice Department announced in August that the Bureau of Prisons would begin phasing out its use of private contract prisons. The Department of Homeland Security, responsible for housing immigration detainees, announced a review of its own use of private facilities, the findings of which were not yet available at time of writing. President-elect Trump's proposal to detain and deport millions of immigrants would make it difficult for the Department of Homeland Security to close any facilities, whether private or public.

Voter Disenfranchisement

In April, Virginia Governor Terry McAuliffe issued an executive order restoring voting rights to all persons in Virginia who had been convicted of a felony and had completed their sentences. This restoration of voting rights would have impacted 206,000 people in Virginia. The state supreme court subsequently invalidated that order, however, ruling that the governor lacked the authority to issue such a blanket restoration of voting rights. The governor responded by creating a process to individually restore voting rights to such individuals, and by late 2016 had restored voting rights to some 67,000 Virginia residents.

Drug Policy

All states and the federal government criminalize possession of illicit drugs for personal use (though some have legalized medical or recreational marijuana). Each year, state law enforcement agencies use these laws to make some 1.3 million arrests. More than one of every nine arrests by state law enforcement agencies is for drug possession, making drug possession the single most arrested crime in the US. As a result, hundreds of thousands of individuals cycle through the criminal justice system every year. Those who are convicted often find that their criminal records lock them out of jobs, housing, education, welfare assistance, voting, and much more, and subject them to discrimination and stigma.

Drug enforcement discriminates against black adults. Black adults use drugs at similar or even lower rates than white adults, yet black adults are more than two-and-a-half times as likely as white adults to be arrested for drug possession in the US.

California, Massachusetts, Nevada, and Maine passed ballot initiatives in 2016 that legalized recreational marijuana, following on the heels of prior legalization initiatives in Colorado and Washington State. Florida, North Dakota, and Arkansas legalized medical marijuana. The Obama administration emphasized the need for more public health approaches to drug use, though it stopped short of calling for decriminalization.

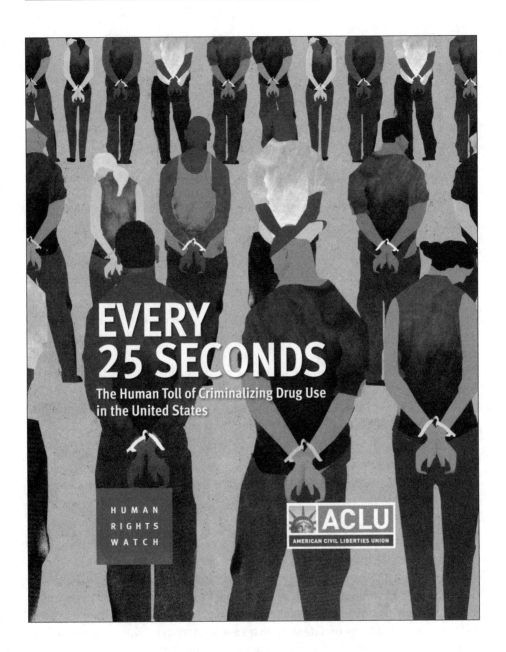

Gun Violence

In June, an apparent politically motivated mass shooting at a gay nightclub in Orlando, Florida that left 49 people dead once again opened up public debate about gun control and the high frequency of mass shootings in the US.

In January, Obama announced a series of steps the executive branch would take to reduce gun violence. However, legislative reforms were stalled in Congress.

Rights of Non-Citizens

The US government continues to detain migrant children from Central America with their mothers, many of them seeking asylum. Although modest reforms announced in 2015 reduced the number of families in detention, the US still detains some families for prolonged periods of time. Human Rights Watch has documented the severe psychological toll of indefinite detention on asylum-seeking mothers and children and the barriers it raises to due process.

Abusive detention conditions are also a concern. Human Rights Watch released an analysis of the US government's own investigations into the deaths of 18 immigrants in custody from 2012 to 2015, revealing dangerously substandard medical care in 16 cases, contributing to the deaths of seven people. Other organizations have documented similar problems in facilities across the country, indicating severely inadequate oversight over a detention system of 200-plus facilities, including privately run facilities and local jails.

In June 2016, the US Supreme Court effectively blocked executive actions by the Obama administration providing a temporary reprieve from deportation to certain unauthorized immigrants. The court issued a split decision that left a lower court's injunction in place.

In November 2016, President-elect Trump reiterated his campaign promises to build a wall on the US-Mexico border, and to quickly detain or deport 2 to 3 million immigrants with criminal records. The Obama administration, which also focused on deporting immigrants with convictions, deported a record 2.5 million people, with and without criminal records, over its two terms. Any push to rapidly deport millions of undocumented immigrants would almost certainly exacerbate abusive conditions of detention in a sprawling system with poor oversight, and further undermine already weak due process protections.

Labor Rights

The US has no national law on paid family leave. A federal bill to establish a paid family leave program is pending in Congress. Meanwhile, a number of states have enacted paid family leave insurance programs. In April 2016, New York State enacted such a program, joining California, New Jersey, and Rhode Island. Under these programs, workers are eligible for paid leave to bond with a new child, to care for a seriously ill loved one, or to assist with family obligations when a family member is called into active military service.

In the US workforce, women who worked full-time, year-round in 2014 earned 79 percent of what men earned, and the gender wage gap was bigger for black and Hispanic women. The Equal Employment Opportunity Commission receives thousands of pregnancy discrimination and sexual harassment claims every year.

Gaps in US law and regulations allow child farmworkers to work at younger ages, for longer hours, and in more hazardous conditions than children working in any other sector. Child farmworkers often work in extreme heat, exposed to toxic pesticides and other dangers. On tobacco farms, child workers are exposed to nicotine, and many report symptoms consistent with acute nicotine poisoning. Some companies ban children under 16 from working on tobacco farms, but these policies leave older children unprotected. The Obama administration failed to change US regulations, and Congress has not amended US labor law to protect child farmworkers. Tobacco companies have not taken sufficient action to eliminate hazardous child labor in their supply chains.

Right to Health

The criminal justice system continues to act as a barrier to adequate health care for those most vulnerable to HIV, particularly people of color, people who use drugs, sex workers, transgender women, and other heavily policed populations.

The US is experiencing what the Centers for Disease Control and Prevention has called an "epidemic" of opioid use, with 78 Americans dying each day from an opioid overdose. Congress responded with the Comprehensive Addiction and Recovery Act, legislation that authorizes increased support for drug dependence prevention, treatment, and overdose prevention programs. Funding, however, remains uncertain, and access to health care remains out of reach for many, partic-

HUMAN
RIGHTS
WATCH

BOOTED

Lack of Recourse for Wrongfully Discharged US Military Rape Survivors

ularly in the 19 states that continue to reject Medicaid expansion under the Affordable Care Act.

In June 2016, the US Supreme Court struck down parts of a Texas law that imposed onerous restrictions on abortion providers. The Texas law required abortion clinics to meet standards for ambulatory surgical centers and required doctors who provide abortions to maintain admitting privileges at local hospitals.

Sexual Assault in the Military

Despite Defense Department reforms, US military service members who report sexual assault frequently experience retaliation, including harassment, poor work assignments, loss of promotion opportunities, disciplinary action, and even criminal charges. In February 2016, the oversight body for US military justice adopted findings and recommendations aimed at ending such retaliation. A Defense Department strategy for combatting retaliation released in April 2016 recognizes the problem, aims to gather and share information about how cases are handled, and emphasizes a range of options for commanders to address retaliation against victims. Various versions of the National Defense Authorization Act would improve transparency and adopt improved protections for whistleblowers, among other steps. At time of writing, the bill was still being negotiated in Congress.

Sexual Orientation and Gender Identity

In 2016, state legislatures introduced a record number of bills seeking to restrict the rights of lesbian, gay, bisexual, and transgender (LGBT) people. North Carolina eliminated local non-discrimination protections for sexual orientation and gender identity and required transgender people to use public facilities that correspond to the sex assigned to them at birth. Mississippi passed a law permitting religious believers to discriminate against LGBT people and unmarried couples. Tennessee passed legislation allowing counselors and therapists to refuse to serve LGBT clients.

In May, the Departments of Education and Labor jointly issued guidance indicating that discrimination on the basis of gender identity constitutes sex discrimination prohibited under federal law. After 22 states and several state and local officials sued to challenge the guidance, a federal court temporarily enjoined the departments from enforcing their interpretation. That litigation had not been resolved at time of writing.

Transgender women in immigration detention have been subjected to sexual assault and mistreatment including indefinite solitary confinement imposed on some purely because authorities lacked appropriate facilities in which to house them.

Violence against Women

In 2016, Obama signed into law the Sexual Assault Survivors' Rights Act, which focuses on collection and preservation of evidence in sexual assault cases. It protects survivors' access to the initial forensic medical examination, and their right to have a rape kit preserved throughout the statute of limitations and be notified if a rape kit will be destroyed.

An estimated 32 percent of women in the US have suffered physical violence from an intimate partner and approximately 19 percent have been raped, with nearly half of these at the hands of an intimate partner. Women in the US are more likely to be killed by a partner, ex-partner, or family member than by any other type of perpetrator.

National Security

The Obama administration made significant gains in releasing detainees at Guantanamo Bay detention facilities to home or third countries, reducing the population from 107 at the end of 2015 to 60 at time of writing. It also continued with plans to hold some 30-40 of the detainees without charge indefinitely, claiming that they cannot be prosecuted but pose too significant a security risk to release. The administration did not adequately explained the basis for these determinations or allow detainees to meaningfully challenge them.

The Obama administration continued to pursue prosecutions against seven men in the fundamentally flawed Guantanamo Bay military commissions—a forum that does not meet international fair trial standards. This includes five men alleged to have played a role in the September 11, 2001 attacks. On the attacks'

**HUMAN
RIGHTS
WATCH**

RUBBER STAMP JUSTICE

US Courts, Debt Buying Corporations, and the Poor

15th anniversary, the case was in its fourth year of pretrial hearings with a trial date still years away. The slow progress is the result of government secrecy about the defendants' torture in Central Intelligence Agency custody, the novel nature of the court's untested rules and procedures, and logistical difficulties associated with holding hearings at Guantanamo Bay.

The US did not initiate any new investigations in 2016 into torture committed by the CIA following the September 11, 2001 attacks, despite overwhelming evidence of violations of federal criminal law. The government has also not provided redress to victims of CIA torture. Both prosecutions and redress are required by international law. However, the Justice Department chose not to assert a national security defense known as the "state secrets privilege" in a lawsuit brought by three men against two CIA contractors for their torture in Afghanistan. Failure to assert the privilege allowed the case, a civil suit for compensation, to proceed further than any previous such case.

The US continued to carry out targeted killings, often with the use of aerial drones, against alleged militants outside conventional war zones, including in Yemen, Pakistan, Libya, and Somalia. In July 2016, the director of national intelligence released figures claiming that the US had killed between 64 and 116 "non-combatants" in such strikes since 2009, a figure that advocacy groups— including Human Rights Watch, which investigated several of the strikes—said appeared to significantly undercount the civilian lives lost. When the government released its figures, Obama issued an executive order promising to offer voluntary payments to survivors and families of civilians killed, without regard to the lawfulness of the strike. It is unclear whether the order has been implemented.

Throughout 2016, the US continued to carry out large-scale warrantless intelligence surveillance programs and failed to address the serious lack of transparency, oversight, and accountability in this area. Federal law enforcement agencies also campaigned for expanded hacking and monitoring powers. The US continued to seek the extradition from Russia of Edward Snowden, the whistle-blower who revealed the scope of US mass surveillance in 2013.

One of the main laws under which the US currently conducts large-scale surveillance, including of people outside its borders, is section 702 of the Foreign Intelligence Surveillance Act. The law is scheduled to sunset at the end of 2017, and congressional debates concerning whether to reform the law are anticipated during the year. In July, a federal appeals court heard a challenge to the constitutionality of section 702 in the context of an Oregon criminal case; the court's decision remained pending at time of writing.

Meanwhile, US global communications surveillance practices under a policy directive known as Executive Order 12333 remain shrouded in secrecy, with neither Congress nor the courts asserting a meaningful oversight role. A longstanding effort by the independent Privacy and Civil Liberties Oversight Board to review some of the government's activities under EO 12333 appeared to generate a backlash: for example, at time of writing, the Senate was considering laws that would prohibit the oversight board from considering the privacy or other rights of anyone other than US citizens and lawful permanent residents.

The Federal Bureau of Investigation (FBI) mounted a campaign to force US technology companies to weaken the encryption they use to protect private communications—a move that would jeopardize human rights globally. The FBI also urged Congress to adopt laws that would allow it to demand individuals' browsing histories and other internet records without a warrant; the measure failed a procedural vote by a narrow margin, raising the risk of a renewed effort in 2017. Federal law enforcement was more successful in obtaining a new administrative rule that expanded its global hacking powers; at time of writing the rule was scheduled to take effect in December 2016, although legislation had been introduced to prevent or delay its final adoption.

Foreign Policy

In February, Obama made an historic trip to Cuba to mark the restart of diplomatic relations. While Obama raised the issue of political prisoners during a joint press conference with Cuban President Raúl Castro, he did not publicly push US concerns about arbitrary detention, blocked websites, and laws used to punish dissent. In March, Obama traveled to Argentina where he announced the declassification of US intelligence and military documents relating to US involvement during the country's "dirty war."

The finalized Trans-Pacific Partnership agreement, which includes side agreements on labor issues in Vietnam, Malaysia, and Brunei, was signed in February by the United States but did not move forward in Congress before the election.

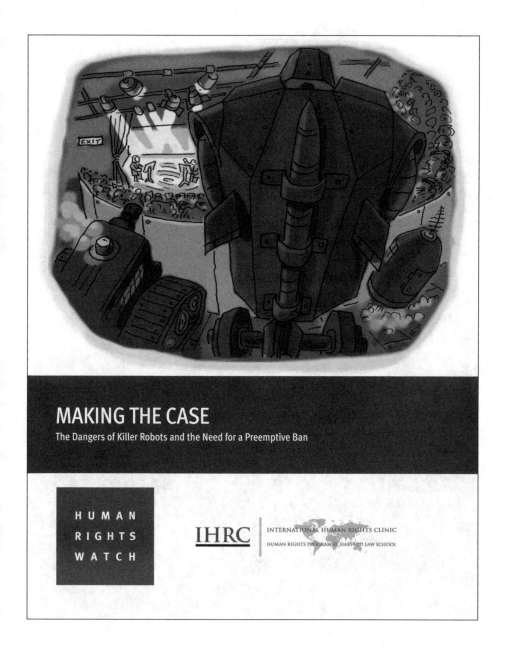

MAKING THE CASE
The Dangers of Killer Robots and the Need for a Preemptive Ban

HUMAN
RIGHTS
WATCH

IHRC | INTERNATIONAL HUMAN RIGHTS CLINIC
HUMAN RIGHTS PROGRAM AT HARVARD LAW SCHOOL

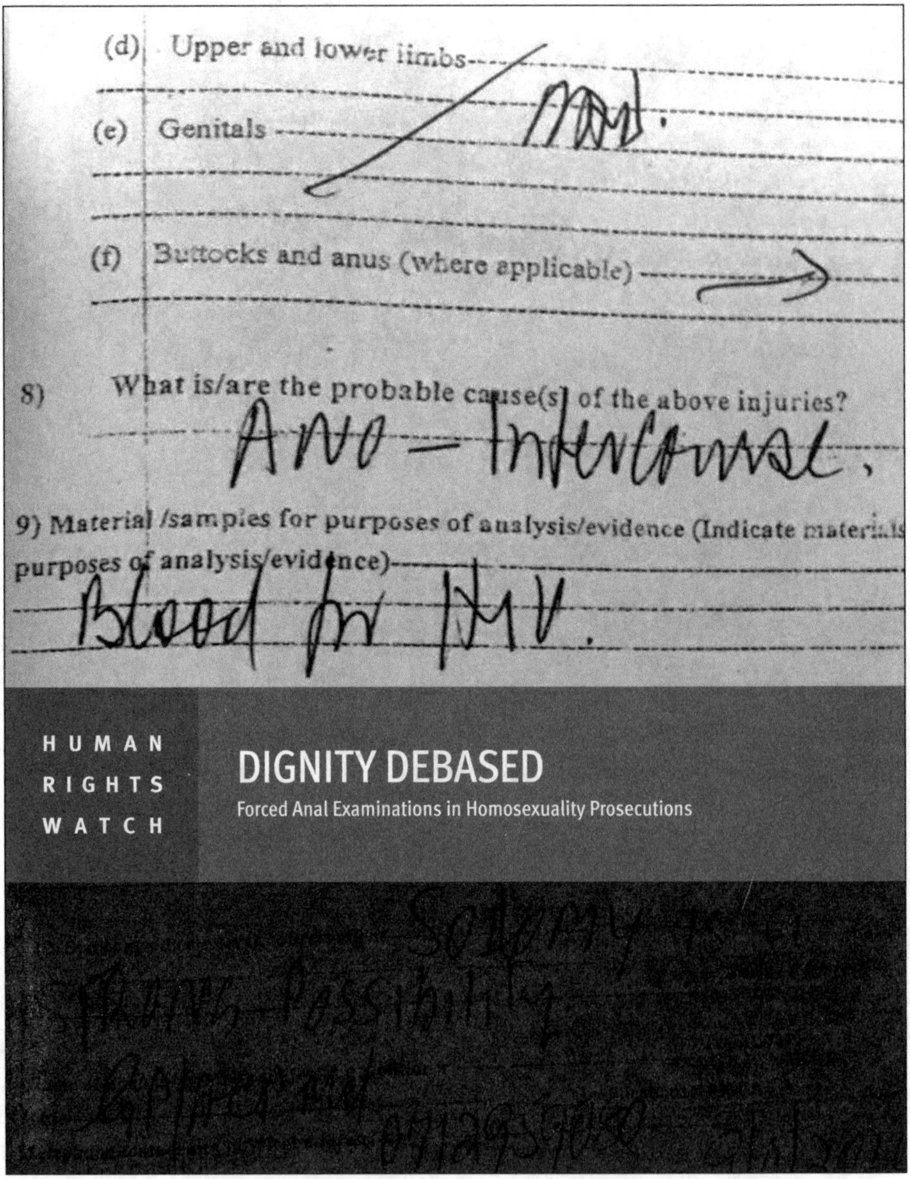

(d) Upper and lower limbs

(e) Genitals — *nAd*.

(f) Buttocks and anus (where applicable) →

8) What is/are the probable cause(s) of the above injuries?

Ano — Intercourse,

9) Material /samples for purposes of analysis/evidence (Indicate materials purposes of analysis/evidence)

Blood for HIV.

HUMAN RIGHTS WATCH

DIGNITY DEBASED

Forced Anal Examinations in Homosexuality Prosecutions

Donald Trump's election victory and his campaign rhetoric against the agreement make it highly unlikely that implementing legislation needed for the agreement will be passed, meaning that the agreement is either dead or will have to significantly renegotiated.

US-led efforts at the United Nations Human Rights Council produced the council's first ever joint statement on China's human rights record in March. However, Obama did not raise major human rights concerns during his visit to China for the G20 summit in September.

Obama traveled to Vietnam in May, where he announced that, despite Vietnam's lack of progress on human rights, the US would lift the ban on lethal arms sales to the country. During Burmese leader Aung Sun Suu Kyi's visit to Washington, DC, in September, the administration announced it would significantly ease remaining sanctions on Burma in the wake of historic democratic elections there.

In his visits to Kenya and Nigeria in August, Secretary of State John Kerry raised concerns about links between human rights violations and insecurity but did little to press partner governments to live up to their rhetorical commitments. After President Kabila of the Democratic Republic of Congo made moves to remain in power for an unconstitutional third term, the US imposed sanctions against several senior Congolese officials.

As violence returned to South Sudan's capital city in July, the US finally began to push for a UN Security Council arms embargo on the warring parties in an effort to stem atrocities.

In September, the Senate introduced a bipartisan resolution to halt weapons sales to Saudi Arabia, as evidence of unlawful airstrikes by Saudi forces in Yemen mounted. Although the resolution did not pass, it was supported by more than a quarter of the Senate, reflecting fissures in what had been steadfast support for Saudi Arabia in the US security establishment.

The US continues to provide significant financial and technical security assistance to Egypt, despite a report from the US General Accountability Office (GAO) showing that both US and Egyptian authorities have been negligent in human rights vetting of security forces and equipment use.

The US hosted the Leaders' Summit on the Global Refugee Crisis on the margins of the UN General Assembly in September, resulting in new commitments from donor countries to roughly double the number of refugees resettled globally and provide an additional $4.5 billion in humanitarian funding over 2015 levels.

In September, Obama waived provisions of the Child Soldiers Prevention Act to allow six countries—the Democratic Republic of Congo, Iraq, Nigeria, Somalia, South Sudan, and Rwanda—to continue to receive US military assistance sanctionable under the law, despite their continued use of child soldiers. Obama also waived the law's restrictions on Burma, even though Burma is not scheduled for US military assistance in fiscal year 2017. The only countries completely restricted were Sudan, Syria, and Yemen, countries to which the United States was not planning to offer military assistance.

The International Criminal Court is analyzing crimes committed in Afghanistan by non-state armed groups, domestic government forces, and international forces, including allegations of disappearances and torture of detainees by US armed forces and the CIA during the Bush administration.

Uzbekistan

Uzbekistan's long-serving authoritarian ruler Islam Karimov died in fall 2016 following almost 27 years of rule. But his death and the installation of former Prime Minister Shavkat Mirziyoyev as president failed to usher in any meaningful improvements in Uzbekistan's abysmal human rights record. The United States and European Union also continued their longstanding policies of muted criticism over the government's abuses.

Authorities maintain rigid control over the population, severely curtailing freedoms of association, expression, and religion. Thousands of individuals remain imprisoned on politically motivated charges, torture is widespread, and authorities regularly harass rights activists, opposition members, and journalists. Muslims and Christians who practice their religion outside strict state controls are persecuted. Authorities force over 1 million adults to harvest cotton every fall under harsh conditions, netting enormous profits for the government.

New Leader, Same Abuses

Karimov's death was confirmed by authorities on September 2, following a stroke. For the previous six days, authorities hid from the public reports he had already died, announcing the death only after foreign leaders publicly expressed condolences. Independent journalists and rights defenders such as Daniil Kislov and Nadejda Atayeva, who reported about the news of Karimov's death and his abusive legacy, were subjected to an orchestrated campaign of online harassment, including death threats, during which they were labelled them as traitors.

Although the constitution required Senate Chairman Nigmatulla Yuldashev, to become interim president for a 3-month period in the event of the president's death or incapacitation, the Senate installed Prime Minister Mirziyoyev in the post, setting presidential elections for December.

In one of Mirziyoyev's first public addresses as interim president he signaled his intent to continue Karimov's repressive policies, vowing to crush any "internal or external threats to stability and sovereignty."

Mirziyoyev was officially declared the winner of the presidential election held on December 4. The Organization for Security and Co-operation in Europe's Office for Democratic Institutions and Human Rights (ODIHR) said that "while the election administration took measures to enhance the transparency of its work and the proper conduct of the election, the dominant position of state actors and limits on fundamental freedoms undermine political pluralism and led to a campaign devoid of genuine competition." ODIHR observers further said that Uzbek "media covered the election in a highly restrictive and controlled environment, and the state-defined narrative did not provide voters the opportunity to hear alternative viewpoints."

Politically Motivated Imprisonment and Harassment of Critics

Authorities have imprisoned thousands of people on politically motivated charges, mostly religious believers, but also rights and opposition activists, journalists, and other perceived critics. Authorities frequently subject detainees to torture and arbitrarily extend their sentences.

Human rights activists in prison include Azam Farmonov, Mehriniso Hamdamova, Zulhumor Hamdamova, Isroiljon Kholdorov, Gaybullo Jalilov, Nuriddin Jumaniyazov, Matluba Kamilova, Ganikhon Mamatkhanov, Chuyan Mamatkulov, Zafarjon Rahimov, Yuldash Rasulov, Fahriddin Tillaev, and Akzam Turgunov. Journalists in prison include Solijon Abdurakhmanov, Muhammad Bekjanov, Gayrat Mikhliboev, Yusuf Ruzimuradov, and Dilmurod Saidov. Opposition activists behind bars include Samandar Kukanov, Kudratbek Rasulov, and Rustam Usmanov. Imprisoned religious figures and other perceived government critics include Aramais Avakyan, Ruhiddin Fahriddinov, Nodirbek Yusupov, Dilorom Abdukodirova, Botirbek Eshkuziev, Bahrom Ibragimov, Davron Kabilov, Erkin Musaev, Davron Tojiev, and Ravshanbek Vafoev.

On October 25, prison authorities released a human rights defender, Bobomurod Razzakov, on medical grounds one year prior to the end of a four-year sentence. But evidence emerged that Razzakov was seriously ill-treated and denied appropriate medical care in prison. In November, following a public appeal for his release by the US State Department and human rights groups, authorities also released the long-serving political activist Samandar Kukanov, behind bars since 1993, reversing an earlier decision to extend his term of imprisonment by an additional three years. Kukanov, also a victim of torture in custody, was seriously ill at the time of his release.

655

With the exception of the rights group Ezgulik, which was allowed to meet with four prisoners in July, August, and October, authorities continue to deny diplomatic missions, the International Committee for the Red Cross, and human rights organizations access to prisons and other detention centers.

On January 11, Human Rights Watch discovered that a prominent religious figure, 52-year-old Akram Yuldashev, one of Uzbekistan's longest held political prisoners, died in prison in 2010 of tuberculosis. He had been due for release in February 2016, but no one knew of his fate because authorities forcibly disappeared him in prison, denying anyone information about his whereabouts or fate since 2009.

In March 2016, long-time rights defender Elena Urlaeva, head of the Tashkent-based Human Rights Alliance of Uzbekistan, checked into the Tashkent Psychiatric Clinic after experiencing multiple traumatic events, including ill-treatment by police. In late April, Urlaeva's doctor informed her she was in good health and would be released on May 2. However, the hospital then refused to release her, arbitrarily detaining her citing "official orders" rather than a medical reason. The hospital released Urlaeva on June 1, after significant international pressure.

After her release, Urlaeva reported ill-treatment during her detention, saying the "hospital staff turned aggressive patients on me, who beat me and dragged me by the hair."

Imprisoned rights defender Ganihon Mamatkhanov's 8-year prison term was due to end on June 4. Days before Mamatkhanov's release, officials accused him of unspecified "violations of prison rules"—a practice authorities have used to arbitrarily extend political prisoners' sentences—and kept him in prison. It is not known by how many years his term has been extended and his current whereabouts are unknown.

In August, a Fergana court sentenced the brother of a Radio Free Europe (RFE) journalist to eight years in prison on drug-related charges, the latest government action involving persons affiliated with RFE's Uzbek Service. In court proceedings, Aziz Yusupov was represented by a lawyer assigned to him by Uzbekistan's National Security Service, whom Yusupov's family said persuaded him to make a false confession to mollify the court. During the trial, no evidence was brought against Yusupov to corroborate the charges.

Forced Labor

The government forces more than 1 million adults every autumn to pick cotton in abusive conditions on pain of punishment. Following a decade of global pressure, authorities did not mobilize children to harvest cotton in 2016, as in 2015, but instead increased the number of forced adult laborers to meet annual production quotas. In several regions, officials also forced children to help toward the end of the harvest.

Teachers, doctors, nurses, civil servants, and private sector employees were forced to pick cotton under threat of dismissal from work or loss of salary and pension and welfare benefits, and authorities detained and threatened citizens attempting to report on these abuses.

Freedom of Religion

Authorities imprison religious believers who practice their faith outside state controls. In September, the Initiative Group of Independent Human Rights Defenders estimated that more than 12,000 persons are currently imprisoned on vague charges related to "extremism" or "anti-constitutional" activity, several hundred of them convicted in the previous year. Authorities banned shared Muslim iftar (breaking of fast) meals in public during Ramadan, severely restricted the religious literature, and continued to ban people under 18 from attending mosques.

Prison authorities arbitrarily extended the prison term of Sunni religious believer Kamol Odilov in late January, just days before he completed his six-year prison term. He and his fellow Muslims had met to discuss the works of the late Turkish Muslim theologian Said Nursi. According to Forum 18, four members of a Sufi Muslim community were imprisoned for four years in Bukhara in June for holding religious meetings at home, as their community does not have state registration.

Sexual Orientation and Gender Identity

Consensual sexual relations between men are criminalized, with a maximum prison sentence of three years. Activists report that police use blackmail and extortion against gay men, threatening to out or imprison them. Lesbian, gay, bisexual, and transgender (LGBT) people face deep-rooted homophobia and discrimination.

Key International Actors

Despite calls by Uzbek rights activists on the US and EU to seize upon the end of Islam Karimov's rule and ensuing transition as an opportunity to push for rights improvements, Washington and Brussels' overall stance on human rights in Uzbekistan remained disappointingly weak. Both failed to articulate publicly clear expectations for reform such as the release of political prisoners or access for United Nations human rights monitors. Since 2002, the government has ignored requests by at least 14 UN rights experts to visit the country. In September, the UN high commissioner for human rights singled out Uzbekistan in a list of country that failed to cooperate with his office for having refuse access to the country.

US Secretary of State John Kerry convened a joint meeting with foreign ministers of the five Central Asian nations in August in Washington following a similar regional meeting in Samarkand in November 2015. While the participating governments issued a general statement reaffirming a commitment to uphold human rights, Secretary Kerry did not publicly express concern about any specific human rights issues with the Uzbek government; it remains unclear whether he did so privately.

In July, however, the State Department downgraded Uzbekistan's placement in the Trafficking in Persons report, a global human trafficking report, from the middle category, Tier II, down to Tier III—the worst category, acknowledging the government's responsibility for widespread adult forced labor. For the eighth consecutive year, the State Department designated Uzbekistan as a "country of particular concern," due to its serial violations of religious freedom, but the White House waived the sanctions envisaged under the statute, citing national security grounds.

Since April 2015, the World Bank has been working with the government to rejuvenate the irrigation system in several districts of Karakalpakstan, an autonomous republic in northwestern Uzbekistan. Recognizing this directly benefits Uzbekistan's cotton industry, the bank agreed with the government that it would comply with national and international forced labor laws and that should there be credible evidence of violations, the bank could suspend the loan.

In the face of overwhelming evidence of forced labor in the project area, instead of suspending its loan, the bank increased its investments in Uzbekistan's agriculture industry, by investing in its joint venture with Indorama Corporation, Indorama Kokand Textile, a leading cotton yarn producer in Uzbekistan. The World Bank's private sector lending arm, the International Finance Corporation (IFC), in December 2015 loaned Indorama US$40 million to expand its textile plant, which uses solely Uzbek cotton.

In December 2015, Germany ended its controversial 13-year military use of Uzbekistan's airbase in Termez. In March, German Foreign Minister Frank-Walter Steinmeier visited Uzbekistan, also in his capacity as chairperson-in-office of the Organization for Security and Co-operation in Europe. He failed to raise serious concerns in public on human rights issues.

UNCHECKED POWER
Police and Military Raids in Low-Income and Immigrant
Communities in Venezuela

**HUMAN
RIGHTS
WATCH**

Venezuela

Under the leadership of President Hugo Chávez and now President Nicolás Maduro, the accumulation of power in the executive branch and erosion of human rights guarantees have enabled the government to intimidate, persecute, and even criminally prosecute its critics.

Severe shortages of medicines, medical supplies, and food have intensified since 2014, and weak government responses have undermined Venezuelans' rights to health and food. Protesters have been arbitrarily detained and subject to abuse by security forces.

Police and military raids in low-income and immigrant communities have led to widespread allegations of abuse.

Other persistent concerns include poor prison conditions, impunity for human rights violations, and continuous harassment by government officials of human rights defenders and independent media outlets.

Prosecution of Political Opponents

Opposition leader Leopoldo López is serving a 13-year sentence in a military prison for his alleged role in inciting violence during a demonstration in Caracas in February 2014, despite the lack of any credible evidence linking him to a crime. Several others arbitrarily arrested in connection with 2014 anti-government protests remain under house arrest or in detention awaiting trial.

In 2016, the Bolivarian National Intelligence Service (SEBIN) detained dozens of people on allegations of planning, fomenting, or participating in violent anti-government actions, including some that were in fact peaceful protests. Many say they have been tortured or otherwise abused in custody, or that they were unable to see their families or lawyers for hours, occasionally days, after arrest. In several cases, prosecutors failed to present any credible evidence linking the accused to crimes. In some, the evidence included possession of political materials, including pamphlets calling for the release of political prisoners.

On August 29, intelligence agents detained Yon Goicoechea, an activist of the Popular Will opposition party, as he was driving to a press conference about an opposition rally scheduled for September 1. Goicoechea's family and lawyer received no official information about his whereabouts for more than 56 hours. A judge subsequently charged Goicoechea with several crimes and ordered his pretrial detention.

Crackdown on Protest Activity

In early 2014, the government responded to massive anti-government protests with brutal force. For several weeks, security forces used excessive force against unarmed protesters and bystanders, and tolerated and sometimes collaborated directly with armed pro-government gangs that attacked protesters with impunity. Detainees were often held incommunicado on military bases for 48 hours or more before being presented to a judge, and in some cases, suffered abuses including severe beatings, electric shocks or burns, and being forced to squat or kneel without moving for hours.

Protesters continue to be subject to prosecution for participating in peaceful demonstrations. José Gregorio Hernández Carrasco, a university student, was detained in May 2016, two days after he participated in an anti-government demonstration in Caracas. He said he was beaten and tortured and finally agreed to sign a confession. The torture techniques included electric shocks, choking him with a plastic bag, and placing a stick on his rectum and threatening to rape him with it. Hernández Carrasco was released in July, but remains subject to criminal prosecution.

In 2016, Venezuelans reported being arrested during street protests over food scarcity—some organized and some spontaneous—and being subject to mistreatment while in detention. Doctors and nurses in public hospitals who have spoken out publicly about the humanitarian crisis report being threatened with the loss of their jobs.

Operation Peoples' Liberation

Beginning in July 2015, President Maduro deployed more than 80,000 members of security forces nationwide in "Operation Peoples' Liberation" (OLP) to address rising security concerns. Police and military raids in low-income and immigrant communities have led to widespread allegations of abuse, including extrajudicial killings, mass arbitrary detentions, maltreatment of detainees, forced evictions, the destruction of homes, and arbitrary deportations.

In February 2016, Attorney General Luisa Ortega Díaz said that 245 people had been killed during OLP raids in 2015, in incidents in which "members of various security forces participated." Dozens more have been killed since in 2016, according to media. Government officials have routinely said that those killed died during "confrontations" with armed criminals. Yet in at least 20 cases, families of victims or witnesses said that there was no confrontation. In several cases, victims were last seen alive in police custody.

Humanitarian Crisis

Severe shortages of medicines and medical supplies make it extremely difficult for Venezuelans to obtain essential medical care. In August, a network of medical residents working in public hospitals throughout the country reported severe shortages of basic medicines in 76 percent of the hospitals surveyed, up from 55 percent in 2014 and 67 percent in 2015.

Official statistics show that infant and maternal mortality rates in 2016 were substantially higher than in previous years. The infant mortality rate for the first five months of 2016 was 18.61 deaths per 1,000—45 percent higher than the 2013 figure. The maternal mortality rate for the first five months of 2016 was 130.70 deaths for every 100,000 births, 79 percent higher than the rate reported for 2009, the most recent year for which such data is available.

Severe shortages of food make it extremely difficult for many people to obtain adequate nutrition. In a 2015 survey by civil society groups and two Venezuelan universities, 87 percent of interviewees nationwide—most from low-income households—said they had difficulty purchasing food. Twelve percent were eating two or fewer meals a day.

The Venezuelan government has downplayed the severity of the crisis. Its own efforts to alleviate the shortages have not succeeded and it has made only limited efforts to obtain available international humanitarian assistance.

Judicial Independence

Since former President Chávez and his supporters in the National Assembly conducted a political takeover of the Supreme Court in 2004, the judiciary has ceased to function as an independent branch of government. Members of the Supreme Court have openly rejected the principle of separation of powers, and publicly pledged their commitment to advancing the government's political agenda.

Since the opposition assumed the majority in the National Assembly in January 2016, the Supreme Court, upon President Maduro's request for a constitutional analysis, has struck down almost every law passed. In October, it removed the budgetary authority from Congress, allowing the president to adopt the 2017 budget by a decree to be approved by the Supreme Court.

Judge María Lourdes Afiuni continues to face criminal prosecution as a result of a 2009 ruling in which she authorized the conditional release of a government critic. Afiuni's ruling was in line with a recommendation by international human rights monitors. After a year in prison and two under house arrest in pre-trial detention, she was released but remains subject to criminal prosecution on charges including abuse of authority.

Freedom of Expression

For more than a decade, the government has expanded and abused its powers to regulate media and has worked aggressively to reduce the number of dissenting media outlets. Existing laws grant the government power to suspend or revoke concessions to private media if "convenient for the interests of the nation," allow for arbitrary suspension of websites for the vaguely defined offense of "incitement," and criminalize expression of "disrespect" for high government officials. While some newspapers, websites, and radio stations criticize the government, fear of reprisals has made self-censorship a serious problem.

Security forces detained, interrogated, and confiscated the equipment of several journalists in 2016. On September 3, Braulio Jatar, a prominent Venezuelan journalist born in Chile who directs an independent digital outlet in Nueva Esparta State, went missing after he covered a spontaneous pot-banging protest against President Maduro in a pro-government neighborhood on Margarita Island. His coverage had received widespread attention in Venezuela and internationally. His family did not know his whereabouts for more than 36 hours. A prosecutor later charged Jatar with money laundering—which carries a sentence of up to 15 years in prison—in connection with approximately US$25,000 cash that he allegedly had in his car. Jatar says the evidence was planted. At time of writing, Jatar was in pretrial detention.

Human Rights Defenders

Government measures to restrict international funding of nongovernmental organizations—combined with unsubstantiated accusations by government officials and supporters that human rights defenders are seeking to undermine Venezuelan democracy—create a hostile environment that undermines the ability of civil society groups to promote human rights.

In May, President Maduro issued a presidential decree that—in addition to declaring a "state of exception" and granting himself the power to suspend rights—instructed the Foreign Affairs Ministry to suspend all agreements providing foreign funding to individuals or organizations when "it is presumed" that such agreements "are used for political purposes or to destabilize the Republic." Maduro has extended the state of exception twice, in September and November.

In 2010, the Supreme Court ruled that individuals or organizations receiving foreign funding can be prosecuted for treason. The National Assembly that year enacted legislation blocking organizations that "defend political rights" or "monitor the performance of public bodies" from receiving international assistance.

Political Discrimination

In June, dozens of workers from the customs and tax agency were fired in apparent retaliation for having supported the recall of President Maduro. Media reports say that hundreds of other referendum supporters nationwide were fired under similar circumstances, and that a government program that distributes food and basic goods at government-capped prices discriminated against government critics.

Prison Conditions

Corruption, weak security, deteriorating infrastructure, overcrowding, insufficient staffing, and poorly trained guards allow armed gangs to exercise effective control over inmate populations within prisons. The Venezuelan Observatory of Prisons, a human rights group, reported that 6,663 people died in prisons between 1999 and 2015. As of July, average overcrowding of 210 percent plagued Venezuelan prisons, according to the Observatory.

In March, four inmates and a prison guard died when detainees and security officers clashed at the Fénix Penitentiary Center in Lara State. Fifty-two detainees, four prison guards, and the prison director were injured. The press has reported other violent prison incidents in 2016, in which at least 20 more people died.

Key International Actors

In May 2016, OAS Secretary General Luis Almagro presented a report on the humanitarian and human rights crisis in Venezuela, and called for invocation of the Inter-American Democratic Charter—an agreement protecting human rights and democratic guarantees in OAS member states. The OAS Permanent Council in June rejected Venezuela's contention that a debate on the report violated its sovereignty, and a majority of member countries voted to move forward and evaluate Venezuela's compliance with the charter. In November, Venezuela walked out of a Permanent Council meeting when the body adopted a resolution supporting dialogue between the government and opposition, arguing the resolution violated its sovereignty.

A dialogue between the government and opposition that began in early 2016, led by former Spanish president José Luis Zapatero, failed to deliver meaningful results. In October, the Vatican announced it would mediate between the sides and subsequently participated in a series of meetings that led to the November release of a handful of political prisoners and a vague joint statement on the need for international assistance to address the humanitarian crisis and for appointment of new members to the National Electoral Council.

In September, Argentina, Brazil, Paraguay, and Uruguay blocked Venezuela from assuming the presidency of the regional trading bloc, Mercosur.

The government withdrew from the American Convention on Human Rights (IAHCR) in 2013, leaving citizens and residents unable to request intervention by the Inter-American Court of Human Rights when local remedies for abuses committed since that date are ineffective or unavailable. The IACHR continues to monitor Venezuela, however, applying the American Declaration of Rights and Duties of Man, which does not require states' ratification.

In August, UN Secretary-General Ban Ki-moon said Venezuela was facing a "humanitarian crisis." The UN high commissioner for human rights has expressed concern regarding deteriorating human rights conditions, including shortages of medicines and food, government intimidation campaigns against human rights defenders, and harsh government responses to peaceful expressions of dissent.

Venezuela's human rights record was scrutinized at the UN Human Rights Council in November. Numerous states urged Venezuela to cooperate with UN special procedures; address arbitrary detention, lack of judicial independence, and shortages of medicine and food; release persons detained for political reasons; respect freedom of expression, association, and peaceful assembly; and ensure that human rights defenders can conduct their work without reprisals.

In 2015, President Barack Obama issued an executive order imposing targeted sanctions against seven Venezuelan government officials. In July 2016, the US Congress extended through 2019 its ability to freeze assets and ban visas of those accused of committing abuses against anti-government demonstrators during the 2014 protests.

As a member of the UN Human Rights Council, Venezuela has regularly voted to prevent scrutiny of human rights violations, opposing resolutions spotlighting abuses in North Korea, Syria, Belarus, and Iran.

Vietnam

The Communist Party of Vietnam (CPV) in 2016 maintained its control over all public affairs and punished those who challenged its monopoly on power. Authorities restricted basic rights, including freedom of speech, opinion, association, and assembly. All religious groups had to register with the government and operate under surveillance. Bloggers and activists faced daily police harassment and intimidation, and were subject to arbitrary house arrest, restricted movement, and physical assaults. Many were detained for long periods without access to legal counsel or family visits. The number of bloggers and activists known to be convicted and sentenced to prison almost tripled from the previous year, from 7 to at least 19.

In January, the CPV held its 12th congress, during which it selected the country's new politburo. Of the 19 members, four, including Vietnam's new president Tran Dai Quang, were from the Ministry of Public Security. In May, Vietnam held a tightly controlled and scripted national election in which all candidates had to be approved by the CPV. Several dozen independent candidates were intimidated and disqualified.

Freedom of Speech and Opinion

The Vietnamese government frequently uses vaguely worded penal code provisions to crackdown on dissent, including "undermining national unity," "conducting propaganda against the state," and "abusing the rights to democracy and freedom to infringe upon the interests of the state."

During the first nine months of 2016, at least 19 bloggers and activists were put on trial and convicted. Others continue to be held without trial, including rights campaigners Nguyen Van Dai, Tran Anh Kim, Le Thanh Tung, and Nguyen Ngoc Nhu Quynh.

In March, the People's Court of Hanoi sentenced prominent blogger Nguyen Huu Vinh (also known as Ba Sam) and his colleague Nguyen Thi Minh Thuy to five and three years respectively under article 258 for running a politically independent website.

Also in March, the People's Court of Ho Chi Minh City sentenced prominent blogger Nguyen Dinh Ngoc (also known as Nguyen Ngoc Gia) to four years in prison for publishing articles on the internet. The same court convicted land rights activists Ngo Thi Minh Uoc to four years, and Nguyen Thi Be Hai and Nguyen Thi Tri, to three years each for staging a peaceful protest outside the United States Consulate in Ho Chi Minh City. In October, Nguyen Dinh Ngoc's sentence was reduced to three years on appeal.

In August, the People's Court of Khanh Hoa sentenced cousins Nguyen Huu Quoc Duy and Nguyen Huu Thien An to three and two years respectively for "conducting propaganda against the Socialist Republic of Vietnam" in accordance with article 88 of the penal code. According to state media, Nguyen Huu Thien An painted reactionary slogans on the outside wall of a police station, while Nguyen Huu Quoc Duy called for the VCP leadership to be removed. The two were also accused of accessing "reactionary" websites.

In September, the People's Court of Dong Da district in Hanoi sentenced land rights activist Can Thi Theu to 20 months in prison for participating in a public protest and boycotting the national election.

State Violence against Activists, Dissidents, and Criminal Suspects

There were frequent physical assaults against human rights bloggers and campaigners at the hands of anonymous men who appear to be acting with state sanction and impunity. During the first seven months of 2016, at least 34 people—including children—reported that unknown assailants beat them.

In February, men threw rocks at the house of former political prisoner, Tran Minh Nhat, and broke his skull. In April, former political prisoner Nguyen Dinh Cuong was taken to a police station in Nghe An province where men in civilian clothes beat ad punched him. In May, police briefly detained 17-year-old rights activist Huynh Thanh Phat for allegedly participating in pro-environment protests. Two men wearing surgical masks and civilian clothes attacked him on the way home from the police station. In June, an unidentified man punched rights activist Nguyen Van Thanh in a café in Da Nang and bruised his face. In July, men in civilian clothes attacked rights activist La Viet Dung with a brick in Hanoi and broke his skull. No one was charged in any of the cases.

Police brutality continued, and detainees were apparently injured and even killed as a result. For example, in March 2016, Y Sik Nie died from alleged torture in Dak Lak province after being arrested for theft. In July, Bui Minh Trang, Bui Minh Truong, and Tran Van Cuong reported that they were detained for five days without a warrant and then beaten in custody by police in Quang Tri province for involvement in a dispute. The three men claimed they were forced to write statements saying they volunteered to spend five days at the police station.

Freedoms of Assembly, Association, and Movement

Vietnam bans all independent political parties, labor unions, and human rights organizations. Authorities require official approval for public gatherings and refuse to grant permission for meetings, marches, or protests they deem politically or otherwise unacceptable.

In May, police used excessive force to disperse pro-environment marches in Hanoi and Ho Chi Minh City. Many protesters reported that they were beaten and detained for hours. Several protesters, including Vo Chi Dai Duong, Dang Ngoc Thuy, Cao Tran Quan, Xuan Dieu, and Nguyen Tan, were taken to administrative detention centers where they were kept for several days without access to legal counsel or due process.

Restrictions on freedom of movement are used to prevent bloggers and activists from attending public events, such as protests, human rights discussions, or trials of fellow activists. In May, police detained prominent rights campaigner Nguyen Quang A and influential blogger Pham Doan Trang to prevent them from attending a private meeting with United States President Barack Obama during his visit to Vietnam. Nguyen Quang A reported that between late March and early August 2016 police detained him six times to prevent him from meeting with foreign diplomats and delegations including Germany, the United States, the European Union, and Australia.

Freedom of Religion

The government monitors, harasses, and sometimes violently cracks down on religious groups that operate outside official, government-registered, and government-controlled religious institutions. Authorities subject to intrusive surveillance unrecognized branches of the Cao Dai church, the Hoa Hao Buddhist church, independent Protestant and Catholic house churches in the central highlands and elsewhere, Khmer Krom Buddhist temples, and the Unified Buddhist Church of Vietnam.

During the first eight months of 2016, the People's Court of Gia Lai province convicted at least nine Montagnards, including Gyun, Thin, Dinh Ku, A Tik, A Jen, Siu Doang, Ksor Pup, Siu Dik, and Ksor Phit, for participating in independent religious groups not approved by the government. They were charged for "undermining national unity" under article 87 and sentenced to between five and eleven years in prison.

Another common form of harassment that authorities continue to use against independent religious groups is forced denunciation of their faith. In April, state media reported that more than 500 followers of the outlawed Dega Protestants "voluntarily renounced" their faith in Chu Puh district, Gia Lai province. This constitutes a violation of freedom of belief, which is not subject to limitation under international human rights law.

Criminal Justice System

Vietnamese courts remained firmly under the political control of the government and the VCP. Trials of rights bloggers and activists consistently failed in 2016 to meet international fair standards. Police regularly intimidated and in some cases detained family members and friends who tried to attend trials.

In March, Hanoi police detained a number of activists, including Nguyen Dinh Ha and Nguyen Quang A, for trying to attend the trial of blogger Nguyen Huu Vinh. In August, police in Khanh Hoa province reportedly dragged Nguyen Thi Nay by the hair and detained her for several hours for trying to approach the court during the trial of her son, Nguyen Huu Quoc Duy.

Drug Detention Centers

Thousands of people who use drugs, including children, continue to be held without due process in government detention centers, where they are forced to work in the name of "labor therapy," a practice that violates prohibitions of forced labor under Vietnamese and international law. According to state media, during the first three months of 2016 alone more than 1,000 people were sent to mandatory centers in and around Ho Chi Minh City. Violations of center rules and failure to meet work quotas are punished by beatings and confinement to disciplinary rooms where detainees are deprived of food and water.

Sexual Orientation and Gender Identity

In November 2015, the National Assembly approved a bill to legalize sex reassignment surgery and to introduce the right to legal gender recognition for transgender people who have undergone such surgery. The law allows people who wish to undergo gender affirming surgeries to do so in Vietnam rather than abroad, and to change the gender marker on official documents—a small, but significant step toward recognizing transgender people's rights. A UNESCO study highlighted bullying—usually in the form of verbal insults from peers and teachers—of lesbian, gay, bisexual, and transgender (LGBT) students in Vietnam's schools.

Key International Actors

The dynamics of Vietnam's foreign relations are complex. Although Hanoi maintains close economic ties to China, one of its largest trade partners, it is engaged in major disputes with Beijing over maritime territory. In recent years, it has forged closer military and economic relations with the US. Vietnam is also an active participant in the Association of Southeast Asian Nations, and sustains ties with Japan, the EU, India, and Australia.

In 2016, as in previous years, the US consistently raised human rights concerns in bilateral meetings and repeatedly called on Vietnam to release political prisoners, but has not directly connected human rights improvements to better diplomatic ties. Even as Vietnam continued to harass and arrest dissidents and failed to implement meaningful reforms, the Obama administration continued to press the US Congress and Vietnam's National Assembly to ratify the Trans Pacific Partnership, and rewarded the government during President Barack Obama's May 2016 visit by lifting a decades-old arms embargo on Vietnam.

The EU and Australia, focusing on commercial relations, made limited efforts to support detained activists or otherwise advocate for improved respect for basic rights in Vietnam. In June, the European Parliament adopted a resolution on the human rights situation in Vietnam. Japan and India continued to remain silent on Vietnam's abysmal rights record.

HUMAN
RIGHTS
WATCH

BOMBING BUSINESSES
Saudi Coalition Airstrikes on Yemen's Civilian Economic Structures

Yemen

The Saudi Arabia-led coalition's aerial and ground campaign against Houthi forces and forces loyal to former President Ali Abdullah Saleh continued in 2016. The campaign began on March 26, 2015, in support of the government of President Abdu Rabu Mansour Hadi and has been supported by the United States and the United Kingdom.

As of October 10, at least 4,125 civilians had been killed and 7,207 wounded since the start of the campaign, the majority by coalition airstrikes, according to the United Nations Office of the High Commissioner for Human Rights (OHCHR).

Dozens of coalition airstrikes indiscriminately or disproportionately killed and wounded thousands of civilians in violation of the laws of war. The coalition also used internationally banned cluster munitions.

Houthi and allied forces committed serious laws-of-war violations by laying banned antipersonnel landmines, mistreating detainees, and launching indiscriminate rockets into populated areas in Yemen and southern Saudi Arabia, killing hundreds of civilians.

Yemeni warring parties began peace talks in Kuwait in April, following a cessation of hostilities, but airstrikes and fighting on the ground continued. This latest round of peace talks broke down in August, subsequent efforts to bring the parties back to negotiations have failed, and coalition airstrikes and ground fighting continue.

None of the states' party to the conflict carried out meaningful investigations into their forces' alleged violations.

Airstrikes

Human Rights Watch has documented 58 apparently unlawful coalition airstrikes since the start of the campaign, which have killed nearly 800 civilians and hit homes, markets, hospitals, schools, civilian businesses, and mosques. Some attacks may amount to war crimes. These include airstrikes on a crowded market in northern Yemen on March 15 that killed 97 civilians, including 25 children, and another on a crowded funeral in Sanaa on October that killed over 100 civilians and wounded hundreds more.

Repeated coalition airstrikes on factories and other civilian economic structures raise serious concerns that the coalition deliberately sought to inflict damage to Yemen's limited production capacity. Human Rights Watch investigated 18 apparently unlawful strikes, some of which used US or UK-supplied weapons, on 14 civilian economic sites. The strikes killed 130 civilians and wounded 173 more. Following the attacks, many of the factories ended production and hundreds of workers lost their livelihoods.

Cluster Munitions

Human Rights Watch has documented the coalition using internationally banned cluster munitions in at least 16 attacks that targeted populated areas, killing and wounding dozens.

Human Rights Watch has identified six types of air-dropped and ground-launched cluster munitions in multiple locations in Yemen, including those produced in the US and Brazil. Amnesty International has further documented the use of UK-made cluster munitions.

In May, the Obama administration suspended transfers of cluster munitions to Saudi Arabia after reports of their use in civilian areas in Yemen. Textron, US-based manufacturer of the CBU-105, announced it would stop production of the weapon in August.

Yemen, Saudi Arabia, and other coalition states are not party to the 2008 Convention on Cluster Munitions. At a meeting in Geneva on May 19, a Yemeni official said the Hadi-led government is considering ratifying the convention following use of the weapons in Yemen.

Landmines

Houthi and allied forces laid numerous landmines, including banned antipersonnel mines, in Yemen's southern and eastern governorates of Aden, Abyan, Marib, Lahj, and Taizz since the beginning of the current conflict. Landmines have killed and wounded dozens of civilians, including children.

Human Rights Watch investigated the cases of five people maimed by antipersonnel mines in Taizz since March 2016, including one man trying to return home with his brother following months of displacement. Landmines killed at least 18 people and wounded over 39 in two districts in Taizz governorate between May 2015 and April 2016, according to a local nongovernmental organization. Medical professionals and Yemenis clearing mines told Human Rights Watch the actual number of mine victims is likely much higher. In June, one doctor said he had treated 50 people in Taizz who had one or more limbs amputed since April who he believed were injured by landmines.

Yemen suffers from a shortage of equipped and trained personnel who can systematically survey and clear mines and explosive remnants of war.

Indiscriminate Attacks

Before and since the coalition air campaign, Houthi and allied forces have used artillery rockets in indiscriminate attacks in the southern cities of Aden, Taizz, Lahj, and al-Dale'a.

Since March 2015, Human Rights Watch has documented seven indiscriminate attacks by Houthi and allied forces in Aden and Taizz that killed 139 people, including at least 8 children.

Shelling by the Houthi-aligned Popular Committees and army units loyal to former president Saleh was responsible for killing 475 civilians and wounding 1,121 between July 1, 2015, and June 30, 2016, according to the UN.

Houthis have also launched artillery rockets into the Najran and Jazan regions in southern Saudi Arabia. Saudi authorities said 29 civilians had been killed and 300 injured in Najran in August alone due to cross-border shelling, Reuters reported.

Attacks on Health and Restrictions on Humanitarian Access

Human Rights Watch has documented numerous airstrikes that unlawfully struck or damaged health facilities in Yemen. On August 15, 2016, a Saudi-led coalition airstrike hit an MSF-supported hospital in Hajja, killing 19 people, and the fourth on an MSF facility. Following the strike, the organization pulled its staff out of six hospitals in northern Yemen.

Houthi and allied forces engaged in military operations around Aden, Taizz, and other areas repeatedly exposed hospitals, patients and health workers to unjustified risk.

According to OHCHR, as of 2016, over 600 health facilities have closed due to damage caused by the conflict, shortage of critical supplies and lack of health workers.

More than 80 percent of the country's total population—20 million people—have been in need of humanitarian assistance. Parties to the conflict have continued to block or restrict critical relief supplies from reaching civilians.

Houthi and allied forces have confiscated food and medical supplies from civilians entering Taizz and blocked humanitarian assistance from reaching the city, contributing to the near collapse of the health system.

The coalition has imposed a naval blockade on Yemen, limiting the importation of vital goods like fuel, which is urgently needed to power generators to hospitals and pump water to civilian residences. In August 2016, the coalition suspended all commercial flights to Sanaa. This is "having serious implications for patients seeking urgent medical treatment abroad," according to the UN.

Aid workers have been kidnapped, unlawfully detained, and killed while engaged in humanitarian operations in Yemen. Humanitarian agencies are frequently denied access to areas controlled by Houthi and Saleh-aligned forces.

Children and Armed Conflict

Among repeated violations against children by parties to the conflict, Human Rights Watch has documented 58 apparently unlawful coalition airstrikes that killed at least 192 children, and multiple airstrikes that struck or damaged schools. The Houthis have also endangered schools and used child soldiers.

The UN secretary-general included the Houthis, government forces, pro-government militias, Al-Qaeda in the Arabian Peninsula (AQAP) and, for the first time, the Saudi Arabia-led coalition on his annual "list of shame" for grave violations against children during armed conflict.

The coalition was responsible for 60 percent of the 785 children killed and 1,168 children wounded, and nearly half of the 101 attacks on schools and hospitals, according to the report.

Houthi forces, government and pro-government forces, and other armed groups have used child soldiers, an estimated one-third of the fighters in Yemen. The UN found in 2015 that 72 percent of 762 verified cases of child recruitment were attributable to the Houthis, with an overall five-fold increase in recruitment of children and a shift towards forced or involuntary recruitment.

Under Yemeni law, 18 is the minimum age for military service. In 2014, the government signed a UN action plan to end the use of child soldiers. Without an effective government in place, the action plan has not been implemented.

On June 6, 2016, the UN secretary-general's office announced it was removing the Saudi-led coalition from its "list of shame," "pending the conclusions of [a] joint review" of the cases included in the report's text after the Saudi government apparently threatened to de-fund UN programs, which could have put children who depend on these programs at risk.

The US again placed Yemen on its list of countries to which arms sales are restricted by the US Child Soldiers Prevention Act, although President Barack Obama granted Secretary of State John Kerry authority to restart aid to Yemen that would otherwise be prohibited by the law.

Terrorism and Counterterrorism

Both AQAP and armed groups loyal to the Islamic State (also known as ISIS) claimed responsibility for numerous suicide and other bombings that killed dozens of civilians.

The US continued its drone attacks on alleged AQAP militants and began to publish basic data related to the strikes. By November, the US reported it had conducted 28 drone strikes in Yemen, killing at least 80 people described as AQAP operatives. The Bureau of Investigative Journalism, a media organization, reported the US had possibly conducted 11 more strikes over the same period.

Arbitrary Detention, Torture, and Enforced Disappearances

After Houthi and allied forces seized control of the capital, Sanaa in late 2014, they cracked down on dissent. Houthi authorities closed several dozen NGOs and barred human rights advocates from traveling. In March, Houthi officials confiscated the passport of prominent rights advocate Abdulrasheed al-Faqih, the second such travel ban the Houthis imposed on a rights advocate. By November, Al-Faqih's passport had yet to be returned.

Houthi and allied forces have committed enforced disappearances, tortured detainees, and arbitrarily detained numerous activists, journalists, tribal leaders, and political opponents. Since August 2014, Human Rights Watch has documented the Sanaa-based authorities' arbitrary or abusive detention of at least 61 people. In 2016, Human Rights Watch documented two deaths in custody and 11 cases of alleged torture or other ill-treatment, including the abuse of a child.

Women's Rights, Sexual Orientation, and Gender Identity

Women in Yemen face severe discrimination in law and practice. They cannot marry without the permission of their male guardian and do not have equal rights to divorce, inheritance, or child custody. Lack of legal protection leaves them exposed to domestic and sexual violence. In the absence of a functioning government, no advances were made to pass a draft constitution that includes provisions guaranteeing equality and prohibiting discrimination based on gender, and a draft Child Rights Law that would criminalize child marriage and female genital mutilation. Forced marriage rates have increased during the ongoing conflict, according to UNFPA.

Under the 1994 penal code, same-sex relations are outlawed with punishments ranging from 100 lashes to death by stoning.

Accountability

None of the warring parties carried out credible investigations into their forces' alleged laws-of-war violations in Yemen.

The coalition-appointed Joint Incidents Assessment Team (JIAT) concluded initial investigations into nine allegedly unlawful strikes. JIAT's results differed drastically from those of the UN, Human Rights Watch and others who documented some of the same strikes. JIAT did not release full investigation reports nor detailed information on their members, their methodology, including how they determine which strikes to investigate, or whether or not they have the power to ensure prosecutions of individuals responsible for alleged war crimes.

The US is not known to have conducted investigations into any alleged unlawful strikes in which its forces may have taken part.

In August, the UN high commissioner for human rights recommended establishing an independent, international mechanism to investigate alleged abuses by all sides in Yemen, finding the coalition-backed Yemeni National Commission was "unable to implement its mandate in accordance with international standards." Three UK parliamentary committees called on the UK to support an independent international inquiry "as a matter of urgency" in September.

In September, the UN Human Rights Council passed a resolution laying out two complementary processes for investigations, through the OHCHR itself, strengthened by the allocation of additional human rights experts, and through the Yemeni National Commission with OHCHR support.

Key International Actors

The US has been a party to the conflict since the first months of fighting, providing targeting intelligence and in-air refuelling. In May, the US said it had deployed some troops in Yemen to aid the United Arab Emirates and its own campaign against AQAP. In October, the US responded to Houthi missile launches, which the Houthis later denied, against US warships with multiple strikes at Houthi-radar sites.

The UK was "providing technical support, precision-guided weapons and exchanging information with the Saudi Arabian armed forces," according to the UK Ministry of Defence. The UK also prepared first drafts of all UN Security Council resolutions on Yemen. The Security Council issued resolutions on the crisis in February and April 2015.

Foreign governments have continued to sell weapons to Saudi Arabia, despite growing evidence the coalition has been committing unlawful airstrikes. US and UK lawmakers, whose governments altogether approved more than $20 billion and $4 billion worth of weapons sales, respectively to Saudi Arabia in 2015 alone, have increasingly challenged the continuation of these sales. Human Rights Watch called on all countries selling arms to Saudi Arabia to suspend weapons sales until it curtails its unlawful airstrikes in Yemen and credibly investigates alleged violations.

On February 25, the European parliament passed a resolution calling on the European Union's High Representative for Foreign Affairs and Security Policy Federica Mogherini "to launch an initiative aimed at imposing an EU arms embargo against Saudi Arabia" due to its conduct in Yemen.

Zimbabwe

During 2016, the government of President Robert Mugabe intensified repression against thousands of people who peacefully protested human rights violations and the deteriorating economic situation. It disregarded the rights provisions in the country's 2013 constitution, and implemented no meaningful human rights reforms.

Police abuse increased, and there was excessive use of force to crush dissent. Human rights defenders, civil society activists, journalists, and government opponents, were harassed, threatened or faced arbitrary arrest by police. Widespread impunity continues for abuses by police and state security agents.

The president publicly attacked judges for "reckless" rulings that allowed public protests against his rule, further eroding judicial independence. He also undermined the independence of the Zimbabwe Human Rights Commission (ZHRC), established as an independent commission under the constitution, when he verbally attacked the institution.

Attacks on Human Rights Defenders

In June 2016, police began a campaign of politically motivated abuses against activists engaged in countrywide protests against poverty, corruption, rights abuses, and lack of electoral reform. Police resorted to heavy-handed tactics, indiscriminately using water cannons, teargas, and batons to violently crush largely peaceful protests.

At various times since June 2016, hundreds of protesters, including student activists, human rights activists, and opposition supporters were arrested, detained, and later released on bail without charge.

For instance, on July 6, police assaulted and arbitrarily arrested, and charged with public violence, hundreds of protesters across the country, including 86 people in Bulawayo, 105 people in Harare, and 16 people in Victoria Falls. The government blocked internet access and WhatsApp text messaging for several hours to obstruct people protesting under the #Tajamuka/Sesijikile campaign led by Promise Mkwananzi and the #ThisFlag campaign led by Pastor Evan

Mawarire. In August, Mawarire and his family fled to the United States after suspected state security agents threatened to kill them.

On August 24 and 26, police arbitrarily arrested over 140 people in Harare on false public violence charges. According to their lawyers, most of those arrested, including security guards, vendors, college students taken from class, did not participate in the protests. Those arrested were later freed on bail after several days in detention.

On September 24, police in Mutare arrested and detained 17 members of the Zimbabwe National Students Union (ZINASU) on charges of allegedly gathering in contravention of the Public Order and Security Act (POSA). After three nights in detention, the Magistrate's Court freed 15 of the 17 ZINASU members and declared their arrest unlawful. At time of writing, two student leaders remain in custody.

Freedom of Expression and Media

Zimbabwe's Constitution guarantees freedom of expression and media, but journalists are subject to arbitrary arrest, harassment, and intimidation when reporting on protests. Reports by the Media Institute of Southern Africa (MISA, Zimbabwe) show that from January 2016, police assaulted, harassed, arrested, or detained at least 31 journalists reporting on protests. They include Garikai Chaunza, Edgar Gweshe, Chris Mahove, James Jemwa, and Khumbulani Zamchiya—whom police arrested in June while they reported on a protest in Harare, detaining them for six hours before releasing them without charge.

On July 6, police briefly detained journalists Elias Mambo, Tafadzwa Ufumeli, Richard Chidza, and Godwin Mangudya at Marimba Station, who were covering protests in Mufakose. Police ordered the journalists to delete from their cameras and mobile phones all pictures and video footage of the protests before releasing them without charge.

On August 3, police used batons to beat up journalists Lawrence Chimunhu, Haru Mutasa, Tsvangirai Mukwazhi, Christopher Mahove, Tendai Musiyazviriyo, Bridget Mananavire, and Imelda Mhetu who were covering a protest in Harare. On August 24, a member of the anti-riot police in Harare harassed and beat journalist Lucy Yasin with a baton as she covered a protest. On the same day the police arrested journalist Tendai Mandimika and detained him for three weeks on false public violence charges before releasing him on bail.

On August 25, the police briefly detained journalists Obey Manayiti and Robert Tapfumaneyi. The following day, police arrested photojournalist James Jemwa while covering protests in Harare. He spent a week in detention on public violence charges before being released on bail.

Women's and Girls' Rights

In January 2016, the Constitutional Court declared child marriage unconstitutional and set 18 as the minimum marriage age. In March, scores of members of parliament from the ruling party and the opposition pledged to protect the rights of girls and to fight to end child marriage. That same month Vice President Emmerson Mnangagwa announced that the government was developing laws to make it a criminal offense.

The government has yet to amend or repeal all existing marriage laws that still allow child marriage. It also has not put in place structures to implement the court's decision and ensure that girls under 18 are not being forced into marriage.

A Human Rights Watch report found that widows are routinely evicted from their marital homes and their property confiscated with little recourse to the formal justice system.

Rule of Law

Authorities continued to ignore human rights provisions in the country's 2013 constitution. The government did not enact new laws or amend existing laws to bring them in line with the constitution and Zimbabwe's international and regional human rights obligations. The government has not repealed or amended the Access to Information and Protection of Privacy Act (AIPPA), the Public Order and Security Act (POSA), and other laws that severely restrict basic rights. In terms of criminal law, sex between men is punishable with up to one year in prison and a fine.

On September 3, President Mugabe interfered with the judiciary's independence by publicly attacking judges for "reckless" rulings that allowed protests against his government. His statements also undermined Zimbabwe's international human rights law obligations to respect due process and judicial independence under the African Charter on Human and Peoples' Rights and the International Covenant on Civil and Political Rights.

On September 9, Mugabe undermined the independence of the Zimbabwe Human Rights Commission when he dismissed its report as "absolutely false" and described its chairperson as "stupid." The commission had published a report showing that partisan government officials had denied food aid to opposition supporters. The commission found the government had violated rights to equality, non-discrimination, and the right to sufficient food. An estimated 4.5 million people needed food aid in 2016.

Authorities have not fully investigated the March 9, 2015 abduction and enforced disappearance of pro-democracy activist and human rights defender Itai Dzamara, who remained missing at time of writing. There has been no progress toward justice for serious past human rights crimes.

Key International Actors

In 2016, Zimbabwe's neighbor and key regional actor South Africa remained silent in the face of a police crackdown in Zimbabwe. In July 2016, Gwede Mantashe, secretary general of South Africa's ruling African National Congress, labelled the Zimbabwe protesters "sponsored elements seeking regime change." On September 21, in an interview with Reuters, President Ian Khama of Botswana said Zimbabwe's 92-year-old President Mugabe should step aside without delay and allow new leadership. The government of Zimbabwe said it was shocked at Khama's comments.

The Southern African Development Community (SADC) failed to raise concerns about deteriorating human rights conditions in Zimbabwe in 2016. When SADC leaders met for their annual summit in Swaziland from August 29 to 31, 2016, they did not press Mugabe's government to prevent abuses and respect human rights in the country.

In February 2016, the European Union renewed sanctions of asset freeze and travel bans against President Mugabe, his wife Grace, and Zimbabwe Defence Industries until February 20, 2017. In September 2016, the European Parliament expressed serious concern about the increase in violence against demonstrators in Zimbabwe and called on the government to respect the right to demonstrate peacefully. It condemned Mugabe's attacks on the judiciary and urged authorities not to interfere with judicial independence. It drew attention to the plight of many women in Zimbabwe and the need to respect their rights.

In August 2016, Australia, Canada, and the United States issued statements in response to protests registering deep concern over use of violence and other human rights violations.

In September 2016, local media reported that the World Bank was preparing an extensive bailout package for Zimbabwe in disregard of the country's deterioration human rights situation. The World Bank however denied the reports, expressing deep care for the people of Zimbabwe, and said direct funding to Zimbabwe would only resume after the country clears its arrears with the bank.